handwritten: 912.4271/ORD £6.99
REFERENCE
QUICK REFERENCE

PHILIP'S

THE STREET ATLAS

Cheshire

Chester, Crewe, Macclesfield, Northwich, Warrington

www.philips-maps.co.uk
First published in 1995 by Philip's
a division of Octopus Publishing Group Ltd
www.octopusbooks.co.uk
Endeavour House 189 Shaftesbury Avenue
London WC2H 8JY
An Hachette UK Company
www.hachette.co.uk

Fifth edition 2010
First impression 2010
CHEEA

ISBN 978-1-84907-127-7 (pocket)

© Philip's 2010

Ordnance Survey®

This product includes mapping data licensed from
Ordnance Survey® with the permission of the
Controller of Her Majesty's Stationery Office.
© Crown copyright 2010. All rights reserved.
Licence number 100011710.

Contents

II	Mobile safety cameras
III	**Key to map symbols**
IV	**Key to map pages**
VI	**Route planning**
VIII	Major administrative and Postcode boundaries
1	**Street maps** at 2⅔ inches to 1 mile
237	**Street map of Chester** at 5⅓ inches to 1 mile
238	**Index** of towns, villages, streets, hospitals, industrial estates, railway stations, schools, shopping centres, universities and places of interest

Digital Data

The exceptionally high-quality mapping found in this atlas is available as digital data in TIFF format, which is easily convertible to other bitmapped (raster) image formats.

The index is also available in digital form as a standard database table. It contains all the details found in the printed index together with the National Grid reference for the map square in which each entry is named.

For further infor...
philips@mapsi...

Mobile safety cameras

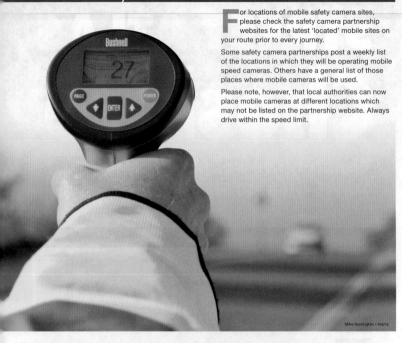

For locations of mobile safety camera sites, please check the safety camera partnership websites for the latest 'located' mobile sites on your route prior to every journey.

Some safety camera partnerships post a weekly list of the locations in which they will be operating mobile speed cameras. Others have a general list of those places where mobile cameras will be used.

Please note, however, that local authorities can now place mobile cameras at different locations which may not be listed on the partnership website. Always drive within the speed limit.

Mike Harrington / Alamy

Useful websites

Cheshire Safer Roads Partnership
www.mysaferroads.org.uk

Derby & Derbyshire Road Safety Partnership
www.slowitdown.co.uk

GanBwyll / GoSafe
www.gosafe.org

Greater Manchester Casualty Reduction Partnership
www.drivesafe.org.uk

Merseyside Road Safety Partnership
www.no-excuses.org.uk

Safer Roads Partnership in West Mercia
www.srpwestmercia.org.uk

Staffordshire Safer Roads Partnership
www.staffordshire.gov.uk/transport/cameras

Further information
www.dvla.gov.uk
www.thinkroadsafety.gov.uk
www.dft.gov.uk
www.road-safe.org

Key to map symbols

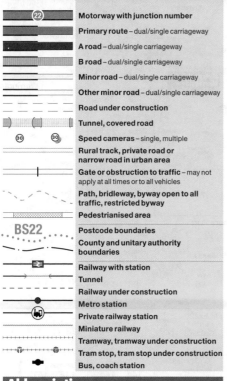

㉒	Motorway with junction number
	Primary route – dual/single carriageway
	A road – dual/single carriageway
	B road – dual/single carriageway
	Minor road – dual/single carriageway
	Other minor road – dual/single carriageway
	Road under construction
	Tunnel, covered road
㉚ ㉚	Speed cameras – single, multiple
	Rural track, private road or narrow road in urban area
	Gate or obstruction to traffic – may not apply at all times or to all vehicles
	Path, bridleway, byway open to all traffic, restricted byway
	Pedestrianised area
BS22	Postcode boundaries
	County and unitary authority boundaries
	Railway with station
	Tunnel
	Railway under construction
	Metro station
	Private railway station
	Miniature railway
	Tramway, tramway under construction
	Tram stop, tram stop under construction
	Bus, coach station

◆	Ambulance station
◆	Coastguard station
◆	Fire station
◆	Police station
✚	Accident and Emergency entrance to hospital
H	Hospital
+	Place of worship
i	Information centre – open all year
☒	Shopping centre
P	Parking
P&R	Park and Ride
PO	Post Office
Ⴟ	Camping site
⚐	Caravan site
►	Golf course
✕	Picnic site
Church	Non-Roman antiquity
ROMAN FORT	Roman antiquity
Univ	Important buildings, schools, colleges, universities and hospitals
	Built-up area
	Woods
River Medway	Water name
	River, weir
	Stream
	Canal, lock, tunnel
	Water
	Tidal water
112 / 58 / 87	Adjoining page indicators

The small numbers around the edges of the maps identify the 1-kilometre National Grid lines

The dark grey border on the inside edge of some pages indicates that the mapping does not continue onto the adjacent page

Abbreviations

Acad	Academy	Meml	Memorial
Allot Gdns	Allotments	Mon	Monument
Cemy	Cemetery	Mus	Museum
C Ctr	Civic centre	Obsy	Observatory
CH	Club house	Pal	Royal palace
Coll	College	PH	Public house
Crem	Crematorium	Rec Gd	Recreation ground
Ent	Enterprise	Resr	Reservoir
Ex H	Exhibition hall	Ret Pk	Retail park
Ind Est	Industrial Estate	Sch	School
IRB Sta	Inshore rescue boat station	Sh Ctr	Shopping centre
Inst	Institute	TH	Town hall / house
Ct	Law court	Trad Est	Trading estate
L Ctr	Leisure centre	Univ	University
LC	Level crossing	W Twr	Water tower
Liby	Library	Wks	Works
Mkt	Market	YH	Youth hostel

The map scale on the pages numbered in blue is 2⅔ inches to 1 mile
4.2 cm to 1 km • 1:23 810

0	¼ mile	½ mile	¾ mile	1 mile

0	250m	500m	750m	1km

The map scale on the pages numbered in red is 5⅓ inches to 1 mile
8.4 cm to 1 km • 1:11 900

0	220yds	440yds	660yds	½ mile

0	125m	250m	375m	500m

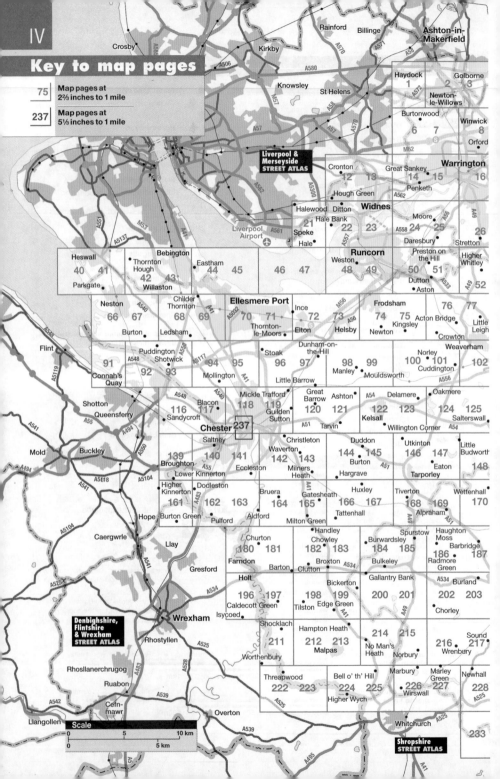

IV

Key to map pages

Scale
0 5 10 km
0 5 km

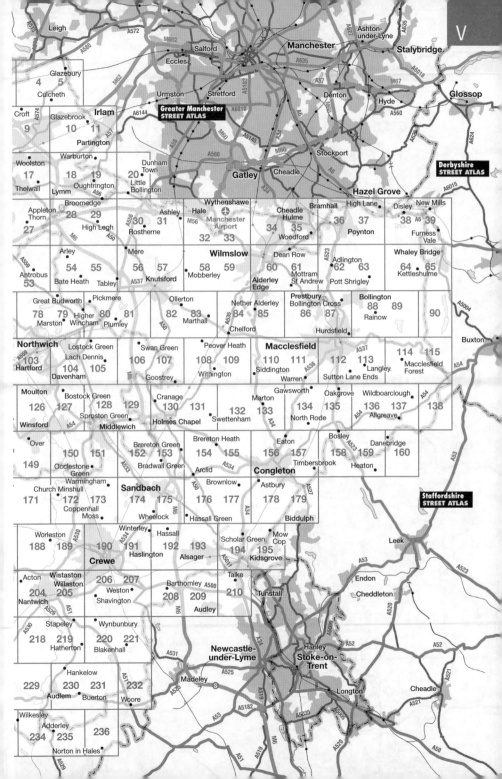

Scale

0 — 5 — 10 km

0 — 5 miles

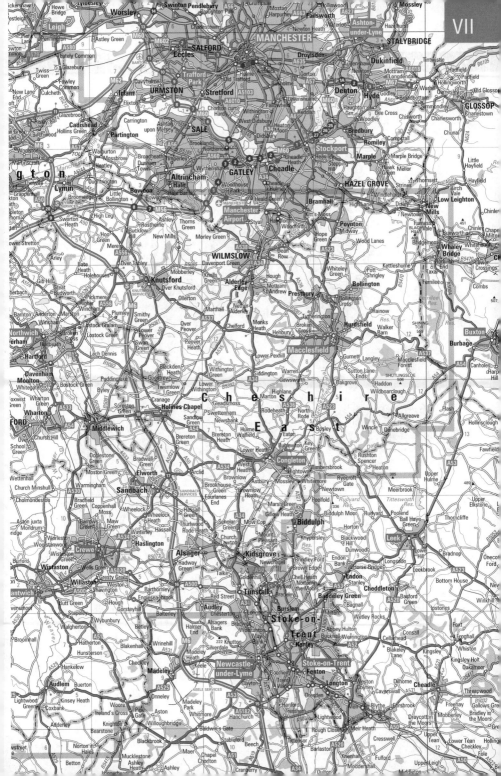

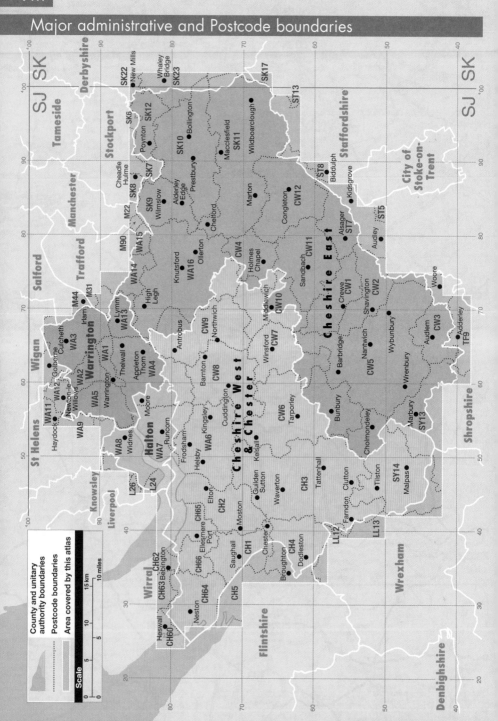

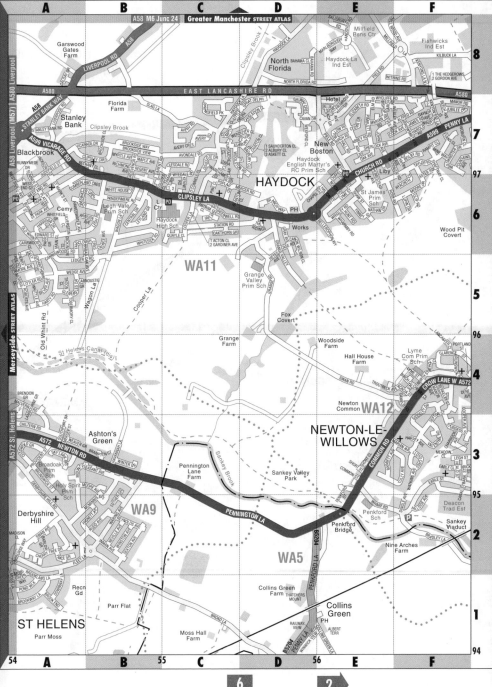

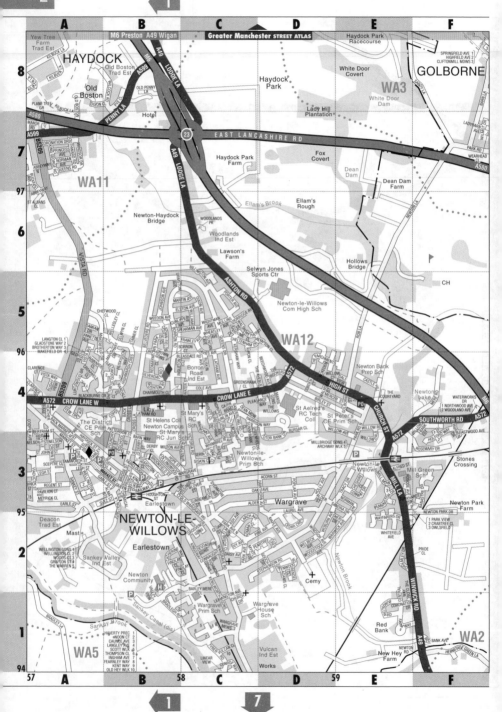

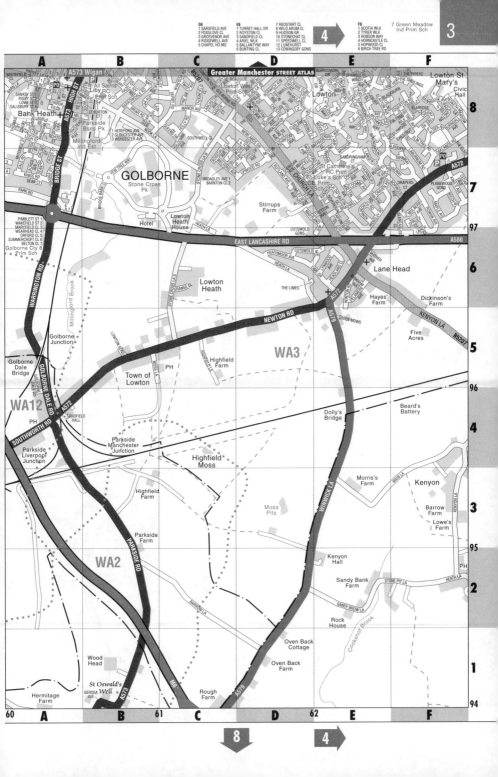

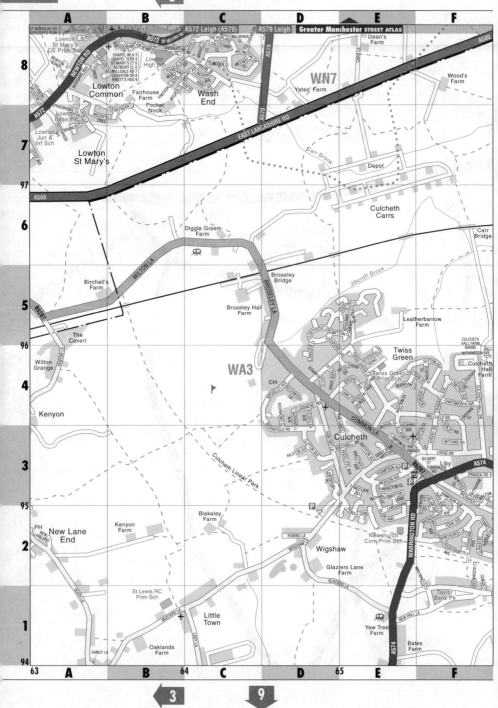

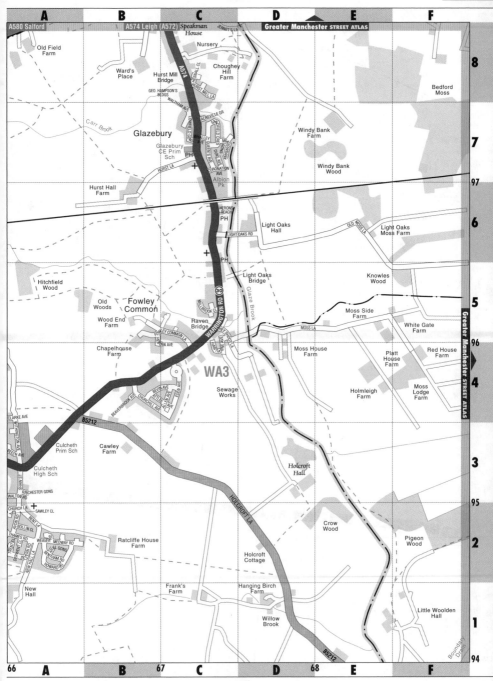

Sutton Moss

Burtonwood Moss

White House Farm

B5204

Higher Farm

8

Bold Moss

Burtonwood Brewery

Yew Tree Farm

YORKSHIRE LA

BRANDY LA

Burtonwood Derby Com Prim Farm Sch

LUMBER LA

GREEN LA

DAHLIA CL
IDA CL
IDA CL
WYS
PEVENSEY WAY
SAMPHIRE GDNS
Bold
Bsns Ctr.

BOLD LA

BACK LA

ALTERTON PK

EPWORTH CL 1
ARNCLIFFE CL 3
DORCHESTER WAY 4

7

PRIMULA CL
MARIGOLD WAY
CROCUS GDNS
LOTUS GDNS

THE PASTURES
ANEMONE
JASMINE GDNS
COLUMBINE WAY
DELAMERE WF
BEGONIA GDNS

1 PEONY GDNS
2 ARABIS GDNS
3 CAMELLIA GDNS

Phipps' Bridge
St Paul of the Cross RC Prim Sch

Burtonwood Ind Ctr

RUSHTON CL

SUNNINGDALE RD

93

B5204
AZALEA GDNS 1
IBERIS GDNS 2
HYDRANGEA WAY 3
LAVENDER GDNS 4
SUNFLOWER CL 5

TRAVERS' ENTRY

NEW BOLD CT

Bold

Haley Head Farm

EXMOUTH
SHERBOURNE
WAY

CHAPEL

KAREN CL

Travers' Farm

Wheatacre Farm

MERCER ST

Lilly Cemy

6

Rose Hill Farm

Bold Ind Pk

DOUGLAS AVE
ROSEHILL AVE

GORSEY LA

ACTON RD
THE MEWS
SHERWOOD
HERBERT ST
HAWKSHEAD RD
CRES

KILSHAW RD
JONES RD

Northfield Riding Ctr

WA9

Moat House

Ashton's Farm

Burtonwood

5

Abbotsfield Farm

Lodge Wood

JOY LA

Clay Lane Farm

Old Lodge Farm

CLAY LA

92

Park Cottage

Maypole Farm

Moat House Farm

WA5

Merseyside STREET ATLAS

4

Nursery

Hollin Wood

Joy Lane Farm

Ivy Cottage

Highfield

Finger Post

BURTONWOOD RD

JOY LA

3

Home Farm

Dog Kennel Plantation

LIMEKILN LA

WRIGHT'S LA

Limekiln Farm

M62

91

M62 Liverpool

M62

2

WA8

Booth's Wood

ORION BVD

1

Old Hall Farm

Duck Wood

OMEGA BVD

90

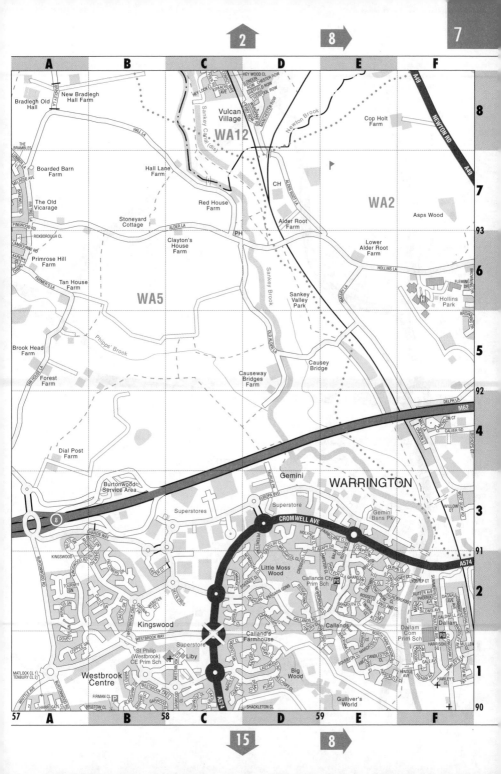

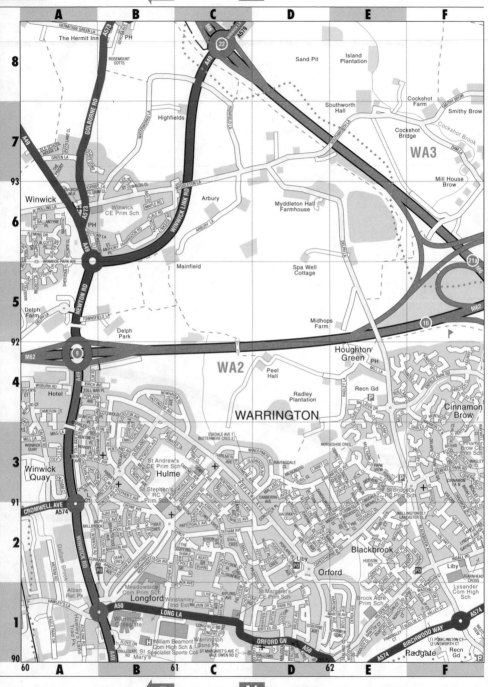

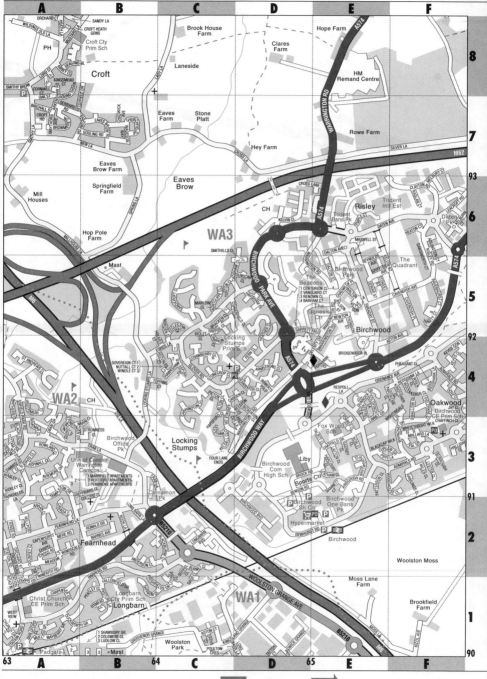

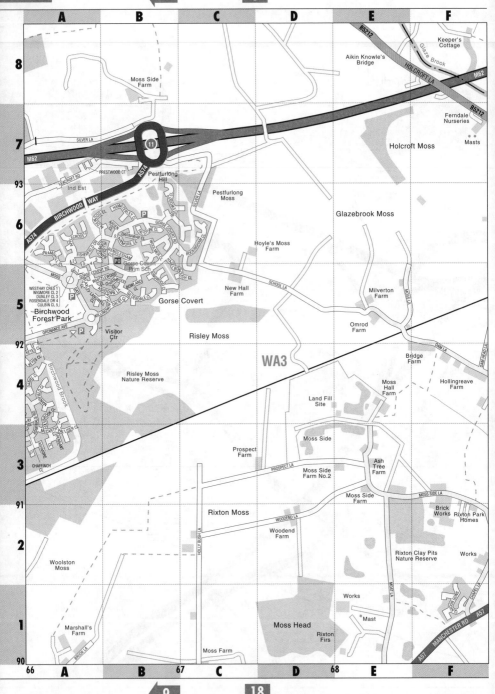

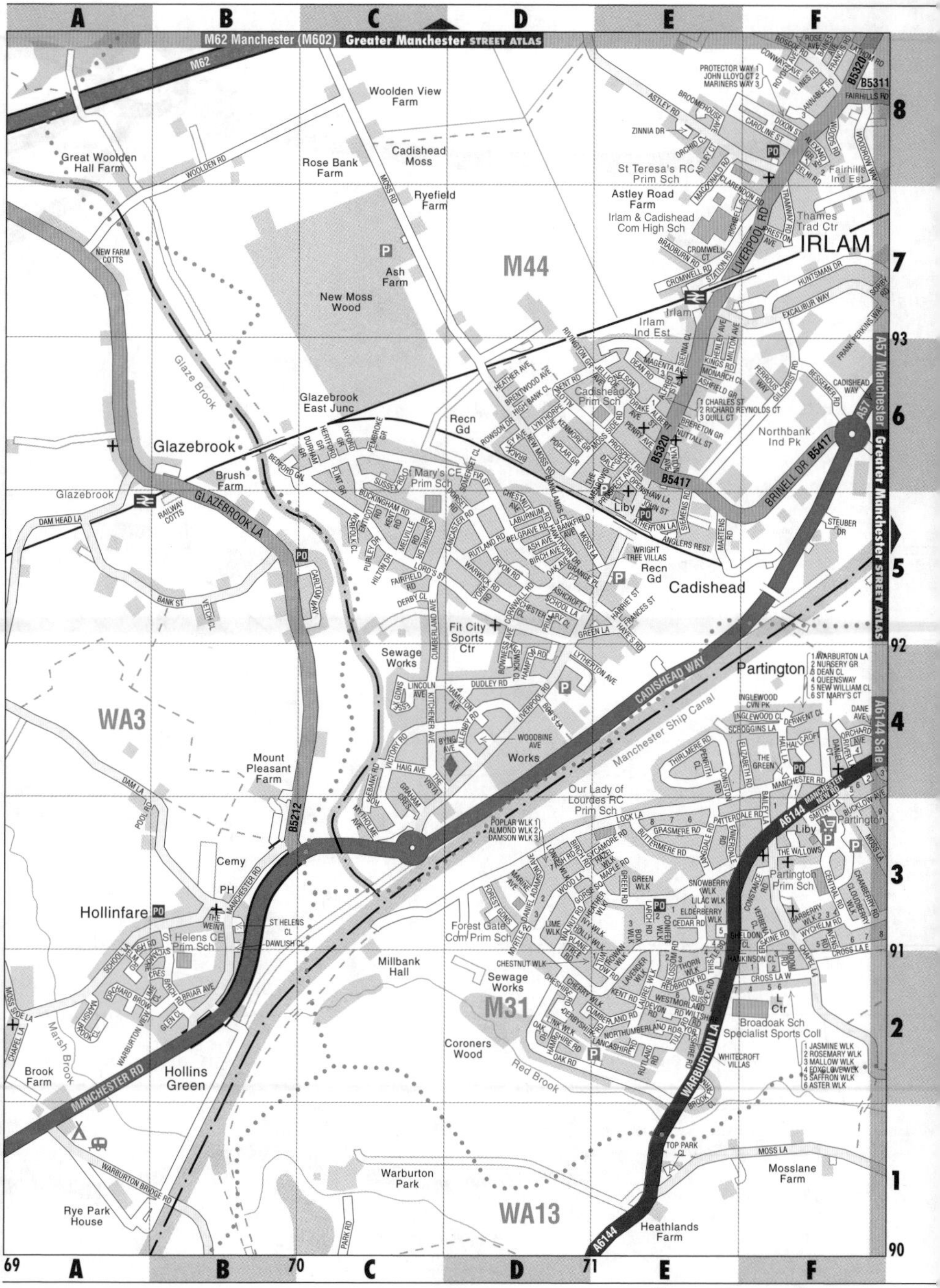

M62 Manchester (M602)
Greater Manchester STREET ATLAS
A57 Manchester
A6144 Sale
A B C D E F
8 7 6 5 4 3 2 1
93 92 91 90
69 70 71
M62
Woolden View Farm
Great Woolden Hall Farm
WOOLDEN RD
Rose Bank Farm
Cadishead Moss
Ryefield Farm
MOSS RD
NEW FARM COTTS
Ash Farm
New Moss Wood
M44
IRLAM
Irlam
Irlam Ind Est
St Teresa's RC Prim Sch
Astley Road Farm
Irlam & Cadishead Com High Sch
Thames Trad Ctr
Fairhills Ind Est
LIVERPOOL RD
B5320
B5311
B5417
ASTLEY RD
PROTECTOR WAY 1
JOHN LLOYD CT 2
MARINERS WAY 3
Glaze Brook
Glazebrook East Junc
Glazebrook
Brush Farm
GLAZEBROOK LA
DAM HEAD LA
RAILWAY COTTS
BANK ST
CARLTON WAY
Recn Gd
St Mary's CE Prim Sch
Cadishead Prim Sch
Northbank Ind Pk
BRINELL DR
1 CHARLES ST
2 RICHARD REYNOLDS CT
3 QUILL CT
Liby
WRIGHT TREE VILLAS
Recn Gd
Cadishead
Fit City Sports Ctr
Sewage Works
CUMBERLAND AVE
DUDLEY RD
CADISHEAD WAY
Partington
1 WARBURTON LA
2 NURSERY GR
3 DEAN CL
4 QUEENSWAY
5 NEW WILLIAM CL
6 ST MARY'S CT
INGLEWOOD CVN PK
Manchester Ship Canal
Works
WOODBINE AVE
WA3
Mount Pleasant Farm
B5212
DAM LA
POOL RD
Our Lady of Lourdes RC Prim Sch
POPLAR WLK 1
ALMOND WLK 2
DAMSON WLK 3
MANCHESTER RD
A6144
Partington Prim Sch
Liby
Cemy
PH
Hollinfare
ST HELENS CL
DAWLISH CL
St Helens CE Prim Sch
Forest Gate Com Prim Sch
Millbank Hall
CHESTNUT WLK
Sewage Works
M31
Broadoak Sch Specialist Sports Coll
L Ctr
WARBURTON LA
WHITECROFT VILLAS
1 JASMINE WLK
2 ROSEMARY WLK
3 MALLOW WLK
4 FOXGLOVE WLK
5 SAFFRON WLK
6 ASTER WLK
Marsh Brook
Brook Farm
Hollins Green
Coroners Wood
Red Brook
MOSS SIDE LA
CHAPEL LA
WARBURTON BRIDGE RD
TOP PARK CL
MOSS LA
Mosslane Farm
Warburton Park
Rye Park House
PARK RD
WA13
Heathlands Farm

19

E2
1 YEW WLK
2 FORSYTHIA WLK
3 BLACKTHORN WLK
4 THISTLE WLK
5 MAGNOLIA CL
6 LOBELIA WLK
7 IRIS WLK

E3
1 PINE WLK
2 MAY WLK
3 HAWTHORN WLK
4 ROSE WLK
5 CARMICHAEL CL
6 MEADOW WLK
7 FIELD WLK
8 GARDEN WLK

F3
1 ALEXANDRA CT
2 ELM CL
3 WINTERGREEN WLK
4 BEECH CL
5 CAMOMILE WLK
6 CHARLOCK WLK
7 WOODRUFF WLK
8 COLUMBINE WLK
9 WORTHINGTON AVE

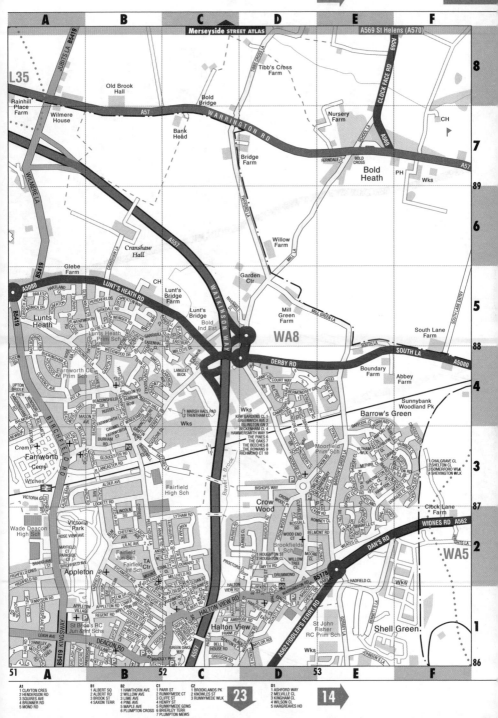

23

14

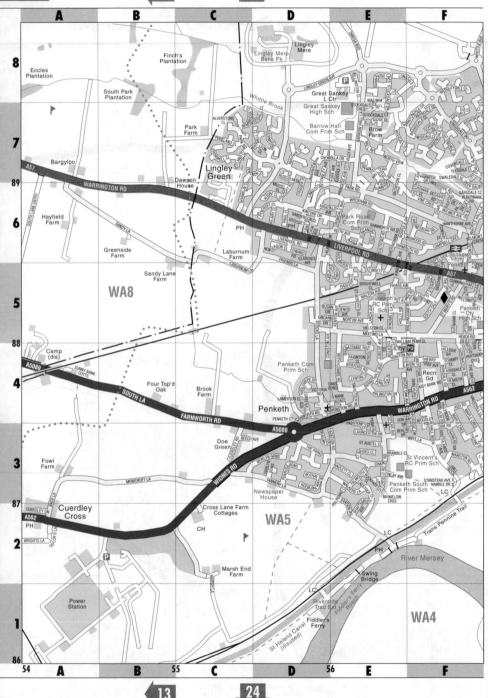

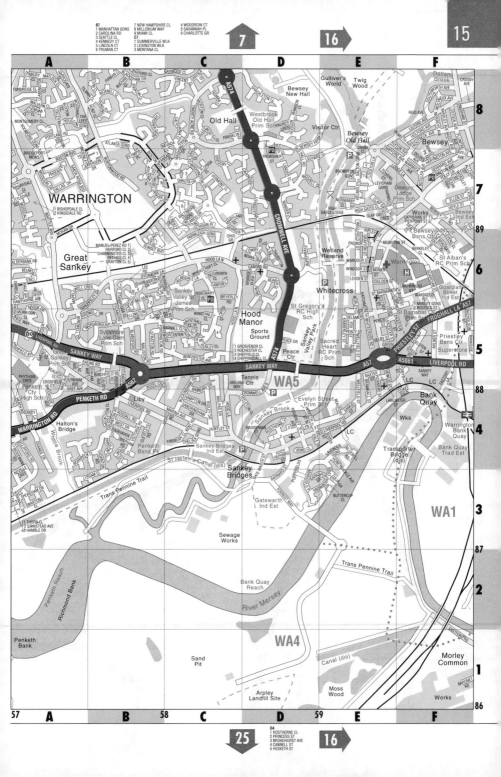

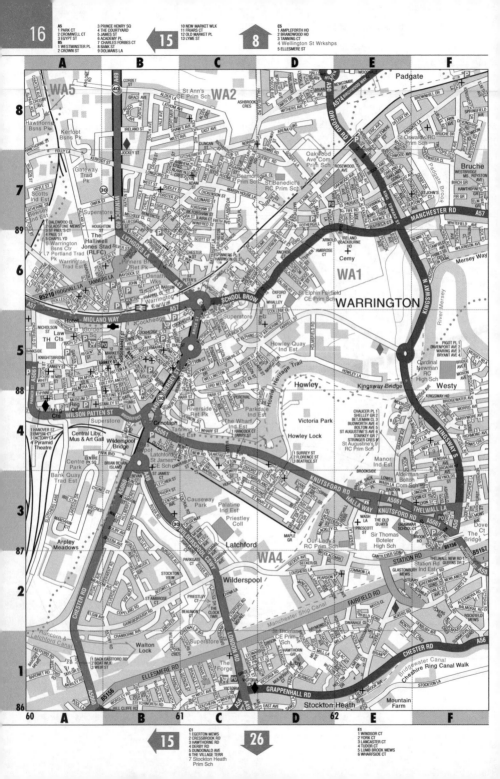

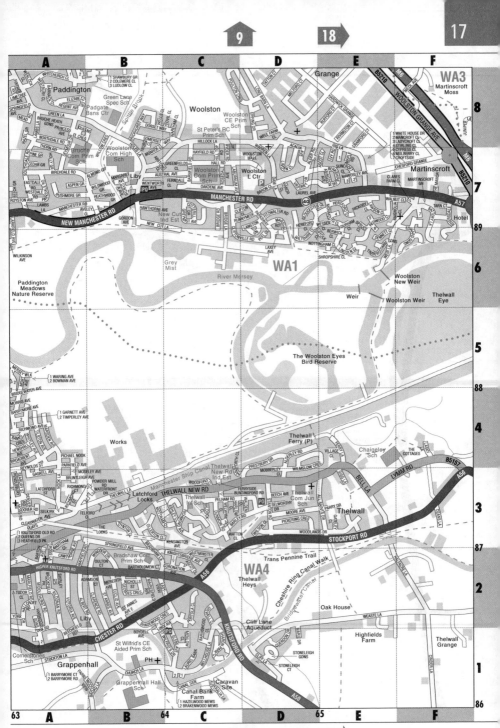

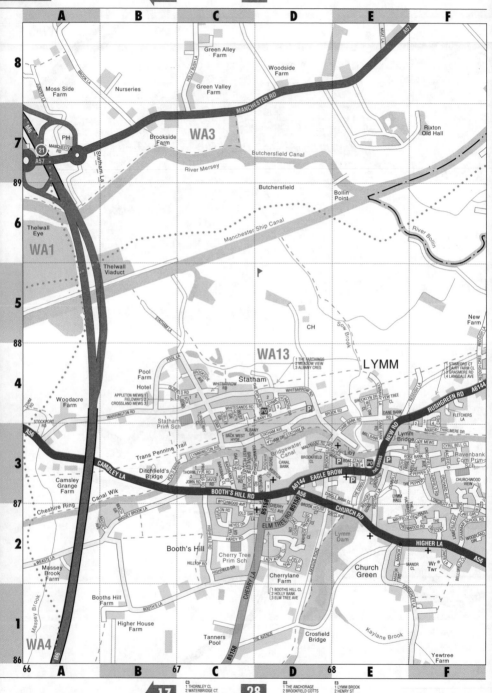

C3
1 THORNLEY CL
2 WATERBRIDGE CT
3 BRIDGEWATER CT

D3
1 THE ANCHORAGE
2 BROOKFIELD COTTS
3 BOOTHS HILL HO

E3
1 LYMM BROOK
2 HENRY ST
3 LEGH ST
4 BRIDGEWATER ST
5 THIRLMERE LODGE
6 THE SQUARE
7 DUKESBRIDGE CT

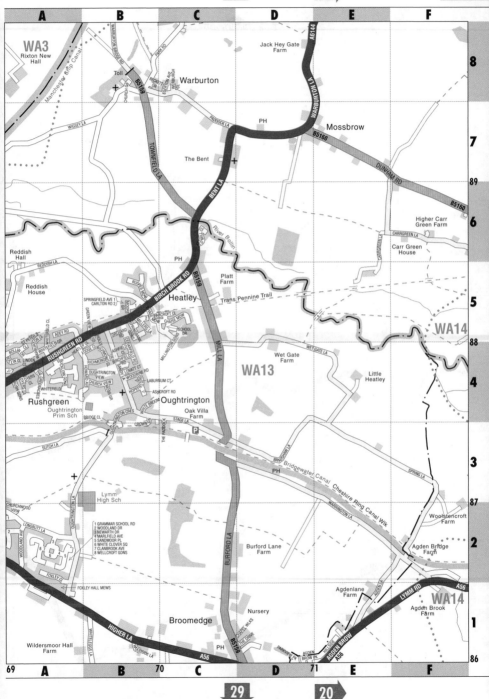

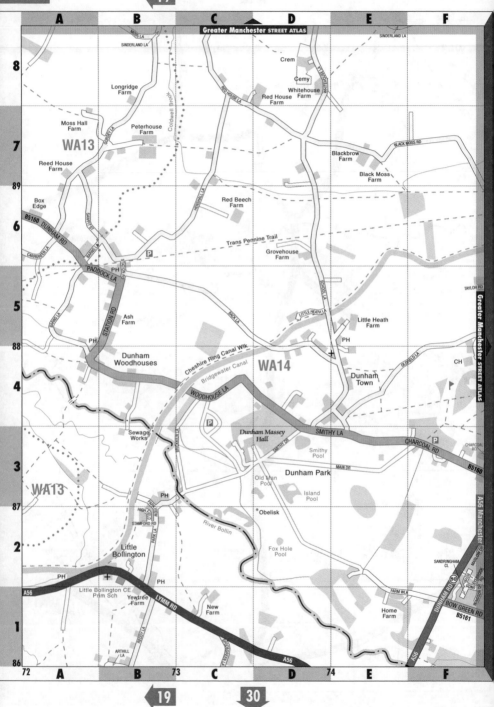

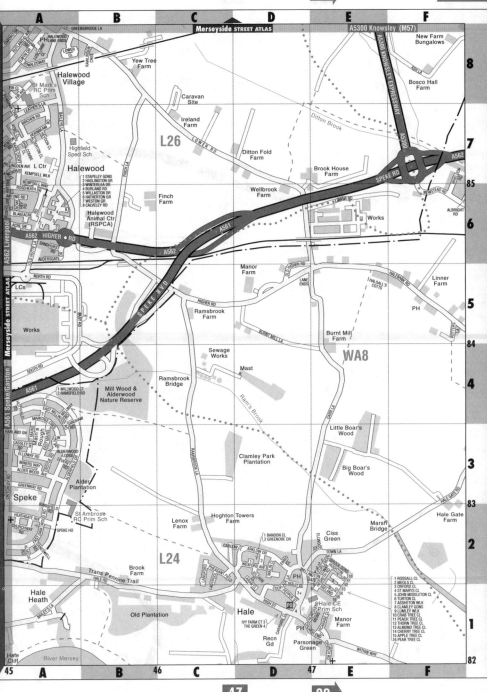

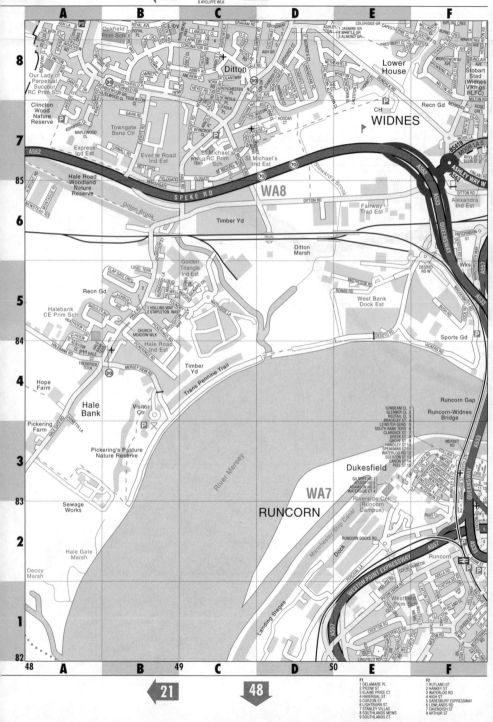

A8
1 MOTTERSHEAD CL
2 VICTORIA CT
3 NAUGHTON RD
A7
1 OLLIER ST
2 THOMAS ST

3 DARLINGTON CT
4 ADELAIDE CT
5 ELEANOR ST
6 MAJOR CROSS ST
7 EMILY ST
8 VICTORIA SQ
9 Moor Lane Bsns Ctr

B8
1 ALBERT SQ
2 DICKSON ST
3 SOUTH ST
4 SALISBURY ST
5 RYLANDS ST
6 HIBBERT ST

7 DEAN CL
8 GLADSTONE ST
9 ELLIOT ST
10 TRAVIS ST
11 GRENFELL ST
12 ALFRED CL
13 QUINN ST

14 MIDWOOD ST
15 Widnes Sh Pk

B7
1 TRINITY PL
2 CHARLOTTE WLK
3 CLARKE GDNS
4 SUTTON S LA

13 **24**

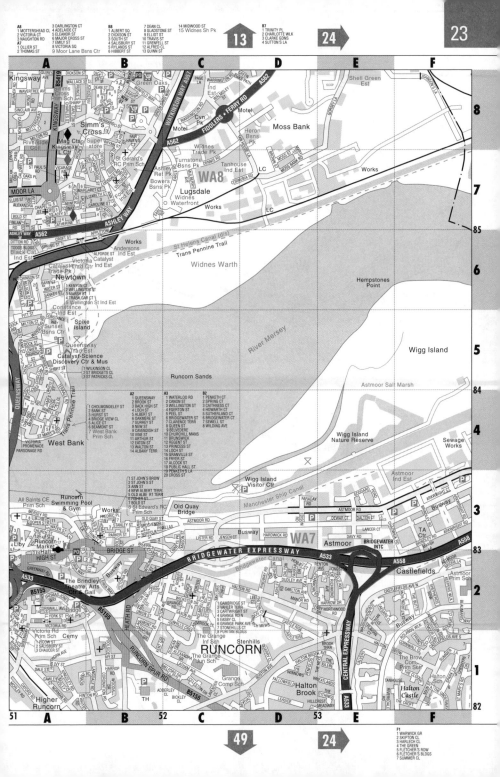

F1
1 WARWICK GR
2 SKIPTON CL
3 HARLECH CL
4 THE GREEN
5 FLETCHER S ROW
6 FLETCHER S BLDGS
7 SUMMER CL

49 **24**

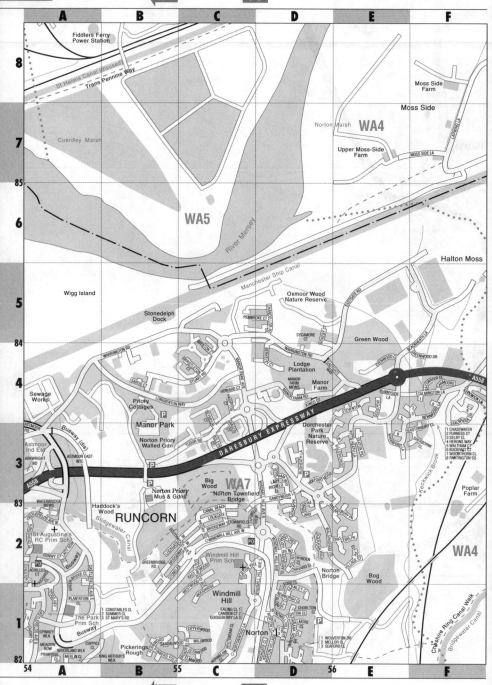

23
14

Fiddlers Ferry
Power Station

St. Helens Canal (disused)

Trans-Pennine Way

8

Moss Side
Farm

Moss Side

Norton Marsh

WA4

7

Cuerdley Marsh

Upper Moss-Side
Farm

MOSS SIDE LA

85

WA5

River Mersey

6

Halton Moss

Manchester Ship Canal

Wigg Island

Oxmoor Wood
Nature Reserve

EASTGATE RD

5

Stonedelph
Dock

PEMBROKE CT

CHANCEL LA RD

SYCAMORE
CT

Green Wood

BLACKHEATH LA

GREENWOOD DR

84

WARRINGTON RD

BIRCHDALE

CREIGHTON RD

BERKELEY CT

WARRINGTON RD

Lodge
Plantation

EASTGATE

OXENWOOD LA

A558

4

Sewage
Works

GARDEN CT

LONGBENTON WAY

STUART RD

HOWARD CT

MANOR PARK RD

MANOR
FARM
MEWS

Manor
Farm

KINGS CT

STEVENTON

SUNNYSIDE
LA

CALMINGTON LA

SYCAMORE

RENWICK LA

Priory
Cottages

TUDOR RD

1 CHASEWATER
2 FURNESS CT
3 SELBY CL
4 HERONS WAY
5 WALTHAM CT
6 BUCKFAST CT
7 WOODTHORN CL
8 PARTINGTON SQ

Manor Park

Busway (die)

Astmoor
Ind Est

ARKWRIGHT
RD

Norton Priory
Walled Gdn

ASTMOOR EAST
INTC

Dorchester
Park
Nature
Reserve

GLASTONBURY CL

SHERBORNE

Poplar
Farm

3

A558

WATERBRIDGE
MEWS

Haddock's
Wood

Bridgewater Canal

Big
Wood

WA7

Norton Townfield
Bridge

LADY
RICHELD
CL

Keckwick Brook

Norton Priory
Mus & Gdns

RUNCORN

CANAL REACH

LOCKGATE

SANDYMOOR

WA4

St Augustine's
RC Prim Sch

BRIDGEWAY

TOWNFIELD

OWNDALE HILL AVE W

SWINDEN

CONWY CT
Busway

GREENBRIDGE
RD

Windmill Hill
Prim Sch

2

ACHILLES
CT

PLANTATION

1 CONSTABLES CL
2 SUMMER CL
3 ST MARY'S RD

Windmill
Hill

Norton
Bridge

Bog
Wood

1

SPINNEY WLK

The Park
Prim Sch

Busway

COPPERWOOD

MILLWOOD

EALING CL
CAMDEN CT
GOOSEBERRY LA

CHORLTON
CL

Norton

1 WOLVERTON DR
2 MELLOR CL
3 SEAFORD CL

Cheshire Ring Canal Walk

Bridgewater Canal

MEADOW
ROW

WOODLAND WLK

PRIMROSE

MERLIN CL

KING ARTHUR'S
WLK

Pickerings
Rough

82

23
50

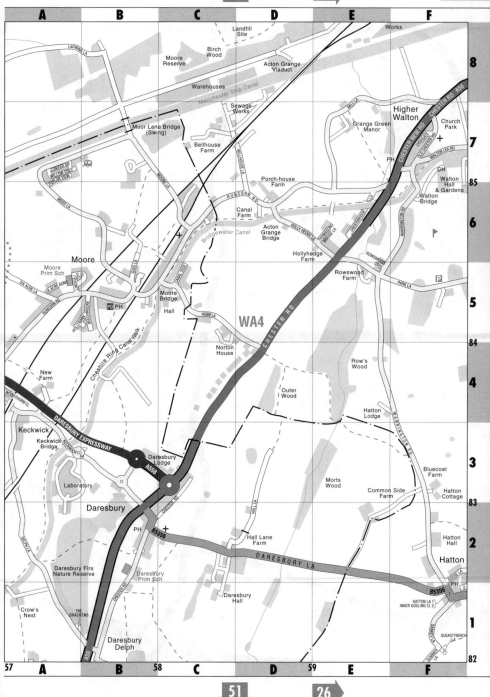

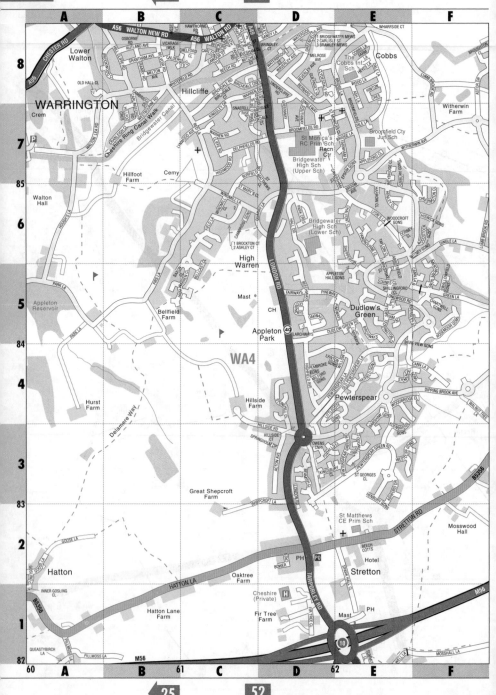

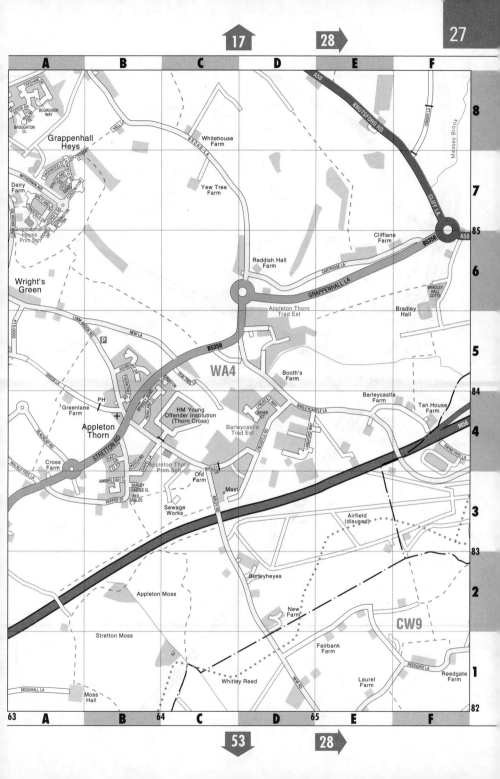

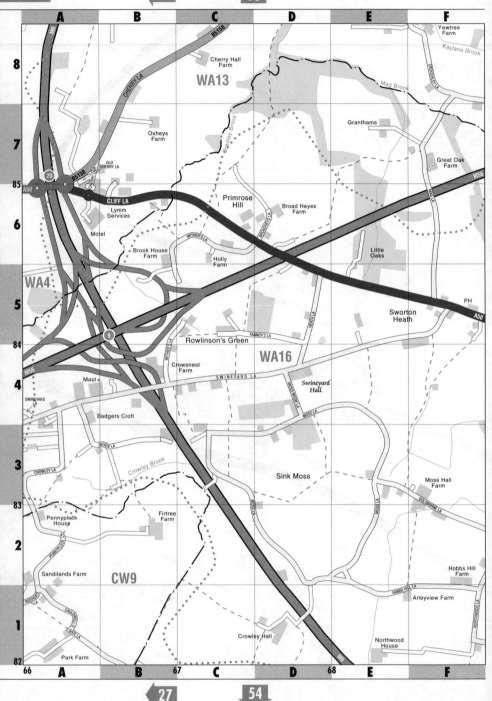

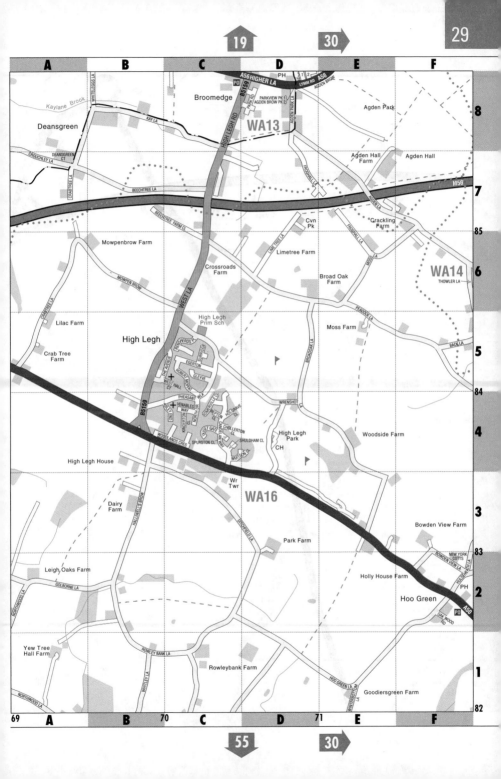

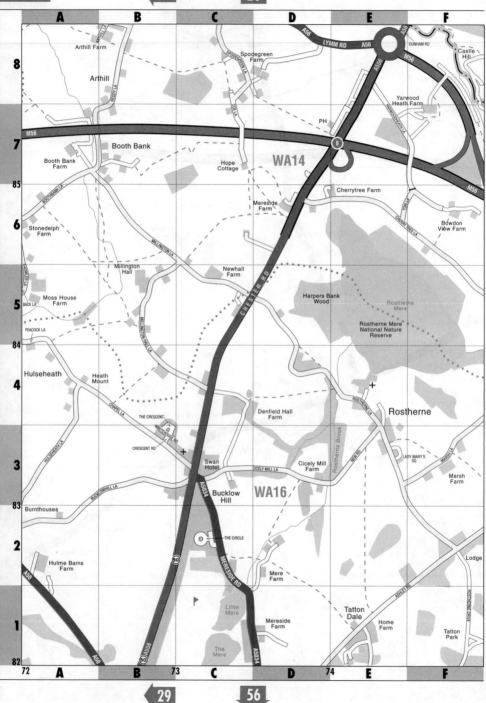

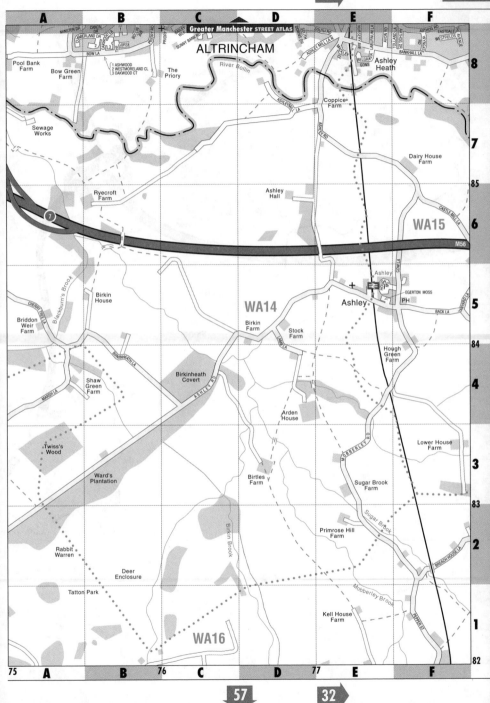

Greater Manchester STREET ATLAS

ALTRINCHAM

River Bollin

Pool Bank Farm

Bow Green Farm

1 ASHWOOD
2 WESTMORELAND CL
3 OAKWOOD CT

The Priory

Ashley Heath

Sewage Works

Coppice Farm

Dairy House Farm

Ryecroft Farm

Ashley Hall

WA15

M56

Blackburn's Brook

Birkin House

WA14

Ashley

PH

Egerton Moss

Briddon Weir Farm

Birkin Farm

Stock Farm

Hough Green Farm

BACK LA

Birkinheath Covert

Shaw Green Farm

Arden House

Lower House Farm

Twiss's Wood

Ward's Plantation

Birtles Farm

Sugar Brook Farm

Sugar Brook

Rabbit Warren

Primrose Hill Farm

Deer Enclosure

Tatton Park

Mobberley Brook

WA16

Kell House Farm

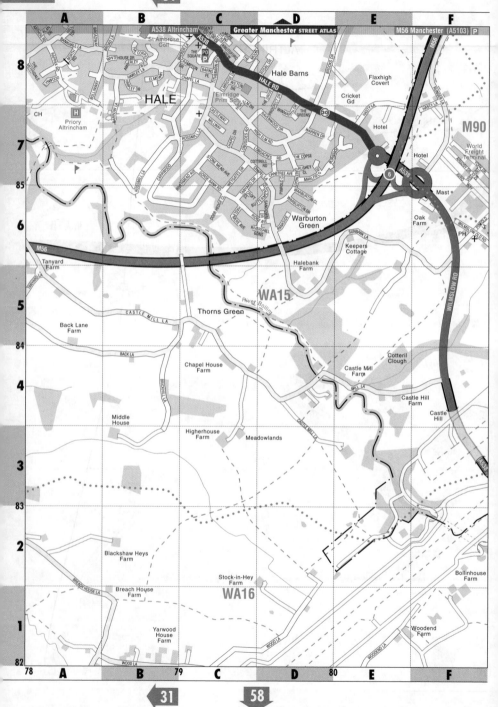

A538 Altrincham

M56 Manchester (A5103) P

8

St Ambrose Golf

THE SQUARE

Hale Barns

HALE RD

Flaxhigh Covert

Cricket Gd

M90

HALE

Elmridge Prim Sch

CH

H

Priory Altrincham

Hotel

World Freight Terminal

7

Hotel

85

6

A538

Mast

Warburton Green

Oak Farm

PH

6

M56

Tanyard Farm

Keepers Cottage

Halebank Farm

WA15

River Bollin

WILMSLOW RD

5

CASTLE MILL LA

Thorns Green

Back Lane Farm

84

BACK LA

BRICKKILN LA

Chapel House Farm

Castle Mill Farm

Cotteril Clough

4

MILL LA

Castle Hill Farm

Castle Hill

Middle House

Higherhouse Farm

Meadowlands

CASTLE MILL LA

3

83

A538

2

Blackshaw Heys Farm

Stock-in-Hey Farm

WA16

Bollinhouse Farm

BREACH HOUSE LA

Breach House Farm

1

Yarwood House Farm

Woodend Farm

WOOD LA

WOODEND RD

82

78

A

B

79

C

80

D

E

F

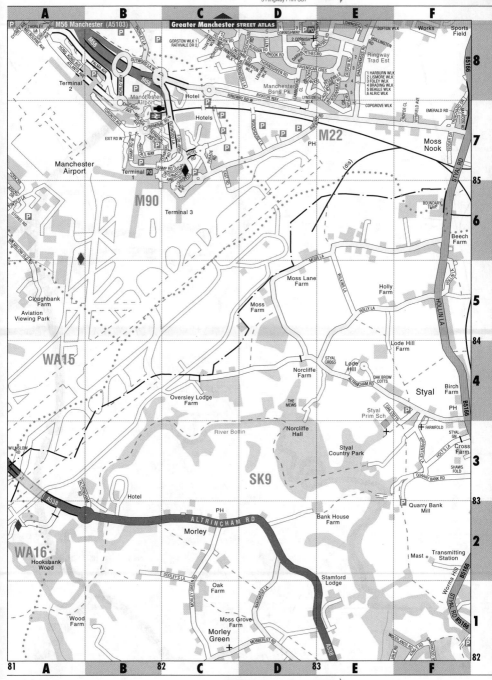

D8
1 ROSSETT AVE
2 WHITEFRIARS WLK
3 AUSTELL RD
4 Cornishway Ind Est
5 Ringway Prim Sch

Greater Manchester STREET ATLAS

M56 Manchester (A5103)

Ringway Trad Est

1 HARBURN WLK
2 LISMORE WLK
3 FOLEY RD
4 BRADING WLK
5 BEAGLE WLK
6 ALRIC WLK

Manchester
Bsns Pk.

Terminal 2

Terminal 1

Hotel

Hotels

M22

Manchester
Airport

Manchester
Airport

Moss
Nook

M90

Terminal 3

Beech
Farm

Cloughbank
Farm

Aviation
Viewing Park

Moss Lane
Farm

Holly
Farm

Moss
Farm

Lode Hill
Farm

WA15

Lode
Hill

Birch
Farm

Norcliffe
Farm

Styal

Oversley Lodge
Farm

THE
MEWS

Styal
Prim Sch

Cross
Farm

River Bollin

Norcliffe
Hall

Styal
Country Park

SK9

Quarry Bank
Mill

Hotel

Bank House
Farm

Morley

ALTRINCHAM RD

WA16

Mast

Transmitting
Station

Hooksbank
Wood

Oak
Farm

Stamford
Lodge

Wood
Farm

Moss Grove
Farm

Morley
Green

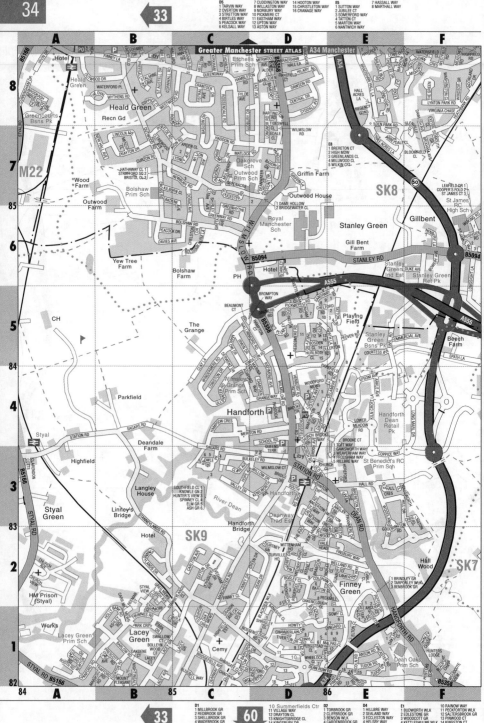

Greater Manchester STREET ATLAS A34 Manchester

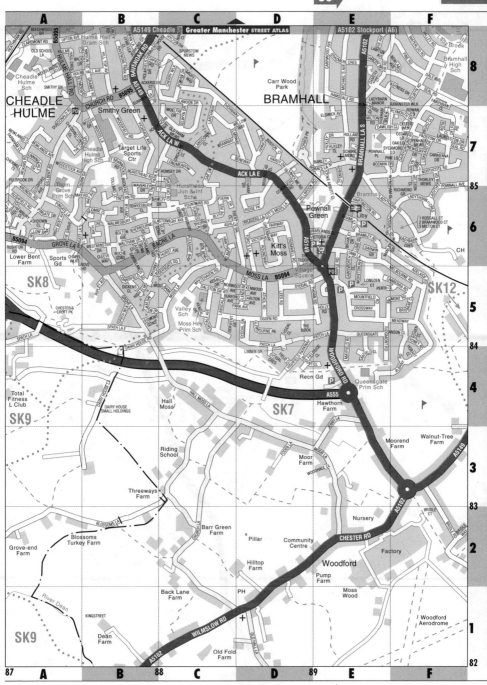

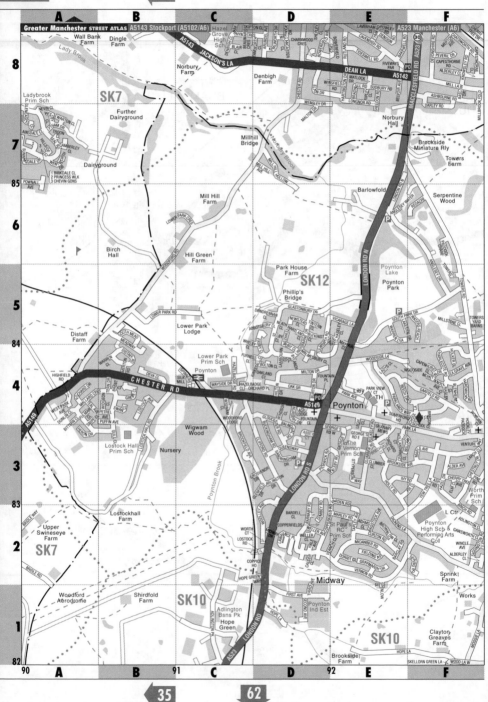

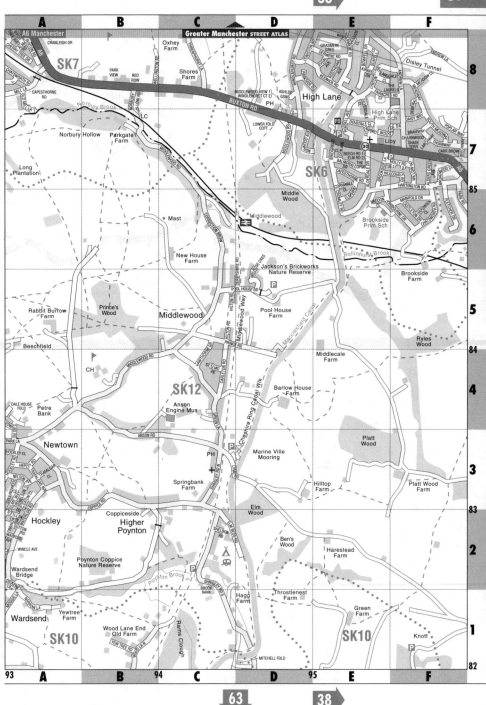

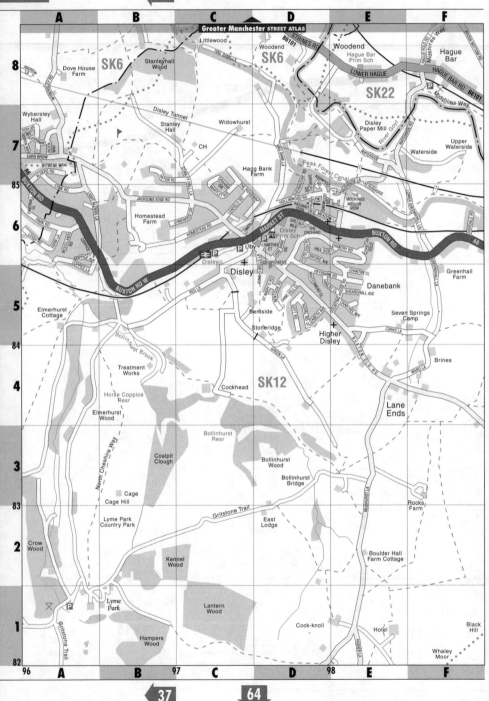

Greater Manchester STREET ATLAS

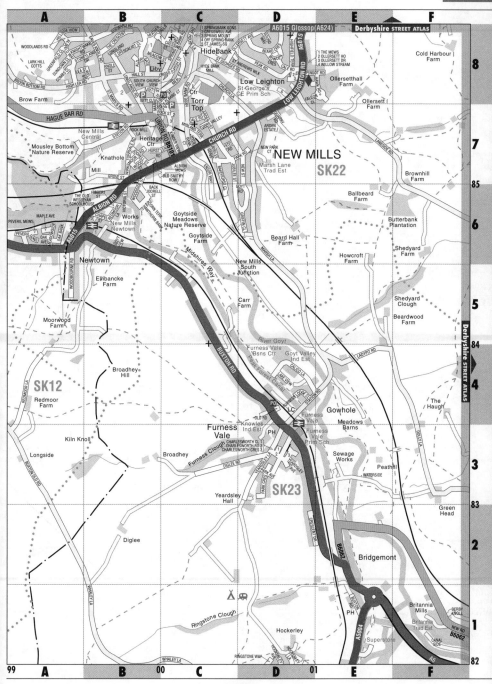

B6
1 Newtown Prim Sch

B8
1 New Mills Prim Sch
2 St Mary's RC Prim Sch

C7
1 FOUNDRY CT
2 LOWER ROCK ST
3 BACK UNION RD
4 LEES MILL

C8
1 New Mills Sch
Bsns & Ent Coll

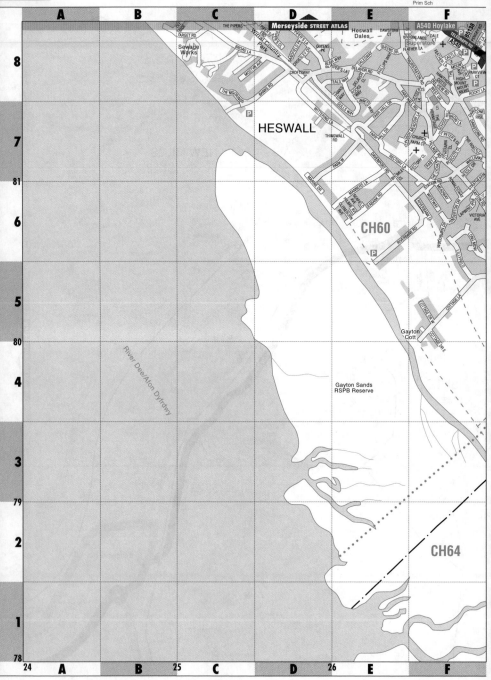

FB
1 STONEWAY CT
2 MAY RD
3 MOUNT CT
4 PYE RD
5 St Peter's CE
   Prim Sch

A540 Hoylake

Heswall Dales

HESWALL

CH60

CH64

Gayton Sands
RSPB Reserve

Gayton Cott

River Dee/Afon Dyfrdwy

Sewage Works

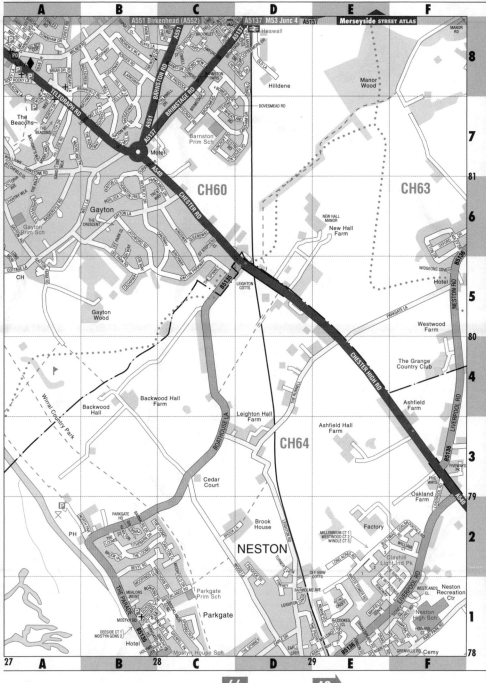

A8
1 DOWNHAM CT
2 BIRCHES HO
3 CHERRY TREE MEWS
4 BEACON CT
5 THE CHASE
6 YEW TREE CT

7 HESWALL POINT

Merseyside STREET ATLAS

A551 Birkenhead (A552)
A5137 M53 Junc 4
Heswall

Hilldene

Manor
Wood

CH60

CH63

The
Beacons

Gayton

NEW HALL
MANOR
New Hall
Farm

Gayton
Wood

Widgeons Covert

Hotel

Westwood
Farm

Leighton
Cotts

The Grange
Country Club

Backwood Hall
Farm

Ashfield
Farm

Backwood
Hall

Leighton Hall
Farm

CH64

Ashfield Hall
Farm

Wirral Country Park

Cedar
Court

Fiveways
Pk

Oakland
Farm

Brook
House

Factory

MILLENNIUM CT 1
WESTWOOD CT 2
WINDLE CT 3

Clayhill
Light Ind Pk

PH

Parkgate
Ho

Westlands
Cl

Neston
Recreation
Ctr

The
Looms

NESTON

Def View
Cotts

Fairholme Ave

Neston
High Sch

Mealors
Went

Parkgate
Prim Sch

Parkgate

DEESIDE CT 1
MOSTYN GDNS 2

Leighton Chase

Cookes

Hotel

Mostyn House Sch

Grenville Rd
Cemy

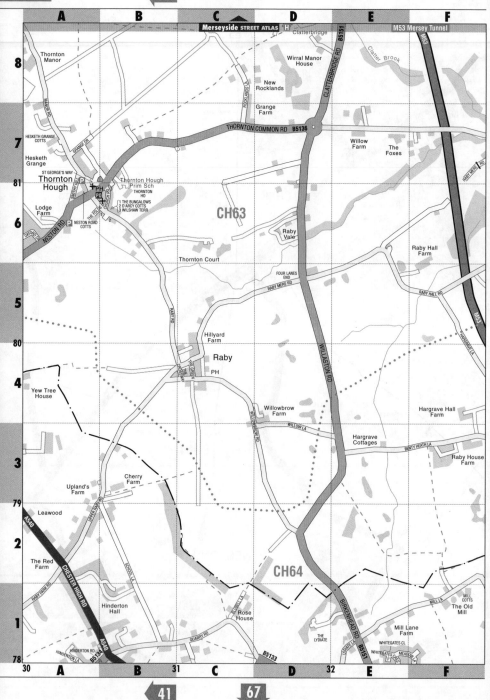

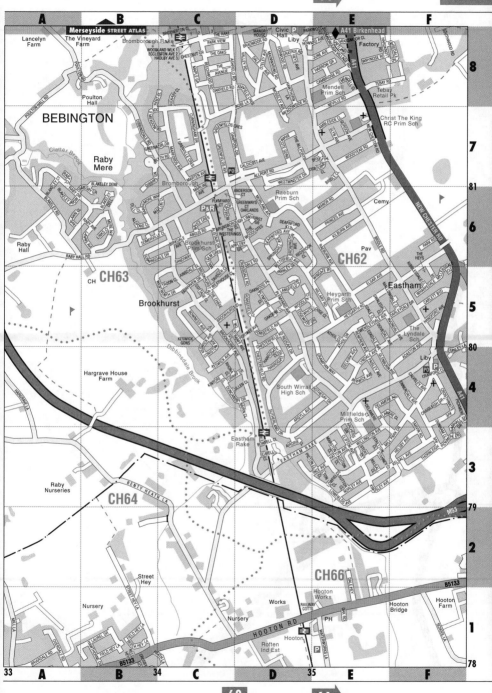

Merseyside STREET ATLAS

BEBINGTON

Raby Mere

CH63

CH64

CH62

CH66

Brookhurst

Eastham

Lancelyn Farm

The Vineyard Farm

Bromborough Rake

Poulton Hall

Clatter Brook

Blakeley Dene

Raby Hall

Hargrave House Farm

Dibbinsdale Brook

Raby Nurseries

Street Hey

Nursery

Nursery

Works

Hooton Works

Roften Ind Est

Hooton

Hooton Bridge

Hooton Farm

Raeburn Prim Sch

Brookhurst Prim Sch

Heygarth Prim Sch

South Wirrall High Sch

Millfields Prim Sch

The Lyndale Sch

Christ The King RC Prim Sch

Mendell Prim Sch

Tebay Retail Pk

Eastham Rake

A41 Birkenhead

NEW CHESTER RD

M53

B5133

HOOTON RD

BENTY HEATH LA

43

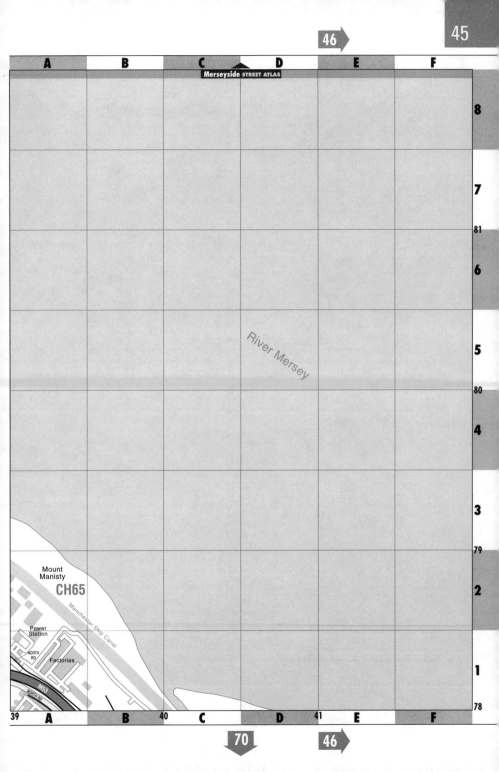

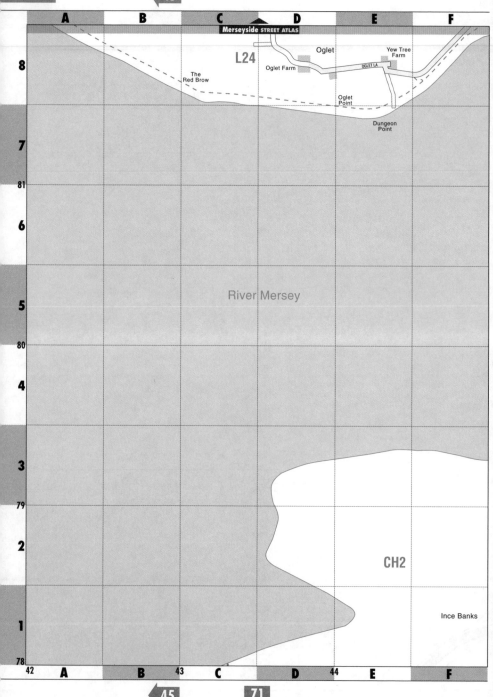

Merseyside STREET ATLAS

Oglet

L24

Yew Tree
Farm

The
Red Brow

Oglet Farm

OGLET LA

Oglet
Point

Dungeon
Point

River Mersey

CH2

Ince Banks

Icehouse
Plantation

Hale Hall

Church Willow
Bed

WITHIN WAY

Hale Park

Willow
Bed

CHURCH RD

L24

Old Pits

LIGHTHOUSE RD

Small Ends

Hale
Head

Lighthouse
(disused)

Hale Head Shore

River Mersey

CH2

WA6

Manchester
Ship Canal

| A | B | C | D | E | F |

8 L24

Docks

Works

1 LINGFIELD HO
2 CUNNINGHAM HO
3 CUNNINGHAM DR

Beacon
Hill

SOUTHLANDS
CT

JOHNS
AVE

ROYDEN AVE

COOMBE DR

HALE VIEW

HILLSIDE AVE

CAMERON AVE

HAZEL AVE

PERRIN AVE

CLARKS TERR

BEACON HILL
VIEW

Recn
Gd

PARK RD

Runcorn Hill
Nature Reserve

HEATH PARK
GR

P

LC

SANDY LA

LANCASTER
AVE

POST OFFICE LA

CANAL SIDE

Weston Point
Prim Sch

7 Weston
Mersey
Locks

Swing
Bridge

WEST RD

BAKER RD

CHURCH
RD

ST LEONARD ST

SYDNEY
ST

SOUTH RD

MATHER AVE

WESTON
CT

WA7

Weston
Point

LYDDALE LA

LC

ROSCOE CRES

CASTNER AVE

CASTNER CT

81 CHESHYRE'S
LA

LYDDALE'S LA

BANKS LA

COLLIER'S
ROW

WESTON
CT
PROSPECT
ROW

60

COMPANY'S CL 1
MONTPELIER AVE 2
LAMBSDALE CL 3

Mast

WESTON
CRES

6 Works

Weaver Navigation

ASHTON CL

CREETA DR

Weston
Village

LAMBSDALE LA

TIDSLEY CRES

BANKES LA

CAVENDISH
FARM RD

A557

5

80 Weaver
Sluices

Weston Marsh
Lock

River Weaver

Works

4

3 Frodsham
Marsh
Farm

ALDER LA

Frodsham Marsh

BROOK FURLONG

79

2 Frodsham Score

Manchester Ship Canal

WA6

1 Jetties

MOORDITCH LA

78

48 | A | B | 49 | C | D | 50 | E | F

River Mersey

Runcorn & Weston Canal (disused)

Manchester Ship Canal

WESTON POINT EXPRESSWAY

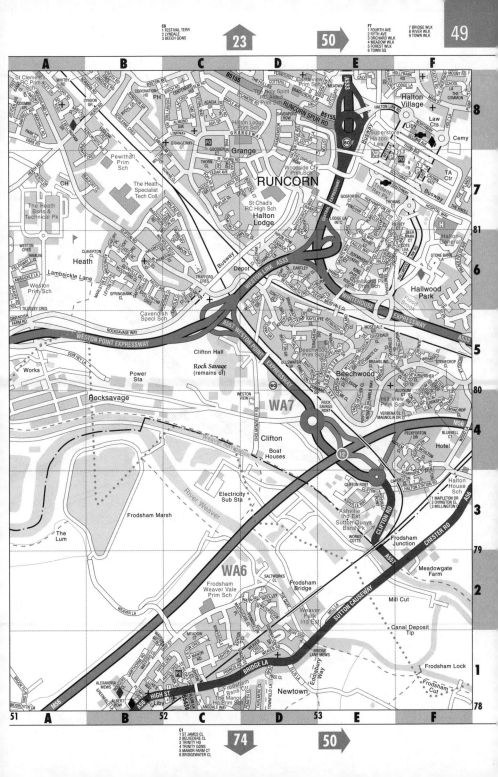

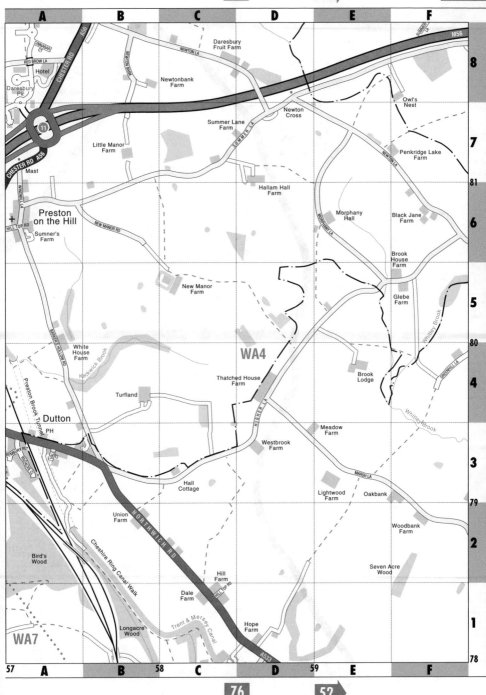

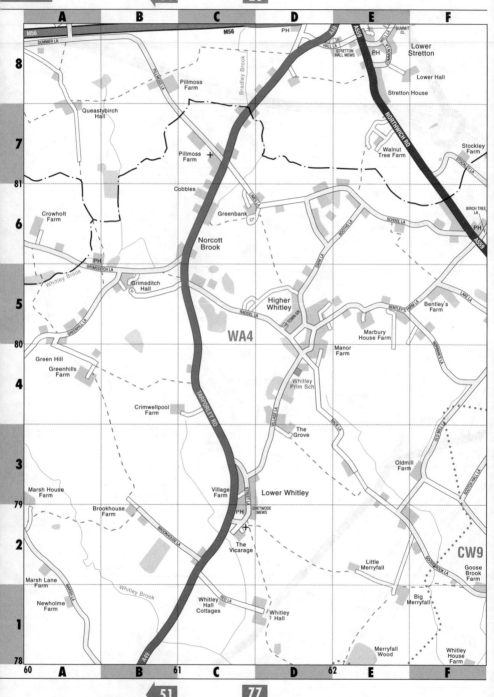

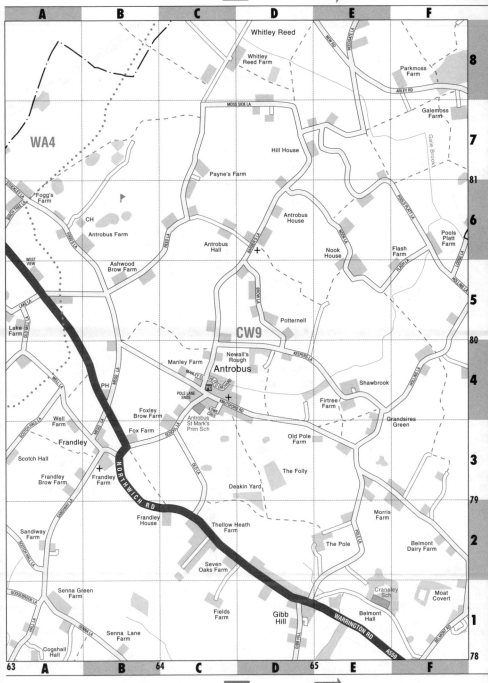

Whitley Reed

Whitley
Reed Farm

Parkmoss
Farm

8

MOSS SIDE LA

ARLEY RD

Galemoss
Farm

WA4

Hill House

7

Payne's Farm

81

Gale Brook

Fogg's
Farm

Antrobus
House

6

CH

Antrobus Farm

Antrobus
Hall

Nook
House

Flash
Farm

Pools
Platt
Farm

Ashwood
Brow Farm

WEST
VIEW

Lake
Farm

Potternell

5

CW9

80

Manley Farm

Newall's
Rough

Antrobus

Shawbrook

4

PH

Pole Lane
Ends

Antrobus
St Mark's
Prim Sch

Firtree
Farm

Grandsires
Green

Well
Farm

Foxley
Brow Farm

Fox Farm

Old Pole
Farm

Frandley

Scotch Hall

The Folly

3

Frandley
Brow Farm

Frandley
Farm

Deakin Yard

79

Sandiway
Farm

Frandley
House

Thellow Heath
Farm

Morris
Farm

Belmont
Dairy Farm

The Pole

2

NORTHWICH RD

Seven
Oaks Farm

Senna Green
Farm

Fields
Farm

Gibb
Hill

Belmont
Hall

Cransley
Sch

Moat
Covert

1

Cogshall
Hall

Senna Lane
Farm

WARRINGTON RD

A559

78

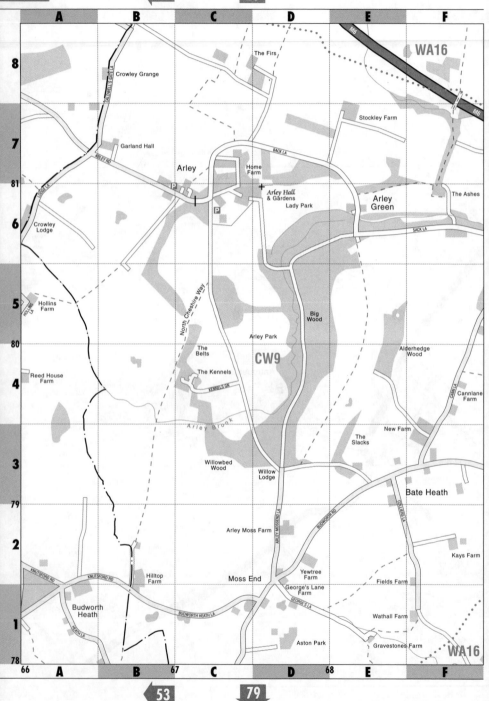

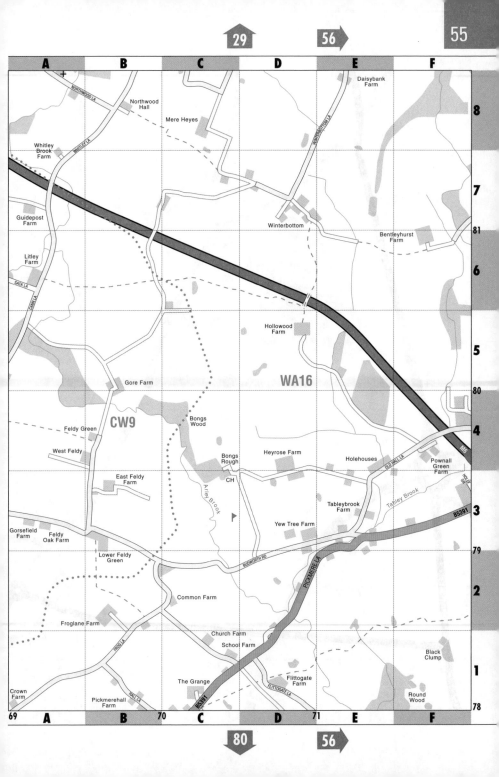

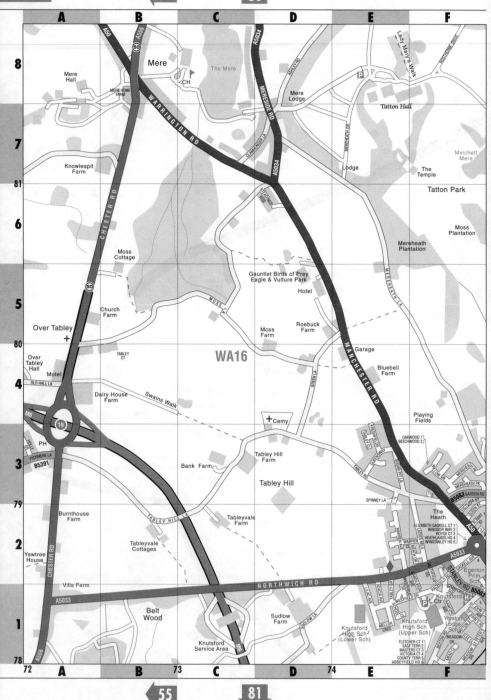

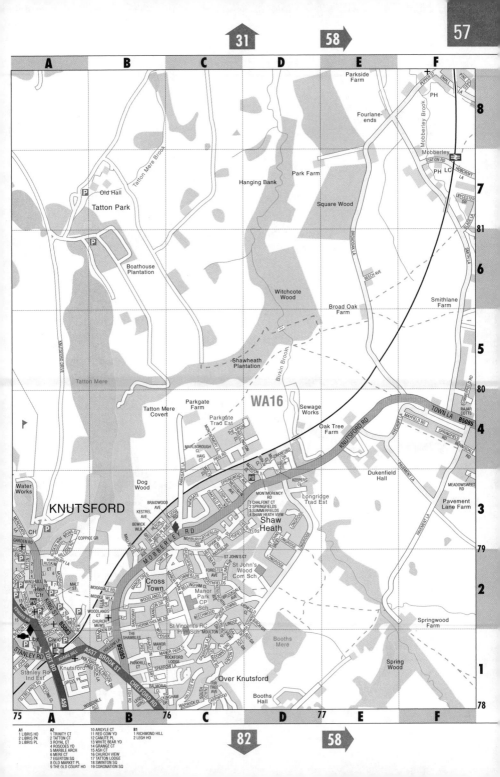

8

Parkside Farm

Fourlane-ends

Mobberley Brook

PH

Mobberley

Station Rd   LC

PH

Horcroft La

Leycester Dr

7

81

Old Hall

Tatton Park

Hanging Bank

Park Farm

Square Wood

Rhododka La

Beech Ave

Smithlane Farm

6

Boathouse Plantation

Witchcote Wood

Broad Oak Farm

Knutsford Drive

5

Shawheath Plantation

Birkin Brook

Tatton Mere

80

Tatton Mere Covert

Parkgate Farm

Parkgate Trad Est

WA16

Sewage Works

Oak Tree Farm

Knutsford Rd

Mayfield Rd

Town La

B5085

Stamfield Rd

Rajar Cotts

4

Water Works

KNUTSFORD

Dog Wood

Braidwood Ave

Kestrel Ave

Bewick Wlk

Montmorency Rd
1 CHALFONT CT
2 SPRINGFIELDS
3 SUMMERFIELDS
4 SHAW HEATH VIEW

Shaw Heath

Longridge Trad Est

Keepers Cl

Dukenfield Hall

Meadowsweet Rd

Pavement Lane Farm

3

79

Mobberley Rd

Cross Town

St John's Ct

St John's Wood Com Sch

Manor Park CP Sch

Springwood Farm

2

Chelford Rd

St Vincent's RC Prim Sch

Booths Mere

Spring Wood

1

Civic Hall
Lib

Stanley Rd Ind Est

Knutsford

A50

Over Knutsford

Fir Tree Ave

Booths Hall

78

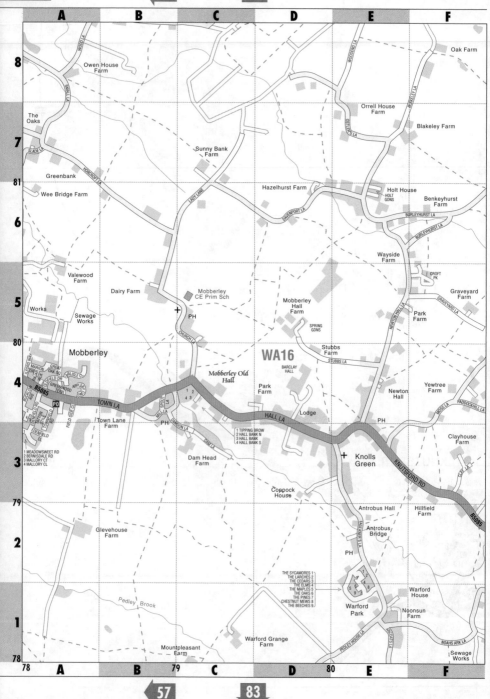

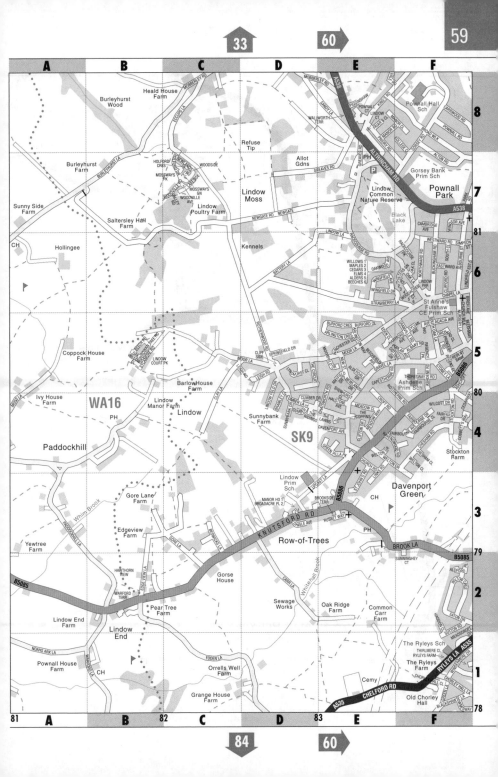

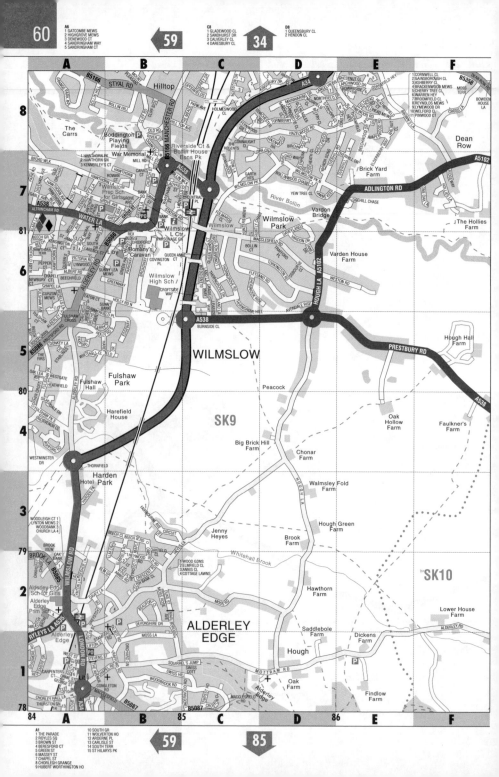

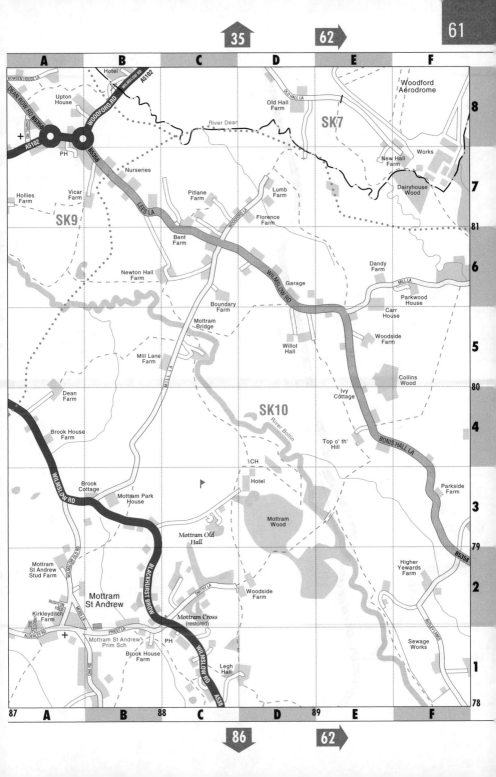

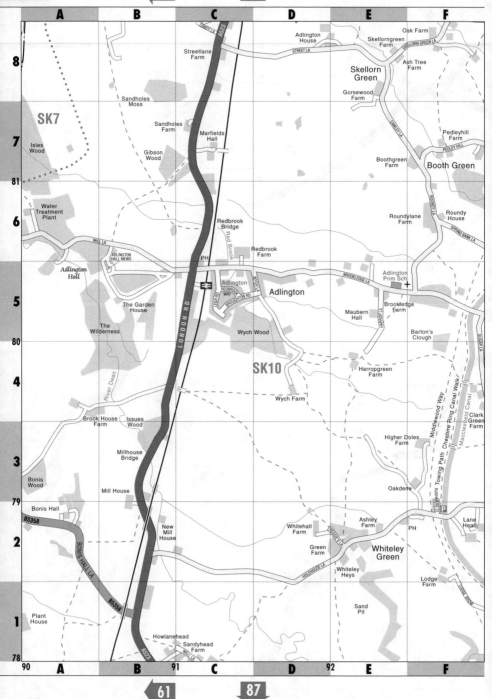

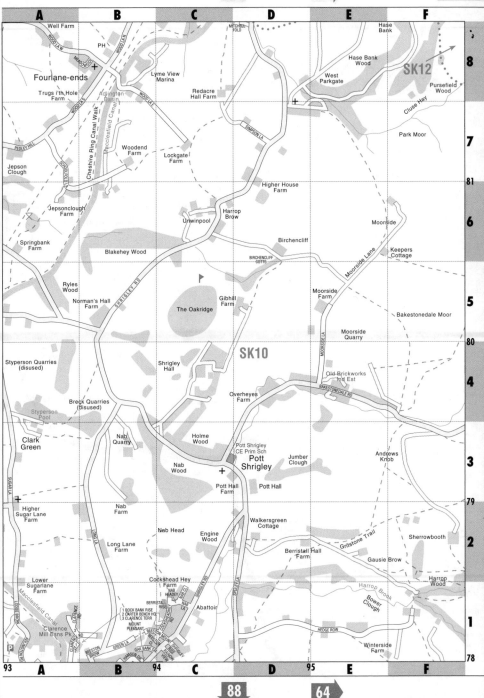

SK12

SK10

Well Farm
PH
Fourlane-ends
Trugs i'th Hole Farm
Lyme View Marina
Mitchell Fold
Hase Bank
Hase Bank Wood
West Parkgate
Cluse Hay
Pursefield Wood
Park Moor
Redacre Hall Farm
Addington Basin
Woodend Farm
Lockgate Farm
Simpson La
Higher House Farm
Moorside
Jepson Clough
Jepsonclough Farm
Springbank Farm
Unwinpool
Harrop Brow
Blakehey Wood
Birchencliff
Birchencliff Cotts
Moorside Lane
Keepers Cottage
Ryles Wood
Norman's Hall Farm
The Oakridge
Gibhill Farm
Moorside Farm
Bakestonedale Moor
Styperson Quarries (disused)
Shrigley Hall
Moorside Quarry
Old Brickworks Ind Est
Breck Quarries (disused)
Bakestonedale Rd
Styperson Pool
Nab Quarry
Overheyes Farm
Clark Green
Holme Wood
Nab Wood
Pott Shrigley CE Prim Sch
Pott Shrigley
Jumber Clough
Andrews Knob
Higher Sugar Lane Farm
Nab Farm
Pott Hall Farm
Pott Hall
Nab Head
Engine Wood
Walkersgreen Cottage
Long Lane Farm
Gritstone Trail
Sherrowbooth
Berristall Hall Farm
Gausie Brow
Lower Sugarlane Farm
Cockshead Hey Farm
Abattoir
Harrop Wood
Macclesfield Canal
1 BOCK BANK RISE
2 CARTER BENCH HO
3 CLARENCE TERR
Mount Pleasant
Harrop Brook
Bower Clough
Clarence Mill Bsns Pk
Hedge Row
Winterside Farm

Cheshire Ring Canal Walk
Macclesfield Canal

93 94 95

78 79 80 81

63
38

	A	B	C	D	E	F

8

Lyme Park

SK12

Higher Moor

Whaley Moor

Knightslow Wood

Handleybarn Farm

Cliff

Knights Low

7

Bow Stones

Bowstonegate

Park Moor

Browside Farm

Holme Wood

Bailey's Farm

Cornfield Farm

81

Sweet Hill

Hole House

6

Handley Fold Farm

Sponds Hill

Gritstone Trail

Lower Cliff Farm

5

Hollow Sponds

Higher Cliff Farm

Sponds

KISHFIELD LA.

B5470

80

Reed Hill

SK23

PADDOCK LA

PADDOCK CL

PLATTS ST

SK10

Kettleshulme

4

Back Sponds

PH

Kettleshulme St James CE Prim Sch

Spout House Farm

Manor Farm

BAKESTONEDALE RD

Brink Farm

The Reed Farm

SIDE END LA

Ellis Bank

Slaters Green Farm

Side End Farm

3

MACCLESFIELD RD

Brink Brow

Gnathole Brook Midfield

Thorneycroft Farm

79

Charles Head

Neighbourway Farm

Whitelands

Carr Clough

2

Charles Head Farm

Todd Brook

Near Carr Farm

Further Harrop Farm

Harrop Wood

Harrop House Farm

Tunstead Knoll Farm

Harrop Brook

Black Brook

1

Dunge Clough

Harrop Fold Farm

B5470

78

96	A		B	97	C		D	98	E		F

63
89

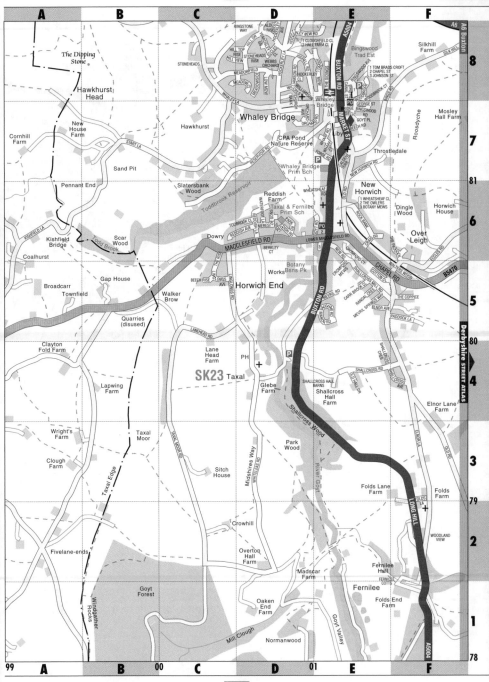

E8
1 MARLOWE RD
2 POPLAR WEINT
3 HADDON HO
4 DENWALL HO
5 ASHFIELD HO
6 HARGREAVE HO

7 THE CROSS
8 The Royal Sh Arc
9 ROKLIS GRANGE
10 SCHOLAR'S CT

F7
1 NORMANS COTTS

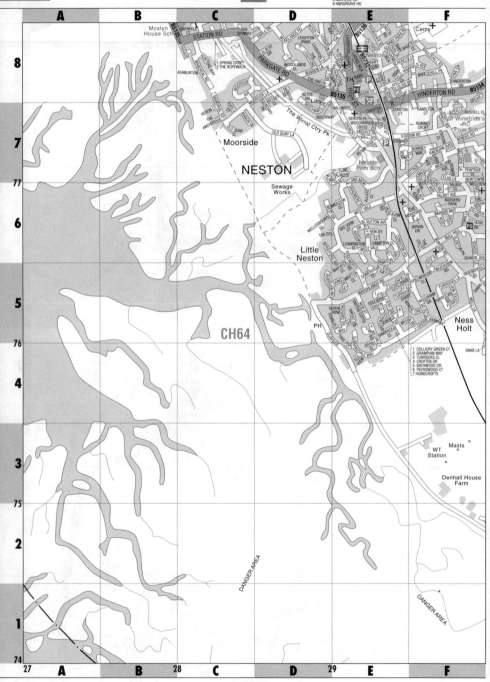

Mostyn House Sch
GRENFELL RD
STATION RD
THE SPINNEY
1 SPRING CROFT
2 THE ROPEWALK
PARKGATE RD
WOODLANDS
LEIGHTON PARK
ASHBURTON
MOORSIDE AVE
NESS
The Wirral Ctry Pk
HALLWOOD
Libr
B5135
HIGH ST
B5136
Neston
Neston Baby Gdns
BLACKEY'S LA
B5138
B5132
B5134
HINDERTON RD
Cemy
St Winefride's RC Prim Sch

Moorside
THE ANCHORAGE
OLD QUAY
OLD QUAY LA
BEECHWAY
SERVITE PL
WOODWARD'S COTTS
STEEPLE RD
CHESTER
STANTON CT
HAMILTON
ROMNEY CT

NESTON
ELGIN WAY
STANLEY
STADIUM RD
ROMNEY WAY
RAEBURN AVE

Sewage Works
FLINT MDW
ALANS MDW
Neston Prim Sch
COTTAGE LA
MORLAND
FLAG LA
TALBOT CT
YEWTREE CL
NEWTOWN
MELLOR

Little Neston
WEST VALE
THE MEADOWS
AVON CL
HENLEY
HAMPTON CL
GIRVIN DR
BADGER BAIT
BADGERS PARK
THE GREEN

LEAMINGTON CL
WEST VALE
WINDTON
BULL HILL
SCHOOL AVE
OLD SCHOOL

SEVEN ROW
COLLIERY GREEN
TURROCKS
WOODHAM
FURROCKS CL
SNAB LA
Ness Holt

PH

DANGER AREA

CH64

1 COLLIERY GREEN CT
2 GRAMPIAN WAY
3 TURROCKS CL
4 CROFTEN DR
5 BATHWOOD DR
6 PEERSWOOD CT
7 HOMECROFTS

WT Station
Masts

Denhall House Farm

DANGER AREA

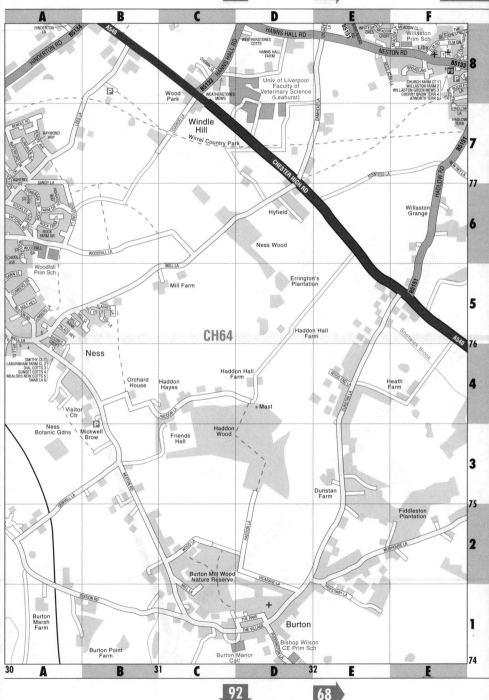

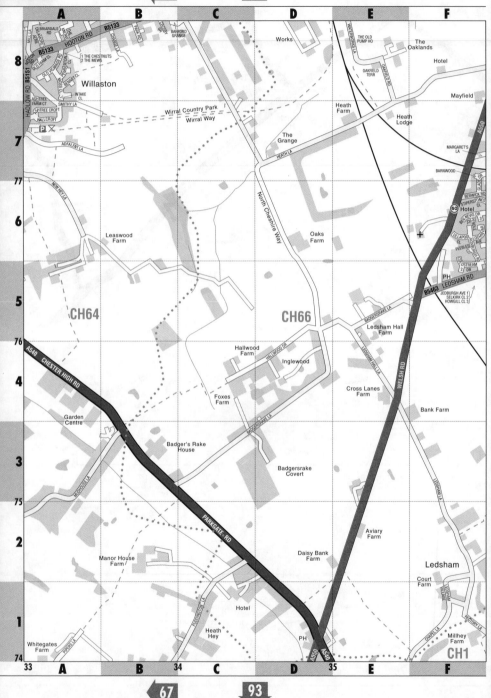

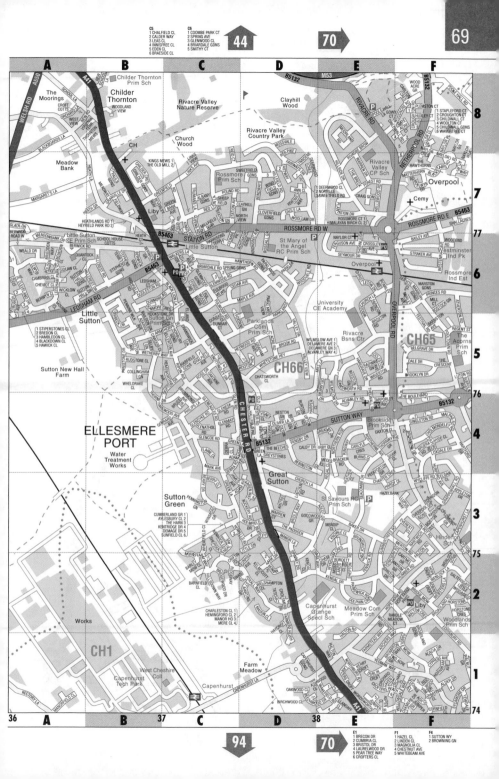

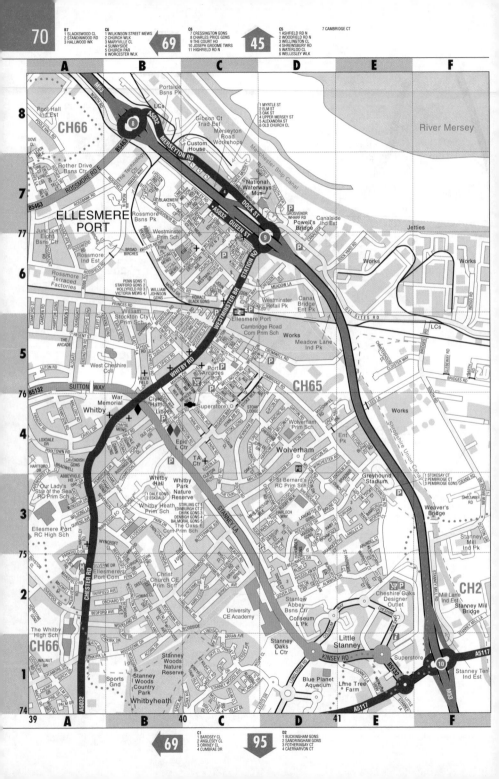

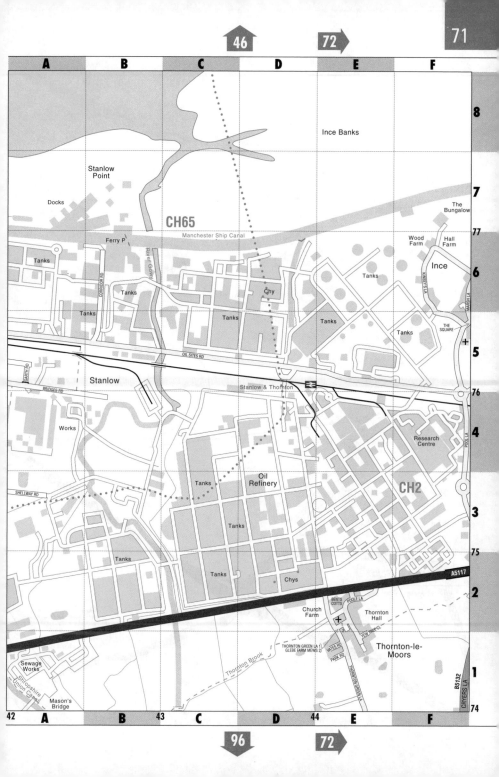

71 47

8

Manchester Ship Canal

Canal Deposit Dump

Works

7

Holme Farm

77

Ince Marshes

Sewage Works

6

KINSEY'S LA

Hoolpool Gutter

MARSH LA

RAKE LA

Ince
PH

THE SQUARE

CH2

Works

Helsby West Cheshire Junction

Hornsmill Brook

5

76

Ince Orchards Ince & Elton
STATION RD

CHERRY TREE CL

M56

WA6

MOUNT PLEASANT

PO

ORCHARD PARK LA
ORCHARD PK

4

Elton Liby
Elton Prim Sch

OLIVE FARM

THE COURTYARD

CHAPEL MEWS
PH

ORK LA
MANN

REDWOOD DR

Sewage Works

Elton

1 BIRCHWOOD CL
2 SORBUS CL

THE PADDOCKS

FARNDALE DR

RYECROFT

WHITEFIELDS

GREENFIELD GDNS

BLACKTHORNE

BIRCHFIELD

MULBERRY

OSIER CL

PARKMOOR

MANOR VIEW

3

MARSHFIELD RD

CHERRY CL

BIRCH GR

FERNDALE AVE

LAWNSWOOD DR

AINSLEY VIEW

MAPLE VIEW

PARKLAND DR

Elton Green

ELM GR

WILLOW GR

LAURELS FARM CT 1
TOWNFIELD VILLAS 2

OLD HALL

75

POND COTTS

A5117

New Dairy Farm

Chester Services

Motel

Lower Hapsford Hall

Sewage Works

2

B5132

GREEN LA

14

Jessamine Farm

HAPSFORD MEWS

DALECROFT

HAPSDALE VIEW

Hapsford

1

M56

COMMON LA

HAPSFORD LA

A5117

CHESTER RD

A56

74

71 97

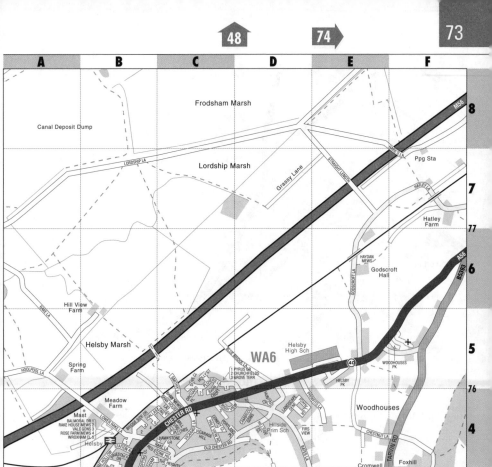

8

Frodsham Marsh

Canal Deposit Dump

LORDSHIP LA

Lordship Marsh

Grassy Lane

STRAIGHT LENGTH

M56

WADE'S LA

Ppg Sta

7

HATLEY LA

Hatley Farm

77

HAYDAN MEWS

Godscroft Hall

6

Hill View Farm

Helsby Marsh

Spring Farm

HOOLPOOL LA

GODSCROFT LA

Helsby High Sch

WA6

WOODHOUSES PK

40

HELSBY PK

Woodhouses

5

76

Meadow Farm

CHESTER RD

Mast

BALMORAL DR 1
RAKE HOUSE MEWS 2
VALE GDNS 3
ROSE FARM MEWS 4
WROXHAM CL 5

Helsby

BLUE BRIDGE LA

1 PYRUS GR
2 CHURCHFIELDS
3 GROVE TERR

Hillside Prim Sch

FIRS VIEW

CHESTNUT LA

Cromwell Court

Foxhill

TARVIN RD

4

STATION RD

HAWKSTONE GR

THE BEECHES
VICARAGE HILL

Old Chester Road

BATE LA

Foxhill Wood

Helsby

Helsby Hill

Liby

KINGS
QUEENS DR
PARKFIELD DR

LOWER ROBIN HOOD LA

Firs Farm

3

75

SPRINGFIELDS 1
GREENWAY CL 2

FRESHMEADOW LA

Helsby Quarry Nature Reserve

HOLLY BANK

FOXGLOVE DELL

Alderhall

THE RIDGEWAY

2

Hornsmill Brook

CROSLAND DR

GEORGE CL

CALLENDER GDNS

MERE VIEW

NESTON CL

THE ARBOUR

WINDSOR DR

STEPHENS

NEWFIELD TERR

THE ROCK

1 CHAPEL VIEW
2 BRITTANNIA RD
3 HOMEWAY
4 HEMLEGH VALE
5 MARLBOROUGH DR
6 BACK CROSLAND TERR
7 LONGSTER CL
8 THE ORCHARD

Rock Farm

BACK LA

BURDING LA

COMMONSIDE

Commonside Farm

Sandstone Trail

1

CROWN BLDGS

RUTHIN WLK 1
BRAMLEY WLK 2
MORTON AVE 3

PH

Horn's Mill Prim Sch

PRIMROSE LA

Walnut Tree Farm

Poplar Tree Farm

B5393 FRODSHAM RD

Alvanley

Alvanley Prim Sch

MANLEY RD

Bowlingalley Farm

Cliff Farm

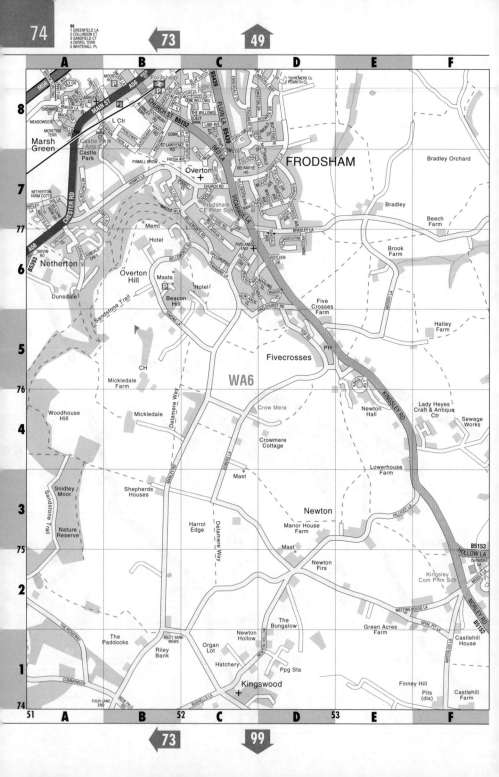

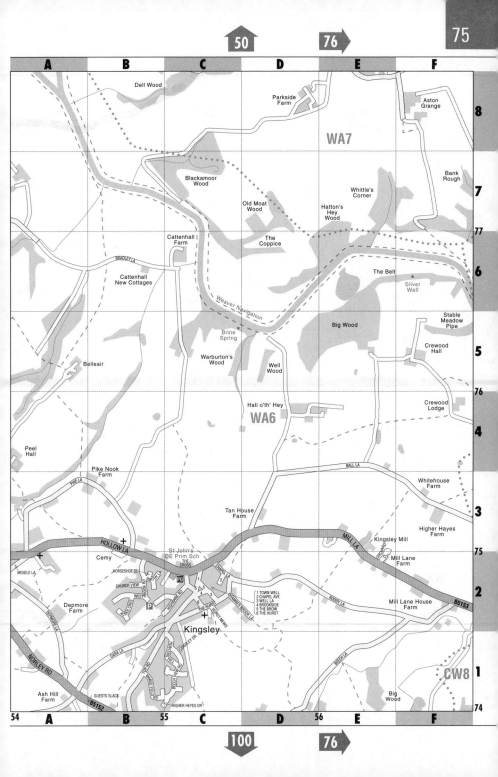

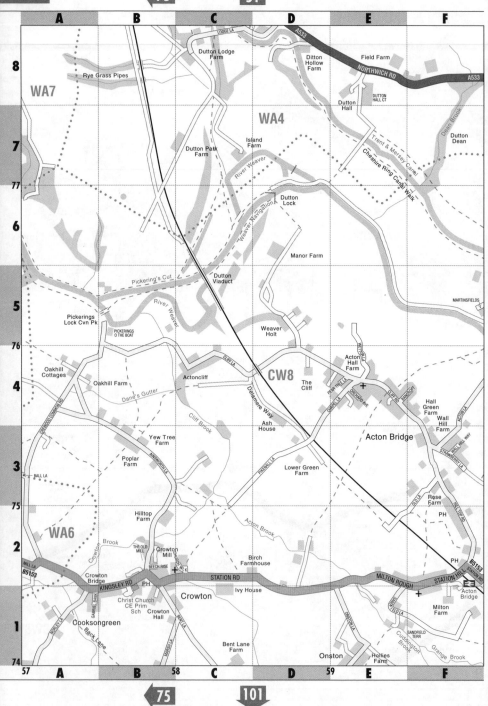

WA7

WA4

8

Rye Grass Pipes

Dutton Lodge Farm

LODGE LA

A533

Ditton Hollow Farm

Field Farm

NORTHWICH RD

A533

Dutton Hall

DUTTON HALL CT

7

Dutton Park Farm

Island Farm

River Weaver

Trent & Mersey Canal

Cheshire Ring Canal Walk

Dutton Dean

Dean Brook

77

Dutton Lock

Weaver Navigation

6

Manor Farm

MARTINSFIELDS

Pickering's Cut

Dutton Viaduct

River Weaver

Weaver Holt

5

Pickerings Lock Cvn Pk

PICKERINGS O THE BOAT

Acton Hall Farm

WELL LA

76

Oakhill Cottages

Oakhill Farm

Dane's Gutter

Actoncliff

GLEB LA

Delamere Way

CW8

The Cliff

PEAR TREE LA

CHAPEL LA

BIRCHDALE AVE

CLIFF RD

BANCROFT

Hall Green Farm

Wall Hill Farm

HESTER LA

4

Cliff Brook

Ash House

Acton Bridge

OAKHILL COMMON RD

Yew Tree Farm

Poplar Farm

AINSWORTH LA

Lower Green Farm

PREHM LA

STRAWBERRY LA

WALL HILL WAY

3

BALL LA

Rose Farm

PH

GLEB LA

HILLTOP RD

75

WA6

Hilltop Farm

Acton Brook

2

Crowton Brook

THE OLD MILL

Crowton Mill

Birch Farmhouse

Milton Farm

PH

MILTON ROUGH

STATION HILL

STATION RD

B5153

BEECH RISE

CHURCH WLK

B5153

MILL LA

Crowton Bridge

KINGSLEY RD

PH

STATION RD

Ivy House

Acton Bridge

SANDFIELD TERR

+

1

Cooksongreen

Christ Church CE Prim Sch

Crowton Hall

Crowton

Bent Lane Farm

Onston

Hollies Farm

Cuddington Brook

Grange Brook

GABRIEL BANK

Back Lane

MARSH LA

KINGSLEY RD

ONSTON LA

GLEB LA

74

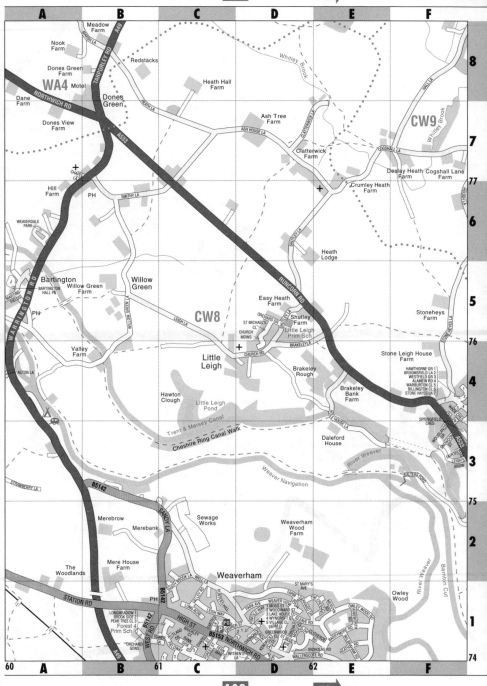

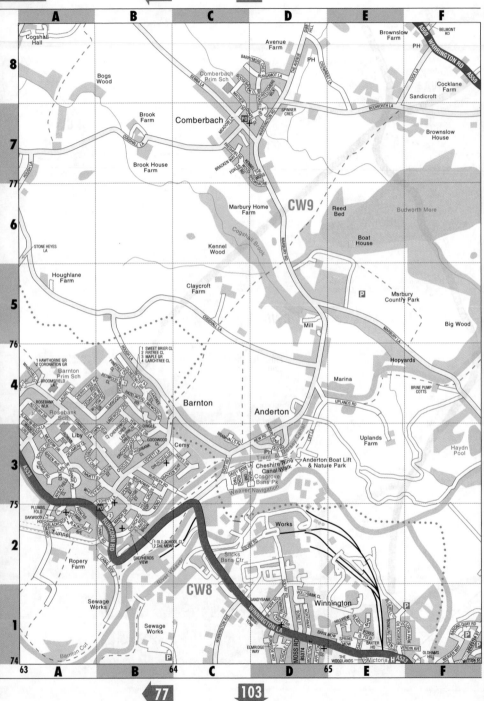

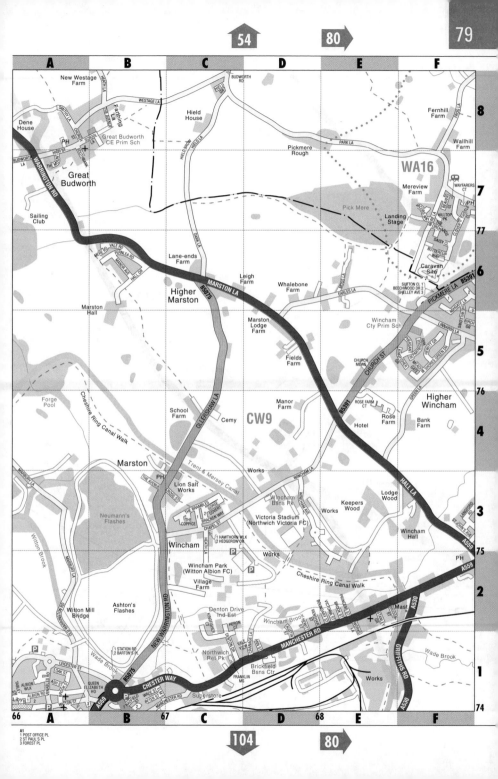

A1
1 POST OFFICE PL
2 ST PAUL'S PL
3 FOREST PL

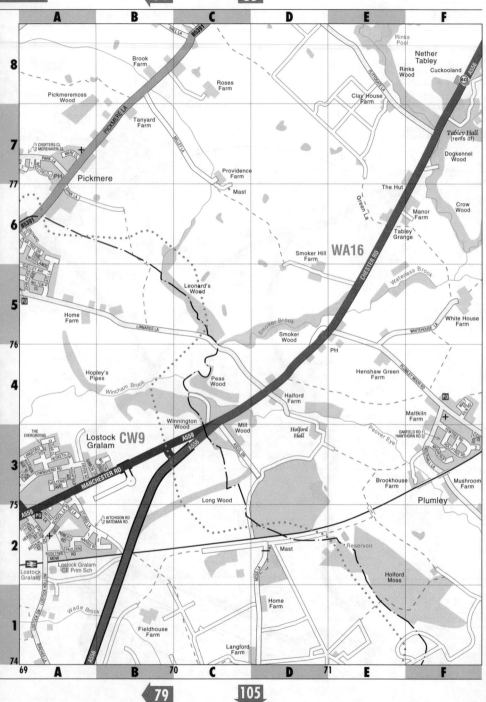

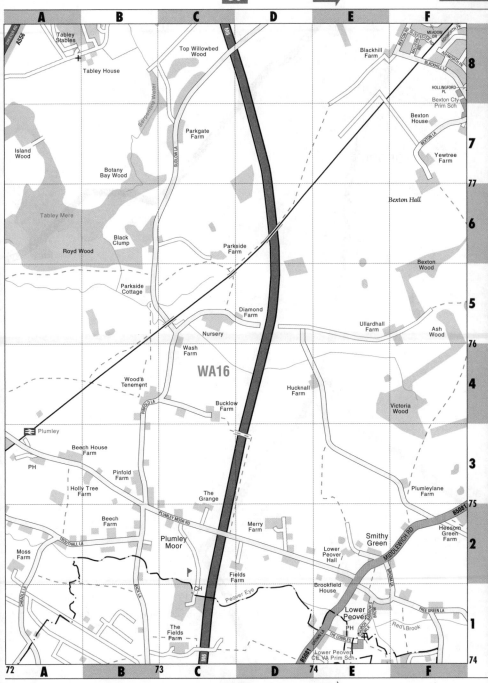

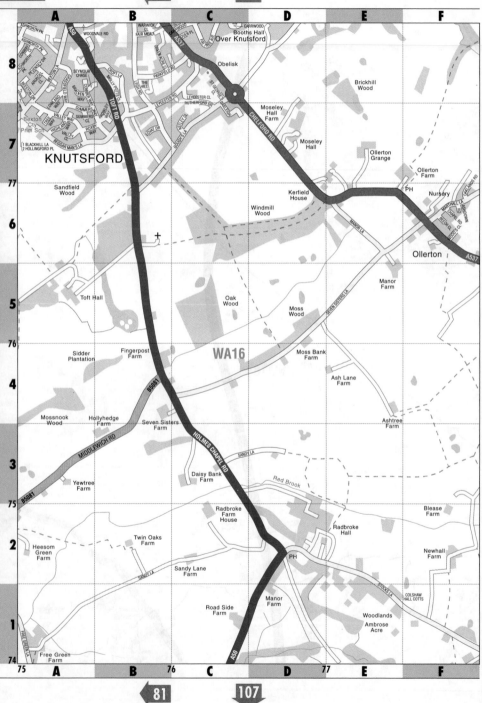

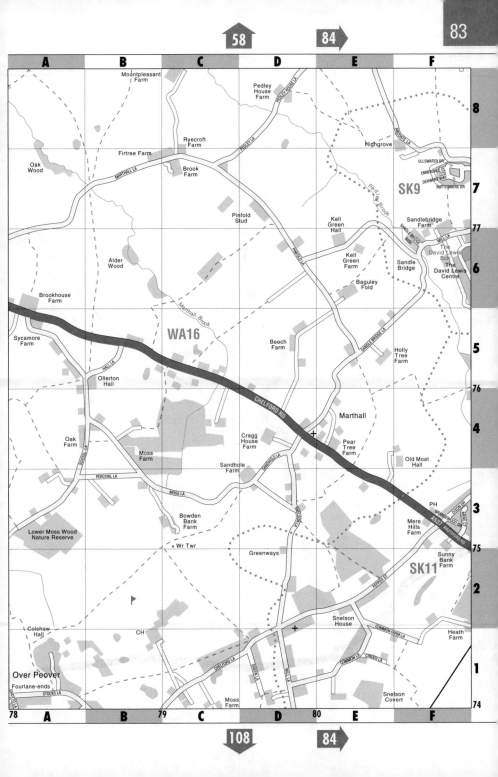

A B C D E F

8

WA16

BUTTERMERE DR

Heathgate Farm

7

Manor Farm

Ivy House

SK9

Sandpit Farm

Little Moss Farm

Tanyard Farm

A535

FODEN LA

Oswald Farm

ABBERLEY HALL

Field's Farm

GREEN LA

PH

WARFORD CRES
MERRYMAN'S LA

77

The David Lewis Sch

Warford Hall Farm

Dane Villa

CHELFORD RD

Walton Farm

ORCHARD CRES

MILL LA
ANCOATS LA
CONISTON DR
WARFORD LA

6

The David Lewis Centre

Warford Hall

Mary Dendy Unit

H

Grogram Cottage

SOSSMOSS LA

WELL ROW

Dog Hole Wood

Stelfoxes

Sossmoss Wood

Dean Green

Gatley Green Farm

SAND LA

5

Peckmill Bottoms

Wyche's Farm

NURSERY LA

76

Peck Mill Farm

Lomas's Bottom

Corbishley Bridge

Sossmoss Hall

SK10

Heawood Hall Farm

4

Firtree Farm

GREEN LA

Callwood's Moss

Corbishley

Heawood Hall

WOODLAND END
MILLBANK
BROOM'S
WOODFIN CT
BRANDS CT
DIXON RD
BUSBY ACRE
HOLE'S LA
WYCH CRES
BRAMPTON RD
WHA
WOODFIN CROFT
CHAPEL CROFT

Line Pits

Roadside Farm

Sandle Heath

Chandler's Farm

BRITTLE LA

3

Chelford CE Prim Sch

P
CASTLE CT

SK11

ALDERLEY RD

Yarwoods

ELMSTEAD RD
ROBIN LA
ROBIN CL

75

A537

Chelford

DIXON CT

Mere Farm

BRITTLE LA

2

KNUTSFORD RD

Chelford

George's Wood

STUB LA

Bollington Pits

COMMON FARM LA

Yewtree Cottages

CHELFORD RDBT

Bloor's Pits

1

PEOVER LA

CHELFORD RD
Knowsley Farm

ASH LA

Dumville's Farm

Fallows Hall Farm

A537

HOLMES CHAPEL RD

A535

PO

Willow Gaff

74

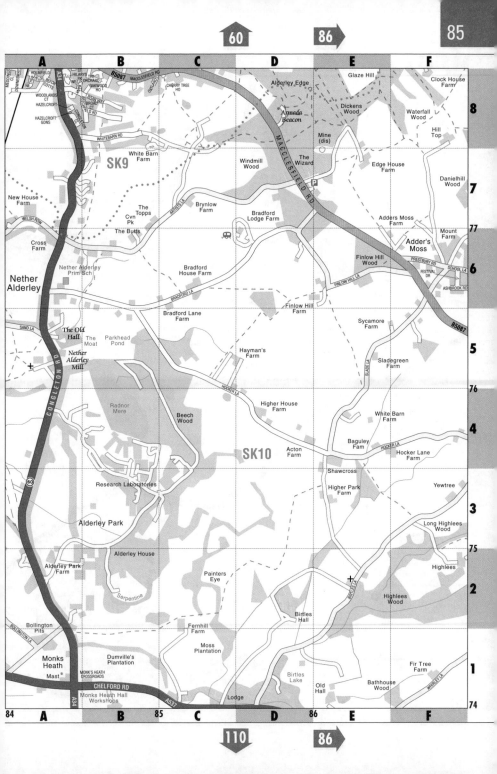

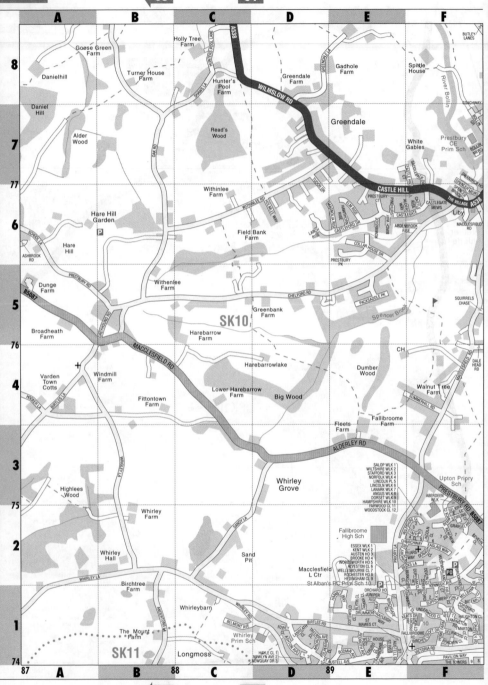

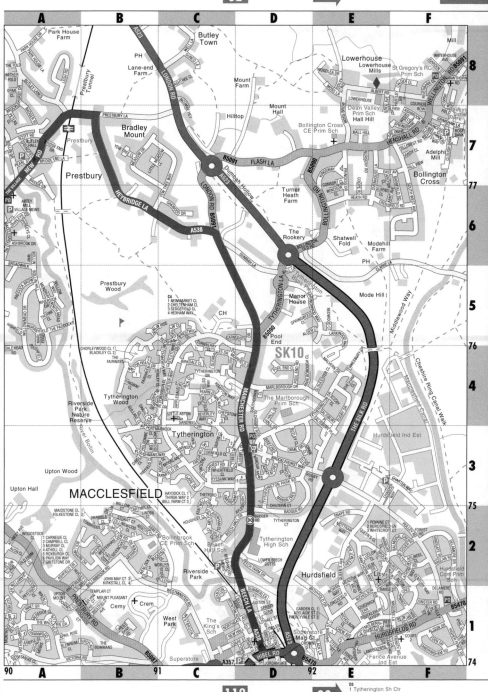

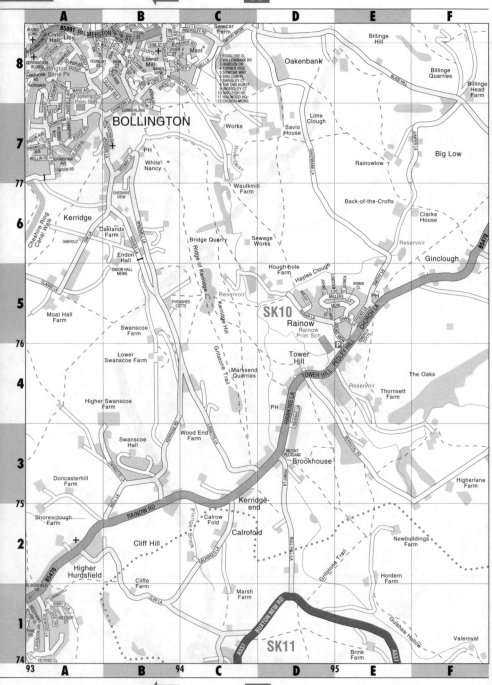

BOLLINGTON

1 FOXGLOVE CL
2 WILLOWBANK DR
3 HANSON DR
4 TURNER RISE
5 SOWCAR WAY
6 SHELDON PL
7 SHRIGLEY CT
8 THE OWLHURST
9 INGERSLEY CT
10 OAKLEIGH HO
11 HALWOOD HO
12 CHURCH MEWS

Round Gons
Civic Hall
Libv
B5091
PALMERSTON ST
QUEEN ST
STORE
INGERSLEY RD
Sawcar Farm
Billinge Hill

Oakenbank

Billinge Quarries

Billinge Head Farm

CORONATION BLDGS
Hawthorn Rd
Thornway
Adlington Bsns Pk
Lower Mill
Nancy View
Mast

Works

Lime Clough

Savio House

BLAZE HILL

St John's CE Prim Sch

CUMBERLAND DR

BOLLINGTON

River Dean

Rainowlow

JUMPER LA

Big Low

White Nancy

Waulkmill Farm

Back-of-the-Crofts

Endor Ave
Swanscoe Ave
Hollin Rd
Grimshaw La
Dawson Rd

PH

Cheshire View

Kerridge

Cheshire Ring Canal Walk

Oaklands Farm

OAKFOLD

Bridge Quarry

Sewage Works

Reservoir

Clarke House

Ginclough

B5470

Endon Hall

ENDON HALL MEWS

Ridge of Kerridge

Hough-hole Farm

Hayles Clough

Reservoir

Clarke La

Moat Hall Farm

FIVEASHES COTTS

Kerridge Hill

NAAR LA

ROBIN CL

SETTLE CL

PH

SK10

Rainow
Rainow Prim Sch

MILLERS

CHURCH LA

Swanscoe Farm

Gritstone Trail

Reservoir

Lower Swanscoe Farm

Marksend Quarries

Tower Hill

The Oaks

Thornsett Farm

Higher Swanscoe Farm

PH

TOWER HILL

HAWKINS LA

PEDLEY HILL

Reservoir

BERRISTAL RD

Swanscoe Hall

Wood End Farm

LIDGETTS LA

CHURCH LA

MOUNT PLEASANT

Brookhouse

Higherlane Farm

Doncasterhill Farm

SWANSCOE LA

MELLA LA

RAINOW RD

Plunge Brook

Calrow Fold

Kerridge-end

Calrofold

BULL HILL LA

Newbuildings Farm

Shoresclough Farm

Cliff Hill

CALROFOLD LA

Gritstone Trail

Hordern Farm

Higher Hursdfield

HURDSFIELD RD

Cliffe Farm

CLIFF LA

Marsh Farm

Valeroyal

B5470

SPRINGHILL
BIBBY LA
HILLSIDE CT
PINE RD

TELFORD CL

BUXTON NEW RD

A537

SK11

Gulshaw Hollow

Brink Farm

A537

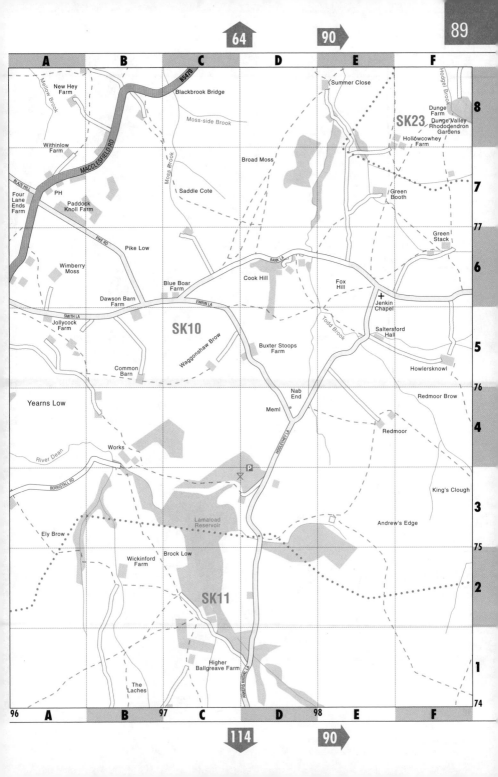

89

65

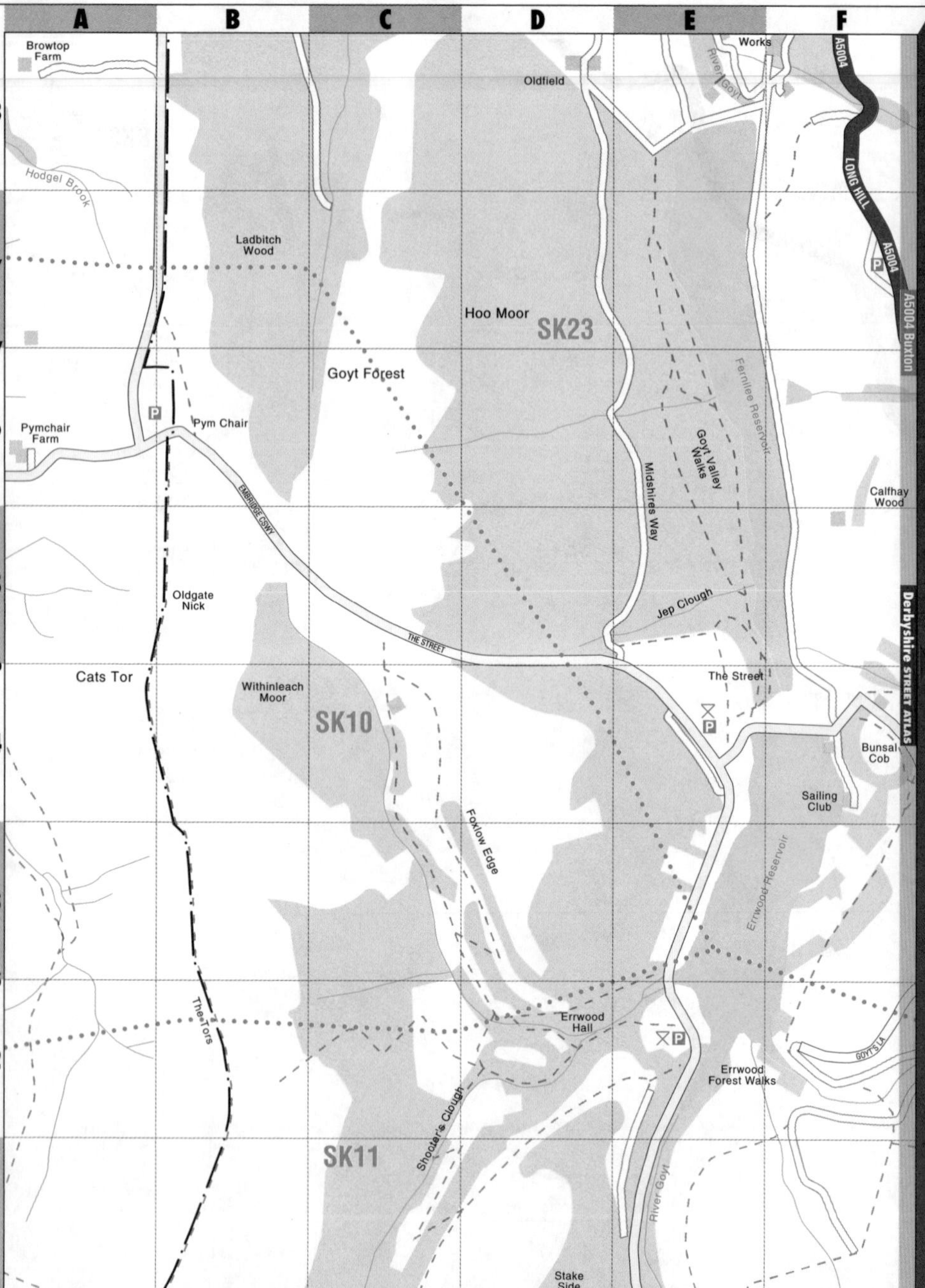

A B C D E F

Browtop Farm

Oldfield

Works

A5004

Hodge Brook

LONG HILL

A5004

8

A5004 Buxton

Ladbitch Wood

7

Hoo Moor

SK23

77

Fernilee Reservoir

Goyt Forest

Goyt Valley Walks

6

Pymchair Farm

P

Pym Chair

Midshires Way

Calfhay Wood

EMBRIDGE CSWY

Derbyshire STREET ATLAS

5

Oldgate Nick

Jep Clough

THE STREET

76

Cats Tor

The Street

Withinleach Moor

P

SK10

Bunsal Cob

4

Foxlow Edge

Sailing Club

Errwood Reservoir

3

75

Errwood Hall

The Tors

2

P

Errwood Forest Walks

GOYT'S LA

Shooter's Clough

River Goyt

SK11

1

River Goyt

74

Stake Side

99 A B 00 C D 01 E F

89

115

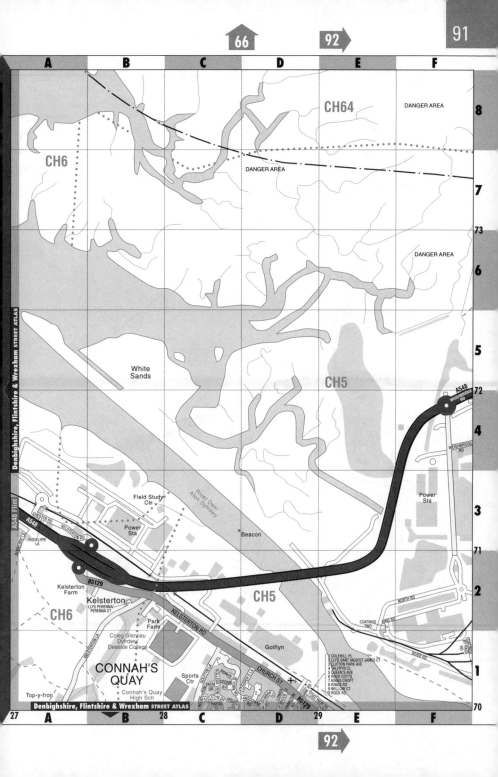

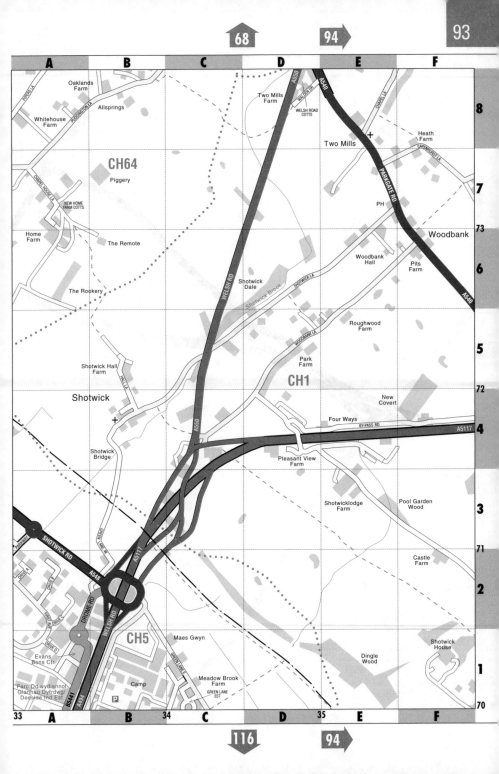

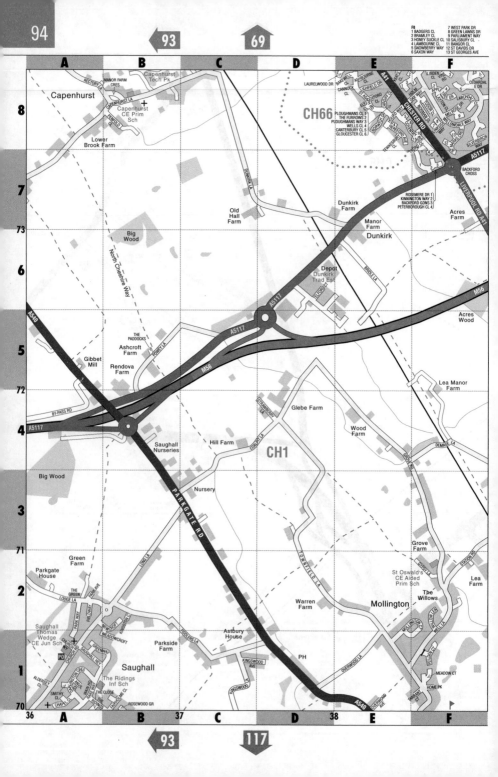

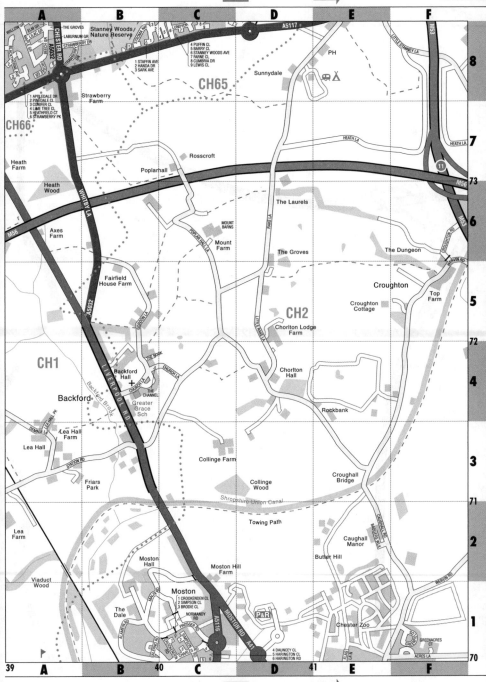

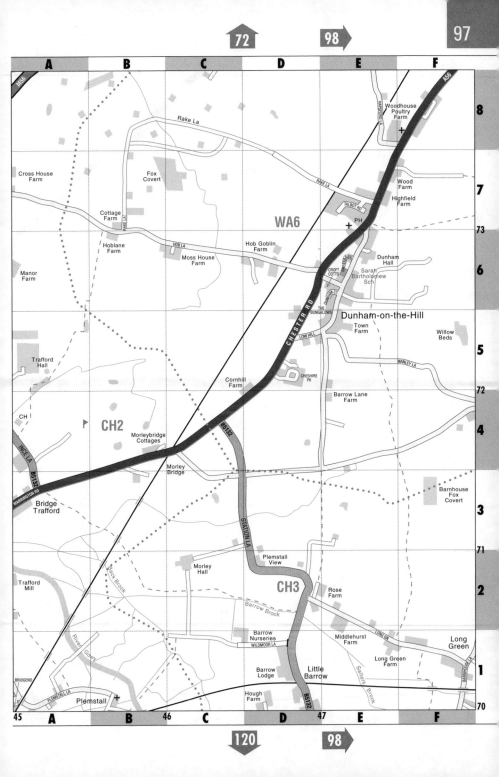

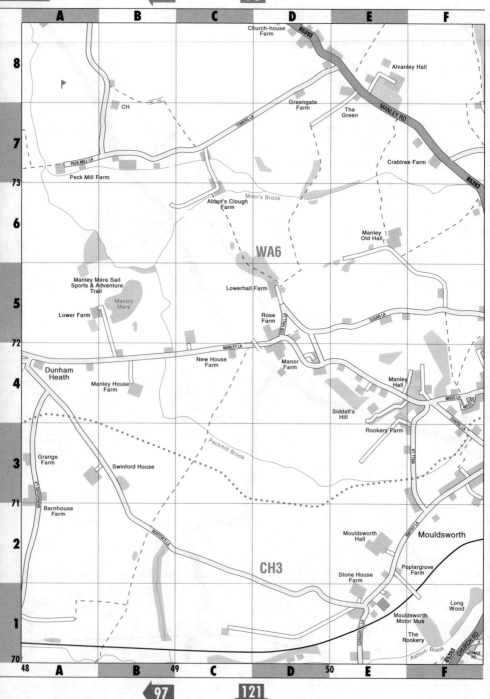

97
73

Church-house Farm
B5393
Alvanley Hall
CH
Greengate Farm
The Green
MANLEY RD
TOWERS LA
PECK MILL LA
Crabtree Farm
Peck Mill Farm
B5393
Moor's Brook
Abbot's Clough Farm
Manley Old Hall
WA6
Manley Mere Sail Sports & Adventure Trail
Lowerhall Farm
Manley Mere
Lower Farm
Rose Farm
SUGAR LA
ROSE FM RD
MANLEY LA
New House Farm
Manor Farm
Manley Hall
MOSS LA
MOSS
Dunham Heath
Manley House Farm
Siddall's Hill
WELL LA
CHARLA
Rookery Farm
Grange Farm
Swinford House
Peckmill Brook
Barnhouse Farm
NORTON'S LA
Mouldsworth Hall
SMITH LA
Mouldsworth
CH3
Stone House Farm
Poplargrove Farm
Long Wood
Mouldsworth Motor Mus
The Rookery
Ashton Brook
B5393
CHURCH RD
GRANGE RD
LONGAR LA

A B C D E F

8 7 73 6 5 72 4 3 71 2 1 70

48 A B 49 C D 50 E F

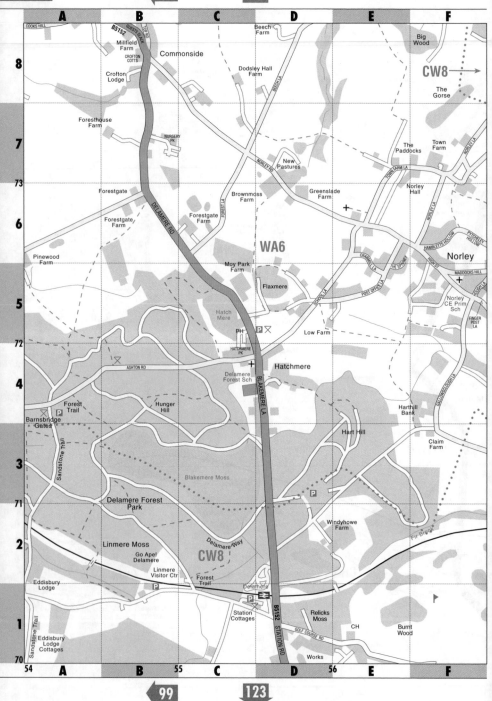

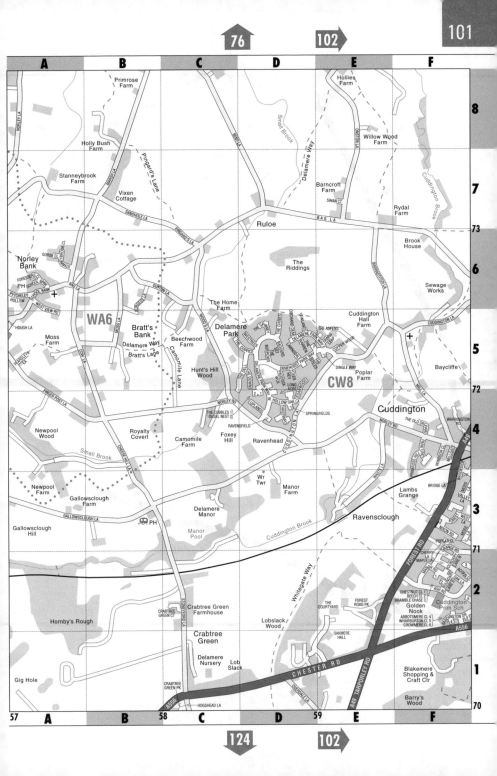

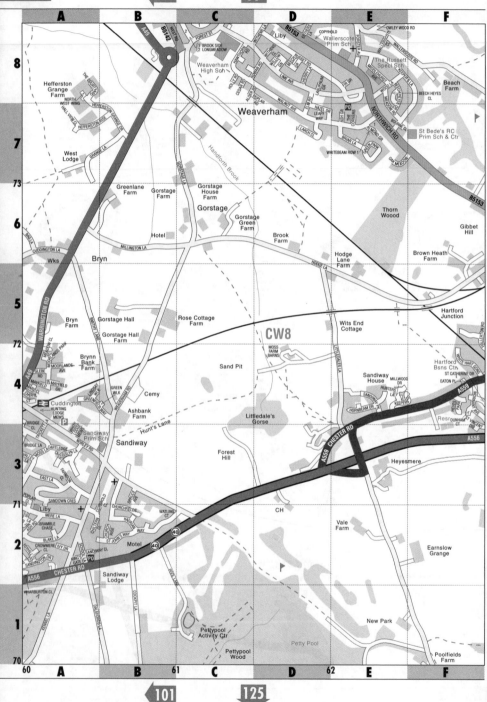

101
77

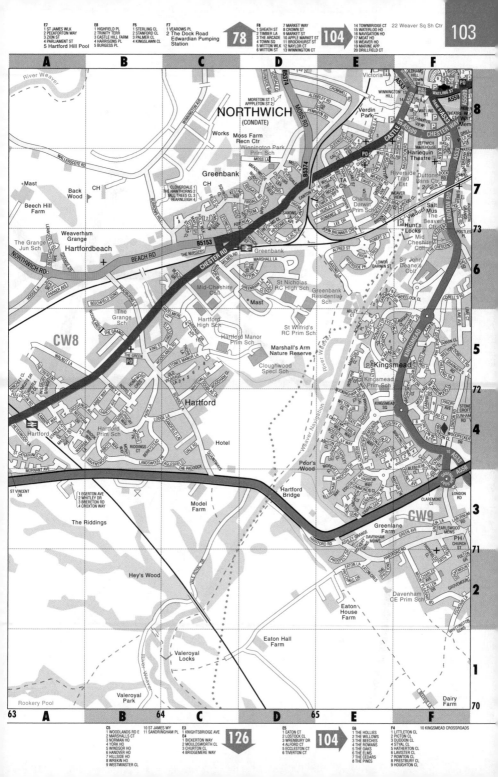

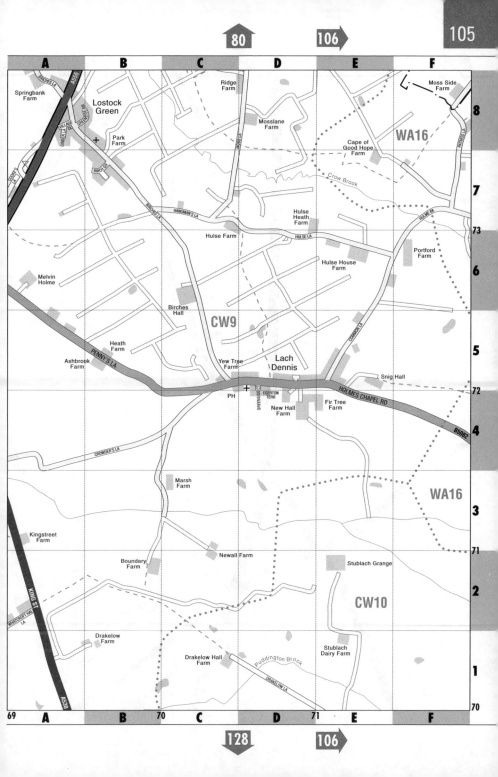

	A	B	C	D	E	F

Cheadle Farm

New Farm

CHEADLE LA

BACK LA

Back Lanes Farm

Backlane Farm

HULME LA

Millgate Farm

Hulme Covert

Bradshaw Brook

Hulme Hall

WA16

HULME HALL LA

Washlone Farm

Highfield House

B5082

Allostock Hall

HOLMES CHAPEL RD

Sculshaw Green Farm

PH

B5081

Shakerley Mere

P

Chestnut House Farm

The Croft

CW10

Stublach Farm

Works

Earnshaw House Farm

B5081

Crown Lane Farm

CROWN LA

B5081

Parkside Farm

PH

Swan Green

PO

BIRCHWOOD DR

Mast

Birch Farm

CHERRY LA

Yewtree Farm

Mill Bank Farm

Foxcovers

Peover Eye

FOXCOVER LA

Heath Farm

Springfield

HEATH LA

SANDY LA

Heath Farm

BAKER'S LA

Springbank Farm

Bradshaw House

Graybrook Farm

Bradshawbrook Farm

Chapel Farm

MIDDLEWICH RD

+

DAME LANE

Old Mill Farm

TOWNFIELD LA

Townfield Farm

HOLE LA

Hole House

Hole House Wood

Axon's Smithy Farm

Chapel House Farm

VAS LA

Allostock

Brookhouse Farm

BROOK VIEW

A50

LONDON RD

PRINCESS RD

Widow's Home Farm

Sandhole Farm

Woodlands Farm

Rudheath Woods

Newplatt Wood

CW4

KING'S LA

King's Lane Farm

NORTHWICH RD

SANDY LA

NEWPLATT LA

NEW PLATT VIEW

Warrington Common

B5082

KNUTSFORD RD

A50

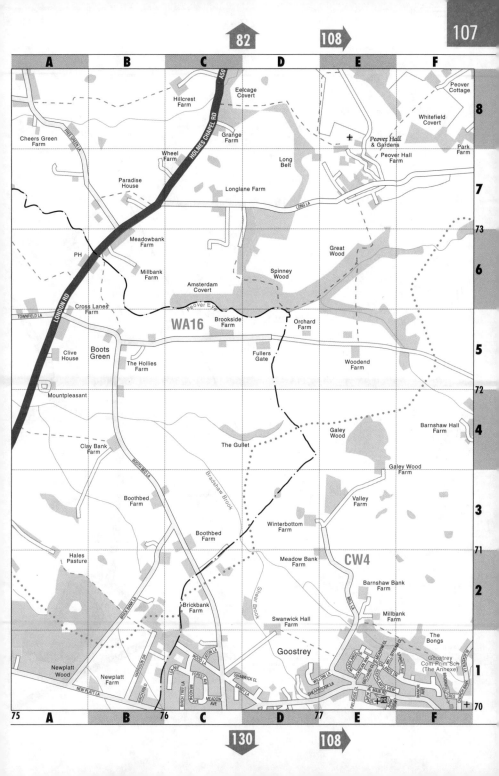

107
83

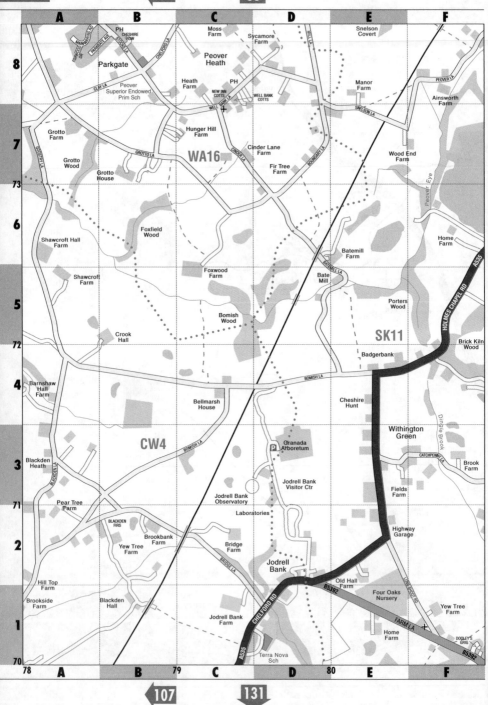

107
131

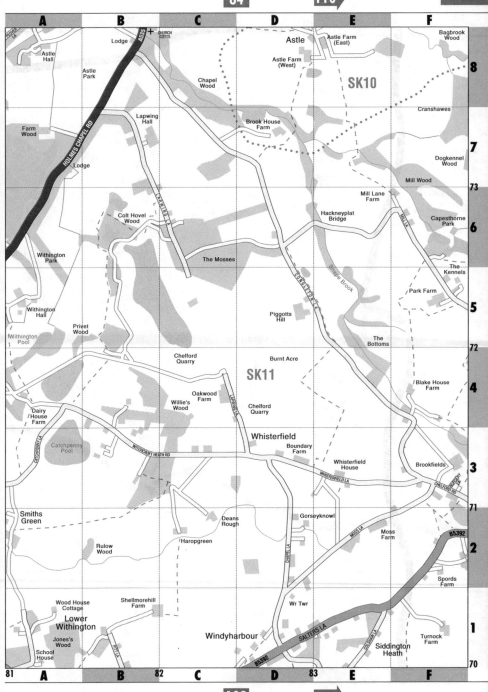

109

85

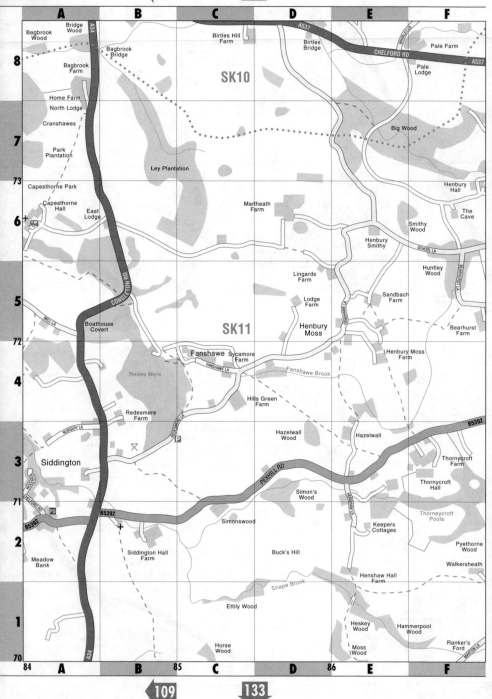

133

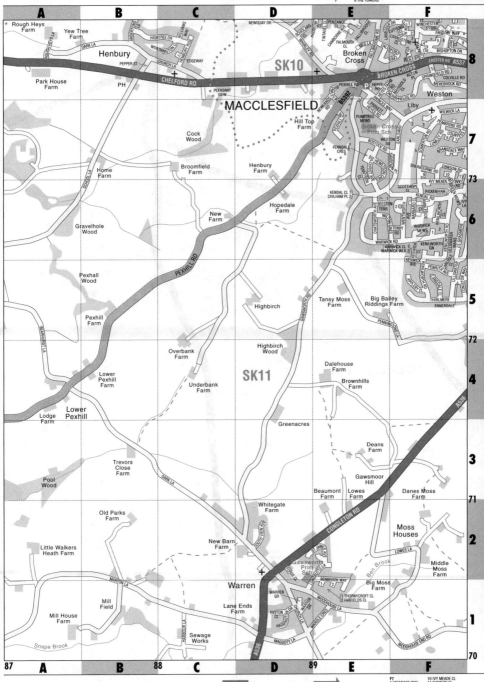

86

112

111

F8
1 ASHBOURNE MEWS
2 SHELBOURNE MEWS
3 ST LUKE'S HO
4 ALDERNEY CL
5 BLANDFORD DR
6 THE TOWERS
7 HEDINGHAM CL
8 MARLBOROUGH HO
9 ABINGDON CL
10 KENNET WAY
11 KENSINGTON SQ
12 WINCHESTER HO

MACCLESFIELD

SK10

SK11

Broken Cross

Weston

Henbury

Rough Heys Farm
Yew Tree Farm
Park House Farm
Home Farm
Gravelhole Wood
Pexhall Wood
Pexhill Farm
Lower Pexhill Farm
Lodge Farm
Lower Pexhill
Pool Wood
Trevors Close Farm
Little Walkers Heath Farm
Old Parks Farm
Mill Field
Mill House Farm
Sewage Works
Lane Ends Farm
Warren
New Barn Farm
Whitegate Farm
Beaumont Farm
Greenacres
Underbank Farm
Overbank Farm
Highbirch
Highbirch Wood
New Farm
Hopedale Farm
Henbury Farm
Hill Top Farm
Broomfield Farm
Cock Wood
Tansy Moss Farm
Big Bailey Riddings Farm
Dalehouse Farm
Brownhills Farm
Deans Farm
Gawsmoor Hill
Lowes Farm
Danes Moss Farm
Moss Houses
Middle Moss Farm
Big Moss Farm
Gawsworth Prim Sch
Broken Cross Prim Sch
Liby

134

112

87   88   89
70   71   72   73

F7
1 VICARAGE WAY
2 DUDLEY WLK
3 PEVERIL WLK
4 PORTLAND WLK
5 SOMERTON CL
6 WARDOUR CL
7 COUNTESS CL
8 WYKEHAM CHASE
9 HILTON CL
10 IVY MEADE CL
11 DAWSON CL

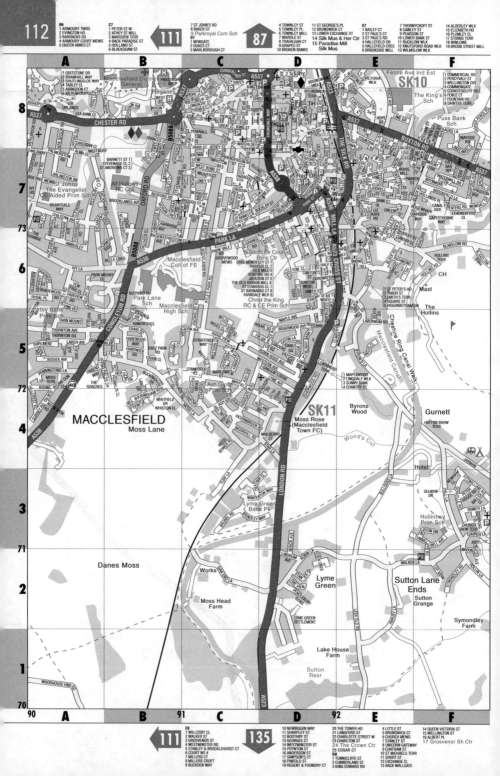

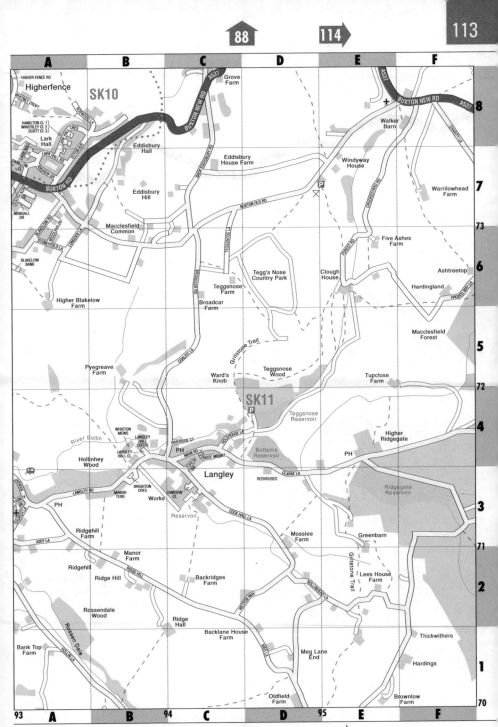

113
89

| | A | B | C | D | E | F |

8

A537

Turnshawflat

The Laches

Ankers Knowl Farm

Fox Stake

Longclough Farm

A537

BUXTON NEW RD

7

73

Hindsclough Farm

Fieldhead Farm

Greenways Farm

Brookhouse

6

HACKED WAY LA

COAL PIT LA

Whitehills

ANKERS LA

Long Clough

Tor Brook

PH

Torgate Farm

5

Chapel House Farm

OVEN LA

Macclesfield Forest

Chambers Farm

72

Toot Hill

Bottom-of-the-Oven

SK11

Torgate Hill

4

Macclesfield Forest

Bollin Brook

Clough Brook

Broughs Place

P

Dryknowle Farm

Trentabank Reservoir

3

71

P

Ferriser

High Ash Farm

2

Nessit Hill

Buxtors Hill

Yarnshaw Hill

Yarnshaw Brook

Dingers Hollow

P

The Vicarage

1

High Moor

Highmoor Brook

Higher Barn

Vicarage Wood

70

| 96 | A | B | 97 | C | D | 98 | E | F |

113
137

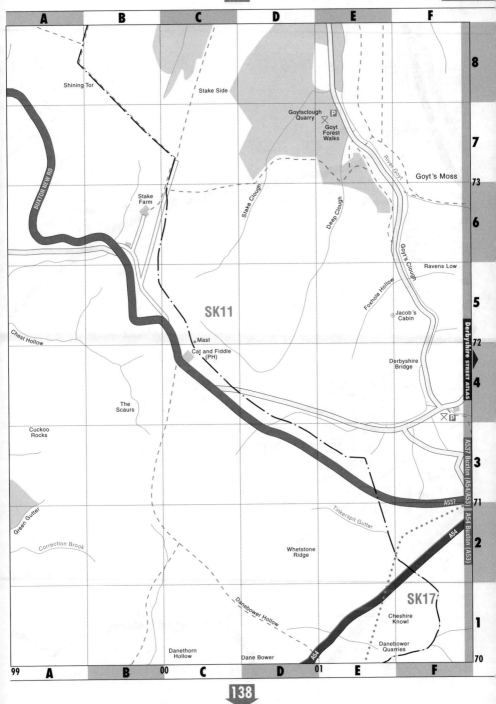

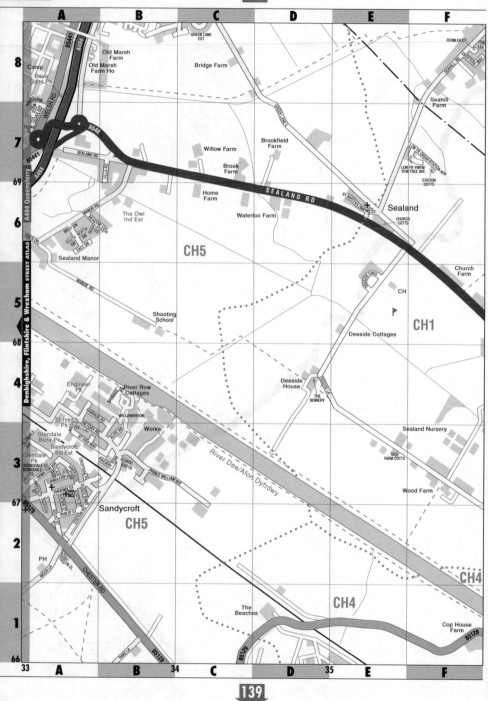

D4
1 CANBERRA WAY
2 BALLERAT CL
3 MAITLAND WAY
4 ROEBOURNE RISE
5 ROSE CL
6 ROSE TERR
7 Western Ave Sh Mall

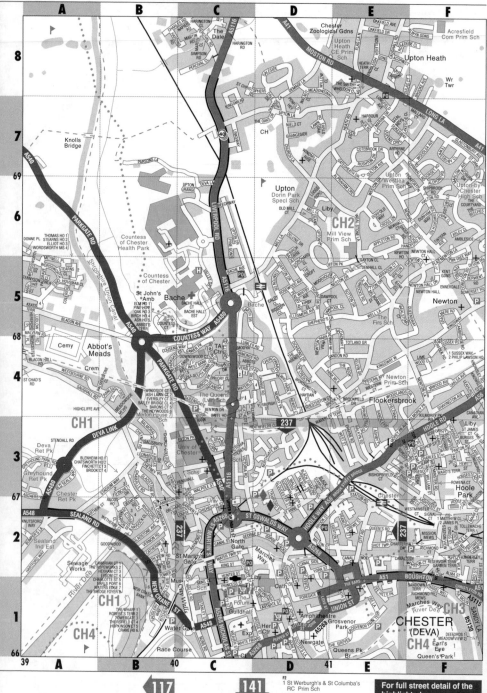

117   95

117   141

F2
1 St Werburgh's & St Columba's
RC Prim Sch

For full street detail of the highlighted area see page 237.

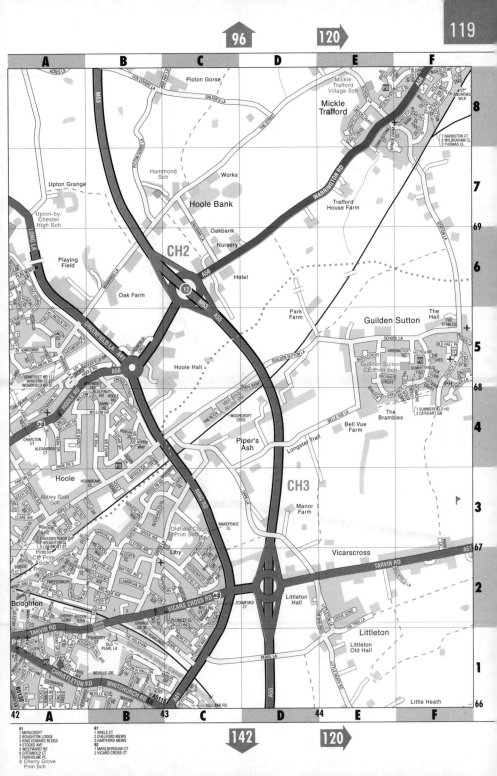

A1
1 MERECROFT
2 BOUGHTON LODGE
3 KING EDWARD BLDGS
4 STOCKS AVE
5 WESTWARD RD
6 COTSWOLD CT
7 FAIRHOLME PL
8 Cherry Grove Prim Sch

B1
1 ARKLE CT
2 CHELFORD MEWS
3 HARTFORD MEWS

B2
1 MARLBOROUGH CT
2 VICARS CROSS CT

119
97

	A	B	C	D	E	F

8

LC

Holme Farm

B5132

PH

Broomhill LA

Broom Hill

Broomhill

Salters Brook

7

CH2

THE AVENUE

ROSS LA

Ardmore

BARROWS LA

The Croft

Heath Farm

69

Ferma La

Barrow Hill

Barrowmore Est

HOLLOWMOOR HEATH

6

GREENFIELDS LODGE

LONG LOOMS

Barrow CE Prim Sch

LAMPITS LA

Great Barrow

HEATH LA

GREYSFIELD FLATS

VILLAGE RD

HAWKINS VIEW

MANOR LA

Longster Trail

FERMA LA

PO

Barrow Hall

Barrow Mill

5

Oxen Bridge

NEW FARM CT

MILL LA

MILL LANE COTTS

+

Hill Farm House

CINDER LA

BARROW LA

68

THE STEADINGS

Milton Brook Lodge

Milton Brook

The Byatts

ROCK LA

CH3

4

Hillview Farm

River Gowy

Stamford Bridge

3

PH

B5132

LANSDOWNE RD

TARVIN RD

The Limes

Holme Bank

CH

Gowy Bank Farm

67

A51

HOLME ST

Nursery

Stamford Heath

Stamford Mill

Abbeyfield

2

GREEN LA

Stamford Mill

MILL LANE

A51

Holme-street Hall

Stamford Hollows Farm

ROCK LA

1

STAMFORD LA

Hollows Farm

Birch Bank Farm

Cotton Hall

66

45	A		B	46	C		D	47	E		F

119
143

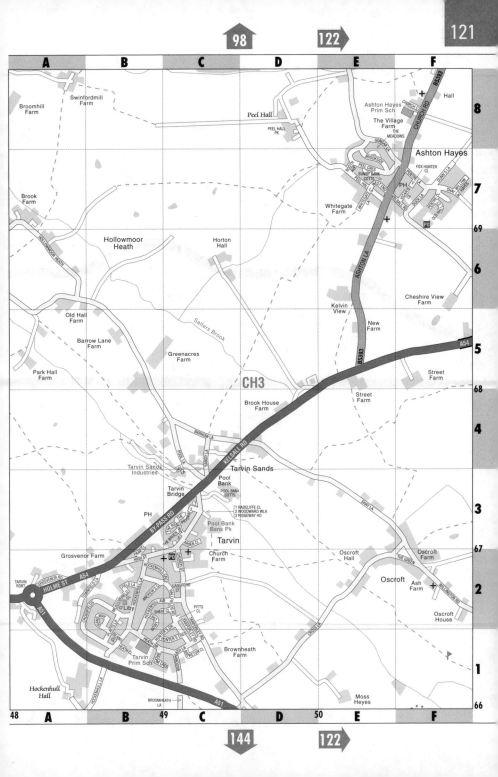

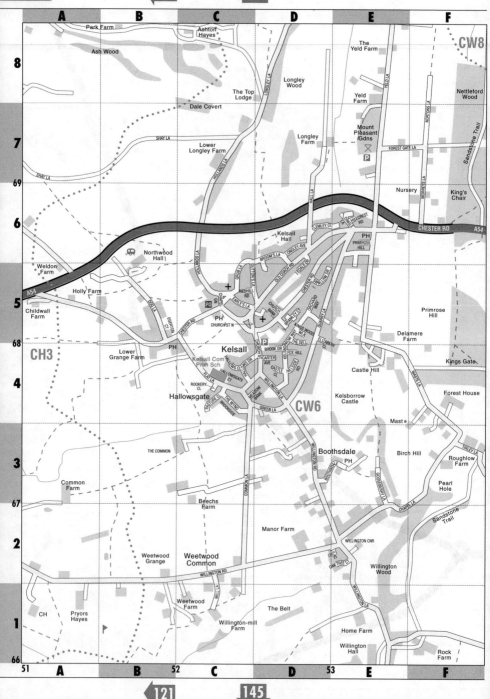

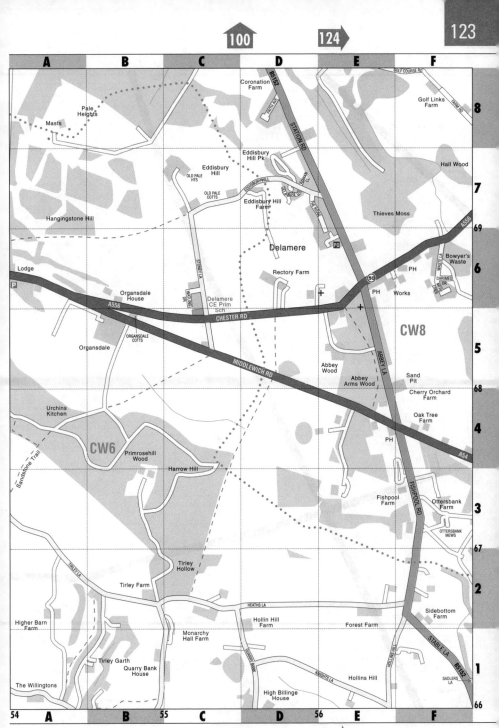

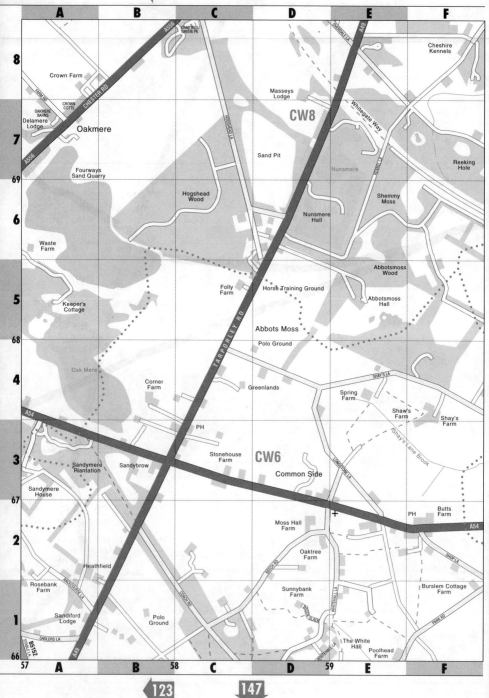

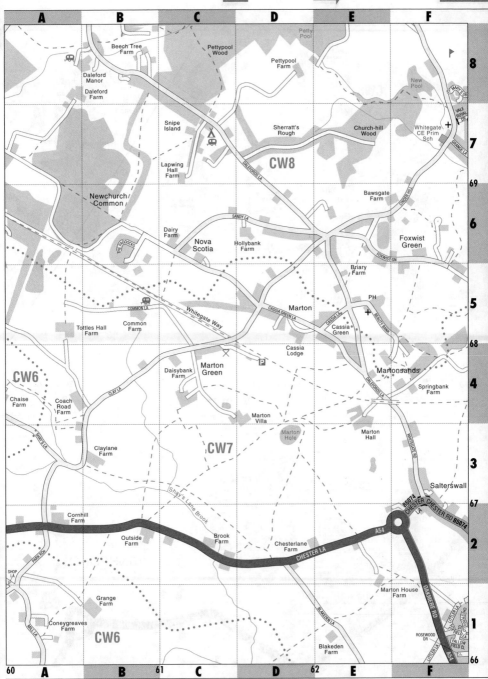

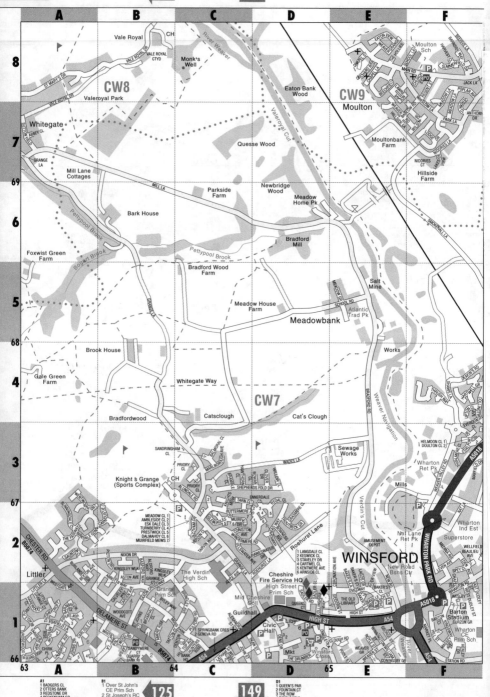

A1
1 BADGERS CL
2 OTTERS BANK
3 REDSTONE DR
4 BECKENHAM GR
5 FINSBURY WLK
6 Greenfields Prim Sch

B1
1 Over St John's CE Prim Sch
2 St Joseph's RC Prim Sch

D1
1 QUEEN'S PAR
2 FOUNTAIN CT
3 THE ROW
4 DINGLE WLK
5 JUBILEE WAY
6 Dingle Recreation Ctr

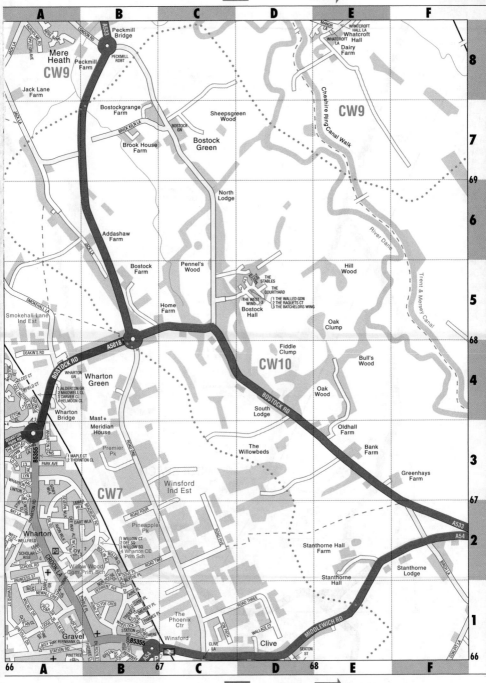

127
105

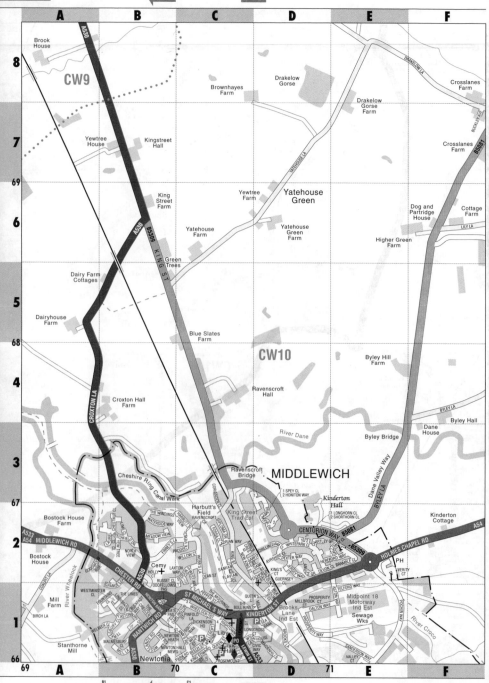

B1
1 Middlewich
Prim Sch

C1
1 LAMBOURNE GR
2 LAWRENCE AVE E
3 LAWRENCE AVE
4 DIERDENS TERR
5 Middlewich
High Sch

127
151

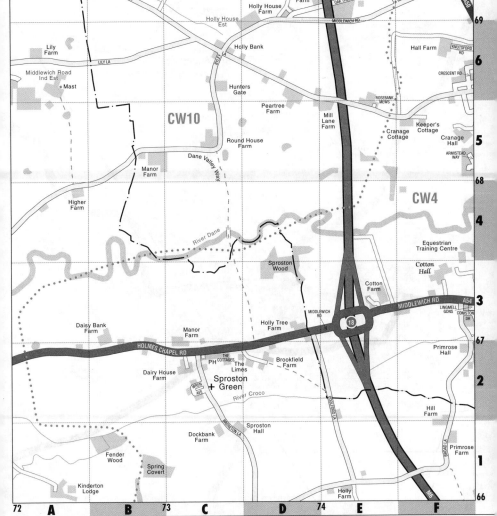

A **B** **C** **D** **E** **F**

8

Warrington Common

B5082

Rudheath Lodge Farm

KNUTSFORD RD

Chestnut Farm

Puddinglake

DRAKELOW LA

Puddinglake Brook

Nook Wood

Oak Tree Farm

KINGS LA

A50

GOOSTREY LA

7

Byley Prim Sch

Byley

Shanty Farm

MOSS LA

Mast

New Farm

Holly House Farm

OAK TREE LA

MIDDLEWICH RD

69

Lily Farm

LILY LA

Holly House Est

Holly Bank

Hall Farm

KNUTSFORD RD

6

Middlewich Road Ind Est

Mast

BYLEY LA

Holly Bank

CRESCENT RD

CW10

Hunters Gate

Peartree Farm

Mill Lane Farm

ROSEBANK MEWS

Cranage Cottage

Keeper's Cottage

Cranage Hall

5

Round House Farm

ARMISTEAD WAY

Dane Valley Way

Manor Farm

68

Higher Farm

River Dane

CW4

4

Equestrian Training Centre

Sproston Wood

Cotton Hall

Cotton Farm

MIDDLEWICH RD

A54

LINGMELL GDNS

CONISTON DR

3

Daisy Bank Farm

Manor Farm

MIDDLEWICH RD

18

Primrose Hall

67

HOLMES CHAPEL RD

Holly Tree Farm

THE COTTAGES

PH

The Limes

Brookfield Farm

Dairy House Farm

WREN AVE

Sproston Green

River Croco

Hill Farm

2

BRERETON LA

Sproston Hall

COLEFORD LA

Dockbank Farm

BYLEY LA

Primrose Farm

Fender Wood

Spring Covert

Holly Farm

M6

1

Kinderton Lodge

66

72 **A** **B** 73 **C** **D** 74 **E** **F**

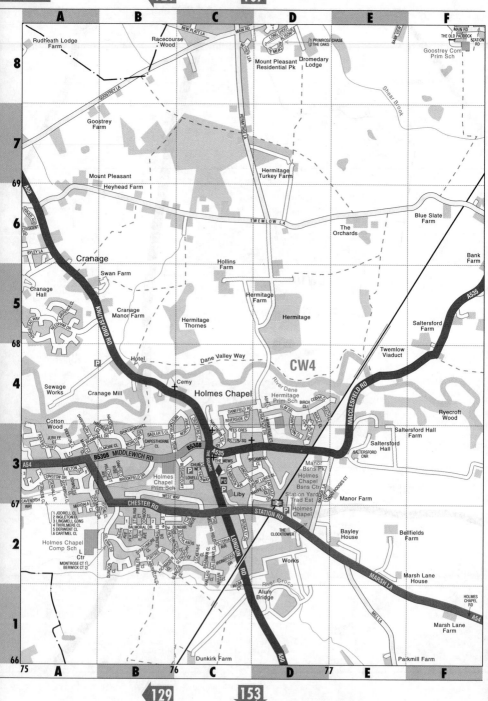

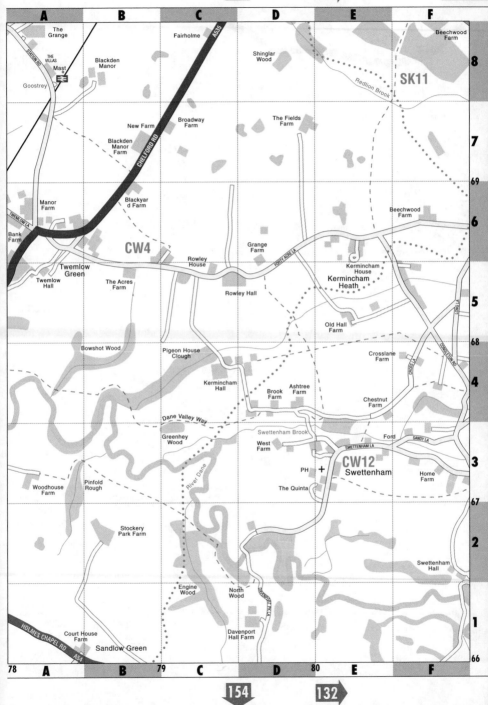

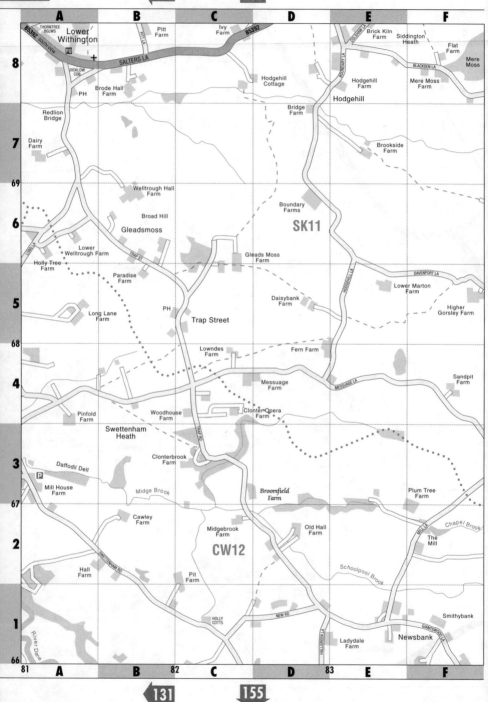

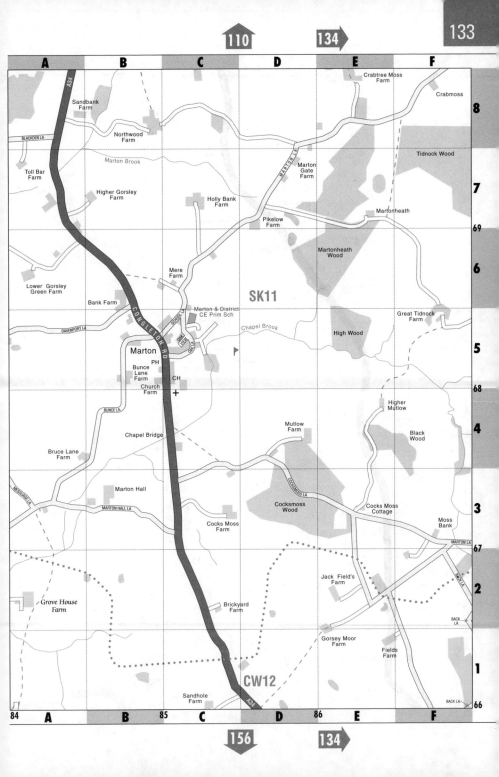

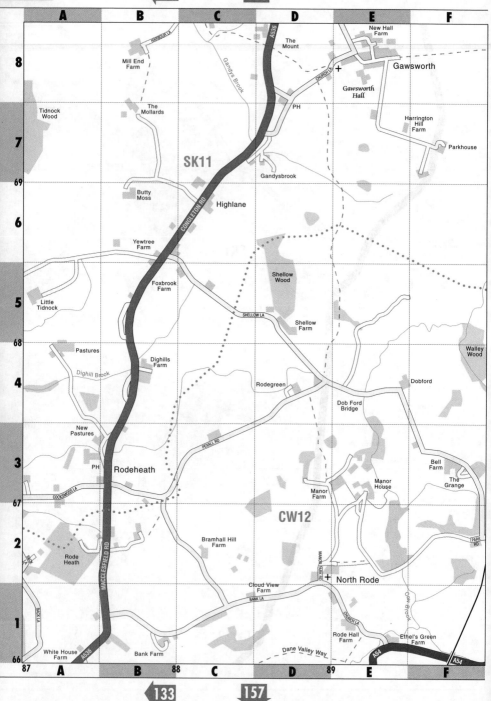

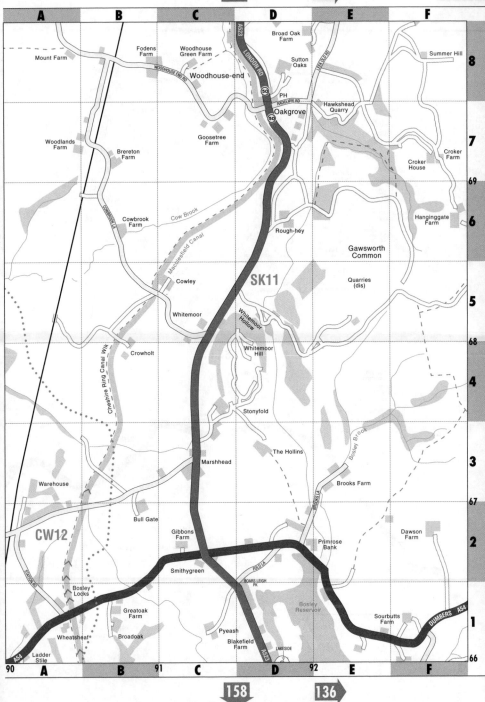

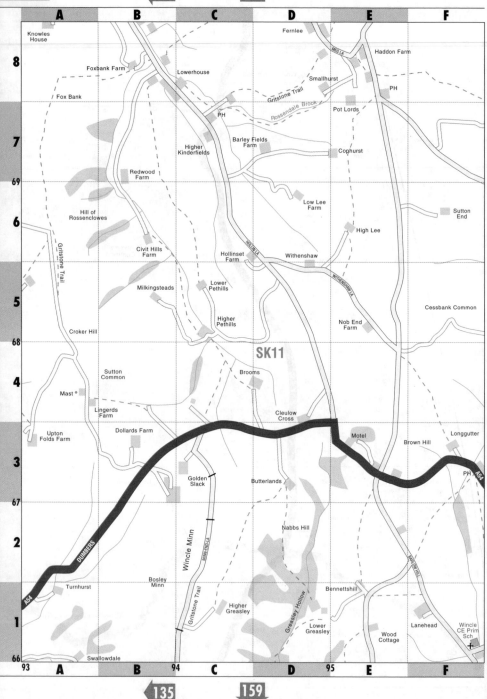

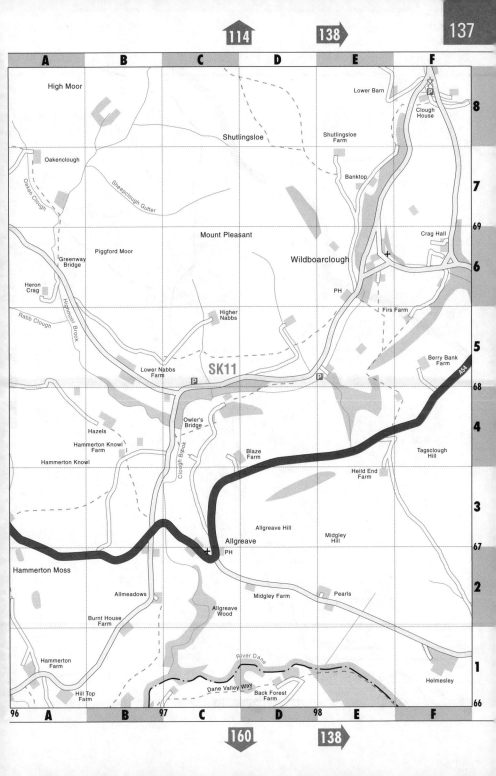

114
138
160
138

High Moor

Oakenclough

Oaken Clough

Shutlingsloe

Lower Barn

Clough House

Shutlingsloe Farm

Banktop

Sheepclough Gutter

Mount Pleasant

Crag Hall

Piggford Moor

Greenway Bridge

Wildboarclough

Heron Crag

Highmoor Brook

PH

Firs Farm

Rabb Clough

Higher Nabbs

SK11

Lower Nabbs Farm

P

P

Berry Bank Farm

A54

Hazels

Owler's Bridge

Hammerton Knowl Farm

Clough Brook

Blaze Farm

Tagsclough Hill

Hammerton Knowl

Heild End Farm

Allgreave Hill

Midgley Hill

Hammerton Moss

Allgreave

PH

Allmeadows

Midgley Farm

Pearls

Burnt House Farm

Allgreave Wood

Hammerton Farm

River Dane

Helmesley

Hill Top Farm

Dane Valley Way

Back Forest Farm

96   97   98

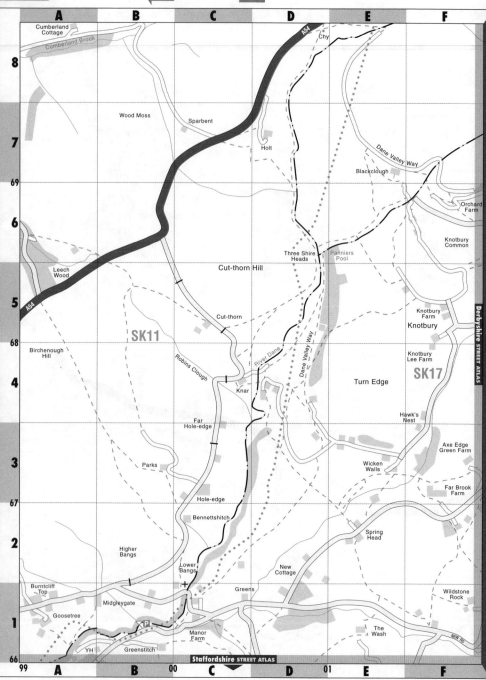

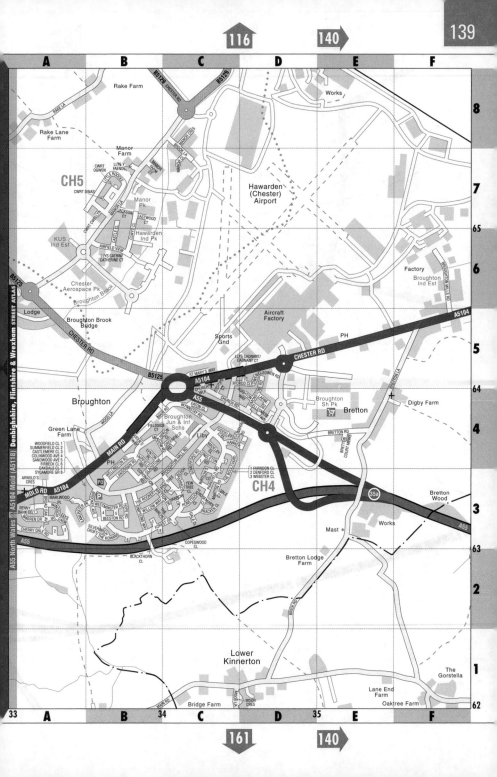

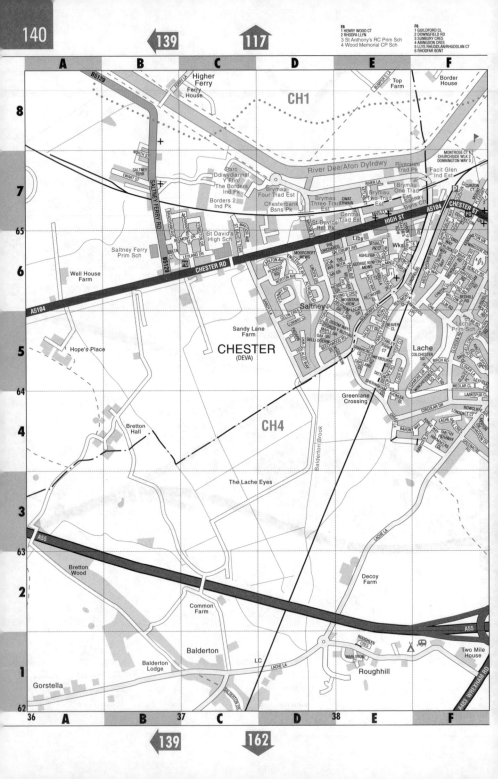

139
117

E6
1 HENRY WOOD CT
2 RHODFA LLYN
3 St Anthony's RC Prim Sch
4 Wood Memorial CP Sch

F6
1 GUILDFORD CL
2 DOWNSFIELD RD
3 SUNBURY CRES
4 ABINGDON CRES
5 LLYS RHUDDLAN/RHUDDLAN CT
6 RHODFAR BONT

CH1

Higher Ferry
Ferry House

Top Farm

Border House

B5129

NORTH ST

SALTNEY TERR

EWART ST

River Dee/Afon Dyfrdwy

Riverside Trad Pk

MONTROSE CT L
CHURCHSIDE WLK 2
DONNINGTON WAY 3

Facit Glen Ind Est

CHESTER ST

Parc Ddiwydiannol y Ffin
The Borders Ind Pk

Brymau Four Trad Est

Brymau Three Trad Est
TRAWAIN

RIVER LA
CWAT

Brymau Two Trad Est

Brymau One Trad Est

SALTNEY FERRY RD

BRADSHAW AVE

Borders 2 Ind Pk

Chesterbank Bsns Pk

Central Trad Est

HIGH ST

A5104

B5729

KINASON DR
KYNASTON AVE

BELMONT DR

LEYLAND DR

M4JOR STER

Saltney Ferry Prim Sch

DELTA CT

HOWARD DR

St David's High Sch

St David's Ret Pk

Liby

WRANLEY
PK CT

Wks

WINDSOR GN
CURZON CT

CHESTER RD

PO

CARLTON AVE

NORTON AVE

SNEYD AVE

MOORCROFT MEWS

THE ORCHARDS
SALISBURY AVE

DEVA AVE
THE NOOK

George Kenyon Mews

ASHLEIGH CL

Prim Sch

Well House Farm

SANDY LA

DELYN CRES

CONWAY CL

AWEL DDEWR

Saltney

IRVING'S CRES

MOUNTAIN VIEW

BEECHWOOD RD

REDWOOD

BEAVER
CT

STANLEY
PARK DR

Lache

Hope's Place

Sandy Lane Farm

CHESTER
(DEVA)

AWEL DU

GELLI DDEWR

CAPEL AVE

WEYBOURNE

Lache
COLCHESTER
SQ

BIRCH RD

LARKSPUR CL

Bretton Hall

CH4

Balderton Brook

Greenlane Crossing

AVONLEA CL

SHERIDAN

CIRCULAR DR

LACHE NL

ROWCLIFFE

LONSDALE CT

GREENACRE RD

The Lache Eyes

A55

Bretton Wood

Decoy Farm

Two Mile House

A55

Common Farm

ROUGHLYN
CRES

MARLSTON

A483 WREXHAM RD

Balderton

LC

LACHE LA

Roughhill

Balderton Lodge

Gorstella

BALNSTON TER

36 **A** 37 **B** **C** 38 **D** **E** **F**

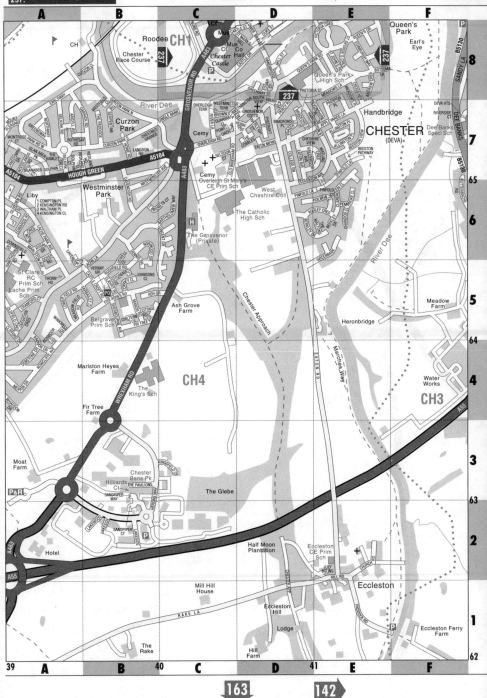

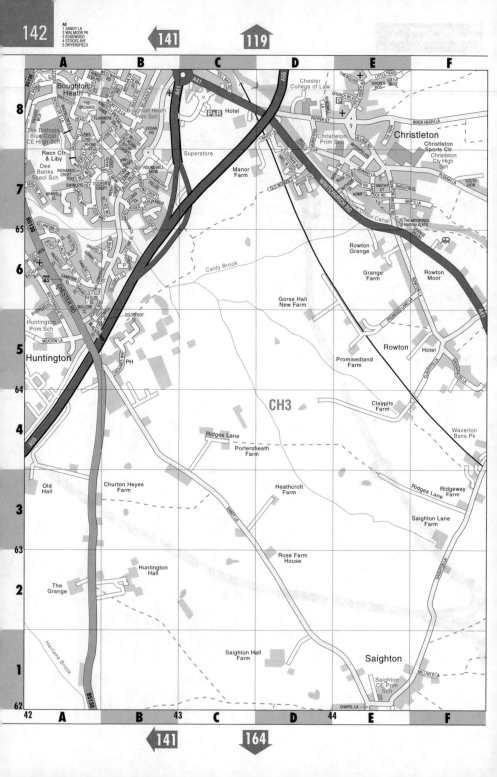

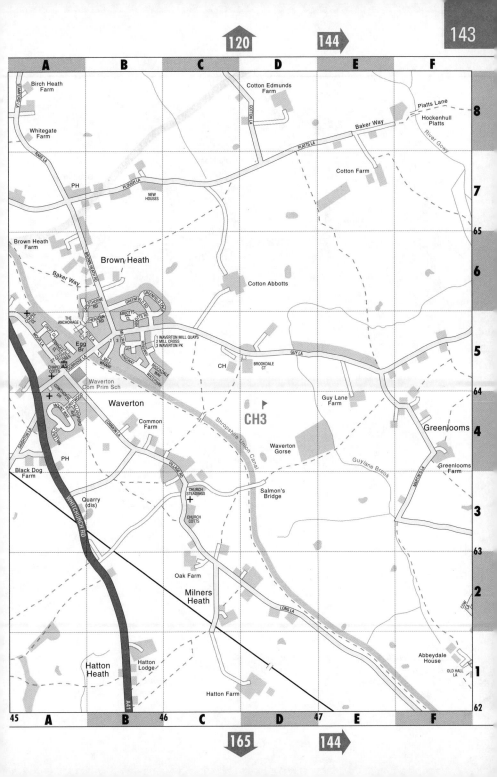

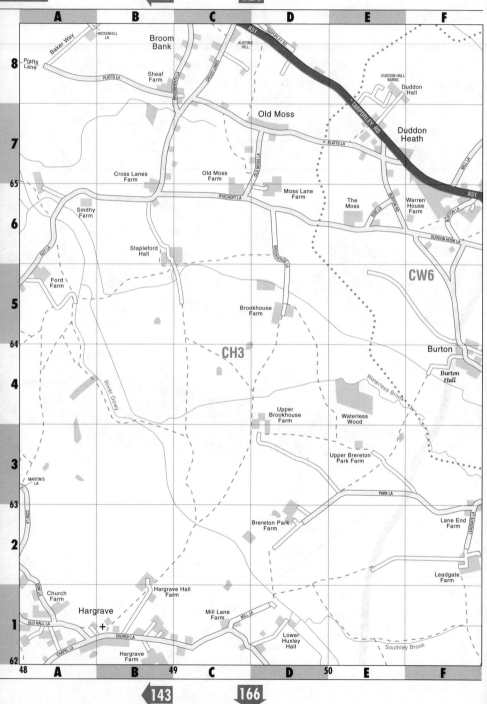

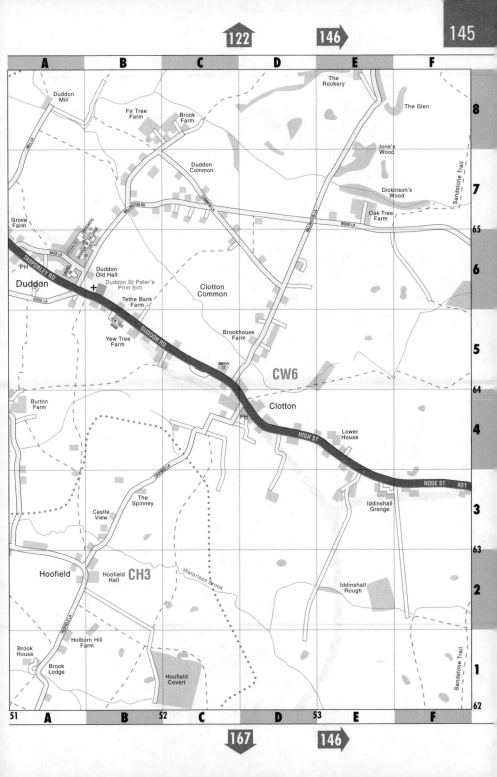

145
123

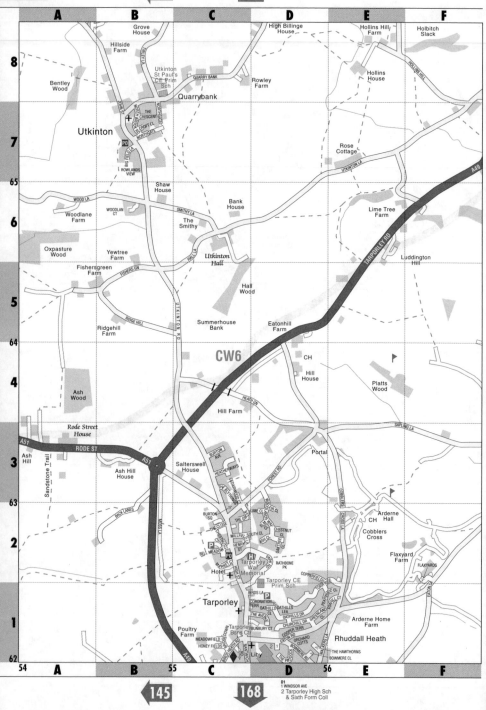

D1
1 WINDSOR AVE
2 Tarporley High Sch
& Sixth Form Coll

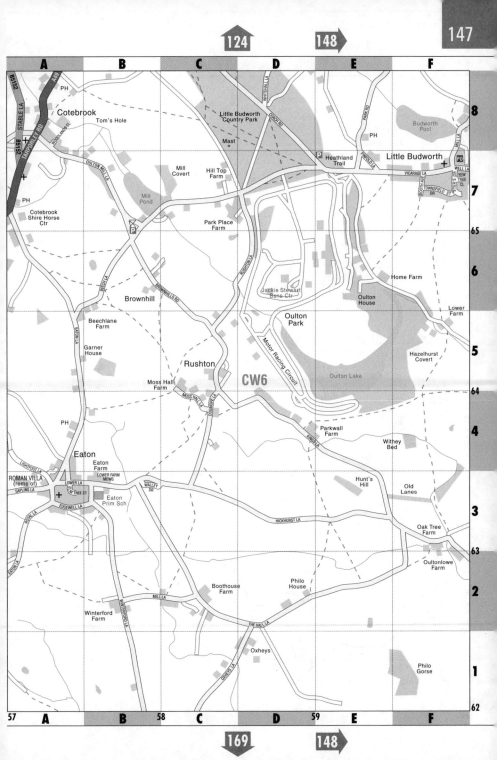

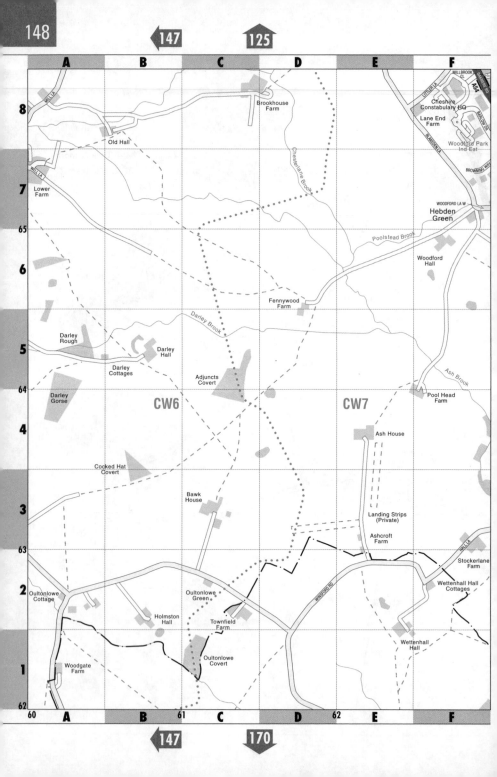

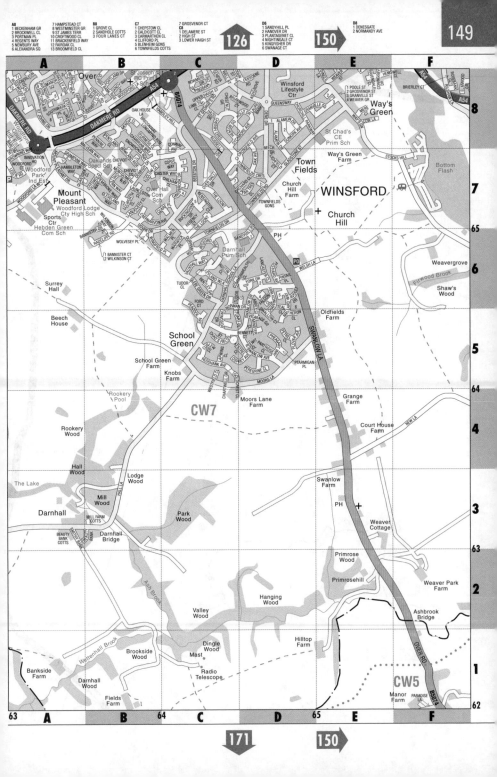

149
127

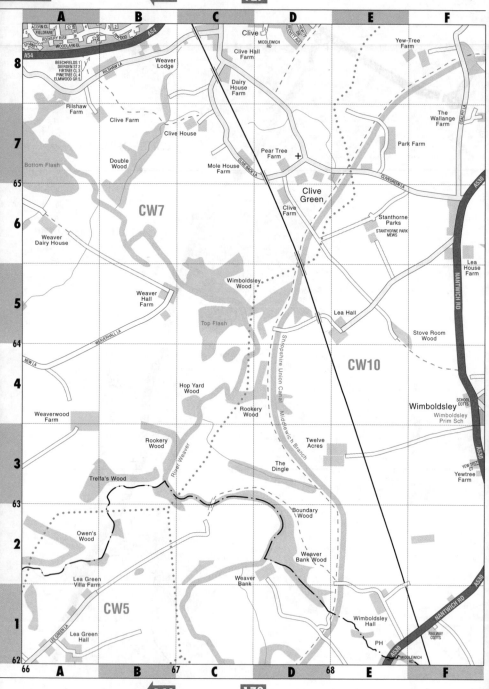

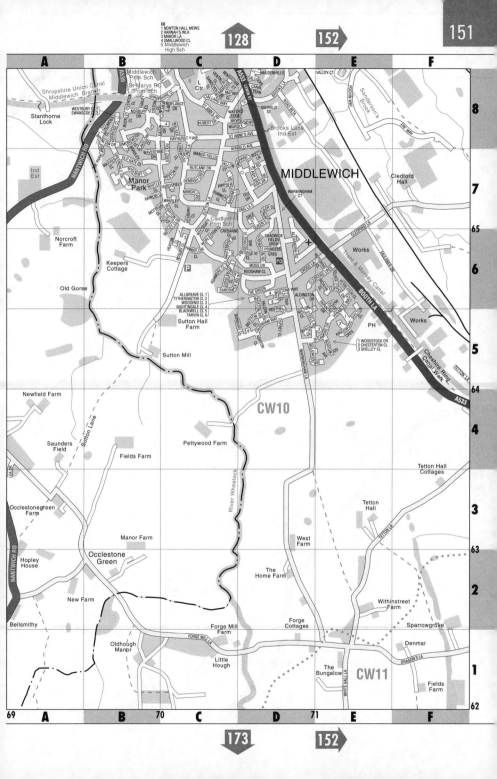

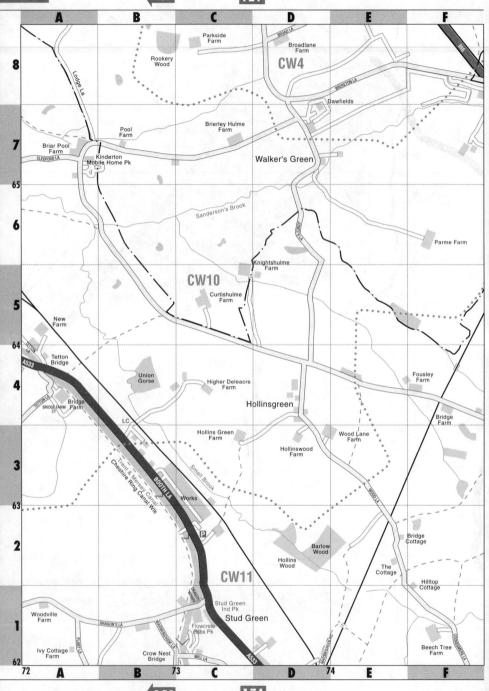

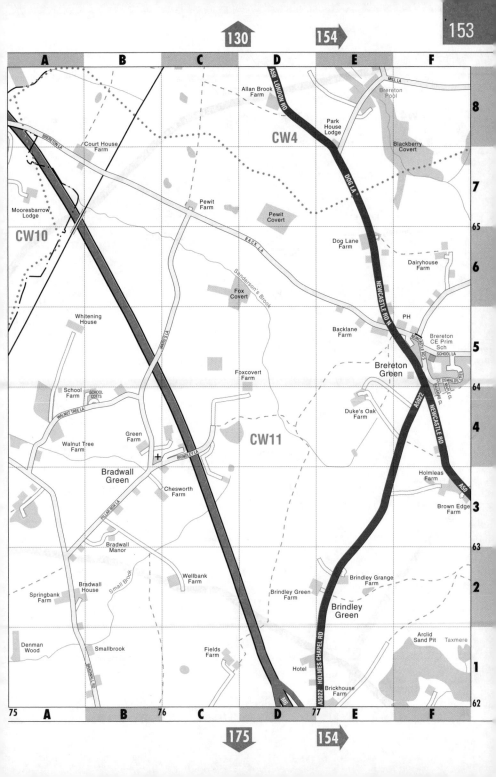

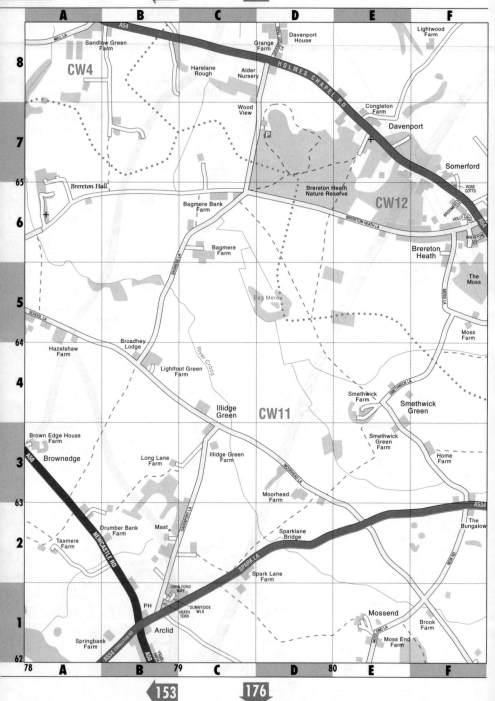

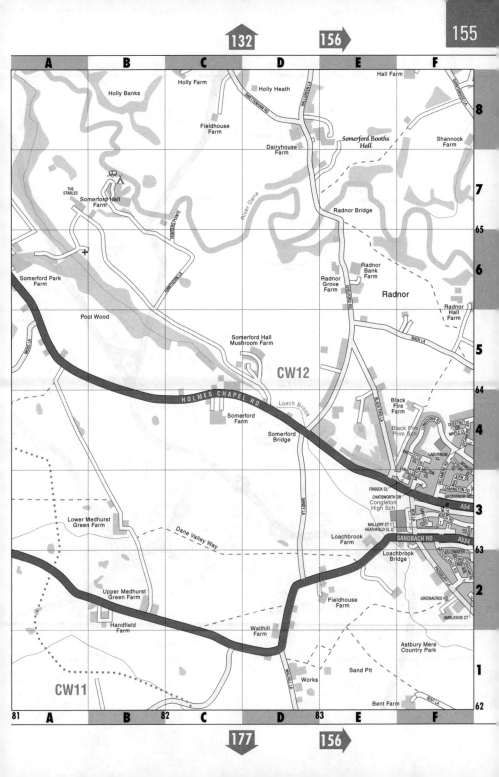

155
133

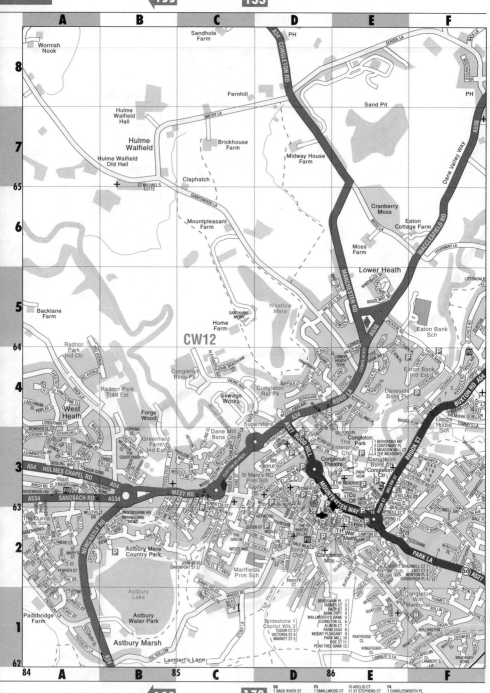

155
178

D3
1 BACK RIVER ST
2 HORACE LAWTON CT
3 WEAVERS COTTS
4 BROOKSIDE RD
5 MEADOW COTTS
6 STONEHOUSE GN

F3
1 SMALLWOOD CT
2 SOMERFORD CT
3 CRANAGE CT
4 GOOSTREY CT
5 MOSTON CT
6 BETCHTON CT
7 RODE CT
8 TETTON CT
9 NEWBOLD CT

10 ARCLID CT
11 ST STEPHENS CT
12 ELWORTH CT

F4
1 CHARLESWORTH PL
2 DODDSWOOD DR
3 BUXTON OLD RD
4 BUCKINGHAM CL
5 Buglawton Ind Est
6 Havannah Bsns Ctr
7 COUNCIL HOS

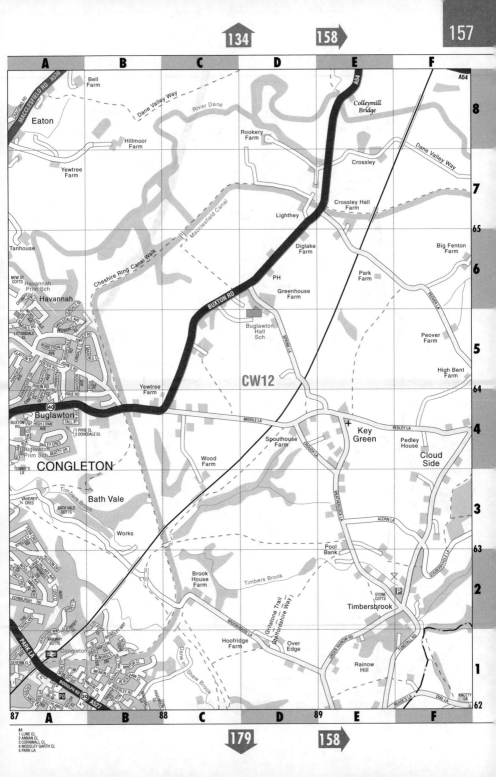

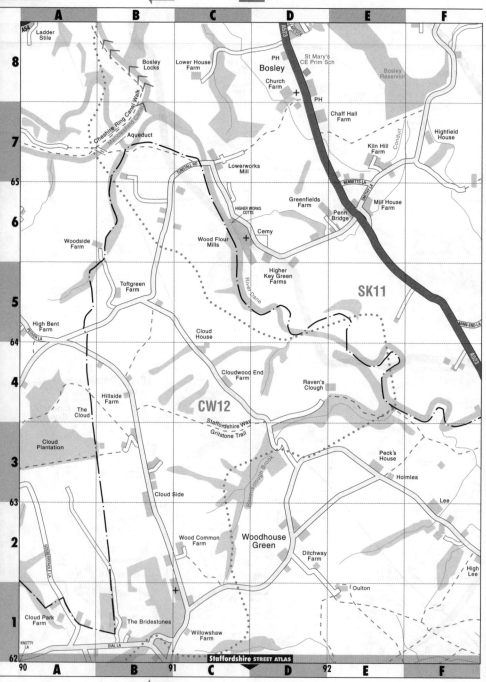

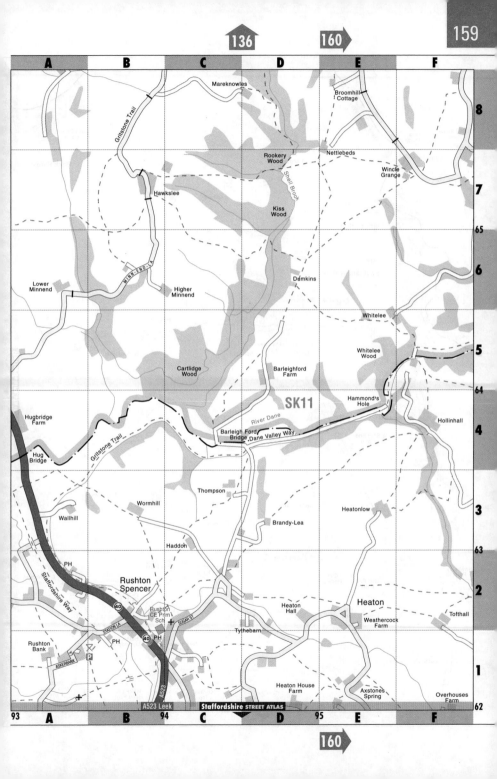

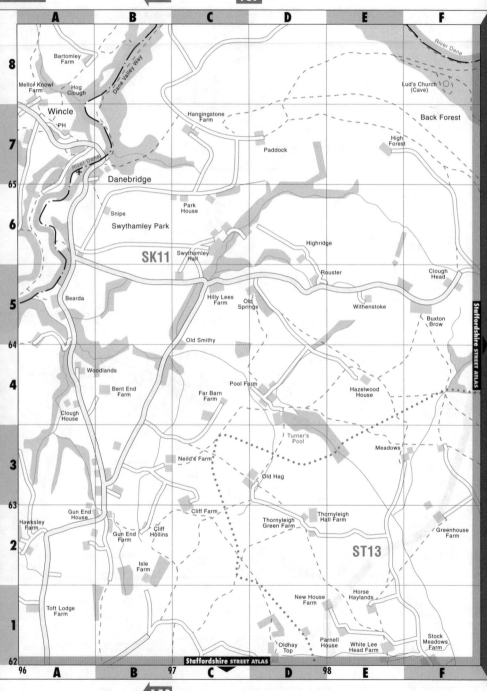
8

Bartomley Farm

Mellor Knowl Farm

Hog Clough

Wincle

PH

River Dane

Danebridge

7

65

Hangingstone Farm

Paddock

Dane Valley Way

High Forest

Lud's Church (Cave)

Back Forest

River Dane

Snipe

Park House

Swythamley Park

6

Swythamley Hall

Highridge

SK11

Rouster

Clough Head

5

Bearda

Hilly Lees Farm

Old Springs

Withenstoke

Buxton Brow

64

Old Smithy

Woodlands

Bent End Farm

Far Barn Farm

Pool Farm

Hazelwood House

4

Clough House

Turner's Pool

Meadows

Neild's Farm

3

Old Hag

63

Gun End House

Cliff Farm

Thornyleigh Green Farm

Thornyleigh Hall Farm

Greenhouse Farm

Hawksley Farm

Gun End Farm

Cliff Hollins

ST13

2

Isle Farm

Horse Haylands

Toft Lodge Farm

New House Farm

White Lee Head Farm

Stock Meadows Farm

1

Oldhay Top

Parnell House

62

96   97   98

A   B   C   D   E   F

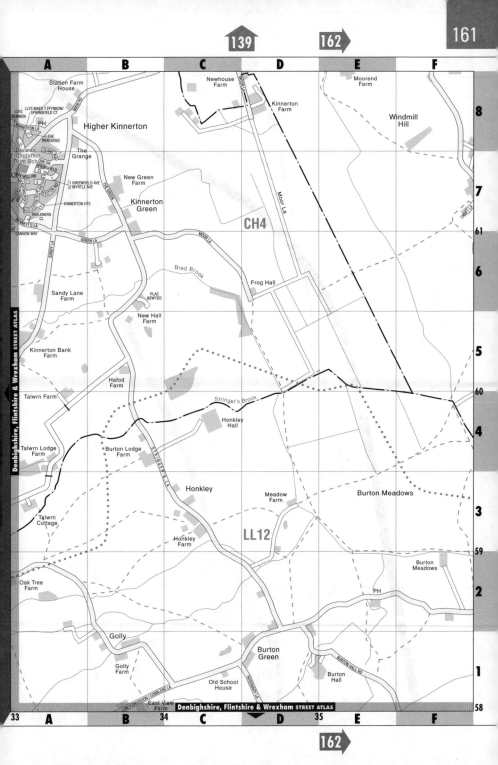

A B C D E F

Station Farm House
Newhouse Farm
Moorend Farm
Windmill Hill

LLYS MAES Y FFYNNON/ SPRINGFIELD CT
LLYS DERWEN
PH
KINNERTON LA
Higher Kinnerton
Kinnerton Farm

THE BRACKENS
Derwen Foundation Prim Sch
The Grange
DEANE RD
OAK RD
SPRINGFIELD CL

Liby
WILLOW
New Green Farm
Kinnerton Green
CH4

1 GREENFIELD AVE
2 MYRTLE AVE

THE GREEN

ECCLESTON
WILLOW
FAULKNERS CL
KINNERTON HTS

BENNETT'S LA
CANNON WAY
GREEN LA
MOOR LA
MOOR La

SANDY LA
Brad Brook
Frog Hall

Sandy Lane Farm
PLAS NEWYDD

New Hall Farm

Kinnerton Bank Farm
Stringer's Brook
Honkley Hall

Hafod Farm

Talwrn Farm

Talwrn Lodge Farm
Burton Lodge Farm
STRINGER'S LA
Honkley
Meadow Farm
Burton Meadows

Talwrn Cottage
LL12
Burton Meadows

Honkley Farm

Oak Tree Farm
PH

Golly
Burton Green
PH
Burton Hall

Golly Farm
BURTON HALL RD

Old School House
Burton Hall

LON Y CRYDDION / COBBLERS LA
East View Farm
ROSSMARY LA

33 A B 34 C D 35 E F

8
7
61
6
5
60
4
3
59
2
1
58

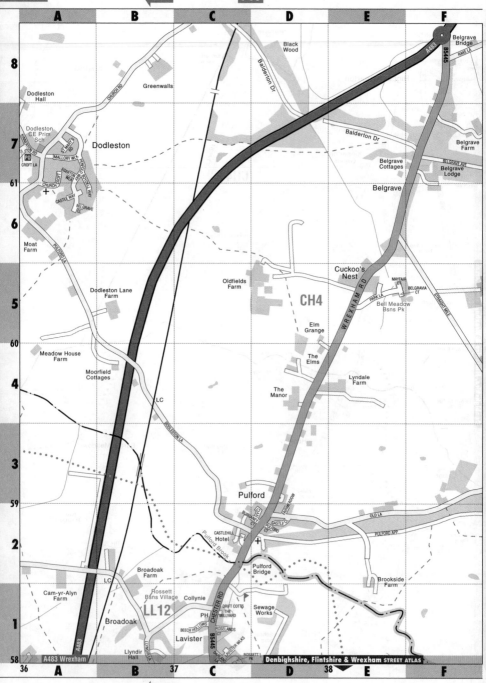

A B C D E F

8

Black Wood

Dodleston
Hall

Greenwalls

Belgrave
Bridge

RAKE LA

CHURCH RD

BALDERTON DR

Balderton Dr

Belgrave
Farm

7

Dodleston
CE Prim
Sch

ST MARY'S

Dodleston

MALLORY WK

PO
CROFT LA

61

CHURCH

+

CASTLE WAY

PENFOLD CROCKETT RW

EGERTON WLK

BELGRAVE
DR

Belgrave
Cottages

BELGRAVE AVE

Belgrave
Lodge

Belgrave

6

Moat
Farm

PULFORD LA

Cuckoo's
Nest

WREXHAM RD

MAYFAIR

PARK LA

BELGRAVIA
CT

STROUGHILL LA

5

Dodleston Lane
Farm

Oldfields
Farm

CH4

Bell Meadow
Bsns Pk

60

Meadow House
Farm

Moorfield
Cottages

Elm
Grange

The
Elms

4

LC

DODLESTON LA

The
Manor

Lyndale
Farm

3

Pulford

59

RUSHMEAD

OLD LA

2

CASTLEHILL
Hotel

Pulford Brook

BURBANKS
CT

THE
CLOSE

CASTLE
CROFT

+

PULFORD APP

Broadoak
Farm

Pulford
Bridge

Brookside
Farm

LC

Rossett
Bsns Village

Collynie

DRIFT COTTS
THE
MILLYARD

Sewage
Works

Cam-yr-Alyn
Farm

LL12

PH

CHESTER RD

ROSELANDS
CT

1

Broadoak

BEECH HOLLOWS

Lavister

B5445

ROSSETT PK

58

A483 Wrexham

Llyndir
Hall

LLYNDIR LA

LAVISTER WLKS

36 A B 37 C D 38 E F

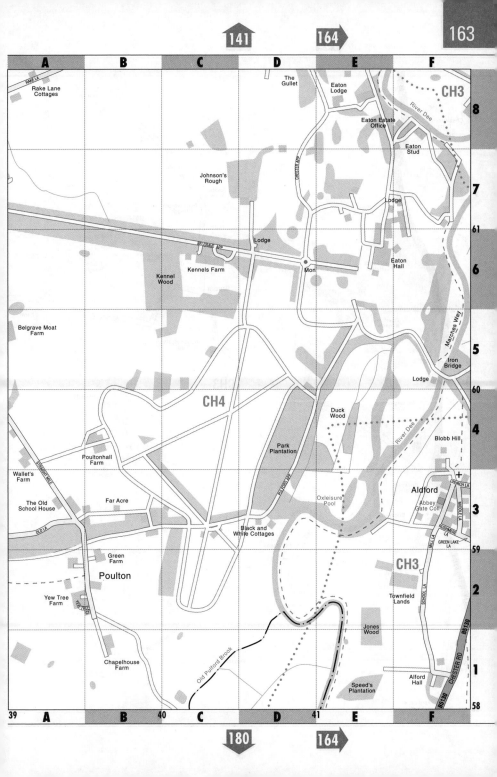

| A | B | C | D | E | F |

8

Cheaveley Bridge

B5130

Cheaveleyhall Farm

Saighton Grange

Abbey Gate Coll

7

Crook of Dee

River Dee

Powsey Brook

Horse Pasture

Smithy Farm

Powseybrook Bridge

61

Lodge

WAVERTON APP

6

Sooty Fields Plantation

BUERTON APP

Chapelhouse Farm

Platt's Rough

Bruera

5

Buerton Kennels

Coldharbour Farm

Coldharbour

PLATT'S LA

CHAPEL LA

Churton Heath Farm

CH4

CH3

60

Penlington's Wood

Newbold

4

HILL COTTS

Lea Newbold Farm

CHURCH LA

Brickyard Farm

3

PH

Bank Farm

Brickyard Plantation

LEA LA

Lea Cottages

59

GREEN LAKE LA

CHESTER RD B5130

2

LOWER LA

Leahall Farm

Wim Bridge

Aldford Brook

Bishop Bennet Way

1

Glebe Farm

The Ponderosa

58

Ford La

Ford Lane Farm

| 42 | A | B | 43 | C | D | 44 | E | F |

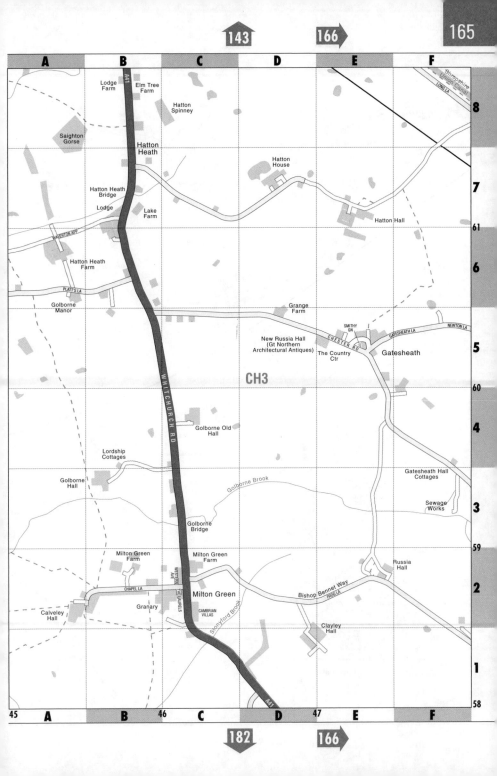

165 144

A B C D E F

8
Golden Nook Farm
The Poplars
LONG LA
Higher Huxley Hall
Green Farm
PH
Huxley Bridge
Pool Bank Farm

7

ORELLA
BELLO
RED LA
River Gowy

61
Nixon's Bridge
Shropshire Union Canal
Mill Farm

6
Poplar Hall Farm
Mast
CROW'S NEST COTTS
Millfields
Works
Dutton's Bridge

Birch Tree Farm
Crow's Nest Bridge

5
Manor Farm
Depot
PH
Newton Hall

60
NEWTON COTTS
Bishop Bennet Way
NEWTON LA
CH3

4
The Cedars
TATTENHALL RD
Cheshire Farm Ice Cream
Yew Tree Farm
Ford Farm
FORD LA
Newton

3
Greaves Farm
Brook Hall
CHESTER RD
Springfield Farm
Oakfield Farm
Keys Brook

59
RAVENSHOLME LA
RAVENSHOLME CT
WOODLANDS
OAKLANDS DR
OAKLANDS AVE
CASTLEFIELDS
KETTSONY DR
HASONS AVE
PARK AVE
KEYSBROOK AVE

2
MILLBROOK RD
Millbrook
Tattenhall Park Prim Sch
Liby
The Rookery
PLANK MOW
MILLBANK COTTS
Whitehead Farm
Owler Hall
TATTENHALL LA

GORSEFIELD
BROCKWAY E
BROCKWAY W
COHERT TCE
BARNFIELD TCE
HALL VIEW
THE NINE HOUSES
PO
PH
BARBOUR SQ
FIELD LA
BURWARDSLEY RD
Fox Covert
Little Owler Farm
BIRDS LA
DERBS LA

1
FROST LA
ROSE CNR
EDGE CROFT
BROXX LA
Tattenhall Hall
Tattenhall
BOLESWORTH RD
Bank House
Broad Oak

58
48 A B 49 C D 50 E F

165 183

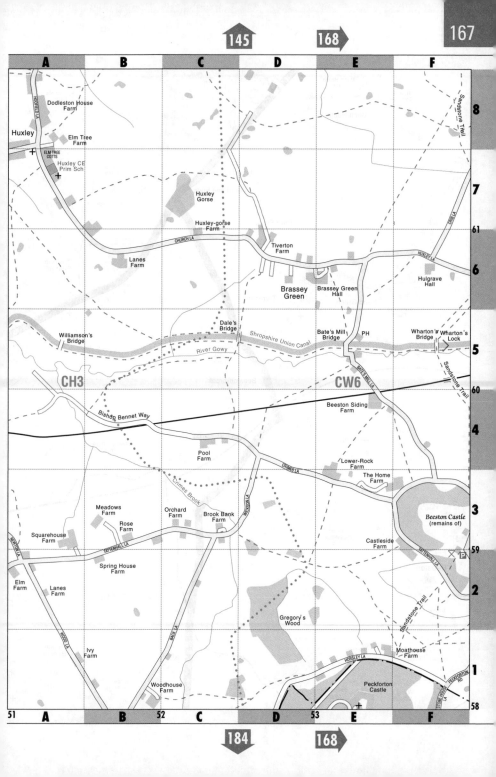

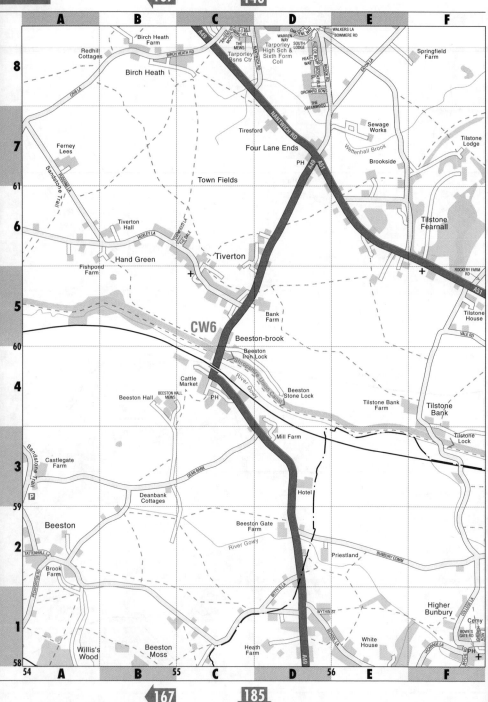

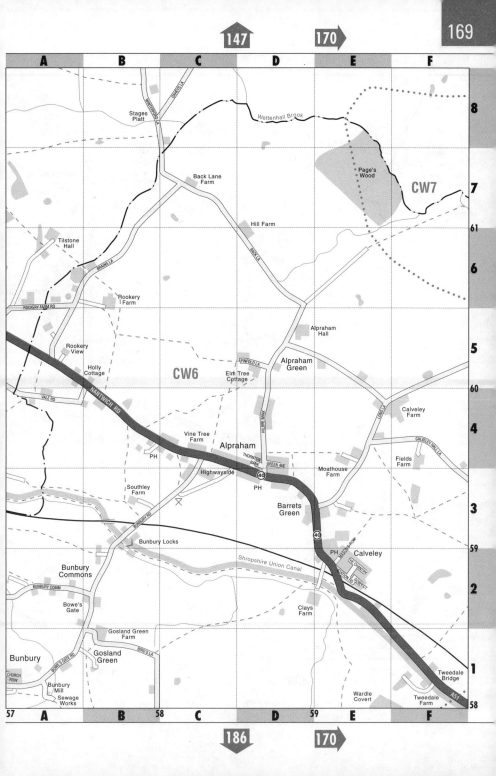

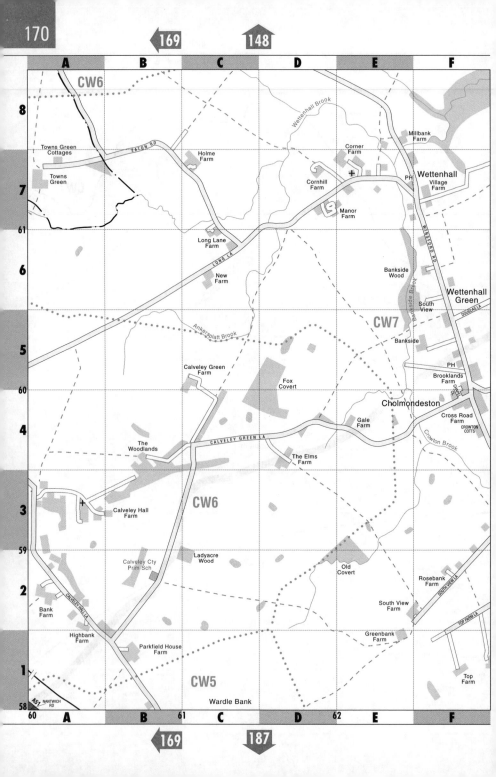

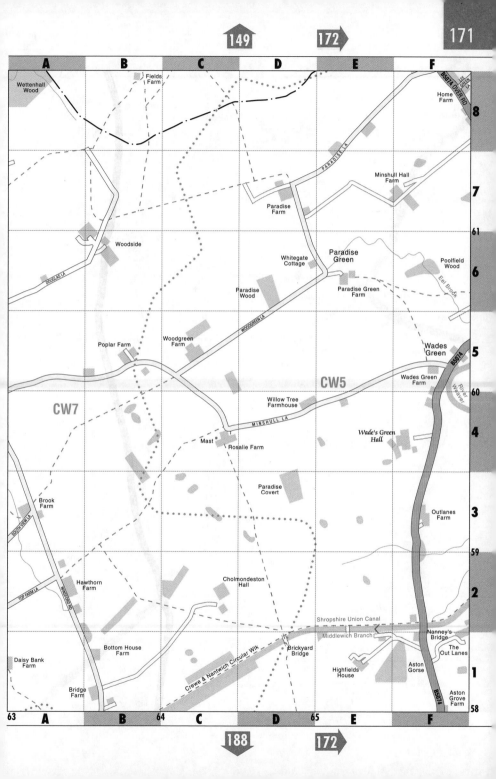

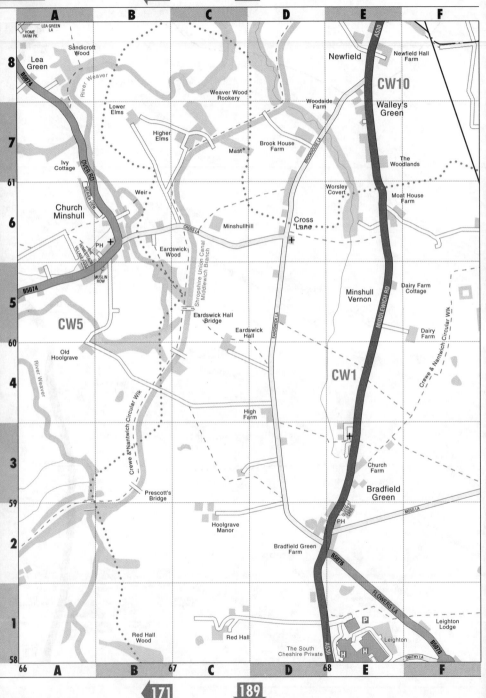

HOME FARM PK
LEA GREEN LA
Sandicroft Wood
Lea Green
Newfield
Newfield Hall Farm

8

River Weaver

CW10

Walley's Green

Weaver Wood Rookery
Lower Elms
Woodside Farm

7

Higher Elms
Brook House Farm
Mast

BROOKHOUSE LA

The Woodlands

Ivy Cottage
OVER RD

61

Weir
Worsley Covert
Moat House Farm

Church Minshull

CROSS LA
Minshullhill
Cross Lane

6

PH
Eardswick Wood

Shropshire Union Canal
Middlewich Branch

MUSLIN ROW
B5074

Minshull Vernon

MIDDLEWICH RD

Dairy Farm Cottage

5

CW5

Eardswick Hall Bridge
Eardswick Hall

EARDSWICK LA

Dairy Farm

Crewe & Nantwich Circular Wlk

60

Old Hoolgrave

CW1

4

River Weaver

High Farm

Church Farm

3

Bradfield Green

Prescott's Bridge

59

GREEN LANE
PH

MOSS LA

2

Hoolgrave Manor

Bradfield Green Farm

B5076

FLOWERS LA

Red Hall Wood

1

Red Hall

Leighton Lodge

P

A530

Leighton

B5076

The South Cheshire Private
H   H

SMITHY LA

58

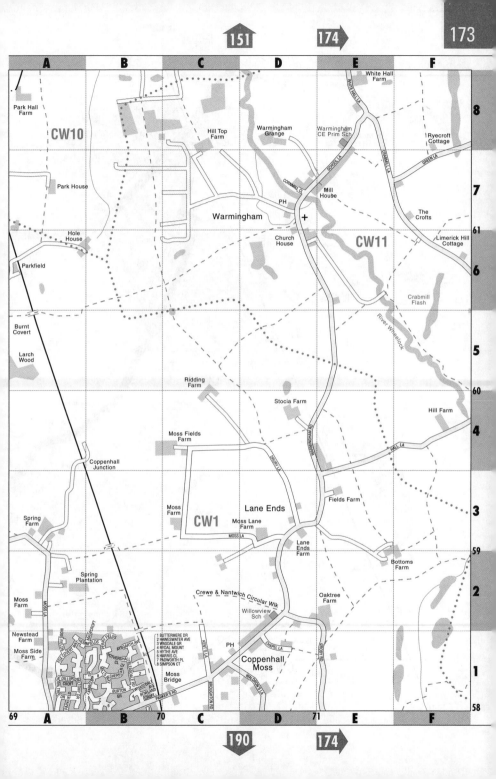

173
152

D6
1 AUSTEN CL
2 SCOTT CL
3 LAWRENCE CL
4 RICHARDSON CL
5 SHELLEY CT
6 THACKERY CT
7 WORDSWORTH CL
8 SOUTHEY CL

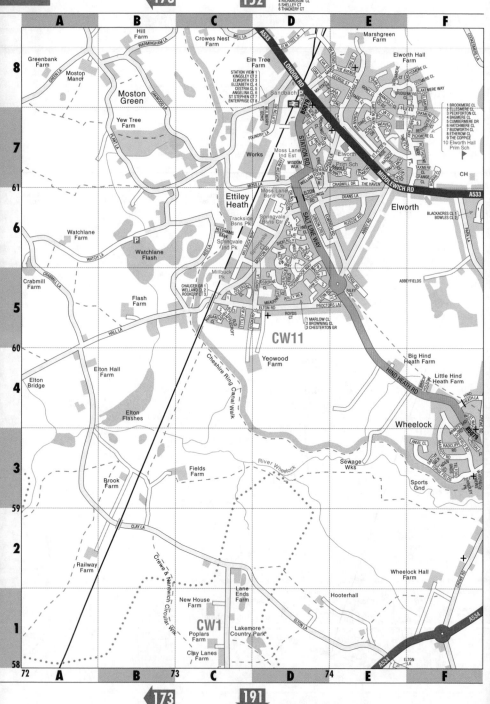

1 BROOKMERE CL
2 ELLESMERE CL
3 PECKFORTON CL
4 BAGMERE CL
5 CUMBERMERE DR
6 HATCHMERE CL
7 BUDWORTH CL
8 ETHEROW CL
9 THE COPPICE
10 Elworth Hall Prim Sch

BLACKACRES CL 1
BOWLES CL 2

1 MARLOW CL
2 BROWNING CL
3 CHESTERTON GR

CHAUCER GR 1
WELLAND CL 2
ROOKERY CT 3

CW11

CW1

173
191

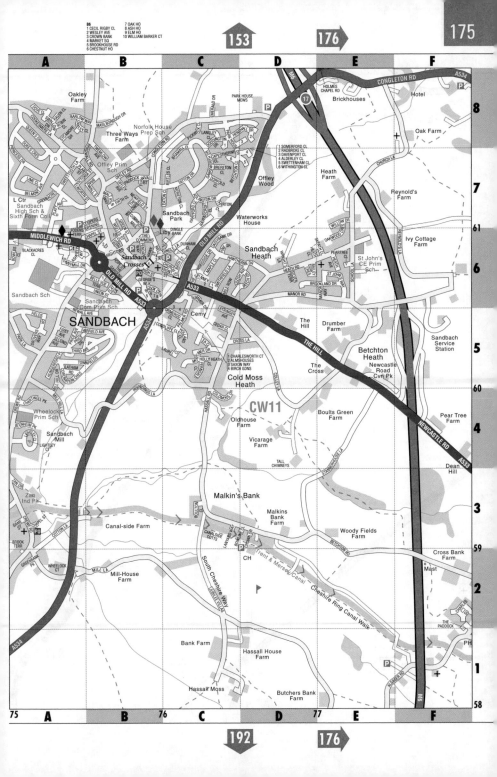

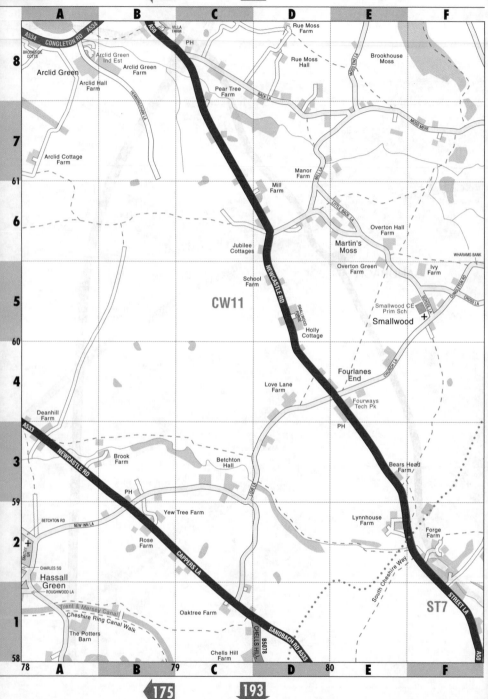

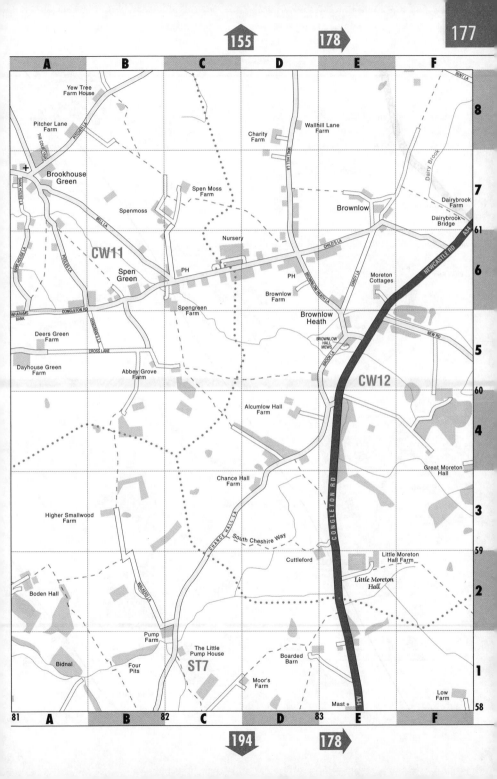

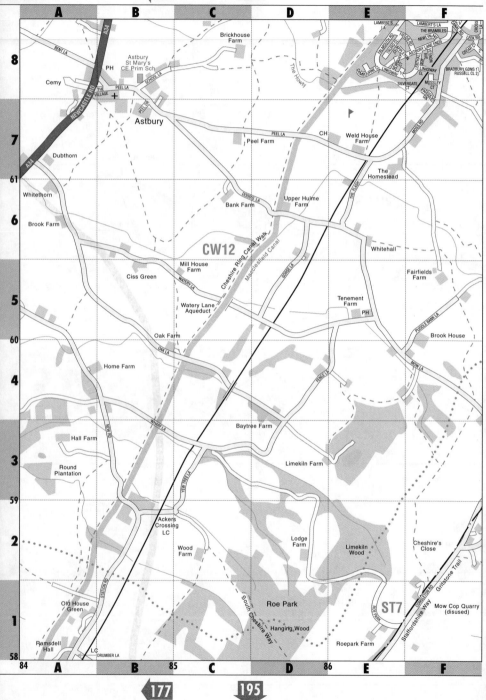

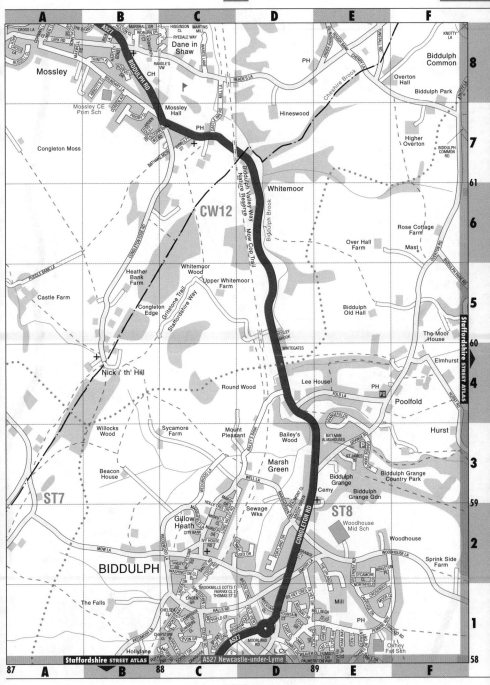

A B C D E F

8

Mossley

Dane in Shaw

KNOTTY LA

Biddulph
Common

Overton
Hall

Biddulph Park

PH

Mossley CE
Prim Sch

Mossley
Hall

Hineswood

Cheshire Brook

7

PH

Higher
Overton

BIDDULPH
COMMON
RD

Congleton Moss

CH

Whitemoor

61

CW12

Bidgulph Brook

6

Rose Cottage
Farm

Whitemoor
Wood

Over Hall
Farm

Mast

Heather
Bank
Farm

Upper Whitemoor
Farm

5

Castle Farm

Congleton
Edge

Biddulph
Old Hall

The Moor
House

60

Nick i' th' Hill

WHITEGATES

Elmhurst

4

Round Wood

Lee House

FOLD LA

PH

Poolfold

Willocks
Wood

Sycamore
Farm

Mount
Pleasant

Bailey's
Wood

Hurst

Beacon
House

Marsh
Green

Bateman
Almshouses

St James
Ct

Biddulph Grange
Country Park

3

ST7

Biddulph
Grange

Cemy

Biddulph
Grange Gdn

ST8

59

Gillow
Heath

CITY BANK

Sewage
Wks

Woodhouse
Mid Sch

Woodhouse

2

BIDDULPH

IVY HOUSE
CL

Sprink Side
Farm

WOODHOUSE LA

MOW LA

The Falls

BROOKMILLS COTTS 1
FAIRFAX CL 2
THOMAS ST 3

Mill

PH

1

Hollylane

CONGLETON RD

Oxhey
Fst Sch

A527 Newcastle-under-Lyme

58

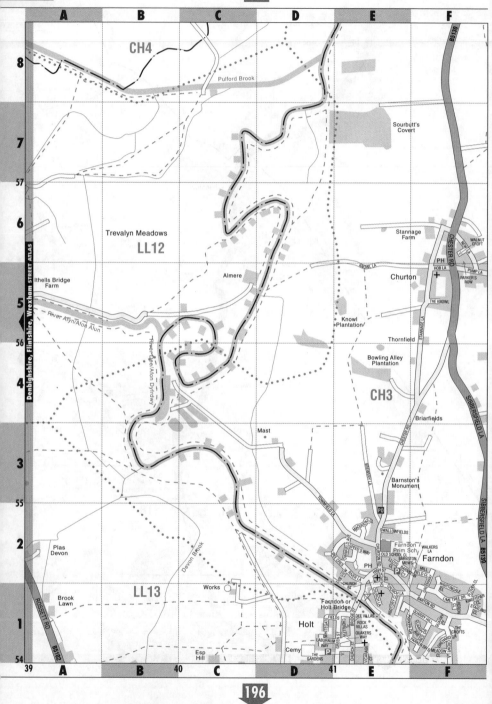

CH4

Pulford Brook

Sourbutt's Covert

Trevalyn Meadows

LL12

Stannage Farm

WALNUT CROFT

Ithells Bridge Farm

Almere

PH

HOB LA

Churton

PARKER'S ROW

PUMP LA

CHESTER RD

BS130

River Alyn/Afon Alun

THE KNOWL

River Dee/Afon Dyfrdwy

Knowl Plantation

Thornfield

STANNAGE LA

Bowling Alley Plantation

CH3

Mast

Briarfields

SIBBERSFIELD LA

CHESTER LA

BREWERY LA

Barnston's Monument

TINKERSFIELD LA

PO

Plas Devon

Devon Brook

SWALLOWFIELDS

MADDOCKS CL

Farndon Prim Sch

WALKERS LA

BARNSTON MEWS

Farndon

BS130

LL13

Works

Brook Lawn

Holt

Farndon or Holt Bridge

MILL

NIGHTINGALE

LIME TREE DR

STARLING

THE CROFTS

Cemy

Esp Hill

LABURNUM WAY

THE GARDENS

GREEN ST

CHURCH ST

ROCK VILLAS

DEE VILLAS

QUAKERS WAY

CHURCH LA

MEADOW CL

CREWE LA

ORCHARD RD

RUSSELL RD

BS102

Denbighshire, Flintshire, Wrexham STREET ATLAS

8

7

57

6

5

56

4

3

55

2

1

54

39   A   B   40   C   D   41   E   F

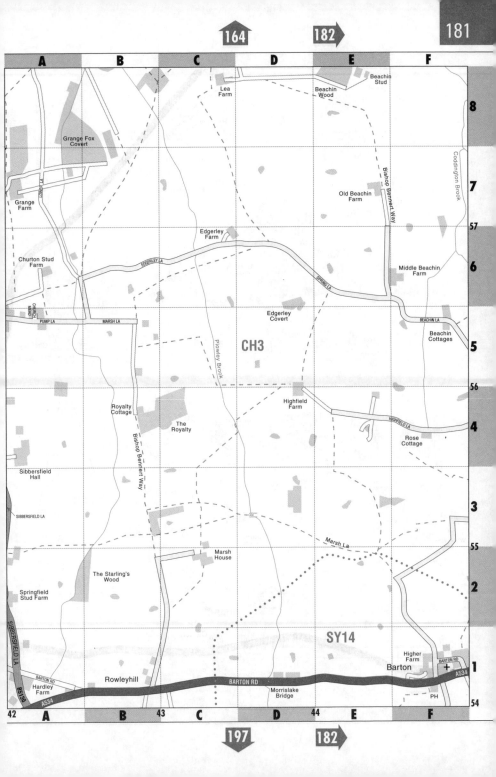

181
165

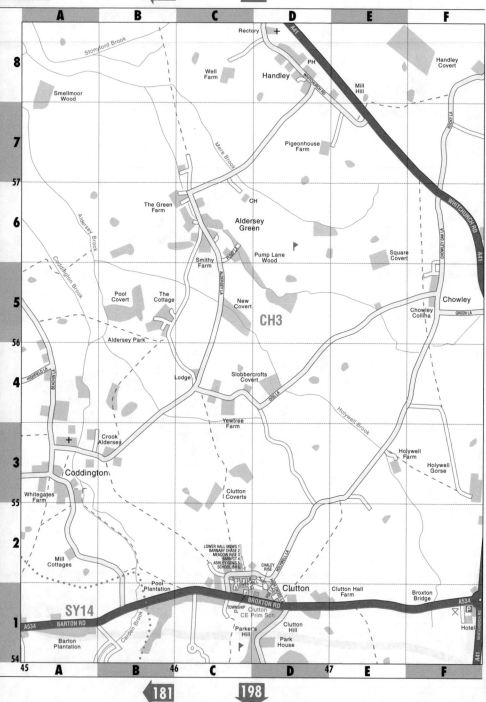

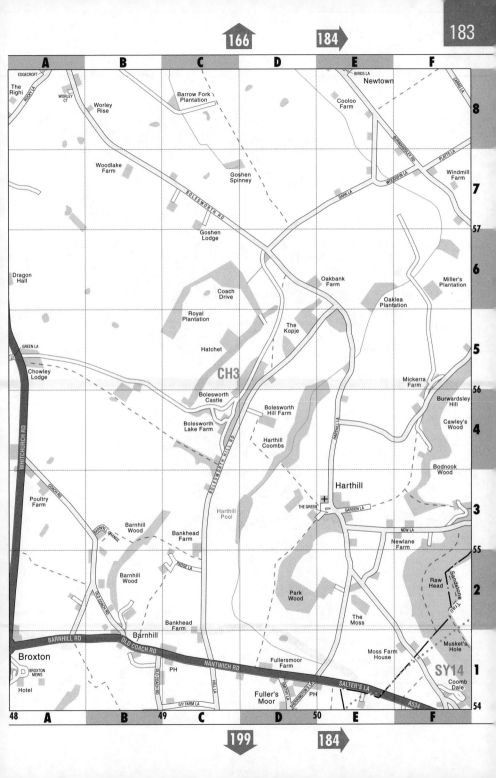

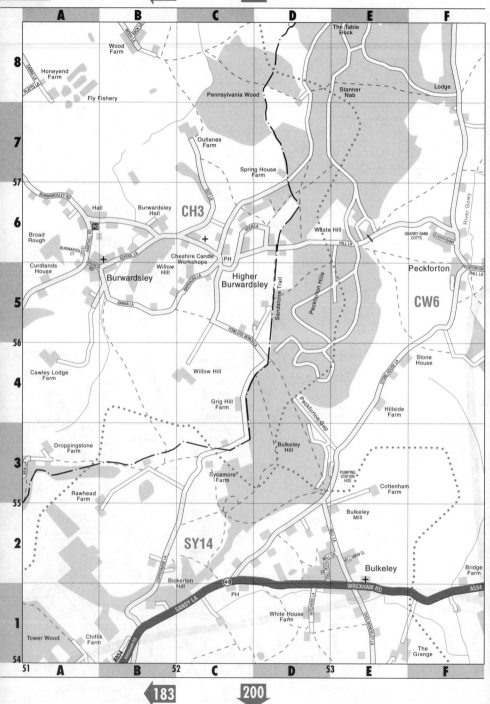

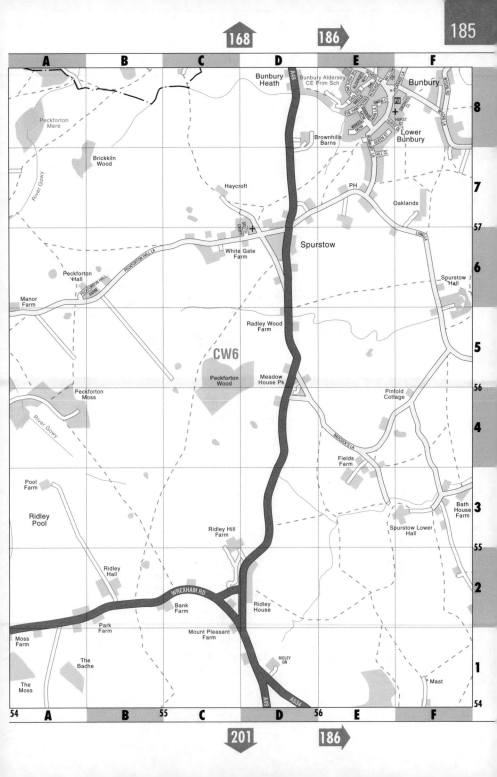

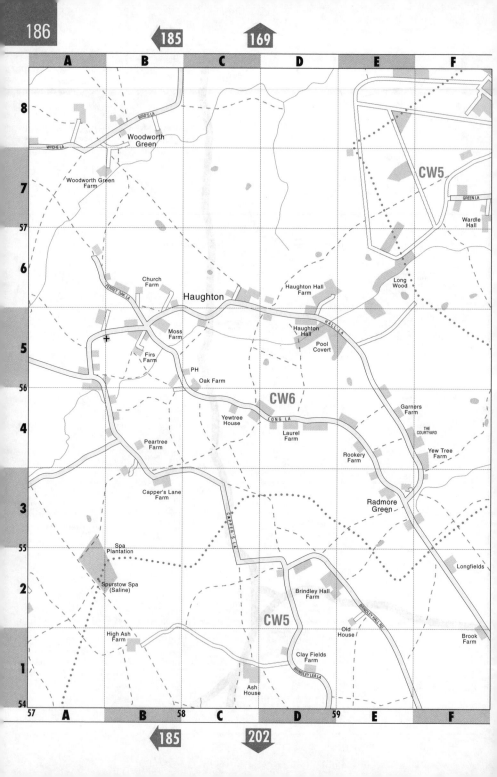

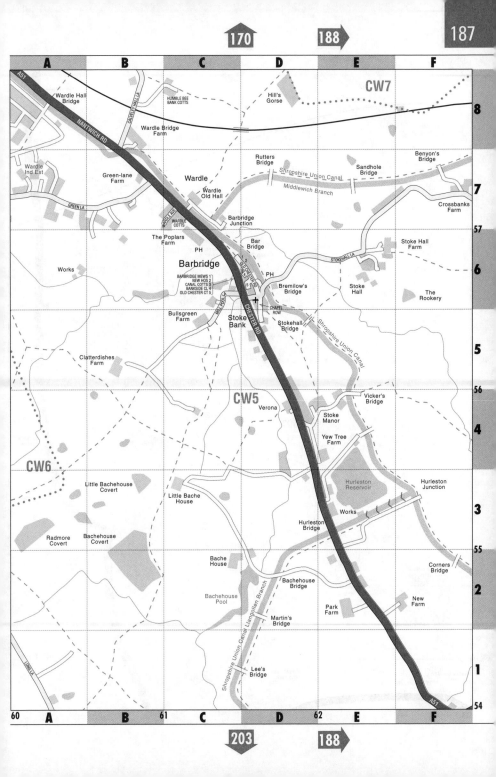

CW7

Wardle Hall Bridge

Hill's Gorse

Rutters Bridge

Shropshire Union Canal
Middlewich Branch

Sandhole Bridge

Benyon's Bridge

Humble Bee Bank Cotts

Wardle Bridge Farm

Wardle Ind Est

Green-lane Farm

Wardle

Wardle Old Hall

Crossbanks Farm

Wardle Cotts

Barbridge Junction

Stoke Hall Farm

The Poplars Farm

PH

Bar Bridge

Stokehall La

Works

Barbridge

BARBRIDGE MEWS 1
NEW HO5 2
CANAL COTTS 3
BANKSIDE CL 4
OLD CHESTER CT 5

PH

Bremilow's Bridge

Stoke Hall

The Rookery

Bullsgreen Farm

Stoke Bank

Chapel Row

Stokehall Bridge

Shropshire Union Canal

Clatterdishes Farm

CW5

Verona

Vicker's Bridge

Stoke Manor

Yew Tree Farm

CW6

Little Bachehouse Covert

Little Bache House

Hurleston Reservoir

Hurleston Junction

Radmore Covert

Bachehouse Covert

Works

Bache House

Hurleston Bridge

Corners Bridge

Bachehouse Pool

Shropshire Union Canal Llangollen Branch

Bachehouse Bridge

Park Farm

New Farm

Martin's Bridge

Lee's Bridge

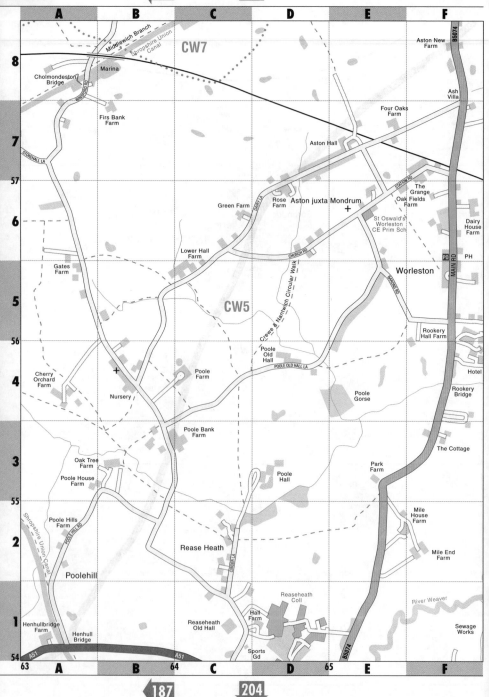

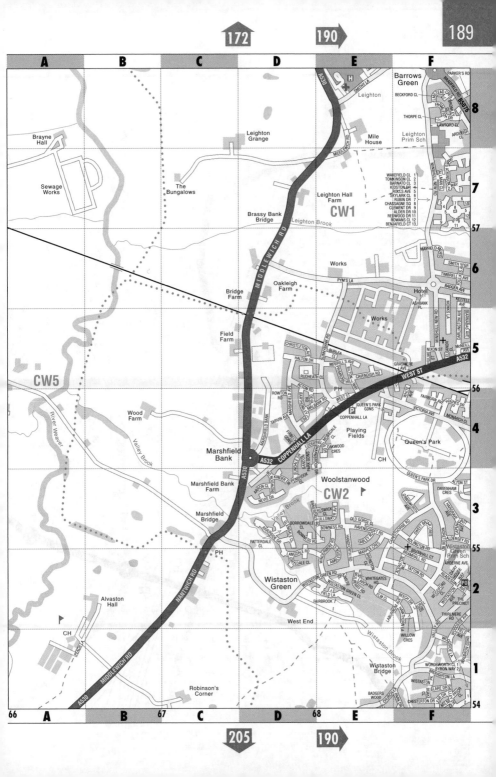

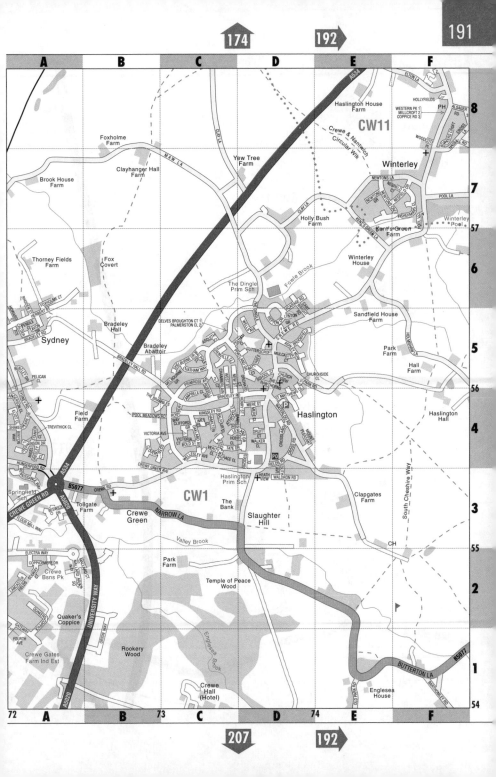

	A	B	C	D	E	F

8

Whitehall Farm

Wheelockheath Farm

Wheelock Heath

Fingerpost Farm

MILL LA

Daisy Bank House

HASSALL RD

Holly Tree Farm
Day Green

COPPICE LA

SANDY LA

School Farm

ALSAGER RD

Hassall Pool

7

POOL LA

HASSALL RD

Walnut Tree Farm

Hassall

CW11

Hassall Hall

57

Bridgehouse Farm

Bostock House

South Cheshire Way

6

Moss Cottage

Green Bank Farm

Dunnock's Fold Farm

5

Castle Farm

RANCORCROFT RD

56

Woodside Farm

Homeshaw Farm

Oakhanger Hall

Moss End Farm

ST7

4

Heathfield Farm

Stockton Farm

SPENCER CT

DELAMERE CT

CRANBERRY

3

Hall o' the Heath

CW1

Gate Farm

Oakhanger Farm

Ashfields

Mast

NURSERY RD

55

Rose Tree Farm

HILLSHAW LA

TAYLOR'S LANE

Peartree Farm

Spartan Wood Farm

White Moss

2

Butterton Lane Farm

BUTTERTON LA

Oakhanger Moss

White Moss Farm

Moss Farm

Mast

CREWE RD B5077

RADWAY GREEN RD

B5078

Radway Green

1

B5017

BUTTERTON LA

Oakhanger

DUNN'S COTTS

FM LN

Mast

M6

LC

Radway Green Bsns & Tech Ctr

CENTRAL AVE

54

CW2

M6

B5078

CW2

	A	B	C	D	E	F
75		76			77	

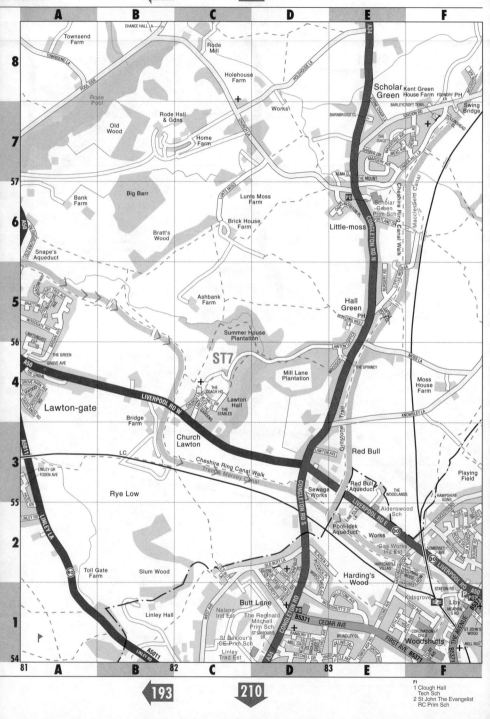

F1
1 Clough Hall
Tech Sch
2 St John The Evangelist
RC Prim Sch

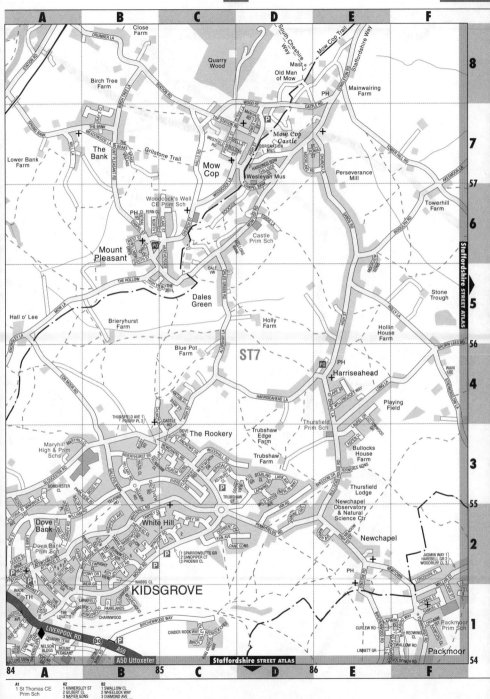

A1
1 St Thomas CE
  Prim Sch

A2
1 KINNERSLEY ST
2 GILBERT CL
3 NAPIER GDNS
4 PEEL CT
5 BANK CT
6 HIGHERLAND CT
7 WESLEY GDNS
8 VICTORIA CT

B2
1 SWALLOW CL
2 WHEELOCK WAY
3 DIAMOND AVE
4 MOSSFIELD CRES
5 LITTLE ROW
6 BRIGHTS AVE
7 BIRCHES WAY
8 SILVERMINE CL
9 MAGPIE CRES

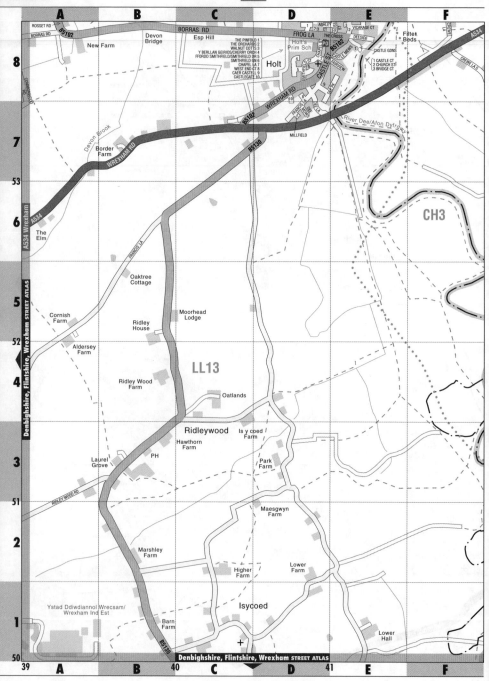

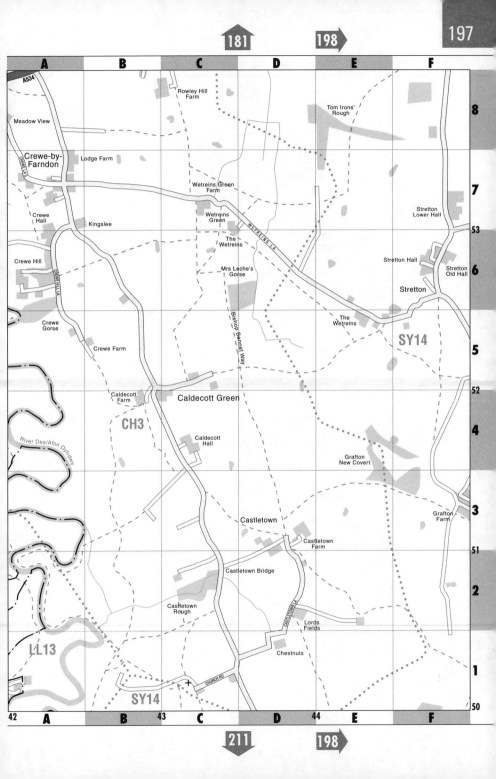

A534

Meadow View

Crewe-by-Farndon

Lodge Farm

Rowley Hill Farm

Tom Irons' Rough

CREWE LA

Crewe Hall

Kingslee

Wetreins Green Farm

Wetreins Green

Stretton Lower Hall

WETREINS LA

The Wetreins

53

Crewe Hill

Mrs Leche's Gorse

Stretton Hall

Stretton Old Hall

Stretton

CREWE HILL LA

Crewe Gorse

The Wetreins

6

Crewe Farm

SY14

Bishop Bennet Way

5

Caldecott Farm

52

Caldecott Green

CH3

River Dee/Afon Dyfrdwy

Caldecott Hall

4

Grafton New Covert

Castletown

Grafton Farm

3

Castletown Farm

51

Castletown Bridge

CASTLETOWN LA

Castletown Rough

Lords Fields

2

LL13

Chestnuts

SY14

CHURCH RD

1

50

197
182

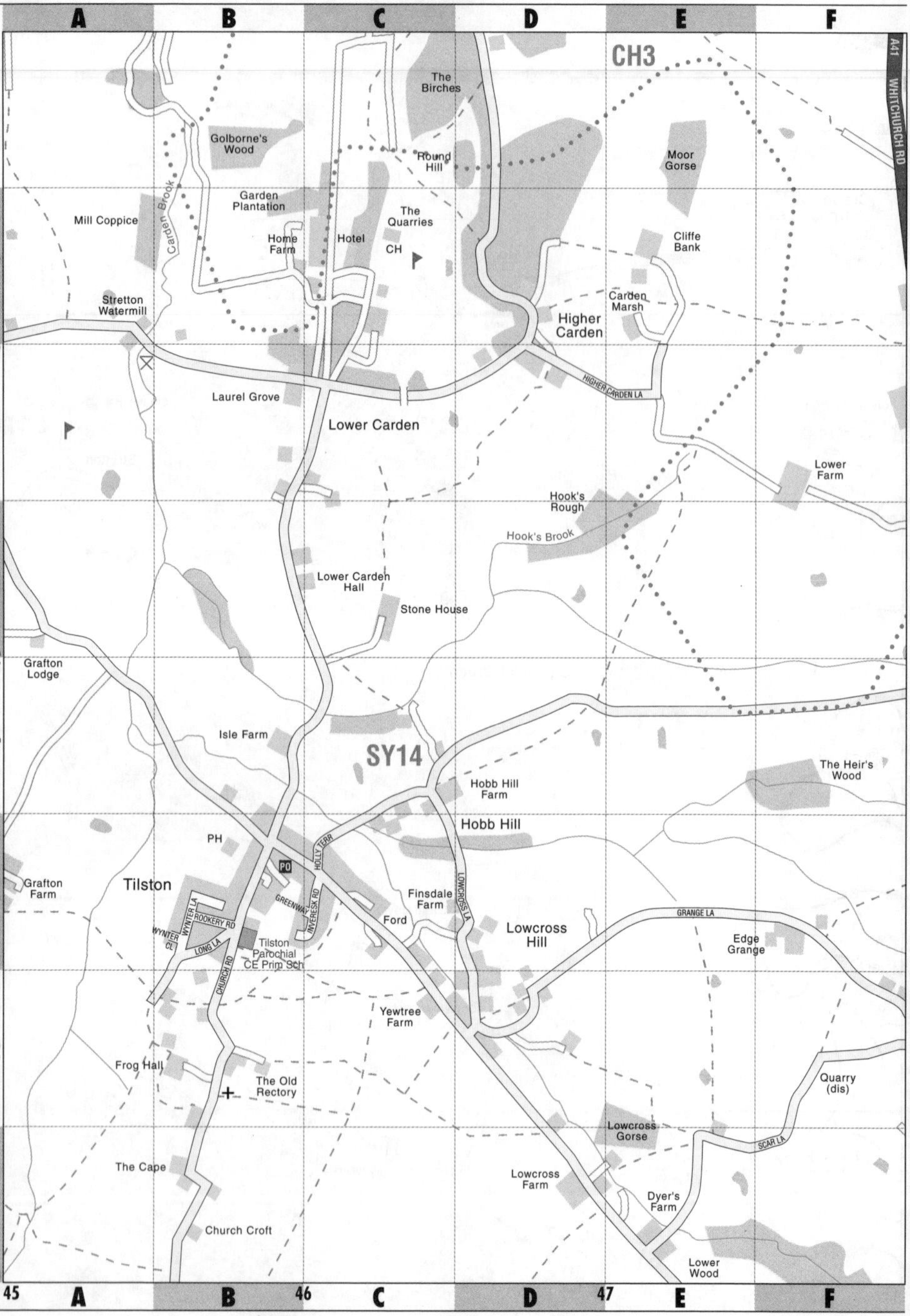

A
B
C
D
E
F
CH3
A41 WHITCHURCH RD
8
7
6
5
4
3
2
1
53
52
51
50
45
46
47
The Birches
Golborne's Wood
Round Hill
Moor Gorse
Garden Plantation
Mill Coppice
Carden Brook
Home Farm
Hotel
The Quarries
CH
Cliffe Bank
Stretton Watermill
Carden Marsh
Higher Carden
HIGHER CARDEN LA
Laurel Grove
Lower Carden
Lower Farm
Hook's Rough
Hook's Brook
Lower Carden Hall
Stone House
Grafton Lodge
Isle Farm
SY14
Hobb Hill Farm
The Heir's Wood
Hobb Hill
PH
PO
HOLLY TERR
Tilston
Grafton Farm
GREENWAY
INVERESK RD
LOWCROSS LA
Finsdale Farm
Ford
Lowcross Hill
GRANGE LA
Edge Grange
WYNTER LA
ROOKERY RD
WYNTER CL
LONG LA
CHURCH RD
Tilston Parochial CE Prim Sch
Yewtree Farm
Frog Hall
The Old Rectory
Quarry (dis)
Lowcross Gorse
SCAR LA
The Cape
Lowcross Farm
Dyer's Farm
Church Croft
Lower Wood

197
212

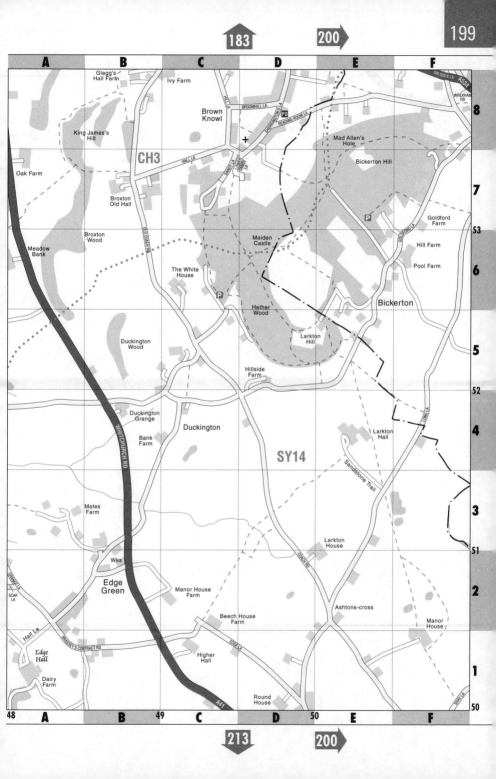

199
184

199
214

	A	B	C	D	E	F

8

WREXHAM RD
A534
Sandstone Trail
BRUNTY BANK
Gallantry Bank
Bickerton Farm
COUNCIL HOS
Gallantry-bank Farm
Bulkeley Hall
Walnut Tree Farm
Manor Farm
CW6

7

Bickerton Holy Trinity CE Prim Sch
LONG LA
GOLF LA
Yewtree Farm
Townsend Farm
BICKERTON LA
Bulkeleyhay
BULKELEY LA

53

Bickerton Hall

6

Manor Farm
Fields Farm
Gate House Farm

Egerton Green

5

Green Farm
Yew Tree Farm
Oak Tree Farm
Bankhouse Farm

52

SY14
Egerton Farm
Park House

4

Bickley Brook
Scotch Farm

Castle Hill

3

Castle Farm
Cholmondeley Park
Cholmondeley Castle
PO
Egerton Cottages

51

BICKERTON RD

2

Egerton Hall
Egerton Bank Farm

1

SPIKE LA
Hampton Grange
Hetherson Green Farm
Cross Lanes Farm
Red Hall

50

GROTSWORTH LA

51	A	B	52	C	D	53	E	F

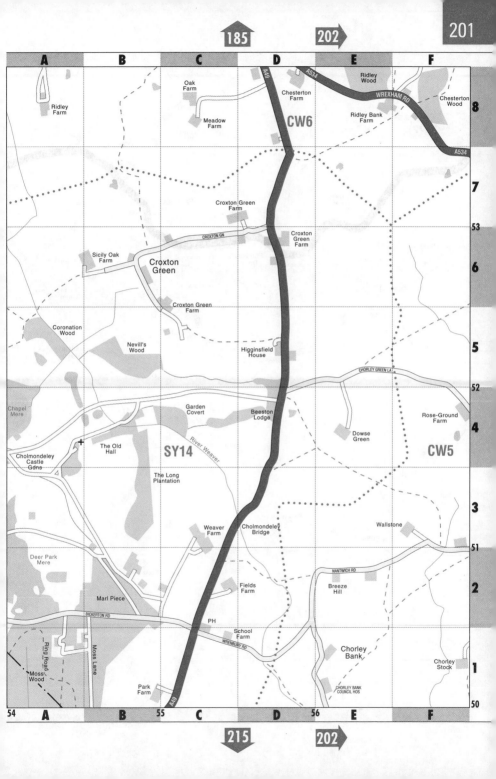

201
186

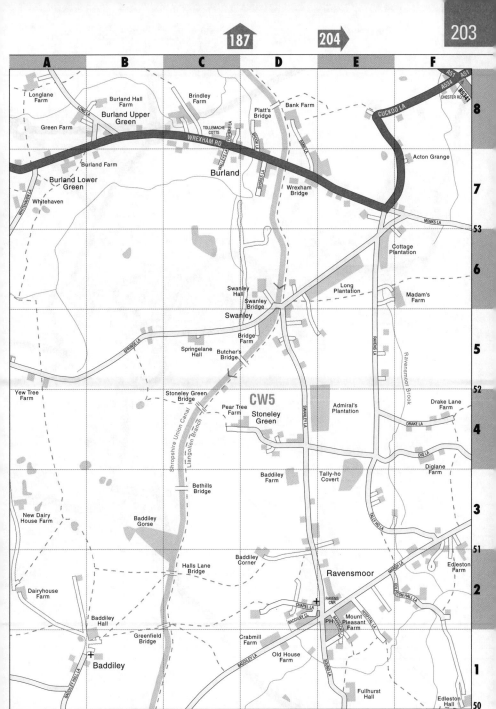

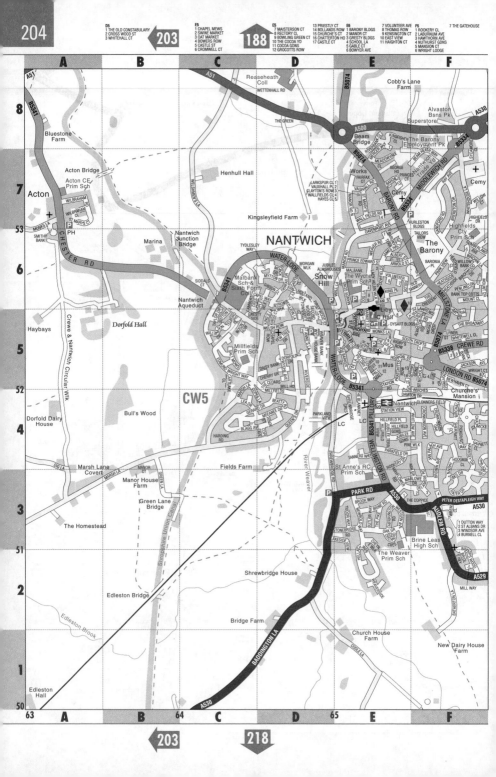

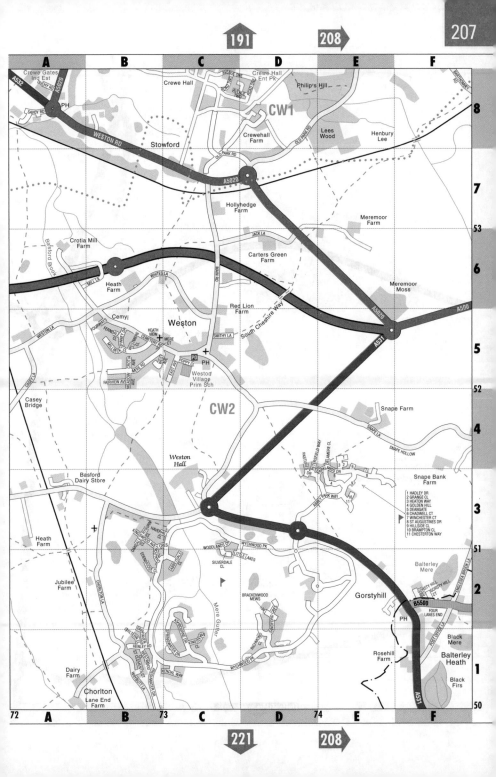

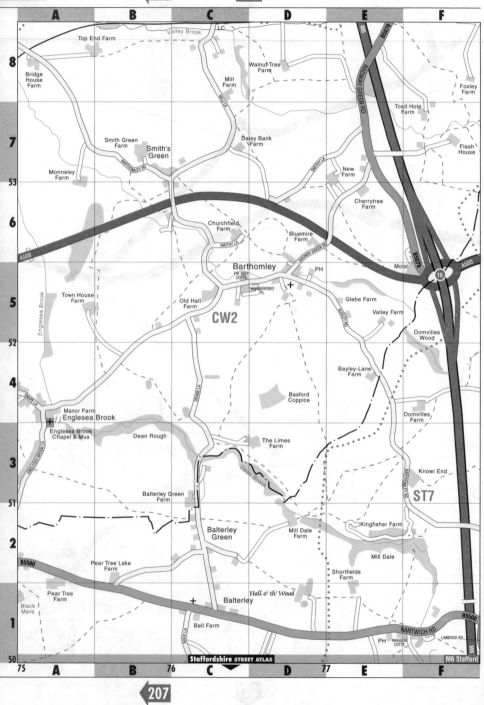

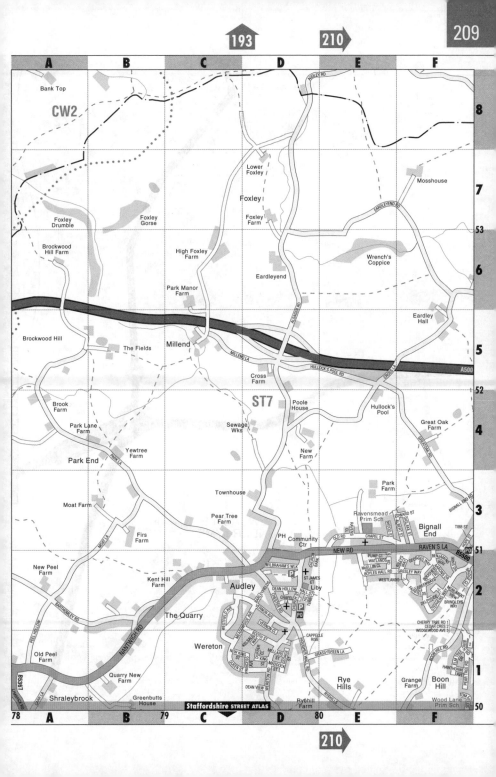

8

7

53

6

5

52

4

3

51

2

1

50

A B C D E F

Sunnyhill Farm

Merelake Way

A5011

West Ave

Nelson Ind Est

Congleton Rd
Linley Trad Est

B5371

FIRST AVE
THE AVENUE

Hartshill Gdns

Maple Ave

Grove Ave
Lower Ash Rd

Hollins

Clough Hall

Walton Way

Swallowmore View 1
Coppice Ho 2
Dumbill Ho 3
Macbeth Ho 4

Coalpit Hill

Sycamore Cl

Park Ave

Kidsgrove Ski Ctr

Foxholes

Merelake Rd

Talke

1 Hollins Grange
2 Gallimore Ho
3 McGowan Ho
4 Hunters Way
5 Brindley Cl

Clough Hall Dr

Newcastle Rd

Bath Pool

New Springs Cottage

Mast

Audley Rd

Church Farm

Liby

Worcester Cl
Swan Bank

Derby

Chester Cl

Bathpool Park

Dunkirk Farm

Lichfield Rd

Wedgwood Rd

Rectory Gdns
Crown Gdns

Ashenough Rd
Park Cres

Bevan Ave

Harecastle Farm

Ashenough

Eardleyend Rd

Diglake Cl

Kent Ho 1
Windsor Ho 2
Norfolk Ho 3
Elizabeth Ct 4
King St 5
Princess St 6
Princess Ct 7
Anne Ct 8

Hurst Cl

Springhead Prim Sch

Long Rd

Harecastle Farm

Dunkirk

Freeport Shopping Mall

Springhead Rd

Target Cl

PH

ST7

Parrot's Drumble

Jamage Ind Est

King Ho

Arbour St

Talke Pits

A500

Woodlands Farm

Bignall Rd

Jamage Rd

Oaktree La

Target Wood

Peacock Hay

Motel

Jamage Farm

Peacock Hay Rd

Bottom Farm

Talke Rd

A500

Colliery (disused)

Diglake

Diglake Farm

Wedgwood's Monument

NEWCASTLE-UNDER-LYME

PH

Crofters La
Red Street

Bell's Hollow

Mitchell's Wood Farm

High Carr

Tibb St

Buffers Green

B5500

Bignall Hill

Audley Rd

ST5

St Chad's Terr
St Chad's CE Prim Sch

Deans La

High Carr Farm

Bridgnorth Gr

Talke Rd

High Carr Network Ctr

Millennium Way
High Carr Bsns Pk

Boon Hill

1 Boon Hill Rd
2 Farm Hollow
3 Diglake Cotts
4 Raven's La

Megacre

Cranberry Dr 1
Huntsbank Dr 2
Wrenbury Cl 3
Warrilow Heath Rd 4
Willotts Hill Rd 5
Haslington Cl 6
Birch House Rd 7
Burford Ave 8

Meremore Dr

Cedar Rd

Parkhouse Ind Est

Cheshire View

Cherry Tree Rd

Wood View Cl
School Cl

Wood Lane

Robin Hood Farm

B5500

Stanley Dr

Crackley Bank Prim Sch

Rosevale Rd

A34

Parkhouse Rd

A34 Newcastle-under-Lyme

ST6

Staffordshire STREET ATLAS A500 Stoke-on-Trent

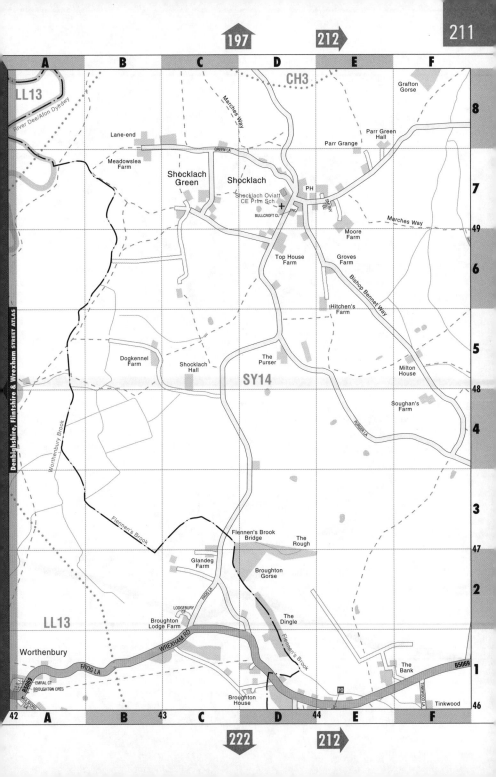

211
198

	A	B	C	D	E	F

New House

Horton Green

8

Kidnal

Kidnal House

Fox Covert

Horton House Farm

Horton Hall

Gatehouse Farm

7

WHITEWOOD LA

Overton Scar

Gam's Wood

49

The Elms

Bishop Bennet Way

Kidnal Hill

Hawthorn Cottage

MEADOWS LA

6

Scar Farm

Meadows Farm

Overton Hall

OVERTON HEATH LA

Bishop Bennet Way

Chorlton Old Hall

Chorlton Hall

5

Overton Heath

LONE LA

48

SY14

Chorlton Lane

4

Chorlton Lodge

Black Lion Farm

Bishop Bennet Way

3

Chorlton House

The Lodge

Field's Farm

Cherry Hill Farm

Cherryhill

The Mount

Cuddington Heath

B5069

47

New Farm

WREXHAM RD

SUNNYSIDE

2

Pitt's Farm

Lane Farm

Heath Farm

Ashley Court Mews

Carding Fields

Old Heys

B5069

1

Cuddington Hall

Greenacres Farm

Cuddington Green

Buenavista

46

FOX LA

45	A		B	46	C		D	47	E		F

211
223

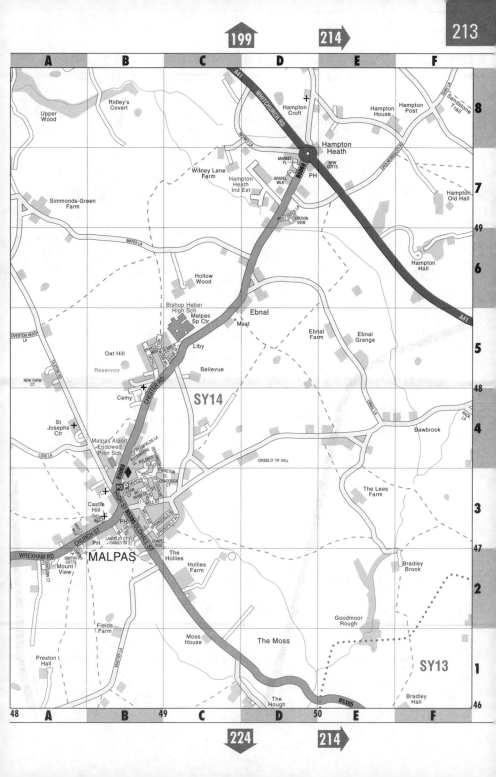

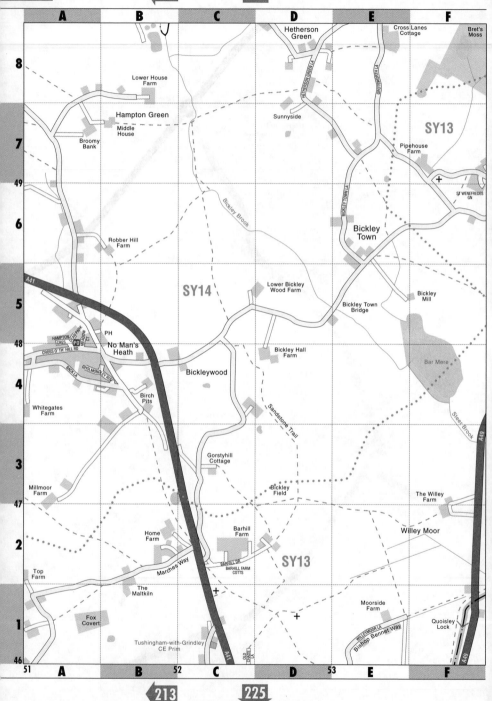

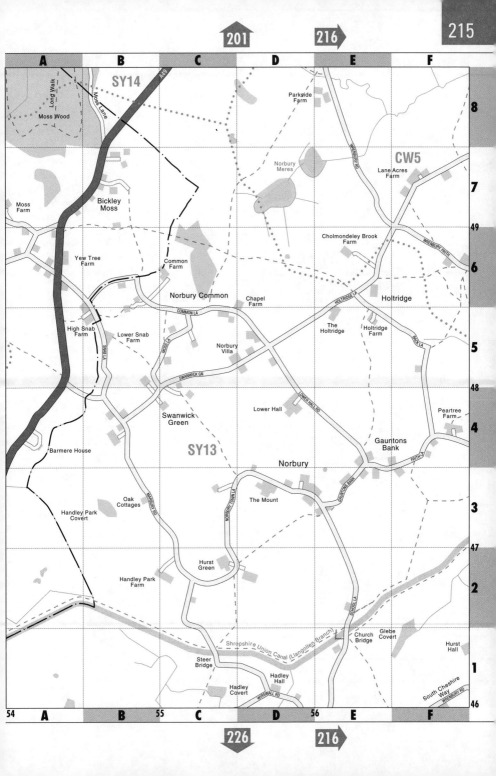

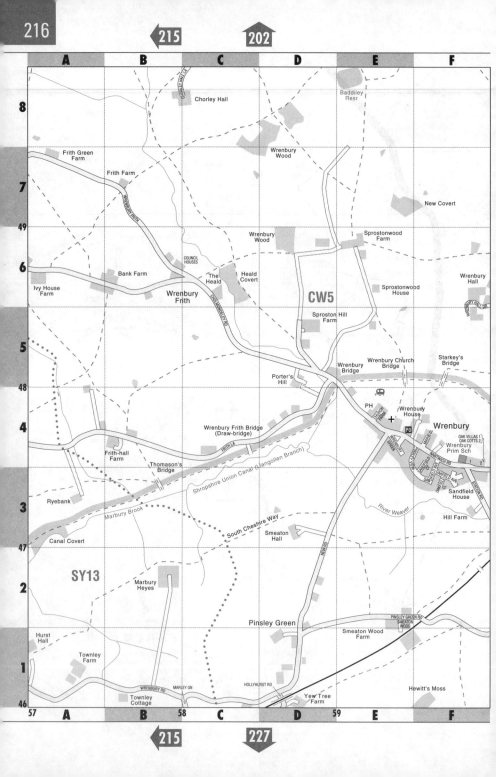

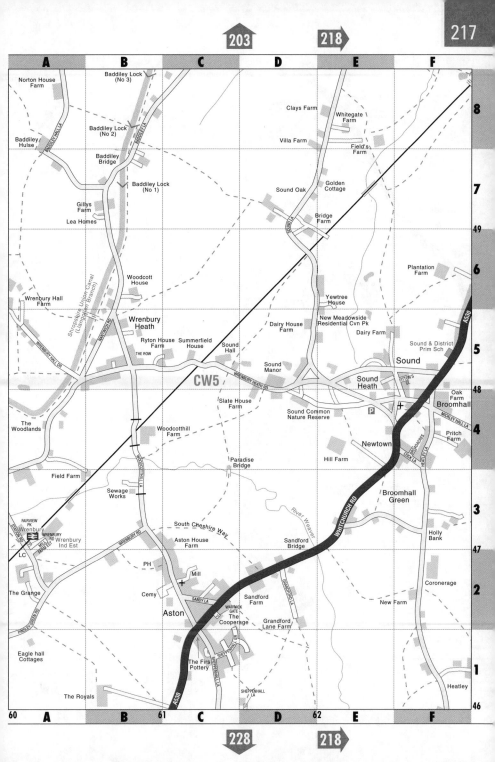

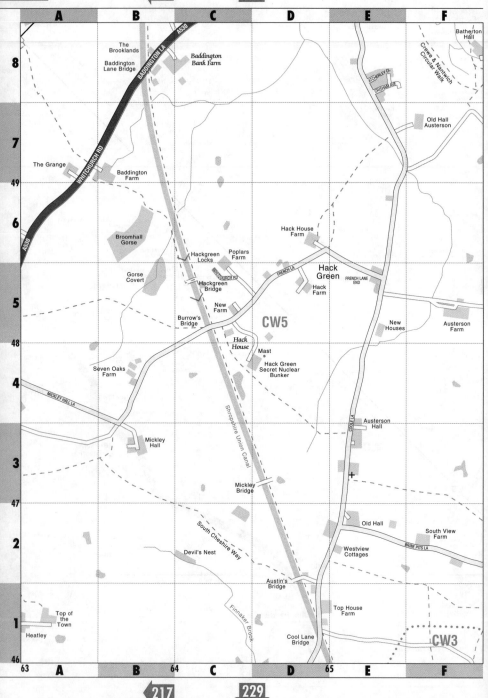

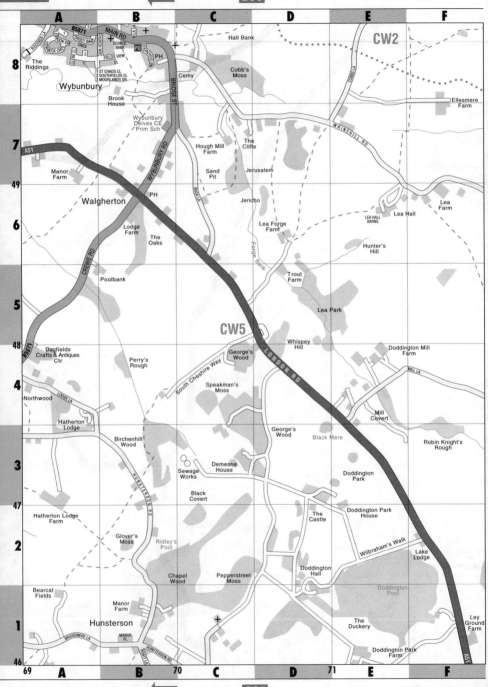

CW2

8
The Riddings
Wybunbury
B5071
MAIN RD
SCHOOL BANK
CHURCH WAY
GREEN LA
FIELDS VIEW CL
1 ST CHADS CL
2 SOUTHFIELDS CL
3 MOORLANDS DR
COHSEY BANK
CRES
CHURCHFIELDS
PO
PH
Hall Bank
Cobb's Moss
Cemy
Brook House
Wybunbury Delves CE Prim Sch
BRIDGE ST
Ellesmere Farm

7
A51
Manor Farm
Walgherton
PH
Hough Mill Farm
The Cliffe
Sand Pit
Jerusalem
WRINEHILL RD
CW2

49
WYBUNBURY RD
BACK LA
Jericho
Lea Forge Farm
Lea Hall
Lea Hall BARNS
Lea Farm

6
Lodge Farm
The Oaks
Hunter's Hill
CREWE RD

5
Poolbank
Forge Bank
Trout Farm
Lea Park

48
CW5
Whispey Hill
Doddington Mill Farm
MILL LA

4
Dagfields Crafts & Antiques Ctr
Perry's Rough
George's Wood
South Cheshire Way
Speakman's Moss
LONDON RD
Mill Covert
Robin Knight's Rough
Northwood
LOOSE LA
Hatherton Lodge

3
HUNSTERSON RD
Birchenhill Wood
Sewage Works
Demesne House
George's Wood
Black Mere
Doddington Park

47
Hatherton Lodge Farm
Black Covert
Doddington Park House

2
Glover's Moss
Ridley's Pool
The Castle
Doddington Hall
Wilbraham's Walk
Lake Lodge
Doddington Pool

1
Bearcat Fields
Manor Farm
Hunsterson
MANOR PL
Chapel Wood
Pepperstreet Moss
The Duckery
Ley Ground Farm

46
BRIDGEMERE LA
HUNSTERSON RD
Doddington Park Farm
A51

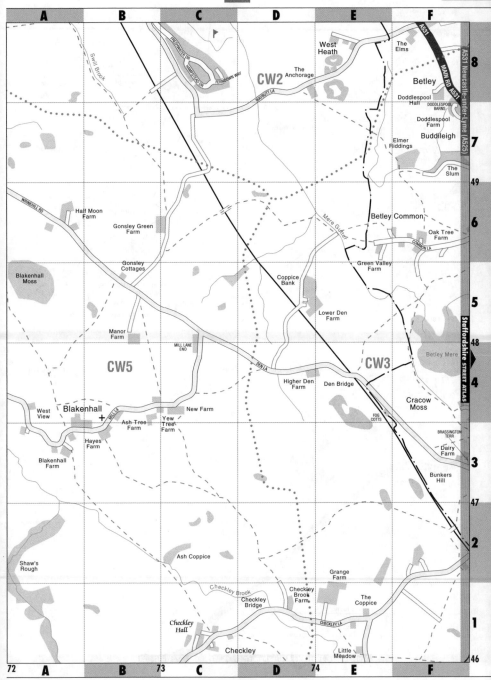

A B C D E F

8

Swill Brook

PRESHALLER DR

HAWTHORNE WAY

FERNDOWN WAY

BABBITT LA

CW2

West Heath

The Anchorage

The Elms

A531

MAIN RD A531

A531 Newcastle-under-Lyme (A525)

Betley

Doddlespool Hall

DODDLESPOOL BARNS

Doddlespool Farm

Buddileigh

7

Elmer Riddings

The Slum

49

WHINEHILL RD

Half Moon Farm

Gonsley Green Farm

Mere Gutter

Betley Common

6

Oak Tree Farm

COMMON LA

Blakenhall Moss

Gonsley Cottages

Green Valley Farm

Coppice Bank

Staffordshire STREET ATLAS

Manor Farm

Lower Den Farm

5

MILL LANE END

48

CW5

DEN LA

CW3

Betley Mere

4

West View

Blakenhall

Higher Den Farm

Den Bridge

Cracow Moss

Ash Tree Farm

Yew Tree Farm

New Farm

MILL LA

FOG COTTS

BRASSINGTON TERR

Dairy Farm

Hayes Farm

Blakenhall Farm

Bunkers Hill

3

47

Shaw's Rough

Ash Coppice

2

Grange Farm

Checkley Brook

Checkley Brook Farm

The Coppice

Checkley Bridge

Checkley Hall

CHECKLEY LA

Checkley

Little Meadow

1

46

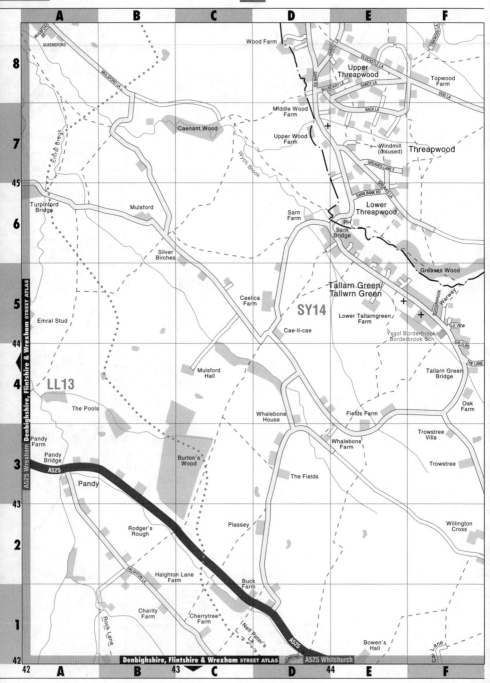

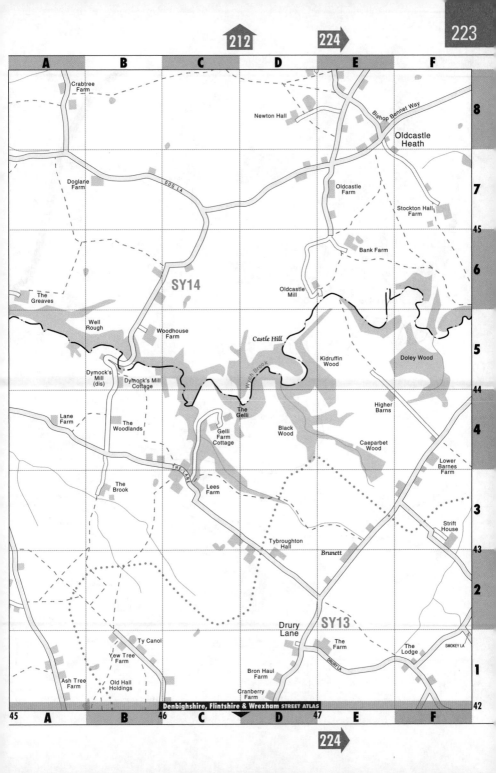

Crabtree Farm

Newton Hall

Bishop Bennet Way

Oldcastle Heath

Doglane Farm

BOG LA

Oldcastle Farm

Stockton Hall Farm

SY14

Bank Farm

The Greaves

Oldcastle Mill

Well Rough

Woodhouse Farm

Castle Hill

Kidruffin Wood

Doley Wood

Wych Brook

Dymock's Mill (dis)

Dymock's Mill Cottage

The Gelli

Higher Barns

Lane Farm

The Woodlands

Gelli Farm Cottage

Black Wood

Caeparbet Wood

Lower Barnes Farm

The Brook

Lees Farm

Strift House

Tybroughton Hall

Brunett

Drury Lane

SY13

Ty Canol

The Farm

The Lodge

SMOKEY LA

Yew Tree Farm

DRURY LA

Ash Tree Farm

Old Hall Holdings

Bron Haul Farm

Cranberry Farm

THE LANE

45 A B 46 C D 47 E F 42

224

45

44

43

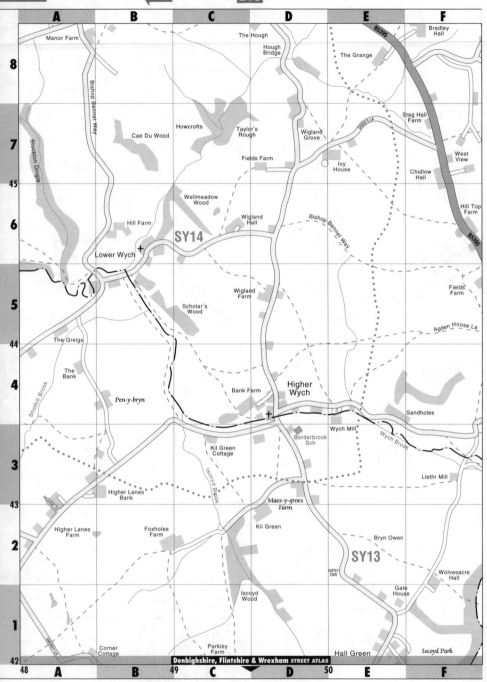

Manor Farm

The Hough

Hough
Bridge

The Grange

Bradley
Hall

B5395

Bishop Bennet Way

Stockton Dingle

Cae Du Wood

Howcrofts

Taylor's
Rough

Wigland
Grove

Stag Hall
Farm

West
View

Chidlow
Hall

Fields Farm

Ivy
House

Wellmeadow
Wood

Hill Farm

Wigland
Hall

SY14

Bishop Bennet Way

Hill Top
Farm

B5395

Lower Wych

Wigland
Farm

Fields
Farm

The Greigs

Scholar's
Wood

Agden House La

The
Bank

Shothill Brook

Pen-y-bryn

Bank Farm

Higher
Wych

Sandholes

Wych Brook

Kil Green
Cottage

Borderbrook
Sch

Wych Mill

Iscoyd Brook

Llethr Mill

Higher Lanes
Bank

Maes-y-groes
Farm

HIGHER LES

Higher Lanes
Farm

Foxholes
Farm

Kil Green

Bryn Owen

SY13

GIPSY
CNR

Wolvesacre
Hall

Iscoyd
Wood

Gate
House

Corner
Cottage

Parkley
Farm

Hall Green

Iscoyd Park

48   A   B   49   C   D   50   E   F

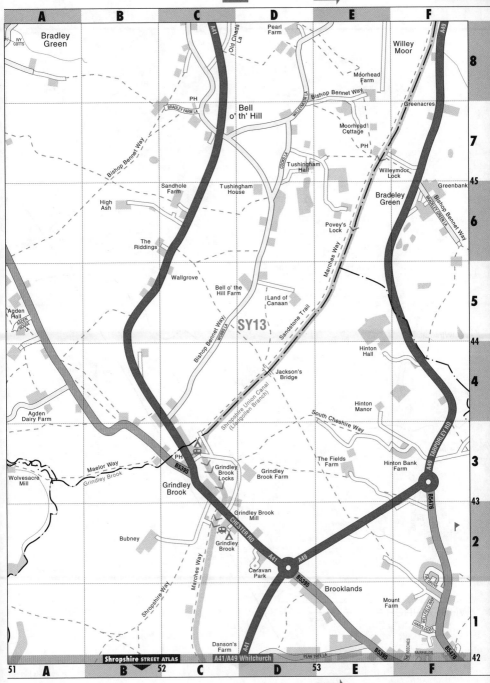

SY13

A41/A49 Whitchurch

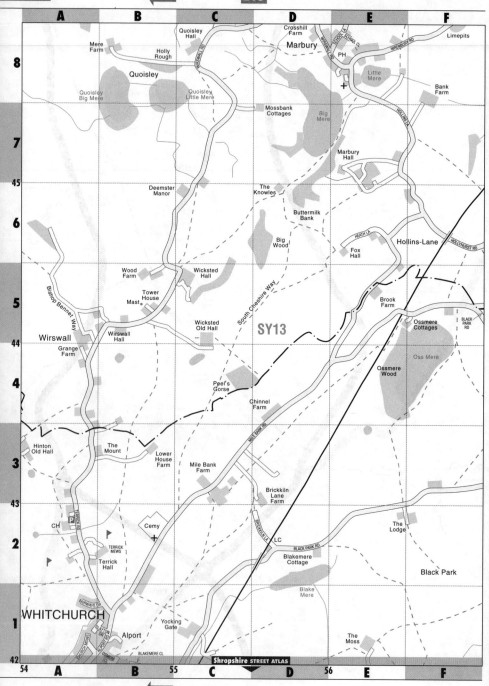

| | A | B | C | D | E | F |

8

Mere Farm

Holly Rough

Quoisley

Quoisley Hall

Quoisley Big Mere

Quoisley Little Mere

Crosshill Farm

Marbury

PH

Little Mere

Limepits

Bank Farm

7

Mossbank Cottages

Big Mere

Marbury Hall

45

Deemster Manor

The Knowles

6

Buttermilk Bank

Big Wood

Hollins-Lane

Fox Hall

HEATH LA

HOLLYHURST RD

5

Wood Farm

Wicksted Hall

Tower House

Mast

South Cheshire Way

SY13

Brook Farm

Ossmere Cottages

BLACK PARK RD

44

Wirswall

Wirswall Hall

Wicksted Old Hall

Oss Mere

Ossmere Wood

4

Grange Farm

Peel's Gorse

Chinnel Farm

3

Hinton Old Hall

The Mount

Lower House Farm

Mile Bank Farm

MILE BANK RD

BRICKKILN LA

Brickkiln Lane Farm

43

CH

P

TERRICK RD

Cemy

LC

BLACK PARK RD

The Lodge

2

TERRICK MEWS

Terrick Hall

Blakemere Cottage

Blake Mere

Black Park

1

WHITCHURCH

FAIRWAYS DR

Alport

Yocking Gate

The Moss

42

BLAKEMERE CL

| 54 | A | B | 55 | C | D | 56 | E | F |

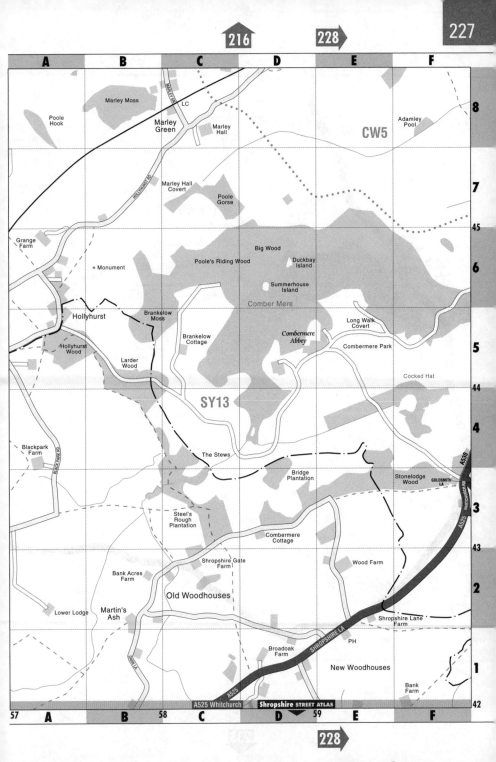

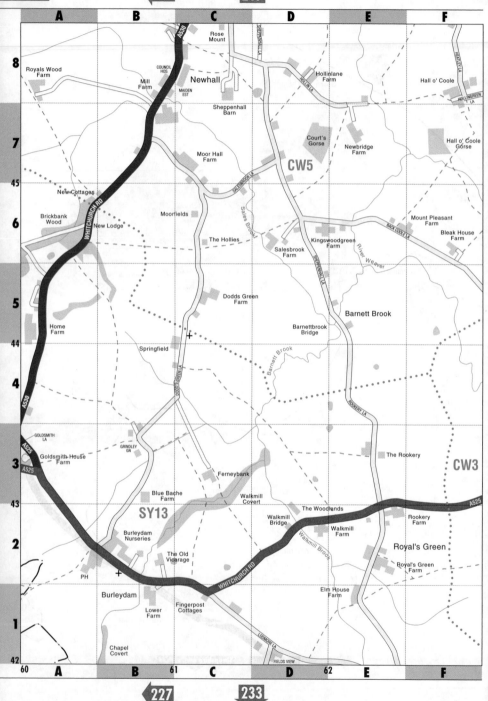

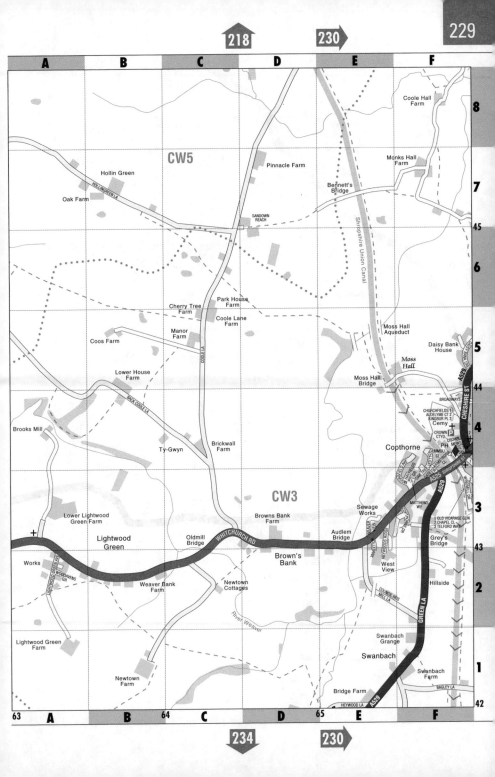

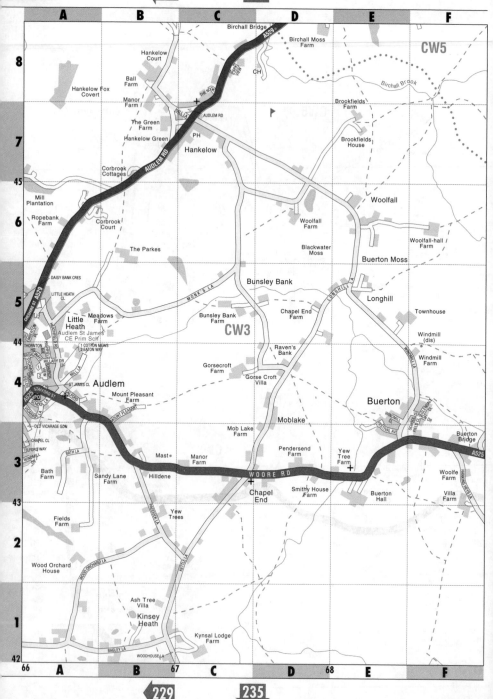

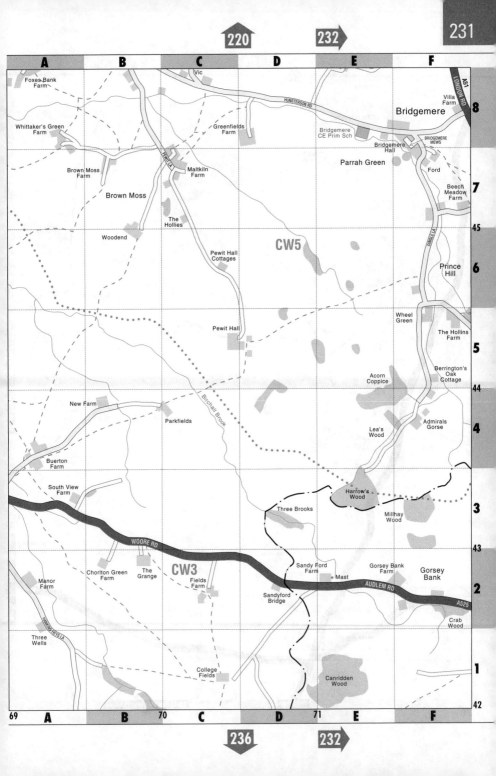

A B C D E F

8 Foxes Bank Farm

Whittaker's Green Farm

Vic

HUNSTERSON RD

Villa Farm

A51 LONDON RD

Bridgemere

Greenfields Farm

Bridgemere CE Prim Sch

Bridgemere Hall

BRIDGEMERE MEWS

Brown Moss Farm

Maltkiln Farm

Parrah Green

Ford

7 Brown Moss

The Hollies

Beech Meadow Farm

45

Woodend

Pewit Hall Cottages

CW5

Prince Hill

6

DUNKIRK LA

Wheel Green

5 Pewit Hall

The Hollins Farm

Berrington's Oak Cottage

Acorn Coppice

44

New Farm

Birchall Brook

4 Parkfields

Lea's Wood

Admirals Gorse

Buerton Farm

South View Farm

Harrow's Wood

3 Three Brooks

Millhay Wood

43

WOORE RD

CW3

Sandy Ford Farm

Gorsey Bank Farm

Gorsey Bank

2 Manor Farm

Chorlton Green Farm

The Grange

Fields Farm

Sandyford Bridge

Mast

AUDLEM RD

A525

HANKEY'S LA

Three Wells

Crab Wood

1

College Fields

Canridden Wood

42

69 A B 70 C D 71 E F

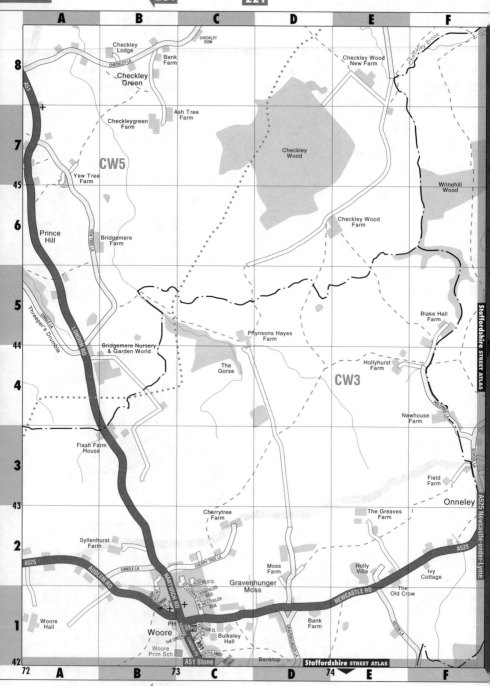

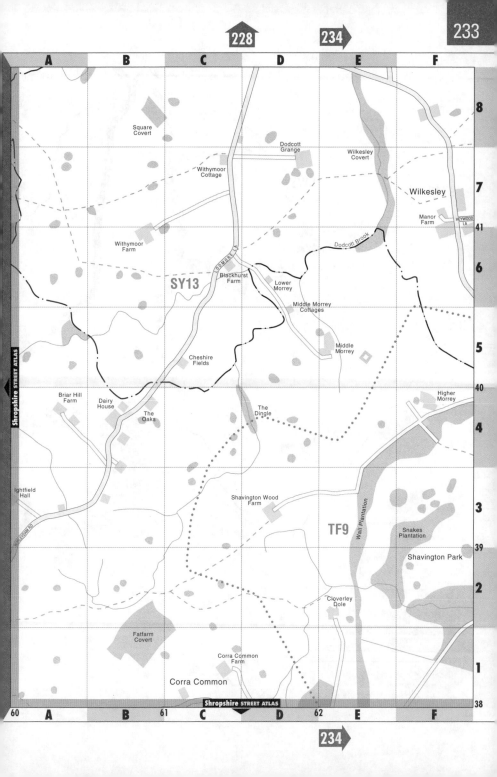

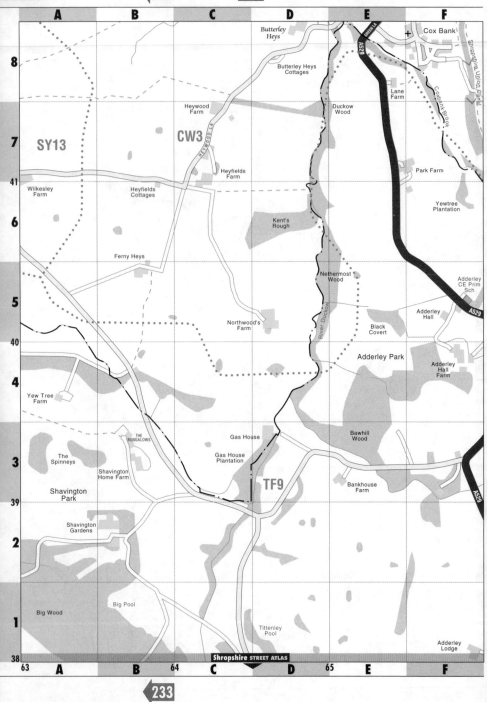

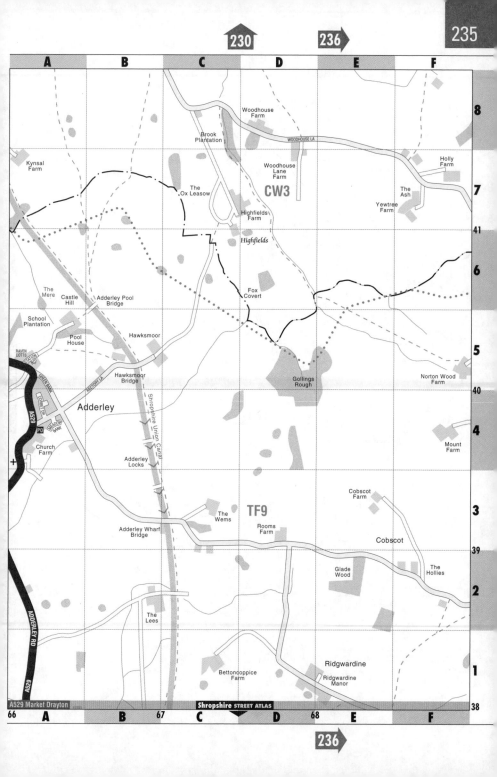

A529 Market Drayton

Shropshire STREET ATLAS

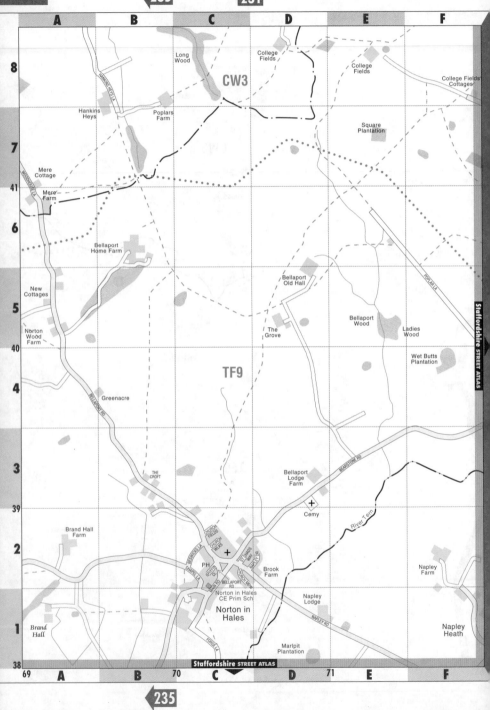

CW3

College
Fields

College
Fields

College Fields
Cottages

Long
Wood

Square
Plantation

Hankins
Heys

Poplars
Farm

8

Mere
Cottage

Mere
Farm

41

7

Bellaport
Home Farm

Bellaport
Old Hall

POPLAR LA

New
Cottages

6

Bellaport
Wood

Ladies
Wood

Norton
Wood
Farm

The
Grove

5

Wet Butts
Plantation

40

TF9

Greenacre

BELLAPORT RD

4

3

THE
CROFT

Bellaport
Lodge
Farm

BEARSTONE RD

River Tern

Cemy

39

Brand Hall
Farm

CHURCH
FIELDS

CHURCH WLK

PH

Brook
Farm

Napley
Farm

2

BERRICKS LA

CHAPEL LA

Norton in Hales
CE Prim Sch

Norton in
Hales

Napley
Lodge

NAPLEY RD

Napley
Heath

1

Brand
Hall

Marlpit
Plantation

38

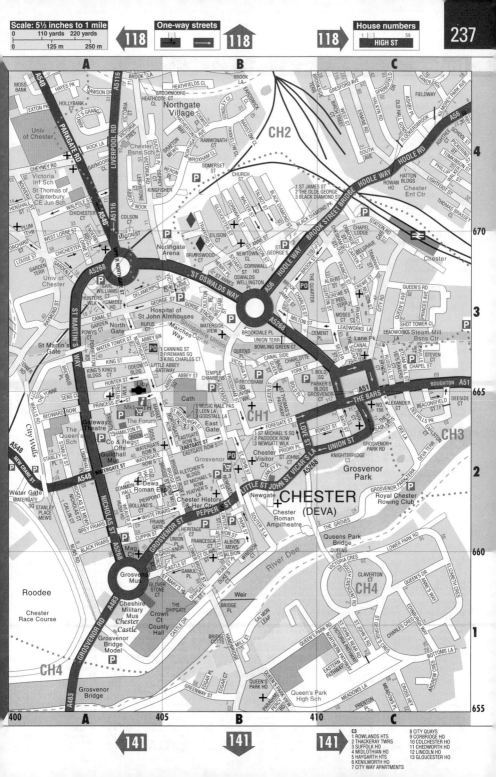

Index

Place name May be abbreviated on the map → **Church Rd** 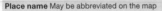 **6** Beckenham BR2..........**53 C6**

Location number Present when a number indicates the place's position in a crowded area of mapping

Locality, town or village Shown when more than one place has the same name

Postcode district District for the indexed place

Page and grid square Page number and grid reference for the standard mapping

Cities, towns and villages are listed in CAPITAL LETTERS

Public and commercial buildings are highlighted in **magenta**   Places of interest are highlighted in blue with a star★

Abbreviations used in the index

Acad	**Academy**	Comm	**Common**	Gd	**Ground**	L	**Leisure**	Prom	**Promenade**
App	**Approach**	Cott	**Cottage**	Gdn	**Garden**	La	**Lane**	Rd	**Road**
Arc	**Arcade**	Cres	**Crescent**	Gn	**Green**	Liby	**Library**	Recn	**Recreation**
Ave	**Avenue**	Cswy	**Causeway**	Gr	**Grove**	Mdw	**Meadow**	Ret	**Retail**
Bglw	**Bungalow**	Ct	**Court**	H	**Hall**	Meml	**Memorial**	Sh	**Shopping**
Bldg	**Building**	Ctr	**Centre**	Ho	**House**	Mkt	**Market**	Sq	**Square**
Bsns, Bus	**Business**	Ctry	**Country**	Hospl	**Hospital**	Mus	**Museum**	St	**Street**
Bvd	**Boulevard**	Cty	**County**	HQ	**Headquarters**	Orch	**Orchard**	Sta	**Station**
Cath	**Cathedral**	Dr	**Drive**	Hts	**Heights**	Pal	**Palace**	Terr	**Terrace**
Cir	**Circus**	Dro	**Drove**	Ind	**Industrial**	Par	**Parade**	TH	**Town Hall**
Cl	**Close**	Ed	**Education**	Inst	**Institute**	Pas	**Passage**	Univ	**University**
Cnr	**Corner**	Emb	**Embankment**	Int	**International**	Pk	**Park**	Wk, Wlk	**Walk**
Coll	**College**	Est	**Estate**	Intc	**Interchange**	Pl	**Place**	Wr	**Water**
Com	**Community**	Ex	**Exhibition**	Junc	**Junction**	Prec	**Precinct**	Yd	**Yard**

Index of towns, villages, streets, hospitals, industrial estates, railway stations, schools, shopping centres, universities and places of interest

238 2nd–Alb

2nd Ave CW12 .... 156 A4
3rd Ave CW12 .... 156 A4
1875 Bakers Ct CH1, CH3 237 C3

A

Aarons Dr ST7 .... 209 F2
Abberley Hall SK9 .... 84 D7
Abbey Cl
  Croft WA3 .... 9 A8
  Whitegate CW8 .... 126 A7
  Widnes WA8 .... 22 C8
  Winsford CW7 .... 149 D5
Abbey Ct SK12 .... 36 D3
Abbeydale Cl
  Cheadle SK8 .... 34 E7
  Chorlton CW2 .... 207 C2
Abbeyfield Ho
  2 Crewe CW2 .... 190 D2
  Ellesmere Port CH65 .... 70 A3
  Knutsford WA16 .... 56 F1
Abbeyfields CW11 .... 174 F5
Abbey Fields CW2 .... 205 E8
Abbey Gate Coll
  Saighton CH3 .... 163 F3
  Saighton CH3 .... 164 E8
Abbey Gate Sch CH2 .... 119 A3
Abbey Gn CH1 .... 237 A3
Abbey Hey WA7 .... 50 C8
Abbey La
  Delamere CW8 .... 123 E5
  Hartford CW8 .... 103 B4
Abbey Mill SK10 .... 87 A6
Abbey Park Way CW2 .... 207 E3
Abbey Pl CW1 .... 190 D6
Abbey Rd
  Golborne WA3 .... 4 C8
  Haydock WA11 .... 1 E7
  Macclesfield SK10 .... 87 B2
  Sandbach CW11 .... 174 E6
  Widnes WA8 .... 22 C8
Abbey Sq CH1 .... 237 B3
Abbey St CH1 .... 237 B3
Abbey Way CW8 .... 103 B4
Abbeyway N WA11 .... 2 A7
Abbeyway S WA11 .... 2 A7
Abbotsbury Cl
  Poynton SK12 .... 36 D5
  Wistaston CW2 .... 206 B8

Abbots Cl SK10 .... 87 B2
Abbots Ct CH2 .... 118 C4
Abbot's Dr CH2 .... 118 C4
Abbotsfield Cl WA4 .... 26 E6
Abbot's Grange CH2 .... 237 A4
Abbots Knoll CH2 .... 118 A4
ABBOT'S MEADS 118 A4
Abbotsmere Cl CW8 .... 101 F2
Abbots Mews CH65 .... 70 B6
ABBOTS MOSS 124 D5
Abbot's Nook CH2 .... 237 A4
Abbots Pk
  Chester CH2 .... 118 C4
  Runcorn WA7 .... 50 E5
Abbot's Terr CH1 .... 118 B5
Abbots Way
  Hartford CW8 .... 103 B4
  Neston CH64 .... 41 E1
Abbotts Cl
  Runcorn WA7 .... 49 A8
  Waverton CH3 .... 143 B5
Abbott's Cl CW12 .... 179 B8
Abbotts Rd CH3 .... 143 B5
Abbotts Way CW7 .... 126 B2
Aberdare Cl WA5 .... 7 E1
Aberdaron Dr CH1 .... 117 E3
Aberdeen Wlk SK10 .... 86 F3
Aberfeldy Cl CW4 .... 130 B2
Abingdon Ave WA1 .... 17 E7
Abingdon Cl 3 SK11 .... 111 F8
Abingdon Cres 4 CH4 .... 140 F6
Abington Cl CW1 .... 190 B6
Abington Wlk WA7 .... 50 C5
Abstone Cl WA1 .... 17 B7

Acacia Ave
  Knutsford WA16 .... 56 E1
  Warrington WA1 .... 17 D7
  Widnes WA8 .... 13 B3
  Wilmslow SK9 .... 59 F5
Acacia Cl CH2 .... 72 C3
Acacia Cres CW1 .... 190 E6
Acacia Dr
  Ellesmere Port CH66 .... 69 F1
  Sandbach CW11 .... 174 F3
Acacia Gdns ST7 .... 195 C3
Acacia Gr WA7 .... 49 C8
Acacia St WA12 .... 1 F4
Academy Pl 6 WA1 .... 16 B5
Academy St WA1 .... 16 B5
Academy Way WA1 .... 16 B5
Acer Ave CW1 .... 190 E7
Achilles Ave WA8 .... 8 B2
Achilles Ct WA7 .... 24 A2

Ackerley Cl WA2 .... 8 F3
Ackers La WA4 .... 16 E1
Ackersley Ct SK8 .... 35 B8
Ackers Rd WA4 .... 16 E1
Ack Lane E SK8 .... 35 C7
Ack Lane W SK8 .... 35 C7
Acorn Bank Cl CW2 .... 206 B7
Acorn Cl
  Cuddington CW8 .... 101 F2
  Winsford CW7 .... 150 A8
Acorn Ct CH2 .... 118 E8
Acorn Dr CH65 .... 70 B1
Acorn La CW12 .... 157 E3
Acorns Prim Sch The
  CH65. .... 69 F5
Acorn St WA12 .... 2 D3
Acorns The CH2 .... 118 E8
Acorn Terr SK22 .... 39 B6
Acreage The
  Bunbury CW6 .... 185 E8
  Goostrey CW4 .... 107 E1
Acrefield Rd WA8 .... 12 B1
Acre Gn L26 .... 21 A6
Acre La
  Bebington CH62 .... 43 D8
  Cheadle SK8 .... 35 C6
  Heswall CH60 .... 41 C8
Acre Rd CH66 .... 69 D5
Acres Cres WA6 .... 75 B2
Acres La CH2 .... 119 A8
Acreville Gr WA3 .... 5 C7
Acton Ave WA4 .... 26 D3
ACTON BRIDGE 76 E3
Acton Bridge Sta CW8 .... 76 F1
Acton CE Prim Sch CW5 204 A7
Acton Cl WA11. .... 1 C6
Acton La CW8 .... 76 F4
Acton Pl SK11 .... 111 F8
Acton Rd
  Burtonwood WA5. .... 6 E6
  Crewe CW2 .... 189 D4
Acton Way ST7 .... 193 D6
Adam Ave
  Ellesmere Port CH66. .... 69 D3
  Ellesmere Port, Great Sutton
  CH66. .... 69 C4
Adam Cl CH66 .... 69 D4
Adams Cl
  Newton-le-Willows WA12 .... 2 D2
  Poynton SK12. .... 36 E2

Adams Hill WA16 .... 57 A1
Adamson Ct WA4 .... 17 B2
Adamson Ho WA7 .... 22 E3
Adamson St WA4 .... 16 B3
Adam St WA2. .... 16 C7
Adaston Ave CH62 .... 43 F4
Adder Hill CH3. .... 142 B7
ADDERLEY 235 A4
Adderley CE Prim Sch
  TF9. .... 234 F5
Adderley Cl WA7. .... 23 C1
Adderley Rd TF9 .... 235 A2
ADDER'S MOSS 85 F6
Addingham Ave WA8. .... 22 C7
Addison Cl CW2. .... 205 F8
Addison Sq WA8 .... 13 A1
Adelaide Ct 4 WA8 .... 23 A7
Adelaide Rd
  Blacon CH1. .... 117 D4
  Bramhall SK7. .... 35 F5
Adelaide Sch CW1 .... 190 C5
Adelaide St
  Crewe CW1. .... 190 C5
  Macclesfield SK10. .... 87 E1
Adela Rd WA7 .... 22 E3
Adey Rd WA13 .... 19 A5
Adfalent La CH64. .... 68 A7
ADLINGTON 62 D5
Adlington Bsns Pk SK10. 36 C1
Adlington Cl SK12. .... 36 F2
Adlington Ct WA3. .... 9 F6
Adlington Dr
  Northwich CW9. .... 104 A5
  Sandbach CW11 .... 175 C7
Adlington Hall Mews
  SK10. .... 62 B5
Adlington Pk SK10. .... 36 C1
Adlington Prim Sch SK10. 62 E5
Adlington Rd
  Bollington SK10. .... 63 A1
  Crewe CW2 .... 189 F3
  Runcorn WA7. .... 24 D2
  Wilmslow SK9 .... 60 E7
Adlington Road Bsns Pk
  SK10. .... 88 A8
Adlington St SK10. .... 112 C8
Adlington Sta SK10. .... 62 C5
Admirals Rd WA3 .... 9 F3
Adshead Ct SK10. .... 88 B7
Adwell Cl WA3. .... 4 A8
Afton WA8. .... 12 A2
Agden Brow WA13 .... 19 E1
Agden Brow Pk WA13 .... 19 D1

Agden Hall Farm WA13. 29 E7
Agden House La SY13 .. 225 A5
Agden La
  Broomedge WA13 .... 19 E1
  Little Bollington WA13. .... 29 E7
Agden Park La WA13 .... 29 D8
Agecroft Rd CW9 .... 104 C7
Aidenswood Sch ST7. .... 194 E2
Ainley Cl WA7 .... 50 A5
Ainscough Rd WA3. .... 9 E3
Ainsdale Cl
  Bebington CH63. .... 43 C5
  Bramhall SK7. .... 36 A7
  Warrington WA5 .... 14 F4
Ainsworth La CW8 .... 76 B3
Ainsworth Rd CW8 .... 77 E1
Aintree Gr CH66 .... 69 D3
Airdrie Cl CH62 .... 43 D3
Aire WA8. .... 12 B2
Aire Cl CH65. .... 70 A7
Airedale Cl WA5 .... 14 F7
Aire Pl CW7 .... 127 B1
Airfield View CH5. .... 139 B6
Aitchison Rd CW9. .... 80 A2
Ajax Ave WA2. .... 8 B2
Ajmere Cl WA2. .... 189 E2
Akesmoor La
  Biddulph ST8 .... 179 B1
  Mow Cop ST7. .... 195 F7
Alamein Cres WA2. .... 16 C7
Alamein Dr CW7 .... 149 D8
Alamein Rd
  Barnton CW8. .... 78 A4
  Chester CH2 .... 95 B1
Alan Dr WA15. .... 32 A8
Alan St CW9 .... 104 B8
Alban Ret Pk WA2 .... 8 A1
Alban St CW1. .... 190 C5
Albany Cres WA13. .... 18 C4
Albany Gdns CH66 .... 69 C7
Albany Gr WA13 .... 18 C4
Albany Rd
  Bramhall SK7. .... 35 F4
  Lymm WA13. .... 18 D4
  Wilmslow SK9 .... 59 F5
Albany Terr 10 WA7 .... 23 A2
Albert Dr
  Neston CH64 .... 66 D8
  Warrington WA5 .... 14 D6
Albert Pl
  Congleton CW12 .... 156 E2
  10 Macclesfield SK11 .... 112 D8
  Northwich CW9 .... 104 B8

Albert Rd
Bollington SK10 . . . 87 E8
Warrington WA4 . . . 17 A2
2 Widnes WA8 . . . 13 B1
Wilmslow SK9 . . . 60 A6
Albert Row WA6 . . . 49 B1
Albert Sq 1 WA8 . . . 23 B8
Albert St
Audley ST7 . . . 209 F3
Chester CH1 . . . 237 C3
Crewe CW1 . . . 190 C5
Irlam M44 . . . 11 E6
Knutsford WA16 . . . 56 F2
Macclesfield SK11 . . . 112 C8
Nantwich CW5 . . . 204 E6
5 Runcorn WA7 . . . 23 A2
Albert Terr WA5 . . . 1 E1
Albion Mews
Chester CH1 . . . 237 B2
New Mills SK22 . . . 39 C7
Albion Pk WA3 . . . 5 C7
Albion Pl CH1 . . . 237 B1
Albion Rd
New Mills SK22 . . . 39 B6
Northwich CW9 . . . 79 A1
Albion St
Chester CH1 . . . 237 B2
Crewe CW1 . . . 190 A3
Albright Rd WA8 . . . 22 A6
Albury Cl WA11 . . . 1 D7
Alcock St 17 WA4 . . . 23 A3
Alconbury Cl WA5 . . . 15 B6
Alcroft Pl WA2 . . . 8 A6
Aldcliffe WA3 . . . 3 F8
Aldelyme Ct CW3 . . . 229 F4
Alder Ave
Poynton SK12 . . . 36 F3
Widnes WA8 . . . 13 B3
Alderbank Rd WA5 . . . 15 A6
Alder Cl
Sandbach CW11 . . . 34 D8
Alder Cres SK22 . . . 16 C8
Alder Ct SK10 . . . 86 F3
Alderdale Dr SK6 . . . 37 E7
Alderdale Gr SK9 . . . 59 E5
Alder Dr
Crewe CW1 . . . 189 F7
Ellesmere Port CH66 . . . 69 F1
Alderfield Dr L24 . . . 21 A3
Alder Gr CH2 . . . 119 B4
Alderleigh La ST7 . . . 195 C4
Alder La
Burtonwood WA2, WA5 . . . 7 C7
Cronton WA8, L35 . . . 12 A5
Frodsham WA6, WA7 . . . 48 D3
Warrington WA3 . . . 16 B8
Alderley Ave WA3 . . . 3 D7
Alderley Cl
Hazel Grove SK7 . . . 36 F8
Poynton SK12 . . . 36 F2
Sandbach CW11 . . . 175 D7
ALDERLEY EDGE . . . 60 A2
Alderley Edge★ SK9, SK10 85 D8
Alderley Edge Prim Sch
SK9 . . . 60 A2
Alderley Edge Sch for Girls
SK9 . . . 60 A2
Alderley Lo SK9 . . . 60 A5
Alderley Pl CH1 . . . 117 E6
Alderley Rd
Alderley Edge SK10, SK9 . . 60 F2
Chelford SK10 . . . 84 C3
Northwich CW8 . . . 103 E8
Prestbury SK10 . . . 86 E3
Warrington WA4 . . . 17 D4
Wilmslow SK9 . . . 60 A6
Alderley Wlk 14 SK11 . . 112 E7
Alderman Bolton Com Sch
WA4 . . . 16 F3
Alderney Cl
Ellesmere Port CH65 . . . 70 C5
2 Macclesfield SK11 . . . 111 F8
Alderney Ho CH2 . . . 119 B4
Alder Rd
Golborne WN7 . . . 3 F8
Warrington WA1 . . . 17 D7
Weaverham CW8 . . . 102 D8
Alder Rise SK23 . . . 65 D8
Alder Root La WA2 . . . 7 D7
Alders SK9 . . . 59 F6
Aldersey Cl
Runcorn WA7 . . . 24 D1
Saughall CH1 . . . 94 A1
ALDERSEY GREEN . . . 182 C6
Aldersey La CH3 . . . 182 C5
Aldersey Rd CW2 . . . 190 A2
Aldersey Way CW6 . . . 185 E8
Aldersgate SK9 . . . 39 B8
Aldersgate Ave WA7 . . . 50 C8
Aldersgate Dr L26 . . . 21 A6
Aldersgate Rd SK8 . . . 35 C5
Alders Green Ave SK6 . . 37 F7
Alders Rd SK12 . . . 38 A7
Alder St WA12 . . . 2 C3
Alders Way SK10 . . . 86 F6
Alderton Cl L26 . . . 21 A7
Alderton Gr CW7 . . . 127 A4
Alder Wood Ave L24 . . . 21 A3
Alderwood Ct WA8 . . . 12 E4
Alderwood Lodge L24 . . . 21 A3
Aldewood Cl WA3 . . . 10 A6
ALDFORD . . . 163 F3
Aldford Cl
Bebington CH63 . . . 43 B6
Hough CW2 . . . 206 E2
Aldford Pl SK9 . . . 59 F2

Aldford Rd CH2 . . . 118 F6
Aldford Sch CH3 . . . 163 F3
Aldford Way CW7 . . . 126 B2
Aldgate CH5 . . . 70 A5
Aldington Dr CW10 . . . 151 D5
Aldridge Dr WA5 . . . 6 F7
Aled Way CH4 . . . 140 D5
Alexander Ct CH3 . . . 237 C2
Alexander Dr WA8 . . . 22 D8
Alexandra Ct
Chester CH2 . . . 119 A4
5 Partington M31 . . . 11 F3
Alexandra Dr
Irlam M44 . . . 11 F8
Runcorn WA7 . . . 23 C1
Alexandra Ind Est WA8 . . 22 F7
Alexandra Mews WA6 . . 49 B1
Alexandra Pl WA1 . . . 190 B5
Alexandra Rd
Middlewich CW10 . . . 151 D6
Warrington, Stockton Heath
WA4 . . . 16 D1
Warrington WA4 . . . 16 F2
Alexandra Sq 6 WA7 . . 23 A3
Alexandra St
Ellesmere Port CH65 . . . 70 C7
Warrington WA1 . . . 16 E7
Widnes WA8 . . . 23 A7
Winsford CW7 . . . 126 C1
Alexandra Stadium The
(Crewe Alexandra FC)
CW2 . . . 190 D2
Alexandria Way CW12 . . 156 F4
Alford Cl 4 CW9 . . . 103 E5
Alforde St WA8 . . . 23 A7
Alfred Cl 7 WA8 . . . 23 B8
Alfred Rd
Golborne WA3 . . . 4 A8
Haydock WA11 . . . 1 F7
Alfred St
Irlam M44 . . . 11 E6
Newton-le-Willows WA12 . . 2 E3
Northwich CW9 . . . 103 E6
Widnes WA8 . . . 23 B8
Algernon St
Runcorn WA7 . . . 22 F3
Warrington, Stockton Heath
WA4 . . . 16 C1
Warrington WA4 . . . 16 D6
Alice Ct WA8 . . . 23 A4
Alison Dr
Goostrey SK11 . . . 130 D8
Macclesfield SK10 . . . 87 F1
Alistair Dr CH3 . . . 43 C6
Allans Cl CH64 . . . 66 E6
Allansford Ave CH3 . . . 143 A4
Allans Mdw CH64 . . . 66 E7
Allcard St WA5 . . . 15 F7
Allen Ave WA3 . . . 5 C2
Allenby Rd M44 . . . 11 D4
Allendale WA7 . . . 50 B6
Allen Dr CW9 . . . 103 F2
Allen Pl CW1 . . . 190 B5
Allen Rd WA7 . . . 48 D1
Allen St
Bollington SK10 . . . 88 B8
Macclesfield SK11 . . . 112 E7
Warrington WA2 . . . 16 A6
Allerton Rd WA8 . . . 13 B1
Allerby Way WA3 . . . 3 E8
ALLGREAVE . . . 137 C3
Allgreave Cl CW10 . . . 151 C6
All Hallows RC Coll
SK11 . . . 112 B7
Allington Pl CH4 . . . 141 E7
Allman Cl CW1 . . . 189 F7
ALLOSTOCK . . . 106 E3
Allotment Rd M44 . . . 11 D6
Allport La CW1 . . . 43 D8
Allport Rd CH62, CH63 . . 43 D7
Allports The CH62 . . . 43 D7
All Saints CE Prim Sch
WA7 . . . 23 A3
All Saints Dr WA4 . . . 17 E3
All Saints RC Prim Sch
WA3 . . . 3 B8
All Saints Upton Prim Sch
WA8 . . . 12 B3
Allysum Ct WA7 . . . 49 F4
Alma Ave CW1 . . . 190 C6
Alma Cl
Macclesfield SK11 . . . 112 A4
Scholar Green ST7 . . . 194 E7
Alma La SK9 . . . 60 A7
Alma Rd SK7 . . . 37 A8
Alma St
Chester CH2 . . . 118 F2
Newton-le-Willows WA12 . . 2 B3
Almeda Rd L24 . . . 21 A4
Almer Dr WA5 . . . 15 C5
Almond Ave
Crewe CW1 . . . 190 D6
Runcorn WA7 . . . 49 C8
Almond Gr
Warrington WA1 . . . 17 B2
Weaverham CW8 . . . 102 C7
Almond Pl ST5 . . . 210 E1
Almond Tree Cl L24 . . . 21 E1
Almond Wlk M31 . . . 11 D3
Almshouses CW11 . . . 175 C6
Alnwick Dr CH65 . . . 70 D2
Alpass Ave WA5 . . . 16 A8
Alpine St WA12 . . . 2 A3
ALPORT . . . 226 B1
Alport Rd SY13 . . . 226 B1
ALPRAHAM . . . 169 D4

Alpraham Cres CH2 . . 118 E6
Alpraham Gn CW6 . . . 169 E5
ALPRAHAM GREEN . . 169 D5
Alric Wlk M22 . . . 33 E8
ALSAGER . . . 193 E5
Alsager Highfields Prim Sch
ST7 . . . 193 D4
Alsager L Ctr ST7 . . . 193 B4
Alsager Rd
Audley ST7 . . . 209 D5
Haslington CW11 . . . 192 C7
Sandbach CW11 . . . 175 E1
Alsager Sch ST7 . . . 193 B4
Alsager Sta ST7 . . . 193 E3
Alsfeld Way SK22 . . . 39 A8
Alton Dr SK10 . . . 87 F1
Alton Rd SK9 . . . 59 F7
Alton St CW2 . . . 190 B3
ALTRINCHAM . . . 31 C8
Altrincham Rd
Styal SK9 . . . 33 D4
Wilmslow SK9 . . . 33 C2
Alt Wlk CW7 . . . 127 A2
Alumbrook Ave CW4 . . 130 C3
Alum Ct CW4 . . . 130 C2
Alun Cres CH4 . . . 141 A5
Alundale Rd CW7 . . . 126 C3
ALVANLEY . . . 73 C1
Alvanley Cl
Macclesfield SK11 . . . 111 F5
Widnes WA8 . . . 22 C8
Alvanley Dr WA6 . . . 73 C2
Alvanley Prim Sch WA6 . . 73 D1
Alvanley Rd
Ellesmere Port CH66 . . . 69 E4
Helsby WA6 . . . 73 C2
Alvanley Rise WA6 . . . 104 A6
Alvanley Terr WA6 . . . 74 B8
Alvanley View . . . 72 B3
Alvanley Way CH66 . . . 69 E4
Alvaston Bsns Pk CW5 . . 204 F5
Alvaston Rd CW5 . . . 204 F5
Alvaston Wlk CW2 . . . 189 F2
Alverstone Cl WA5 . . . 14 C7
Alverton Cl WA8 . . . 22 D8
Alverton Cl SK10 . . . 86 F1
Alveston Dr SK9 . . . 60 C8
Alvingham Cl 11 CW9 . . 104 B8
Alvis Rd CH5 . . . 116 B3
Alwyn Gdns CH2 . . . 118 F8
Alyndale Rd CH4 . . . 140 D6
Alyn Rd CH2 . . . 96 F1
Amberleigh 4 WA4 . . . 27 B3
Amberley Dr WA15 . . . 32 B8
Amberley Rd SK11 . . . 112 A6
Ambleside Cl
Bebington CH62 . . . 43 E7
Crewe CW2 . . . 189 E2
Macclesfield SK11 . . . 111 F6
Runcorn WA7 . . . 49 E5
Winsford CW7 . . . 126 C3
Ambleside Cres WA2 . . 8 D3
Ambleside Wlk 2 SK9 . . 34 E1
Ambleside Rd CH65 . . . 70 C2
Ambrose Ct WA1 . . . 16 B6
Ambuscade Cl CW1 . . 190 E5
Amelia Cl WA8 . . . 13 B4
Amelia St WA2 . . . 16 C7
Amersham Cl SK10 . . . 87 C3
Amis Gr WA3 . . . 3 E8
Ampleforth Ho 11 WA1 . . 16 C5
Amusement Depot WA7 . . 126 E2
Amy St CW2 . . . 190 C3
Anchorage The
1 Lymm WA13 . . . 18 D3
Neston CH64 . . . 66 C7
Warrington CH3 . . . 143 A5
Anchor Cl WA7 . . . 50 D6
Anchor Ct WA1 . . . 16 A6
Ancoats La WA16, SK9 . . 83 F8
Anderson Cl
Crewe CW1 . . . 191 A4
Warrington WA2 . . . 9 B2
Anderson Ct CH62 . . . 43 B6
Andersons Ind Est WA4 . . 23 B6
Anderson St 8 SK10 . . 112 C8
ANDERTON . . . 78 D4
Anderton Boat Lift & Nature
Park★ CW9 . . . 78 D3
Anderton Grange CW9 . . 103 F7
Andertons La SK10, SK11 . . 86 B1
Anderton Way SK9 . . . 34 D3
Andover Cl WA2 . . . 8 E1
Andover Rd WA11 . . . 1 E8
Andrew Cl WA8 . . . 22 C8
Andrew Cres CW2 . . . 237 C1
Andrew Gr SK10 . . . 113 A7
Andrew La SK6 . . . 37 F8
Andrew's Cl CH3 . . . 121 B2
Andrew's Wlk CH60 . . . 41 B8
Andromeda Way WA9 . . 6 B7
Anemone Way WA9 . . . 6 A7
Angela St CH5 . . . 116 A2
Angelina CW11 . . . 174 D7
Anglers Rest M44 . . . 11 E5
Anglesey Cl 2 CH65 . . 70 C1
Anglesey Dr SK12 . . . 36 F6
Anglesey Water SK12 . . 36 E6
Angus Gr CW10 . . . 128 D2
Angus Rd CH63 . . . 43 C6
Angus Wlk SK10 . . . 86 F2
Ankers Knowl La SK11 . . 114 D8
Ankers La SK11 . . . 114 D6
Annable Rd M44 . . . 11 F8
Annan Cl 2 CW12 . . . 157 A1
Ann Cl CH66 . . . 69 D7
Anne St WA7 . . . 210 D6
Anne's Way CH4 . . . 237 C1
Annette Ave WA12 . . . 2 A5
Annie St WA2 . . . 16 C6

Annions La CW5 . . . 205 F1
Annis Cl SK9 . . . 60 B2
Annis Rd SK9 . . . 60 B2
Ann St
Northwich CW9 . . . 79 D1
Runcorn WA7 . . . 23 B3
Ann Street W WA8 . . . 23 B7
Ansdell Rd WA8 . . . 13 C2
Anson Cl SK7 . . . 35 F5
Anson Engine Mus★
SK12 . . . 37 C4
Anson Rd
Handforth SK9 . . . 34 E1
Poynton SK12 . . . 37 B3
Anthony Dr CW9 . . . 126 F7
Anthony's Way CH60 . . 41 A7
Antons Ct L26 . . . 21 A6
Antons Rd L26 . . . 21 A6
Antony Rd WA4 . . . 16 B1
Antrim Cl WA11 . . . 1 C6
Antrim Dr CH66 . . . 69 F2
Antrim Rd WA2 . . . 8 A2
ANTROBUS . . . 53 C4
Antrobus St CW12 . . . 156 D3
Anvil Cl
Elton CH2 . . . 72 B4
Haslington CW11 . . . 174 F3
Saughall CH1 . . . 94 A1
Appleby Cl
Macclesfield SK11 . . . 111 F5
Widnes WA8 . . . 22 C8
Appleby Cres WA16 . . 58 A4
Appleby Gr CH62 . . . 43 D6
Appleby Rd WA2 . . . 8 C3
Appleby Wlk 5 WA8 . . 22 C8
Applecroft ST5 . . . 210 E1
Applecross Cl WA3 . . . 10 A6
Appledale Cl SK10 . . . 87 C4
Appledale Dr CH66 . . . 95 A8
Applefield CW8 . . . 103 D7
Appleford Cl WA4 . . . 26 E7
Apple Market St 10 CW9 . . 103 F8
APPLETON . . . 13 A2
Appleton Cl CW12 . . . 178 E8
Appleton Dr CH65 . . . 69 F3
Appleton Hall Gdns 4 . . 26 E5
Appleton Mews WA13 . . 18 C4
APPLETON PARK . . . 26 D5
Appleton Rd
Chester CH2 . . . 118 E6
Widnes WA8 . . . 13 B1
Appleton St
Widnes WA8 . . . 23 B7
Winnington CW8 . . . 78 D1
APPLETON THORN . . . 27 B4
Appleton Thorn Prim Sch
WA4 . . . 27 C4
Appleton Thorn Trad Est
WA4 . . . 27 C5
Appleton Village 13 . . . 13 B1
Appleton Wlk 8 SK9 . . 34 E1
Apple Tree Cl L24 . . . 21 E1
Appletree Gr WA7 . . . 8 F2
Apple Tree Gr CH66 . . . 94 F8
Appleyards La CW7 . . . 141 E7
Apprentice La SK9 . . . 33 F3
April Rise SK10 . . . 87 A1
Arble Gdns WA9 . . . 6 B7
Aragon Cl WA4 . . . 24 C3
Aragon Gn CW1 . . . 117 E6
Aran Cl L24 . . . 21 D1
Arbour Cl
Macclesfield SK10 . . . 87 D3
Northwich CW9 . . . 104 C8
Arbour Cres SK10 . . . 87 D3
Arbour Mews SK10 . . . 87 D3
Arbour St ST7 . . . 210 D5
Arbour The WA2 . . . 73 A2
Arbury La WA2 . . . 8 C6
Arcade The
Ellesmere Port CH65 . . . 70 A5
3 Northwich CW9 . . . 103 F8
Archer Ave WA4 . . . 16 D2
Archer Cl SK10 . . . 87 E7
Archers Gn CH2 . . . 43 E3
Archers Green Rd WA5 . . 7 B3
Archers Way
Blacon CH1 . . . 118 A2
Ellesmere Port CH65 . . . 70 A5
Arches Com Prim Sch The
CH1 . . . 117 C5
Archway Wlk WA12 . . . 2 E3
ARCLID . . . 154 B1
Arclid Cl SK9 . . . 34 E1
Arclid Ct 10 SK12 . . . 156 F3
ARCLID GREEN . . . 176 A8
Arclid Green Ind Est
CW11 . . . 176 B8
Arden WA8 . . . 12 A2
Ardenbrook Rise SK10 . . 86 F6
Arden Cl
Gatley SK8 . . . 34 C7
Tarvin CH3 . . . 121 C3
Warrington WA3 . . . 10 B6
Arden Ct CW12 . . . 179 B7
Arden Ct CH64 . . . 66 E6
Arden Est SK22 . . . 39 C7
Arden Mdw CW6 . . . 168 C8
Arden Sq CW7 . . . 191 A2
Arden St SK22 . . . 39 C7
Arderne Ave CW2 . . . 190 A2
Arderne Ho CH2 . . . 118 F7
Arderne Pl 12 SK9 . . . 60 A1
Ardern Lea WA6 . . . 73 D1
Ardleigh Cl CW1 . . . 189 F8
Arena Gdns WA3 . . . 16 D8
Argosy Dr M90 . . . 32 F7

Argyle Ct 10 WA16 . . . 57 A2
Argyll Ave
Bebington CH62 . . . 43 D4
Chester CH4 . . . 141 A3
Argyll Cl SK10 . . . 87 A1
Ariel Gdns WA3 . . . 5 A2
Ariel Wlk WA3 . . . 3 E8
Arizona Cres WA5 . . . 15 B7
Arkenshaw Rd WA3 . . . 9 A7
Arkenstone Cl WA8 . . . 12 C2
Arkle Ave SK8, SK9 . . . 34 E4
Arkle Ct 1 CH3 . . . 119 B1
Arklow Dr L24 . . . 21 D2
Arkwright Cl CW7 . . . 149 A8
Arkwright St WA2 . . . 23 F3
Arkwright Rd WA7 . . . 23 F3
ARLEY . . . 54 C7
Arley Ave WA4 . . . 26 D8
Arley Cl
Alsager ST7 . . . 193 C3
Chester CH2 . . . 118 F6
Macclesfield SK11 . . . 112 A7
Arley Ct CW9 . . . 103 E5
Arley Dr WA8 . . . 12 B2
Arley End WA16 . . . 29 C4
ARLEY GREEN . . . 54 D6
Arley Hall & Gardens★
CW9 . . . 54 D6
Arley Mossend La CW9 . . 54 D2
Arley Pl CW2 . . . 206 A8
Arley Rd
Antrobus CW9 . . . 54 B7
Appleton Thorn WA4 . . 27 C3
Northwich CW9 . . . 104 C8
Arley Wlk CW11 . . . 174 D5
Arlington Cl CW12 . . . 206 C8
Arlington Cres SK9 . . . 59 E5
Arlington Dr
Golborne WN7 . . . 4 C8
Macclesfield SK11 . . . 112 A7
Poynton SK12 . . . 36 D3
Warrington WA3 . . . 14 E4
Arlington Way SK9 . . . 59 E5
Armistead Way CW4 . . 130 A5
Armitstead Rd CW11 . . 174 F4
Armitt St SK11 . . . 112 C7
Armour Ave WA2 . . . 8 B2
Armoury Court Mews 4
SK11 . . . 112 B6
Armoury Twrs 1 SK11 . . 112 B6
Armstrong Cl
Audlem CW3 . . . 229 F4
Warrington WA3 . . . 9 E5
Armthorpe Dr CH66 . . . 69 C5
Arncliffe Dr WA5 . . . 6 F6
Arndale WA7 . . . 49 E5
Arnhem Cres WA2 . . . 16 C7
Arnold Pl WA8 . . . 22 C7
Arnold's Cres WA3 . . . 139 A3
Arnold St
Nantwich CW5 . . . 204 E6
Warrington WA1 . . . 16 D6
Arnside Ave
Congleton CW12 . . . 156 A2
Haydock WA11 . . . 1 B6
Arnside Cl
High Lane SK6 . . . 37 E8
Winsford CW7 . . . 126 D2
Arnside Gr WA4 . . . 16 B2
Arpley Rd WA1 . . . 16 B4
Arpley St WA1 . . . 16 A4
Arradon Ct CH2 . . . 118 E5
Arran Ave CH65 . . . 70 C1
Arran Cl
Holmes Chapel CW4 . . 130 C2
Warrington WA2 . . . 9 A2
Arran Dr WA6 . . . 74 C6
Arrivals Way M90 . . . 33 B7
Arron Cl CW2 . . . 189 D3
Arrowcroft Rd CH3 . . . 119 F5
Arrowsmith Dr ST7 . . . 193 B3
Arrowsmith Rd WA11 . . 1 F7
ARTHILL . . . 30 B8
Arthill La
Little Bollington WA14 . . 20 B1
Rostherne WA14 . . . 20 B1
Arthog Dr WA15 . . . 31 F8
Arthog Rd WA15 . . . 32 A8
Arthur St
Chester CH1 . . . 118 A2
3 Crewe CW2 . . . 190 D2
Lostock Gralam CW9 . . 80 A2
11 Runcorn WA7 . . . 23 A2
Warrington WA2 . . . 16 A6
Artists La SK10 . . . 85 C7
Artle Rd CW2 . . . 206 C8
Arundel Ave
Knutsford WA16 . . . 82 A8
Macclesfield SK10 . . . 87 F2
Wistaston CW2 . . . 205 E8
Arundel Cl CH65 . . . 70 E3
Arundell Cl WA5 . . . 6 F6
Arundel Rd SK8 . . . 35 A6
Ascol Dr WA16 . . . 80 C3
Ascot Ave WA7 . . . 49 B6
Ascot Cl
Congleton CW12 . . . 156 D4
Macclesfield SK10 . . . 87 C3
Warrington, Martinscroft
WA1 . . . 17 E7
Warrington WA4 . . . 17 C2
Ascot Ct CW9 . . . 104 C8
Ascot End CH66 . . . 69 E3

Ascot Ho CH1 . . . . 118 B2
Ash Ave
  Irlam M44 . . . . 11 D5
  Newton-le-Willows WA12 . . 2 C2
Ashbank CW9 . . . . 104 D7
Ashbank Pl CW1 . . . . 189 F6
Ashberry Cl SK9 . . . . 60 D8
Ashberry Dr WA4 . . . . 27 B5
Ashbourne Ave WA7 . . . . . 49 B6
Ashbourne Cl CH66 . . . . . . 94 E8
Ashbourne Dr
  Chorlton CW2 . . . . 207 C1
  High Lane SK6 . . . . 37 F6
Ashbourne Mews **1**
  SK10 . . . . 111 F8
Ashbourne Rd
  Hazel Grove SK7 . . . . 36 F8
  Warrington WA5 . . . . 15 B5
Ashbrook Ave WA7 . . . . . . 49 F3
Ashbrook Cres WA2 . . . . . 16 D8
Ashbrook Dr SK10 . . . . 87 A6
Ashbrook Rd
  Bollington SK10 . . . . 87 F7
  Nether Alderley SK10 . . . . 85 F6
Ashburton CH64 . . . . 66 C8
Ashbury Dr WA7 . . . . 24 D2
Ashby Dr CW11 . . . . 1 D7
Ashby Dr CW11 . . . . 174 C5
Ashby Pl CH2 . . . . 237 C4
Ash Cl
  Ellesmere Port CH66 . . . . 69 F1
  Holmes Chapel CW4 . . . 130 D4
  Malpas SY14 . . . . 213 C5
  Tarporley CW6 . . . . 146 D2
Ashcroft Ave CW2 . . . . . . 206 B3
Ashcroft Cl SK9 . . . . 59 F5
Ashcroft Cl M44 . . . . 11 D5
Ashcroft Rd WA13 . . . . . . 19 B4
Ash Ct **12** WA16 . . . . 57 A2
Ashdene Prim Sch SK9 . . 59 F5
Ashdene Rd SK9 . . . . 59 F5
Ashdown Cl SK8 . . . . 35 A6
Ashdown La WA3 . . . . 10 B5
Ashdown WA16 . . . . 82 F6
Ashenhurst Rd ST7 . . . . . 193 F3
Ashenough Rd ST7 . . . . . 210 D6
Asher Ct WA4 . . . . 27 D4
Ashfield Cl WA13 . . . . 19 B4
Ashfield Cres
  Bebington CH62 . . . . 43 D8
  Blacon CH1 . . . . 117 D5
Ashfield Dr SK10 . . . . 87 A2
Ashfield Gdns WA4 . . . . . . 16 F3
Ashfield Gr M44 . . . . 11 E6
Ashfield Ho **5** CH64 . . . 66 E8
Ashfield Rd
  Bebington CH62 . . . . 43 C8
  Ellesmere Port CH65 . . . . 70 C5
Ashfield Road N **1** CH65 70 C5
Ashfield St CW10 . . . . 151 D8
Ashfield Way CW11 . . . . . 175 A6
Ashford Cl SK9 . . . . 34 C4
Ashford Dr WA4 . . . . 26 E3
Ashford Rd SK9 . . . . 60 A4
Ashford Way **1** WA8 . . 13 D1
Ashgate La CW9 . . . . 79 F6
Ash Gr
  Chester CH4 . . . . 141 B5
  Congleton CW12 . . . . . . 156 A3
  Ellesmere Port CH66 . . . . 69 C6
  Gatley SK8 . . . . 34 B8
  Golborne WA3 . . . . 3 B8
  Handforth SK9 . . . . 34 C3
  Knutsford WA16 . . . . 57 D1
  Macclesfield SK11 . . . . . 112 C4
  Middlewich CW10 . . . . . . 151 D7
  Nantwich CW5 . . . . 204 F3
  Rode Heath ST7 . . . . 193 F7
  Runcorn WA7 . . . . 49 C8
  Warrington WA4 . . . . 16 D3
  Weaverham CW8 . . . . . . 102 E7
  Widnes WA8 . . . . 22 D8
Ashgrove CW7 . . . . 149 D8
Ash Grove Prim Sch
  SK11 . . . . 112 C4
Ash Ha La
  Hoole Bank CH2 . . . . . . 119 C8
  Picton CH2 . . . . 96 C2
Ash Ho
  Chester CH2 . . . . 118 C5
  8 Sandbach CW11 . . 175 B6
Ash House La CW8 . . . . . . 77 D7
Ash La
  Warrington WA4 . . . . 26 E8
  Widnes WA8 . . . . 22 A8
Ashlands WA6 . . . . 74 C7
Ash Lawn Ct CH2 . . . . . . 118 C4
Ashlea Dr CW5 . . . . 205 E5
Ashleigh Cl CH4 . . . . 140 E6
ASHLEY 31 E5
Ashley Cl WA3 . . . . 17 C3
Ashley Ct
  Frodsham WA6 . . . . 74 A8
  Holt LL13 . . . . 196 D8
  Warrington WA4 . . . . 26 C6
Ashley Dr
  Bramhall SK7 . . . . 35 C6
  Hartford CW8 . . . . 103 A6
Ashley Gdns
  Clutton CH3 . . . . 182 C1
  High Lane SK6 . . . . 37 D8
Ashley Gn WA8 . . . . 22 D8
Ashley Grange CW9 . . . . 103 E3
ASHLEY HEATH 31 E8

Ashley Mdw CW1 . . . . 191 D5
Ashleymill La WA14 . . . . . . 31 D7
Ashley Mill Lane N WA14 . 31 E8
Ashley Rd
  Ashley, Ashley Heath WA14,
    WA15 . . . . 31 E7
  Ashley WA14, WA15, WA16 . 31 C4
  Handforth SK9 . . . . 34 B1
  Mere WA16 . . . . 56 D8
  Runcorn WA7 . . . . 23 D2
Ashley Ret Pk WA8 . . . . . . 23 B7
Ashley Sch WA8 . . . . 12 D1
Ashley Sta W14 . . . . 31 E5
Ashley Way WA8 . . . . 23 B7
Ashley Way W WA8 . . . . . . 22 F7
Ash Lo SK12 . . . . 36 D4
Ashmead Cl ST7 . . . . 193 E3
Ashmead Mews ST7 . . . . 193 E3
Ashmore Cl
  Middlewich CW10 . . . . . . 151 C6
  Warrington WA3 . . . . 10 A3
Ashmore's La ST7 . . . . . . 193 D3
Ash Mount CW3 . . . . 232 B1
Ashmuir Cl
  Blacon CH1 . . . . 117 E3
  Crewe CW1 . . . . 190 B6
Ashness Dr SK7 . . . . 35 E8
Ash Priors WA8 . . . . 12 D3
Ash Rd
  Crewe CW1 . . . . 190 D6
  Cuddington CW8 . . . . . . 101 F2
  Elton CH2 . . . . 72 C3
  Haydock WA11 . . . . 1 E7
  Hollinfare WA3 . . . . 11 A2
  Lymm WA13 . . . . 18 C3
  Partington M31 . . . . 11 D3
  Poynton SK12 . . . . 36 F3
  Warrington WA5 . . . . 14 F4
  Winwick WA2 . . . . 8 B6
Ashridge St WA7 . . . . 22 F3
Ash St CW9 . . . . 79 A1
Ash Terr WA11 . . . . 112 C4
Ashton Ave SK10 . . . . 86 D1
Ashton Cl
  Bebington CH62 . . . . 43 E3
  Congleton CW12 . . . . . . 157 B1
  Frodsham WA6 . . . . 49 C1
  Middlewich CW10 . . . . . . 151 D5
  Northwich CW9 . . . . 103 E4
  Runcorn WA7 . . . . 48 F6
Ashton Cres WA6 . . . . 49 C1
Ashton Dr WA6 . . . . 49 C1
ASHTON HAYES 121 F8
Ashton Hayes Prim Sch
  CH3 . . . . 121 F8
Ashton La CH3 . . . . 121 E6
ASHTON'S GREEN 1 B3
Ashton St WA2 . . . . 16 B6
Ashtree Cl
  Neston CH64 . . . . 67 A7
  Prestbury SK10 . . . . 87 C8
Ashtree Croft CH64 . . . . . . 68 A7
Ashtree Ct CH2 . . . . 237 C4
Ashtree Dr CH64 . . . . 67 A7
Ashtree Farm Ct CH64 . . . 68 A7
Ash View ST7 . . . . 195 B2
Ashville Ct CW2 . . . . 206 B7
Ashville Ind Est WA7 . . . . 49 E3
Ashville Point WA7 . . . . . . 49 E3
Ashville Way WA7 . . . . 49 E3
Ash Way CH60 . . . . 41 B6
Ashwood WA14 . . . . 31 B8
Ashwood Ave
  Golborne WA3 . . . . 3 D8
  Warrington WA1 . . . . 16 E7
Ashwood Cl
  Barnton CW8 . . . . 78 B4
  Ellesmere Port CH66 . . . . 69 D1
  Widnes WA8 . . . . 22 A7
Ashwood Cres CW8 . . . . . 78 B3
Ashwood Ct CH2 . . . . 119 A3
Ashwood Farm Ct CH2 . . . 96 B6
Ashwood La CH2 . . . . 96 B5
Ashwood Rd SK12 . . . . 38 D6
Ashworth Pk WA16 . . . . . . 81 F8
Asiatic Cotts CH5 . . . . . . 116 B3
Askerbank La SK11 . . . . . 159 A1
Askett Cl WA11 . . . . 1 C7
Askrigg Ave CH66 . . . . 69 B5
Aspen Cl
  Ellesmere Port CH66 . . . . 69 E1
  Harrisehead ST7 . . . . . . 195 E3
  Heswall CH60 . . . . 41 D8
Aspen Gr
  Saughall CH1 . . . . 117 B7
  Warrington WA1 . . . . 17 A7
Aspens The CW8 . . . . 101 E5
Aspen Way
  Chester CH2 . . . . 119 B4
  High Lane SK6 . . . . 38 A7
Aspinall Cl WA2 . . . . 9 A3
Aspull Cl WA3 . . . . 9 C4
Asquith Cl CW1 . . . . 191 C5
Assheton Cl WA12 . . . . 2 A4
Assheton Wlk L24 . . . . 21 E2
ASTBURY 178 B7
Astbury Cl
  Crewe CW1 . . . . 190 A7
  Golborne WA3 . . . . 4 B8
  Kidsgrove ST7 . . . . 195 C3
Astbury Dr CW8 . . . . 78 A4
Astbury Lane Ends CW12 178 B3
ASTBURY MARSH 156 B1

Astbury Mere Ctry Pk*
  CW12 . . . . 156 B2
Astbury St Mary's CE Prim
  Sch CW12 . . . . 178 B8
Astbury St CW12 . . . . 156 C2
Aster Cres WA7 . . . . 49 F4
Aster Rd WA11 . . . . 1 F7
Aster Wlk M31 . . . . 11 F2
Astle Cl CW10 . . . . 151 C7
Astle Ct SK11 . . . . 84 A3
Astle La SK10 . . . . 84 E1
Astley Cl
  Knutsford WA16 . . . . 82 C7
  Warrington WA4 . . . . 16 B3
  Widnes WA8 . . . . 12 C3
Astley Ct M44 . . . . 11 E8
Astley Rd M44 . . . . 11 E8
ASTMOOR 23 E3
Astmoor Bridge La WA7 . . 23 F2
Astmoor East Intc WA7 . . 24 A3
Astmoor Ind Est WA7 . . . . 23 F3
Astmoor La WA7 . . . . 23 F1
Astmoor Prim Sch WA7 . . 23 E2
Astmoor Rd WA7 . . . . 23 E3
Aston
  Nantwich 217 C2
  Runcorn 50 D1
Aston Ave
  Warrington WA3 . . . . 9 F4
  Winsford CW7 . . . . 126 B2
Aston by Sutton Prim Sch
  WA7 . . . . 50 C2
Aston Cl WA1 . . . . 9 C1
Aston Fields Rd WA7 . . . . 50 E4
Aston Forge WA7 . . . . 50 F5
Aston Gn WA7 . . . . 50 E6
ASTON HEATH 50 E2
ASTON JUXTA
  MONDRUM 188 D6
Aston La
  Aston WA7 . . . . 50 C2
  Runcorn WA7 . . . . 50 F5
  Woore CW3 . . . . 232 E1
Aston Lane N WA7 . . . . . . 50 E4
Aston Lane S WA7 . . . . . . 50 E3
Aston Rd ST5 . . . . 210 D1
Aston St
  19 Handforth SK9 . . . . 34 D5
  Middlewich CW10 . . . . . . 128 E1
Astor Dr WA4 . . . . 26 F8
Atcherley Cl CW5 . . . . . . 218 E8
Atelbrae Cl CH8 . . . . 103 F7
Atherton La M44 . . . . 11 E5
Atherton Rd CH65 . . . . 69 F4
Athey St Mill **2** SK11 . 112 C7
Athey St SK11 . . . . 112 C8
Athlone Rd WA2 . . . . 8 A1
Athol Cl
  Bebington CH62 . . . . 43 E5
  Newton-le-Willows WA12 . . 1 F4
Atholl Ave CW2 . . . . 190 C1
Atholl Cl SK10 . . . . 87 A1
Atholl Rd SK7 . . . . 35 D5
Atkin Cl CW12 . . . . 156 A3
Atlanta Ave M90 . . . . 33 A8
Atlanta Gdns WA5 . . . . . . 15 B8
Atlantic Trad Pk CW7 . . . 126 E5
Atlas Way CH66 . . . . 69 F7
Atterbury Cl WA8 . . . . 12 C2
Attlee Ave WA3 . . . . 5 C4
Attwood Cl CW1 . . . . 191 C6
Attwood Rise ST7 . . . . . . 195 A2
Attwood St ST7 . . . . 195 A2
Atworth Terr CH64 . . . . . . 67 F8
Auburn Cl WA8 . . . . 12 C3
Auckery Ave CH66 . . . . . . 69 D3
Auckland Rd CH1 . . . . . . 117 D4
AUDLEM 230 B4
Audlem Cl WA7 . . . . 49 F4
Audlem Dr CW9 . . . . 104 A6
Audlem Rd
  Hankelow CW3 . . . . 230 C7
  Hatherton CW5 . . . . 219 D3
  Nantwich CW5 . . . . 204 F3
Audlem St James' CE Prim
  Sch CW3 . . . . 230 A5
AUDLEY 209 C2
Audley Cres CH4 . . . . 141 E6
Audley Rd
  Alsager ST7 . . . . 193 E1
  Barthomley CW2 . . . . . . 208 E3
  Newcastle-under-Lyme ST7,
    ST5 . . . . 210 B2
  Talke ST7 . . . . 210 B6
Audley St CW1 . . . . 190 D5
Audley Street W CW1 . . . 190 D5
Audre Cl WA5 . . . . 14 D6
Aughton Way CH4 . . . . . . 139 D4
Augusta Cl SK10 . . . . 87 B4
Augusta Ho CH1 . . . . 117 F6
Austell Rd **6** M22 . . . . 33 D8
Austen Cl **1** CW11 . . . 174 D6
Austen Dr WA2 . . . . 8 A6
Austen Ho SK10 . . . . 86 F1
Austin CW7 . . . . 149 C6
Austins Hill CH3 . . . . 144 C8
Austin St CW9 . . . . 79 D1
Austral Ave WA1 . . . . 17 C1
Australia La WA4 . . . . 17 C1
Autumn Ave WA16 . . . . . . 57 C2
Avebury Cl
  Golborne WA3 . . . . 3 E8
  Widnes WA8 . . . . 13 F3
Aveley Cl WA1 . . . . 17 B7
Avens Rd M31 . . . . 11 F3
Avenue One CW1 . . . . . . 207 C8

Avenue The
  Alderley Edge SK9 . . . . . . 60 A1
  Alsager ST7 . . . . 193 D4
  Altrincham WA15 . . . . 31 F8
  Basford CW6 . . . . 203 C2
  Combarbach CW9 . . . . . . 78 D8
  Great Barrow CH3 . . . . . 120 F7
  High Legh WA16 . . . . 29 C5
  Kidsgrove ST7 . . . . 194 F1
  Lymm WA13 . . . . 18 D1
  Marston CW9 . . . . 79 B3
  Newton-le-Willows WA12 . . 2 D4
  Northwich CW9 . . . . 79 B8
  Sandbach CW11 . . . . . . 174 E8
  Tarporley CW6 . . . . 146 D1
Avenue Two CW1 . . . . . . 207 C8
Avery Cl WA2 . . . . .8 E2
Avery Cres WA11 . . . . 1 C7
Avery Rd WA11 . . . . 1 C7
Avery Sq WA11 . . . . 1 C7
Aviemore Dr WA2 . . . . 9 A3
Avocet Cl
  Newton-le-Willows WA12 . . 2 C4
  Warrington WA2 . . . . 8 D3
Avocet Dr CW7 . . . . 149 D6
Avon WA8 . . . . 12 A2
Avon Ave WA5 . . . . 14 F4
Avon Cl
  Kidsgrove ST7 . . . . 195 B2
  Macclesfield SK10 . . . . . . 87 A2
  Neston CH64 . . . . 66 E6
Avon Ct ST7 . . . . 193 C5
Avondale CH65 . . . . 70 B2
Avondale Ave CH62 . . . . . 43 F5
Avondale Dr WA8 . . . . 12 B1
Avondale Rd WA11 . . . . . . 1 C7
Avondale Rise SK9 . . . . . . 60 D6
Avon Dr
  Congleton CW12 . . . . . . 156 F1
  Crewe CW1 . . . . 191 A5
Avonlea Cl CH4 . . . . 140 E4
Avon Rd
  Altrincham WA15 . . . . 31 E8
  Culcheth WA3 . . . . 5 A2
  Gatley SK8 . . . . 34 C7
Avonside Way SK11 . . . . 112 C5
Avon Wlk CW7 . . . . 127 A2
Avro Way M90 . . . . 32 F7
Axminster Wlk SK7 . . . . . . 35 E7
Aycliffe Wlk **6** WA8 . . . 22 C8
Aylesbury Cl
  Ellesmere Port CH66 . . . . 69 C3
  Macclesfield SK10 . . . . . . 87 D3
Aylesby Cl WA16 . . . . 57 B1
Aylsham Cl WA8 . . . . 12 C4
Ayrshire Cl CW10 . . . . . . 128 D2
Ayrshire Way CW12 . . . . 157 A1
Aysgarth Ave CW1 . . . . . 173 B1
Azalea Gdns WA9 . . . . 6 A7
Azalea Gr WA7 . . . . 49 F4

B

Babbacombe Rd WA5 . . . . 14 E4
Babbage Rd CH5 . . . . 116 A4
BACHE 118 B5
Bache Ave CH2 . . . . 118 B5
Bache Dr CH2 . . . . 118 C5
Bachefield Ave CH3 . . . . 142 A6
Bache Hall Ct CH2 . . . . . 118 C5
Bache Hall Est CH2 . . . . 118 C5
Bachelor's Ct CH3 . . . . . 142 A8
Bachelor's La CH3 . . . . . 142 A8
Bache Sta CH2 . . . . 118 D5
Back Bridge St CW1 . . . . 190 C5
Back Brook Pl WA4 . . . . . 16 C5
Back Coole La CW3 . . . . . 229 B4
Back Crosland Terr WA6 . 73 B2
Back Cross La
  Congleton CW12 . . . . . . 179 A8
  Newton-le-Willows WA12 . . 2 B4
Back Eastford Rd WA4 . . . 16 A1
Back Edisbury Rd SK11 . 113 C7
BACKFORD 95 A4
Backford Cl WA7 . . . . 50 C5
Backford Cross CH66 . . . . 94 F7
Backford Gdns CH66 . . . . 94 F7
Back Forshaw St WA2 . . . 16 C7
Back Heathcote St ST7 . . 195 A2
Back High St **3** WA2 . . . 2 A3
Back Jodrell St SK22 . . . . 39 B7
Back La
  Alpraham CW6 . . . . 169 D6
  Altrincham WA15 . . . . 32 B4
  Bate Heath CW9 . . . . 54 D7
  Betley CW2 . . . . 208 C1
  Brereton Green CW11 . . 153 D6
  Burtonwood WA5 . . . . 6 D7
  Congleton CW12 . . . . . . 156 A4
  Duddon CW6 . . . . 145 A6
  Helsby WA6 . . . . 73 D2
  Higher Whitley WA4 . . . . 52 E4
  High Legh WA14 . . . . 29 F5
  Marton CW12, SK11 . . . 133 F2
  No Man's Heath SY14 . . 214 A4
  Norbury SY13 . . . . 215 F5
  Partington WA14 . . . . 20 C5
  Plumley WA16 . . . . 81 B1
  Shavington CW2 . . . . . . 206 D4
  Smallwood CW11 . . . . . . 176 D8
  Swan Green WA16 . . . . . 106 B8
  Tattenhall CH3 . . . . 167 C2
  Threapwood SY14 . . . . . 222 E7
  Warrington WA5 . . . . 14 A3
  Wybunbury CW5 . . . . . . 220 C6
Backlands CW1 . . . . 190 C6
Back Lanes CW6 . . . . 146 B2
Back Market St WA12 . . . . . 2 A3

Back Paradise St **4**
  SK11 . . . . 112 C7
Back Park St CW12 . . . . . 156 E2
Back Queen St CH1 . . . . . 237 B3
Back River St **3** CH66 . 156 D3
Back Union Rd **3** SK22 . 39 C7
Back Wallgate **13** SK11 . 112 D8
Badbury Cl WA11 . . . . 1 D7
Badcock's La CW6 . . . . . 185 E4
BADDILEY 203 B1
Baddiley Cl CW5 . . . . 203 D2
Baddiley Hall La CW5 . . . 217 A8
Baddiley La CW5 . . . . 203 D1
Baddington La CW5 . . . . . 204 C1
Badger Ave CW1 . . . . 190 B5
Badger Bait CH64 . . . . 66 F6
Badger Cl WA7 . . . . 50 A6
Badger Ho SK10 . . . . 87 D2
Badger Rd
  Macclesfield SK10 . . . . . . 87 D2
  Prestbury SK10 . . . . 87 A7
Badgers Cl
  Christleton CH3 . . . . 142 E7
  1 Ellesmere Port CH66 . 94 F8
  1 Winsford CW7 . . . . 126 A1
Badgers Croft ST5 . . . . . 210 E1
Badgers Pk CH64 . . . . 66 F6
Badgersrake La CH66 . . . 68 D3
Badgers Set CW8 . . . . . . 101 D5
Badgers Wlk CH2 . . . . 95 E2
Badgers Wood CW2 . . . . 205 D8
Bag La
  Cuddington CW8, WA6. . 101 E7
  Norley WA6 . . . . 101 A6
Bagley La CW3 . . . . 230 B1
Bagmere Cl
  Brereton Green CW11 . . 153 F4
  Sandbach CW11 . . . . . . 174 F7
Bagmere La CW11 . . . . . 154 B5
Bagnall Cl WA5 . . . . 15 C5
Bagot Ave WA5 . . . . 15 F8
Bagstock Ave SK12 . . . . . 36 E2
Baguley Ave WA8 . . . . 22 A5
Bahama Cl WA11 . . . . 1 D8
Bahama Rd WA11 . . . . 1 D8
Baildon Gn CH66 . . . . 69 B5
Bailey Ave CH65 . . . . 69 F6
Bailey Bridge Cl CH2 . . . 118 D4
Bailey Bsns Pk SK10 . . . . 87 F7
Bailey Cl CW1 . . . . 190 C7
Bailey Cres
  Congleton CW12 . . . . . . 157 A4
  Sandbach CW11 . . . . . . 175 D6
Bailey Ct
  Alsager ST7 . . . . 193 E3
  1 Macclesfield SK10 . 112 E7
Bailey's Bank ST8 . . . . . . 179 D3
Baileys La WA4 . . . . 13 A5
Baileys La L26 . . . . 21 A7
Baileys La L26 . . . . 21 A1
Bainbridge Ave WA3 . . . . . 3 F8
Bainbridge Cres WA5 . . . . 14 E8
Baines Ave M44 . . . . 11 F8
Bakehurst Cl SK22 . . . . . . 39 C7
Baker Cl CW2 . . . . 190 A2
Baker Dr CH66 . . . . 69 E3
Baker Rd WA4 . . . . 48 D7
Baker's Cl CW7 . . . . 126 E1
Baker's Ct CW7 . . . . 126 E1
Baker's La
  Swan Green WA16 . . . . . 106 D6
  Winsford CW7 . . . . 126 E1
Bakers Pl WA2 . . . . 16 B7
Baker St **8** SK11 . . . . . 112 C7
Bakers Villas The CW12 . 156 D2
Bakestondale Rd SK10 . . 63 E4
Bakewell Cl CH66 . . . . 94 E8
Bakewell Rd
  Burtonwood WA5 . . . . 7 A7
  Hazel Grove SK7 . . . . 36 E8
Bala Cl WA5 . . . . 7 E2
BALDERTON 140 C1
Baldock Cl WA4 . . . . 17 C3
Balfour Cl CW1 . . . . 191 C4
Balfour St WA7 . . . . 22 F1
Balham Cl WA8 . . . . 13 A4
Balharry Ave WA11 . . . . . . 1 E7
Ballantyne Pl WA2 . . . . . . 8 A6
Ballantyne Way **5** WA3 . 3 E8
Ballater Cres WA3 . . . . . 119 B2
Ballater Dr WA2 . . . . 8 E4
Balleral Cl **2** CH1 . . . . 117 D4
Balliol Cl SK11 . . . . 112 F3
Ball La
  Bollington SK10 . . . . 87 D5
  Kingsley WA6 . . . . 75 E4
BALL O' DITTON 12 E2
Ball Pathway WA8 . . . . . . 12 E1
Balmoral Ave
  Crewe CW2 . . . . 190 B1
  Northwich CW9 . . . . 104 A5
Balmoral Cl
  Knutsford WA16 . . . . 57 B1
  Winsford CW7 . . . . 126 C3
Balmoral Cres SK10 . . . . . 87 F2
Balmoral Dr
  Helsby WA6 . . . . 73 B4
  High Lane SK6 . . . . 37 E7
  Holmes Chapel CW4 . . . 130 B2
  Poynton SK12 . . . . 36 D3
Balmoral Gdns
  Congleton CW12 . . . . . . 156 F4
  Ellesmere Port CH65 . . . . 70 D3
Balmoral Pk CH1 . . . . 118 B3
Balmoral Pl CW5 . . . . 205 D4

Balmoral Rd
Warrington WA4 . . . . 16 F2
Widnes WA8 . . . . 13 A4
Balmoral Way SK9 . . . . 60 A6
BALTERLEY 208 C1
BALTERLEY GREEN 208 C2
BALTERLEY HEATH 207 F1
Baltimore Gdns WA5 . . . . . 15 C7
Bamburgh Ct CH65 . . . . 70 E3
Bamford Cl
Bollington SK10 . . . . 88 A7
Gatley SK8 . . . . 34 D8
Runcorn WA7 . . . . 49 C7
Bamford St SK10 . . . . 87 E1
Banastre Dr WA12 . . . . 2 F3
Banbury Cl SK10 . . . . 87 E2
Banbury Dr WA5 . . . . 15 C5
Banbury St ST7 . . . . 194 D1
Bancroft CW8 . . . . 76 F4
Bancroft Rd WA8 . . . . 13 D2
Bandon Cl L24 . . . . 21 D2
Banff Ave CH63 . . . . 43 D5
Bangor Cl 11 CH66 . . . . 94 F8
Bank Cl
Chester CH2 . . . . 118 E5
Macclesfield SK11 . . . . 112 E7
Neston CH64 . . . . 67 A6
Bank Cott CW12 . . . . 156 E2
Bank Ct 5 ST7 . . . . 195 A2
Bankes' La
Runcorn, Weston Point WA7 . . . . 48 E6
Runcorn, Weston WA7 . . . . . 48 F5
Bankfield Ave
Irlam M44 . . . . 11 D5
Wistaston CW2 . . . . 206 A7
Bankfield Rd WA8 . . . . 12 C1
Bankfield Sch WA8 . . . . 12 D1
Bankfields Dr CH62 . . . . 44 B5
Bank Gdns WA5 . . . . 14 E4
Bankhall La WA14, WA15 . . 31 F8
BANK HEATH 3 A8
Bankhey CH64 . . . . 66 F5
Bank Ho CW7 . . . . 126 C1
Bankhouse Dr CW12 . . . . . 157 A5
Bank House La
Helsby WA6 . . . . 73 C4
Smallwood CW11 . . . . 177 A6
Bank La
Burland CW5 . . . . 203 D8
Congleton CW12 . . . . 134 C1
Rainow SK10 . . . . 89 D6
Banklands Cl M44 . . . . 11 D5
Bank Mews WA6 . . . . 73 C4
Bank Pl SK9 . . . . 60 B7
BANK QUAY 15 F4
Bank Quay Trad Est WA1 . . 15 F4
Bank Rd CH5 . . . . 91 D1
Banks Cl CW12 . . . . 156 C3
Banks Cres WA4 . . . . 16 F4
Bankside
Altrincham WA15 . . . . 32 D6
Runcorn WA7 . . . . 50 E7
Warrington WA1 . . . . 16 A5
Bank Side CW8 . . . . 77 C1
Bankside Cl
Barbridge CW5 . . . . 187 D6
Handforth SK9 . . . . 34 D1
Bankside Ct ST7 . . . . 193 E5
Bank Sq SK9 . . . . 60 B7
Banks Rd CH60 . . . . 40 D8
Bank St
Congleton CW12 . . . . 156 E2
Hollinfare WA3 . . . . 11 B5
Kidsgrove ST7 . . . . 195 C4
Macclesfield SK11 . . . . 112 E7
Newton-le-Willows WA12 . . . . 1 F3
8 Warrington WA1 . . . . 16 B5
Widnes WA8 . . . . 23 A4
BANK THE 195 B7
Bank The ST7 . . . . 195 B7
Bank Top Cotts CW5 . . . . 204 F6
Bank View CW4 . . . . 107 E1
Banky Fields CW12 . . . . . . 156 C2
Banky Fields Cres CW12 . 156 C1
Bannacks Cl CW5 . . . . 205 D6
Bannister Ct CW7 . . . . 149 B7
Bannister Gr CW7 . . . . 149 B6
Barbauld St WA1 . . . . 16 B5
Barber Dr ST7 . . . . 194 E7
Barberry Wlk M31 . . . . 11 F3
Barber's La
Antrobus CW9 . . . . 53 D6
Northwich CW8 . . . . 103 E8
Barber St SK11 . . . . 112 E6
Barbondale Cl WA5 . . . . . . 14 F7
Barbour Sq CH3 . . . . 166 B1
BARBRIDGE 187 C6
Barbridge Mews CW5 . . . 187 D6
Barbridge Rd ST5 . . . . 210 D2
Barclay Hall WA16 . . . . 58 D4
Barclay Rd SK12 . . . . 36 E2
Bardell Cl SK12 . . . . 36 D2
Bardsey Cl 1 CH65 . . . . . . 70 C1
Bardsley Ave WA5 . . . . 7 F1
Barford Cl WA5 . . . . 7 B1
Barford Dr
Golborne WA3 . . . . 4 A8
Handforth SK9 . . . . 34 C1
Barford Grange CH64 . . . . 68 B8
Barham Ct WA3 . . . . 9 D4
Barhill Dr SY13 . . . . 214 C2
Barhill Farm Cotts SY13 . 214 C2
Barington Dr WA7 . . . . 50 E7
Baristow Cl CH2 . . . . 237 B4
Barker's Hollow Rd WA4 . 51 A5
Barker St
Crewe CW2 . . . . 190 D1
Barker St *continued*
Nantwich CW5 . . . . 204 E5
Barkhill Rd CH3 . . . . 119 B3
Bark St CW12 . . . . 156 E2
Barley Castle Cl WA4 . . . . . 27 B3
Barleycastle La WA4 . . . . . 27 D4
Barleycastle Trad Est WA4 . . . . 27 D4
Barley Croft
Alsager ST7 . . . . 193 E2
Chester CH3 . . . . 142 A7
Barleycroft Terr ST7 . . . . 194 F7
Barley Dr SK7 . . . . 35 E7
Barleyfields ST7 . . . . 209 D2
Barley Mere Cl WA12 . . . . . 2 C2
Barley Mow Cl CH66 . . . . . 69 C2
Barley Rd WA4 . . . . 17 C3
Barleywood Cl CW2 . . . . . 206 B8
Barlow Dr CW7 . . . . 148 F8
Barlow Gr WA9 . . . . 1 A2
Barlow Hill SK11 . . . . 136 F2
Barlow Rd
Handforth SK9 . . . . 34 B1
Moulton CW9 . . . . 126 F7
Barlow Way CW11 . . . . 175 A8
Barmouth Cl WA5 . . . . 7 E2
Barnabas Ave CW1 . . . . . . 189 F5
Barnaby Chase CH3 . . . . . 182 C2
Barnaby Rd SK12 . . . . 36 D2
Barnack Cl WA1 . . . . 17 A8
Barnacre Dr CH64 . . . . 41 B2
Barnard Cl SK11 . . . . 111 F6
Barnard St WA5 . . . . 15 D3
Barnato Cl CW1 . . . . 189 F7
Barnbridge Cl ST7 . . . . . . 194 E7
Barnbrook Cl CW7 . . . . . . 126 A1
Barncroft WA7 . . . . 50 D7
Barn Croft WA6 . . . . 73 C4
Barncroft Cl SK11 . . . . 84 A3
Barn Croft Rd L26 . . . . 21 A7
Barn Ct CH3 . . . . 182 C2
Barnes Ave WA2 . . . . 9 B2
Barnes Cl
Blacon CH1 . . . . 117 F6
Haslington CW1 . . . . 191 C4
Warrington WA5 . . . . 15 A5
Widnes WA8 . . . . 13 D2
Barnes Rd WA8 . . . . 13 C2
Barneston Rd WA8 . . . . 13 E3
Barnett Ave WA12 . . . . 1 E3
BARNETT BROOK 228 E5
Barnett Gr CW12 . . . . 156 A3
Barnett St SK11 . . . . 112 B7
Barnett Wlk CW2 . . . . 206 C8
Barnfield CH3 . . . . 166 A2
Barnfield Ave WA7 . . . . 50 D7
Barnfield Cl CH66 . . . . 69 C2
Barnfield Rd
Bollington SK10 . . . . 87 F6
Warrington WA1 . . . . 17 C7
Barnham Cl WA3 . . . . 3 A8
BARNHILL 183 B1
Barnhill Grange CH3 . . . . 183 B3
Barnhill Rd CH3 . . . . 183 A1
Barnhouse La
Great Barrow CH3 . . . . 120 E7
Mouldsworth CH3 . . . . 98 A3
Barn La WA3 . . . . 2 F8
Barn Mdw CW8 . . . . 78 E1
Barnmoore Cl SY14 . . . . . 213 B4
Barn Rd CW12 . . . . 156 D4
Barnside Way
Macclesfield SK10 . . . . 87 C3
Moulton CW9 . . . . 126 F8
Barns La WA14 . . . . 20 A5
Barns Pl WA15 . . . . 32 C8
Barn St WA8 . . . . 23 A6
Barnstaple Way WA5 . . . . . 14 E4
Barns The CW10 . . . . 127 D5
Barnston Ave CH65 . . . . . . 69 F5
Barnston Ct
Farndon CH3 . . . . 180 E2
Mickle Trafford CH2 . . . . . . 119 F8
Barnston Mews CH3 . . . . 180 E2
Barnston Prim Sch CH60 . 41 C7
Barnston Rd CH60 . . . . 41 C8
Barnston Towers Cl CH60 . 41 C8
Barnston Twrs CH60 . . . . . 41 C8
Barnswood Cl WA4 . . . . . . 17 C1
BARNTON 78 C4
Barnton Cl WA3 . . . . 3 D7
Barnton Prim Sch CW8 . . . 78 A4
Barn Way WA12 . . . . 2 B3
Barnwell Ave WA3 . . . . 4 D4
Barnwell Cl CW2 . . . . 206 B8
Barnwood CH66 . . . . 68 F7
Baron Cl WA1 . . . . 17 D7
Baronet Mews WA4 . . . . . . 16 A1
Baronet Rd WA4 . . . . 16 A1
Baron Gn SK8 . . . . 34 D7
Baronia Pl CW5 . . . . 204 F6
Barons Cl WA7 . . . . 23 F1
Baron's Cl WA8 . . . . 22 C8
Barons Ct CH2 . . . . 118 C4
Barons Quay Rd CW9 . . . . 78 F1
Barons Rd
Shavington CW2 . . . . 206 B4
Worleston CW5 . . . . 188 E5
Barony Bldgs 1 CW5 . . . . 204 E6
Barony Ct CW5 . . . . 204 E7
Barony Employment Pk The CW5 . . . . 204 F8
Barony Rd CW5 . . . . 204 E7
Barony Terr CW5 . . . . 204 E6
BARONY THE 204 F6
Barony Way CH4 . . . . 140 E4
Barracks La
Burwardsley CH3 . . . . 184 C5
Barracks La *continued*
Macclesfield SK10 . . . . 112 F8
Ravensmoor CW5 . . . . 203 E2
Barracks Sq 3 SK11 . . . . 112 B6
Barrastitch La CW8 . . . . . 101 E6
Barratt Rd ST7 . . . . 193 F3
Barrel Well Hill CH2 . . . . . 118 F1
BARRETS GREEN 169 D3
Barrie Gdns ST7 . . . . 210 C8
Barrie Gr CW1 . . . . 190 E4
Barrington Dr CW10 . . . . 151 C7
Barrow Ave WA2 . . . . 8 E2
Barrow CE Prim Sch CH3 . . . . 120 D6
Barrowdale Rd WA3 . . . . 3 B8
Barrow Hall Com Prim Sch WA5 . . . . 14 E7
Barrow Hall Farm CH3 . . 120 E5
Barrow Hall La WA5 . . . . . 14 E7
Barrow La
Altrincham WA15 . . . . 32 B7
Golborne WA2 . . . . 3 C2
Great Barrow CH3 . . . . 120 C5
Tarvin CH3 . . . . 121 C4
Barrow Mdw SK8 . . . . 34 E8
Barrowmore Est CH3 . . . . 120 F7
Barrow's Brow WA16 . . . . . 81 E1
Barrows Cl CW1 . . . . 190 A8
BARROWS GREEN 189 F8
BARROW'S GREEN 13 E4
Barrow's Green La WA8 . . 13 E3
Barrow's Row WA8 . . . . 13 B4
Barrule Cl WA4 . . . . 26 D7
Barry Cl CH65 . . . . 95 C8
Barrymore Ave WA4 . . . . . 16 F4
Barrymore Cres CW9 . . . . . 78 D8
Barrymore Ct WA4 . . . . 17 A1
Barrymore Rd
Runcorn WA7 . . . . 49 B7
Warrington WA4 . . . . 17 A1
Weaverham CW8 . . . . 77 E1
Barrymore Way CH63 . . . . 43 B6
Barry St WA4 . . . . 16 C4
Barsbank Cl WA13 . . . . 18 C3
Barsbank La WA13 . . . . 18 C3
Barshaw Gdns WA4 . . . . . . 26 E4
Bars The CH1, CH3 . . . . . . 237 C2
Bartholomew Ct WA4 . . . . 17 B2
Bartholomew Way CH4 . . 141 C6
BARTHOMLEY 208 C5
Barthomley Cres CW2 . . . 189 D4
Barthomley Rd
Barthomley CW2 . . . . 208 B7
Betley ST7 . . . . 208 F3
BARTINGTON 77 A5
Bartington Hall Pk CW8 . . 77 A5
Bartlegate WA7 . . . . 50 B5
BARTON 181 F1
Barton Ave WA4 . . . . 17 A2
Barton Cl
Handforth SK9 . . . . 34 D2
Runcorn WA7 . . . . 50 D7
Barton Ct
Warrington WA2 . . . . 16 B6
Winsford CW7 . . . . 126 F1
Barton Rd
Barton CH3, SY14 . . . . 181 D1
Barton SY14 . . . . 181 F1
Congleton CW12 . . . . 156 F3
Farndon CH3 . . . . 180 F1
Barton's Pl CW9 . . . . 79 B1
Barton St SK11 . . . . 112 C7
Barton Stadium (Winsford United FC) CW7 . . . . . . 126 F1
Barwood Ave ST7 . . . . 194 A5
Barwoods Dr CH4 . . . . 140 F6
BASFORD 206 E5
Basford Rd CW2 . . . . 206 D8
Basford Way CW7 . . . . 126 B2
Baskervyle Cl CH60 . . . . . . 41 A6
Baskervyle Rd CH60 . . . . . 41 A6
Baslow Dr
Gatley SK8 . . . . 34 C8
Hazel Grove SK7 . . . . 36 F8
Bassett Cl CW5 . . . . 205 D6
Batchelors Wing The CW10 . . . . 127 D5
BATE HEATH 54 F3
Bateman Almshouses ST8 . . . . 179 E3
Bateman Cl CW1 . . . . 190 B4
Bateman Rd CW9 . . . . 80 B2
Batemans Ct CW2 . . . . 206 B8
Batemill Cl SK10 . . . . 86 F1
Batemill La WA16, SK11 . . 108 E5
Bates La WA6 . . . . 73 D4
Bate's Mill La CW6 . . . . . . 167 E5
Bath Cres SK8 . . . . 35 B6
Batherton Cl WA8 . . . . 23 B7
Batherton La CW5 . . . . . . 204 F2
Bath La CW3 . . . . 230 A3
Bath St
Chester CH1 . . . . 237 C2
Sandbach CW11 . . . . 175 C6
Warrington WA1 . . . . 16 A5
BATH VALE 157 A3
Bath Vale Cotts CW12 . . . 157 A3
Bathwood Dr CH64 . . . . . . 66 E5
Batterbee Ct CW1 . . . . . . 191 D5
Battersby La WA2 . . . . 16 C6
Battersea Ct WA8 . . . . 12 F3
Battery La
Warrington WA1 . . . . 17 F7
Wilmslow SK9 . . . . 59 D6
Bawtry Ct WA2 . . . . 8 E1
Baxter Cl WA7 . . . . 50 D7
Baxter Ho CW8 . . . . 78 E1
Baxter St WA5 . . . . 15 E5
Baycliffe WA13 . . . . 18 D2
Bayley Rd CW5 . . . . 205 D6
Baynard Dr WA8 . . . . 22 C5
Bayswater Cl WA7 . . . . 24 F4
Baytree Cl CH66 . . . . 69 F1
Bayvil Cl WA7 . . . . 50 E7
Beach Gr CW8 . . . . 103 C6
Beachin La CH3 . . . . 182 A4
Beach Rd CW8 . . . . 103 B6
Beacon Ct 4 CH60 . . . . 41 A8
Beacon Hill View WA7 . . . . 48 D7
Beacon La CH60 . . . . 41 A7
Beaconsfield Cres WA8 . . 13 A4
Beaconsfield Gr WA8 . . . . 13 B4
Beaconsfield Rd
Runcorn WA7 . . . . 22 E1
Widnes WA8 . . . . 13 B4
Beaconsfield St CH3 . . . . 237 C2
Beacons The CH60 . . . . 41 A7
Beacons The WA3 . . . . 9 D5
Beadnell Dr WA5 . . . . 14 F3
Beagle Point CW7 . . . . 126 A1
Beagle Wlk M22 . . . . 33 E8
Beames Ho CW1 . . . . 190 B4
Beam Heath Way CW5 . . 204 F7
Beamish Cl WA4 . . . . 26 D3
Beamont St WA8 . . . . 23 A4
Beam St CW5 . . . . 204 E6
Beard Cres SK22 . . . . 39 D8
Beardsmore Dr WA3 . . . . 3 E8
Bearhurst La SK11 . . . . . . 111 A5
Bearstone Rd TF9 . . . . 236 E3
Beasley Cl CH66 . . . . 69 D3
Beata Rd ST5 . . . . 210 F1
Beatrice St WA4 . . . . 16 D3
Beatty Ave WA2 . . . . 8 C1
Beatty Dr CW12 . . . . 157 A4
Beatty Rd CW5 . . . . 204 D4
Beaufort Chase SK9 . . . . . . 34 F1
Beaufort Cl
Alderley Edge SK9 . . . . 60 B2
Runcorn WA7 . . . . 49 B7
Warrington WA5 . . . . 15 A5
Widnes WA8 . . . . 22 A8
Beaufort St WA5 . . . . 15 E4
Beaulieu Ave CW7 . . . . . . 126 F2
Beaumaris Cres SK7 . . . . . 36 C8
Beaumaris Dr CH65 . . . . . . 70 D2
Beaumaris Way WA7 . . . . . 23 F2
Beaumont Cl
Biddulph ST8 . . . . 179 D3
Chester CH4 . . . . 140 E6
Wistaston CW2 . . . . 205 F8
Beaumont Ct
Handforth SK9 . . . . 34 C5
Warrington WA4 . . . . 16 C2
Beaumont Prim Sch WA2 . 16 C7
Beauty Bank
Whitegate CW7 . . . . 125 E5
Winsford CW7 . . . . 149 B3
Beauty Bank Cotts CW7 . 149 A3
Beaverbrook Ave WA3 . . . . . 5 B4
Beaver Cl
Chester CH4 . . . . 140 E5
Pickmere WA16 . . . . 79 F7
Beaver Ctr The CW9 . . . . . 103 F7
BEBINGTON 43 A7
Bebington Rd CH66 . . . . . . 69 D4
Becconsall Cl CW1 . . . . . . 190 A8
Becconsall Dr CW1 . . . . . 190 A8
Bechers WA8 . . . . 12 B3
Beckenham Cl WA8 . . . . . . 13 D4
Beckenham Gr 4 CW7 . . 126 A1
Beckett Ave CW7 . . . . 150 D8
Beckett Dr
Lymm WA13 . . . . 19 B8
Winwick WA2 . . . . 8 A5
Beckett's La CH3 . . . . 142 B8
Beckford Cl CW1 . . . . 189 F8
Becks La SK10 . . . . 86 F2
Bedells La SK9 . . . . 60 A6
Bedford Ave CH65 . . . . 70 A2
Bedford Avenue E CH65 . . 70 B2
Bedford Ct CW2 . . . . 190 D1
Bedford Gdns CW2 . . . . . . 190 C1
Bedford Gn M44 . . . . 11 B6
Bedford Gr ST7 . . . . 193 B5
Bedford Pl CW2 . . . . 190 C1
Bedford Rd
Kidsgrove ST7 . . . . 195 A3
Macclesfield SK11 . . . . 112 B7
Bedford Rise CW7 . . . . . . 149 C6
Bedford St
Crewe CW2 . . . . 190 C1
Warrington WA4 . . . . 26 C8
Bedward Row CH1 . . . . . . 237 A2
Beech Ave
Culcheth WA3 . . . . 5 A3
Frodsham WA6 . . . . 74 C8
Golborne WA3 . . . . 3 F7
Haydock WA11 . . . . 1 F7
Mobberley WA16 . . . . 57 E6
Rode Heath ST7 . . . . 193 F8
Warrington, Thelwall WA4 . . 17 D3
Warrington WA5 . . . . 14 C3
Beech Bank SK10 . . . . 87 D1
Beech Cl
Alderley Edge SK9 . . . . 60 B3
Congleton CW12 . . . . 156 A4
Cuddington CW8 . . . . 101 F2
Holmes Chapel CW4 . . . . . 130 D4
Newton-le-Willows WA12 . . . 2 C2
Ollerton WA16 . . . . 82 F6
4 Partington M31 . . . . 11 F3
Beech Cotts
Alderley Edge SK9 . . . . 85 A8
Stretton WA4 . . . . 26 E1
Beech Cres SK12 . . . . 36 E4
Beechcroft Ave CW2 . . . . 206 B7
Beechcroft Dr CH65 . . . . . . 70 B2
Beech Ct WA8 . . . . 12 B3
Beech Dr
Crewe CW2 . . . . 189 F2
Knutsford WA16 . . . . 57 C2
Talke ST7 . . . . 210 E8
Beeches SK9 . . . . 59 F6
Beeches The
Chester CH2 . . . . 119 A6
Ellesmere Port CH66 . . . . . . 69 D4
Helsby WA6 . . . . 73 C4
Mobberley WA16 . . . . 58 E1
Nantwich CW5 . . . . 204 F5
3 Northwich CW9 . . . . 103 E6
Whitchurch SY13 . . . . 225 F1
Widnes WA8 . . . . 13 D4
Beech Farm Dr SK10 . . . . . 87 D2
Beechfield
Moulton CW9 . . . . 126 E8
Wilmslow SK9 . . . . 60 A6
Beechfield Ave SK9 . . . . . . 59 E5
Beechfield Cl CH60 . . . . 41 A7
Beechfield Dr CW10 . . . . . 128 B2
Beechfield Gdns CW8 . . . 103 B6
Beechfield Rd
Alderley Edge SK9 . . . . 85 B8
Cheadle SK8 . . . . 35 B8
Ellesmere Port CH65 . . . . . . 70 B5
Warrington WA4 . . . . 17 A2
Beechfields CW7 . . . . 150 B8
Beech Gdns 3 WA7 . . . . . . 49 C8
Beech Gr
Chester CH2 . . . . 119 A3
Crewe CW1 . . . . 190 E5
Ellesmere Port CH66 . . . . . . 95 A8
Lymm WA13 . . . . 18 B2
Macclesfield SK11 . . . . 112 E5
Sandbach CW11 . . . . 175 D6
Warrington, Latchford WA4 . 16 D3
Warrington WA1 . . . . 17 A7
Weaverham CW8 . . . . 102 D8
Wilmslow SK9 . . . . 60 A6
Winsford CW7 . . . . 149 D8
Beech Hall Dr SK10 . . . . . . 87 C2
Beech Hall Sch SK10 . . . . . 87 C2
Beech Heyes Cl CW8 . . . . 102 E8
Beech Heyes Dr CW8 . . . . 102 E8
Beech Hey La CH64 . . . . . . 43 B1
Beech Hollows LL12 . . . . . 162 C1
Beech La
Barnton CW8 . . . . 78 A3
Cotebrook CW6 . . . . 147 B6
Macclesfield SK10 . . . . 87 D1
Norley WA6 . . . . 75 E1
Wilmslow SK9 . . . . 60 A6
Beechlands Ave CH3 . . . . 119 A1
Beechmill Dr WA3 . . . . 4 E3
Beechmoore WA4 . . . . 25 B5
Beechmuir CH1 . . . . 117 E3
Beech Rd
Alderley Edge SK9 . . . . 60 B3
Aston WA7 . . . . 50 B4
Heswall CH60 . . . . 41 C8
High Lane SK6 . . . . 37 F7
Little Budworth CW6 . . . . . 124 D2
Paddockhill WA16 . . . . 59 B5
Runcorn WA7 . . . . 49 C8
Warrington WA4 . . . . 26 C8
Whaley Bridge SK23 . . . . . . 65 E7
Beech Rise
Crowton CW8 . . . . 76 B2
Horwich End SK23 . . . . 65 C5
Beech St CW10 . . . . 128 C1
Beech Street W CW1 . . . . 190 C4
Beech Tree Cl CW5 . . . . . 205 D5
Beechtree Farm Cl WA16 . 29 C7
Beechtree La WA13 . . . . . . 29 B7
Beech View Rd WA6 . . . . . 75 C1
Beechway
Bollington SK10 . . . . 88 A7
Chester CH2 . . . . 118 C6
High Lane SK6 . . . . 37 F7
Neston CH64 . . . . 66 D7
Wilmslow SK9 . . . . 59 F5
Beechways WA4 . . . . 26 D5
Beechways Dr CH64 . . . . . . 66 D7
BEECHWOOD 49 E5
Beechwood
Knutsford, Cross Town WA16 . . . . 57 C2
Knutsford WA16 . . . . 56 F3
Beechwood Ave
Hartford CW8 . . . . 103 A6
Newton-le-Willows WA12 . . . 2 D4
Runcorn WA7 . . . . 49 E5
Warrington, Padgate WA1 . . 16 E7
Warrington WA5 . . . . 14 F5
Beechwood Cl CW5 . . . . . 205 A4
Beechwood Dr
Alsager ST7 . . . . 193 B4
Eaton (nr Congleton) CW12 . . . . 156 F8
Ellesmere Port CH66 . . . . . . 69 D1
Higher Wincham CW9 . . . . . 79 F6
Wilmslow SK9 . . . . 60 E8
Beechwood Gr SK8 . . . . . . 35 A8
Beechwood La WA3 . . . . 4 D4
Beechwood Mews SK10 . . 87 C2
Beechwood Prim Sch
Crewe CW1 . . . . 190 C5
Runcorn WA7 . . . . 49 E5
Beechwood Rd
Bebington CH62 . . . . 43 C8
Saltney CH4 . . . . 140 E5

Beecroft Cl WA5 . . . . 7 D1
Beehive La CW9 . . . . 126 F8
BEESTON 168 A2
BEESTON-BROOK 168 C5
Beeston Brow SK10 . . . . . . 88 B8
Beeston Castle* CW6 . . 167 F3
Beeston Cl
  Bollington SK10 . . . . 63 C1
  Holmes Chapel CW4 . . . . 130 A3
  Middlewich CW10 . . . . . . 151 D5
  Warrington WA3 . . . . 9 D4
Beeston Ct WA7 . . . . 24 C4
Beeston Dr
  Alsager ST7 . . . . 193 C3
  Knutsford WA16 . . . . 82 A8
  Winsford CW7 . . . . 149 C7
Beeston Gn CW66 . . . . 69 E5
Beeston Hall Mews CW6 . 168 B4
BEESTON MOSS 168 B1
Beeston Mount SK10 . . . . . 63 C1
Beeston Pathway CH4 . . . 141 E7
Beeston Rd
  Broughton CH4 . . . . 139 B3
  Handforth SK9 . . . . 34 D5
  Higher Kinnerton CH4 . . . 161 A7
Beeston St CW8 . . . . 103 E7
Beeston View CH4 . . . . . . 141 E7
Beggar Man's La WA16 . . 82 A7
Begonia Gdns WA9 . . . . 6 A7
Beilby Rd WA11 . . . . 1 E7
Belfry Cl SK9 . . . . 60 D8
Belfry Dr SK10 . . . . 87 C4
BELGRAVE 162 E6
Belgrave App CH3 . . . . . . 163 C6
Belgrave Ave
  Alsager ST7 . . . . 193 C3
  Congleton CW12 . . . . 156 D3
  Eccleston CH4 . . . . 162 F7
  Saltney CH4 . . . . 140 E6
  Warrington WA1 . . . . 16 F8
Belgrave Cl
  Dodleston CH4 . . . . 162 A6
  Golborne WN7 . . . . 4 C8
  Widnes WA8 . . . . 13 E3
Belgrave Dr CH65 . . . . 69 F5
Belgrave Prim Sch CH4 . 141 B5
Belgrave Rd
  Chester CH3 . . . . 142 B8
  Crewe CW2 . . . . 190 B2
  Irlam M44 . . . . 11 D5
  Macclesfield SK11 . . . . . . 112 C4
  Northwich CW9 . . . . 104 A4
Belgrave St CH1 . . . . 237 C3
Belgravia Ct
  Pulford CH4 . . . . 162 E5
  Widnes WA8 . . . . 12 F3
Belgravia Gdns WA15 . . . 31 E8
Bellaport Rd TF9 . . . . 236 A4
Bellard Dr CH2 . . . . 119 A4
Bell Ave SK11 . . . . 112 F3
Bellcast Cl WA4 . . . . 26 C5
Bellemonte Rd WA6 . . . . . 74 C6
Bellerophon Way WA11 . . 1 E6
Belleville Ave M22 . . . . 33 E8
Bellevue La WA4 . . . . 119 E4
Belle Vue Terr CW11 . . . . 175 B6
Bell Farm Ct SK10 . . . . . . 87 C3
Bellflower Cl WA4 . . . . 12 E4
Bellhouse La
  Higher Walton WA4 . . . . . . 25 D7
  Warrington WA4 . . . . 17 C1
Bell House Rd WA8 . . . . . 13 C1
Bellingham Cl WA16 . . . . . 57 C2
Bellingham Dr WA7 . . . . . . 49 A8
Bell La
  Smallwood CW11 . . . . . . 177 B7
  Warrington WA4 . . . . 17 E3
Bell Meadow Bsns Pk
  CH4 . . . . 162 E5
Bell Meadow Ct CW6 . . . 146 C2
BELL O' TH' HILL 225 D7
Bellsfield Cl WA13 . . . . . . 18 F2
Bell's Hollow ST5 . . . . . . 210 E3
Belmont Ave
  Macclesfield SK10 . . . . . . 86 C1
  Sandbach CW11 . . . . 175 A7
  Warrington WA4 . . . . 16 F3
Belmont Cres WA5 . . . . . . 15 A6
Belmont Dr CH4 . . . . 140 C6
Belmont Rd
  Bramhall SK7 . . . . 35 F5
  Great Budworth CW9 . . . . 53 F1
  Northwich CW9 . . . . 104 C7
  Widnes WA8 . . . . 13 C2
Belton Cl WA3 . . . . 3 A7
Beltony Dr CW1 . . . . 173 A1
Belvedere **9** WA7 . . . . . . 23 A3
Belvedere Cl **2** WA6 . . . 49 C1
Belvedere Dr CH1 . . . . . . 117 E4
Belvedere Rd WA12 . . . . . . 2 B5
Belvedere Terr ST7 . . . . . 193 F7
Belvoir Ave SK7 . . . . 36 E8
Belvoir Rd
  Warrington WA4 . . . . 26 B8
  Widnes WA8 . . . . 13 B1
Bembridge Cl
  Warrington WA5 . . . . 14 C7
  Widnes WA8 . . . . 12 F4
Bembridge Ct CW10 . . . . 151 C8
Bembridge Dr CW10 . . . . 151 C8
Benbrook Gr SK9 . . . . 34 E2
Benbrook Way SK11 . . . . 111 E1
Bendee Ave CH64 . . . . 67 A7
Bendee Rd CH64 . . . . 67 A7

Benjafield Ct CW1 . . . . . . 189 F7
Benjamins Way ST7 . . . . . 209 F2
Bennet Cl CH64 . . . . 68 A8
Bennet Rd CW9 . . . . 104 D6
Bennett Ave WA1 . . . . 16 F6
Bennett Cl CW1 . . . . 190 E4
Bennett Ct CW7 . . . . 149 D5
Bennetts La SK11 . . . . . . 158 E7
Bennett's La
  Higher Kinnerton CH4 . . . 161 A7
  Widnes WA8 . . . . 13 E1
Bennett St WA1 . . . . 16 B5
Ben Nevis Dr CH66 . . . . . . 68 F6
Benson Rd WA3 . . . . 9 D3
Benson Wlk **3** SK9 . . . . 34 D2
Bentham Ave WA2 . . . . 8 C3
Bentham Rd WA3 . . . . 5 A2
Bentinck St WA7 . . . . 22 F3
Bent La
  Astbury CW12 . . . . 178 A8
  Culcheth WA3 . . . . 5 A2
  Lymm WA13 . . . . 19 C6
  Norley CW8 . . . . 101 C8
Bentley Dr CW1 . . . . 191 A5
Bentley Gr CW7 . . . . 149 C6
Bentley's Farm La WA4 . . 52 E5
Benton Dr CH2 . . . . 118 C4
Bents Cotts CH2 . . . . 71 E2
Bents Rd SK12 . . . . 38 D5
Benty Heath La CH64,
  CH66 . . . . 43 B3
Beresford Ct **4** SK9 . . . 60 A1
Beresford St WA1 . . . . 16 E7
Berisford Ho CW12 . . . . . 156 E3
Berkeley Ave CW7 . . . . . . 193 D5
Berkeley Cl
  Golborne WN7 . . . . 4 C8
  Warrington WA5 . . . . 15 F6
Berkeley Cres CW2 . . . . . 206 A8
Berkeley Ct
  Newton-le-Willows WA12 . . 1 F4
  Runcorn WA7 . . . . 24 D4
Berkeley Prim Sch The
  CW2 . . . . 206 B7
Berkeley Rise CW7 . . . . . 149 A8
Berkley Dr SK23 . . . . 65 D6
Berkley Dr CH4 . . . . 141 D6
Berkshire Cl SK10 . . . . . . 86 E2
Berkshire Dr
  Congleton CW12 . . . . 156 D4
  Irlam M44 . . . . 11 C5
Bermondsey Gr WA8 . . . . 13 D4
Bernard Ave WA4 . . . . 26 D8
Bernisdale Rd WA16 . . . . . 57 F4
Bernsdale Cl CH5 . . . . . . 116 A3
Bernsdale Ct/Llys Bernsdale
  CH5 . . . . 116 A3
Berristall Rise SK10 . . . . . 63 C1
Berristal Rd SK10 . . . . 88 E3
Berry Cl
  Ellesmere Port CH66 . . . . 69 C3
  Wilmslow SK9 . . . . 60 A5
Berry Dr CH66 . . . . 69 C3
Berry Rd WA8 . . . . 12 D1
Berryste
ad CW8 . . . . 103 B4
Bertram St WA12 . . . . 2 A4
Berwick Ave CH62 . . . . . . 43 E4
Berwick Cl
  Macclesfield SK10 . . . . . . 86 F2
  Warrington WA7 . . . . 17 E6
Berwick Ct CW4 . . . . 130 B2
Berwick Gdns CH66 . . . . . 69 B6
Berwick Gr CH66 . . . . 69 B6
Berwick Rd CH66 . . . . 69 A6
Berwick Road W CH66 . . . 69 A6
Berwyn Cl CH66 . . . . 69 A6
Bessancourt CW4 . . . . . . 130 C3
Bessemer Rd M44 . . . . 11 F6
Beswick Dr CW1 . . . . 191 A4
Beswicks La
  Norton in Hales TF9 . . . . 236 C2
  Row-of-Trees SK9 . . . . . . 59 C3
Beswicks Rd CW8 . . . . 78 E1
Beswick St SK11 . . . . 112 B7
Betchton Cl CW11 . . . . . . 175 C7
Betchton Ct **6** CW12 . . 156 F3
BETCHTON HEATH. 175 E5
Betchton Rd CW11 . . . . . . 175 E3
Betchworth Cres WA7 . . . 49 D6
Betchworth Way SK10 . . . 87 C4
Bethany Cl WA11 . . . . 1 B7
Betjeman Cl WA4 . . . . 16 D7
Betjeman Way CW1 . . . . . 190 F5
BETLEY 221 F8
Betley Cl CW9 . . . . 104 A5
Betley St CW1 . . . . 190 C4
Betsyfield Dr WA3 . . . . 9 A7
Bettisfield Ave CH62 . . . . . 43 D6
Betty's La
  Beeston CW6 . . . . 168 D1
  Woore CW3 . . . . 232 C1
Bevan Ave ST7 . . . . 210 E6
Bevan Cl WA5 . . . . 14 D5
Bevan Ct WA4 . . . . 16 B3
Bevan View WA5 . . . . 15 F7
Beverley Ave WA4 . . . . 26 D8
Beverley Dr CH60 . . . . 41 B6
Beverley Rd WA5 . . . . 15 C6
Beverley Way
  Ellesmere Port CH66 . . . . 69 B7
  Macclesfield SK10 . . . . . . 87 C4
Bevin Ave WA3 . . . . 5 A4
Bevyl Rd CH64 . . . . 41 B2
Bewick Wlk WA8 . . . . 57 B3
Bewley Ct CH3 . . . . 142 A4
BEWSEY 15 F8
Bewsey Bsns Ctr WA5 . . . 15 F6

Bewsey Farm Cl WA5 . . . . 15 D8
Bewsey Ind Est WA5 . . . . 16 A7
Bewsey Lodge Prim Sch
  WA5 . . . . 15 F7
Bewsey Park Cl WA5 . . . . 15 F7
Bewsey Rd WA2, WA5. . . . 16 A6
Bexhill Ave WA2 . . . . 8 B4
Bexington Dr CW1 . . . . . . 190 B8
Bexton Ave CW7 . . . . 126 A2
Bexton Cty Prim Sch
  WA16 . . . . 81 F7
Bexton La WA16 . . . . 82 A8
Bexton Rd WA16 . . . . 56 F1
Bibby Ave WA1 . . . . 16 E6
Bibby's La SK10 . . . . 88 A1
Bibby St ST7 . . . . 193 E7
BICKERTON 199 E6
Bickerton Ave WA6 . . . . . . 74 D7
Bickerton Cl WA3 . . . . 9 F6
Bickerton Holy Trinity CE
  Prim Sch SY14. . . . . . . 200 A7
Bickerton Rd ST4 . . . . 201 B2
Bickerton Way **1** CW9 . 103 E4
Bickley Cl
  Hough CW2 . . . . 206 E2
  Northwich CW9 . . . . 103 E5
  Runcorn WA7 . . . . 23 C1
  Warrington WA2 . . . . 8 F3
BICKLEY MOSS. 215 B7
Bickley Town La SY14 . . . 214 C6
BICKLEYWOOD 214 C4
Bicknell Cl WA5 . . . . 15 B8
Bida La CW12 . . . . 179 B8
BIDDULPH 179 B2
Biddulph Common Rd
  ST8. . . . . 179 F7
Biddulph Grange ST8 . . 179 E1
Biddulph Grange Ctry Pk★
  ST8 . . . . 179 E2
Biddulph Grange Gdn★
  ST8 . . . . 179 E3
Biddulph Park Rd ST8. . . 179 F5
Biddulph Rd
  Congleton CW12 . . . . 179 B8
  Harriseahead ST7 . . . . . . 195 F6
Biddulph St CW12. . . . . . . 179 C7
Biddulph Valley Ltr
  ST8 . . . . 179 D1
Biddulph Valley Way Nature
  Reserve★ CW12 . . . . . . 179 D7
Bideford Rd WA5 . . . . 14 E4
Bidston Cl CH2 . . . . 118 D5
Bidston Gn CH66 . . . . 69 D4
Bidvale Way CW1 . . . . . . 190 D7
Big Field La CW6 . . . . 146 B7
Biggin Ct WA2 . . . . 8 E1
Biggs Way CW12 . . . . 156 E5
BIGNALL END 209 F3
Bignall End Rd
  Audley ST7 . . . . 210 A3
  Newcastle-under-Lyme
    ST7 . . . . 210 A4
Billinge Ave WA12 . . . . 2 C5
Billington Cl
  Barnton CW8 . . . . 77 F4
  Crewe CW2 . . . . 190 A2
  Warrington WA5 . . . . 14 E8
Billington Rd WA8 . . . . . . 12 B3
Bilton Cl WA8 . . . . 13 E2
Bilton Way CW7 . . . . 189 E5
Bings Rd SK23 . . . . 65 F8
Bingswood Ave SK23 . . . . 65 F8
Bingswood Rd SK23 . . . . . 65 E7
Bingswood Trad Est SK23 . 65 E8
Binney Rd CW9 . . . . 104 B8
Binyon Way CW1 . . . . 191 A4
Birchall Ave WA3 . . . . 4 E4
BIRCHALL MOSS 219 E1
Birchall Moss La CW5 . . 219 E1
Birchall Wlk CW7 . . . . . . 206 D8
Birch Ave
  Alsager ST7 . . . . 193 E2
  Crewe CW1 . . . . 190 F5
  Macclesfield SK10 . . . . . . 87 B1
  Wilmslow SK9 . . . . 59 F6
  Winsford CW7 . . . . 127 A1
Birch Brook Rd WA13 . . . 19 C5
Birch Cl
  Crewe CW1 . . . . 190 F5
  Holmes Chapel CW4 . . . 130 D3
Birch Cres WA12. . . . . 1 F4
Birch Ct CW12 . . . . 155 F3
Birchdale Cres WA4 . . . . . 26 C8
Birchdale Ct WA4 . . . . 26 C8
Birchdale Rd
  Warrington, Paddington
    WA1 . . . . 17 A7
  Warrington WA4 . . . . 26 C8
Birchenall Cl ST7 . . . . 195 B1
Birchen Cl **2** L26 . . . . . . 21 A7
Birchenwood Rd ST6,
  ST7. . . . . 195 B1
Birchenwood Way ST7 . . 195 B1
Birches Cl CH60 . . . . 41 A8
Birches La CW5 . . . . 105 B7
Birches The
  Broughton CH4 . . . . 139 B3
  Crewe CW2 . . . . 206 C8
  Neston CH64 . . . . 41 F2
Birches Way **7** ST7 . . . . 195 B2

Birchfield Ave
  Rode Heath ST7 . . . . 193 F7
  Widnes WA8 . . . . 13 A2
Birchfield Rd
  Lymm WA13 . . . . 19 B4
  Warrington WA5 . . . . 15 B5
  Widnes, Appleton WA8 . . 13 A1
Birch Fold CW4 . . . . 107 B1
Birchgate Cl SK10 . . . . . . 86 E1
Birch Gdns CW11 . . . . . . 175 C5
Birch Gr
  Ellesmere Port CH66 . . . . 70 A1
  Higher Wincham CW9 . . . 79 F5
  Knutsford WA16 . . . . 57 D2
  Lostock Green CW9. . . . . 105 B7
  Warrington, Bruche WA1 . 16 F7
  Warrington, Latchford WA4. 16 D3
Birchhall Cl CW5 . . . . 204 F4
Birch Heath CW3 . . . . 168 B8
Birch Heath La CH3 . . . . . 142 F8
Birch Heath Rd CW6 . . . . 168 C8
Birch Hill WA6 . . . . 99 C8
Birch Ho CH2 . . . . 118 C5
Birch House Rd ST5. . . . . 210 D1
Birchin Cl CW5 . . . . 205 A6
Birchin La CW5 . . . . 205 A6
Birch La
  Hough CW2 . . . . 206 F2
  Winsford CW10 . . . . 127 F2
Birchmuir CH1. . . . . 117 E3
Birchmuir Cl CW1 . . . . . . 190 B6
Birch Rd
  Audley ST7 . . . . 209 F1
  Chester CH4 . . . . 140 F5
  Congleton CW12 . . . . 155 F3
  Haydock WA11. . . . . 1 E7
  Hollinfare WA3 . . . . 11 B2
  Partington M31 . . . . 11 D3
  Poynton SK12 . . . . 36 F2
  Runcorn WA7 . . . . 49 C8
  Widnes WA8 . . . . 13 B3
Birch Rise CH2 . . . . 118 D6
Birch Tree Ave SK7 . . . . . 37 A8
Birch Tree Ct CH2 . . . . . . 237 C4
Birch Tree La
  Antrobus WA4 . . . . 53 A6
  Goostrey CW4 . . . . 107 C1
  The Bank ST7. . . . . 195 B8
Birch Tree Rd **6** WA3 . . . . 3 F8
Birch Valley Rd ST7 . . . . . 195 C1
Birchway
  Bollington SK10 . . . . 88 A8
  Bramhall SK7 . . . . 35 D7
  Heswall CH60 . . . . 41 C5
  High Lane SK6. . . . . 37 F7
  Birch Way SK10 . . . . 86 E6
Birchways WA4 . . . . 26 E5
BIRCHWOOD. 9 E5
Birchwood Bvd WA3 . . . . . . 9 D7
Birchwood CE Prim Sch
  WA3 . . . . 9 F3
Birchwood Com High Sch
  WA3 . . . . 9 E2
Birchwood Dr
  Ellesmere Port CH66. . . . . 69 D1
  Elton CH2 . . . . 72 C3
Birchwood Com High Sch
  WA3 . . . . 9 E2
Birchwood Dr
  Nantwich CW5. . . . . 204 F6
  Swan Green WA16 . . . . . 106 D7
  Wilmslow SK9 . . . . 60 D8
BIRCHWOOD FOREST
  PARK. 10 A5
Birchwood L & Tennis Ctr
  WA3 . . . . 9 E2
Birchwood Office Pk WA2 . 9 B3
Birchwood One Bsns Pk
  WA3 . . . . 9 E2
Birchwood Park Ave WA3 . 9 D5
Birchwood Sh Ctr WA3 . . . 9 D2
Birchwood St WA3. . . . . . . 9 D2
Birchwood Way WA2, WA3 . 9 B3
Birds La
  Tarporley CW6 . . . . 146 C1
  Tattenhall CH3 . . . . 166 E1
Bird's La CW6 . . . . 186 B8
Birdwell Dr WA5 . . . . 15 A5
Birkdale Ave CH63 . . . . . . 43 C6
Birkdale Cl
  Bramhall SK7. . . . . 36 A7
  Macclesfield SK10 . . . . . . 87 C4
Birkdale Ct **3** CW9 . . . . 104 B8
Birkdale Dr ST7 . . . . 195 C3
Birkdale Gdns CW7 . . . . . 126 A2
Birkdale Rd
  Warrington WA5 . . . . 14 F4
  Widnes WA8 . . . . 13 B5
Birkenhead Rd CH64 . . . . 42 E1
Birkenhead St CW9 . . . . . 104 C8
Birkett Ave CH65. . . . . 70 C2
Birkin Cl WA16. . . . . 57 D4
Birkinheath La WA14 . . . . 31 B4
Birley St WA12 . . . . 2 D4
Birstall Cr WA7 . . . . 49 D7
Birtles Cl CW11 . . . . 175 C7
Birtles Hall SK10 . . . . 85 D2
Birtles La SK10 . . . . 85 E2
Birtles Rd
  Macclesfield SK10 . . . . . . 86 D1
  Warrington WA2 . . . . 8 D1
Birtles Way **4** SK9 . . . . 34 D5
Birtley Ct WA8 . . . . 12 B1
Birtwistle Rd CW9 . . . . . . 104 D6
Bisham Pk WA7 . . . . 24 D2
Bishopdale Cl WA5. . . . . . 14 F7
Bishopgates Dr CW9 . . . . 103 E4

Bishop Heber High Sch
  SY14 . . . . 213 C5
Bishop Rd SK10 . . . . 88 A7
Bishop Reeves Rd WA11. . 1 E7
Bishops' Blue Coat CE High
  Sch The CH3. . . . . 142 A8
Bishop's Cl ST7 . . . . 210 D8
Bishops Ct
  Broughton CH4 . . . . 139 C4
  Warrington WA2 . . . . 8 A7
Bishopsfield Cl CH2. . . . . 118 F3
Bishops Gate CH2. . . . . . 119 A3
Bishops Gdns CH65 . . . . . 70 A5
Bishop St CH2 . . . . 118 F3
Bishops Way WA8 . . . . . . 13 D3
Bishops Wood CW5 . . . . 204 F2
Bishopton Dr SK11 . . . . . 111 F8
Bishop Wilson CE Prim Sch
  CH64 . . . . 67 D1
Bispham Rd WA5 . . . . 15 B4
Bittern Cl
  Poynton SK12 . . . . 36 A4
  Runcorn WA7 . . . . 50 D8
  Warrington WA2 . . . . 8 D3
Bittern Gr SK10 . . . . 87 A1
Blackacres Cl CW11 . . . . 174 F6
Blackbird Way ST7 . . . . . 195 F1
Blackboards La CH66 . . . . 69 A8
BLACKBROOK
  Haydock. 1 A7
  Warrington 8 E2
Blackbrook Ave WA2. . . . . 8 F2
Blackbrook Cl WA8 . . . . . 12 C3
Blackburn Cl WA3 . . . . 3 E8
Blackburn Ave CW8 . . . . . 22 B5
Blackburne Cl WA2 . . . . . . 9 C2
Blackburne Dr WA12 . . . . . 2 A4
Blackcap Rd WA4 . . . . 27 A4
Blackcap Wlk WA3 . . . . 9 E3
Black Cat Ind Est WA8 . . . 23 A6
Blackcroft Ave CW8 . . . . . 78 A2
Blackden Firs CW4 . . . . . 108 B2
Blackden La
  Goostrey CW4 . . . . 108 A3
  Siddington SK11 . . . . 132 F8
Blackden Wlk SK9 . . . . . . 34 D1
Black Diamond Pk CH1. . 237 B4
Black Diamond St CH1 . . 237 B4
Blackdown Cl CH66 . . . . . 69 A5
Blackeys La CH64 . . . . 66 E8
Black Firs La CW12 . . . . . 155 F4
Black Firs Prim Sch
  CW12 . . . . 155 F4
Black Friars CH1. . . . . 237 A2
Blackheath La WA7 . . . . . 24 F5
Blackhill La WA16 . . . . 81 F8
Blackhurst Brow SK10 . . . 61 B2
Blackhurst Farm Rd
  CW5 . . . . 202 C3
Blackhurst St WA1 . . . . . . 16 B5
Black La SK10 . . . . 87 E1
Blackledge Cl WA3 . . . . . . 9 A3
Blackley Cl
  Macclesfield SK10 . . . . . . 87 B4
  Warrington WA4 . . . . 16 D3
Black Lion La CH66. . . . . . 69 C6
Black Moss Rd WA14 . . . . 20 F7
BLACK PARK. 226 F2
Black Park Rd SY13 . . . . 226 D2
Black Rd SK11 . . . . 112 F7
Blackshaw Cl CW12 . . . . 157 B1
Blackshaw Dr WA5 . . . . . . 7 B1
Blackshaw La SK9 . . . . . . 59 F1
Blackshaw St **6** SK11 . . 112 C7
Blackwall CH66 . . . . 69 F7
Blackthorn Cl
  Broughton CH4 . . . . 139 B3
  Huntington CH3 . . . . 142 A5
  Wistaston CW2 . . . . 206 B8
Blackthorne Ave CH66. . . . 95 A8
Blackthorne Rd WA4 . . . . 26 C3
Blackwell Cl CW10 . . . . . 151 D6
BLACON. 117 F3
Blacon Ave CH1. . . . . 118 A5
Blacon Cty High Sch
  CH1. . . . . 117 D4
Blacon Hall Rd CH1 . . . . 117 F5
Blacon Point Rd CH1 . . . 117 E3
Bladon Cres ST7 . . . . 193 C5
Blagg Ave CW5 . . . . 204 C4
Blair Cl SK7 . . . . 36 C8
Blair Dr WA8 . . . . 12 C3
Blairgowrie Dr SK10 . . . . . 87 B4
Blaizefield Cl CW3 . . . . . . 232 C2
Blakeacre Rd L26 . . . . 21 A6
Blake Cl
  Blacon CH1 . . . . 117 F6
  Crewe CW2 . . . . 189 F1
Blakeden La CW7 . . . . . . 148 F8
Blakehill Dr WA5 . . . . 15 B6
Blake La CW8. . . . . 102 A2
Blakeley Brow CH63 . . . . . 43 A6
Blakeley Cl CH63 . . . . 43 A7
Blakeley Dell CH63 . . . . . . 43 B6
Blakeley Dene CH63 . . . . . 43 B7
Blakeley La WA16 . . . . 58 F8
Blakeley Rd CH63 . . . . 43 A6
Blakelow Bank SK11 . . . . 112 F6
Blakelow Cl CW10. . . . . . 151 B8
Blakelow Cres CW5 . . . . 205 F3
Blakelow Dr CW5 . . . . 205 D4
Blakelow Rd SK11 . . . . . . 112 F6
Blakemere Cl SY13 . . . . . 226 B1
Blakemere Ct CH65 . . . . . 70 C7
Blakemere Dr CW9 . . . . . 103 E5
Blakemere La WA6 . . . . . 100 D4

Blakemere Sh & Craft Ctr
  CW8 . . . . **101** F1
Blakemere Way CW11 . . **174** F8
BLAKENHALL **221** A4
Blake St CW12 . . . . **156** C3
Blandford Dr
  5 Macclesfield SK11 . . . . **111** F8
  Northwich CW9 . . . . . . **103** E3
Blandford Rd WA5 . . . . . . **15** B5
Blankney Rd CH4 . . . . . **161** A7
Blantyre St WA7 . . . . **22** F3
Blaze Farm★ SK11 . . . . **137** D4
Blaze Hill SK10 . . . . **88** E8
Bleadale Cl SK9 . . . . **34** D1
Bleasdale Rd
  Crewe CW1 . . . . **173** B1
  Newton-le-Willows WA12 . . **2** C4
Bleeding Wolf La ST7 . . **194** E5
Blenheim Cl
  Macclesfield SK10 . . . . . . **87** A1
  Northwich CW9 . . . . . . **103** F4
  Poynton SK12 . . . . **36** F4
  Warrington WA2 . . . . **8** F2
  Wilmslow SK9 . . . . **60** D7
  Wistaston CW2 . . . . . . **206** A3
Blenheim Ct ST7 . . . . . **193** D5
Blenheim Gdns **5** CW7 . . **149** C7
Blenheim Ho CH1 . . . . . **118** B3
Blenheim Pk CW11 . . . . **175** A4
Bloomfield Cl SK8 . . . . . . **34** E7
Bloomsbury Way WA8 . . **12** D3
Blossom Hts CW8 . . . . . **103** D7
Blossom Rd M31 . . . . **11** E2
Blossoms La SK7 . . . . **35** A2
Blossom Way/Ffordd Y
  Blodau CH4 . . . . **140** D5
Blount Cl CW1 . . . . **190** B4
Bluebell Cl CH64 . . . . . . **42** C1
Bluebell Ave WA11 . . . . . . **1** E7
Bluebell Cl
  Huntington CH3 . . . . . . **142** B6
  Macclesfield SK10 . . . . . . **87** D3
  Winnington CW8 . . . . **78** E1
Bluebell Cl WA7 . . . . **49** F4
Bluebell La SK10 . . . . . . **87** C3
Bluebell Mews **4** SK10 . . **87** D3
Bluebell Rd WA5 . . . . . . **15** E4
Bluebell Way
  Alsager ST7 . . . . **193** B3
  Handforth SK9 . . . . **34** C1
Blue Bridge La WA6 . . . . **73** C5
Bluecoat St WA2 . . . . **16** B7
Blue Hatch WA6 . . . . **74** C8
Blue Planet Aquarium★
  CH65 . . . . **70** C1
Blue Ridge Cl WA5 . . . . . **14** E7
Blundell Rd WA8 . . . . **22** D8
Blunstone Cl CW2 . . . . . **190** A2
Blyth Cl
  Macclesfield SK10 . . . . . . **86** E1
  Runcorn WA7 . . . . **50** D5
Blythe Ave
  Bramhall SK7 . . . . **35** C6
  Congleton CW12 . . . . . . **156** A2
  Widnes WA8 . . . . **13** B5
Blythe Pl CW7 . . . . **127** B2
Blythings The CW6 . . . . **146** C3
Blyth Rd CH63 . . . . **43** C7
Boardmans Pl CW9 . . . . **104** A5
Boars Leigh Pk SK11 . . **135** D1
Boathorse Rd ST7 . . . . . **210** F8
Boathouse La CH64 . . . . **41** C3
Boat Stage WA13 . . . . . . **18** E3
Boat Wlk WA4 . . . . **16** A1
Bob's La M44 . . . . **11** D4
Boddington Dr WA4 . . . . **27** A7
Boden Dr CW5 . . . . **205** D4
Boden St SK11 . . . . **112** D8
Bodiam Ct CH65 . . . . **70** E2
Bodmin Ave SK10 . . . . . . **86** E1
Bodmin Cl WA7 . . . . **50** B6
Bodmin Dr SK7 . . . . **35** E7
Bodnant Cl CW1 . . . . . . **190** A8
BOLD **6** B6
Bold Bsns Ctr WA9 . . . . . . **6** B7
Bold Cross WA8 . . . . **13** E7
BOLD HEATH **13** E7
Bold Ind Est WA8 . . . . . . **13** C5
Bold Ind Park WA9 . . . . . . **6** B6
Bold La WA5, WA9 . . . . . . **6** C7
Bold Pl CW1 . . . . **237** B3
Bold Sq CH1 . . . . **237** C3
Bold St
  Haslington CW1 . . . . . . **191** C4
  Runcorn WA7 . . . . **23** B3
  Sandbach CW11 . . . . . . **175** B6
  Warrington WA1 . . . . . . **16** A5
  Widnes WA8 . . . . **13** B2
Bolesworth Hill Rd CH3 . **183** C4
Bolesworth Rd
  Chester CH2 . . . . **118** F6
  Tattenhall CH3 . . . . **183** C7
Boleyn Cl CH1 . . . . **117** E6
Boleyn Ct WA7 . . . . **24** C3
Bolland's Ct CH1 . . . . . . **237** A2
Bollands Row **14** CW5 . . **204** E5
Bolleyn Wood Ct SK9 . . . **34** B1
Bollin Ave
  Altrincham WA14 . . . . . . **31** B8
  Winsford CW7 . . . . **127** B2
Bollinbarn SK10 . . . . **87** B2
Bollinbarn Dr SK10 . . . . . **87** A2
Bollinbrook CE Prim Sch
  SK10 . . . . **87** B2
Bollinbrook Rd SK10 . . . . **87** B2
Bollin Cl
  Alsager ST7 . . . . **192** F3

Bollin Cl *continued*
  Culcheth WA3 . . . . **5** A2
  Lymm WA13 . . . . **19** A4
  Sandbach CW11 . . . . . . **174** E7
  Winsford CW7 . . . . **127** B2
Bollin Ct SK9 . . . . **60** C6
Bollin Dr
  Congleton CW12 . . . . . . **156** F1
  Lymm WA13 . . . . **19** A4
Bollin Gr
  Biddulph ST8 . . . . **179** E1
  Prestbury SK10 . . . . **87** A3
BOLLINGTON **88** B7
Bollington Ave CW9 . . . **104** A5
BOLLINGTON CROSS . . . **87** F7
Bollington Cross CE Prim
  Sch SK10 . . . . **87** F7
Bollington Ho CW12 . . . **156** F1
Bollington La SK10 . . . . . **84** E2
Bollington Rd SK10 . . . . . **87** D6
Bollinhead La SK11 . . . . **113** D2
Bollin Hill
  Prestbury SK10 . . . . **87** A5
  Wilmslow SK9 . . . . **60** B8
Bollin Mews SK10 . . . . . . **86** F1
Bolliway WA15 . . . . **32** A8
Bollin Way SK10 . . . . **87** A6
Bollin Wlk SK9 . . . . **60** C7
Bollinwood Chase SK9 . . . **60** D7
Bolshaw Cl CW1 . . . . . . **190** A7
Bolshaw Farm La SK8 . . . **34** C6
Bolshaw Prim Sch SK8 . . . **34** C6
Bolshaw Rd SK8 . . . . **34** C6
Bolton Ave
  Cheadle SK8 . . . . **35** B6
  Warrington WA4 . . . . . . **16** F4
Bolton Cl
  Golborne WA3 . . . . **4** B8
  Poynton SK12 . . . . **36** D4
Bomish La CW4, SK11 . . **108** C3
Bond Cl WA5 . . . . **15** D4
Bond St
  Macclesfield SK11 . . . . . **112** C7
  Winnington CW8 . . . . . . **78** D1
Bonis Hall La SK10 . . . . . **61** F4
BOON HILL **210** A2
Boon Hill Rd ST7 . . . . . . **209** F1
Booth Ave
  Ashton Hayes CH3 . . . . . **121** E7
  Little Budworth CW6 . . . **147** F7
  Sandbach CW11 . . . . . . **175** C6
BOOTH BANK **30** B7
Boothbank La WA14 . . . . **30** B6
Booth Bed La WA16, CW4 **107** B4
Boothby St **12** SK10 . . . **112** C8
Boothfields WA16 . . . . . . **57** C2
BOOTH GREEN **62** F7
Booth La
  Middlewich CW10 . . . . . **151** E6
  Middlewich, Stud Green CW10,
  CW11 . . . . **152** B3
Booth Rd
  Handforth SK9 . . . . **34** A1
  Hartford CW8 . . . . **103** A4
BOOTHSDALE **122** D3
Boothsdale CW6 . . . . . . **122** D3
BOOTH'S HILL **18** C2
Booths Hill Cl WA13 . . . . **18** C2
Booths Hill Ho **3** WA13 . . **18** C3
Booth's Hill Rd WA13 . . . **18** C3
Booths La WA3 . . . . **52** E6
Booth's La WA13 . . . . **18** B1
Boothsmere Cl CW11 . . . **174** F8
Booth St
  Audley ST7 . . . . **209** D1
  Congleton CW12 . . . . . . **156** C2
  Warrington WA5 . . . . . . **15** E4
BOOTS GREEN **107** B5
Borderbrook SY14 . . . . . **222** F5
Borderbrook Sch
  Higher Wych SY14 . . . . . **224** D3
  Tallarn Green/Tallwrn Green
  SY14 . . . . **222** F5
Border Rd CH60 . . . . **41** B8
Borders 2 Ind Pk CH4 . . . **140** C7
Border Way CH3 . . . . . . **119** C1
Borough Rd CW12 . . . . . **156** F3
Borras Rd LL13 . . . . **196** A8
Borron Cl WA12 . . . . **2** B4
Borron Rd WA12 . . . . **2** B5
Borron Road Ind Est WA12 **2** C4
Borrowdale Ave WA4 . . . . . **8** C3
Borrowdale Cl
  Crewe CW2 . . . . **189** E3
  Frodsham WA6 . . . . **74** D8
Borrowdale Rd WA8 . . . . . **22** C8
Bosden Cl SK9 . . . . **34** D5
BOSLEY **158** D8
Bosley Brook CW12 . . . . **179** D5
Bosley Cl
  Handforth SK9 . . . . **34** D2
  Middlewich CW10 . . . . . **151** C6
Bosley Dr SK12 . . . . **37** A3
Bosley View **5** CW11 . . **157** B1
Bostock Gn
  Bostock Green CW9 . . . . **127** C2
  Ellesmere Port CH65 . . . . **69** F6
BOSTOCK GREEN **127** C2
BOSTOCK HALL **127** D5
Bostock Rd
  Macclesfield SK11 . . . . . **111** E7
  Winsford CW7 . . . . **127** A2
Bostock St WA5 . . . . **15** E6
Boston Ave WA7 . . . . **23** D1

Boston Bvd WA5 . . . . **15** A7
Boston Cl
  Bramhall SK7 . . . . **35** D7
  Culcheth WA3 . . . . **4** F4
Boswell Ave WA4 . . . . . . **16** B2
Botany Bsns Pk SK23 . . . **65** D6
Botany Mews SK23 . . . . . **65** E6
Boteler Ave WA5 . . . . . . **15** F7
Bottoms La CH4 . . . . . . **141** F8
Boughey Rd ST7 . . . . . . **209** F2
BOUGHTON **119** A2
Boughton CH2, CH3 . . . . **118** F2
Boughton Hall Ave CH3 . . **119** A2
Boughton Hall Dr CH3 . . **119** B1
BOUGHTON HEATH **142** A8
Boughton Heath Prim Sch
  CH3 . . . . **142** B8
Boughton Lodge **2** CH3 . **119** A1
Boulevard The
  Broughton CH4 . . . . **139** C3
  Ellesmere Port CH65 . . . . **69** F4
Boulting Ave WA5 . . . . **7** F1
Boulton Cl CW11 . . . . . . **175** C3
Boundary Ct CH3 . . . . . . **119** B1
Boundary La
  Chester CH4 . . . . **140** E5
  Congleton CW12 . . . . . . **179** B8
  Heswall CH60 . . . . **41** A8
  Over Peover WA16, SK11 . **108** D7
  Siddington SK11 . . . . . . **132** E8
  Threapwood SY14 . . . . . **222** E8
Boundary Lane N CW8 . . **101** C1
Boundary Lane S CW8 . . **101** F2
Boundary Pk CH64 . . . . . . **66** D7
Boundary St
  Northwich CW9 . . . . **79** E2
  Warrington WA1 . . . . . . **16** E7
Boundary Terr SK9 . . . . . . **33** F6
Bourchier Way WA4 . . . . . **27** A8
Bourne Ave WA3 . . . . **3** D8
Bourne Cl CW8 . . . . **102** E7
Bournemouth Cl WA7 . . . . **50** D6
Bourne Rd ST7 . . . . **194** F2
Bourne St
  Mow Cop ST7 . . . . **195** C7
  Wilmslow SK9 . . . . **59** F6
Bouverie St CH1 . . . . . . **237** A4
Boverton Cl WA5 . . . . **7** E1
Bowden Cl
  Congleton CW12 . . . . . . **156** A3
  Culcheth WA3 . . . . **4** F4
Bowden Cres SK22 . . . . . . **39** D8
Bowden Dr CW9 . . . . . . **104** C8
Bowden House La SK9 . . . **61** A8
Bowden View La WA16 . . . **29** F2
Bowdon Cl WA1 . . . . **16** F8
Bowen Cl
  Bramhall SK7 . . . . **35** F5
  Widnes WA8 . . . . **12** D4
Bowen Cooke Ave CW1 . . **190** A5
Bowen St CW2 . . . . **190** A3
Bower Cres WA4 . . . . **26** D2
Bowerfield Ave SK7 . . . . . **36** D8
Bowerfield Cres SK7 . . . . **36** E8
Bower Rd CH60 . . . . **41** C8
Bowers Bsns Pk WA8 . . . . **23** C7
Bowers Row **11** CW5 . . **204** E5
Bower St WA8 . . . . **13** C1
Bowery Ave SK8 . . . . **34** F6
Bowey The CH1 . . . . **116** D4
Bowe's Gate Rd CW6 . . . **169** A1
Bowfell Cl CH2 . . . . **63** D3
Bowfell Dr SK6 . . . . **37** E8
Bow Green Rd WA14 . . . . **20** F1
Bowkers Croft CW1 . . . . **191** F8
Bow La WA14 . . . . **31** B8
Bowland Cl
  Runcorn WA7 . . . . **49** E5
  Warrington WA3 . . . . . . **10** B5
Bowland Croft CW1 . . . . **173** B1
Bowland Rise CW7 . . . . . **149** B7
Bowles Cl CW11 . . . . . . **175** A4
Bowling Cl CW11 . . . . . . **175** D3
Bowling Green Ct
  Chester CH3 . . . . **237** B3
  6 Nantwich CW5 . . . . **204** E5
  Winnington CW8 . . . . **78** E1
Bowman Ave WA5 . . . . . . **17** A5
Bowmans The SK10 . . . . . **87** B1
Bowmere Cl
  Biddulph ST8 . . . . **179** C1
  Tarporley CW6 . . . . **146** D1
Bowmere Dr CW7 . . . . . . **149** C8
Bowmere Rd CW6 . . . . . **146** D1
Bowness Ave
  Bebington CH63 . . . . **43** C5
  Irlam M44 . . . . **11** D4
  Warrington WA2 . . . . **8** C2
Bowness Cl CW4 . . . . . . **130** A3
Bowness Ct CW12 . . . . . **156** A1
Bowness Rd CW2 . . . . . . **189** E3
Bowood Ct WA2 . . . . **8** A4
Bowring Dr CH64 . . . . . . **41** B1
Bowyer Ave **6** CW5 . . . **204** E6
Boxgrove Cl WA8 . . . . . . **13** B3
Box La CW12 . . . . **155** F3
Boxmoor Cl CH4 . . . . . . **141** A5
Box Tree Mews SK11 . . . **112** A7
Box Wlk M31 . . . . **11** E3
Boydell Ave
  Warrington WA4 . . . . . . **17** B2
  Warrington, Westy WA4 . . **16** F4
Boydell Way CW4 . . . . . . **162** A6
Boyle Ave WA2 . . . . **8** E1
Boyles Hall Rd ST7 . . . . . **209** E2
Bracken Cl
  Broughton CH4 . . . . **139** C3

Bracken Cl *continued*
  Macclesfield SK10 . . . . . . **86** F1
  Rode Heath ST7 . . . . . . **193** F8
  Warrington WA3 . . . . **9** C5
Brackendale
  Elton CH2 . . . . **72** B3
  Runcorn WA7 . . . . **49** D8
Brackenfield Way **11**
  CW7 . . . . **149** A8
Bracken Rd CH66 . . . . . . **69** E4
Brackens The
  Daresbury WA4 . . . . **25** A1
  Higher Kinnerton CH4 . . **161** A8
Bracken Way
  Barnton CW8 . . . . **78** B3
  Comberbach CW9 . . . . . . **78** C7
  Frodsham WA6 . . . . **74** C6
  Knutsford WA16 . . . . **82** A8
  Wincham CW9 . . . . **79** C3
Brackenwood Cl CW2 . . **206** B8
Brackenwood Dr WA8 . . . **22** A8
Brackenwood Mews
  Chorlton CW2 . . . . **207** D2
  Wilmslow SK9 . . . . **60** A6
Brackley Ave M44 . . . . . . **11** D6
Brackley St
  Runcorn WA7 . . . . **22** F3
  Warrington WA4 . . . . . . **16** C1
Bradburn Rd M44 . . . . . . **11** E7
Bradburns La CW8 . . . . . **103** B6
Bradbury Gdns CW12 . . . **156** F1
Bradbury Rd CW7 . . . . . . **127** B2
Braddon Cl CW9 . . . . . . **103** F4
BRADELEY GREEN **225** E6
Bradeley Green La SY13 . **225** F6
Bradeley Hall Rd CW1 . . **191** B5
Bradeley Rd CW1 . . . . . . **191** C4
BRADFIELD GREEN **172** E3
Bradfield Rd CW1 . . . . . . **190** B7
Bradford La SK10 . . . . **85** C6
Bradford Pl CH4 . . . . . . **141** D7
Bradford Rd CW9 . . . . . . **126** E4
Bradford St CH4 . . . . . . **141** D7
Bradgate Rd SK8 . . . . **34** D8
Bradgate Cl WA5 . . . . **14** F5
Brading Wlk M22 . . . . . . **33** E8
Bradleigh Rd WA12 . . . . . . **2** B1
Bradley Cl CW10 . . . . . . **151** B2
BRADLEY GREEN **225** A8
Bradley Hall Cotts WA4 . . **27** F6
Bradley La
  Frodsham WA6 . . . . **74** D7
  Newton-le-Willows WA5,
  WA12 . . . . **2** A1
BRADLEY MOUNT **87** B7
Bradley St SK11 . . . . . . **112** E6
Bradley Way WA8 . . . . . . **13** B1
Bradmoor Rd CH62 . . . . . **43** D8
Bradshaw Ave CH4 . . . . **140** B7
Bradshaw Com Prim Sch
  WA4 . . . . **17** B2
Bradshaw Hall La
  Cheadle SK8 . . . . **34** E8
  Gatley SK8 . . . . **34** D8
Bradshaw La
  Lymm WA13 . . . . **19** D3
  Warrington WA4 . . . . . . **17** B3
Bradshaw Pl CW12 . . . . **156** E2
Bradshaw St WA8 . . . . . . **13** A2
BRADWALL GREEN **153** B3
Bradwall Rd CW11 . . . . . **175** B7
Bradwall Rd CW11 . . . . . **175** B8
Bradwell Cl CH65 . . . . . . **70** A4
Bradwell Ct CW12 . . . . . **156** F2
Bradwell Dr SK8 . . . . **34** C7
Bradwell Gr CW12 . . . . . **156** F2
Bradwell Rd
  Golborne WA3 . . . . **3** E7
  Hazel Grove SK7 . . . . . . **36** E8
Braemar Ave CW9 . . . . . **104** C7
Braemar Cl
  Chester CH3 . . . . **119** C3
  Holmes Chapel CW4 . . . **130** C2
  Warrington WA2 . . . . **9** A3
  Wistaston CW2 . . . . **205** E8
Braemar Ct CH65 . . . . . . **70** E3
Braeside
  6 Ellesmere Port CH66 . . **69** C5
  Macclesfield SK11 . . . . . **112** F6
Braidwood Ave M44 . . . . . **57** C3
Brains La CW6 . . . . **169** B6
Braintree Rd M22 . . . . . . **33** E8
Braithwaite Cl WA7 . . . . . **49** D5
Braithwaite Rd WA3 . . . . . **3** D8
Brakeley La CW8 . . . . **77** D4
Brakenwood Mews WA4 . . **17** C1
Brake The ST7 . . . . **195** B7
Brake Village ST7 . . . . . . **195** B7
Bramall Cl CW11 . . . . . . **175** C7
Bramble Chase CW8 . . . **101** F2
Bramble Cl
  Chester CH3 . . . . **142** A7
  Macclesfield SK10 . . . . . . **87** B2
  Middlewich CW10 . . . . . **128** E2
  Warrington WA5 . . . . . . **14** E3
  Winsford CW7 . . . . **126** C3
Brambles The
  Burtonwood WA5 . . . . **7** A7
  Congleton CW12 . . . . . . **178** F8
  Haslington CW1 . . . . . . **191** B4
  Wincham CW9 . . . . **79** C3
Bramble Way WA7 . . . . . . **49** E4
Brambling Cl WA3 . . . . **9** F8
BRAMHALL **35** D8
Bramhall Cl CW2 . . . . . . **126** B1
Bramhall Ct CW2 . . . . . . **189** F2

Bramhall Dr
  Bebington CH62 . . . . **43** F4
  Holmes Chapel CW4 . . . **130** A3
Bramhall High Sch SK7 . . **35** F8
Bramhall Lane S SK7 . . . . **35** E7
Bramhall Rd CW7 . . . . . **189** F2
Bramhalls Pk CW9 . . . . . . **78** D3
Bramhall St WA5 . . . . **15** E5
Bramhall Sta SK7 . . . . . . **35** E6
Bramhall Way SK10 . . . . **112** A8
Bramley Cl
  Bramhall SK7 . . . . **35** E6
  2 Ellesmere Port CH66 . . **94** F8
  Wilmslow SK9 . . . . **59** D4
Bramley Ct CW6 . . . . . . **122** D5
Bramley Dr SK7 . . . . **35** E6
Bramley Mews WA4 . . . . **26** C8
Bramley Rd SK7 . . . . **35** E6
Bramley Wlk WA6 . . . . . . **73** A1
Brampton Ave SK10 . . . . . **87** A2
Brampton Cl CW2 . . . . . **207** E3
Brampton Ct CW9 . . . . **1** B3
Bramshill Cl WA3 . . . . . . **10** A6
Bramway
  Bramhall SK7 . . . . **35** C7
  High Lane SK6 . . . . **37** F7
Bramwood Ct SK7 . . . . . . **35** E6
Brancaster Dr WA3 . . . . . . **4** A7
Branceth Ct CH65 . . . . . . **70** C3
Branch Way WA11 . . . . . . **1** D6
Brancote Gdns CH62 . . . . **43** D7
Branden Dr WA16 . . . . . . **57** B1
Brandon WA8 . . . . **12** B2
Brandon Cl SK9 . . . . **34** D2
Brandwood Ave WA2 . . . . . **8** B2
Brandwood Ho **2** WA1 . . **16** C5
Bransdale Cl WA5 . . . . . . **14** F3
Bransdale Way SK11 . . . **111** F7
Brantfield Cl WA2 . . . . **8** E2
Brassey Ct CW5 . . . . . . **205** C6
BRASSEY GREEN **167** D6
Brassey's Contract Rd
  SY14 . . . . **199** A1
Brassey St CH3 . . . . **118** F1
Brassey Way CW5 . . . . . **205** D5
Brassington Terr CW3 . . . **221** F3
Brathay Cl WA2 . . . . **8** C3
BRATT'S BANK **101** B5
Brattswood Dr ST7 . . . . . **194** A5
Bray Cl
  Crewe CW1 . . . . **190** C5
  Runcorn WA7 . . . . **49** D6
Bray Rd CH4 . . . . **141** C7
Breach House La WA16 . . **32** A1
Bread St SK11 . . . . **112** C7
Brecivale Cl SK12 . . . . . . **36** E3
Breck Rd WA8 . . . . **13** B1
Breck The CH66 . . . . **69** E7
Brecon Cl SK12 . . . . **36** F4
Brecon Ct WA5 . . . . **7** E2
Brecon Dr **1** CH66 . . . . **69** E1
Breconway CW7 . . . . **149** B8
Brecon Way WA2 . . . . **8** D3
Bredon Cl CH66 . . . . **69** A6
Breen Cl CH3 . . . . **166** B1
Breezehill Cl CH64 . . . . . . **66** F8
Breezehill Pk CH64 . . . . . **66** F8
Breezehill Rd CH64 . . . . . **66** F8
Brendon Ave WA2 . . . . **8** A3
Brendon Gr WA9 . . . . **1** A4
Brennus Pl CH1 . . . . **237** A3
Brent Cl SK12 . . . . **36** B4
Brentfield WA8 . . . . **12** D2
Brentnall Cl WA5 . . . . **15** C5
Brentwood Ave M44 . . . . **11** D6
Brentwood Rd CH1 . . . . . **117** E5
Brereton CE Prim Sch
  CW11 . . . . **153** F5
Brereton Cl
  Chester CH3 . . . . **121** C1
  Crewe CW2 . . . . **189** E2
  Malpas SY14 . . . . **213** B3
  Runcorn WA7 . . . . **50** A8
  Sandbach CW11 . . . . . . **175** C7
Brereton Dr
  Brereton Green CW12 . . **154** F6
  8 Cheadle SK8 . . . . . . **34** E8
Brereton Gr CW5 . . . . . . **204** F7
Brereton Gr M44 . . . . **11** E6
BRERETON GREEN **153** E5
BRERETON HEATH **154** F6
Brereton Heath La CW11,
  CW12 . . . . **154** E6
Brereton Heath Nature
  Reserve★ CW12 . . . . . **154** D6
Brereton La CW4 . . . . . . **130** A3
Brereton Rd
  Handforth SK9 . . . . **34** B3
  Hartford CW8 . . . . **103** A4
Bretland Dr WA4 . . . . **27** A7
Breton Cl CH2 . . . . **118** C5
BRETTON **139** E4
Bretton Court Mews
  CH4 . . . . **139** B3
Bretton Dr CH4 . . . . **139** B3
Bretton La CH4 . . . . **139** E4
Bretton Rd CH4 . . . . **139** E4
Bretton Wlk M22 . . . . . . **33** D8
Brewery La CH3 . . . . **180** E3
Brian Ave
  Warrington, Stockton Heath
  WA4 . . . . **16** E1
  Warrington WA2 . . . . . . **16** D8
Brian Bevan Island WA1 . . **16** F6
Briar Ave WA3 . . . . **11** B2

Briar Cl WA16. . . . . 57 A3
Briardale Cl CW2 . . . . . . 205 F8
Briardale Gdns 4 CH66 . . 69 C6
Briardale Rd
 Ellesmere Port CH66. . . . . . 69 C6
 Willaston CH64 . . . . 43 A1
Briar Dr CH60. . . . . 41 A8
Briarfield Ave WA8. . . . . . 12 A1
Briarfield Rd
 Ellesmere Port CH65. . . . . . 70 B5
 Heswall CH60 . . . . 41 B8
Briar La CW4 . . . . 102 E7
Briarlands Cl SK7. . . . . . . 35 D6
Briar Rd WA3 . . . . 3 B8
Briarstead Cl SK7 . . . . . . 35 D7
Briarswood
 Biddulph ST8 . . . . 179 D1
 Kidsgrove ST7 . . . . 195 B1
Briarswood Ct CH1. . . . . 237 B3
Briar Wlk WA3. . . . . 3 B8
Briarwood
 Runcorn WA7. . . . . 50 B8
 Wilmslow SK9 . . . . 60 C7
Briarwood Ave
 Macclesfield SK11. . . . . . 112 D5
 Warrington WA1 . . . . 16 E7
Briarwood Ct CW7 . . . . . 149 C8
Brick Bank CW5 . . . . 204 F5
Brick Bank La WA16,
 CW4. . . . . 107 B2
Brickfield Bsns Ctr CW9 . . 79 D1
Brickfield La CH3 . . . . . . 119 F2
Brickhill La WA15. . . . . . . 32 B4
Brickhurst Way WA1 . . . . 17 B8
Brickkiln La
 Little Bollington WA14. . . . 20 C3
 Whitchurch SY13. . . . . . . 226 D2
Brick Kiln La CW10. . . . . 127 B7
Brickley Ct CW8 . . . . 77 C1
Brick Rd CH4 . . . . 139 D2
Brick St
 Newton-le-Willows WA12 . . . 1 F3
 Warrington WA1 . . . . 16 C5
Bridestone Sh Ctr CW2 156 D2
Bridewell Ct WA8. . . . . . . 13 B3
Bridge Ave WA4 . . . . 16 F4
Bridge Avenue E WA4 . . . 16 F5
Bridge Bank Cl WA3 . . . . . 3 B7
Bridge Cl
 Audley ST7. . . . . 209 F2
 Cuddington CW8 . . . . 102 A3
 Lymm WA13. . . . . 19 B4
 Wistaston CW2 . . . . 206 A7
Bridge Cotts CH4 . . . . . . 237 B1
Bridge Ct
 Chester CH2 . . . . 119 A2
 Holt LL13 . . . . 196 E8
 Neston CH64 . . . . 66 E7
Bridgedown CW6 . . . . . . 146 C1
Bridge Dr
 Christleton CH3 . . . . 142 D7
 Handforth SK9. . . . . 34 D3
Bridge End Dr SK10 . . . . . 87 A7
Bridge End La SK10 . . . . . 87 A7
Bridge Farm Ct CW10 . . 152 A4
Bridgefield Ave SK9. . . . . 34 C1
Bridgefoot WA1 . . . . 16 B4
Bridge Foyer The CH1. . . 118 B2
Bridge Gn SK10 . . . . 87 A7
Bridge La
 Cuddington CW8 . . . . 101 F3
 Frodsham WA6 . . . . 49 D1
 Goostrey CW4 . . . . 108 C2
 Warrington WA4 . . . . 26 E7
 Warrington, Woolston WA1 . 17 C7
Bridge Lane Mews WA6. . 49 D1
Bridgeman Rd CH1. . . . . 117 E3
Bridgeman St WA5 . . . . . . 15 D4
Bridge Mdw WA6 . . . . 17 C7
Bridge Ret Pk WA7 . . . . . . 23 A2
Bridge Row CW12. . . . . . 156 F4
Bridge Sh Ctr The WA4 . . 16 F3
Bridge Side Dr WA6. . . . . 73 B4
Bridges Rd CH65 . . . . 70 F5
Bridge St
 Chester CH1 . . . . 237 B2
 Congleton CW12 . . . . 156 D2
 Golborne WA3 . . . . 3 A7
 Holt LL13 . . . . 180 E1
 Macclesfield SK11. . . . . . 112 C7
 Neston CH64 . . . . 66 E7
 Newton-le-Willows WA12 . . . 2 B3
 Northwich CW9 . . . . 79 E2
 Runcorn WA7. . . . . 23 B2
 Saltney CH4. . . . . 140 C7
 Warrington WA1 . . . . 16 B5
 Whaley Bridge SK23 . . . . . 65 E7
 Wybunbury CW5 . . . . 220 B8

Bridge Street Row E
 CH1 . . . . 237 B2
Bridge Street Row W
 CH1 . . . . 237 B2
Bridge Terr CH3 . . . . 119 B2
BRIDGE TRAFFORD 97 A3
Bridge View Cl WA8. . . . . 23 A4
Bridgewater Ave WA4 . . . 16 F4
Bridgewater Cl
 Congleton CW12 . . . . 157 B1
 7 Frodsham WA6 . . . . 49 C1
 Gatley SK8. . . . . 34 D7
Bridgewater Ct
 3 Lymm WA13. . . . . 18 C3
 6 Runcorn WA7 . . . . 23 B2
Bridgewater Dr CH3. . . . 119 C2
Bridgewater Expressway
 WA7 . . . . 23 C2
Bridgewater Grange WA7 50 F5
Bridgewater High Sch
 (Lower Sch) WA4 . . . . . . 26 D6
Bridgewater High Sch
 (Upper Sch) WA4 . . . . . . 26 D7
Bridgewater Intc WA7. . . . 23 E3
Bridgewater Mews WA4 . . 26 C8
Bridgewater Pl WA3 . . . . . . 9 E4
Bridgewater St
 4 Lymm WA13. . . . . 18 C3
 6 Runcorn WA7 . . . . 23 A4
Bridgeway E WA7 . . . . 24 C2
Bridgeway W WA7 . . . . . . 24 C2
Bridge Wlk 7 WA7 . . . . . . 49 F7
Bridgewood Dr CH66. . . . 69 C2
Bridgfield Cl SK6 . . . . 37 E7
Bridgnorth Gr ST5 . . . . . 210 E2
Bridle Cl CH62. . . . . 43 E7
Bridle Ct
 Bramhall SK7. . . . . 35 F2
 Crewe CW2 . . . . 190 B4
Bridle Hey CW5. . . . . 204 F2
Bridle La CH1. . . . . 94 E6
Bridlemere Ct WA1 . . . . . . 16 E8
Bridle Pk CH62 . . . . 43 E7
Bridle Rd
 Bebington CH62. . . . . 43 E6
 Crewe CW2 . . . . 190 B4
 Woodford SK7 . . . . 35 A7
Bridle Way
 Ellesmere Port CH66. . . . . . 69 D3
 Woodford SK7 . . . . 36 A2
Brieden Way CH66. . . . . . 69 A6
Brierley Bsns Ctr CW1. . 190 D4
Brierley Ct CW7. . . . . 149 F8
Brierley Prim Sch CW1. . 190 D4
Brierley Rd CW12 . . . . . . 157 B1
Brierley St CW1. . . . . 190 D4
Brierley Terr 6 WA8. . . . . 13 C1
Briers Cl WA2 . . . . 8 F3
Brieryhurst Rd ST7. . . . . 195 B3
Briggs Ave CW2 . . . . 190 D1
Brighton Cres SK11 . . . . 113 B3
Brighton St WA5 . . . . 15 E6
Brights Ave 6 ST7. . . . . . 195 B2
Bright St CW1 . . . . 190 B5
Brightwell Cl WA5 . . . . . . 14 E5
Brimelow Cres WA5. . . . . 14 E8
Brimstage Cl CH60 . . . . . . 41 C8
Brimstage Gn CH60. . . . . 41 B8
Brimstage Rd CH60 . . . . . 41 C7
Brindley
 Warrington WA4 . . . . 16 F4
 Winsford CW7 . . . . 126 C1
Brindley Cl
 Kidsgrove ST7 . . . . 194 E1
 Talke ST7 . . . . 210 E8
Brindley Ct WA4 . . . . 26 D8
Brindley Gr SK9 . . . . 34 E2
BRINDLEY GREEN 157 C2
Brindley Hall Rd CW5 . . 186 E2
Brindley La CW11. . . . . . 153 C4
Brindley Lea La CW5. . . . 186 D1
Brindley Pk CW11. . . . . . 174 F3
Brindley Rd WA7. . . . . 23 F3
Brindley St WA7 . . . . 22 F3
Brindleys Way ST7 . . . . . 209 F2
Brindley Theatre, Arts Ctr &
 Gall The * WA7 . . . . 23 A2
Brindley Way
 Congleton CW12 . . . . 157 B1
 Macclesfield SK11. . . . . . 112 C3
Brindley Wharf WA4 . . . . 50 F6
Brine Leas High Sch
 CW5 . . . . 204 F3
Brinell Dr M44. . . . . 11 F6
Brine Pits La CW5. . . . . . 218 F2
Brine Pump Cotts CW9 . . 78 F4
Brine Rd CW5 . . . . 204 E3
Brines Brow La CH3. . . . . 99 D2
Brinley Cl CH62. . . . . 43 D5
Brinton Cl WA8. . . . . 22 E8
Brisbane Cl SK7 . . . . 35 F2
Brisbane Rd CH1. . . . . . . 117 C4
Bristol Ave WA7 . . . . 50 E6
Bristol Cl
 Blacon CH1. . . . . 117 C4
 Gatley SK8. . . . . 34 C7
Bristol Dr 3 CH66 . . . . . . 69 E1
Bristow Cl WA5 . . . . 15 B8
Britannia Dr CW9 . . . . . . 104 E8
Britannia Trad Est SK23 . 39 F1
Britannia Gdns CW11 . . . 174 F5
Britannia Rd WA6 . . . . 73 B2
Brixham Ave SK8 . . . . 34 F7
Brixham Wlk SK7 . . . . 35 E7
Broadacre CW9 . . . . 78 D6
Broadacres Pl SK9 . . . . . . 59 D3
Broadacres CW5 . . . . 217 F4

Broadbent Ave WA4. . . . . 16 F4
Broad Birches CH65. . . . . 70 A6
Broadcar Rd SK11. . . . . . 113 C6
Broad Ct SK9 . . . . 85 B8
Broadfields WA7. . . . . 50 C8
Broadheath Terr WA8 . . . 12 D1
Broadheys La WA16. . . . . 28 D6
Broadhurst Ave
 Culcheth WA3 . . . . 4 F2
 8 Warrington WA5. . . . . . 15 D4
Broadhurst La CW12 . . . 156 C3
Broad La
 Altrincham WA15. . . . . 32 B8
 Appleton Thorn WA4 . . . . . 27 C8
 Burtonwood WA5 . . . . 6 E8
 Haydock WA5, WA9. . . . . . . 1 C1
 Heswall CH60 . . . . 40 C8
 Holmes Chapel CW4 . . . . 129 F1
 Stapeley CW5. . . . . 205 A1
Broadlake CH64. . . . . 67 F8
Broadland Gdns CH66 . . . 69 F2
Broadland Rd CH66 . . . . . 69 F2
Broadleigh Way CW2 . . . 206 C8
Broadley Ave WA3 . . . . 3 C7
Broadmead
 Chester CH3 . . . . 119 C2
 Heswall CH60 . . . . 41 C7
BROADOAK 162 B1
Broad Oak Ave
 Broughton CH4 . . . . 139 A3
 Haydock WA11. . . . . 1 A6
 Warrington WA5 . . . . 14 E4
Broadoak La
 High Legh WA16 . . . . 29 D5
 Mobberley WA16. . . . . 57 E6
Broadoak Prim Sch WA9 . . 1 A3
Broadoak Sch Specialist
 Sports Coll M31 . . . . 11 F2
Broad St CW1. . . . . 190 C6
Broadwalk SK10 . . . . 87 A5
Broadway
 Altrincham WA15. . . . . 32 A8
 Barnton WA8 . . . . 78 B3
 Widnes WA8 . . . . 12 A1
 Wilmslow SK9 . . . . 60 B6
Broadway E CH2 . . . . 118 C5
Broadways CW3 . . . . 230 A4
Broadway W CH2 . . . . . . 118 C5
Broadway The CW5 . . . . 204 F5
Broad Wlk SK9. . . . . 59 F8
Brock Cl SK6 . . . . 37 F7
Broady Ct 2 CW2 . . . . . . 190 D2
Brock Dr SK8 . . . . 35 B8
Brock Gdns CW1. . . . . 21 E2
Brock Hollow CW11. . . . . 174 F4
Brockhurst Mews CW9 . . 104 A6
Brockhurst St CW9. . . . . 104 A6
Brockbank Dr CW8 . . . . . 103 E7
Brocklehurst Ave SK10 . . 87 F2
Brocklehurst Ct 2 SK10 . 87 D3
Brocklehurst Dr SK10 . . . 87 A7
Brocklehurst Manor SK10 87 E1
Brocklehurst Mews 3
 SK10 . . . . 87 D3
Brocklehurst Way SK10 . . 87 D3
Brock Rd WA3. . . . . 9 D3
Brocks Croft Gdns ST8 . 179 C1
Brock St SK10 . . . . 87 D1
Brockton CV4 . . . . 26 C6
Brockway E CH3 . . . . 166 A1
Brockway W CH3 . . . . . . 166 A1
Brockwell Cl 2 CW7. . . . 149 A8
Brodie Cl CH2 . . . . 95 C1
Brogden Ave WA3. . . . . 4 E4
Broken Banks 10 SK11. . 112 D7
BROKEN CROSS
 Macclesfield 111 E8
 Northwich 104 C7
Broken Cross SK11. . . . . 111 F8
Brokencross Pl CW9 . . . 104 C7
Broken Cross Prim Sch
 SK11. . . . . 111 E7
Bromborough Rake Sta
 CH62. . . . . 43 C8
Bromborough Sta CH63 . . 43 C7
Bromborough Village Rd
 CH62 . . . . 43 E8
Bromley Ave WA3 . . . . 3 D7
Bromley Cl
 Crewe CW1 . . . . 189 F8
 Heswall CH60 . . . . 40 E7
 Warrington WA2 . . . . 8 F3
Bromley Dr CW4 . . . . 130 C2
Bromley Rd
 Congleton CW12 . . . . 156 F3
 Macclesfield SK10 . . . . . . 111 E8
Brompton Gdns WA5. . . . 15 E7
Brompton Way
 Ellesmere Port CH66. . . . . . 69 E1
 Handforth SK9. . . . . 34 C5
Bromilows Cotts ST8. . . . 179 C1
Bronington Ave CH62 . . . 43 D6
Bronte Cl WA2. . . . . 8 A6
Brook Acre Prim Sch WA2 . 8 E1
Brookash Rd M22 . . . . 34 A8
Brook Ave
 Handforth SK9. . . . . 34 D4
 Shavington CW2 . . . . 206 C5
 Warrington, Stockton Heath
 WA4 . . . . 16 E1
 Warrington, Westy WA4 . . 16 F5
Brook Bank SK12 . . . . 37 C2
Brook Bottom Rd SK22 . . 39 A8
Brook Cl
 Crewe CW1 . . . . 190 F4
 Cronton WA8 . . . . 12 C6
Brook Ct
 Chester CH1 . . . . 118 B3

Brook Ct continued
 Sandbach CW11 . . . . 175 B6
Brookdale WA8. . . . . 12 A3
Brookdale Ave WA16. . . . . 57 C2
Brookdale Ct CH3 . . . . . . 143 D5
Brookdale Pk CW2 . . . . . 190 A3
Brookdale Pl CH1 . . . . . . 237 B3
Brookdale Way CH3 . . . . 143 B5
Brook Dr
 Kelsall CW6 . . . . 122 D4
 Warrington WA5 . . . . 15 A5
Brooke Ave CH2 . . . . 118 F8
Brooke Ct SK9 . . . . 34 E4
Brooke Dr SK9. . . . . 34 D4
Brooke Ho SK10 . . . . 86 F1
Brook End WA9. . . . . 1 A1
Brookes Ave CH4 . . . . . . 139 B3
Brooke Way SK9 . . . . 34 D4
Brook Farm Cl M31. . . . . 11 E2
Brookfield CH1. . . . . 191 D5
Brookfield Ave
 Poynton SK12. . . . . 36 C3
 Runcorn WA7 . . . . 23 E2
Brookfield Cl
 Lymm WA13. . . . . 18 D3
 Tarporley CW6 . . . . 168 D8
Brookfield Cotts 2 WA13 . 18 D3
Brookfield Cres CW4 . . . 107 F1
Brookfield Ct CW1 . . . . . 190 B5
Brookfield Dr
 Alsager ST7 . . . . 193 C5
 Chester CH2 . . . . 118 E4
 Holmes Chapel CW4 . . . . 130 B3
Brookfield La SK11. . . . . 112 F7
Brookfield Pk WA4. . . . . . 17 A2
Brookfield Rd
 Comberbach CW9 . . . . . . 78 D8
 Culcheth WA3 . . . . 4 D3
 Lymm WA13. . . . . 18 D3
Brookfields Sch WA8. . . . 13 D2
Brookfields Ave WA16 . . . 57 C1
Brookfield Wlk WA12 . . . . 2 B3
Brook Furlong WA6 . . . . . 74 F3
Brook Hey CH64 . . . . 41 B2
Brook Ho WA4. . . . . 16 F3
Brookhouse Rd
 Alsager ST7 . . . . 193 D3
 8 Sandbach CW11 . . . . . 175 B6
BROOKHOUSE 43 C5
Brookhurst Ave CH63 . . . 43 C5
Brookhurst Cl CH63. . . . . 43 C5
Brookhurst Prim Sch
 CH63. . . . . 43 C6
Brookhurst Rd CH63 . . . . 43 C5
Brook La
 Alderley Edge SK9 . . . . . . 59 F3
 Astbury CW12 . . . . 177 E5
 Broughton CH5 . . . . 139 C7
 Burland CW5 . . . . 203 D8
 Chester CH2 . . . . 118 E4
 Faddiley CW5. . . . . 202 F8
 Knutsford WA16. . . . . 57 B1
 Neston CH64 . . . . 41 C2
 Northwich CW9 . . . . 104 D7
 Warrington WA3 . . . . 18 A8
Brookland Ave CW2. . . . . 205 F8
Brookland Dr CW11 . . . . 175 E6
Brookland La WA9 . . . . 1 A1
BROOKLANDS. 225 E1
Brooklands Ave SK11. . . 112 B7
Brooklands Dr
 Goostrey CW4 . . . . 107 F1
 Northwich CW9 . . . . 104 A4
Brooklands Gdns CH64. . 41 C1
Brooklands Gr CW1 . . . . 190 A6
Brooklands Pk 1 WA8 . . 13 C2
Brooklands Rd
 Congleton CW12 . . . . 155 F2
 Neston CH64 . . . . 41 C1
Brooklands The CW2 . . . 206 E3
Brooklands The CW2. . . . 206 E3
Brookledge La SK10. . . . . 62 E5
Brooklet Rd CH60. . . . . . . 41 C8
Brooklyn Dr
 Ellesmere Port CH65. . . . . . 69 F5
 Lymm WA13. . . . . 18 E4
Brooklyn St CW2. . . . . . . 190 C2
Brookmills Cotts ST8 . . . 179 C1
Brookmoore Ct CH2 . . . . 237 A4
Brook Pl
 Chester CH1 . . . . 237 B3
 Warrington WA4 . . . . 16 E3
Brook Rd
 Ellesmere Port CH66. . . . . . 69 D5
 Lymm WA13. . . . . 18 E4
Brooks Dr WA15 . . . . 32 D8
Brookside
 Ashton Hayes CH3. . . . . . 121 E7
 Chester CH3 . . . . 142 A8
 Cuddington CW8 . . . . 101 F3
 Kelsall CW6 . . . . 122 D4
 Kingsley WA6. . . . . 75 C2
 Warrington WA4 . . . . 16 E3
Brook Side CW8 . . . . 102 C8

Brookside Ave
 Lymm WA13. . . . . 18 C4
 Poynton SK12. . . . . 36 E3
 Sutton Lane Ends SK11 . . 112 F2
 Warrington, Stockton Heath
 WA4 . . . . 16 D1
 Warrington WA5 . . . . 15 A4
Brookside Cl WA11. . . . . . . 1 B7
Brookside Cotts CW11. . 176 A8
Brookside Ct SK10 . . . . . . 87 A1
Brookside Gn CW2 . . . . . 206 C8
Brookside La SK6. . . . . . . 37 E7
Brookside Mill 6 SK11 . . 112 E7
Brookside Miniature Rly *
 SK12 . . . . 36 F7
Brookside Prim Sch
 Ellesmere Port CH66. . . . . . 69 E4
 High Lane SK6. . . . . 37 E6
Brookside Rd
 4 Congleton CW12 . . . . . 156 D3
 Frodsham WA6 . . . . 74 A8
Brookside Terr
 Chester CH2 . . . . 237 C4
 Wilmslow SK9 . . . . 59 E3
Brookside View WA11. . . . 1 B7
Brookside Way WA11 . . . . 1 B7
Brooks La
 Bosley SK11. . . . . 135 E2
 Middlewich CW10 . . . . . . 128 D1
Brook Slack CW6 . . . . . . 124 D1
Brooks Lane Ind Est
 CW10 . . . . 128 D1
Brook St
 Chester CH1 . . . . 237 B3
 Congleton CW12 . . . . 156 F3
 Crewe CW2 . . . . 190 D3
 Golborne, Bank Heath WA3 . 3 A8
 Knutsford WA16. . . . . 57 B1
 Macclesfield SK11. . . . . . 112 E7
 Neston CH64 . . . . 66 B8
 Northwich CW9 . . . . 79 A1
 Northwich, Lostock Gralam
 CW9 . . . . 79 E2
 2 Runcorn WA7 . . . . 23 A2
 3 Widnes WA8. . . . . 13 B1
Brook Street Bridge CH1,
 CH2 . . . . 237 C4
Brook Street Mill 19
 SK11 . . . . 112 E7
Brook Terr
 Runcorn WA7 . . . . 23 E1
 Sandbach CW11 . . . . 175 A3
BROOKVALE 50 B5
Brookvale Avenue N WA7 50 B6
Brookvale Avenue S WA7 . 50 B6
Brookvale Cl WA5 . . . . 6 F6
Brookvale Prim Sch WA7 . 50 B5
Brook View
 Alderley Edge SK9 . . . . . . 60 A3
 Allostock WA16 . . . . 106 F3
Brookview Cl CW2 . . . . . 206 C8
Brook Villas ST7 . . . . 193 C4
Brook Way
 Hartford CW8 . . . . 103 B4
 Nantwich CW5. . . . . 204 E3
 Warrington WA5 . . . . 15 A5
Brookway La WA9 . . . . 1 A1
Brook Well CH4. . . . . 66 F5
Brookwood Cl WA4 . . . . . 26 B8
Broom Ave WA4 . . . . 26 E6
BROOMEDGE 27 C8
Bromehouse Ave M44. . . 11 E8
Broomfield CW12 . . . . . . 154 F6
Broomfield Cl
 Chelford SK11 . . . . 84 A3
 Wilmslow SK9 . . . . 60 E8
 13 Winsford CW7 . . . . . . 149 A8
Broomfield Cty Jun Sch
 WA4 . . . . 26 E7
Broomfields WA4 . . . . 26 E7
Broomfields La CW8 . . . . 77 F4
Broomfields Rd WA4 . . . . 26 D7
BROOMHALL 217 F4
BROOMHALL GREEN . . . 217 F3
Broomheath La
 Tarvin, Broom Bank CH3 . . 144 C7
 Tarvin CH3. . . . . 121 C1
Broomhill La
 Brown Knowl CH3 . . . . . . 199 D8
 Great Barrow CH3 . . . . . . 120 E8
Broom La WA16. . . . . 81 F2
Broomlands CH60. . . . . . . 40 E8
Broomlands Cotts WA5 . 219 E1
Broom Rd M31. . . . . 11 F2
Broomsfield La CW8 . . . . 78 A4
Broom's La CW6 . . . . 122 D6
Broom St CW1. . . . . 190 A6
Broseley Ave WA3 . . . . 4 D4
Broseley La WA3 . . . . 4 D4
Brotherton Cl CH62 . . . . . 43 C8
Brotherton Way WA12. . . . 2 B4
Brough St W SK11 . . . . . 112 C7
BROUGHTON 139 A4
Broughton Ave WA3 . . . . . 3 D7
Broughton Cres CW2. . . . 190 F1
Broughton Hall Rd CH4 . 139 C4
Broughton Ind Est CH4 . . 139 D3
Broughton Inf Sch CH4. . 139 C4
Broughton Jun Sch CH4 139 C4
Broughton La CW2. . . . . 189 F1
Broughton Mills Rd CH4. 139 D4
Broughton Rd
 Adlington SK10 . . . . 62 C5
 Crewe CW2 . . . . 190 C8

Broughton Sh Pk CH4. . . . . . 139 E4
Broughton Way WA1 . . . . 22 B5
Brow Com Prim Sch The
WA7 . . . . 23 F1
Brow La
Antrobus CW9 . . . . 53 D5
Heswall CH60 . . . . 40 F7
Browmere Dr WA3 . . . . 9 A7
Brown Ave
Lawton-gate ST7 . . . . . 194 A5
Nantwich CW5 . . . . 204 F4
BROWNEDGE 154 A3
BROWN HEATH 143 B6
Brown Heath Rd CH3 . . . 143 B6
BROWNHILL 147 B6
Brownhill Dr WA1 . . . . 16 F8
Brownhills Rd CW6 . . . . . 147 C6
Browning Ave WA8 . . . . . . 22 F8
Browning Cl
Blacon CH1 . . . . 117 F6
Sandbach CW11 . . . . 174 D5
Browning Dr
Ellesmere Port CH65 . . . . 69 F4
Winwick WA2 . . . . 8 A6
Browning Gn [2] CW5 . . . 204 F4
Browning St ST7 . . . . 210 C8
Browning St CW1 . . . . . . 190 C4
Browning Way CW7 . . . . . 149 A2
BROWN KNOWL 199 C8
Brown Lees CE CW2 . . . . 190 B1
Brown Lees Rd ST7 . . . . . 195 F4
BROWNLOW 177 E7
Brownlow Cl SK12 . . . . 36 E2
Brownlow Hall Mews
CW12 . . . . 177 E8
BROWNLOW HEATH 177 D5
Brownlow Heath CW12 . . 177 E5
Brownlow Heath La
CW12 . . . . 177 D6
BROWN MOSS 231 B7
BROWN'S BANK 229 D2
Brown's La
Chester CH4 . . . . 141 C7
Wilmslow SK9 . . . . 60 E8
Brown St
[3] Alderley Edge SK9 . . . . 60 A1
Congleton CW12 . . . . 156 E3
Macclesfield SK11 . . . . . . 112 C7
Widnes WA8 . . . . 23 D7
Brow The WA6 . . . . 75 C2
BROXTON 183 A1
Broxton Ave CW10 . . . . . . 151 D6
Broxton Cl WA8 . . . . 12 C3
Broxton Mews CH3 . . . . . . 183 A1
Broxton Rd
Clutton CH3 . . . . 182 D1
Ellesmere Port CH66 . . . . 69 E5
Bruce Ave WA2 . . . . 8 D1
Bruce Cres CH63 . . . . 43 C6
Bruce Dr CH66 . . . . 69 C4
BRUCHE 16 F7
Bruche Ave WA1 . . . . 16 F8
Bruche Com Prim Sch
WA1 . . . . 17 A7
Bruche Dr WA1 . . . . 16 F8
Bruche Heath Gdns WA1 . 17 A8
Bruen The CH3 . . . . 121 C3
BRUERA 164 D6
Bruera Rd CH65 . . . . 69 F4
Brunel Ct CW9 . . . . 104 E5
Brunel Rd SK11 . . . . 112 C2
Brunner Gr CW5 . . . . 205 A5
Brunner Rd WA8 . . . . 23 A8
Brunsborough Cl CH62 . . . 43 C6
Brunswick [1] SY14 . . . . . . 23 A3
Brunswick Cres CH66 . . . . 69 E3
Brunswick Ct [5] SK11 . . . 112 D7
Brunswick Hill SK10 . . . . 112 D8
Brunswick Rd WA12 . . . . . . 1 F4
Brunswick St
Congleton CW12 . . . . 156 F3
[5] Macclesfield SK10 . . . 112 D8
St Helens WA9 . . . . 1 A3
Brunswick Terr SK10 . . . . 112 D8
Bruntleigh Ave WA4 . . . . . 17 A3
Brunty Bank SY14 . . . . . . 200 A8
Bryant Ave WA4 . . . . 16 F5
Brymau Four Trad Est
CH4 . . . . 140 D7
Brymau One Trad Est
CH4 . . . . 140 D7
Brymau Three Trad Est
CH4 . . . . 140 D7
Brymau Two Trad Est
CH4 . . . . 140 E7
BRYN 102 A6
Brynlow Dr CW10 . . . . . . 151 B8
Brynmore Dr SK11 . . . . . . 112 F7
Brynn St WA8 . . . . 23 B8
Brynton Cl SK10 . . . . 87 C1
Brynton Rd SK10 . . . . 87 C1
Buchanan Cl WA8 . . . . 12 F3
Buchan Gr CW2 . . . . 190 B3
Buckbean Way CW4 . . . . . 107 E1
Buckden Way [3] SK10 . . 112 C8
Buckfast Ave WA11 . . . . . . 2 A7
Buckfast Cl
Cheadle SK8 . . . . 35 B6
Macclesfield SK10 . . . . . . 87 C2
Poynton SK12 . . . . 36 D5
Warrington WA5 . . . . 14 E3
Buckfast St WA7 . . . . 24 E3
Buckfast Way CW10 . . . . . 128 B1
Buckingham Ave
Chester CH3 . . . . 119 B2
Widnes WA8 . . . . 13 A4

Buckingham Cl
[4] Congleton CW12 . . . . 156 F4
Wistaston CW2 . . . . 205 E8
Buckingham Dr
Knutsford WA16. . . . . 57 B1
Macclesfield SK11 . . . . . . 112 B5
Northwich CW9 . . . . 103 E4
Warrington WA5 . . . . 15 C4
Winsford CW7 . . . . 149 C7
Buckingham Gdns [1]
CH65 . . . . 70 D2
Buckingham Rd
Irlam M44 . . . . 11 C6
Poynton SK12 . . . . 36 D3
Wilmslow SK9 . . . . 59 F6
Buckingham Rise SK11 . . 112 B4
Buck La CW2 . . . . 206 E8
Buckland Cl WA8 . . . . 22 D7
Buckley Ave CW10 . . . . . . 128 C7
Buckley Cl CW10 . . . . 151 B8
Buckley Ct CH64 . . . . 67 F8
Buckley St
Macclesfield SK11 . . . . . . 112 D7
Warrington WA2 . . . . 16 B6
Bucklow Ave
Mobberley WA16. . . . . 58 A4
Partington M31 . . . . 11 F3
Bucklow Gdns WA13 . . . . . 19 A4
BUCKLOW HILL 30 C3
Bucklow Hill La WA16. . . . . 30 B3
Bucklow Wlk [1] SK11 . . . 112 F7
BUCKOAK 99 A5
Buckton St WA1 . . . . 16 D7
BUDDILEIGH 221 F7
Bude Cl
Alsager ST7 . . . . 193 B3
Bramhall SK7 . . . . 35 F7
Crewe CW1 . . . . 190 B8
Bude Rd WA8 . . . . 12 E2
Budworth Ave
Warrington WA4 . . . . 16 F4
Widnes WA8 . . . . 12 D2
Budworth Cl
Runcorn WA7 . . . . 49 D7
Sandbach CW11 . . . . 174 F7
BUDWORTH HEATH 54 A1
Budworth Heath La CW9 . 54 C1
Budworth La CW9 . . . . 78 E7
Budworth Rd
Bate Heath CW9 . . . . 54 E2
Ellesmere Port CH66 . . . . 69 E2
Over Tabley WA16 . . . . . . 55 C2
Budworth Wlk [1] SK9 . . . 34 E1
BUERTON 230 E4
Buerton App CH3 . . . . 164 B6
BUERTON MOSS 230 E6
Buffs La CH64 . . . . 41 B8
Buggen La CH64 . . . . 66 D8
BUGLAWTON 157 A4
Buglawton Hall Sch
CW12 . . . . 157 D5
Buglawton Ind Est [5]
CW12 . . . . 156 F4
Buglawton Prim Sch
CW12 . . . . 157 A4
Buildwas Rd CH64 . . . . 41 F2
BULKELEY 184 E1
Bulkeley La SY14 . . . . 200 C8
Bulkeley Rd
Handforth SK9 . . . . 34 D3
Poynton SK12 . . . . 36 E3
Bulkeley St
Chester CH3 . . . . 119 A1
Crewe CW1 . . . . 190 A1
Bullcroft St CW14 . . . . . . 211 D7
Bull Hill CH64. . . . . 66 F6
Bull–Hill–La SK10, SK11 . . 88 D2
Bullocks House Rd ST7. . . 195 E3
Bullocks La SK11 . . . . 112 E3
Bull Ring CW9 . . . . 103 F8
Bull Ring The CW10 . . . . . 128 C3
Bumper's La CH1 . . . . 117 F1
BUNBURY 185 F8
Bunbury Aldersey CE Prim
Sch CW6 . . . . 185 E8
Bunbury Cl
Middlewich CW10 . . . . . . 151 D5
Northwich CW9 . . . . 104 A5
Stoak CH2 . . . . 96 A7
Bunbury Comm CW6 . . . . 168 C2
BUNBURY COMMONS . . . 169 A2
Bunbury Dr WA7 . . . . 49 C6
Bunbury Gn CH65 . . . . 70 D2
BUNBURY HEATH 185 D8
Bunbury La CW6 . . . . 185 E8
Bunbury Mill[*] CW6 . . . . 169 E3
Bunbury Rd CH65 . . . . 69 B3
Bunce La SK11 . . . . 133 B4
Bunce St CH1 . . . . 237 A1
Bungalow WA12 . . . . 2 E1
Bungalows The
Adderley TF9 . . . . 234 B3
Dunham-on-the-Hill WA6. . 97 E6
Thornton Hough CH63. . . . 42 B6
BUNSLEY BANK 230 D5
Bunting Cl [6] WA3 . . . . . . 3 E8
Buntingford Rd WA4 . . . . . 17 C3
Bunts La CW12 . . . . 156 E1
Burdett Rd CH66 . . . . 69 E2
Burfield Dr WA4 . . . . 26 D7
Burford Ave
Bramhall SK7 . . . . 35 D5
Newcastle-under-Lyme
ST5 . . . . 210 D1
Burford Cl CW8 . . . . 103 A4
Burford Cres SK9 . . . . 59 E5
Burford La WA13 . . . . 19 C2

Burgamot La CW9. . . . . . . 78 D8
Burganey Ct CH4 . . . . 162 D2
Burgess Ave WA4 . . . . 16 B2
Burgess Cl CW5 . . . . 205 B4
Burgess Dr CH1 . . . . 117 A5
Burgess La WA6 . . . . 101 B6
Burgess Pl [6] CW8 . . . . . 103 E8
Burgess St SK10 . . . . 112 F8
Burges St CW2 . . . . 218 F3
Burjen Way CW1 . . . . 190 B6
Burkhardt Dr WA12 . . . . . . 2 E3
BURLAND 203 C7
Burland Cl WA7 . . . . 22 F1
Burland Gr CW7 . . . . 126 A2
BURLAND LOWER
GREEN 203 A7
Burland Rd
Halewood L26 . . . . 21 A6
Newcastle-under-Lyme
ST5 . . . . 210 D2
BURLAND UPPER
GREEN 203 B8
Burlea Cl CW2 . . . . 189 E5
Burlea Dr CW2 . . . . 206 B5
BURLEYDAM 228 B1
Burleydam Rd SY13 . . . . . 233 A4
Burleyhurst La SK9, WA16. . 59 B7
Burley La WA4 . . . . 27 C4
Burmarsh La WA8 . . . . 22 B5
Burnell Cl CW5 . . . . 204 F3
Burnell Rd CH65 . . . . 70 C4
Burnet Cl WA2 . . . . 9 C2
Burnfell WA3 . . . . 3 F7
Burnham Cl
Culcheth WA3 . . . . 4 E4
Warrington WA5 . . . . 14 F5
Widnes WA8 . . . . 12 C3
Burnham Rd CH4 . . . . 140 F6
Burnsall Ave WA3 . . . . 3 F8
Burnsall Dr WA8 . . . . 12 C3
Burns Ave
Ellesmere Port CH66 . . . . 69 E4
Rode Heath ST7 . . . . 193 E8
Burns Cres WA8 . . . . 22 F8
Burns Dr CW1 . . . . 190 F4
Burns Gr WA2 . . . . 8 C2
Burnside WA15 . . . . 32 D7
Burnside Ave WA4 . . . . . . 16 D1
Burnside Cl SK9 . . . . 60 C6
Burnside Way
Northwich CW8 . . . . 103 D8
Winnington CW8 . . . . 78 D1
Burns Rd CW12 . . . . 157 A2
Burns Way CW1 . . . . 117 E6
Burnt Acre SK11 . . . . 84 B3
Burnt Mill La WA8 . . . . . . 21 D5
Burnwood Gr ST7 . . . . . . 195 B2
Burran Rd M22 . . . . 33 D8
Burrough Cl WA3 . . . . 9 F3
Burrows Hill CH4 . . . . . . 103 B7
Burrows La WA6 . . . . 73 F2
Burrows St WA11 . . . . 1 A6
Burrows The CW8 . . . . . . 101 D5
Bursar Cl WA12 . . . . 2 C4
Burslam St CW12 . . . . . . 156 E2
BURTON
Duddon 144 F4
Neston 67 D1
Burton Ave CW6 . . . . 146 C2
Burton Cl
Culcheth WA3 . . . . 4 F3
Widnes WA8 . . . . 12 F3
Burton Dr SK12 . . . . 36 D4
Burton Gn CH66 . . . . 69 D4
Burton Gr CW1 . . . . 173 B1
BURTON GREEN 161 D1
Burton Hall Rd LL12. . . . . 161 E1
Burton La CW6 . . . . 144 F6
Burton Manor Coll CH64 . 67 D1
Burton Mere Fisheries RSPB
Reserve[*] CH64 . . . . 92 C8
Burton Mill Wood Nature
Reserve[*] CH64 . . . . 67 C2
Burton Rd
Blacon CH1 . . . . 117 C5
Duddon CW6 . . . . 144 E6
Neston CH64 . . . . 66 F6
Warrington WA3 . . . . 9 D1
Burton Sq CW6 . . . . 146 C2
BURTONWOOD 6 E6
Burtonwood Com Prim Sch
WA5 . . . . 6 E7
Burtonwood Ind Ctr WA5. . 6 E7
Burtonwood Rd
Warrington, Great Sankey
WA5 . . . . 15 C6
Warrington, Kingswood WA5. 7 A2
BURWARDSLEY 184 B5
Burwardsley Ct CH3. . . . . 184 A6
Burwardsley Rd CH3 . . . . 166 D1
Burwardsley Way CW9. . . 103 E4
Bushell Cl CH64 . . . . 66 F7
Bushell Rd CH64 . . . . 66 F7
Bushells La WA6 . . . . 99 B8
Bush Rd
Christleton CH3 . . . . 142 E7
Widnes WA8 . . . . 22 F5
Bush Way CH60 . . . . 40 D8
Butler Way CW5 . . . . 204 E3
Butley Cl
Macclesfield SK10 . . . . . . 87 D3
Middlewich CW10 . . . . . . 151 C2
Butley Hall SK10 . . . . 87 A7
Butley Lanes SK10 . . . . . . 61 F1
BUTLEY TOWN 87 C8
Buttercup Cl WA5 . . . . 15 E3

Buttercup Way WA16. . . . . 79 F6
Buttermarket St WA1 . . . . 16 B5
Buttermere Ave
Ellesmere Port CH65 . . . . 70 C3
Warrington WA2 . . . . 8 C3
Buttermere Cl WA8 . . . . . . 74 D8
Buttermere Cres WA2 . . . . 8 C3
Buttermere Ct CW12 . . . . 156 A2
Buttermere Dr
Alderley Edge SK9 . . . . . . 83 F7
Altrincham WA15. . . . . 32 D6
Crewe CW1 . . . . 173 B1
Buttermere Gr WA7 . . . . . . 49 D5
Buttermere Rd
Partington M31 . . . . 11 E3
Winsford CW7 . . . . 126 C2
BUTTERS GREEN 210 A2
Butterton La CW1 . . . . . . 192 B2
BUTT GREEN 205 B3
BUTT LANE 194 D1
Butts Gn WA5. . . . . 7 A3
Butts The
Alsager ST7 . . . . 193 D4
Runcorn WA7 . . . . 23 F2
Buxton Ave CW1 . . . . 190 E4
Buxton Cl WA5 . . . . 15 A8
Buxton New Rd
Buxton SK11 . . . . 115 A6
Macclesfield Forest SK11 . 114 D7
Macclesfield SK11 . . . . . . 88 E1
Buxton Old Rd
Congleton CW12 . . . . 157 C6
Disley SK12 . . . . 38 E4
Macclesfield SK11 . . . . . . 113 D7
Buxton Rd
Congleton CW12 . . . . 157 C6
High Lane SK6, SK7, SK12. . 37 D8
Horwich End, New Horwich
SK23 . . . . 65 E6
Macclesfield SK10, SK11 . 113 A7
New Mills SK22, SK23 . . . 39 C4
Whaley Bridge SK23 . . . . 39 E1
Buxton Road W SK12 . . . . 38 B5
Bye Pass The CH3. . . . . . . 119 E2
Byland Ave SK11 . . . . 35 B6
Byland Cl WA8 . . . . 13 C5
Bylands Cl [4] CW10 . . . . 128 C6
Bylands Cl SK12 . . . . 36 D4
BYLEY 129 A7
Byley La
Cranage CW4, CW10. . . . 129 C6
Middlewich CW10 . . . . . . 128 E3
Byley Prim Sch CW10 . . . 129 B7
Byley Way CW7 . . . . 126 B1
Byng Ave M44 . . . . 11 D4
By–Pass Rd
Chester CH4 . . . . 93 E4
Tarvin CH3 . . . . 121 B3
Byron Cl
Blacon CH1 . . . . 117 F6
Crewe CW1 . . . . 190 F4
Rode Heath ST7. . . . . 193 E7
Sandbach CW11 . . . . 174 D6
Byron Ct WA2 . . . . 8 C2
Byron's La SK11 . . . . 112 E5
Byrons St SK11 . . . . 112 D6
Byron Wa7 . . . . 23 A1
Byron Way CW7 . . . . 190 A1
Byron Wlk CW5 . . . . 204 D6
Bythom Cl CH3 . . . . 142 E7

C

Cabot Cl WA5. . . . . 7 C1
Cabul Cl WA2 . . . . 16 D7
CADISHEAD. 11 E6
Cadishead Prim Sch M44. 11 E6
Cadishead Way M44 . . . . . 11 E6
Cadnant Cl CH1 . . . . 117 D3
Cadnant Ct/Llys Cadnant
CH4 . . . . 139 C5
Cadshaw Cl WA3 . . . . 9 D5
Caer Castell LL13 . . . . . . 196 D8
Caerleon Cl CW7 . . . . 149 A8
Caerllew LL13 . . . . 180 E1
Caernarvon Ave CW7 . . . . 149 B7
Caernarvon Cl WA7 . . . . . . 23 F2
Caernarvon Ct [4] CH65. . 70 D2
Caesars Cl WA7 . . . . 23 E2
Cairn Brae WA12. . . . . 2 C4
Cairns Cres CH1 . . . . 117 D4
Cairo St WA1 . . . . 16 B5
Caister Way CW7 . . . . 149 C7
Caithness Ct [3] WA7 . . . . 23 B2
Calamine St SK11 . . . . . . 112 E6
Calday Gr WA11 . . . . 1 A8
Caldbeck Ave WA2 . . . . . . 8 D2
CALDECOTT GREEN 197 C4
Caldicott Cl [2] CW7 . . . . 149 C7
Caldicott Ave WA5 . . . . . . 7 F2
Caldwell Cl WA5. . . . . 205 B4
Caldwell Rd WA5 . . . . 23 A7
Caldwell's Gate La CW9 . . 54 B8
Caldy Cl CH3 . . . . 118 D5
Caldy Dr CH66 . . . . 69 D4
Caldy Rd
Alsager ST7 . . . . 193 C4

Caldy Rd continued
Handforth SK9 . . . . 34 D3
Caldy Valley Rd
Chester CH3 . . . . 142 B7
Huntington CH3 . . . . 142 A6
Cale Rd SK22 . . . . 39 D8
Calico La SK23. . . . . 39 E4
California Cl WA5 . . . . 15 C8
Callands Cty Prim Sch
WA5 . . . . 7 E2
Callands Rd WA5 . . . . 7 D2
Callender Gdns WA6 . . . . . 73 A2
Callin Ct CH1 . . . . 237 A2
Calmington La WA7 . . . . . . 24 F4
CALROFOLD 88 C2
Calrofold Dr ST5 . . . . 210 D1
Calrofold La SK10 . . . . 88 C2
Calstock Cl WA3 . . . . 14 E3
CALVELEY 169 E2
Calveley Ave CH62 . . . . . . 43 F4
Calveley Cl CW9 . . . . 103 C5
Calveley Cty Prim Sch
CW6 . . . . 170 B2
Calveley Green La CW6,
CW7. . . . . 170 C4
Calveley Hall La CW5,
CW6 . . . . 170 A2
Calveley Rd
Halewood L26 . . . . 21 A6
Macclesfield SK10 . . . . . . 86 F1
Calveley Way CW7 . . . . . . 126 A1
Calverley Cl [3] SK9 . . . . . 60 C8
Calverly Cl WA7. . . . . 50 C5
Calvers WA7 . . . . 23 E1
Camberley Cl SK7 . . . . 36 A7
Camberwell Park Rd WA8 13 A4
Camborne Cl SK10 . . . . . . 111 E8
Camborne Cl
Congleton CW12 . . . . 178 E8
Runcorn WA7 . . . . 50 C6
Cambourne Rd WA5 . . . . . 6 F6
Cambrai Ave WA4 . . . . 16 C2
Cambrian Ave CH3 . . . . . . 119 B2
Cambrian Cl CH66 . . . . . . 69 A6
Cambrian Rd CH1 . . . . . . 118 B2
Cambrian Villas CH3 . . . . 165 C3
Cambrian Way CW7 . . . . . 149 B8
Cambridge Ave
Macclesfield SK11 . . . . . . 112 B7
Wilmslow SK9 . . . . 59 F7
Winsford CW7 . . . . 126 A1
Cambridge Cl
Biddulph ST8 . . . . 179 C1
Warrington WA4 . . . . 26 B7
Cambridge Ct [7] CH65 . . 70 C5
Cambridge Gdns
Helsby WA6 . . . . 73 D4
Warrington WA4 . . . . 26 C6
Cambridge Rd
Bebington CH62 . . . . 43 E8
Chester CH2 . . . . 118 F5
Ellesmere Port CH65 . . . . 70 D5
Macclesfield SK11 . . . . . . 112 B7
Cambridge Road Com Prim
Sch CH65 . . . . 70 C5
Cambridge St
Runcorn WA7 . . . . 23 C2
Widnes WA8 . . . . 23 B7
Camden Ct WA7 . . . . 24 D1
Camden Rd CH65 . . . . 70 A5
Camden St CW1 . . . . 190 D2
Camellia Gdns WA9 . . . . . . 6 B7
Camelot Cl WA12 . . . . 1 F4
Camelot Gr [2] CW7 . . . . 206 C4
Camelot Way WA7 . . . . . . 50 A8
Cameron Ave
Runcorn WA7 . . . . 48 E8
Shavington CW2 . . . . 206 B3
Cameron Ct WA2 . . . . 8 A4
Cameron Rd WA8 . . . . 23 A8
Camm St CW2 . . . . 190 D2
Camomile Wlk [8] M31 . . . 11 F3
Campbell Ave WA4 . . . . . . 49 A8
Campbell Cl
Congleton CW12 . . . . 157 A4
Haslington CW1 . . . . 191 C4
Macclesfield SK10 . . . . . . 87 A1
Northwich CW9 . . . . 103 F4
Campbell Cres WA5 . . . . . 14 F6
Campden Way SK9 . . . . . . 34 D4
Campion Cl
Huntington CH3 . . . . 142 A6
Warrington WA3 . . . . 9 C4
Campsey Ash WA8 . . . . . . 12 F4
Camrose Cl WA7 . . . . 49 C6
Camsley La WA13 . . . . 18 B3
Canaan WA3. . . . . 4 C8
Canada St WA1 . . . . 9 A2
Canadian Ave CH2 . . . . . . 119 A3
Canal Bank WA13 . . . . 18 D3
Canal Bridge Ent Pk
CH65. . . . . 70 D6
Canal Cotts CW5 . . . . 187 D6
Canal Rd CW12 . . . . 156 F1
Canal Reach WA7 . . . . 24 C2
Canalside CH65 . . . . 70 D6
Canal Side
Barnton CW8 . . . . 78 B2
Chester CH1 . . . . 237 C3
Macclesfield SK11 . . . . . . 112 F7
Moore WA4 . . . . 25 C5
Runcorn WA7 . . . . 48 D7
Warrington WA4 . . . . 17 C1

Canal Side *continued*
Whaley Bridge SK23 39 F1
Canalside Cotts CW11 175 C3
Canal Side Cotts WA7 50 F6
Canalside Ind Est CH65 70 D7
Canal St
Chester CH1 237 A3
Congleton CW12 156 E2
Macclesfield SK10 112 E8
Newton-le-Willows WA12 1 F3
Runcorn WA7 23 B2
Whaley Bridge SK23 65 E8
Canal Terr CW10 151 D8
Canberra Ave WA2 8 D3
Canberra Rd SK7 35 F5
Canberra Sq WA2 8 D2
Canberra Way [1] CH1 117 D4
Candelan Way WA16 29 C4
Candle La CW3 232 B2
Candleston Cl WA5 7 E1
Candy La SK10 62 C8
Canford Cl
Crewe CW1 190 B8
Warrington WA5 15 C6
Cannell Ct WA7 50 A6
Cannell St [4] WA5 15 D4
Canning St CH1 237 A3
Canniswood Rd WA11 1 A6
Cann La CW9 55 A6
Cann Lane N WA4 26 E5
Cann Lane S WA4 26 F4
Cannock Cl CH66 94 E8
Cannonbury Cl WA7 50 A8
Cannon St CH65 70 A5
Cannon Way CH4 161 A7
Canon Dr WA14 31 B8
Canons Rd WA5 15 D6
Canon St WA7 22 F3
Canon Wilson Cl WA11 1 D6
Canterbury Cl CH66 94 E8
Canterbury Rd
Blacon CH1 117 F5
Widnes WA8 22 C8
Canterbury St WA4 16 C4
Cantilever Gdns WA4 16 E2
Cantley Cl WA7 49 D6
Canton Pl CW8 103 D7
Canton St SK11 112 D6
Canton Wlks SK11 112 D6
Canute Pl [12] WA16 57 A2
Capeland Cl CH4 140 E5
Capel Way CW5 204 D6
CAPENHURST 94 A8
Capenhurst Ave
Crewe CW2 190 A3
Warrington WA2 9 A2
Capenhurst CE Prim Sch CH1 94 B8
Capenhurst Cl SK12 36 F4
Capenhurst Gdns CH66 69 D1
Capenhurst Grange Specl Sch CH66 69 E2
Capenhurst La
Capenhurst CH1 94 B8
Ellesmere Port CH65 70 A3
Woodbank CH1 93 F7
Capenhurst Sta CH1 69 C1
Capenhurst Tech Pk CH1 69 B1
Capesthorne Cl
Alsager ST7 193 C3
Hazel Grove SK7 36 F8
Holmes Chapel CW4 130 B3
Northwich CW9 103 F4
Sandbach CW11 175 C7
Widnes WA8 22 E8
Capesthorne Hall* SK11 110 A6
Capesthorne Rd
Crewe CW2 189 F3
Hazel Grove SK7 36 F8
High Lane SK6 37 E7
Warrington WA2 8 D2
Waverton CH3 143 B6
Wilmslow SK9 59 E5
Capesthorne Way SK11 112 F7
Capitol Wlk CW12 156 D2
Cappelle Rise ST7 209 D1
Capper Cl ST7 195 A2
Cappers La CW11 176 C2
Capper's La CW5, CW6 186 C3
Carden Ave CW7 126 B1
Cardenbrook Gr [4] SK9 34 D2
Carden Cl WA3 9 D4
Cardeston Cl WA7 49 F3
Cardiff Cl CH66 94 E8
Cardigan Cl
Macclesfield SK11 112 A8
Warrington WA5 7 D2
Cardinal Newman RC High Sch WA4 16 F5
Cardway Bsns Pk ST7 193 F3
Carey St WA8 13 B1
Carina Pk WA5 7 B2
Carisbrook Ave SK10 87 E2
Carisbrook Dr CW7 149 C7
Carisbrooke Cl CW2 205 E8
Carleton Rd SK12 37 C4
Carlett Bvd CH62 43 F5
Carlingford Rd WA4 26 B7
Carlisle Cl
Macclesfield SK11 111 F5
Mobberley WA16 58 A4
Winsford CW7 126 A1
Carlisle Rd CH1 117 E5
Carlisle St
[13] Alderley Edge SK9 60 A1
Crewe CW2 190 B2
Warrington WA4 26 C8
Carlow Cl L24 21 D2
Carlton Ave
Bramhall SK7 35 D5
Handforth SK9 34 C2
Runcorn WA7 23 D2
Saltney CH4 140 D6
Carlton Cl
Mickle Trafford CH2 119 E8
Neston CH64 41 C2
Carlton Cres CH66 69 F8
Carlton Pl CH2 119 A4
Carlton Rd
Lymm WA13 19 B5
Northwich CW9 104 B7
Carlton St
Warrington WA4 26 C8
Widnes WA8 23 A8
Carlton Way M44 11 C5
Carlyle Cl ST7 193 E8
Carlyle Cres CH66 69 E4
Carmarthen Cl
Warrington WA5 7 D2
[3] Winsford CW7 149 C7
Carmel Cl CH1 117 D3
Carmel Ct WA8 13 B4
Carmenna Dr SK7 35 F7
Carmichael Cl [6] M31 11 E3
Carnegie Cl SK10 87 A1
Carnoustie Cl
Wilmslow SK9 60 D8
Winsford CW7 126 B2
Carnoustie Dr SK10 87 D5
Carnoustie Gr WA11 1 A5
Carol Dr CH60 41 C8
Carolina Rd [2] WA5 15 B7
Caroline Ho CH1 117 F6
Caroline St
Irlam M44 11 F8
Widnes WA8 23 B7
Carol St WA4 16 D4
Carpenter Gr WA2 9 A1
Carpenters Ct SK9 60 A1
Carr Brook Cl SK23 65 E5
Carr Brow SK6 38 A7
Carrgreen La WA13 19 F6
Carriage Cl L24 21 D1
Carriage Dr
Biddulph ST8 179 E1
Frodsham WA6 74 A6
Northwich CW8 103 C5
Carriage Ho CW1 190 A5
Carrick Dr CH65 70 B2
Carrick Rd CH4 141 B7
Carrington Cl WA3 9 C4
Carrington Way CW1 190 B8
Carrington Wlk WA1 16 C6
Carr La
Alderley Edge SK9 59 D2
Audley ST7 209 A1
Golborne WA3 4 A7
Golborne, Wash End WN7 4 E8
Hale L24, WA8 21 E4
Carr Mill Mews SK9 34 B1
Carroll Dr CW2 205 F8
Carrs Ct SK9 60 B7
Carrs La CH3 166 F1
Carr St ST7 195 F1
Carrwood
Altrincham WA15 32 B7
Knutsford WA16 57 C1
Carr Wood Ave SK7 35 E8
Carrwood Cl WA11 1 A6
Carrwood Rd SK9 59 F8
Carsdale Rd M22 33 E8
Car St CH1 237 C3
Carter Ave CW6 122 D4
Carter Bench Ho SK10 63 A1
Carter Cl CW5 204 D6
Carter La SK11 84 B4
Carter St CH1 237 C3
Cartier Cl WA5 7 C1
Cartlake Cl CW5 204 C5
Cartledge Cl CW8 102 A3
Cartmel Ave WA2 8 C3
Cartmel Cl
Holmes Chapel CW4 130 A3
Macclesfield SK10 87 B2
Warrington WA5 7 E2
Winsford CW7 126 D2
Cartmel Dr CH66 69 F2
Cartmell Cl WA7 49 B6
Cartridge La WA4 27 E6
Cartwright Rd CW1 191 D5
Cartwright St
Runcorn WA7 23 C2
Warrington WA5 15 E6
Carver Ave CW4 130 A6
Carver Cl CW7 127 A4
Case Rd WA11 1 D6
Casey La CW2 206 F4
Cassia Green La CW7 125 D5
Cassia La CW7, CW8 125 E5
Cassley Rd L24 21 A3
Casson St CW1 190 B5
Castle Bank CW8 103 E7
Castle Cl
Broughton CH5 139 B6
Kelsall CW6 122 D4
Pulford CH4 162 D2
Castle Croft Rd CH4 141 B5
Castle Ct
Holt LL13 196 E8
[17] Nantwich CW5 204 E5
Northwich CW8 103 E7
Castle Dr
Chester CH1 237 B1
Ellesmere Port CH65 70 A3
Heswall CH60 40 F8
Castle Farm SY14 200 E3
CASTLEFIELDS 23 F2
Castlefields CH3 166 C3
Castlefields Avenue E WA7 24 A2
Castlefields Avenue N WA7 23 F2
Castlefields Avenue S WA7 24 A1
Castleford Dr SK10 86 E6
Castlegate
Prestbury SK10 86 E6
Wrexham LL13 196 D8
Castlegate Mews SK10 86 F6
Castle Gdns LL13 196 E8
Castle Gn WA5 7 B2
Castlehill CH4 162 C2
Castle Hill
Newton-le-Willows WA12 2 E4
Prestbury SK10 86 E6
Castle Hill Ct SK10 86 F7
Castle Hill Farm [3] CW8 103 E8
Castle Ho ST7 195 C3
Castle Inn Rd CW12 179 C7
Castlemead Wlk CW9 103 E4
Castlemere Cl CH4 139 A3
Castlemere Dr CW1 190 C7
Castle Mews LL13 196 E8
Castle Mill La WA15 32 B5
Castle Park Arts Ctr WA6 74 A8
Castle Prim Sch ST7 195 D6
Castle Rd
Mow Cop ST7 195 D7
Runcorn WA7 49 F8
Castle Rise
Prestbury SK10 86 F6
Runcorn WA7 23 D2
Castle St
Chester CH1 237 B1
[1] Crewe CW1 190 C4
Holt LL13 196 D8
Macclesfield SK11 112 D8
[5] Nantwich CW5 204 E5
Northwich CW8 103 F8
Widnes WA8 13 D1
Castleton Dr SK6 37 F6
CASTLETOWN 197 D3
Castletown Cl SK10 87 C4
Castletown La CH3 197 D2
Castleview Prim Sch WA7 49 D8
Castleview Rd ST7 195 B3
Castleway WA15 32 C7
Castle Way CH4 162 A6
Castner Ave WA7 48 E7
Catalan Cl CW7 127 A1
Catalyst Ind Est WA8 23 A6
Catalyst - Science Discovery Ctr & Mus* WA8 23 A5
Catalyst Trade Pk WA8 23 A6
Catchpenny La SK11 108 F3
Catford Cl WA8 12 C2
Catfoss Cl WA2 8 E1
Cathcart Gn CH3 119 F5
Catherine Ct/Llys Catrin CH5 139 B6
Catherine St
Chester CH1 118 B2
Crewe CW2 190 D2
Macclesfield SK11 112 C8
Warrington WA5 16 A7
Widnes WA8 23 A7
Catherine Way WA12 2 B2
Catholic High Sch The CH4 141 D6
Catterall Ave WA2 8 D2
Caughall Rd CH2 95 E2
Caunce Ave
Golborne WA3 3 A7
Haydock WA11 1 B6
Newton-le-Willows WA12 2 C1
Causeway Ave WA4 16 C3
Causeway Park WA4 16 C3
Cavalier Dr CH1 117 E6
Cavan Dr WA11 1 D7
Cavell Dr CH65 70 A4
Cavendish Ave WA3 9 F5
Cavendish Cl
[5] Macclesfield SK10 87 D3
Warrington WA5 15 D7
Winsford CW7 149 A8
Cavendish Cres ST7 193 D5
Cavendish Ct
Chester CH4 141 A5
Widnes WA8 12 F1
Cavendish Farm Rd WA7 49 A5
Cavendish Gdns CH65 70 A4
Cavendish Mews SK9 60 A6
Cavendish Pl WA3 9 F5
Cavendish Rd
Chester CH4 141 B6
Crewe CW2 189 E5
Hazel Grove SK7 36 E8
Cavendish Specl Sch WA7 49 C5
Cavendish St [7] WA7 22 F2
Cavendish Way CW4 130 A3
Caversham Cl WA4 26 E6
Cawdor Dr CH3 119 A2
Cawdor St
Runcorn WA7 22 F3
Warrington WA4 26 C8
Cawfield Ave WA8 12 D1
Cawley Ave WA3 4 E4
Cawley La SK10 62 E7
Cawley St
[8] Macclesfield SK11 112 E7
Runcorn WA7 23 A1
Cawood Cl CH66 69 B5
Cawthorne Ave WA4 17 A2
Caxton Cl
Ellesmere Port CH66 69 E4
Widnes WA8 12 C3
Cecil Rd ST8 179 C2
Cecil Rigby Cl [1] CW11 175 B6
Cecil St CH3 119 A1
Cedab Rd CH65 70 C6
Cedar Ave
Alsager ST7 193 D3
Aston WA7 50 B4
Connah's Quay CH5 91 C1
Connah's Quay, Garden City CH5 116 A7
Ellesmere Port CH66 69 D6
Golborne WA3 3 F7
Kidsgrove ST7 194 D1
Runcorn WA7 49 C7
Widnes WA8 13 B2
Cedar Cl
Connah's Quay CH5 116 A7
Holmes Chapel CW4 130 D4
Lostock Gralam CW9 80 A3
Middlewich CW10 151 E6
Poynton SK12 36 E3
Sandbach CW11 175 C5
Cedar Cres
Audley ST7 209 F1
Newton-le-Willows WA12 2 D2
Cedar Ct
Alsager ST7 193 E4
Congleton CW12 178 F8
Culcheth WA3 4 F1
Willaston CW5 205 D6
Cedardale Dr CH66 94 F8
Cedardale Pk WA8 13 E4
Cedar Dr
Barnton CW8 78 A4
Chester CH2 119 B4
Cedarfield Rd WA13 19 B4
Cedar Gr
Chester CH2 119 B4
Haydock WA11 1 E7
Macclesfield SK11 112 D5
Nantwich CW5 205 A5
Neston CH64 66 F8
Warrington, Latchford WA4 16 D3
Warrington WA1 17 A7
Winsford CW7 127 A1
Cedar Ho CH3 142 B8
Cedar Lo SK7 35 F7
Cedar Mews CH1 117 E4
Cedar Pk CH3 119 C2
Cedar Rd
Newcastle-under-Lyme ST5 210 D1
Partington M31 11 E3
Warrington WA5 14 F6
Weaverham CW8 102 C8
Cedars SK9 59 F6
Cedar St WA12 2 C2
Cedars The
Alsager ST7 193 D3
Mobberley WA16 58 E2
Nantwich CW5 204 D5
[7] Northwich CW9 103 E6
Cedarway
Bollington SK10 88 A7
Heswall CH60 41 B5
Wilmslow SK9 59 F5
Cedar Way CW2 206 B7
Cedarways WA4 26 D5
Cedarwood CH4 101 D5
Cedarwood Ct CW6 146 C3
Celandine Cl CH3 142 A7
Celandine Way WA9 6 B7
Celyn Cres CH4 140 D5
Cement Pl CH1 237 B3
Cemetery Rd CW2 207 B5
Cemlyn Cl CH1 117 E3
Centenary Ho WA7 49 C8
Centenary Pl CW12 156 E3
Central Ave
Alsager CW2 192 F1
Ellesmere Port CH65 70 C4
Warrington, Latchford WA4 16 B3
Warrington WA2 16 C8
Central Dr
Barnton CW8 78 A3
Gatley SK8 34 D8
Haydock WA11 1 B6
Central Expressway WA7 49 E7
Central Gr CW9 104 D6
Central Pl SK9 60 B7
Central Rd
Northwich CW9 104 D7
Partington M31 11 F3
Warrington WA4 16 C3
Central St ST7 195 B6
Central Trad Pk CH4 140 E7
Central Way
Newton-le-Willows WA12 2 E2
Warrington WA2 16 B6
Centre Ct ST7 193 E4
Centre Park WA1 16 A4
Centre Park Sq WA1 16 A4
Centurion Cl WA3 9 D4
Centurion Row WA7 23 F2
Centurion Way CW10 128 D2
Century Rd ST5 210 F2
Century Way SK10 87 F2
Cestria Cl CW11 174 D7
Chads Gn CW5 206 A1
Chadwell Ct CW2 207 E4
Chadwick Ave
Croft WA3 9 B7
Warrington WA4 16 E1
Chadwick Cl SK9 34 C1
Chadwicke Cl CW5 204 F4
Chadwick Fields Orch CW10 151 D6
Chadwick Pl WA3 9 E5
Chadwick Rd
Middlewich CW10 151 C6
Runcorn WA7 23 E3
Chadwick Terr SK10 87 E1
Chaffinch Cl
Congleton CW12 156 E1
Warrington WA3 9 F3
Chaffinch Way CW7 149 D6
Chaigeley Sch WA4 17 E4
Chain Maker's Row CH4 140 E7
Chaise Mdw WA13 19 C5
Chaley Rise CH3 182 D1
Chalfield Ave CH66 69 C5
Chalfield Cl
[1] Ellesmere Port CH66 69 C5
Wistaston CW2 206 B7
Chalfont Cl WA4 26 E6
Chalfont Cres CW2 207 B2
Chalfont Ct WA16 57 C3
Chalgrave Cl WA8 13 F3
Chalkwell Dr CH60 41 C7
Challinor St CH3 119 A1
Chamber Brook La WA6 75 C2
Chamberlain Ct CW1 191 C4
Chamberlain Dr SK9 34 D1
Chambers St CW2 190 D2
Chance Hall La CW12, ST7 177 C3
Chancel La SK9 60 B8
Chancellor Rd WA7 24 D5
Chancery La
Alsager ST7 193 B3
Bollington SK10 88 B7
Chandlers Ct WA7 22 E1
Chandler Way WA3 3 E8
Chandos Cl CH4 141 E6
Change La CH64 68 B8
Channel The CH1 95 B4
Chantler Ave WA4 16 E4
Chantry Ave CW8 103 B4
Chantry Cl SK12 38 E5
Chantry Ct
Chester CH1 117 E2
Crewe CW1 190 D4
Macclesfield SK11 112 D5
Chantry Fold SK12 38 E6
Chantry Rd SK12 38 E6
Chantry The CW6 169 E2
Chantry Wlk CH60 41 A6
Chapel Ave WA6 75 C2
Chapel Bank ST7 195 D6
Chapel Cl
Audlem CW3 229 F3
Cholmondeston CW7 170 F4
Comberbach CW9 78 D7
Ellesmere Port CH65 70 C7
Mount Pleasant ST7 195 B6
Saughall CH1 94 A1
Waverton CH3 143 A5
Chapel Cotts CH3 143 A5
Chapel Croft SK11 84 B3
Chapel Cross Rd WA2 9 A2
Chapel Ct
Northwich CW9 103 F7
Wilmslow SK9 60 A6
Chapel Dr WA15 32 C7
Chapelfields WA6 74 A8
Chapel Gn CW6 122 C5
Chapel House La CH64 93 A7
Chapel House Mews [5] WA3 3 D8
Chapel La
Acton Bridge CW8 76 E4
Aldford CH3 164 D5
Allostock WA16 106 E3
Altrincham WA15 32 C7
Appleton Thorn WA4 27 B4
Audley ST7 209 D2
Burtonwood WA5 6 F6
Chester CH3 119 A1
Crewe CW1 173 D1
Dutton WA4 77 B7
Hargrave CH3 144 A1
Harriseahead ST7 195 E4
Hollins Green WA3 10 F1
Holt LL13 196 D8
Kelsall CW6 122 E2
Kingsley WA6 75 C2
Ledsham CH66 68 F1
Manley WA6, CH3 98 F3
Mere WA16 30 B4
Milton Green CH3 165 B2
Moulton CW9 126 E8
Norton in Hales TF9 236 C2
Partington M31 11 F2
Rainow SK10 88 E5
Ravensmoor CW5 203 D2
Rode Heath ST7 193 F7
Saighton CH3 142 E1
Threapwood SY14 222 E8
Warrington WA4 26 C8
Widnes WA8 12 C4
Wilmslow SK9 60 A6
Windyharbour SK11 109 D2
Woodbank CH1 93 E8
Chapel Lodge CH1 237 C3
Chapelmere Cl CW11 174 E7
Chapelmere Ct CW1 190 C7

Chapel Mews
Alsager ST7 . . . . 193 C3
Ellesmere Port CH65 . . . . . 70 B4
Elton CH2 . . . . 72 B3
▮ Nantwich CW5 . . . . 204 E5
Chapel Rd
Alderley Edge SK9 . . . . 60 A1
Horwich End SK23 . . . . 65 E5
Ollerton WA16 . . . . 82 E2
Warrington WA5 . . . . 14 E3
Wilmslow SK9 . . . . 61 A8
Winsford CW7 . . . . 126 F1
Chapel Rise SY14 . . . . . 213 B3
Chapel Row
Barbridge CW5 . . . . 187 D6
Nantwich CW5 . . . . 204 D5
Chapel St
▮ Alderley Edge SK9 . . . . . 60 A1
Audley ST7 . . . . 209 E3
Bollington SK10 . . . . 88 B8
Chester CH3 . . . . 237 C3
Congleton CW12 . . . . 156 D2
Crewe CW2 . . . . 190 D3
Haydock WA11 . . . . 1 E6
Holt LL13 . . . . 196 D8
Kidsgrove ST7 . . . . 194 D2
Macclesfield SK11 . . . . 112 D6
Moulton CW9 . . . . 126 E8
Mount Pleasant ST7 . . . . . 195 B6
New Mills SK22 . . . . 39 B6
Newton-le-Willows WA12 . . 2 B3
Northwich CW8 . . . . 103 F7
Sandbach CW11 . . . . 175 B6
Sandbach, Wheelock
  CW11 . . . . 175 A3
Weaverham CW8 . . . . 77 C1
Whaley Bridge SK23 . . . . . . 65 E8
Widnes WA8 . . . . 23 A7
Wincham CW9 . . . . 79 C3
Chapel Terr WA3 . . . . 4 B8
Chapel View
Bebington CH62 . . . . 44 A6
Helsby WA6 . . . . 73 B2
Chapel Wlk WA3 . . . . 4 B8
Chapel Wlks
Broomedge WA13 . . . . 19 D1
Cheadle SK8 . . . . 35 B6
Chapel Yd WA2 . . . . 16 A6
Chapman Cl WA8 . . . . . . 12 D4
Charcoal Rd WA14 . . . . . 20 F3
Charity La
Macclesfield Forest
  SK11 . . . . 114 B6
Macclesfield SK11 . . . . 113 F8
Charlcote Cres CW2 . . . 206 C8
Charlecote Rd SK12 . . . . . 36 F4
Charles Ave
Davenham CW9 . . . . 103 F2
Warrington WA5 . . . . 14 F6
Charles Cres CH4 . . . . . 237 C1
Charles Ct CW2 . . . . 190 C3
Charles Darwin Prim Sch
  CW8 . . . . 103 E7
Charles Forbes Ct ▮
  WA1 . . . . 16 B5
Charles Price Gdns ▮
  CH65 . . . . 70 C6
Charles Rd CH2 . . . . 95 C1
Charles Sq CW11 . . . . . . 175 F2
Charles St
Chester CH1 . . . . 237 B3
Chester, Hoole Park CH2 . . 118 F3
▮ Crewe CW1 . . . . 190 C4
Irlam M44 . . . . 11 E6
Widnes WA8 . . . . 23 A8
Charleston Cl CH66 . . . . . 69 D2
Charleston Gr WA5 . . . . . 15 B6
Charlesworth Cl SK23 . . . 39 D3
Charlesworth Cres SK23 . 39 D3
Charlesworth Ct CW1 . . . 175 C6
Charlesworth Pl ▮
  CW12 . . . . 156 F4
Charlesworth Rd SK23 . . . 39 D3
Charlesworth St CW1 . . . 190 D6
Charlock Wlk ▮ M31 . . . . 11 F3
Charlotte Cl CH1 . . . . . . 237 B3
Charlotte Gr ▮ WA5 . . . . 15 C7
Charlotte St
Chester CH1 . . . . 237 B3
Macclesfield SK11 . . . . 112 D7
Charlotte Street W ▮
  SK11 . . . . 112 C8
Charlotte Wlk ▮ WA8 . . . 23 B7
Charlton Cl WA7 . . . . 50 A7
Charlton Ct CH2 . . . . 119 A4
Charlton St
▮ Macclesfield SK11 . . . . . 112 C8
Warrington WA4 . . . . 16 F3
Charminster Cl WA5 . . . . 15 B5
Charmouth Cl WA2 . . . . . . 8 B4
Charnock Ave WA12 . . . . . 1 F3
Charnock Rd WA3 . . . . 4 F3
Charnwood
High Lane SK6 . . . . 37 F7
Kidsgrove ST7 . . . . 195 B1
Charnwood Cl
Macclesfield SK10 . . . . 87 A1
Warrington WA3 . . . . 10 B5
Charnwood Cres SK7 . . . . 36 D8
Charon Way WA5 . . . . 7 B3
Charter Ave WA5 . . . . 14 E8
Charter Cres CH66 . . . . . 69 E3
Charterhall Dr CH2 . . . . . 118 F2
Charterhouse Cl CH65 . . . 70 E5
Charter Rd SK10 . . . . 88 A7
Charter St WA5 . . . . 87 F3
Chartley Gr CW10 . . . . . 128 D2
Chartwell Gdns WA4 . . . . 26 F5

Chartwell Gr CW7 . . . . . 149 C5
Chartwell Pk CW11 . . . . . 175 A4
Chase Dr CH66 . . . . 69 E2
Chase Mdw WA13 . . . . . . 19 B5
Chaser Ct CH1 . . . . 117 F3
Chase The
Bebington CH63 . . . . 43 C5
▮ Heswall CH60 . . . . 41 A8
Chasewater WA7 . . . . 24 F4
Chase Way CH66 . . . . 69 E2
Chassagne Sq CW1 . . . . 189 F7
Chatburn Ct WA3 . . . . 4 F2
Chater Dr CW5 . . . . 204 F3
Chatfield Dr WA3 . . . . 9 E3
Chatham St ▮ SK11 . . . . 112 D8
Chatham Way CW1 . . . . . 191 C5
Chatsworth Ave
Culcheth WA3 . . . . 4 F4
Macclesfield SK11 . . . . 111 E6
Chatsworth Cl
Ellesmere Port CH66 . . . . . 69 C5
Northwich CW9 . . . . 104 A5
Wistaston CW2 . . . . 206 A7
Chatsworth Dr
Chester CH2 . . . . 119 A5
Congleton CW12 . . . . 155 F3
Widnes WA8 . . . . 13 C3
Chatsworth Ho CH1 . . . . . 118 B3
Chatsworth Rd
Hazel Grove SK7 . . . . 36 F8
High Lane SK6 . . . . 37 F6
Wilmslow SK9 . . . . 59 E4
Chatteris Pk WA7 . . . . 24 E2
Chatterton Dr WA7 . . . . . . 50 E8
Chatterton Ho ▮ CW5 . . . 204 E5
Chaucer Cl CH1 . . . . 117 E6
Chaucer Gr CW11 . . . . . . 174 C5
Chaucer Pl WA4 . . . . 16 F4
Chaucer St WA7 . . . . 23 A1
CHEADLE HULME 35 A8
Cheadle Hulme High Sch
  SK8 . . . . 35 B7
Cheadle Hulme Sch SK8 . . 35 A8
Cheadle La WA16 . . . . 81 A1
Cheadle Wood SK8 . . . . . . 34 E8
CHECKLEY 221 C1
Checkley Dr ST8 . . . . 179 D1
CHECKLEY GREEN 232 B8
Checkley La CW3, CW5 . . 221 E1
Checkley Rd ST5 . . . . 210 C1
Checkley Row CW5 . . . . . 232 C8
Cheddar Gr WA5 . . . . 6 F7
Cheddington Cl SK3 . . . . . 34 E8
Chedlee Dr SK8 . . . . 34 E8
Chedworth Dr WA8 . . . . . . 12 C4
Chedworth Ho ▮ CH1 . . . 237 C3
Cheerbrook Rd CW5 . . . . 205 D4
Cheese Hill La WA6, CW8 . 101 B4
CHELFORD 84 B2
Chelford Ave WA3 . . . . 3 D8
Chelford CE Prim Sch
  SK11 . . . . 84 A3
Chelford Cl
Chester CH1 . . . . 117 F1
Warrington WA4 . . . . 26 C8
Chelford Dr CW9 . . . . 103 F5
Chelford La WA16 . . . . 83 C1
Chelford Mews ▮ CH3 . . 119 B1
Chelford Rd
Chelford, Marthall WA16,
  SK11 . . . . 83 D4
Chelford SK10, SK11 . . . . . 84 D1
Congleton CW12 . . . . 155 E6
Goostrey CW4 . . . . 131 B7
Handforth SK9 . . . . 34 D5
Macclesfield SK10, SK11 . 111 C8
Monks Heath SK10 . . . . . . 85 B1
Nether Alderley SK9 . . . . . . 84 C7
Ollerton WA16 . . . . 82 D7
Prestbury SK10 . . . . 86 D5
Whisterfield SK11 . . . . 109 F3
Chelford Rdbt SK11 . . . . . 84 B1
Chelford Sta SK11 . . . . . . 84 A2
Chells Hill CW11 . . . . 176 C1
Chell St CW1 . . . . 190 B5
Chelsea Cl ST8 . . . . 179 C1
Chelsea Gdns WA5 . . . . . . 15 C4
Chelston Dr SK8 . . . . 34 C6
Cheltenham Cl
▮ Macclesfield SK10 . . . . . 87 C4
Warrington WA5 . . . . 15 A8
Cheltenham Cres
Crewe CW1 . . . . 190 B7
Runcorn WA7 . . . . 49 B6
Cheltenham Dr WA12 . . . . . 2 C5
Cheltenham Rd CH65 . . . . 70 D3
Chemical St WA12 . . . . 2 B3
Cheney Wlk CW2 . . . . . . 206 D8
Chepstow Cl
Biddulph ST8 . . . . 179 C1
Macclesfield SK10 . . . . 87 C4
Warrington WA5 . . . . 7 E3
▮ Winsford CW7 . . . . 149 C7
Cherington Cl SK9 . . . . . . 34 F3
Cherington Cres SK11 . . . 112 B7
Cheriton Way CW2 . . . . . 206 A8
Cherrington Rd CW1 . . . . 190 E6
Cherry Blossom Rd WA7 . . 49 F4
Cherry Brow Terr CH64 . . 67 F8
Cherry Cl
Newcastle-under-Lyme
  ST5 . . . . 210 D1
Newton-le-Willows WA12 . . . 1 F4
Willaston CH64 . . . . 67 C8
Cherry Cnr WA13 . . . . 28 A7
Cherry Cres CW7 . . . . . . 149 C8
Cherry Dale Rd WA4 . . . . 139 A3
Cherryfields Rd SK11 . . . 111 F8

Cherry Gdns CH3 . . . . . . 119 A1
Cherry Gr
Ellesmere Port CH66 . . . . . 70 A1
Nantwich CW5 . . . . 204 F3
Cherry Grove Prim Sch ▮
  CH3 . . . . 119 A1
Cherry Grove Rd CH3 . . . 119 A1
Cherry La
Congleton CW12 . . . . 179 E8
Cuddington CW8 . . . . 101 F2
Lawton Heath ST7 . . . . . . 193 E6
Lymm WA13 . . . . 18 C1
Weaverham CW8 . . . . 102 D8
Cherry Orch/Y Berllan
  Geirios LL13 . . . . 196 D8
Cherry Rd CH3 . . . . 119 A1
Cherrysutton WA8 . . . . . . 12 B3
Cherrysutton Mews WA8 . 12 B4
Cherry Tree Ave
Barnton CW8 . . . . 78 A4
Lawton-gate ST7 . . . . 194 A5
Lymm WA13 . . . . 18 D2
Poynton SK12 . . . . 36 F3
Runcorn WA7 . . . . 49 C8
Warrington WA5 . . . . 14 F4
Cherry Tree Cl
Elton CH2 . . . . 72 B4
Hale L24 . . . . 21 E1
Haydock WA11 . . . . 1 A5
▮ Wilmslow SK9 . . . . 60 E8
Cherry Tree Ct CW5 . . . . 205 A4
Cherry Tree Dr
Hazel Grove SK7 . . . . 37 A8
St Helens WA9 . . . . 1 A2
Cherry Tree Ho SK9 . . . . . 85 C8
Cherry Tree La
Rostherne WA14 . . . . 30 E6
Woore CW3 . . . . 232 C2
Cherry Tree Mews ▮
  CH60 . . . . 41 A8
Cherry Tree Prim Sch
  WA13 . . . . 18 C2
Cherry Tree Rd
Audley ST7 . . . . 209 F1
Crewe CW1 . . . . 190 E6
Golborne WA3 . . . . 3 F8
Newcastle-under-Lyme
  ST5 . . . . 210 E1
Whitchurch SY13 . . . . 225 D2
Winsford CW7 . . . . 125 F2
Woodford SK7 . . . . 35 E2
Cherry Tree Way CW12 . . 156 E2
Cherry Wlk
Cheadle SK8 . . . . 35 C8
Partington M31 . . . . 11 D2
Swan Green WA16 . . . . . . 106 D7
Cherrywood Cres CW8 . . . 78 B4
Cherwell Cl
Cheadle SK8 . . . . 35 A7
Warrington WA2 . . . . 8 D2
Cheryl Ct CW8 . . . . 102 A4
Cheryl Dr WA8 . . . . 13 D1
Chester Aero Pk CH4 . . . 118 A3
Chester Roman
  Amphitheatre *
  CH1 . . . . 237 B2
Chester Row WA12 . . . . . . 7 D8
Chester's Croft Pk SK8 . . . 35 A5
Chester Sq CW1 . . . . 190 C4
Chester St
Chester CH4 . . . . 140 F7
▮ Crewe CW1 . . . . 190 C4
Widnes WA8 . . . . 13 B1
Chester Sta CH1 . . . . 237 C3
Chesterton Cl CW10 . . . . 151 E5
Chesterton Ct CH2 . . . . . 118 D4
Chesterton Dr
Crewe CW2 . . . . 189 F1
Winwick WA2 . . . . 8 A5
Chesterton Gr CW11 . . . . 174 D5
Chesterton Way CW2 . . . 207 B3
Chester Trad Pk CH1 . . . . 117 F2
Chester Visitor Ctr *
  CH1 . . . . 237 B2
Chester Way CW9 . . . . . . 104 A8
Chester West Employment
  Pk CH1 . . . . 117 E2
Chester Zoo * CH2 . . . . . 95 E1
Chester Zoological Gdns *
  CH2 . . . . 118 D8
Chestnut Ave
▮ Ellesmere Port CH66 . . . 69 F1
Irlam M44 . . . . 11 D5
Macclesfield SK10 . . . . 87 E2
Rode Heath ST7 . . . . 193 F7
Shavington CW2 . . . . 206 C5
Warrington WA5 . . . . 14 F6
Widnes WA8 . . . . 13 B2
Chestnut Cl
Chester CH2 . . . . 119 A3
Cuddington CW8 . . . . 101 F2
Middlewich CW10 . . . . 128 B2
Tarporley CH6 . . . . 146 C2
Willaston WA8 . . . . 60 E8
Chestnut Ct
Tarporley CW6 . . . . 146 C2
Widnes WA8 . . . . 12 D1
Chestnut Dr
Alsager ST7 . . . . 193 E2
Congleton CW12 . . . . 156 A4
Holmes Chapel CW4 . . . . 130 D3
Poynton SK12 . . . . 36 F3
Chestnut Gr
Barnton CW8 . . . . 78 B4
Bebington CH62 . . . . 43 D8
Crewe CW1 . . . . 190 E5
Golborne WA3 . . . . 3 F8
Newcastle-under-Lyme
  ST5 . . . . 210 E1
Winsford CW7 . . . . 149 C8
Chestnut Grange CH4 . . . 141 B7
Chestnut Ho ▮ CW11 . . . 175 B6
Chestnut La WA3 . . . . 3 E4
Chestnut Lodge Sch WA8 . 13 B3
Chestnut Mews WA16 . . . 58 E1
Chestnuts The CH64 . . . . . 67 F8
Chestnut Wlk M31 . . . . . . 11 D2

Chester La CW7 . . . . 125 D2
Chester New Rd WA4 . . . . 25 F7
Chester Race Course *
  CH1 . . . . 237 A1
Chester Rd
Aston CW5 . . . . 204 A6
Aston WA7 . . . . 50 B4
Audley ST7 . . . . 209 D2
Barbridge CW5 . . . . 187 D5
Broughton CH4 . . . . 139 D5
Churton CH3 . . . . 180 F6
Connah's Quay CH6 . . . . . . 91 A3
Cuddington CW8 . . . . 101 D1
Daresbury WA4 . . . . 25 B1
Delamere CW6, CW8 . . . . 123 C5
Dunham-on-the-Hill CH2,
  WA6 . . . . 97 D5
Ellesmere Port, Great Sutton
  CH66 . . . . 69 D4
Ellesmere Port, Whitby CH65,
  CH66 . . . . 70 A2
Frodsham WA6 . . . . 74 A7
Gatesheath CH3 . . . . 165 E5
Grappenhall WA4 . . . . 17 B1
Hartford CW8 . . . . 102 E3
Hartford, Greenbank CW8 . 103 C6
Hazel Grove SK7 . . . . 36 D8
Helsby WA6 . . . . 73 C4
Heswall CH60, CH64 . . . . . 41 C6
Higher Walton WA4 . . . . . . 25 F5
Holmes Chapel CW4 . . . . 130 B2
Huntington CH3 . . . . 142 A6
Kelsall CW6 . . . . 122 D5
Lavister LL12 . . . . 162 C1
Macclesfield SK11 . . . . 112 B8
Malpas SY14 . . . . 213 B4
Mere WA16 . . . . 56 B6
Middlewich CW10 . . . . 128 B2
Neston CH64 . . . . 66 E7
Over Tabley WA16 . . . . 56 A2
Plumley WA16 . . . . 80 E5
Poynton SK12 . . . . 36 B4
Rostherne WA14, WA16 . . . 30 C5
Runcorn WA7 . . . . 50 A6
Saltney CH4 . . . . 140 C6
Sandycroft CH5 . . . . 116 A2
Talke ST7 . . . . 210 D7
Warrington WA4 . . . . 16 D4
Whitchurch SY13 . . . . 225 D2
Winsford CW7 . . . . 125 F2
Woodford SK7 . . . . 35 E2
Chester Ret Pk CW4 . . . . 118 A3

Chetton Dr WA7 . . . . 50 E7
Chetwode Mews WA4 . . . 52 C2
Chetwode St CW1 . . . . . . 190 C5
Chetwood Cl WA12 . . . . . . 2 B5
Chetwood Dr WA8 . . . . . . 12 F4
Cheveley Cl SK10 . . . . 87 C2
Chevin Gdns SK7 . . . . 36 A7
Cheviot Ave WA2 . . . . 8 A3
Cheviot Cl CH66 . . . . 69 A6
Cheviot Ct CW7 . . . . 149 B7
Cheviot Sq CW7 . . . . 149 B7
Chevron Cl CH1 . . . . 117 E4
Chevron Hey CH1 . . . . . . 117 E4
Cheyne Wlk CW5 . . . . . . 204 E3
Cheyney Rd CH1 . . . . 118 B3
Chicago Ave M90 . . . . 33 B7
Chicago Pl WA5 . . . . 15 B6
Chichester Cl
Grappenhall Heys WA4 . . . 27 A7
Runcorn WA7 . . . . 50 D6
Chichester Ct CH1 . . . . . . 237 A3
Chichester St CH1 . . . . . . 237 A3
Chidlow Cl
Hough CW2 . . . . 206 E2
Widnes WA2 . . . . 23 A5
Chilco Cl CH66 . . . . 69 F2
Childer Cres CH66 . . . . . . 69 B7
Childer Gdns CH66 . . . . . 69 B7
CHILDER THORNTON 69 B8
Childer Thornton Prim Sch
  CH66 . . . . 69 B8
Child's La CW12 . . . . 177 E6
Childwall Ct CH66 . . . . . . 69 F8
Childwall Gdns CH66 . . . . 69 F8
Childwall Rd CH66 . . . . . . 69 F8
Chilham Cl CW7 . . . . 149 C7
Chilham Pl SK11 . . . . 111 F6
Chilington Ave WA8 . . . . . 22 D8
Chillingham Cl CW10 . . . . 128 D2
Chiltern Ave SK11 . . . . . . 112 A7
Chiltern Cl
Chester CH4 . . . . 141 B5
Crewe CW2 . . . . 207 B1
Cuddington CW8 . . . . 102 A2
Chiltern Cres WA2 . . . . 8 A3
Chiltern Ct SK10 . . . . 87 D3
Chiltern Pl WA2 . . . . 8 A3
Chiltern Rd
Culcheth WA3 . . . . 4 E4
St Helens WA9 . . . . 1 A3
Warrington WA4 . . . . 8 A3
Chilton Dr CW7 . . . . 149 B7
Chilton Dr CH66 . . . . 69 F2
Chilwell Cl WA8 . . . . 12 D4
Chilworth Cl CW2 . . . . . . 206 C8
China La WA4 . . . . 16 C2
Chines The CW8 . . . . 101 D5
Chippingdale Cl WA5 . . . . 15 C5
Chipstead Cl CW8 . . . . . . 103 A4
Chirk Cl CH2 . . . . 103 F6
Chirk Gdns CH65 . . . . 70 D3
Chirk Pl CW7 . . . . 126 A1
Chirton Cl WA11 . . . . 1 D7
Chisledon Cl WA11 . . . . . . 1 D7
Chislet Ct WA8 . . . . 12 E4
Chiswick Cl WA7 . . . . 50 D7
Chiswick Gdns WA4 . . . . . 26 F6
Chollerton Cl WA16 . . . . . 29 C6
Cholmley Dr WA12 . . . . . . 2 B4
Cholmondeley Castle Gdns *
  SY14 . . . . 201 A4
Cholmondeley La SY14 . . 200 F2
Cholmondeley Rd
Ellesmere Port CH65 . . . . . 69 F4
Hampton Heath SY14 . . . . 213 E7
Runcorn WA7 . . . . 49 D4
Wrenbury CW5 . . . . 216 C5
Cholmondeley St
Macclesfield SK11 . . . . 112 D6
Widnes WA8 . . . . 23 A4
CHOLMONDESTON 170 C4
Cholmondley Rise SY14 . . 214 B4
Chorlegh Grange ▮ SK9 . . 60 A1
Chorley Bank 201 E2
CHORLEY BANK 201 E2
Chorley Bank Council Hos
  CW5 . . . . 201 E1
CHORLEY GREEN 202 A1
Chorley Green La CW5,
  SY14 . . . . 201 E5
Chorley Hall Cl WA5 . . . . . 59 F1
Chorley Hall La
Alderley Edge SK9 . . . . 60 A1
Faddiley CW5 . . . . 202 C2
Chorley's La WA8 . . . . 13 E3
Chorley St WA12 . . . . 1 B6
Chorley Stock La CW5 . . . 202 C2
Chorleywood Cl SK10 . . . . 87 B4
CHORLTON 207 B1
Chorlton Cl WA7 . . . . 24 D1
Chorlton La CW2 . . . . 207 B2
CHORLTON LANE 212 B4
CHOWLEY 182 F5
Chowley Oak La CH3 . . . . 182 F6
Chrimes Dr CH9 . . . . 123 F6
Christchurch Ave CW2 . . . 190 A1
Christ Church CE Prim Sch
  Crewe CW1 . . . . 76 B1
Ellesmere Port CH65 . . . . . 70 B7
Warrington WA2 . . . . 9 A1
Christie Cl CH66 . . . . 44 A2
Christie St WA8 . . . . 13 D1
CHRISTLETON 142 E8
Christleton Ave
Crewe CW2 . . . . 189 D5
Northwich CW9 . . . . 104 A4

Christleton Ct WA7 . . . . 24 C4
Christleton Cty High Sch
CH3 . . . . 142 F7
Christleton Dr CH66 . . . . . 69 E6
Christleton Prim Sch
CH3 . . . . 142 E8
Christleton Rd CH3 . . . . . 119 A1
Christleton Sports Ctr
CH3 . . . . 142 E8
Christleton Way SK9 . . . . . 34 D5
Christopher Dr CH62 . . . . . 44 A5
Christ the King RC & CE Prim
Sch SK11 . . . . 112 D6
Christ The King RC Prim Sch
CH62 . . . . 43 E7
Church Ave SK9 . . . . 34 A2
Church Bank
Audley ST7 . . . . 209 D2
Goostrey CW4 . . . . 107 F1
Kelsall CW6 . . . . 122 D5
Tattenhall CH3 . . . . 166 B2
Church Bk SK23 . . . . 65 D7
Church CI
Handforth SK9 . . . . 34 D3
Weaverham CW8 . . . . 77 D1
Church College CI CH1 . . . 118 B3
Church Cotts
Astle SK11 . . . . 109 B8
Rainow SK10 . . . . 88 E5
Sealand CH1 . . . . 116 E6
Waverton CH3 . . . . 143 C3
Church Croft CH4 . . . . . . 162 A6
Church Ct
Ashton Hayes CH3 . . . . . 121 F8
Farndon CH3 . . . . 180 E2
Church Dr
Newton-le-Willows WA12 . . 2 C1
Warrington WA2 . . . . 9 A1
Church End L24 . . . . 21 D1
Church End Mews L24 . . . . 21 D1
Church's Ct 18 CW5 . . . . . . 204 E5
Church's Mansion ★
CW5 . . . . 204 F5
Church Farm CW5 . . . . . . 216 E4
Church Farm Ct
Heswall CH60 . . . . 40 F7
Willaston CH64 . . . . 67 F8
Churchfield Rd WA6 . . . . . . 74 C8
Churchfields
Audlem CW3 . . . . 230 A4
Barnton CW8 . . . . 78 B3
Croft WA3 . . . . 9 B7
Cuddington CW8 . . . . . . 102 B2
Helsby WA6 . . . . 73 C4
Knutsford WA16 . . . . 57 C2
Widnes WA8 . . . . 13 B5
Wybunbury CW5 . . . . . . 220 B8
Church Fields TF9 . . . . . . 236 C2
Church Gn WA13 . . . . 19 B8
CHURCH GREEN 18 E2
Church Hall CI CH1 . . . . . 117 F4
CHURCH HILL 149 D6
Church Hill WA6 . . . . 57 A2
Churchill Ave WA3 . . . . 5 B4
Churchill CI CW12 . . . . . . 156 A3
Churchill Dr CW6 . . . . . . 146 D1
Churchill Mans 16 SK6 . . . 23 A3
Churchill Parkway CW7 . 149 D8
Churchill Way
Macclesfield SK11 . . . . . 112 D8
Neston CH64 . . . . 66 E8
Church La
Alderley Edge SK9 . . . . . . 60 A2
Aldford CH3 . . . . 163 F3
Backford CH1 . . . . 95 B4
Bebington CH62 . . . . 44 A4
Bramhall SK7 . . . . 35 C2
Chester CH2 . . . . 118 D7
Congleton CW12 . . . . . . 134 E1
Culcheth WA3 . . . . 4 F3
Ellesmere Port CH66 . . . . 69 D3
Farndon CH3 . . . . 180 E1
Golborne WA3 . . . . 3 D7
Guilden Sutton CH3 . . . . 119 F5
Hargrave CH3 . . . . 144 B1
Henbury SK11 . . . . 111 C8
Huxley CH3, CW6 . . . . . . 167 C6
Lawton-gate ST7 . . . . . . 194 C4
Mobberley WA16 . . . . 58 C5
Mow Cop ST7 . . . . 195 E7
Nantwich CW5 . . . . 204 E5
Neston CH64 . . . . 66 E7
New Mills SK22 . . . . 39 C8
Rainow SK10 . . . . 88 E5
Sandbach CW11 . . . . . . 175 E7
Scholar Green ST7 . . . . . 194 C7
Smallwood CW11 . . . . . . 176 E4
Stoak CH2 . . . . 96 A7
Sutton Lane Ends SK11 . 112 F3
Warren SK11 . . . . 134 D8
Warrington WA4 . . . . 17 B1
Weaverham CW8 . . . . . . 77 D1
Wistaston CW2 . . . . 205 E8
CHURCH LAWTON 194 C3
Church Mdw TF9 . . . . . . 236 C2
Church Mdws
Little Leigh CW8 . . . . 77 D5
Whitchurch SY13 . . . . . . 226 A1
Church Mead CH3 . . . . . 181 A5
Church Meadow La CH60 . 40 F7
Church Meadow Wlk
WA8 . . . . 22 B5
Churchmere CI CW1 . . . . 190 C7
Church Mews
Bollington SK10 . . . . 88 B8

Church Mews *continued*
Higher Wincham CW9 . . . . 79 E5
Knutsford WA16 . . . . 57 B2
6 Macclesfield SK11 . . . 112 D8
CHURCH MINSHULL 172 A6
Church Par 5 CH65 . . . . . 70 C6
Church Rd
Alsager ST7 . . . . 193 C4
Ashton Hayes CH3 . . . . . 121 F8
Barnton CW8 . . . . 78 B2
Broughton CH4 . . . . 139 C4
Burwardsley CH3 . . . . . . 184 A5
Cheadle SK8 . . . . 35 B8
Dodleston CH4 . . . . 162 B8
Eccleston CH4 . . . . 141 E2
Frodsham WA6 . . . . 74 C7
Hale L24 . . . . 47 E8
Handforth SK9 . . . . 34 D3
Haydock WA11 . . . . 1 E7
Little Leigh CW8 . . . . 77 D4
Lymm WA13 . . . . 18 E2
Mouldsworth CH3 . . . . . . 98 F1
New Mills SK22 . . . . 39 C7
Northwich CW9 . . . . 104 A8
Saughall CH1 . . . . 94 A1
Shocklach CH3 . . . . 197 C1
Thornton Hough CH63 . . . 42 B6
Tilston SY14 . . . . 198 B2
Wilmslow SK9 . . . . 59 E4
Worleston CW5 . . . . 188 D6
Church Rise CW8 . . . . . . 102 B2
Church Row CW6 . . . . . . 168 F1
Churchside CI CW1 . . . . . 191 D5
Churchside Wlk CH4 . . . . 140 F7
Church St
Audley ST7 . . . . 209 D2
Audley, Wood Lane ST7 . 210 A1
Bollington SK10 . . . . 88 B8
Chester CH1 . . . . 237 B4
Connah's Quay CH5 . . . . . 91 D1
Davenham CW9 . . . . 104 A3
Ellesmere Port CH65 . . . . 70 C6
Farndon LL13 . . . . 180 E2
Frodsham WA6 . . . . 74 B8
Great Budworth CW9 . . . . 79 A8
Higher Wincham CW9 . . . . 79 E5
Kelsall CW6 . . . . 122 D4
Kidsgrove, Butt Lane ST7 194 D1
Kidsgrove, The Rookery
ST7 . . . . 195 C4
Macclesfield SK10, SK11 . 112 D8
Malpas SY14 . . . . 213 B3
Moulton CW9 . . . . 126 F8
Mount Pleasant ST7 . . . . 195 C6
Newton-le-Willows WA12 . . 2 E4
Runcorn WA7 . . . . 23 A3
Sandbach CW11 . . . . . . 175 C6
Tarvin CH3 . . . . 121 C2
Warrington WA1 . . . . 16 C5
Weaverham CW8 . . . . 77 D1
Widnes WA8 . . . . 23 A2
Wilmslow SK9 . . . . 60 B7
Winsford CW7 . . . . 126 E1
Church Steadings CH3 . . 143 C3
Church Street N CW6 . . . 122 C5
Church Street W SK11 . . . 112 C8
Church Terr SK9 . . . . 34 D4
Church View
Audlem CW3 . . . . 230 A4
Handforth SK9 . . . . 34 A2
Haslington CW1 . . . . 191 D5
Kingsley WA6 . . . . 75 B2
16 Knutsford WA16 . . . . . 57 A2
Lymm WA13 . . . . 19 B4
New Mills SK22 . . . . 39 C8
Church View Terr WA11 . 112 F3
Church View Wlk CW2 . . . 205 E8
Churchward CI CH2 . . . . . 118 D4
Churchway SK10 . . . . 86 F2
Church Way
Alvanley WA6 . . . . 73 A1
Blacon CH1 . . . . 117 E5
Chester CH1 . . . . 94 A1
Wybunbury CW5 . . . . . . 220 B8
Churchway Rd L24 . . . . . . 21 A2
Church Wlk
Broughton CH4 . . . . 139 C5
Crowton CW8 . . . . 76 C2
2 Ellesmere Port CH65 . . . 70 C6
Holmes Chapel CW4 . . . 130 C3
Knutsford WA16 . . . . 57 A2
Lower Peover WA16 . . . . . 81 E1
Malpas SY14 . . . . 213 B3
Northwich CW9 . . . . 104 A8
Wilmslow SK9 . . . . 59 F6
Winwick WA2 . . . . 8 A6
Church Wlks
Christleton CH3 . . . . 142 E8
Norton in Hales TF9 . . . . 236 C2
Churchwood View WA13 . . 18 F3
Churchyard Side CW5 . . . 204 E5
CHURTON 180 E5
Churton CI
Chester CH2 . . . . 119 A2
Farndon CH3 . . . . 180 E2
Churton St CH3 . . . . 119 A2
Cicely Mill La WA16 . . . . . 30 D3
Cinder CI CH3 . . . . 119 F5
Cinder Hill CW7 . . . . 125 F6
Cinder-Hill La ST7 . . . . . 194 F7
Cinder La
Chelford SK11 . . . . 83 E1
Guilden Sutton CH3 . . . . 119 F5
Lostock Green CW9 . . . . 105 A8

Cinder La *continued*
Nantwich CW5 . . . . 188 C2
Over Peover WA16 . . . . . 108 C7
Warrington WA4 . . . . 17 F1
Cinder Rock Way ST7 . . . 195 C1
Cinnabar Ct WA4 . . . . 16 E4
CINNAMON BROW 8 F4
Cinnamon Brow CE Prim Sch
WA2 . . . . 8 F3
Cinnamon La WA2 . . . . 8 F2
Cinnamon Lane N WA2 . . . 8 F3
Cinnamon Pk WA2 . . . . 9 B3
Circle Ave CW5 . . . . 205 E5
Circle The
Crewe CW2 . . . . 190 D1
Mere WA16 . . . . 30 C2
Circuit The
Alderley Edge SK9 . . . . . . 60 B3
Cheadle SK8 . . . . 35 A7
Wilmslow SK9 . . . . 59 D5
Circular Dr CH4 . . . . 140 F4
City Bank ST8 . . . . 179 C2
City Quays 8 CH1 . . . . . . 237 C3
City Rd CH1 . . . . 237 C3
City Walls Rd CH1 . . . . . . 237 A2
City Way Apartments 7
CH1 . . . . 237 C3
Civic Way
Ellesmere Port CH65 . . . . 70 B4
Middlewich CW10 . . . . . 128 C1
Clair Ave CH5 . . . . 116 A3
Clamhunger La WA16 . . . . 56 D7
Clamley Gdns L24 . . . . . . 21 E2
Clanbrook Ave WA13 . . . . 19 A2
Clanfield Ave WA8 . . . . . . 12 C3
Clap Gate Cres WA5 . . . . . 15 E7
Clap Gates Cres WA5 . . . . 15 E7
Clap Gates Rd WA5 . . . . . 15 E7
Clare Ave
Chester CH2 . . . . 119 A3
Handforth SK9 . . . . 34 C3
Clare Dr
Crewe CW2 . . . . 189 F1
Ellesmere Port CH65 . . . . 70 B1
Macclesfield SK10 . . . . . . 87 C3
Clare Ho CH1 . . . . 117 F6
Claremont Ave WA8 . . . . . 13 C4
Claremont CI CW9 . . . . . 103 F3
Claremont Dr WA8 . . . . . . 13 B4
Claremont Rd
Cheadle SK8 . . . . 35 A8
Crewe CW2 . . . . 190 B2
Runcorn WA7 . . . . 23 B2
Clarence Ave
Chester CH2 . . . . 119 B2
Warrington WA4 . . . . 14 D6
Widnes WA8 . . . . 13 A4
Clarence Ct
Newton-le-Willows WA12 . . 2 A4
Wilmslow SK9 . . . . 60 A6
Clarence Gr CW1 . . . . . . 190 B5
Clarence Mill Bsns Pk
SK10 . . . . 63 A1
Clarence Rd
Bollington SK10 . . . . 63 A1
Warrington WA1 . . . . 17 B2
Clarence St
Newton-le-Willows WA12 . . 1 F4
Runcorn WA7 . . . . 22 F3
Warrington WA1 . . . . 16 E7
Clarence Terr
7 Runcorn WA7 . . . . 23 A3
Clarendon CI
Chester CH4 . . . . 141 E6
Runcorn WA7 . . . . 50 D7
Clarendon Cotts SK9 . . . . 34 A3
Clarendon CI WA2 . . . . 7 F4
Clarendon Dr SK10 . . . . . . 88 A1
Clarendon Rd M44 . . . . . . 11 F7
Clare PI CW7 . . . . 149 C2
Clares Farm CI WA1 . . . . . 17 F7
Clare St
Harriseahead ST7 . . . . . 195 E4
Mount Pleasant ST7 . . . . 195 C6
Clarke Ave
Culcheth WA3 . . . . 5 A4
Warrington WA4 . . . . 16 D2
Clarke Gdns 3 WA8 . . . . . 23 B7
Clarke La
Bollington SK10 . . . . 87 E5
Langley SK11 . . . . 113 D3
Clarke Terr SK11 . . . . . . 112 D8
CLARK GREEN 63 A3
Clarks Terr WA7 . . . . 48 D8
Clary Mdw CW8 . . . . 78 E1
Clatterbridge Hospl CH63 42 D8
Clatterbridge Rd CH63 . . . 42 D8
Clatterwick La CW8 . . . . . 77 D7
Claude St WA1 . . . . 16 C6
Claughton Ave CW2 . . . . 190 C1
Claverton CI WA7 . . . . 49 B8
Claverton Ct CH4 . . . . . . 237 C1
Claydon Gdns WA3 . . . . . . 10 F1
Clay Heyes SK11 . . . . 84 A3
Clayhall Gn CH66 . . . . 69 D7
Clayhill Light Ind Pk CH64 41 F2
Clay La
Bickerton SY14 . . . . 200 B7
Burtonwood WA5 . . . . 6 E5
Handforth SK9 . . . . 34 C5
Haslington CW1, CW11 . 191 D7
Over Peover WA16 . . . . . 108 B8
Sandbach CW11, CW1 . . 174 B2
Wilmslow SK9 . . . . 59 C4
Winsford CW7 . . . . 125 B4

Claypit Rd CH4 . . . . 141 B5
Claypits La CH3 . . . . 142 F5
Clayton Ave
Congleton CW12 . . . . . . 157 A5
Golborne WA3 . . . . 3 E8
Clayton-By-Pass CW12 . . 156 C3
Clayton CI CW1 . . . . 190 A7
Clayton Cres
Runcorn WA7 . . . . 22 F1
Widnes WA8 . . . . 12 F1
Clayton Dr SY13 . . . . 226 B1
Clayton Rd WA3 . . . . 9 F6
Clayton's Row CW5 . . . . . 204 E7
Cleadon Way WA8 . . . . . . 12 E4
Clearwater Quays WA4 . . . 17 A3
Cleaver Mews SK11 . . . . 112 C5
Cleaver Rd CH1 . . . . 117 E4
Cledford Cres CW10 . . . . 151 E6
Cledford La CW10 . . . . . 151 E7
Cledford Prim Sch
CW10 . . . . 151 C7
Cledwen Rd/Ffordd Cledwen
CH4 . . . . 139 D5
Cleethorpes Rd WA7 . . . . 50 C7
Cleeves CI WA1 . . . . 16 C5
Cleeve Way SK8 . . . . 35 B6
Clegge St WA2 . . . . 16 B7
Clelland St WA4 . . . . 16 C3
Clement Dr CW1 . . . . . . 189 F7
Clemley CI CW6 . . . . 122 D6
Clerewood Ave SK8 . . . . . 34 B7
Clevedon CI SK11 . . . . . . 112 A7
Cleveland Dr CH66 . . . . . 69 A6
Cleveland Rd WA2 . . . . 8 B3
Cleveland Way CW7 . . . . 149 B2
Cleveleys Ave WA8 . . . . . . 13 D2
Cleveleys Rd WA5 . . . . . . 15 B4
Cleves CI CH1 . . . . 117 D6
Cliffbrook Gr 2 SK9 . . . . . 34 D2
Cliffe Rd
Crewe CW1 . . . . 190 B7
Neston CH64 . . . . 66 F5
Warrington WA4 . . . . 26 C7
Cliffe St 3 WA8 . . . . 13 C1
Cliff La
Acton Bridge CW8 . . . . . . 76 C4
Lymm WA13 . . . . 28 B6
Macclesfield SK10, SK11 . 88 B1
Warrington WA4 . . . . 17 D1
Clifford Dr CH4 . . . . 140 F5
Clifford Gr CW1 . . . . 191 C4
Clifford PI 4 CW7 . . . . . 149 C7
Clifford Rd
Macclesfield SK11 . . . . . 112 A8
Poynton SK12 . . . . 36 D3
Warrington WA5 . . . . 15 A4
Wilmslow SK9 . . . . 59 F6
Cliff Rd
Acton Bridge CW8 . . . . . . 76 E4
Wilmslow SK9 . . . . 60 B8
Cliff Side
Wilmslow/Alderley Edge
SK9 . . . . 59 D5
Wilmslow SK9 . . . . 60 B8
Cliff View WA6 . . . . 74 A8
CLIFTON 49 D4
Clifton Ave
Bebington CH62 . . . . 43 E3
Crewe CW2 . . . . 190 B3
Warrington WA4 . . . . 4 D3
Clifton CI WA1 . . . . 17 D7
Clifton Cres WA6 . . . . 49 C1
Clifton Ct WA7 . . . . 49 B6
Clifton Dr
Blacon CH1 . . . . 117 E3
Northwich CW9 . . . . 104 A5
Wilmslow SK9 . . . . 59 E4
Clifton Gdns CH65 . . . . . . 70 C3
Clifton La WA7 . . . . 49 C2
Cliftonmill Mdws WA3 . . . . 2 F8
Clifton Park Ave CH5 . . . . 91 D1
Clifton Rd
Runcorn, Clifton WA7 . . . . 49 E3
Runcorn, Heath WA7 . . . . 49 B6
Sandbach CW11 . . . . . . 174 D7
Clifton Rdbt WA7 . . . . 49 E3
Clifton St
Alderley Edge SK9 . . . . . . 60 A1
Crewe CW2 . . . . 190 B3
Warrington WA4 . . . . 16 C4
Cliftonville Rd WA1 . . . . . . 17 D6
Clincton CI WA8 . . . . 22 A8
Clincton View WA8 . . . . . . 22 A8
Clincton Wood Nature
Reserve ★ WA8 . . . . 22 A7
Clipsley Cres WA11 . . . . . . 1 B7
Clipsley La WA11 . . . . 1 C6
Clitheroe Rd CW8 . . . . . . 77 E1
CLIVE 127 D1
Clive Ave WA2 . . . . 8 C1
Clive Back La CW7 . . . . . 150 D7
Cliveden Rd CH4 . . . . 140 F5
CLIVE GREEN 150 D8
Clivegreen La CW10 . . . . 150 E7
Clive La CW7 . . . . 150 C8
Clock Face Rd WA8 . . . . . 13 E8
Clocktower The CW4 . . . . 130 D2
Clock Twr The WA1 . . . . . . 16 C2
Cloister Way CH65 . . . . . . 70 E5
Clonners Field CW5 . . . . 205 A4
Closeburn Ave CH60 . . . . 40 E6
Close La
Alsager ST7 . . . . 192 F3
Mow Cop ST7 . . . . 195 D7
Close The
Alsager ST7 . . . . 193 A3
Hartford CW8 . . . . 103 D6
Newton-le-Willows WA12 . . 2 E1

Close The *continued*
Saughall CH1 . . . . 94 A1
Tarporley CW6 . . . . 146 C2
CLOTTON 145 D4
Cloudberry Wlk M31 . . . . . 11 E3
CLOUD SIDE 157 F4
Cloud The ★ CW12 . . . . . 158 A4
Cloud View CW12 . . . . . . 157 A2
Clough Ave
Handforth SK9 . . . . 34 B2
Warrington WA2 . . . . 8 B2
Clough Bank SK10 . . . . . . 87 F7
Clough Field CI SK23 . . . . 65 D8
CLOUGH HALL 210 F8
Clough Hall Dr ST7 . . . . . 210 E6
Clough Hall Rd ST7 . . . . . 210 F8
Clough Hall Tech Sch 1
ST7 . . . . 194 F1
Clough La CW8 . . . . 103 D6
Clough Rd CW7 . . . . 126 E1
Cloughside SK12 . . . . 38 E6
Clough The WA7 . . . . 23 F1
Clough Wlk CW2 . . . . 206 D8
Cloughwood Specl Sch
CW8 . . . . 103 D5
Clovelly Ave WA5 . . . . 14 E7
Clovelly Gr WA7 . . . . 50 C5
Clover Ave WA6 . . . . 74 D7
Clover Ct WA7 . . . . 50 B5
Cloverdale CW8 . . . . 103 C7
Cloverdale Rd SK11 . . . . 112 B5
Clover Dr
Pickmere WA16 . . . . 79 F7
Winsford CW7 . . . . 126 D3
Cloverfield
Lymm WA13 . . . . 18 F4
Runcorn WA7 . . . . 50 C7
Cloverfield Gdns CH66 . . . 69 D7
Cloverfields CW1 . . . . . . 191 B4
Clover La CH4 . . . . 140 F5
Clover PI CH4 . . . . 140 F5
Clowes Ave ST7 . . . . 193 F2
Clowes St SK11 . . . . 112 B8
Clumber CI SK12 . . . . 36 E3
Clumber Rd SK12 . . . . . . 36 E3
CLUTTON 182 D1
Clutton CE Prim Sch
CH3 . . . . 182 D1
Clwyd CI CH5 . . . . 139 B6
Clwyd Way CH66 . . . . 69 A6
Clyde Ave ST8 . . . . 179 E1
Clyde Cres CW7 . . . . 127 B1
Clyde Gr CW2 . . . . 190 A3
Clydesdale CH65 . . . . 70 B3
Clydesdale Ave CW2 . . . . 190 B3
Clydesdale Rd WA4 . . . . . 26 D8
Coach Ho The ST7 . . . . . 194 C4
Coach Rd
Broxton CH3 . . . . 183 A3
Edge Green SY14 . . . . . 199 D2
Little Budworth CW6 . . . . 147 D8
Coachway SK10 . . . . 86 F7
Coalbrookdale Rd CH64 . . 41 F1
COALPIT HILL 210 C8
Coalpit Hill ST7 . . . . 210 C8
Coalpit La
Clive Green CW10 . . . . . 150 F7
Langley SK11 . . . . 113 C5
Coalport Dr CW7 . . . . . . 126 A3
Coare St SK10 . . . . 87 D1
Coastguard La CH64 . . . . 41 B1
Coatings By Pass Rd CH5 . 91 F1
Coatings Two CH5 . . . . . . 91 E2
Cobal Ct WA6 . . . . 74 B8
Cobbett's Way WA9 . . . . . 59 F4
Cobblers Cross La CW6 . 146 E2
Cobblers La/Lon Y Cryddion
LL12 . . . . 161 B1
Cobbles The
Chester CH4 . . . . 141 D7
Cuddington CW8 . . . . . . 101 D4
Lower Peover WA16 . . . . . 81 E1
Cobblestone Ct CH2 . . . . 119 E8
COBBS 26 E8
Cobbs Inf Sch The WA4 . . 26 E8
Cobbs La
Hough CW2 . . . . 206 D2
Warrington WA4 . . . . 26 E8
Cobden St
Newton-le-Willows WA12 . . 2 D4
Warrington WA2 . . . . 16 B6
Cob Hall La WA6 . . . . 98 D5
Cob Moor Rd ST7 . . . . . . 195 A4
COBSCOT 235 E3
Cock Hall La SK11 . . . . . 113 D3
Cockhedge La WA1 . . . . . 16 C5
Cockhedge Sh Pk WA1 . . . 16 B5
Cockhedge Way WA1 . . . . 16 C5
Cockington CI CW9 . . . . . 104 A4
Cock La
Great Budworth CW9 . . . . 78 F8
Sound CW5 . . . . 217 F4
Cocklade La L24 . . . . 21 D1
Cock Lane Ends WA8 . . . . 22 B4
Cockpit La CW8 . . . . 102 B1
Cockshades Farm CW5 . . 206 C2
Cocksheadhey Rd SK10 . . 63 C1
Cocksmoss La
Congleton SK11 . . . . . . 134 A3
Marton SK11 . . . . 133 D3
Cocoa Gdns SK11 . . . . . . 204 E5
Cocoa Yd The 10 CW5 . . . 204 E5
CODDINGTON 182 A3
Coe La WA14 . . . . 30 C7
Cogshall La
Anderton CW9 . . . . 78 C5
Comberbach CW9 . . . . . . 78 B2

Colchester Ho 10 CH1....237 C3
Colchester Sq CH4....140 F5
COLDHARBOUR....164 F5
Coldmoss Dr CW11....175 C4
COLD MOSS HEATH....175 C5
Coldstream Cl WA2....8 E3
Coldstream Dr CH66....68 F5
Cole Ave WA12....2 C4
Colebrook Cl WA3....10 A4
Coleclough Pl WA3....4 F1
Coleg Glannau Dyfrdwy/
  Deeside Coll CH5....91 B1
Colehill Bank CW12....156 E2
Colehill Pl CH5....91 D1
Colemere Cl WA1....17 A8
Colemere Ct CH65....70 C7
Coleridge Cl
  Blacon CH1....118 A5
  Sandbach CW11....174 C5
Coleridge Gr WA8....12 E1
Coleridge Way CW1....190 F5
Colinwood Ave CH4....139 B3
Coliseum L Pk CH65....70 D2
Coliseum Way CH65....70 D2
Collar House Dr SK10....86 E6
College Cl
  Warrington, Fearnhead
    WA2....9 B2
  Warrington WA1....16 D5
  Wilmslow SK9....59 F8
College Ct SK11....112 B5
College Fields
  Crewe CW2....190 A1
  Widnes WA8....12 F5
College Gn CH4....141 D7
College La CW6....168 F1
College Rd ST7....193 B5
College View CH5....91 C1
Collegiate Rd WA2....8 B3
Colleys La CW11....175 D5
Colleys La CW5....205 B7
Colliers La CW9....54 E2
Collier's Row WA7....48 E7
Collier St WA7....22 F3
Colliery Green Cl CH64....66 E5
Colliery Green Ct CH64....66 E5
Colliery Green Dr CH64....66 E5
Collinbrook Ave CW2....190 B1
Collingham Way CW7....126 D1
Collingtree Ave CW7....127 A3
Collingwood Cl
  Macclesfield SK10....87 B2
  Poynton SK12....37 A3
Collingwood Rd WA12....2 B3
COLLINS GREEN....1 E1
Collins Green La WA5....1 E1
Collinson Ct 2 WA6....74 B8
Collins St CW2....190 A3
Colne Rd WA5....6 F6
Colorado Cl WA5....15 C7
Colshaw Dr SK9....34 D2
Colshaw Hall Cotts WA16....82 F1
Colshaw La SK11....109 E1
Colson Ct CW2....237 A4
Coltsfoot Cl CH3....142 B5
Columbine Cl
  Huntington CH3....142 A6
  Widnes WA8....12 B4
Columbine Way WA9....6 B7
Colville Cl 8 M31....11 F3
Colville Ct WA2....8 A3
Colville Rd SK11....111 F8
Colwyn Cl
  Ellesmere Port CH65....70 D3
  Warrington WA5....7 E2
Colwyn Rd SK7....35 F8
Combermere Abbey*
  SY13....227 D5
COMBERBACH....78 C7
Comberbach Dr CW5....205 A4
Comberbach Prim Sch
  CW9....78 C8
Combermere Pl 8 CW1....190 B5
Comber Way WA16....82 A8
Comboy Dr CW9....104 C6
Combs Cl SK22....39 A8
Commercial Ave WA8....34 F5
Commercial Rd SK10....112 E8
Common Farm La SK11....83 E1
Commongate SK10....112 E8
Commonhall St CH1....237 A2
Common La
  Betley CW3....221 F6
  Chelford SK11....83 E1
  Culcheth WA3....4 E4
  Duddon CW6....145 C7
  Hapsford WA6....72 D1
  Kelsall CW6....122 C3
  Lach Dennis CW9....105 E5
  Norbury SY13....215 C5
  Stretton WA4....52 E8
  Warrington WA4....14 F6
  Waverton CH3....143 B4
  Winsford CW7....125 B5
Common Rd WA12, WA5....1 E3
COMMONSIDE....100 B8
COMMON SIDE....124 D3
Commonside WA6....73 E1
Commons Mill CW11....175 B7
Common St CW11....175 B6
Common The
  Kelsall CW6....122 B3
  Runcorn WA7....49 F8
Commonwealth Cl CW7....149 D6
Commonwood Rd LL13....196 A8

Company's Cl WA7....48 F6
Compass Cl WA7....50 D5
Compton Cl WA11....1 C7
Compton Pl
  Chester CH4....141 A6
  Ellesmere Port CH65....70 B5
Concorde Pl WA2....8 D2
Concourse Way WA9....1 A2
Condliffe Cl CW11....175 C5
Conery Cl WA6....73 C4
Coney Gr WA7....50 B5
CONGLETON....157 A4
Congleton Bsns Ctr
  CW12....156 E3
Congleton Bsns Pk
  CW12....156 C4
Congleton Cl SK9....85 A8
CONGLETON EDGE....179 B5
Congleton Edge Rd
  CW12....179 A5
Congleton High Sch
  CW12....155 F3
Congleton La SK11....109 D5
Congleton L Ctr CW12....156 E3
Congleton Mus* CW12....156 E2
Congleton Rd
  Alderley Edge SK9....60 A1
  Biddulph ST8....179 D2
  Broughton CH4....139 C4
  Kidsgrove ST7....194 D1
  Macclesfield SK11....133 B5
  Marton SK11....133 A5
  Mow Cop ST7....178 F1
  North Rode SK11....134 C6
  Sandbach, Arclid Green
    CW11....175 E8
  Sandbach CW11....175 B8
  Scholar Green CW12, ST7....177 E3
  Siddington SK11....110 B8
  Smallwood CW11....177 A6
  Swettenham CW12....131 F4
  Warren SK11....111 E2
Congleton Ret Pk CW12....156 E4
Congleton Road N ST7....194 E6
Congleton Road S ST7....194 D3
Congleton Sta CW12....157 A1
Congleton Theatre*
  CW12....156 E3
Congleton War Memorial
  Hospl CW12....156 F1
Conifer Cl CH66....95 A8
Conifer Cl
  Moore WA4....25 A7
  Warrington WA5....14 F7
Conifers The ST7....193 B3
Conifer Wlk M31....11 E3
Coningsby Dr CW7....126 E1
Coningsby Gdns 18 WA3....3 E8
Coniston Ave
  Bebington CH63....43 C4
  Congleton CW12....155 F2
  Warrington WA5....14 D4
  Winsford CW7....126 C2
Coniston Cl
  Alderley Edge SK9....84 A7
  Hooton CH66....44 B2
  Nantwich CW5....205 A6
  Runcorn WA7....49 D6
Coniston Dr
  Frodsham WA6....74 D8
  Handforth SK9....34 C4
  Holmes Chapel CW4....130 A3
Coniston Rd
  Chester CH2....118 F5
  High Lane SK6....37 D8
  Neston CH64....66 E6
  Partington M31....11 E4
Coniston Way SK11....111 F5
CONNAH'S QUAY....91 B1
Connah's Quay High Sch
  CH5....91 C1
Connah's Quay Sports Ctr
  CH5....91 C1
Connaught Ave WA1....16 E7
Connaught Cl SK9....60 C8
Connaught Dr WA12....2 C2
Conrad Cl CW1....190 E4
Conroy Way WA12....7 C8
Consort Cl SK10....87 E7
Constable Dr SK9....60 E8
Constables Cl WA7....24 A1
Constance Ind Est WA8....23 A6
Constance Rd M31....11 F3
Constance Way WA8....23 A5
Convamore Rd SK7....35 D7
Conway Ave
  Irlam M44....11 F8
  Warrington WA5....7 C7
  Winsford CW7....149 C7
Conway Cl
  Crewe CW1....190 C8
  Knutsford WA16....82 A8
  Saltney CH4....140 D5
Conway Cres SK10....87 F1
Conway Ct CH65....70 D3
Conway Dr WA12....2 C2
Conwy Ct WA7....24 A2
Coogee Ave WA5....14 E2
Cook Ave WA11....1 F7
Cookes Cl CH4....41 E1
Cooke's La CW9....104 F6
Cookesmere La CW11....175 A8
Cooks Hill WA6....99 F8
Cooks La ST3....225 D7
COOKSONGREEN....76 A1
Cook St CH65....70 C6

Coole La
  Hack Green CW5....218 E3
  Newhall CW3....229 C5
Coombe Dr WA7....49 A8
Coombe Park Ct 1 CH66....69 C6
Coombe Pk CH66....69 C6
Co-operative St SK12....38 D6
Cooper Ave
  Newton-le-Willows WA12....1 F3
  Warrington WA2....8 B2
Coope Rd SK10....87 E6
Cooper La WA11....1 C6
Cooper's Croft CH3....142 A7
Cooper's Fold SK8....34 F6
Coopers La CH5....91 D1
Coopers Opening CW11....175 B7
Coopers Pl WA4....16 C1
Cooper St
  Congleton CW12....156 E3
  Runcorn WA7....23 A3
  Widnes WA8....13 B1
Cooper Terr CW6....146 D1
Cope Ave CW5....204 C4
Copeland Cl WA7....49 E5
Copeland Rd WA4....16 B2
Copes La CW5....204 C4
Copeswood Cl CH4....139 C3
Copgrove Wlk M22....33 E7
Copley Wlk CW5....204 D5
Cop Mdw SK11....112 F2
COPPENHALL....190 D7
Coppenhall Gr CW2....190 A4
Coppenhall Heyes CW2....190 A4
Coppenhall L Ctr CW1....190 E5
COPPENHALL MOSS....173 D1
Copper Beech CH3....139 C3
Copperfield Cl WA3....9 C5
Copperfield Rd
  Cheadle SK8....35 B5
  Poynton SK12....36 D2
Copperfields
  Poynton SK12....36 D2
  Tarporley CW6....146 D2
  Wilmslow SK9....60 C8
Copperhill Rd CW12....179 B7
Coppermine La SY14....184 B2
Copper St SK11....112 E6
Copperwood WA7....24 C1
Copper Wood CW1....189 F7
Coppice Ave SK12....38 A6
Coppice Cl
  High Lane SK12....38 A6
  Runcorn WA7....24 A1
  Willaston SK8....205 D6
Coppice Dr
  Elton CH2....72 C4
  Warrington WA5....7 A1
Coppice Gn
  Elton CH2....72 C4
Coppice Gr WA16....57 A3
Coppice Ho
  Poynton SK12....36 D2
  Talke ST7....210 C8
Coppice La SK12....38 A5
Coppicemere Dr CW1....191 A2
Coppice Rd
  Haslington CW11....192 A8
  Poynton SK12....37 B3
  Talke ST7....210 C8
  Willaston SK8....205 D6
Coppice Rise SK11....112 D5
Coppice The
  Altrincham WA15....32 B8
  Cuddington CW8....101 D5
  Horwich End SK23....65 F5
  Nantwich CW5....204 F3
  Sandbach CW11....174 F2
  Wincham CW9....79 C3
Coppice Way SK9....34 E3
Coppins Cl
  Chester CH3....119 A2
  Helsby WA6....73 B4
Coppins The
  Warrington WA4....8 C2
  Wilmslow SK9....59 E4
Copse The
  Altrincham WA15....32 D7
  High Lane SK6....37 E7
  Newton-le-Willows WA12....2 A4
  Runcorn WA7....50 A6
COPTHORNE....229 F4
Copthorne Cl CW12....156 F2
Copthorne Dr CW1....229 F3
Copyhold CW8....102 D8
Corbet Ave WA2....16 B8
Corbet Dr TF9....235 A4
Corbet St WA2....16 B8
Corbridge Ho 9 CH1....237 C3
Corfe Way CW7....149 C7
Coriander Cl CW10....128 C3
Corks La SK12....38 E5
CORLTON....207 B1
Cormorant Cl CW1....190 F4
Cormorant Dr WA7....22 E2
Cornbrook Rd SK11....112 C4
Corner Croft SK9....60 A4
Cornerhouse La WA8....12 D3
Corners The CW8....102 E7
Cornerstones Sch WA4....17 A2
Cornfield Cl
  Ellesmere Port CH66....69 F1
  Macclesfield SK10....87 C3
Cornforth Way WA8....12 F3
Cornhill Cl ST5....210 D1
Cornish Cl M22....33 D8
Cornishway M22....33 D7

Cornishway Ind Est 4
  M22....33 D8
Cornmill Cl CW11....173 D7
Cornmill Ct WA3....9 A8
Cornubia Rd WA8....23 D7
Cornwall Ave WA7....23 A2
Cornwall Cl
  8 Congleton CW12....157 A1
  High Lane SK6....37 E7
  Macclesfield SK10....88 E1
  Runcorn WA7....23 F1
Cornwall Gr CW1....190 B5
Cornwall Ho CH1....237 B3
Cornwall Rd
  Chester CH2....118 F7
  Gatley SK8....34 B8
  Irlam M44....11 D5
  Widnes WA8....13 B3
Cornwall St
  Chester CH1....237 B4
  Warrington WA1....16 E1
Cornwell Cl SK9....60 E8
Coronation Ave
  Alsager ST7....193 A3
  Glazebury WA3....5 C7
  Warrington WA1....17 C2
  Winsford CW7....126 C6
Coronation Bldgs SK10....88 A8
Coronation Cres
  Crewe CW1....190 E6
  Sandbach CW11....175 A5
Coronation Dr
  Frodsham WA6....49 D1
  Haydock WA11....2 A7
  Newton-le-Willows WA12....2 F4
  Widnes WA8....22 C8
Coronation Gr CW8....78 A4
Coronation Ho WA7....49 C8
Coronation Mill ST7....195 D7
Coronation Rd
  Broughton CH4....139 B3
  Congleton CW12....156 F3
  Ellesmere Port CH65....70 C4
  Middlewich CW10....151 D6
  Runcorn, Higher Runcorn
    WA7....23 B1
  Runcorn, Preston Brook
    WA7....50 F6
Coronation Sq 19 WA16....57 A2
Coronation St
  Chester CH4....140 F7
  Crewe CW1....190 D5
  Macclesfield SK10....112 D6
Coronation Terr CW6....146 D1
Coroner's La WA8....13 A4
Coronet Ave CW9....103 F3
Coronet Way WA8....22 B8
CORRA COMMON....233 C1
Correction Brow SK12....37 C6
Corridor Rd WA7....71 B6
Corwen Cl WA5....14 D5
Cosgrove Bsns Pk CW9....78 D3
Cossack Ave WA2....8 C1
COTEBROOK....147 A8
Cotebrook Dr CH2....118 E7
Cotebrook Rd CW6....104 C8
Cotebrook Shire Horse Ctr*
  CW6....147 A7
Cote Lea Ct WA7....49 F6
Cotes Pl CH1....117 E3
Cotgreaves Ct CH4....141 B5
Cotswold Ave WA3....3 D6
Cotswold Cl
  Chester CH4....118 F6
  Cuddington CW8....102 A2
  Macclesfield SK10....86 E1
Cotswold Cl 6 CH3....119 A1
Cotswold Gr WA9....1 A3
Cotswold Pl WA2....8 A4
Cotswold Rd WA2....8 B3
Cotswold Way CW7....149 B7
Cottage Cl
  Bebington CH63....43 C5
  Neston CH64....66 F7
Cottage Dr E CH60....40 F5
Cottage Drive W CH60....40 F5
Cottage Gr SK9....59 F5
Cottage La
  Heswall CH60....40 F5
  Macclesfield SK10....112 F7
Cottage Lawns SK9....60 B2
Cottage Mews CH4....141 B5
Cottage St SK11....112 B8
Cottages The
  Lawton Heath ST7....193 D6
  Sproston Green CW4....129 F2
  Warrington WA4....17 C4
Cottam Dr WA2....9 A8
Cotterdale Cl WA5....14 F7
Cotterill Dr WA1....49 D8
Cotterill Dr WA1....17 C7
Cotterill St CW2....190 D2
Cottesmore Dr CH60....41 D8
Cottesmore Gdns WA15....32 C8
Cotton Cl SK23....65 E5
Cotton La
  Christleton CH3....120 D2
  Runcorn WA7....49 D8
  Sandbach CW11....175 A3
Cotton Mews CW3....230 A4
Cottons Bridge WA4....50 F5
Cottonwood Gr ST7....195 E4
Cottrell Rd WA15....32 D7
Coulton Rd WA8....13 F3

Col–Cra 249

Council Hos
  Audlem CW3....229 E2
  Bickerton SY14....200 A8
  7 Congleton CW12....156 F2
  Nantwich CW5....228 B8
Council Houses CW5....216 B6
Countess Ave SK8....34 E5
Countess Ct 7 SK11....111 F7
Countess Ct CH1....118 B5
Countess of Chester Health
  Pk CH2....118 B6
Countess of Chester Hospl
  CH2....118 C5
Countess Rd SK11....111 F7
Countess Way CH2....118 C5
Counting House Rd SK12....38 E5
Country Ctr The* CH3....165 E5
Courier Row SK10....87 F7
Court 2 SK10....87 F1
Court Ho The 8 CH66....70 C6
Courtney Gn SK9....34 D2
Courtney Rd CH4....140 E5
Court No 4 6 SK10....112 C8
Court The CH64....66 F6
Courtyard The
  Bostock Green CW10....127 D5
  Chester CH2....118 F6
  Congleton CW12....156 B8
  Cuddington CW8....101 E2
  Elton CH2....72 B4
  Haughton CW6....186 F4
  Newton-le-Willows WA12....2 E4
  Smallwood CW11....177 A7
  4 Warrington WA1....16 B5
  Weaverham CW8....102 A8
  Willaston CH64....67 F8
Cousens Way CH1....118 B4
Covell Rd SK12....36 D5
Coventry Ave CH66....94 E8
Coverdale Cl WA5....14 F7
Coverdale Fold CW11....174 D5
Covert Cl CW7....149 B8
Covert Gdns ST7....210 D8
Covert Rise CH3....166 A2
Covington Pl SK9....60 B6
Cowanway WA8....12 F5
Cowbrook La SK11....135 B6
Cowdell St WA2....16 B7
Cowfields CW5....204 E6
Cowhey Cl CH4....141 B5
Cow Hey La WA6, WA7....49 A5
Cow La
  Ashley WA15....31 F6
  Bollington SK10....88 B7
  Hargrave CH3....144 A2
  Macclesfield SK11....112 D6
  Norley WA6....101 A5
  Wilmslow SK9....60 C7
  Winsford CW7....149 E8
Cowley Cl CW1....190 E1
Cowper Cl CW2....206 A8
Cowthorne Dr CH3....143 A4
COX BANK....234 F8
CPA Pond Nature Reserve*
  SK23....65 D7
Crab La WA2....9 B3
Crabmill Dr CW11....174 E2
Crabmill La
  Norley WA6....100 E6
  Warmingham CW11....173 E7
Crabtree Ave
  Altrincham WA15....32 D7
  Disley SK12....38 E5
Crabtree Cl WA12....2 E3
Crab Tree Cl CW4....21 E2
Crabtree Cnr SK12....38 D6
Crabtree Fold WA7....50 C8
Crabtree Gr CW1....190 E6
CRABTREE GREEN....101 C1
Crabtree Green Pk CW8....124 C8
Crabtree La WA13....29 A7
Crabwall Pl CH1....117 F5
Crackley Bank Prim Sch
  ST5....210 E1
Craddock St SY14....213 B3
Cradley WA8....12 C2
Cragside Way SK9....60 C6
Craig Cl SK11....112 B5
Craig Dr SK23....65 E6
Craig Gdns CH66....69 E7
Craigleigh Gr CH62....43 F4
Craig Rd
  Congleton CW12....156 F4
  Macclesfield SK11....112 B5
Craigside ST8....179 C1
Craig Wlk ST7....193 F2
Craithie Rd CH3....119 A2
Crampton Dr WA15....32 C8
CRANAGE....130 A6
Cranage Cl WA7....49 D7
Cranage Ct 3 CW12....156 F3
Cranage La CW9....79 D1
Cranage Rd CW2....190 A3
Cranage Way 16 SK9....34 D5
Cranberry Cl ST7....193 A3
Cranberry La ST7....193 A3
Cranberry Moss La ST7....193 A3
Cranberry Moss Nature
  Reserve* ST7....193 A3
Cranberry Prim Sch ST7....193 A3
Cranberry Rd M31....11 F3
Cranborne Ave WA4....16 B1

Cranborne Rd CW1 . . . . . . 190 D6
Cranebrook Cl CW1 . . . . . . 190 A8
Crane Ho CH1 . . . . 118 B1
Cranfield Dr ST7 . . . . 193 A3
Cranford Ave
  Knutsford WA16 . . . . 56 F1
  Macclesfield SK11 . . . . 112 F7
Cranford Cl CH62 . . . . 43 F4
Cranford Ct
  Chester CH4 . . . . 141 A5
  Warrington WA1 . . . . 17 E8
Cranford Dr WA16 . . . . 57 D4
Cranford Mews ST1 . . . . . . 193 A3
Cranford Rd SK9 . . . . 34 A1
Cranford Sq WA16 . . . . 56 F1
Cranham Ave WA3 . . . . 3 E7
Cranleigh Al WA4 . . . . 26 B7
Cranleigh Cres CH1 . . . . . 118 B4
Cranleigh Dr SK7 . . . . 37 A8
Cranmere Cl CW9 . . . . 104 A4
Cranshaw La WA8 . . . . 13 B6
Cransley Sch CW9 . . . . 53 E1
Cranswick Gr CH66 . . . . . . 69 C5
Crantock Dr SK8 . . . . 34 C8
Cranwell Ave WA3 . . . . 4 F4
Crauford Rd CW2 . . . . 157 A8
Craven Ave
  Warrington WA3 . . . . 3 E7
Craven Ct WA2 . . . . 7 F4
Crawford Ave WA8 . . . . 12 B2
Crawford Pl WA7 . . . . 49 B6
Crawley Ave WA2 . . . . 8 A3
Crayford Ave CW12 . . . . . . 157 A5
Cresanne Cl CW10 . . . . 151 C7
Crescent Dr
  Furness Vale SK23 . . . . 39 D2
  Helsby WA6 . . . . 73 B3
Crescent Rd
  Alderley Edge SK9 . . . . 60 B2
  Congleton CW12 . . . . 156 C2
  Cranage CW4 . . . . 129 F6
  Ellesmere Port CH65 . . . . . 70 D6
  Rostherne WA16 . . . . 30 B3
Crescent The
  Chester CH2 . . . . 118 D4
  Congleton CW12 . . . . 156 C2
  Ellesmere Port CH65 . . . . . 69 F5
  Hartford CW8 . . . . 103 A5
  Heswall, Gayton CH60 . . . . 41 B6
  Lymm WA13 . . . . 18 F2
  Macclesfield SK10 . . . . 87 E1
  Middlewich CW10 . . . . 128 B1
  Mottram St Andrew SK10 . . 61 A1
  Nantwich CW5 . . . . 204 F6
  New Mills SK22 . . . . 39 B8
  Northwich CW9 . . . . 103 F6
  Rostherne WA16 . . . . 30 B3
  Utkinton CW6 . . . . 146 B7
  Weaverham CW8 . . . . 102 E8
Cressbrook Rd **2** WA4 . . 16 C1
Cressington Gdns 7
  CH65 . . . . 70 C6
Cresswell Ave
  Newcastle-under-Lyme
    ST5 . . . . 210 A1
  New Mills SK22 . . . . 39 C8
Cresswellshawe Rd ST7 . 193 D4
Cresswell St SK22 . . . . 39 C8
Cresta Dr WA7 . . . . 48 F6
Crestwood Cl CW2 . . . . . . 206 B7
Crew Ave SK10 . . . . 87 E1
CREWE 190 E5
Crewe Bsns Pk CW1 . . . . . 190 F2
CREWE-BY-FARNDON . . . 197 A7
Crewe Gates Farm Ind Est
  CW1 . . . . 207 A8
Crewe Gates Ind Est
  CW1 . . . . 207 A8
CREWE GREEN 191 B3
Crewe Green Ave CW1 . . . 191 B4
Crewe Green Rd CW1 . . . . 191 A3
Crewe Hall Ent Pk CW1 . . 207 D8
Crewe Her Ctr* CW1 . . . . 190 D3
Crewe Hill La CW3 . . . . . . 197 A6
Crewe La CH3 . . . . 180 F1
Crewe Lane S CH3 . . . . 197 A7
Crewe Rd
  Alsager ST7 . . . . 193 B3
  Crewe, Crewe Green CW1 . 191 B3
  Crewe CW1 . . . . 190 F2
  Haslington CW1, ST7 . . . . 191 D5
  Hatherton CW5 . . . . 219 F3
  Lawton-gate ST7 . . . . 193 F4
  Nantwich CW2, CW5 . . . . . 205 D6
  Sandbach CW11 . . . . 175 A5
  Shavington CW2 . . . . 206 C6
Crewe St
  Chester CH1 . . . . 237 C3
  Crewe CW1 . . . . 190 D4
  Crewe Sta CW1 . . . . 190 E2
Crewood Common Rd
  CW8 . . . . 76 A3
Crib La CW6 . . . . 168 A8
Criftin Cl CH66 . . . . 69 C2
Crimes La CH3, CW6 . . . . . 167 D4
Crisham Ave CW5 . . . . 218 E8
Crispin Rd M22 . . . . 33 E8
Critchley Rd L24 . . . . 21 A3
Croasdale Dr WA7 . . . . 49 E5
Crocus Gdns WA9 . . . . 6 A7
Crocus St CW8 . . . . 78 B3
Croesmere Dr CH66 . . . . . . 69 D2
CROFT 9 B8
Croft Cl
  Altrincham WA15 . . . . 32 C6

Croft Cl *continued*
  Congleton CW12 . . . . 156 F2
  Utkinton CW6 . . . . 146 B7
  Waverton CH3 . . . . 143 A5
Croft Cotts
  Dunham-on-the-Hill WA6 . . 97 E6
  Ellesmere Port CH66 . . . . . 69 A8
Croft Ct CH65 . . . . 70 E3
Croft Cty Prim Sch WA3 . . . 9 A8
Croften Dr CH64 . . . . 66 E5
Crofters Cl
  6 Ellesmere Port CH66 . . 69 E1
  Pickmere WA16 . . . . 80 A7
  Wistaston CW2 . . . . 206 B8
Crofters Ct
  Holmes Chapel CW4 . . . . . 130 C3
  Newcastle-under-Lyme
    ST5 . . . . 210 D3
Crofters Gn SK9 . . . . 59 F6
Crofters Heath CH66 . . . . . 69 E1
Crofters Lea CW8 . . . . 103 D7
Crofters Pk CH5 . . . . 116 A3
Crofters Way CH1 . . . . 116 F8
Croft Gdns WA4 . . . . 27 A7
Croft Heath Gdns WA3 . . . . 9 A8
Croft Ho WA3 . . . . 9 A7
Croft La
  Dodleston CH4 . . . . 162 A7
  Knutsford WA16 . . . . 82 B8
Crofton Cl WA4 . . . . 27 C5
Crofton Cotts WA6 . . . . . . 100 B8
Crofton Gdns WA3 . . . . 4 E3
Crofton Rd WA7 . . . . 22 E1
Croft Pk WA16 . . . . 58 F5
Croft Rd SK9 . . . . 59 E4
Croftside WA1 . . . . 17 F7
Croftside Way SK9 . . . . 60 C6
Croft St
  Golborne WA3 . . . . 3 A8
  Widnes WA8 . . . . 23 A6
Crofts The CH3 . . . . 180 F1
Croftsway CH60 . . . . 40 D8
Croft The
  Chester CH2 . . . . 118 D5
  Norton in Hales TF9 . . . . . 236 B3
  Runcorn WA7 . . . . 23 F1
Croftwood Cl **10** CW7 . . . 149 A8
Cromdale Way WA5 . . . . . . 14 E6
Cromer Dr CW1 . . . . 190 B8
Cromford Cl SK23 . . . . 65 E6
Cromford Mews SK23 . . . . 65 E5
Cromley Rd SK6 . . . . 37 E6
Crompton Cl CW12 . . . . . . 157 A6
Crompton Dr WA2 . . . . 8 A6
Crompton Rd SK11 . . . . . . 112 C7
Crompton Way WA3 . . . . 4 B8
Cromwell Ave WA5 . . . . 15 D6
Cromwell Avenue S WA5 . . 15 D4
Cromwell Cl CW12 . . . . 2 A4
Cromwell Ct
  Irlam M44 . . . . 11 E7
  6 Nantwich CW5 . . . . . . 204 E5
  2 Warrington WA1 . . . . . 16 A5
Cromwell Dr CW2 . . . . 206 C4
Cromwell Rd
  Bramhall SK7 . . . . 35 D6
  Ellesmere Port CH65 . . . . . 70 D5
  Irlam M44 . . . . 11 E7
  Northwich CW8 . . . . 103 E8
Cromwell St WA8 . . . . 23 A6
Cronkinson Ave CW5 . . . . 204 F4
Cronkinson Oak CW5 . . . . 204 F4
CRONTON 12 D5
Cronton CE Prim Sch
  WA8 . . . . 12 C6
Cronton Farm Ct WA8 . . . . 12 E4
Cronton La WA8 . . . . 12 F5
Cronton Park Ave WA8 . . . 12 C6
Cronton Park Cl WA8 . . . . . 12 C6
Cronton Rd L35, WA8 . . . . . 12 C5
Cronulla Dr WA5 . . . . 14 E7
Crooked La CH3, CW6 . . . 145 C4
Crookedyard Rd SK11 . . . 113 E7
Crookenden Cl CH2 . . . . . . 95 C1
Crookenden Rd CH2 . . . . . . 95 C1
Crook La CW7 . . . . 127 A2
Croppers Rd WA2 . . . . 8 F3
Crosby Ave WA5 . . . . 14 E8
Crosby Dr CH64 . . . . 43 B1
Crosfield Ct WA5 . . . . 15 A5
Crosfield St WA1 . . . . 16 A5
Crosland Dr WA6 . . . . 73 A2
Crossall St SK11 . . . . 112 C7
Crossdale Rd CH62 . . . . 43 D5
Crossfield Ave
  Culcheth WA3 . . . . 4 F2
  Lymm WA13 . . . . 18 F3
  Winsford CW7 . . . . 149 D7
Crossfield Rd
  Bollington SK10 . . . . 87 E6
  Handforth SK9 . . . . 34 D4
Crossfields CH3 . . . . 121 B2
Crossgates WA8 . . . . 13 F3
Cross Gn CH2 . . . . 118 E6
Cross Hey CH4 . . . . 237 C1
Crossings Ho CW1 . . . . . . 190 A5
Crossings The WA12 . . . . . . 2 C3
Crosskeys Cl CW6 . . . . 145 A6
Cross La
  Audley ST7 . . . . 209 E5
  Church Minshull CW1,
    CW5 . . . . 172 C6
  Congleton CW12 . . . . 157 A1
  Croft WA3 . . . . 9 D7
  Haslington CW11 . . . . 191 F8
  Middlewich CW10 . . . . 151 D6

Cross La *continued*
  Neston CH64 . . . . 66 E5
  Newton-le-Willows WA12 . . 2 B4
  Sandbach CW11 . . . . 175 D5
  Smallwood CW11 . . . . 176 F5
  Swettenham CW12 . . . . . . 131 F4
  Tarvin CH3 . . . . 121 E2
  Warrington WA4 . . . . 17 A3
  Wilmslow SK9 . . . . 60 F8
Crossland Mews WA13 . . . 18 C4
Crosslands
  Congleton CW12 . . . . 157 A1
  Haslington CW11 . . . . 191 D4
Crossland Terr WA6 . . . . . . 73 B2
CROSS LANE 172 D6
Cross Lane CW11 . . . . 177 B5
Cross Lane E M31 . . . . 11 F3
Cross Lanes CH3 . . . . 144 C8
Cross Lane S WA3 . . . . 9 E6
Cross Lane W M31 . . . . 11 F2
Crossledge CW12 . . . . 156 B3
Crossley Ave CH66 . . . . 69 E6
Crossley Cres CH2 . . . . . . 119 B5
Crossley Dr CH60 . . . . 40 D8
Crossley Pk WA6 . . . . 99 C7
Crossley St WA1 . . . . 16 C5
Cross o' th' Hill SY14 . . . . 213 D4
Cross o' th' Hill Rd SY14. 214 A4
Cross Rd
  Gatley SK8 . . . . 34 B7
  Haslington CW11 . . . . 191 D4
Cross St
  Alsager ST7 . . . . 193 C3
  Barnton CW8 . . . . 78 B3
  Chester CH2 . . . . 118 F2
  Congleton CW12 . . . . 156 D3
  Crewe CW1 . . . . 190 D3
  Golborne WA3 . . . . 3 A7
  Haslington CW11 . . . . 191 D4
  Holt LL13 . . . . 196 E8
  Macclesfield SK11 . . . . . . 112 E6
  Marston CW9 . . . . 79 C3
  Neston CH64 . . . . 66 E8
  New Mills SK22 . . . . 39 C8
  20 Runcorn WA7 . . . . 23 A3
  Warrington WA2 . . . . 16 B7
  Widnes WA8 . . . . 13 C1
Cross The
  Holt LL13 . . . . 196 E8
  Kingsley WA6 . . . . 75 C2
  Lymm WA13 . . . . 18 E3
  7 Neston CH64 . . . . 66 E8
CROSS TOWN 57 B2
Crossway
  Bramhall SK7 . . . . 35 E5
  Crewe CW1 . . . . 190 D6
  Widnes WA8 . . . . 22 D8
Crossways ST8 . . . . 179 E1
Crossways Rd ST7 . . . . 194 A4
Crossway The CH63 . . . . . . 42 C4
Cross Wood St **5** CW5 . 204 D5
Crosthwaite Ave CH62 . . . . 43 F4
Croston Cl
  Alderley Edge SK9 . . . . 60 C1
  Widnes WA8 . . . . 12 C3
Crotia Ave CW7 . . . . 207 B5
Crouch La CW12 . . . . 157 D4
Crouchley Hall Mews
  WA13 . . . . 18 F1
Crouchley La WA13 . . . . . . 18 F1
CROUGHTON 95 F5
Croughton Rd
  Ellesmere Port CH66 . . . . . 69 F8
  Stoak CH2 . . . . 96 A7
  Stoak, Croughton CH2 . . . . 95 F6
Crowbrook Gr **7** SK9 . . . . 34 D1
Crowder's La CW9 . . . . 105 B4
Crowe Ave WA2 . . . . 8 B7
Crowland Gdns SK8 . . . . . . 35 B6
Crow Lane E WA12 . . . . 2 C4
Crow Lane W WA12 . . . . 2 A4
Crowley La CW9, WA16 . . . 28 A7
Crowmere Cl CW8 . . . . 102 A2
Crown Ave WA8 . . . . 22 B8
Crown Bank
  3 Sandbach CW11 . . . . . 175 B6
  Talke ST7 . . . . 210 D6
Crown Bank Cres ST7 . . . 210 D6
Crown Bldgs WA6 . . . . 73 B1
Crown Cotts CH4 . . . . 124 A7
Crown Ctr The **24** SK11 . 112 C8
Crown Ctyd CW3 . . . . 229 F4
Crown Dr CW11 . . . . 175 D3
Crownest La WA6 . . . . 78 E8
Crown Fields Cl WA12 . . . . 2 B5
Crown Gate WA7 . . . . 49 F7
Crown Gdns
  Newton-le-Willows WA12 . . 2 B4
  Talke ST7 . . . . 210 D6
Crown Gn WA13 . . . . 19 B4
Crown La WA16 . . . . 106 D8
Crown Mews CW3 . . . . 229 F4
Crown Park Dr WA12 . . . . . . 2 B5
Crown St W SK11 . . . . 112 C7
Crown St
  Newton-le-Willows WA12 . . 2 A4
  8 Northwich CW8 . . . . . 103 F8
  2 Warrington WA1 . . . . . 16 B7
Crow's Nest Cotts CH3 . . 166 C6
CROWTON 76 C1
Crowton Cotts CW7 . . . . . 170 F4
CROW WOOD 13 D3
Crow Wood La WA8 . . . . . . 13 D3
Crow Wood Pl WA8 . . . . . . 13 D3
Croxton Gn SY14 . . . . 201 C6
CROXTON GREEN 201 C6
Croxton La CW10 . . . . 128 A4

Croxton Way CW8 . . . . . . 103 A4
Croyde Cl M22 . . . . 33 F7
Croyde Rd L24 . . . . 21 A3
Crum Hill **2** CW9 . . . . 104 A8
Cryers La
  Elton CH2 . . . . 72 A2
  Thornton-le-Moors CH2 . . . 96 F8
Cty High Sch Leftwich The
  CW9 . . . . 104 A4
Cuckoo La
  Acton CW5 . . . . 203 E8
  Neston CH64 . . . . 67 C7
Cuckooland* WA16 . . . . . . 80 F8
CUCKOO'S NEST 162 E5
Cuckstoolpit Hill SK10 . . 112 E8
CUDDINGTON 101 F4
CUDDINGTON GREEN . . 212 B1
CUDDINGTON HEATH . . 212 E2
Cuddington La
  Cuddington CW8 . . . . 101 D4
  Sandiway CW8 . . . . 102 A6
Cuddington Prim Sch
  CW8 . . . . 101 F2
Cuddington Way **3** SK9 . . 34 D5
CUERDLEY CROSS 13 A2
Cuerdley Gn WA5 . . . . 14 A2
Cuerdley Rd WA5 . . . . 14 C3
Cuerdon Dr WA4 . . . . 17 D1
CULCHETH 4 E3
Culcheth Hall Dr WA3 . . . . . 4 F4
Culcheth Hall Farm Barns
  WA3 . . . . 5 A3
Culcheth High Sch WA3 . . . 5 A3
Culcheth Prim Sch WA3 . . . 5 A3
Culford Cl WA7 . . . . 24 D1
Culland St CW2 . . . . 190 C2
Cullen Cl CH63 . . . . 43 C4
Cullen Rd WA7 . . . . 48 D7
Cumber Cl SK9 . . . . 59 D4
Cumber Dr SK9 . . . . 59 D4
Cumber La SK9 . . . . 59 D4
Cumberland Arena CW1 190 D5
Cumberland Ave
  Irlam M44 . . . . 11 C5
  Nantwich CW5 . . . . 204 F6
Cumberland Cl
  Crewe CW1 . . . . 190 D5
  Talke ST7 . . . . 210 E2
Cumberland Cres WA11 . . 1 A6
Cumberland Dr
  Altrincham WA14 . . . . 31 B8
  Bollington SK10 . . . . 88 B8
Cumberland Gr CH66 . . . . 69 C3
Cumberland Rd
  Congleton CW12 . . . . 156 A3
  Partington M31 . . . . 11 E2
Cumberland St
  2 Macclesfield SK10 . . . 112 D8
  Warrington WA4 . . . . 16 C3
Cumbermere Dr CW11 . . . 174 E2
Cumbers Dr CH64 . . . . 67 A5
Cumbers La CH64 . . . . 67 A5
Cumbrae Dr **2** CH65 . . . . 70 C1
Cumbria Cl **2** CH66 . . . . . 69 E1
Cundiff Cl SK11 . . . . 112 E6
Cunliffe Ave WA12 . . . . 2 B5
Cunliffe Cl WA7 . . . . 50 A7
Cunningham Cl WA5 . . . . . 14 F5
Cunningham Dr
  Bebington CH63 . . . . 43 C7
  Gatley M22 . . . . 34 A8
  Runcorn WA7 . . . . 22 E1
Cunningham Ho WA7 . . . . . 48 E8
Cunningham Rd WA8 . . . . . 22 D8
Cuppin St CH1 . . . . 237 A2
Curlender Way L24 . . . . 21 E2
Curlew Cl
  Golborne WA3 . . . . 3 D8
  Macclesfield SK10 . . . . 87 C5
  Winsford CW7 . . . . 149 C5
Curlew Gr WA3 . . . . 9 E3
Curlew Rd ST7 . . . . 195 E1
Currans Rd WA7 . . . . 8 B2
Curzon Ave ST7 . . . . 193 D5
Curzon Cl CH4 . . . . 141 B8
Curzon Ct CH4 . . . . 140 F7
Curzon Dr WA4 . . . . 27 A7
Curzon Gr CW7 . . . . 126 F3
Curzon Mews SK9 . . . . 60 A5
Curzon Park N CH4 . . . . . . 141 B7
Curzon Park S CH4 . . . . . . 141 B7
Curzon Rd
  Gatley SK8 . . . . 34 B7
  Poynton SK12 . . . . 36 E2
Curzon St
  Chester CH4 . . . . 140 F7
  5 Runcorn WA7 . . . . 22 F1
Cwat Erwain CH4 . . . . 140 E7
Cwrt Cwellyn CH5 . . . . 139 B7
Cwrt Dinas CH5 . . . . 139 B7
Cwrt Ogwen CH5 . . . . 139 B7
Cwrt Y Terfyn CH4 . . . . . . 140 F6
Cygnet Cl CH66 . . . . 69 C6
Cygnet Ct WA1 . . . . 16 A3
Cyman Cl CH1 . . . . 117 D3
Cynthia Ave WA1 . . . . 17 B7
Cynthia Rd WA7 . . . . 22 F1
Cypress Ave
  Ellesmere Port CH66 . . . . . 69 F1
  Widnes WA8 . . . . 13 B2
Cypress Cl WA1 . . . . 17 C7
Cypress Gr WA7 . . . . 49 C7
Cypress Way SK6 . . . . 38 A7
Cyril Bell Cl WA13 . . . . 18 F3
Cyril St WA2 . . . . 16 B7

D

Daffodil Cl WA8 . . . . 13 E4
Daffodil Gdns WA9 . . . . 6 A7
Dagfields Crafts & Antiques
  Ctr* CW5 . . . . 220 A4
Dagnall Ave WA5 . . . . 7 F2
Dahlia Cl WA9 . . . . 6 A7
Daintry St SK11 . . . . 112 E7
Daintry Terr SK10 . . . . 112 E8
Dairy Bank CH2 . . . . 72 B4
Dairybrook Gr **7** SK9 . . . . 34 E1
Dairy Farm Cl WA13 . . . . . . 18 F4
Dairyground Rd SK7 . . . . . 35 F7
Dairy House La SK7 . . . . . . 35 B6
Dairy House Rd SK7 . . . . . . 35 B5
Dairy House Small Holdings
  SK7 . . . . 35 B4
Dairy House Way CW2 . . . 189 F2
Dairy La SK7 . . . . 188 D6
Dairylands Rd ST7 . . . . . . 193 F4
Daisy Ave WA12 . . . . 2 C2
Daisy Bank
  Alsager ST7 . . . . 193 A4
  Nantwich CW5 . . . . 204 D5
Daisy Bank Cres CW3 . . . 229 F5
Daisybank Dr
  Congleton CW12 . . . . 156 D4
  Sandbach CW11 . . . . 175 C6
Daisy Bank La CW9 . . . . . . 78 C3
Daisy Bank Mill Cl WA3 . . . 4 E3
Daisy Bank Rd
  Lymm WA13 . . . . 18 C3
  Warrington WA5 . . . . 14 F4
Daisy Cl WA16 . . . . 79 F6
Daisy Way SK6 . . . . 37 F7
Dakota Dr WA5 . . . . 15 C7
Dalby Cl WA3 . . . . 10 B5
Dalby Ct CW9 . . . . 104 E5
Dale Ave
  Bebington CH62 . . . . 43 D8
  Bramhall SK7 . . . . 35 F8
  Ellesmere Port CH66 . . . . . 69 C6
Dale Cl
  Warrington WA5 . . . . 15 D4
  Widnes WA8 . . . . 22 A8
Dale Cres CW12 . . . . 156 F2
Dalecroft WA6 . . . . 72 E1
Dale Ct
  Heswall CH60 . . . . 40 E8
  Middlewich CW10 . . . . 151 D7
Dale Dr
  Chester CH2 . . . . 118 D8
  Ellesmere Port CH65 . . . . . 69 F5
Daleford Manor CW8 . . . . 125 B8
Dalefords La
  Cuddington CW8 . . . . 102 A1
  Whitegate CW8 . . . . 125 D7
Dale Gdns CH65 . . . . 70 B3
Dale Gr
  Congleton CW12 . . . . 157 A2
  Irlam M44 . . . . 11 E6
Dale Head Rd SK10 . . . . . . 86 F4
Dale House Fold SK12 . . . . 37 A4
Dale La WA4 . . . . 26 E7
Dale Pl CW12 . . . . 156 F2
Dale Rd
  Bebington CH62 . . . . 43 D6
  Golborne WA3 . . . . 3 A7
  New Mills SK22 . . . . 39 C7
  Warrington WA5 . . . . 14 C8
Dalesford Cres SK10 . . . . 111 E8
DALES GREEN 195 C5
Dales Green Rd ST7 . . . . . 195 C5
Daleside CH2 . . . . 118 D8
Dale's Sq CW9 . . . . 103 F6
Dale St
  Chester CH3 . . . . 119 A1
  Macclesfield SK10 . . . . 112 E8
  Runcorn WA7 . . . . 23 A1
Dalesway Ch60 . . . . 40 E8
Dale The
  Neston CH64 . . . . 66 E6
  Tiverton CW6 . . . . 168 C6
  Warrington WA5 . . . . 14 F5
Dale View
  Kidsgrove ST7 . . . . 195 C5
  Newton-le-Willows WA12 . . 2 E4
Dale Way CW11 . . . . 190 A5
Dalewood Cl WA2 . . . . 16 A6
Dalewood Cres CH2 . . . . . . 72 A3
DALLAM 7 F2
Dallam Com Prim Sch WA5 7 F1
Dallam La WA2 . . . . 16 A7
Dallas Dr WA5 . . . . 15 A7
Dallimore Way **8** CH2 . . . 95 C1
Dalton Dr SK7 . . . . 35 C5
Dalton Ave
  Warrington, Birchwood
    WA3 . . . . 9 E6
  Warrington WA5 . . . . 15 F7
Dalton Bank WA1 . . . . 16 C6
Dalton Cl CH1 . . . . 117 E3
Dalton Ct
  Runcorn WA7 . . . . 23 E3
  Sandbach CW11 . . . . 174 E7
Dalton St
  Runcorn WA7 . . . . 23 D2
  Warrington WA3 . . . . 9 E5
Dalton Way CW10 . . . . 128 D3
Dalton's La CW7 . . . . 50 E7
Dam La WA3 . . . . 15 A7
Damery Ct SK7 . . . . 35 E8
Damery Rd SK7 . . . . 35 E8
Damhead La CH64 . . . . 41 E7
Dam Head La WA3 . . . . 11 A5

Damian Dr WA12. . . . . 2 A5
Dam La
  Hollinfare WA3 . . . . 11 A4
  Mobberley WA16. . . . . . . 58 C3
  Warrington WA1 . . . . 17 D7
  Winwick WA3. . . . . 8 F7
Dams La WA16. . . . . 106 D5
Damson Dr CW5 . . . . 204 E4
Damson La WA16. . . . . . . 58 C3
Damson Wlk M31 . . . . . . 11 D3
Danby Cl
  Runcorn WA7. . . . . 49 D6
  Warrington WA5 . . . . 15 E7
Dane Ave M31 . . . . 11 F4
DANEBANK 38 E5
Dane Bank Ave
  Congleton CW12 . . . . . . 156 E4
  Crewe CW2 . . . . 190 A2
Dane Bank Dr SK12 . . . . 38 D6
Dane Bank Rd
  Lymm WA13. . . . . 18 E4
  Northwich CW9 . . . . 104 B7
Dane Bank Road E WA13 . 18 E4
DANEBRIDGE 160 B7
Dane Cl
  Alsager ST7 . . . . 193 A3
  Chester CH4 . . . . 140 F5
  Sandbach CW11 . . . . . . 174 E7
Dane Dr
  Biddulph ST8 . . . . 179 E1
  Wilmslow SK9 . . . . 60 D6
Danefield Ct SK8. . . . . . . 34 D8
Danefield Rd
  Holmes Chapel CW4 . . . 130 C4
  Northwich CW9 . . . . 104 B7
Dane Gdns ST7 . . . . 195 C2
Dane Gr CH2 . . . . 119 F8
Dane Hill Cl SK12. . . . . . . 38 D5
DANE IN SHAW 179 C8
Dane Mill Bsns Ctr
  CW12. . . . . 156 C3
Dane Pl
  Crewe CW1 . . . . 190 D6
  Winsford CW7. . . . . 127 B1
Danescroft WA8 . . . . 12 B3
Daneside Bsns Pk CW12. 156 E4
Danes Sq SK11. . . . . 112 D5
Dane St
  Congleton CW12 . . . . . . 156 C3
  Middlewich CW10 . . . . . 128 D2
  Northwich CW9 . . . . 104 B8
Daneswell Rd L24. . . . . . . 21 A2
Daniel Adamson Ave M31 11 D3
Daniel Cl WA3 . . . . 10 A4
Daniel Ct M31 . . . . 11 F4
Daniell Way CH3. . . . . . . 142 A7
Danily Ct SY14. . . . . 213 B3
Dan's Rd WA8 . . . . 13 E2
Dapplebeath Rd CW2 . . 190 A1
Darby Cl CH64 . . . . 66 E5
D'Arcy Cotts CH63 . . . . . . 42 B6
Darent Rd WA11 . . . . 1 B7
DARESBURY 25 B2
Daresbury Cl
  Holmes Chapel CW4 . . . 130 A3
  4 Wilmslow SK9. . . . . . . 60 C8
Daresbury Ct WA8 . . . . . . 13 E3
DARESBURY DELPH 25 B1
Daresbury Expressway
  WA4. . . . . 25 A3
Daresbury Firs Nature
  Reserve★ WA4. . . . . 25 A2
Daresbury Pk WA4 . . . . . . 25 D2
Daresbury Pk WA4 . . . . . . 51 A8
Daresbury Prim Sch WA4. 25 B2
Darian Ave M22. . . . . 33 D8
Dario Gradi Dr CW2. . . . 190 D1
Dark Ark La CH3, WA6. . . . 99 B3
Darkie Mdw CW6 . . . . . . 185 E8
Dark La
  Henbury SK11 . . . . 111 B8
  Higher Whitley WA4. . . . . 52 D6
  Kingsley WA6. . . . . 75 B1
  Marston CW9 . . . . 79 C2
  Tattenhall CH3. . . . . 183 E7
  Warren SK11. . . . . 111 C3
  Whitchurch SY13. . . . . . 227 B1
Darland La LL12 . . . . 162 C1
Darley Ave
  Crewe CW2 . . . . 190 A3
  Warrington WA2 . . . . 8 E1
Darley Cl WA8 . . . . 12 B3
Darleydale Dr CH62 . . . . . 43 F5
Darley Rd SK7 . . . . 36 F7
Darlington Ave CW1 . . . 189 F5
Darlington Cres CH1 . . . . 94 A1
Darlington Ct **3** SK8 . . . . . 23 A7
Darlington St CW10 . . . . 128 C1
Darnaway Cl WA1. . . . . . . 10 B6
DARNHALL 149 A3
Darnhall Prim Sch CW7. 149 D6
Darnhall School La CW7. 149 C6
Dart Cl
  Alsager ST7 . . . . 193 A4
  Biddulph ST8 . . . . 179 D1
Dartnall Cl SK12 . . . . 38 A6
Dart Wlk CW7 . . . . 127 B2
Darwen Gdns WA2. . . . . . . 8 E1
Darwin Gr SK7 . . . . 35 E6
Darwin Rd CH1 . . . . 117 C4
Darwin St CW8 . . . . 103 E7
Daryl Rd CH60 . . . . 41 A8
Dashwood Cl WA4 . . . . . . 27 A7
Daten Ave WA3 . . . . 9 E6
Daten Pk WA3 . . . . 9 F6
Dauncey Cl CH2. . . . . 95 C1
Davehall Ave SK9 . . . . 60 A7
DAVENHAM 104 A2

Davenham Ave WA1. . . . . 16 E8
Davenham CE Prim Sch
  CW9. . . . . 103 F2
Davenham Cres CW2 . . . 190 A3
Davenham Ct CW9 . . . . . 104 A3
Davenham Mdws CW9. . . 103 F3
Davenham Rd
  Davenham CW9. . . . . . . 104 E3
  Handforth SK9. . . . . 34 D4
Davenham Rdbt CW9 . . . 103 F3
Davenham Way CW10 . . 151 D5
DAVENPORT 154 E7
Davenport Ave
  Crewe CW2 . . . . 206 D8
  Nantwich CW5. . . . . 204 E7
  Warrington WA4 . . . . 16 F5
  Wilmslow SK9 . . . . 59 E4
Davenport Cl CW11 . . . . 175 D8
DAVENPORT GREEN . . . 59 F3
Davenport La
  Brereton Green CW11. . . 154 C2
  Marton SK11 . . . . 132 F5
  Mobberley WA16. . . . . . . 58 D6
Davenport Park La
  CW12. . . . . 131 D2
Davenport Rd CH60 . . . . . 40 E7
Davenport Row WA7 . . . . 49 D8
Davenport St
  Congleton CW12 . . . . . . 156 C2
  Crewe CW1 . . . . 190 C6
  Macclesfield SK10 . . . . . 112 E8
Daven Prim Sch CW12 . . 156 E2
Davenport La CW12. . . . . 156 E1
Davey La SK9. . . . . 60 B2
Daveylands SK9 . . . . 60 B2
David Lewis Ctr The★
  SK9. . . . . 84 A6
David Lewis Sch The SK9. 83 F6
David Rd WA13 . . . . 18 E3
David's Ave WA5. . . . . 15 B5
Davidson Ave CW12. . . . 157 A5
David St CW8 . . . . 103 E7
Davies Ave
  Gatley SK8. . . . . 34 B6
  Newton-le-Willows WA12 . . 2 C4
  Warrington WA4 . . . . 16 F4
Davies Cl WA8 . . . . 23 A4
Davies Rd SK10. . . . . 112 E8
Davies Way WA13. . . . . . . 18 E3
Davis Cl ST7 . . . . 193 E3
Davy Rd WA7 . . . . 23 E3
Dawlish Ave SK8. . . . . 34 F7
Dawlish Cl
  Bramhall SK7. . . . . 35 E7
  Hollinfare WA3 . . . . 11 B3
Dawn Cl WA4. . . . . 67 A5
Dawn Gdns CH65. . . . . . . 70 B4
Dawpool Cl CH2 . . . . 118 D5
Dawpool Dr CH62 . . . . . . 43 C7
Dawson Cl
  Langley SK11. . . . . 113 C3
  11 Macclesfield SK11 . . . 111 F7
Dawson Dr CH2. . . . . 237 A4
Dawson Rd
  Bollington SK10. . . . . 88 A7
  Gatley SK8 . . . . 34 D8
  Macclesfield SK10 . . . . . 111 F7
Dawstone Ct CH60 . . . . . . 40 F8
Dawstone Rd CH60. . . . . . 41 A7
Dawstone Rise CH60 . . . . 40 F7
DAY GREEN. 192 F8
Deacon Rd WA8 . . . . 13 B1
Deacons Cl WA3 . . . . 9 A8
Deacon Trad Est WA12 . . . 2 A2
Deadman's La CW5 . . . . . 205 B2
Deakin's Rd CW7 . . . . . . 126 F4
Deal Cl WA5 . . . . 15 F6
Dean Bank CW6 . . . . 168 C3
Dean Cl
  Bollington SK10. . . . . 88 A7
  Handforth SK9. . . . . 34 C1
  Partington M31 . . . . 11 F4
  Sandbach CW11 . . . . . . 174 E8
  7 Widnes WA8. . . . . 23 B8
Dean Cres WA2 . . . . 8 B2
Dean Ct
  Bollington SK10. . . . . 88 B8
  Golborne WA3 . . . . 3 A7
Dean Dr SK9. . . . . 34 D2
Deane Ct CW5 . . . . 205 B4
Deanery Cl CH2 . . . . 118 C4
Deangate CH2 . . . . 207 E3
Dean Hollow ST7 . . . . . . 209 D2
Dean La SK7 . . . . 36 E8
Dean Mdw WA12. . . . . 2 C4
Dean Oaks Prim Sch SK9. 34 E1
Dean Pk SY14. . . . . 214 A5
Dean Rd
  Golborne WA3 . . . . 3 A7
  Handforth SK9. . . . . 34 E3
  Irlam M44 . . . . 11 E6
DEAN ROW 60 F8
Dean Row Ct **9** SK9 . . . 34 D1
Dean Row Rd SK9. . . . . . . 61 A8
Deans Cl
  Chester CH2 . . . . 118 C6
  Tarvin CH3. . . . . 121 B1
Deansfield Way CH2 . . . . 72 A3
Deansgate CH65 . . . . 70 A5
DEANSGREEN. 29 A8
Deansgreen WA13. . . . . . 29 A7
Deans La
  Sandbach CW11 . . . . . . 174 E6
  Warrington WA4 . . . . 17 F3
Dean's La
  Barthomley CW2 . . . . . . 208 C4

Dean's La continued
  Newcastle-under-Lyme
  ST5 . . . . 210 D2
Deans Rd CH65 . . . . 70 F3
Dean St
  Middlewich CW10 . . . . . 128 C2
  Northwich CW9 . . . . 104 C8
  Widnes WA8 . . . . 23 B8
  Winsford CW7. . . . . 126 D1
Deansway WA8 . . . . 22 C8
Deans Way
  Higher Kinnerton CH4 . . 161 A7
  Tarvin CH3. . . . . 121 B2
Dean Valley Prim Sch
  SK10. . . . . 87 E8
Dean View ST7 . . . . 209 D1
Deanwater Cl WA3 . . . . . . 9 D4
Deanwater Ct SK8 . . . . . . 34 D7
Deanway SK9 . . . . 34 C1
Deanway Trad Est SK9 . . 34 D3
Dearnford Ave CH62 . . . . 43 D6
Dearnford Cl CH62 . . . . . 43 D6
Debra Cl CH66 . . . . 69 C4
Debra Rd CH66 . . . . 69 C4
Decade Cl ST5 . . . . 210 F2
Dee Banks
  Chester CH3 . . . . 142 A8
  Huntington CH3 . . . . . . 141 F7
Dee Banks Specl Sch
  CH3. . . . . 142 A7
Dee Cl
  Biddulph ST8 . . . . 179 E1
  Sandbach CW11 . . . . . . 174 E8
  Talke ST7 . . . . 210 E7
Dee Cres CH3. . . . . 180 E2
Deefords CH3. . . . . 118 F1
Dee Fords Ave CH3 . . . . . 119 A1
Dee Hills Pk CH3. . . . . . . 237 C2
Dee La
  Chester CH1, CH3 . . . . . 237 C2
  Holt LL13 . . . . 196 D3
Dee Mdws LL13. . . . . 196 D7
Dee Park Cl CH60 . . . . . . 41 B8
Dee Park Rd CH60 . . . . . . 41 B5
Deepdale WA8 . . . . 12 C3
Deep Dale WA5. . . . . 14 F6
Dee Pk LL13. . . . . 196 D8
Dee Point Cty Prim Sch
  CH1. . . . . 117 D3
Dee Rd CH2 . . . . 96 F1
Dee Park Ct WA7. . . . . . . 49 F6
Deerwood Cl
  Ellesmere Port CH66. . . . 69 D7
  Macclesfield SK10 . . . . . 86 F1
Deerwood Cres CH66. . . . 69 D7
Deeside
  Ellesmere Port CH65. . . . 70 B2
  Holt LL13 . . . . 196 E8
Dee Side CH60. . . . . 40 C8
Deeside Cl CH5 . . . . 70 B2
Deeside Coll/Coleg Glannau
  Dyfrdwy CH5. . . . . 91 B1
Deeside Cres CH1. . . . . . 116 C5
Deeside Ct
  Chester CH3 . . . . 237 C2
  Neston CH64 . . . . 41 B1
Deeside Ind Pk/Parc
  Ddiwydiannol Glannau
  Dyfrdwy CH5. . . . . 92 E2
Deeside La CH1. . . . . 116 D4
Dee Sq CW7 . . . . 127 B2
Dee View Dr SK9 . . . . 34 C1
Dee View Cotts CH64. . . . 41 D1
Dee View Rd
  Connah's Quay CH5. . . . . 91 E1
  Heswall CH60 . . . . 40 F8
Dee Villas LL13 . . . . 180 E1
Dee Way CW7 . . . . 127 A2
Deirdre Ave WA8 . . . . 13 A1
De Lacy Row WA7. . . . . . . 24 A2
Delafield Cl WA2. . . . . 8 F3
Delaisy Way CW7. . . . . . . 127 A1
Delaman Pl **1** WA7 . . . . . 22 F1
DELAMERE 123 D6
Delamere CE Prim Sch
  CW6. . . . . 123 C5
Delamere Cl
  Barnton CW8 . . . . 78 A3
  Bebington CH62 . . . . 43 E4
  Chorlton CW2 . . . . 207 E4
  Sandbach CW11 . . . . . . 174 F8
Delamere Ct
  Alsager ST7. . . . . 192 F4
  Bebington CH62 . . . . 43 E4
  7 Crewe CW1 . . . . 190 C4
Delamere Dr
  Ellesmere Port CH66. . . . 69 E5
  Macclesfield SK10 . . . . . 87 F2
Delamere Forest Pk★
  CW8 . . . . 100 B3
Delamere Forest Sch
  WA6 . . . . 100 C4
Delamere Gr CW8. . . . . . 123 D7
Delamere Ho WA6 . . . . . . 74 C7
Delamere La CH3 . . . . 99 C2
DELAMERE PARK. 101 C5
Delamere Park Way E
  CW8. . . . . 101 D5
Delamere Park Way W
  CW8. . . . . 101 D5

Delamere Rd
  Congleton CW12 . . . . . . 155 F3
  Handforth SK9 . . . . 34 E4
  Macclesfield SK10 . . . . . . 87 F1
  Nantwich CW5. . . . . 204 F3
  Norley WA6 . . . . 100 B6
Delamere Rise CW7. . . . . 126 B1
Delamere St
  Chester CH1 . . . . 237 A3
  Crewe CW1 . . . . 190 C4
  Warrington WA5 . . . . 15 E5
  Winsford CW7 . . . . 126 B1
Delamere Sta CW8. . . . . 100 D1
Delamere's Acre CH64 . . . 68 A8
Delavor Cl CH60 . . . . 40 E8
Delavor Rd CH60. . . . . 40 E8
Delenty Dr WA3. . . . . 9 E4
Delery Dr WA3. . . . . 16 E8
Delfur Rd SK7 . . . . 35 E6
Delhi Rd M44 . . . . 11 F8
Dell Cl CH63 . . . . 43 B6
Dell Dr WA2 . . . . 9 A2
Dell La CH60. . . . . 41 B7
Dell The
  Cuddington CW8 . . . . . . 101 D5
  Guilden Sutton CH3 . . . . 119 F5
  Kelsall CW6 . . . . 122 D5
Delmar Rd WA16. . . . . 57 C1
Delphfields Rd WA4. . . . . 26 C7
Delphield WA7. . . . . 50 D8
Delph La
  Daresbury WA4 . . . . 25 A2
  Warrington, Houghton Gn
  WA2 . . . . 8 E6
  Warrington WA5 . . . . 8 A5
Delphside Cl SK11. . . . . . 209 F2
Delta Cres WA5. . . . . 7 C2
Delta Ct CH4. . . . . 140 B6
Delves Ave WA5 . . . . 15 F7
Delves Broughton Ct
  CW1. . . . . 191 D5
Delves Cl CW2 . . . . 206 B4
Delves Wlk CH3. . . . . 142 B7
Delvine Dr CH2 . . . . 118 D6
Demage Dr CH66. . . . . 69 D3
Demage La
  Backford CH1 . . . . 94 F4
  Chester CH2 . . . . 118 D8
Demage La S CH2 . . . . . . 118 D7
Denbigh Cl
  Hazel Grove SK7. . . . . . . 36 C8
  Helsby WA6. . . . . 73 A1
Denbigh Cres CW10 . . . . 151 C7
Denbigh Ct CH65 . . . . 70 D3
Denbigh Dr CW7 . . . . 149 B7
Denbigh Gdns CH65 . . . . 70 C3
Denbigh St CH1. . . . . 118 B3
Denbury Ave WA4. . . . . . . 16 F2
Dene Dr CW2 . . . . 190 A2
Dene Dr CW7 . . . . 149 D8
Denehurst Cl WA5 . . . . . . 14 F4
Denehurst Park Way
  CW8. . . . . 101 D5
Denesgate **1** CW7 . . . . . 149 D8
Deneside Ave CW1 . . . . . 190 C6
Deneway
  Bramhall SK7. . . . . 35 D7
  High Lane SK6. . . . . 37 F8
Denewood Ct **3** SK9 . . . . 60 A6
Denford Cl CH4 . . . . 139 C4
Denford Pl ST7 . . . . 193 D6
Denhall Cl CH2 . . . . 118 E5
Denhall La CH64 . . . . 67 A3
Denham Ave WA5. . . . . . . 15 B5
Denham Dr SK7 . . . . 35 E8
Denison Rd SK7. . . . . 36 E8
Den La CW3, CW5 . . . . . . 221 D4
Dennett Cl WA1. . . . . 17 E6
Dennis Dr CH4. . . . . 141 B6
Dennison Rd SK8 . . . . 35 B8
Dennis Rd WA8 . . . . 23 C7
Dennis Round Ct ST7. . . 193 C3
Densham Ave WA2. . . . . . . 8 B4
Denston Cl CW2 . . . . 190 B1
Denstone Dr CH4 . . . . . . 141 A4
Dentdale Wlk M22 . . . . . . 33 C8
Dentith Dr CH1 . . . . 117 E5
Denton Cl CW7 . . . . 126 C1
Denton Dr CW9 . . . . 79 C1
Denton Drive Ind Est
  CW9. . . . . 79 C2
Denton St WA8 . . . . 13 C1
Denver Ave CW2 . . . . 190 B3
Denver Dr WA5. . . . . 15 B7
Denwall Ho **4** CH64. . . . . 66 E8
Depenbeck Cl SY14 . . . . 213 B4
Depmore La WA6 . . . . 75 A2
Derby Cl
  Irlam M44 . . . . 11 C5
  Newton-le-Willows WA12 . . 2 B3
Derby Dr WA1 . . . . 16 F7
Derby Knoll SK23. . . . . . . 39 F1
Derby Rd
  Golborne WA3 . . . . 3 C8
  Talke ST7 . . . . 210 D7
  4 Warrington WA4 . . . . . 16 C1
  Widnes, Barrow's Green
  WA8 . . . . 13 D4
  Widnes, Lunts Heath WA8 . 13 B4
Derby Row WA7 . . . . 7 D8
DERBYSHIRE HILL 1 A2
Derbyshire Hill Rd WA9 . . 1 A2
Derbyshire Rd
  Partington M31 . . . . 11 E2
  Poynton SK12. . . . . 37 D5

Derby St
  Congleton CW12 . . . . . . 156 D3
  Crewe CW1 . . . . 190 B5
  Newton-le-Willows WA12 . . 2 B3
Dereham Way WA7 . . . . . 24 D3
Derek Ave WA2. . . . . 8 E1
Derfel Terr **4** WA6 . . . . . 74 B8
Derrington Ave CW2 . . . . 190 C3
Derwen Foundation Prim
  Sch CH4. . . . . 161 A7
Derwent Cl
  Alsager ST7 . . . . 193 A4
  Culcheth WA3. . . . . 5 A2
  Holmes Chapel CW4 . . . 130 A3
  Macclesfield SK11. . . . . 112 A6
  Partington M31 . . . . 11 F4
  Willaston CW5 . . . . 205 D6
Derwent Cres ST7. . . . . . 195 C2
Derwent Dr
  Biddulph ST8 . . . . 179 E1
  Bramhall SK7. . . . . 35 C5
  Congleton CW12 . . . . . . 156 F1
  Handforth SK9. . . . . 34 C5
  Hooton CH66 . . . . 44 B2
Derwent Rd
  Chester CH2 . . . . 119 A5
  High Lane SK6. . . . . 37 E8
  Warrington WA4 . . . . 16 B2
  Widnes WA8 . . . . 12 C1
Derwent Way
  Alderley Edge SK9. . . . . . 83 F7
  Neston CH64 . . . . 44 E2
Desoto Rd WA8. . . . . 22 E5
Desoto Road E WA8 . . . . 22 F6
Desoto Road W WA8 . . . . 22 F6
De Trafford Mews **9** WA9. 34 D2
Deva Ave CH4 . . . . 140 D6
Deva Bsns Pk CH5 . . . . . 116 A8
Deva Cl SK12 . . . . 36 B4
Deva Ct CH2 . . . . 118 F2
Deva Hts CH3. . . . . 141 F7
Deva La CH2. . . . . 118 C6
Deva Link CH1 . . . . 118 B3
Deva Rd CW2 . . . . 189 D4
Deva Ret Pk CH1. . . . . . . 118 A3
Deva Terr CH3 . . . . 237 C2
Devon Cl
  Macclesfield SK10 . . . . . . 86 F2
  Middlewich CW10 . . . . . 128 D2
Devon Gr ST8. . . . . 179 C1
Devon Pl
  Congleton CW12 . . . . . . 156 E4
  Widnes WA8 . . . . 13 B3
Devon Rd
  Chester CH2 . . . . 118 F5
  Irlam M44 . . . . 11 D5
  Partington M31 . . . . 11 E2
Devonshire Dr SK9. . . . . . 60 B2
Devonshire Gdns WA12. . . 2 C2
Devonshire Pl CH4 . . . . . 141 E7
Devonshire Rd
  Broughton CH4 . . . . 139 C4
  Hazel Grove SK7. . . . . . . 36 F8
  Warrington WA1 . . . . 16 F8
Dewar Ct WA7 . . . . 23 E3
Dewa Roman Experience★
  CH1. . . . . 237 A2
Dewar St WA3 . . . . 9 E5
Dewes St CW1 . . . . 190 B5
Dewhurst Rd WA3 . . . . 9 D2
Dexter Way CW10 . . . . . 128 D2
Dial Cotts CH64. . . . . 67 A5
Dial La CW12, SK11 . . . . 158 B1
Dial Rd WA15 . . . . 32 C8
Dial St WA1 . . . . 16 C5
Diamond Ave **3** ST7 . . . . 195 B2
Dibbinsdale Rd CH63. . . . 43 B7
Dibbins Gn CH63. . . . . . . 43 B7
Dickens Cl
  Cheadle SK8 . . . . 35 B5
  Sandbach CW11 . . . . . . 174 D6
Dickens La SK12 . . . . 36 E2
Dickenson Cl WA11. . . . . . 1 A6
Dickinson Way ST7 . . . . . 193 A3
Dicklow Cob SK11 . . . . . . 132 A8
Dickson Cl WA8 . . . . 23 B8
Dicksons Dr CH2. . . . . . . 118 D4
Dickson St
  Widnes, Kingsway WA8. . . 23 A8
  2 Widnes WA8. . . . . 23 B8
Dierden St CW7 . . . . 127 B1
Dierdens Terr **4** CW10 . . 128 C1
Dig La
  Acton CW5. . . . . 203 F4
  Frodsham WA6. . . . . 74 A7
  Shavington CW5 . . . . . . 206 B2
  Warrington WA2 . . . . 9 B3
Diglake Cl ST7 . . . . 210 C6
Diglake Cotts ST7 . . . . . . 210 A2
Diglake St ST7 . . . . 209 F3
Diglee Rd SK23 . . . . 39 C3
Dingle Cl CW11 . . . . 173 A1
Dimelow Ct SY14 . . . . . . 213 A2
Dinas Cl CH1 . . . . 117 E7
Dingle Ave
  Newton-le-Willows WA12 . . 1 F2
  Row-of-Trees SK9 . . . . . . 59 D3
Dingle Bank
  Chester CH4 . . . . 141 C7
  Sandbach CW11 . . . . . . 175 C6
Dingle Bank Cl WA13. . . . 18 E3
Dinglebrook Gr **5** SK9 . . 34 D1

Dingle Cl SK10 . . . . 87 B3
Dingle La
　Bridgemere CW5 . . . . 231 F6
　Kelsall CW6 . . . . 122 E6
　Sandbach CW11 . . . . . . 175 C6
　Warrington WA4 . . . . 26 F6
　Winsford CW7 . . . . 126 E1
Dingle Prim Sch The
　CW1 . . . . 191 D6
Dingle Rch Ctr **6** CW7 126 D1
Dingle The
　Barnton CW8 . . . . 78 B4
　Haslington CW1 . . . . . . 191 D5
　Lymm WA13 . . . . 18 E3
Dingleway WA4 . . . . 26 D8
Dingle Way CW8 . . . . 101 E5
Dingle Wlk **4** CW7 . . . 126 D1
Dinnington Dr WA12 . . . . . 12 E3
Diploma Dr CW10 . . . . . . 128 C2
Dipping Brook Ave WA4. . 26 F4
DISLEY 38 C5
Disley Prim Sch SK12 . . . . 38 D6
Disley Sta SK12 . . . . 38 D6
Distaff Rd SK12 . . . . 36 B4
District CE Prim Sch The
　WA12 . . . . 2 A4
Ditchfield La WA16 . . . . . 29 D3
Ditchfield Pl WA8 . . . . . . 22 B8
Ditchfield Rd
　Warrington WA5 . . . . 14 E3
　Widnes WA8 . . . . 22 B8
DITTON 22 C8
Ditton CE Prim Sch WA8 . 12 A1
Ditton Prim Sch WA8 . . . . 12 E1
Ditton Rd WA8 . . . . 22 D6
Dixon Ave WA12 . . . . 2 C5
Dixon Cl WA11 . . . . 2 A8
Dixon Dr SK11 . . . . 84 B3
Dixon Rd CW12 . . . . 157 A5
Dixon's Hos CH3 . . . . . . 142 E8
Dixon St
　Irlam M44 . . . . 11 F8
　Warrington WA1 . . . . 16 A5
Dobb Hedge Cl WA15 . . . 32 C6
Dobell's Rd CW9 . . . . 103 F5
Dobers La WA6 . . . . 74 C4
Dobson Ct SY14 . . . . 213 B3
Dock Rd
　Northwich CW9 . . . . 103 F7
　Widnes WA8 . . . . 23 A5
Dock Road Edwardian
　Pumping Station The* **2**
　CW9 . . . . 103 F7
Dock St
　Ellesmere Port CH65 . . . 70 C7
　Widnes WA8 . . . . 23 A5
Dock Yard Rd CH65 . . . . . 70 E6
Doddington Dr CW11 . . . 175 C8
Doddington Rd CW2 . . . . 190 A3
Doddlespool Barns WA3. 221 F7
Dodd's Green La CW5,
　SY13 . . . . 228 C4
Dodd's La
　Astbury CW12 . . . . 178 C6
　Higher Wych SY13, SY14. 224 E7
Doddswood Dr **2** CW12 156 F4
Dodgsley Dr WA6 . . . . 75 C1
Dodleston La CH4 . . . . . 162 D3
DODLESTON 162 B7
Dodleston CE Prim Sch
　CH4. . . . . 162 A3
Dodleston La CH4 . . . . . 162 C3
Deeford Cl WA3 . . . . 4 C5
Doe's Meadow Rd CH63 . 43 B7
Dog La
　Brereton Green CW4,
　CW11 . . . . 153 E2
　Kelsall CW6 . . . . 122 B5
　Nantwich CW5 . . . . 204 E6
　Tattenhall CH3 . . . . 182 E4
　Threapwood SY14 . . . . 223 C7
Dogmore La CW9 . . . . . . 147 C4
Dolly La SK23 . . . . 39 F3
Dolmans Cl **9** WA1 . . . 16 B5
Dolphin Cres CH66 . . . . . 69 E2
Dolphin Ct CH4 . . . . 141 A7
Dombey Rd SK12 . . . . 36 D2
Domestic App M90 . . . . . 33 C6
Domville Cl WA13 . . . . . . 18 E2
Donagh Cl SK10 . . . . 86 F2
DONES GREEN 77 B8
Donkey La SK9 . . . . 60 A5
Donne Pl CH1 . . . . 117 F6
Donnington Way CH4 . . . 140 F7
Don Wlk CH65 . . . . 70 A7
Dood's La WA4 . . . . 27 A5
Dooley's Grig SK11 . . . . 108 F1
Dooley's La SK9 . . . . 34 C2
Dorac Ave SK8 . . . . 34 C7
Dorchester Cl
　Kidsgrove ST7 . . . . 195 A3
　Wilmslow SK9 . . . . 60 D8
Dorchester Pk WA7 . . . . . 24 E3
Dorchester Pk Nature
　Reserve* WA7. . . . . 24 D3
Dorchester Rd
　Chester CH4 . . . . 140 F5
　Warrington WA5 . . . . 15 C5
Dorchester Way
　Burtonwood WA5. . . . . . . .6 F6
　Macclesfield SK10 . . . . . 87 C4
Doreen Ave CW12 . . . . . 179 B8
Dorfold Cl CW11 . . . . 175 C7
Dorfold Dr CW5. . . . . 204 D5
Dorfold Hall* CW5 204 B5

Dorfold St CW1. . . . . 190 C4
Dorfold Way CH2 . . . . 118 E6
Doric Ave WA6 . . . . 74 D7
Dorin Park Specl Sch
　CH2. . . . . 118 D6
Dormer Cl CH3 . . . . 143 A5
Dorney Cl WA4 . . . . 26 E6
Dornoch Ct CW4 . . . . 130 B2
Dorothea St WA2 . . . . 16 C7
Dorric Way CW1 . . . . 190 C7
Dorrington Cl WA7. . . . . . 50 E8
Dorrit Cl SK12 . . . . 36 E2
Dorset Cl CW12 . . . . 156 E4
Dorset Dr ST8 . . . . 179 C1
Dorset Gdns WA7 . . . . 50 A6
Dorset Pl
　Chester CH2 . . . . 119 A5
　Kidsgrove ST7 . . . . 195 A2
Dorset Rd
　Chester CH2 . . . . 118 F7
　Irlam M44 . . . . 11 D5
Dorset Way WA1 . . . . 17 B8
Dorset Wlk SK10 . . . . 86 F2
Douglas Ave WA3 . . . . .6 B6
Douglas Cl
　Northwich CW8 . . . . 103 C5
　Widnes WA8 . . . . 13 F3
Douglas La CW7 . . . . 171 A6
Douglas Pl CH4 . . . . 140 E6
Doulton Cl CW1 . . . . 126 F3
Doune Cl CH65 . . . . 70 D3
Dounrey Cl WA2 . . . . .9 A2
DOVE BANK. 195 A2
Dove Bank Prim Sch
　ST7 . . . . 195 A2
Dove Cl
　Ellesmere Port CH66 . . . 70 A8
　Elton CH2 . . . . 72 C4
　Helsby WA6 . . . . 73 C5
　Sandbach CW11 . . . . . . 175 A8
　Warrington WA3 . . . . .9 F4
Dovecote Cl CW2 . . . . . . 206 B8
Dovecote Dr WA11 . . . . . . 1 C7
Dovecote Gn WA5 . . . . . . .7 A1
Dovedale Ave CH62 . . . . . 43 E5
Dovedale Cl
　Congleton CW12 . . . . . 157 A4
　High Lane SK6 . . . . 37 E7
　Warrington WA2 . . . . .8 E3
Dovedale Ct WA8 . . . . 12 B3
Dove Gr ST8 . . . . 179 D1
Dove Ho ST7 . . . . 195 C3
Dove Pl CW7 . . . . 127 B2
Dover Cl WA7 . . . . 50 E6
Dover Ct CH65 . . . . 70 D2
Dover Ct WA4. . . . . 16 F3
Dover Dr
　Ellesmere Port CH65. . . . 70 D2
　Winsford CW7 . . . . 149 B6
Dover Rd
　Chester CH4 . . . . 141 A6
　Macclesfield SK10 . . . . . 87 F2
　Warrington WA3 . . . . 17 A3
Dover St WA7 . . . . 23 B3
Dovesmead Rd CH60 . . . . 41 C7
Doward St WA8 . . . . 13 C2
Downes Cl SK10 . . . . 87 A1
Downesway SK9 . . . . 59 F1
Downham Ave WA3 . . . . . .4 F2
Downham Ct **1** WA8 . . . 41 A8
Downham Dr CH60 . . . . . . 41 A8
Downham Pl CH1 . . . . . . 117 E4
Downham Road S CH60 . . 41 A8
Downing Cl SK11 . . . . 112 F3
Downs End WA16 . . . . 57 C1
Downsfield Rd CH4 . . . . . 141 A6
Downside WA8 . . . . 12 B3
Downs Rd WA7 . . . . 23 A1
Downs The CW8 . . . . 101 D5
Downswood Ct CH2. . . . . 118 C4
Downswood Dr CH2. . . . . 118 C4
Downway La WA9 . . . . .1 A1
Dragon's La
　Middlewich CW11 . . . . . 151 F1
　Sandbach CW11 . . . . . . 152 B1
Dragons Wharf CW11 . . . 152 C1
Dragon Yd WA3 . . . . 13 B4
Drake Ave M44 . . . . 11 E6
Drake Cl WA3 . . . . .7 D1
Drake La CW5 . . . . 203 F4
Drakelow La CW10 . . . . . 128 F8
Drake Rd CH4 . . . . 41 E1
Drakes Way SY14 . . . . . . 213 B5
Drapers Ct WA3. . . . . .3 F7
Draycott Dr ST5 . . . . 210 D2
Drayton Cl
　12 Handforth SK9 . . . . 34 D1
　Runcorn WA7. . . . . 22 F1
Drayton Cres CW1 . . . . . 190 F5
Drayton Dr SK8 . . . . 34 B7
Drenfell Rd ST7 . . . . 194 F7
Drift Cotts LL12 . . . . 162 C1
Drillfield Ct **20** CW9 . . 103 B8
Drillfield Rd CW9 . . . . . . 103 A8
Drill Field Rd CW9 . . . . . 103 F8
Drive A CH5 . . . . 93 A2
Drive B CH5 . . . . 93 A2
Drive C CH5 . . . . 93 A2
Drive D CH5 . . . . 93 A1
Drive The
　Altrincham WA15. . . . . . . 32 D8
　Bollington SK10 . . . . 87 F7
　Broomedge WA13 . . . . . . 19 D1
　Holmes Chapel CW4 . . . 130 B3
Drovers Way CW11. . . . . . 175 A5
Droxford Ct SK9 . . . . 60 B6

Druitt Ct CW1. . . . . 191 D4
Drumber La ST7 . . . . 195 B8
Drumber The CW7 . . . . . . 126 D1
Drumble Field SK11. . . . . . 84 A3
Drummond Ave CH66 . . . 69 C4
Drummond Ct WA8 . . . . . 13 D2
Drummond Way SK10 . . . 86 E1
Druridge Dr WA5 . . . . 14 F4
Drury Cl CW1 . . . . 190 F5
Drury La
　Knutsford WA16. . . . . . . 57 A2
　Tallarn Green/Tallwrn Green
　SY13 . . . . 223 E1
　Warmingham CW1. . . . . 173 D4
DRURY LANE. 223 D1
Dryden Cl CW2 . . . . 190 A1
Dryden Pl WA2 . . . . .8 C2
Dryersfield **5** CH3 . . . 142 A8
Dryhurst Dr SK12 . . . . 36 D6
Dryhurst La SK12 . . . . 38 D6
Dublin Croft CH66. . . . . . . 69 E1
Duchess Pl CH2 . . . . 237 A4
Duchy Rd CW4. . . . . 207 A8
DUCKINGTON 199 C4
Duck La CH3. . . . . 121 F7
Duckworth Gr WA2 . . . . . . 9 A1
DUDDON 145 A6
Duddon Cl
　Duddon CW6 . . . . 145 B6
　3 Northwich CW9 . . . 103 F4
Duddon CW6 . . . . 145 B6
Duddon Hall Barns CW6. 144 E8
Duddon Hook La CW6 . . . 144 F6
Duddon Rd CW6 . . . . 145 B5
Duddon St Peter's Prim Sch
　CW6 . . . . 145 B6
Dudleston Rd CH66 . . . . . 69 B6
Dudley Ave WA7 . . . . 23 D2
Dudley Cres CH65 . . . . . . 44 B3
Dudley Rd
　Ellesmere Port CH65 . . . 70 B5
　Irlam M44 . . . . 11 D4
Dudley St WA2 . . . . 16 B7
Dudley Wlk **2** SK21. . . 111 F7
Dudlow Green Rd WA4. . . 26 E5
Dudson Cl CW1. . . . . 207 C1
Dufton Wlk M22 . . . . 33 E8
Duke Ave
　Cheadle SK8 . . . . 34 F6
　Glazebury WA3 . . . . .5 C7
Duke Cl WA7 . . . . 22 F2
Dukesbridge Ct **7** WA13 . 18 E3
Duke's Cres CW1 . . . . . . 175 A7
Dukes Ct **3** SK11 . . . . 112 D7
Duke's Ct CH1 . . . . 237 B1
DUKESFIELD 22 E3
Duke St
　Alderley Edge SK9 . . . . . 60 B2
　Chester CH1. . . . . 237 B1
　Congleton CW12 . . . . . 156 D2
　Crewe CW2 . . . . 190 C3
　Macclesfield SK11 . . . . . 112 D7
　Newton-le-Willows WA12 . .2 B3
Dukesway CH2 . . . . 118 E7
Dukes Way CW9 . . . . 103 E5
Dukes Wharf WA7 . . . . . . 50 E6
Dulas Ct CH2 . . . . 118 E8
Dulverton Ave CH3 . . . . . 119 C2
Dumbah La SK10. . . . . . . 87 D6
Dumbers WA7 . . . . 136 A2
Dumbill Ho ST7 . . . . 210 C8
Dunbar Cl
　Connah's Quay CH5. . . . 91 D1
　Ellesmere Port CH66 . . . 69 C5
Dunbar Cheap CW4 . . . . 130 C2
Dunbar Ct CH66. . . . . 69 C5
Duncan Ave
　Newton-le-Willows WA12 . 2 C5
　Runcorn WA7. . . . . 23 C1
Duncansby Cres WA5 . . . 14 E6
Duncansby Dr CH63 . . . . 43 C4
Duncan St WA2 . . . . 16 C7
Dundalk Rd WA8 . . . . 22 C8
Dundee Ct WA2 . . . . .8 E4
Dundee CH65 . . . . 70 E3
Dundonald Ave **8** WA4 . 16 C1
Dundonald Rd SK8 . . . . . 35 A7
Dundrennan Cl SK12 . . . . 36 D5
Dunge Valley Rhododendron
　Gdns* SK23. . . . . 89 F8
Dunham Cl
　Alsager ST7 . . . . 193 C3
　Bebington CH62. . . . . . . 43 F3
　Sandbach CW11 . . . . . . 175 C6
Dunham Cres CW2 . . . . . 206 B8
Dunham Ct
　Dunham-on-the-Hill WA6. 97 E6
　Hartford CW8 . . . . 102 F4
DUNHAM HEATH 98 A4
Dunham Massey Hall*
　WA14 . . . . 20 D3
DUNHAM-ON-THE-HILL. . 97 E5
Dunham Pk (Deer Pk)*
　WA14 . . . . 20 D3
Dunham Rd
　Altrincham, Bowgreen
　WA14 . . . . 20 F1
　Handforth SK9 . . . . 34 D5
　Mossbrow WA13 . . . . . . 19 E7
　Northwich CW9 . . . . 104 A4
DUNHAM TOWN 20 E4
Dunham Way SK9 . . . . 34 D5
DUNHAM WOODHOUSES . 19 B6
DUNKIRK. 94 E6
Dunkirk La CH1 . . . . 210 A6
Dunkirk Ave CW7 . . . . . . 149 D8
Dunkirk Dr CH65 . . . . 70 B1

Dunkirk La
　Capenhurst CH1 . . . . 94 C7
　Ellesmere Port CH65. . . . 70 A1
Dunkirk Trad Est CH1 . . . 94 D6
Dunley Cl WA3. . . . . 10 A5
Dunlin Ave WA12 . . . . .2 C4
Dunlin Cl
　Poynton SK12. . . . . 36 A4
　Runcorn WA7. . . . . 49 F5
　Warrington WA3 . . . . .9 F7
Dunlin Rise SK10. . . . . . . 87 B5
Dunlop St WA4 . . . . 16 B3
Dunmail Gr WA7 . . . . 49 E5
Dunmore Cl CW10 . . . . . 151 C7
Dunmore Cres CH66 . . . . 69 B6
Dunmore Rd CH66 . . . . . . 69 B6
Dunmow Rd WA4 . . . . 17 C3
Dunnillow Field CW5. . . . 205 A4
Dunnock Cl WA2. . . . . 13 E2
Dunnock Gr WA3 . . . . .9 E4
Dunnocksfold Rd ST7 . . . 193 A4
Dunnockswood ST7. . . . 193 A4
Dunn's Cotts CW1 . . . . . 192 C1
Dunn's La CH3 . . . . 121 F7
Dunoon Cl CW4. . . . . 130 B2
Dunraven Rd CH64 . . . . . 67 A7
Dunscar Cl WA3 . . . . .9 D5
Dunsford WA8 . . . . 12 B3
Dunsmore Cl WA11 . . . . . .1 C7
Dunstan La CH64. . . . . . . 67 E3
Dunster Cl CW9. . . . . 104 A4
Dunster Gr CH60 . . . . 41 B7
Dunster Rd SK10. . . . . . . 87 F1
Dunwood Dr ST7. . . . . . . 193 D6
Dunwoody Way CW1,
　CW2. . . . . 190 B4
Durban Ave CH3 . . . . 142 D7
Durber Cl ST7 . . . . 209 D1
Durham Cl
　Macclesfield SK10 . . . . . 86 F2
　Warrington WA1 . . . . 17 E7
Durham Ct CH65 . . . . 70 E3
Durham Dr CW7 . . . . 149 C6
Durham Gr M44. . . . . 11 C6
Durham Rd
　Blacon CH1 . . . . 117 F5
　Widnes WA8 . . . . 13 B3
Durlston Cl WA8 . . . . 12 C2
Durrell Way WA3 . . . . .3 F8
DUTTON 51 A4
Dutton Cl WA1. . . . . 16 C5
Dutton Gn CH2. . . . . 70 F3
Dutton Hall Cl WA4 . . . . . 76 E8
Dutton La CW8, WA6. . . . 101 B6
Duttons Bsns Ctr CW9. . . 103 F7
Dutton's La CW6. . . . . . . 122 C5
Dutton Way
　Crewe CW1 . . . . 190 B6
　Nantwich CW5. . . . . 204 E3
Duxford Ct WA7 . . . . .8 E1
Dyar Terr CW8 . . . . 78 D1
Dye House La WA6. . . . . . 73 C5
Dyers Cl WA13 . . . . 19 A4
Dyers La WA13 . . . . 19 A4
Dykin Cl WA3 . . . . 13 E3
Dykin Rd WA3 . . . . 13 E3
Dysart Bldgs CW5. . . . . . 204 E5
Dyserth Rd CH1 . . . . 117 D3
Dystelegh Rd SK12. . . . . . 38 D6

E

Eadie Gr CW1. . . . . 190 A7
Eaglais Way SK10. . . . . . . 86 F2
Eagland Pl CW12. . . . . . . 156 E4
Eagle Brow WA13 . . . . . . 18 D3
Eagle La CH66 . . . . 69 D7
Eagle Mount WA4. . . . . . . 16 C2
Eagle Park Dr WA2. . . . . . .8 A1
Eaglesfield CW8 . . . . 103 C4
Eagles Way WA7 . . . . 49 E6
Ealing Cl WA7 . . . . 24 D1
Ealing St WA5 . . . . 15 B5
Eanleywood Farm Cl WA7 50 C7
Eanleywood La WA7 . . . . . 50 C7
Eardley Cres CW12 . . . . . 156 E4
Eardley Pl **6** CW1 . . . . 190 B5
Eardleyend Rd ST7. . . . . 209 E7
Eardswick Cl CW2 . . . . . 206 B8
Eardswick La CW1 . . . . . 172 D5
Eardswick Rd CW10 . . . . 151 C6
Earle Cl WA12 . . . . .1 F3
Earle Cres CH64 . . . . 41 D1
Earle Dr CH64 . . . . 41 D1
Earle Rd WA8 . . . . 23 C7
Earles La CW9 . . . . 79 E6
Earle's La CW6 . . . . 122 C5
Earl St
　Crewe CW1 . . . . 190 D4
　Newton-le-Willows WA12 . 2 A3
EARLESTOWN 2 B2
Earlestown Sta WA12 . . . . .2 B3
Earl Rd SK8, SK9. . . . . . . 34 E5
Earls Gdns CH65 . . . . 70 B5
Earls Oak CH2 . . . . 118 D7
Earl's Port CH1 . . . . 118 B2
Earls Rd CW2 . . . . 206 B4
Earl St WA12 . . . . 16 B7
Earlston Ct CH3 . . . . 237 C2
Earlsway
　Chester CH4 . . . . 141 A8
　Macclesfield SK11 . . . . . 111 F7
Earls Way
　Northwich CW9 . . . . 103 E4
　Runcorn WA7. . . . . 49 E6
Earlswood Mews CW9. . . 103 F3

Easby Cl
　Cheadle SK8 . . . . 35 B6
　Poynton SK12. . . . . 36 D4
　Runcorn WA7. . . . . 23 C2
Easenhall Cl WA8 . . . . . . 13 C5
East Ave
　Bollington SK10 . . . . 87 F7
　Gatley SK8 . . . . 34 D8
　Northwich CW9 . . . . 104 D8
　Warrington, Great Sankey
　WA5 . . . . 15 A4
　Warrington, Stockton Heath
　WA4 . . . . 16 D1
　Warrington WA2 . . . . 16 C8
　Weston CW2 . . . . 207 C5
Eastbury Cl WA8 . . . . 13 C5
Eastcott Cl CW12 . . . . . . 155 F4
East Cl ST7. . . . . 193 E4
Eastdale WA15. . . . . 31 F8
Eastdale Rd WA1 . . . . 17 A7
East Dam Wood Rd L24 . . 21 A2
East Dudley St CW7 . . . . 126 F1
Eastern Ave 7 B2
Eastern Pathway CH4 . . 237 C1
Eastern Rd CW5 . . . . 205 F5
Eastfields Gr CH1 . . . . . . 117 A8
Eastford Rd WA4 . . . . 16 A1
Eastgate SK10 . . . . 112 E8
Eastgate Rd
　Holmes Chapel CW4 . . . 130 D3
　Runcorn WA7. . . . . 24 E5
Eastgate Row N CH1 . . . 237 B2
Eastgate Row S CH1 . . . 237 B2
Eastgate St CH1 . . . . 237 B2
Eastgate Way WA7 . . . . . 24 D4
East Gn CH5 . . . . 116 A6
EASTHAM 43 F5
Eastham Ctry Pk* CH62. . 44 A8
Eastham Ho CH62 . . . . . . 44 A4
Eastham Mews CH62. . . . 44 A4
Eastham Rake CH65, CH64 43 D3
Eastham Rake Sta CH63. . 43 D3
Eastham Village Rd CH62. 44 A5
Eastham Way **11** SK9 . 34 D5
East La
　Cuddington CW8 . . . . . 102 A3
　Runcorn WA7. . . . . 49 F7
East Lancashire Rd WA11,
　WA12, WA3 . . . . .2 C7
East Mill Dr CW9 . . . . 104 A8
East Milwood Rd L24 . . . . 21 A3
East Park Rd SK11 . . . . . 112 B5
East Rd
　Halewood L24, L26 . . . . 21 A5
　Middlewich CW10 . . . . . 128 B1
　Wythenshawe M90 . . . . . 33 C7
East Side
　Nantwich CW5 . . . . 204 E6
　East Terr WA16 . . . . 56 F1
East View
　11 Nantwich CW5 . . . 204 E6
　Warrington WA4 . . . . 17 B2
Eastward Ave SK9. . . . . . . 59 F6
Eastway
　Ellesmere Port CH66. . . . 69 D7
　Widnes WA8 . . . . 12 D1
Eastwood WA7 . . . . 24 C2
Eastwood Ave WA12 . . . . .2 E3
Eastwood Ct CH5 . . . . . . 139 B7
Eastwood Rd WA5 . . . . . . .6 F7
EATON
　Congleton 157 A8
　Tarporley 147 A4
Eaton Ave CH4. . . . . 141 D7
Eaton Bank Ind E 156 F4
Eaton Bank Ind Est
　CW12 . . . . 156 F5
Eaton Bank Sch CW12. . . 156 F5
Eaton Cl
　Broughton CH4 . . . . 139 C4
　Poynton SK12. . . . . 37 A3
　Sandbach CW11 . . . . . . 175 C4
Eaton Cres CW9 . . . . 103 E2
Eaton Ct
　1 Northwich CW9 . . . 103 E5
　Wilmslow SK9 . . . . 60 A6
Eaton Dr
　Alderley Edge SK9 . . . . . 59 F2
　Middlewich CW10 . . . . . 151 B8
Eaton Gr CH4 . . . . 140 E6
Eaton La
　Davenham CW9 . . . . . . 103 C2
　Eaton CW6. . . . . 147 A5
　Goostrey CW4 . . . . 107 C1
　Macclesfield SK11 . . . . . 112 D5
　Tarporley CW6 . . . . 168 E8
Eaton Mews CH4. . . . . . . 141 D7
Eaton Pl CW8 . . . . 102 F4
Eaton Prim Sch CW6 . . . 147 B3
Eaton Rd
　Alsager ST7 . . . . 193 D4
　Chester CH4 . . . . 141 E4
　Tarporley CW6 . . . . 146 D1
　Wettenhall CW7. . . . . . . 170 B8
Eaton St
　Crewe CW2 . . . . 190 C4
　12 Runcorn WA7. . . . . 23 A2
Eaton View CW9 . . . . 126 E8
Eaton Way WA3. . . . . 230 A4
Eaves Brow Rd WA3. . . . . .9 B7
Eaves Knoll Rd SK22 . . . . 39 B8
EBNAL 213 D5
Ebnal La SY14 . . . . 213 E4
Ebury Pl CH4 . . . . 141 D7
Eccles Cl SK23 . . . . 65 D8
Eccles Rd SK23 . . . . 65 F6
ECCLESTON 141 E1

Eccleston Ave
Bebington CH62. . . . . 43 C8
Chester CH4 . . . . 141 D6
Ellesmere Port CH66. . . . . 69 C5
Eccleston CE Prim Sch
CH4. . . . . 141 E2
Eccleston Cl WA3 . . . . 9 C5
Eccleston Ct **5** CW9 . . . . 103 E5
Eccleston Dr WA7. . . . . . . 23 C1
Eccleston Rd CH4 . . . . . . 161 A7
Eccleston Way **3** SK9 . . . 34 D4
Eccups La SK9. . . . . 59 C8
Echo Cl CH4 . . . . 140 E5
Ecton Ave SK10. . . . . . . 113 A7
Ecton Cl CW7 . . . . 127 A4
Edale Cl
Bebington CH62. . . . . 43 E5
Gatley SK8. . . . . 34 D7
Edale Dr CW6. . . . . 122 D5
Edburton Ct A3 . . . . 3 A8
Eddisbury Cl SK11 . . . . . 112 F7
Eddisbury Dr ST5 . . . . . . 210 D2
Eddisbury Hill CW6, CW8 123 D7
Eddisbury Hill Pk CW8 . . 123 D7
Eddisbury Rd CH66. . . . . . 69 F1
Eddisbury Sq WA6 . . . . . . 74 B8
Eddisbury Terr SK11 . . . . 112 F7
Eddisbury Way CW9 . . . . 103 E3
Eddisford Dr WA3. . . . . . . 4 D4
Edelsten Dr WA5 . . . . 15 F5
Eden Ave
Fowley Common WA3 . . . . . 5 C4
High Lane SK6 . . . . 37 E7
Winsford CW7 . . . . 126 C5
Edenbridge Cl CW2 . . . . . 207 B2
Edenbridge Gdns WA4 . . . 26 E3
Eden Cl
Biddulph ST8 . . . . 179 E1
5 Ellesmere Port CH66 . 69 C5
Kidsgrove ST7 . . . . 195 B2
Wilmslow SK9 . . . . 59 E5
Edendale WA8 . . . . 12 B2
Eden Dr SK10. . . . . 87 F1
Edenfield Cl WA16 . . . . . . 58 A3
Edenfield Rd WA16 . . . . . 58 A4
Edenhall Cl CW4 . . . . . . 130 A3
Eden Park Rd SK8. . . . . . . 34 E8
Edgar Ct
Chester CH4 . . . . 237 B1
25 Macclesfield SK11 . . 112 C8
Edgar Pl CH4 . . . . 237 B1
Edgars Dr WA2 . . . . 9 A1
Edgecroft CH3 . . . . 166 A1
Edge Gr CH2. . . . . 118 F2
EDGE GREEN 199 B2
Edgehill Chase SK9 . . . . . 60 E7
Edge La SK14 . . . . 199 C1
Edgerley La A3 . . . . 181 B6
Edgerton Rd WA3 . . . . 3 E8
Edge View La SK9 . . . . . . 59 B2
Edgeview Rd CW12. . . . . 179 B7
Edgeway
Henbury SK11 . . . . 111 C8
Wilmslow SK9 . . . . 60 B5
Edgewell La WA6 . . . . . . 147 A3
Edgewood **8** CH3. . . . . 142 A8
Edgewood Ct WA8 . . . . . . 22 B7
Edgewood Dr
Bebington CH62. . . . . 43 D5
Wistaston CW2 . . . . 206 A7
Edgworth St WA2 . . . . . . 16 A6
Edinburgh Cl
Congleton CW12 . . . . . . 156 F2
Widnes WA8 . . . . 22 A8
Wistaston CW2 . . . . 205 E8
Edinburgh Way CH4. . . . . 237 C1
Edison Rd WA7 . . . . 23 D3
Edith St WA7 . . . . 22 F3
Edlestone Gr **9** SK9 . . . . 34 E1
Edleston Hall La CW5 . . . 203 F2
Edleston Pl SK10 CW2 . . 190 B3
Edleston Rd CW2 . . . . . . 190 D3
Edmund Wright Way
CW5 . . . . 204 C5
Edna St CH2 . . . . 118 F3
Edward Gdns WA1 . . . . . 17 F6
Edward Rd WA5 . . . . 14 D6
Edwards Ave CW2. . . . . . 206 C5
Edwards Ct CW2. . . . . . . 206 C5
Edwards Rd CH4 . . . . . . 141 A6
Edward St
Audley ST7. . . . . 209 F3
Crewe CW2. . . . . 190 D2
Ellesmere Port CH66. . . . . 70 C7
Haydock WA11. . . . . 1 A6
Macclesfield SK11 . . . . . 112 B7
Northwich CW9 . . . . . . 104 C8
Widnes WA8 . . . . 13 D1
Edwards Way
Alsager ST7 . . . . 193 A6
Widnes WA8 . . . . 22 C8
Egdon Cl WA8 . . . . 13 E2
Egerton Av WA16 . . . . . . 29 C5
Egerton Ave
Hartford CW8 . . . . 103 A4
Partington WA13 . . . . 19 C8
Warrington WA1 . . . . 16 F7
Egerton Ct
Egerton Ct CW6. . . . . . . 122 B5
Egerton Dr CH2. . . . . . . 118 D5
EGERTON GREEN 200 C5
Egerton Mews **1** WA4 . . 16 C1
Egerton Moss WA15. . . . . 31 E5
Egerton Prim Sch WA16. . 56 F2

Egerton Rd
Blacon CH1 . . . . 117 E5
Handforth SK9. . . . . 34 B1
Lymm WA13. . . . . 18 C2
Egerton Sq **7** WA16 . . . . 57 A2
Egerton St
Chester CH1 . . . . 237 C3
Congleton CW12 . . . . . . 156 C2
Ellesmere Port CH65. . . . . 70 C6
Runcorn WA7. . . . . 22 F3
Warrington, Howley WA1 . . 16 D5
Warrington, Stockton Heath
WA4 . . . . 16 C1
Egerton Terr CW9. . . . . . 105 D4
Egerton Wlk CH4 . . . . . . 162 A7
Eggbridge La CH3. . . . . . 143 A5
Egremont Ct WA4. . . . . . . 16 C3
Egypt St
3 Warrington WA1. . . . . 16 A5
Widnes WA8 . . . . 22 F7
Eilison Ct CH1 . . . . 237 B3
Elaine Cl
Ellesmere Port CH66. . . . . 69 C4
Widnes WA8 . . . . 13 C1
Elaine Price Ct **3** WA7 . . 22 F7
Elaine St WA1 . . . . 16 D7
Elanor Rd CW1 . . . . 174 D7
Elcombe Ave WA3 . . . . 3 E7
Elderberry Way SK9 . . . . . 60 E8
Elderberry Wlk M31. . . . . 11 E3
Elder Dr CH4 . . . . 140 E5
Eldon Rd SK10. . . . . 111 F8
Eldon St WA1 . . . . 16 D6
Eldon Terr CH64. . . . . . . 66 E7
Eleanor Cl CW1 . . . . 189 F5
Eleanor St
Ellesmere Port CH65. . . . . 70 C6
5 Widnes WA8 . . . . . . 23 A7
Electra Way CW1 . . . . . . 191 A2
Electricity St CW2. . . . . . 190 C3
Elgar Ave CH62 . . . . 43 E5
Elgar Cl CH3. . . . . 119 B3
Eliot Cl WA7 . . . . 191 A4
Elizabethan Way CW9 . . . 104 E6
Elizabeth Ave SK12. . . . . 38 D5
Elizabeth Cl
Kelsall CW6. . . . . 122 D5
Sandbach CW11. . . . . . . 174 D7
Elizabeth Cres CH4. . . . . 237 C1
Elizabeth Ct
Talke ST7 . . . . 210 D5
3 Widnes WA8 . . . . . . 23 B7
Elizabeth Dr WA1 . . . . . . 17 A8
Elizabeth Gaskell Ct
WA16. . . . . 56 F2
Elizabeth Ho **5** SK11 . . 112 E7
Elizabeth Rd
Haydock WA11. . . . . 1 E7
Partington M31 . . . . 11 F4
Elizabeth St
Congleton CW12 . . . . . . 156 C2
Crewe CW1 . . . . 190 B5
Macclesfield SK11 . . . . . 112 D7
Elizabeth Terr WA8 . . . . . 12 D1
Elkan Cl WA8 . . . . 13 E2
Elkan Rd WA8 . . . . 13 E2
Elk View SY14 . . . . 222 F5
Ella Gr WA16 . . . . 57 B2
Elland Dr CH66 . . . . 69 C5
Ellen Brook Rd M22 . . . . . 33 D8
Ellen St WA5 . . . . 15 F7
Ellerby Cl WA7 . . . . 50 D7
Ellerton Ave CH66. . . . . . 69 C5
Ellerton Cl WA8 . . . . 12 D5
Ellesmere Ave
Broughton CH4 . . . . 139 D4
Chester CH2 . . . . 118 D5
Ellesmere Cl CW11. . . . . 174 E8
Ellesmere Pl **11** CW1. . . 190 B5
ELLESMERE PORT 70 A7
Ellesmere Port Com Hospl
CH65. . . . . 70 A2
Ellesmere Port Greyhound
Stad CH65. . . . . 70 E3
Ellesmere Port RC High Sch
CH65. . . . . 70 A3
Ellesmere Port Sta CH65 . 70 E3
Ellesmere Rd
Culcheth WA3. . . . . 4 E3
Northwich CW9 . . . . . . 104 A4
Warrington WA4 . . . . 16 B1
Ellesmere St
Runcorn WA7. . . . . 23 B2
3 Warrington WA1. . . . . 16 C5
Warrington WA1 . . . . 16 C5
Ellesworth Cl WA5 . . . . . 15 C8
Ellingham Way CW9. . . . . 103 E3
Ellington Dr WA5 . . . . . . 15 B5
Elliot Ho CH1 . . . . 118 A5
Elliot St **9** WA8 . . . . . . 23 B8
Elliott Ave WA1. . . . . 16 E4
Ellis La WA6 . . . . 49 D1
Ellison St
Crewe CW1 . . . . 190 B6
Widnes WA8 . . . . 22 F7
Elloway Rd L24 . . . . 21 A3
Ellwood Cl L24 . . . . 21 E2
Ellwood Gn CW2 . . . . . . 206 B3

Elm Ave
Newton-le-Willows WA12 . . 2 C2
Widnes WA8 . . . . 13 B2
Elm Beds Rd SK12. . . . . . 37 C2
Elm Cl
Crewe CW2 . . . . 189 E2
2 Partington M31 . . . . . 11 F3
Poynton SK12. . . . . 36 F3
Tarporley CW6. . . . . 146 D2
Elm Cres CW9. . . . . 60 B3
Elm Ct CW1. . . . . 190 D6
Elm Dr
Crewe CW1 . . . . 190 E6
Holmes Chapel CW4 . . . . 130 D3
Macclesfield SK10. . . . . . 87 E2
Elmfield Cl SK9 . . . . 60 B2
Elmfield Rd SK9 . . . . 60 B2
Elm Gn CH64 . . . . 67 F8
Elm Gr
Alderley Edge SK9 . . . . . . 60 B2
Alsager ST7 . . . . 193 E4
Ellesmere Port CH66. . . . . 70 A1
Handforth SK9. . . . . 34 C3
Saltney CH4. . . . . 140 E5
Warrington WA1 . . . . 16 F7
Widnes WA8 . . . . 13 B1
Winsford CW7 . . . . 127 A1
Elm Ho
Chester CH2 . . . . 118 C5
5 Sandbach CW11. . . . 175 B6
Elmore Cl
Holmes Chapel CW4 . . . . 130 B3
Runcorn WA7. . . . . 24 D1
Elm Rd
Congleton CW12 . . . . . . 156 B3
Haydock WA11. . . . . 1 E7
High Lane SK6. . . . . 37 F7
Hollinfare WA3 . . . . 11 A2
Middlewich CW10 . . . . . 151 D7
Runcorn WA7. . . . . 49 C8
Warrington WA5 . . . . 14 F4
Weaverham CW8. . . . . . 102 D7
Willaston CH64 . . . . 67 F8
Elmridge Ct WA3 . . . . 3 F8
Elmridge Dr WA3 . . . . 3 F8
Elmridge Prim Sch WA15. 32 C8
Elmridge Way CW8 . . . . . 78 D1
Elm Rise
Frodsham WA6 . . . . 74 C7
Prestbury SK10 . . . . 86 E6
Elms SK9 . . . . 59 F6
Elmsett Cl WA5 . . . . 14 E5
Elm Sq CH4. . . . . 140 F6
Elm St
Ellesmere Port CH65. . . . . 70 C7
Northwich CW9 . . . . 79 B1
Elmstead Cres CW1 . . . . 189 F8
Elmstead Rd SK11. . . . . . 84 A3
Elms The
Golborne WA3. . . . . 3 F8
Mobberley WA16. . . . . . . 58 E2
6 Northwich CW9 . . . . 103 E6
Runcorn WA7. . . . . 23 A2
Tallarn Green/Tallwrn Green
SY14 . . . . 222 F5
Elmsway
Altrincham WA15. . . . . . . 32 B8
Bollington SK10. . . . . . . 88 A8
Bramhall SK7. . . . . 35 C7
High Lane SK6. . . . . 37 E6
Elm Terr CW1. . . . . 190 E6
Elm Tree Ave
Lymm WA13. . . . . 18 D2
Warrington WA1 . . . . 16 F8
Elm Tree Cotts CH1 . . . . 167 A7
Elm Tree Cl WA5 . . . . . . 147 A3
Elm Tree Ct ST7 . . . . . . 209 F1
Elm Tree La CW11 . . . . . 174 D8
Elm Tree Rd
Golborne WA3. . . . . 3 F8
Lymm WA13. . . . . 18 D2
Elmuir CH1 . . . . 117 E3
Elmwood WA7 . . . . 24 C1
Elmwood Ave
Chester CH2 . . . . 118 C4
Warrington WA1 . . . . 16 F7
Elmwood Cl ST7 . . . . . . 194 A4
Elmwood Gr CW7 . . . . . . 149 F8
Elmwood Rd CH66 . . . . . 78 B4
Elnor Ave SK23 . . . . 65 E5
Elnor La SK23 . . . . 65 F4
Elphins Dr WA4 . . . . 16 C2
Elsby Rd ST7 . . . . 193 F2
Elston Ave WA12. . . . . 2 C5
Elstree Ave CH3. . . . . . . 119 B3
Elstvick Ave SK7. . . . . . . 35 E7
Eltham Cl WA3 . . . . 13 E3
Eltham Wlk WA8 . . . . . . 13 E3
ELTON 72 C3
Elton Cl
Bebington CH62. . . . . 43 E3
Golborne WA3. . . . . 3 E7
Handforth SK9. . . . . 34 E1
Warrington WA3 . . . . 9 C4
Elton Crossings Rd
CH2. . . . . 174 D6
Elton Dr SK7. . . . . 36 D8
ELTON GREEN 72 B3
Elton La
Haslington CW11, CW1. . . 174 D1
Winterley CW11. . . . . . . 191 F8
Elton Prim Sch CH2. . . . . 72 B4
Elton Rd CW11. . . . . 174 D5
Elton Shopping Precinct
CH2. . . . . 72 B3

Elvington Cl
Congleton CW12 . . . . . . 156 E2
Runcorn WA7. . . . . 49 F4
Elwood Way CW5 . . . . . . 205 B4
ELWORTH 174 E6
Elworth Ave WA8 . . . . . . 13 A5
Elworth CE Prim Sch
CW11 . . . . 174 E7
Elworth Ct
8 Congleton CW12 . . . . 156 F3
Sandbach CW11. . . . . . . 174 D7
Elworth Hall Prim Sch
CW11. . . . . 174 E7
Elworth Rd CW11 . . . . . . 174 E6
Elworth St CW11 . . . . . . 175 A7
Elworth Way **8** SK9. . . . 34 D4
Elwyn Dr L26 . . . . 21 A8
Ely Cl CH66 . . . . 94 E8
Ely Pk WA7 . . . . 24 E2
Embassy Cl CH1 . . . . . . 117 C4
Emberton Pl CW3 . . . . . 230 A5
Embleton Ct WA7 . . . . . . 49 D5
Embridge Cswy SK10. . . . 90 B5
Emerald Dr CW11 . . . . . 175 C8
Emerald Rd M22 . . . . . . 33 F7
Emily St **7** WA8 . . . . . . 23 A7
Emmett St CW8 . . . . 78 A3
Empire Ct WA16 . . . . . . 16 A4
Empress Dr CW2 . . . . . . 190 B3
Emral Ct SY14 . . . . 211 A1
Emslie Ct CH44 . . . . 66 C7
Enderby Rd CH1 . . . . . . 237 A3
Endon Ave SK10 . . . . . . 88 A7
Endon Hall Mews SK10. . . 88 B5
Endsleigh Cl CH2 . . . . . . 118 E8
Endsleigh Gdns CH2 . . . . 118 E8
Enfield Cl CW2 . . . . 206 B3
Enfield Park Rd WA2 . . . . . 9 A3
Enfield Rd CH65 . . . . . . 70 B5
Engineer Pk CH5 . . . . . . 116 A4
Englefield Ave CH4 . . . . 140 D6
Englefield Cl CW1 . . . . . 190 A8
ENGLESEA BROOK 208 A4
Englesea Brook Chapel &
Mus* CW2 . . . . 208 A3
Englesea Brook La CW2 . 208 A3
Englesea Gr CW2 . . . . . 190 B1
Ennerdale
Chester CH2 . . . . 118 F5
Macclesfield SK11 . . . . . 111 F5
Ennerdale Ave
Bebington CH62. . . . . 43 F4
Warrington WA2 . . . . 8 B3
Ennerdale Cl
Alderley Edge SK9 . . . . . . 83 F7
Winsford CW7 . . . . 126 D3
Ennerdale Dr
Congleton CW12 . . . . . . 156 B2
Frodsham WA6 . . . . 74 C8
Ennerdale Rd
Crewe CW2 . . . . 189 D3
Partington M31 . . . . 11 E3
Ennis Cl L24 . . . . 21 D2
Ensor Way SK22 . . . . 39 C7
Enterprise Ctr CW1 . . . . 174 D7
Enterprise Ctr The CW12 156 A3
Enterprise Way WA3 . . . . . 4 A7
Enticott Rd M44 . . . . 11 C5
Enville St WA4 . . . . 16 C4
Epic L Ctr CH65 . . . . 70 C4
Epping Dr WA1 . . . . 17 D8
Epsom Ave SK8, SK9 . . . . 34 E4
Epsom Gdns WA4 . . . . . . 26 E7
Epsom Gdns WA4 . . . . . . 26 E7
Epworth Cl WA5 . . . . 6 F7
ERF Way CW10 . . . . 151 E8
Eric Ave WA1 . . . . 16 E8
Eric Dr CW11 . . . . 174 D7
Eric St WA8 . . . . 13 C2
Erindale Cres WA6. . . . . . 74 A6
Ermine Rd CH2 . . . . 237 C4
Ernest St CW2 . . . . 190 C1
Erneley Cl CW5 . . . . 204 D6
Errington Ave CH65 . . . . . 70 C6
Errwood Forest Walks*
SK17. . . . . 90 E2
Erskine Rd M31. . . . . . . 11 F3
Erwood St WA2 . . . . 16 B6
Escalade CH65 . . . . 70 B3
Eskdale Ave
Bebington CH62. . . . . 43 E5
Bramhall SK7. . . . . 35 C5
Warrington WA2 . . . . 8 C3
Eskdale Cl WA7 . . . . 49 D5
Esk Dale Cl CW7 . . . . . . 126 C2
Esk Rd CW7 . . . . 127 A2
Essex Cl CW12 . . . . 156 E5
Essex Dr
Biddulph ST8 . . . . 179 D2
Kidsgrove ST7 . . . . 194 F2
Essex Gdns M44 . . . . . . 11 C4
Essex Rd CH2. . . . . 119 A5
Essex Wlk SK10. . . . . 86 F1
Esthers La CW8 . . . . 102 A3
Etchells Prim Sch SK8 . . . 34 C8
Ethelda Dr CH2 . . . . 119 A5
Etherow Cl CW11 . . . . . 174 E7
Ethos Ct CH1 . . . . 237 C3
Eton Cl CH63 . . . . 41 F6
Eton Rd CH65. . . . . 70 C4
Ettiley Ave CW11 . . . . . . 174 C5
ETTILEY HEATH 174 C6
Ettrick Pk CH3. . . . . 119 E2
Euclid Ave WA4 . . . . 17 B2
Europa Bvd WA5 . . . . 7 D3
Europa Way CH65 . . . . . . 70 C6
Eustace St WA2. . . . . . . 16 A6

Evans Bsns Ctr CW5. . . . . 93 A1
Evans Cl WA11. . . . . 1 F7
Evansleigh Dr CH5 . . . . . 116 A3
Evans Pl WA4. . . . . 16 D3
Evans St CW1. . . . . 190 C6
Eva St CW11. . . . . 174 D8
Evelyn St WA5 . . . . 15 F8
Evelyn Street Prim Sch
WA5 . . . . 15 E4
Evenwood Cl WA7 . . . . . . 24 E4
Everdon Cl CW7 . . . . . . 126 F4
Everest Cl CH66. . . . . . . 69 F3
Everest Rd ST7 . . . . 195 C3
Everglade Cl SK11 . . . . . 112 B5
Evergreens The CW9. . . . . 80 A3
Evergreen Way WA9 . . . . . 6 A7
Everite Rd WA8 . . . . 22 B7
Everley Cl WA7 . . . . 50 C5
Eversley CH2. . . . . 118 C4
Eversley Cl CH2 . . . . 118 C4
Evesham Cl
Macclesfield SK10. . . . . . 87 E4
Warrington WA4 . . . . 26 C8
Evesham Dr SK9 . . . . . . 34 C2
Evington Ho **2** SK11. . . 112 B6
Ewart St CH4 . . . . 140 B7
Ewloe Ct CH65. . . . . 70 D2
Ewrin La SK10 . . . . 89 D5
Excalibur Ind Est ST7 . . . 193 E3
Excalibur Ind Est ST7. . . 193 E2
Excalibur Way M44. . . . . 117 D7
Exchange Cl SK11 . . . . . 112 D8
Exchange St SK11 . . . . . 112 D8
Exeter Cl SK8 . . . . 34 F8
Exeter Pl CH1 . . . . 117 F5
Exeter Rd CH65 . . . . 70 C5
Exeter Wlk SK7 . . . . 35 F7
Exit Rd W M90. . . . . 33 B7
Exmouth Cres WA7 . . . . . 50 E6
Exmouth Way WA5. . . . . . 6 F6
Express Ind Est WA8 . . . 22 A7
Exton Pk CH1 . . . . 237 A4
Eyam Rd SK7 . . . . 36 E8
Eyebrook Rd WA14. . . . . 20 F2
Eyre Pl CH65. . . . . 70 B6
Eyston Cl CW9 . . . . 103 E5

F

Facit Glen Ind Est CH4 . . 140 F7
Factory La
Warrington WA1, WA5. . . . 15 F4
Widnes WA8 . . . . 13 B3
Factory Rd CH5 . . . . 116 A3
FADDILEY 202 D7
FADDILEY BANK. 202 C6
Fairacre Dr CW10 . . . . . 151 E6
Fairacres Rd SK6. . . . . . . 37 E8
Fairbourne Ave
Alderley Edge SK9 . . . . . . 60 B3
Wilmslow SK9 . . . . 59 F4
Fairbourne Cl
Warrington WA5 . . . . 7 E3
Wilmslow SK9 . . . . 59 F4
Fairbourne Dr SK9 . . . . . 59 F4
Fairbrook CW2. . . . . 189 E2
Fairbrother Cres WA2. . . . 8 D2
Fairburn Ave CW2 . . . . . 189 F4
Fairburn Cl WA8 . . . . . . 13 E3
Fairclough Ave WA1 . . . . 16 C4
Fairclough Cres WA11. . . . 1 A6
Fairclough St
Burtonwood WA5. . . . . . . 6 E6
Newton-le-Willows WA12 . . 2 B3
Fairfax Cl ST8 . . . . 179 C1
Fairfax Ct CW5. . . . . 204 E7
Fairfax Dr
Nantwich CW5. . . . . 204 D6
Runcorn WA7. . . . . 23 D2
Wilmslow SK9 . . . . 59 F4
Fairfield Ave
Bollington SK10. . . . . . . 88 A8
Ellesmere Port CH65. . . . . 70 A2
Sandbach CW11. . . . . . . 175 B5
Fairfield Gdns Ave WA16 . 16 E2
Fairfield High Sch WA8 . . 13 B3
Fairfield Jnr Sch WA8 . . . 13 B2
Fairfield Rd
Broughton CH4 . . . . 139 B4
Chester CH2 . . . . 119 A4
Irlam M44 . . . . 11 C5
Lymm WA13. . . . . 18 F3
Northwich CW9 . . . . . . 104 A4
Warrington WA1 . . . . 16 E4
Widnes WA8 . . . . 13 B2
Fairfields
Audley ST7. . . . . 209 F2
Whitchurch SY13 . . . . . . 225 F1
Fairfield St WA1 . . . . 16 D6
Fairford Cl WA5 . . . . 15 B6
Fairford Rd CH4 . . . . . . 140 D6
Fairford Way SK9 . . . . . . 60 D7
Fairhaven CW2 . . . . 207 B1
Fairhaven Cl
Bramhall SK7. . . . . 35 F8
Macclesfield SK10. . . . . . 88 A8
Warrington WA5 . . . . 15 B4
Fairhaven Dr CH63 . . . . . 43 C5
Fairhaven Rd WA8 . . . . . 13 C2

Fair Haven's Ct WA8 . . . . . 23 B8
Fairhills Ind Est M44 . . . . 11 F8
Fairhills Rd M44 . . . . 11 F8
Fairholme Ave CH64 . . . . 41 C1
Fairholme Cl CH4 . . . . . . 96 B1
Fairholme Pl 7 CH3 . . . . 119 A1
Fairholme Rd CW9 . . . . . 127 A8
Fair Isle Cl CH65 . . . . 70 C1
Fairlawn Cl CH63 . . . . 43 A6
Fair Mead WA6 . . . . 82 B8
Fairmeadow CH4 . . . . . . 162 D2
Fairoak Cl 12 CW7 . . . . . 149 A8
Fairoak Ct WA7 . . . . 50 F3
Fairoak La WA7 . . . . 50 F3
Fair Oak Rd ST5 . . . . . . 210 D1
Fairview LL13 . . . . 196 E8
Fairview Ave
  Alsager ST7 . . . . 193 D4
  Weston CW2 . . . . 207 B5
Fair View Cl CW8 . . . . . . 77 F3
Fairview Rd
  Ellesmere Port CH65 . . . . 70 A2
  Macclesfield SK11 . . . . 112 A6
Fairway
  Bramhall SK7 . . . . 35 D6
  Sandycroft CH5 . . . . . . 116 A2
Fairways
  Frodsham WA6 . . . . 74 D7
  Warrington WA4 . . . . . . 26 D5
Fairways Dr
  Ellesmere Port CH66 . . . . 69 D7
  Whitchurch SY13 . . . . . 226 A1
Fairways The
  Macclesfield SK10 . . . . . 87 B4
  Winsford CW7 . . . . 126 A2
Fairway The ST7 . . . . . . 193 C4
Fairway Trad Est WA8 . . . 22 E6
Fairywell Cl SK9 . . . . 34 D1
Falcon Cl
  Middlewich CW10 . . . . . 151 D5
  New Mills SK22 . . . . 39 D8
  Winsford CW7 . . . . 149 D6
Falcondale Rd WA2 . . . . . . 8 B6
Falcon Dr CW1 . . . . 190 B8
Falconers Gn WA5 . . . . . . 7 B2
Falcon Rd CH66 . . . . 69 F3
Falcons Way WA7 . . . . . . 49 E6
Falkirk Ave WA8 . . . . 12 F3
Fallibroome Cl SK10 . . . . 111 E8
Fallibroome High Sch
  SK10 . . . . 86 E2
Fallibroome Rd SK10 . . . 111 E8
Fallon Ct CW10 . . . . 151 C7
Fallowfield WA7 . . . . 23 D1
Fallowfield Cl CW7 . . . . 125 F1
Fallowfield Ct CW1 . . . . 190 A6
Fallowfield Gr WA5 . . . . . . 9 B1
Falmouth Cl SK10 . . . . . 111 E8
Falmouth Dr WA5 . . . . . . 14 E3
Falmouth Pl WA7 . . . . . . 50 E6
Falmouth Rd
  Congleton CW12 . . . . . 178 E8
  Crewe CW1 . . . . 190 A6
Falstone Cl WA3 . . . . 10 B6
Falstone Dr WA7 . . . . 50 E7
Fanner's La WA16 . . . . . . 28 D5
Fanny's Croft ST7 . . . . . 193 D2
FANSHAWE 110 C4
Fanshawe La SK11 . . . . . 110 E5
Fanshawe Wlk SK12 . . . . 206 C8
Faraday Rd
  Ellesmere Port CH65 . . . . 70 A4
  Runcorn WA7 . . . . 23 D3
Faraday St WA3 . . . . 9 E5
Farams Rd ST7 . . . . 193 E7
Farbailey Cl CH4 . . . . . . 141 B5
Farcroft Cl WA13 . . . . . . 19 C5
Farfields Cl SK11 . . . . . . 111 E1
Farley Cl CW10 . . . . 151 B8
Farmdale Dr CH2 . . . . . . 72 A3
Farm Dr CH5 . . . . 91 C1
Farmer Cl CW2 . . . . 190 A4
Farmers Heath CH66 . . . . 69 D2
Farmer's La WA5 . . . . 7 A6
Farmfield Dr SK10 . . . . . . 87 C3
Farmfields Rise CW3 . . . 232 C1
Farmfold SK9 . . . . 33 F3
Farm Hollow ST7 . . . . . . 210 A2
Farm La
  High Lane SK12 . . . . 38 A6
  Warrington WA4 . . . . . . 26 E8
  Withington Green SK11 . 108 E1
Farmleigh Dr CW1 . . . . . 189 F8
Farmleigh Gdns WA5 . . . . 15 C6
Farm Rd
  Northwich CW9 . . . . . . 104 E7
  Oakmere CW8 . . . . 124 A8
  Weaverham CW8 . . . . . . 77 D1
Farmside Cl WA5 . . . . . . 15 F7
Farmstead Way CH66 . . . 69 E1
Farm Way WA12 . . . . 2 B3
Farm Wlk WA14 . . . . 20 E1
Farndale WA8 . . . . 13 A5
Farndale Cl
  Warrington WA5 . . . . . . 14 F7
  Wistaston CW2 . . . . . . 206 A6
Farndale Wlk SK11 . . . . 112 D6
Farndon Cl CW9 . . . . . . 180 F2
Farndon Ct
  Broughton CH4 . . . . . . 139 C4
  Cuddington CW8 . . . . . 102 A3
Farndon Prim Sch CH3 . . 180 E2
Farndon Rd CH66 . . . . . . 69 E6
Farne Cl CH65 . . . . 95 C8

Farnham Ave SK11 . . . . 112 A6
Farnham Cl
  Cheadle SK8 . . . . 35 A7
  Warrington WA4 . . . . . . 26 E7
Farnhill Cl WA7 . . . . 50 D8
Farnley Cl WA7 . . . . 24 D1
FARNWORTH 13 A3
Farnworth CE Prim Sch
  WA8 . . . . 13 A4
Farnworth Cl WA8 . . . . . . 13 B4
Farnworth Ct WA8 . . . . . . 13 B3
Farnworth Rd WA8 . . . . . 14 C4
Farnworth St WA8 . . . . . . 13 B4
Farrant St WA8 . . . . 23 B8
Farrell Rd WA4 . . . . 26 C8
Farrell St WA1 . . . . 16 D5
Farr Hall Dr CH60 . . . . . . 40 E7
Farr Hall Rd CH60 . . . . . . 40 E7
Farrier Ct CW1 . . . . 190 D7
Farriers Way CW7 . . . . . 126 A1
Farringdon Rd WA2 . . . . . 8 B6
Farthing La CW9 . . . . 79 B8
Farthings The WA13 . . . . 18 D4
Farwood Cl SK10 . . . . . . 86 F2
Faulkner Dr CW10 . . . . . 151 E6
Faulkners Cl CH4 . . . . . . 161 A7
Faulkners La WA16 . . . . . 58 E2
Faulkner St CH2 . . . . . . 118 F3
Fawns Keep SK9 . . . . 60 D7
Fawns Leap CW5 . . . . . . 101 E5
Fearndown Way SK10 . . . 87 C4
FEARNHEAD 9 B2
Fearnhead Cross WA2 . . . . 8 F2
Fearnhead La WA2 . . . . . . 9 A2
Fearnleigh CW8 . . . . 103 C2
Fearnley Way WA12 . . . . . 2 C1
Feather La CH60 . . . . 40 F8
Feather's La CH1 . . . . . . 237 B2
Feilden Ct CH1 . . . . 94 F1
Felix Rd CW8 . . . . 103 E8
Felskirk Rd M22 . . . . 33 C8
Fence Ave SK10 . . . . 112 E8
Fence Ave Ind Est SK10 . 112 E8
Fence Ct SK10 . . . . 112 E8
Fence La CW12 . . . . 178 D4
Fenham Dr WA5 . . . . 14 F4
Fennel St WA1 . . . . 16 C5
Fenton Cl
  Congleton CW12 . . . . . 157 A1
  Widnes WA8 . . . . 12 C3
Fenwick La WA7 . . . . 49 D6
Fenwick Rd CH66 . . . . . . 69 C5
Ferguson Ave CH66 . . . . . 69 E6
Ferguson Dr WA2 . . . . 8 D1
Ferma La CH3 . . . . 120 D6
Fernbank Cl
  Crewe CW1 . . . . 190 F3
  Warrington WA3 . . . . 9 A4
  Winsford CW7 . . . . 127 B1
Fernbank Rise SK8 . . . . . 88 B8
Fern Cl
  Mount Pleasant ST7 . . . 195 C6
  Warrington WA3 . . . . 9 D4
Fern Cres CW12 . . . . . . 157 A3
Fern Ct CW1 . . . . 190 E3
Ferndale Ave CH2 . . . . . . 72 A3
Ferndale
  Bold Heath WA8 . . . . . . 13 C4
  Sandbach CW11 . . . . . 175 C5
  Warrington WA1 . . . . . . 17 C7
  Weston CW2 . . . . 207 B5
Ferndale Cres SK11 . . . . 111 F7
Ferndale Gdns ST1 . . . . 195 E3
Ferndown Way CW2 . . . . 221 E8
Fernhill Rd CH1 . . . . 117 E6
Fernhurst WA7 . . . . 49 D8
FERNILEE 65 E1
Fernilee Cotts SK23 . . . . . 65 E1
Fernilee Ct CH1 . . . . 118 F8
Fern Lea Dr SK11 . . . . . 112 A8
Fernleaf Cl ST7 . . . . 193 F8
Fernlea Rd
  Heswall CH60 . . . . 41 A8
  Marston CW9 . . . . 79 B6
Fernleigh Cl
  Middlewich CW10 . . . . . 151 E6
  Winsford CW7 . . . . 126 A1
Fern Rd CH65 . . . . 70 B2
Fernway CW7 . . . . 127 B1
Fern Way CW8 . . . . 77 C1
Fernwood WA7 . . . . 24 B1
Fernwood Gr SK9 . . . . . . 60 C8
Fernyess La CH64 . . . . . . 67 E7
Ferret Oak La CW6 . . . . 186 B6
Ferrous Way M44 . . . . . . 11 F6
Ferry Ct CH5 . . . . 116 A6
Ferry La
  Sealand CH1 . . . . 117 C1
  Warrington WA4 . . . . . . 17 E4
Ferry Rd CH62 . . . . 44 A4
Festival Ave
  Buerton WA5 . . . . 230 E3
  Warrington WA5 . . . . 8 D2
Festival Cres WA2 . . . . . . 8 D2
Festival Dr SK8 . . . . 83 F6
Festival Hill CH65 . . . . . . 69 F5
Festival Rd CH65 . . . . . . 69 F5
Festival Terr 1 WA7 . . . . 49 E8
Festival Way WA7 . . . . . . 49 E8
Fforadd Cledwen/Cledwen Rd
  CH4 . . . . 139 D5
Ffordd Smithfield/Smithfield
  Dr LL13 . . . . 196 D8
Ffordd Y Blodau/Blossom
  Way CH4 . . . . 140 D5
Fiddlers Ferry Rd WA8 . . . 23 C8
Fiddler's Ferry Rd WA8 . . . 13 D1

Fiddlers La CH1 . . . . 94 C1
Field Ave CW2 . . . . 189 F1
Fieldbank Rd SK11 . . . . 112 B8
Field Cl
  Bollington SK10 . . . . . . 87 F7
  Bramhall SK7 . . . . 35 D4
  Northwich CW8 . . . . . . 103 C7
  Tarvin CH3 . . . . 121 B2
Fieldfare CW7 . . . . 150 A8
Fieldfare Cl
  Golborne WA3 . . . . 3 D8
  Warrington WA3 . . . . 9 F4
Fieldgate WA8 . . . . 22 B6
Fieldhead Mews SK9 . . . . 60 E8
Fieldhead Rd SK9 . . . . . . 60 E8
Field Hey La CH64 . . . . . 43 B1
Fieldhouse Row WA7 . . . . 49 D7
Fielding Ave SK12 . . . . . 36 E2
Field La
  Crewe CW2 . . . . 189 E2
  Tarvin CH3 . . . . 121 B2
  Tattenhall CH3 . . . . . . 166 B1
  Warrington WA4 . . . . . . 26 D6
Fields Cl ST7 . . . . 193 E4
Fields Dr CW11 . . . . 175 A5
Fieldsend Dr WN7 . . . . . . 4 C8
Fieldside CW6 . . . . 145 B6
Fieldside Cl
  Bramhall SK7 . . . . 35 D4
  Goostrey CW4 . . . . 107 E1
Field Side Cl WA16 . . . . . 58 A4
Fields View CW5 . . . . . . 139 B4
Fields Rd
  Alsager ST7 . . . . 193 E3
  Congleton CW12 . . . . . 178 F8
  Haslington CW1 . . . . . . 191 D4
Fields The CW5 . . . . 205 D5
Fields View SY13 . . . . . . 228 D1
Fields View CW5 . . . . . . 220 B8
Fieldsway WA7 . . . . 49 A6
Field View ST8 . . . . 179 D1
Fieldview Dr WA2 . . . . 8 C1
Field View Dr SK11 . . . . 112 E5
Fieldway
  Chester CH2 . . . . 118 C4
  Ellesmere Port CH66 . . . 69 B7
  Frodsham WA6 . . . . 74 C7
  Saughall CH1 . . . . 94 A2
  Weaverham CW8 . . . . . . 78 C2
  Widnes WA8 . . . . 13 E2
Field Way ST7 . . . . 193 E4
Fife Rd WA1 . . . . 16 E7
Fifth Ave
  Kidsgrove ST7 . . . . 194 F1
  2 Runcorn WA7 . . . . . . 49 F7
Fildes Cl WA5 . . . . 15 C5
Filkin's La CH3 . . . . 119 A1
Fillmore Gr WA8 . . . . 12 F3
Finchdale Gdns WA3 . . . . 4 B8
Finchett Cl CH1 . . . . 118 B3
Finchett Dr CH1 . . . . . . 118 B3
Finch La CH3 . . . . 21 B7
Finchley Cl WA12 . . . . 2 C2
Finger Post La WA6 . . . . 101 A4
Finlan Rd WA8 . . . . 22 F7
Finlay Ave WA5 . . . . 14 E3
Finlow Hill La SK10 . . . . 85 E6
Finney Cl SK9 . . . . 34 C2
Finney Dr SK9 . . . . 34 C2
Finney Gr WA11 . . . . 1 E6
FINNEY GREEN 34 E2
Finney La SK8 . . . . 34 B8
Finney's La CW10 . . . . . 128 B2
Finningley Ct WA2 . . . . . . 8 E1
Finsbury Cl WA5 . . . . . . 15 C4
Finsbury Pk WA8 . . . . . . 13 C5
Finsbury Way SK9 . . . . . 34 E2
Finsbury Wlk CW7 . . . . 149 A8
Fir Ave
  Bramhall SK7 . . . . 35 E8
  Halewood L26 . . . . 21 A8
Firbank Cl WA2 . . . . 24 D1
Firbeck Cl
  Broughton CH4 . . . . . . 139 B3
  Congleton CW12 . . . . . 155 F3
Firbeck Gdns CH4 . . . . . 189 D4
Fir Cl
  Halewood L26 . . . . 21 A8
  Poynton SK12 . . . . 36 F3
  Tarporley CW6 . . . . . . 146 D2
Fir Ct SK10 . . . . 86 F1
Firdale Rd CW8 . . . . 103 D7
Firecrest Ct WA1 . . . . . . 16 A3
Firemans Sq CH1 . . . . . 237 A3
Fir Gr
  Macclesfield SK11 . . . . 112 D5
  Warrington WA1 . . . . . . 16 E7
  Weaverham CW8 . . . . . 102 E8
Fir La CW8 . . . . 102 A2
Firman Cl WA5 . . . . 15 B8
Fir Rd SK7 . . . . 35 E8
Firsway Pk CW5 . . . . . . 217 C1
Firs La WA5 . . . . 26 B6
Firs Pottery The* CW5 . . 217 C1
Firs Sch The CH2 . . . . . 118 C5
Fir St
  Irlam M44 . . . . 11 D6
  Widnes WA8 . . . . 13 C2
First Ave
  Connah's Quay CH5 . . . . 93 A2
  Crewe CW1 . . . . 190 F2
  Kidsgrove ST7 . . . . 194 E1
  Poynton SK12 . . . . 36 D1
  Sandbach CW11 . . . . . 175 A5
First Dig La CW5 . . . . . . 219 C8

Firs The SK9 . . . . 60 A5
First Wood St CW5 . . . . 204 D5
Firs View WA6 . . . . 73 D4
Firth Bvd WA2 . . . . 16 C7
Firth Cl CW11 . . . . 175 B7
Firth Fields CW9 . . . . . . 103 F2
Firthfields Cl CW9 . . . . . 103 F2
Fir Tree Ave
  Chester CH4 . . . . 141 B5
  Golborne WA3 . . . . 3 D8
  Knutsford WA16 . . . . . . 82 C8
Firtree Cl
  Barnton CW8 . . . . 78 B4
  Winsford CW7 . . . . 127 B1
Fir Tree Cl WA4 . . . . 26 D1
Fir Tree Cotts CW2 . . . . 208 C5
Firtree Gr CH66 . . . . 95 A8
Fir Tree La
  Burtonwood WA5 . . . . . . 7 A7
  Chester CH3 . . . . 119 C2
  Faddiley CW5 . . . . 202 B3
Fir Tree Wlk WA3 . . . . 3 F8
Fir Way CH60 . . . . 41 B5
Firwood Rd ST8 . . . . 179 E1
Firwood Wlk CW2 . . . . . 190 C1
Fisher Ave WA3 . . . . 8 B2
Fisherfield Dr WA3 . . . . . 10 A6
Fishermans Cl CW11 . . . 191 F7
Fisher Rd CH1 . . . . 117 E4
Fishers Gn CW6 . . . . . . 146 B5
Fishers La CW5 . . . . 203 C8
Fisher St WA7 . . . . 23 B3
Fishpool Rd CW8 . . . . . . 123 F3
Fishwicks Ind Est WA11 . . 1 F8
Fistral Ave SK8 . . . . 34 C8
Fit City Sports Ctr M44 . . 11 D5
Fitton's Cl CW5 . . . . 217 F5
Fitton St CW9 . . . . 80 A2
Fitz Cl SK10 . . . . 87 D3
Fitz Cres SK10 . . . . 87 D3
Fitzherbert St WA2 . . . . . 16 C7
Fitzwalter Rd WA1 . . . . . 17 D7
Fitzwilliam Ave SK11 . . . 112 F3
Fiveashes Cotts SK10 . . . 88 B5
Five Ashes Rd CH4 . . . . 141 B5
FIVECROSSES 74 C6
Five Ways CW6 . . . . 41 F3
Fiveways Par SK7 . . . . . . 36 E8
Fiveways Pk CH64 . . . . . 41 F3
Flacca Ct CH3 . . . . 166 B1
Flag La
  Crewe CW1, CW2 . . . . . 190 C4
  Neston CH64 . . . . 66 F7
Flag Lane N CH2 . . . . . . 118 E8
Flag Lane S CH2 . . . . . . 118 E8
Flander Cl WA8 . . . . 12 C2
Flashes La CH64 . . . . . . 67 B5
Flash La
  Antrobus CW9 . . . . 53 F5
  Bollington SK10 . . . . . . 87 D7
Flat La
  Kelsall CW6 . . . . 122 C4
  Sandbach CW11 . . . . . 175 B6
Flatt La CH65 . . . . 70 B5
Flatts La SK23 . . . . 64 F4
Flavian Cl WA1 . . . . 128 C2
Flavian St WA7 . . . . 23 E2
Flaxley Cl WA3 . . . . 10 A5
Flaxmere Dr CH3 . . . . . . 142 B8
Flaxyards CW6 . . . . 146 F2
Fleet La WA9 . . . . 1 A2
Fleet St CW5 . . . . 70 A5
Fleetwood Cl WA5 . . . . . . 15 B4
Fleetwood Dr WA12 . . . . . 2 B4
Fleetwood Wlk WA7 . . . . 50 C6
Fleming Dr WA2 . . . . 8 C8
Fleming St CH65 . . . . . . 70 C6
Flers Ave WA4 . . . . 16 C4
Fletcher Ct WA16 . . . . . . 56 F1
Fletcher Dr SK12 . . . . . . 37 F6
Fletcher Gr CW9 . . . . . . 104 C6
Fletcher's Bldgs
  Chester CH1 . . . . 237 B2
  6 Runcorn WA7 . . . . . . 23 B2
Fletchers La 3 WA4 . . . . 18 F4
Fletcher's Row 5 WA7 . . . 23 F1
Fletcher St
  Crewe CW1 . . . . 190 B5
  Warrington WA4 . . . . . . 16 B3
Fletsand Rd SK9 . . . . . . 60 D6
Flint Cl CH64 . . . . 66 E6
Flint Ct CH65 . . . . 70 D2
Flint Dr CH64 . . . . 66 E6
Flint Rd WA8 . . . . 22 C4
Flint Mdw CH64 . . . . 66 E7
Flint St SK10 . . . . 112 E8
Flittogate La WA16 . . . . . 80 E8
Flixton Dr CW2 . . . . 190 A2
FLOOKERSBROOK 118 E4
Flookersbrook CH1 . . . . 237 C4
Florence St WA4 . . . . 16 D3
Florida Cl WA5 . . . . 7 C1
Flour Mill Way CW1 . . . . 191 A3
Flowcrete Bsns Pk
  CW11 . . . . 152 C1
Flowerscroft CW5 . . . . . 205 A4
Flowers La CW1 . . . . . . 172 E1
Flower St CW8 . . . . 103 E7
Floyd Dr WA2 . . . . 8 B1
Fluin La WA6 . . . . 74 C8
Flying Fields Dr SK11 . . 112 A5
Foden Ave ST7 . . . . 194 A3
Foden La
  Alderley Edge SK9 . . . . 59 C1
  Bramhall SK7 . . . . 35 D3

Foden St SK10 . . . . 87 D1
Fodens Terr CW11 . . . . . 175 A6
Foden Wlk 7 SK9 . . . . . . 34 D2
Fog Cotts CW3 . . . . 221 E4
Fogg's La CW9, WA5 . . . . 53 A6
Fold La
  Biddulph ST8 . . . . 179 E4
  Bosley SK11 . . . . 135 D2
Folds La SK23 . . . . 65 F3
Folds The CH63 . . . . 42 A6
Fold The SK10 . . . . 87 A8
Foley Wlk M22 . . . . 33 E8
Fol Hollow CW12 . . . . . . 156 B1
Folkestone Cl SK10 . . . . . 87 B2
Folkstone Way WA7 . . . . 50 C7
Folly La WA5 . . . . 15 F7
Forbes Cl WA3 . . . . 9 E3
Forbes Pk SK7 . . . . 35 D7
Ford Cl CW1 . . . . 190 B5
Ford Ct CW7 . . . . 149 C6
Fordington Rd WA5 . . . . 15 B5
Ford La
  Crewe CW1 . . . . 190 B6
  Tattenhall CH3 . . . . . . 166 F4
Fords La SK7 . . . . 195 D6
Ford's La SK7 . . . . 35 D6
Ford St WA1 . . . . 16 D6
Fordton L Ctr WA2 . . . . . . 8 A3
Foregate St CH1 . . . . . . 237 B2
Foreland Cl WA5 . . . . . . 14 C7
Forest Ave CW4 . . . . . . 107 C1
Forest Cl
  Cuddington CW8 . . . . . 101 F3
  Rainow SK10 . . . . 88 E5
Forest Dr
  Broughton CH4 . . . . . . 139 C3
  Langley SK11 . . . . 113 C4
Forester Ave WA16 . . . . . 57 C2
Foresters Cl WA4 . . . . . 101 A6
Forest Gate Com Prim Sch
  M31 . . . . 11 D3
Forest Gate La CW6 . . . . 122 E7
Forest Gdns M31 . . . . . . 11 D3
Forest Ho SK10 . . . . 87 F2
Forest La WA6 . . . . 100 C6
Forest Pl 3 CW9 . . . . . . 79 A1
Forest Prim Sch CW8 . . . 77 C1
Forest Rd
  Cuddington CW8 . . . . . 101 F2
  Delamere CW6 . . . . . . 124 B1
  Ellesmere Port CH66 . . . 69 E7
  Heswall CH60 . . . . 41 A8
  Macclesfield SK11 . . . . 113 E6
  Tarporley CW6 . . . . . . 146 D3
Forest Road Pk CW8 . . . 101 E2
Forest St
  Chester CH1 . . . . 237 C2
  Weaverham CW8 . . . . . 102 C8
Forest Wlk 5 WA7 . . . . . 49 F7
Forge Cl
  Cronton WA8 . . . . 12 C5
  Warren SK11 . . . . 111 D2
Forge Fields CW11 . . . . 174 F3
Forge La
  Congleton CW12 . . . . . 156 B3
  Norton in Hales TF9 . . . 236 C1
Forge Mill La CW10 . . . . 151 C1
Forge Rd
  Ellesmere Port CH66 . . . 69 C6
  Warrington WA5 . . . . . . 14 F5
  Whaley Bridge SK23 . . . 65 E8
Forge Sh Ctr The WA4 . . . 16 C1
Forge Way CW1 . . . . . . 140 F4
Formby Dr WA5 . . . . 14 F4
Formby Dr SK8 . . . . 34 B8
Forrest Way WA5 . . . . . . 15 D3
Forshaw's La WA5 . . . . . . 6 E8
Forshaw St WA2 . . . . 16 C8
Forster Ave CW8 . . . . . . 102 E8
Forster St WA2 . . . . 16 B7
Forsythia Wlk 2 M31 . . . 11 E2
Forty Acre La CW4,
  CW12 . . . . 131 D6
Forum Sh Ctr The CH1 . . 237 A2
Forwood Rd CH62 . . . . . . 43 D8
Fossa Cl CW10 . . . . 128 C2
Foster Rd CW12 . . . . . . 156 E2
Foster St WA8 . . . . 13 B1
Fothergill St WA1 . . . . . . 16 D6
Fotheringay Ct 3 CH65 . . 70 D2
Foulkes Ave CW1 . . . . . 189 F6
Foundry Bank CW12 . . . 156 E3
Foundry Ct 1 SK22 . . . . . 39 C7
Foundry Ind Est WA8 . . . 23 B7
Foundry La
  Sandbach CW11 . . . . . 174 D7
  Scholar Green ST7 . . . . 194 F7
  Widnes WA8 . . . . 22 C5
Foundry St
  Bollington SK10 . . . . . . 88 B8
  Newton-le-Willows WA12 . . 2 B3
  Warrington WA2 . . . . . . 16 B6
Fountain Cl SK12 . . . . . . 36 D4
Fountain Ct
  Biddulph ST8 . . . . 179 D1
  2 Winsford CW7 . . . . . 126 D1
Fountain Ho SK10 . . . . . 112 E8
Fountain La
  Davenham CW9 . . . . . . 103 F2
  Frodsham WA6 . . . . 74 B8
Fountains Ave WA11 . . . . . 1 F7
Fountains Cl
  Middlewich CW10 . . . . . 128 B1
  Runcorn WA7 . . . . 50 C5
Fountain Sq SK12 . . . . . . 38 D6

Fountains Rd SK8 . . . . 35 C6
Fountain St
　Congleton CW12 . . . . .156 D2
　Macclesfield SK10 . . . . . . .112 E8
Fountains Wlk WA3 . . . . . . .4 B8
FOURLANE-ENDS 63 A8
FOUR LANE ENDS 168 D7
Four Lane Ends
　Alvanley WA6 . . . . .74 B1
　Warrington WA3 . . . . .9 D3
Four Lanes Ct **3** CW7 . . . 149 B8
FOURLANES END 176 E4
Four Lanes End
　Betley CW2 . . . . .207 F2
　Thornton Hough CH63 . . . 42 D5
Fourseasons Cl CW2 . . . . . 206 B8
Fourth Ave
　Connah's Quay CH5 . . . . . 92 E2
　Crewe CW1 . . . . .190 F1
　Kidsgrove ST7 . . . . .194 F1
　1 Runcorn WA7 . . . . .49 F7
Fourways WA7 . . . . .207 B5
Fourways Tech Pk CW1 . . 176 E4
Fowey Cl SK10 . . . . .86 D1
Fowler Cl CW2 . . . . .190 D1
Fowler Rd CH1 . . . . .117 D4
Fowlers Bench La CH3 . . . .184 C5
Fowler St SK10 . . . . .87 D1
FOWLEY COMMON 5 C7
Fowley Common La WA3 . . 5 C5
Foxall Way WA5 . . . . .69 D2
Fox Bench Cl WA8 . . . . . . .12 F4
Fox Bench Cl SK7 . . . . .35 C6
Foxcote WA8 . . . . .12 B2
Foxcote Cl CH1 . . . . .117 D5
Fox Cover CH3 . . . . 119 F5
Fox Cover Rd CH60 . . . . . . 41 D7
Fox Covert WA7 . . . . .50 C7
Foxcovert La WA16 . . . . . . 106 E7
Fox Covert La
　Hoole Bank CH2 . . . . 119 B8
　Picton CH2 . . . . .96 A1
Fox Covert Way CW1 . . . . . 173 A1
Foxdale Ct WA4 . . . . .26 C7
Foxdene CW6 . . . . .69 D5
Foxendale Cl CW8 . . . . . . .103 D7
Foxes Fold CW8 . . . . .78 E1
Foxes Hey CW8 . . . . .105 D5
Foxes Hollow CW1 . . . . . . .190 E7
Foxes Wlk CH3 . . . . .142 A7
Foxfield Cl WA2 . . . . .8 E3
Foxfield La CW7 . . . . .126 A1
Fox Gdns
　Lymm WA13 . . . . .18 C4
　Talke ST7 . . . . .210 D8
Foxglove Cl
　Bollington SK10 . . . . .88 C8
　2 Golborne WA3 . . . . . . .3 D8
　Huntington CH3 . . . . .142 A6
　Wistaston CW2 . . . . .206 B7
Foxglove Ct WA6 . . . . .74 C8
Foxglove Dell WA6 . . . . . . 73 D2
Foxglove Way CH64 . . . . . .66 E5
Foxglove Wlk M31 . . . . . . .57 C1
Fox Gr WA16 . . . . .57 C1
Fox Hill CW6 . . . . 122 D4
Foxhill Cl CW8 . . . . .102 A2
Foxhill Ct CW6 . . . . .146 E1
Foxhill Gr WA6 . . . . 73 D4
Foxhills Cl WA3 . . . . .26 D3
Foxholme Ct CW1 . . . . . . .191 A6
Fox Hunter Cl CH3 . . . . . . 121 F7
Fox La
　Clutton CH3 . . . . 182 D1
　Waverton CH3 . . . . 143 B5
Foxlea CW9 . . . . .78 C7
Fox Lea CH1 . . . . 117 A8
FOXLEY 209 D7
Foxley Cl WA13 . . . . 19 A2
Foxley Hall Mews WA3 . . . 19 A1
Foxley Heath WA8 . . . . . . 22 E8
Fox's Dr CH5 . . . . 116 A6
Fox St
　Congleton CW12 . . . . 156 F3
　Runcorn WA7 . . . . .23 A1
　Warrington WA5 . . . . 15 E5
Foxwist Cl CH2 . . . . .237 B4
Foxwist Gn CW8 . . . . .125 E6
FOXWIST GREEN 125 E6
Foxwood Dr WA16 . . . . . . 108 A8
　Fox Wood Sch WA3 . . . . . 9 E3
Francesca Ct CH1 . . . . . . .237 B2
Frances St
　Crewe CW2 . . . . .190 D2
　Irlam M44 . . . . .11 E5
　Macclesfield SK11 . . . . . .112 B8
Francis Cl WA8 . . . . .22 C3
Francis Ct CH1 . . . . .237 C3
Francis La LL13 . . . . 196 D7
Francis' La LL13 . . . . 196 B6
Francis Rd
　Frodsham WA6 . . . . .49 C1
　Irlam M44 . . . . .11 F8
　Warrington WA4 . . . . 16 B1
Francis St CH1 . . . . .237 C3
FRANDLEY 53 A3
Frank Bott Ave CW1 . . . . . 190 A7
Franklin Cl
　Macclesfield SK11 . . . . . .112 B8
　Warrington WA5 . . . . 15 C8
Franklin Mews CW9 . . . . . .71 C1
Franklyn Ave CW2 . . . . . . 190 B3
Fox Perkins Way M44 . . . . 11 F7
Frank St WA8 . . . . .23 C3
Frank Webb Ave CW1 . . . . 190 A6
Frappel Ct WA2 . . . . .16 B6
Fraser Ct CH4 . . . . .141 D7
Fraser Rd WA5 . . . . 14 D6

Frawley Ave WA12 . . . . . . .2 C5
Freckleton Cl WA5 . . . . . . .15 B4
Frederick St
　Warrington WA4 . . . . 16 E3
　Widnes WA8 . . . . .23 B8
Frederick Terr WA8 . . . . . .22 A4
Fredric Pl WA7 . . . . .23 B3
Freedom Dr ST7 . . . . .195 E3
Free Green La WA16 . . . . . 107 A8
Freeport Shopping Mall
　ST7 . . . . .210 C6
French La CW5 . . . . .218 C5
French Lane End CW5 . . . .218 C5
French St WA8 . . . . .13 D1
Freshfield SK8 . . . . .34 B8
Freshfield Dr SK10 . . . . . . .87 C3
Freshfields
　Comberbach CW8 . . . . . .78 C2
　Knutsford WA16 . . . . 56 E3
　Wistaston CW2 . . . . .206 A7
Freshfields Dr WA2 . . . . . . 9 C1
Freshmeadow La WA6 . . . .73 B2
Freshwater Cl WA5 . . . . . . 14 D7
Freshwater Dr CW2 . . . . . .221 C8
Freshwater View CW8 . . . .103 F8
Friars Ave WA3 . . . . .14 E5
Friars Cl
　Rainow SK10 . . . . .88 D3
　Wistaston CW2 . . . . .205 F8
Friar's Cl SK9 . . . . .59 E8
Friars Ct **11** WA1 . . . . . . .16 B5
Friars Gate
　Chester CH1 . . . . .237 B2
　Warrington WA1 . . . . 16 B4
Friars La WA1 . . . . .16 B4
Friars Way WA6 . . . . .86 F2
Frida Cres CW9 . . . . .103 E6
Friends La WA5 . . . . .14 D6
Friesian Gdns ST5 . . . . . . .210 C2
Frith Ave CW8 . . . . .123 D8
Frith La CW5 . . . . 216 C4
Frith Terr SK11 . . . . .112 D4
Frobisher Ct WA5 . . . . .64 E8
Frobisher Rd CH64 . . . . . . .66 E8
Froda Ave WA6 . . . . .74 B7
FRODSHAM 74 D7
Frodsham Bsns Ctr WA6 . . .49 C1
Frodsham CE Prim Sch
　WA6 . . . . .74 C7
Frodsham L Ctr WA6 . . . . .74 B8
Frodsham Manor House Prim
　Sch WA6 . . . . .49 C1
FRODSHAM MARSH 48 B2
Frodsham Rd WA6 . . . . . . .73 D1
FRODSHAM SCORE 48 B2
Frodsham Sq CH1 . . . . . . .237 B3
Frodsham St CH1 . . . . . . .237 B3
Frodsham StaWA6 . . . . . . .74 B8
Frodsham Way WA9 . . . . . .34 E4
Frodsham Weaver Vale Prim
　Sch WA6 . . . . .49 C2
Froghall La
　High Legh WA16 . . . . 29 D7
　Warrington WA2, WA5 . . . 15 F5
Frog La
　Holt LL13 . . . . .196 B8
　Milton Green CH3 . . . . . .165 E2
　Pickmere WA16 . . . . 30 D1
　Worthenbury LL13, SY14 . . 211 B1
Frome Ct CW11 . . . . 175 C6
Front St CW11 . . . . .175 C6
Frosts Mews CW5 . . . . . . .70 B6
Fryer Rd CW9 . . . . .80 A3
Fryer St **16** WA7 . . . . . . .23 A3
Fuchsia Cl CH66 . . . . .69 F1
Fulbeck WA8 . . . . .12 C2
Fulbeck Cl CW2 . . . . 206 B8
Fulbrook Dr SK8 . . . . .35 A6
Fuller Dr CW2 . . . . .206 B7
FULLER'S MOOR 188 C6
Fullerton Rd CW6 . . . . . . .103 A4
Fulmar Cl SK12 . . . . .36 A4
Fulmards Cl SK9 . . . . .60 C7
Fulshaw Ave SK9 . . . . .60 A6
Fulshaw Cross SK9 . . . . . . .60 A5
Fulshaw Ct SK9 . . . . .60 A5
FULSHAW PARK 60 B5
Fulshaw Pk SK9 . . . . .60 A5
Fulshaw Pk S SK9 . . . . .60 A4
Fulton Gr CW9 . . . . .103 F2
Fulwood Gdns CH66 . . . . . .69 C6
Fulwood Mews CH66 . . . . . 69 C6
Fulwood Rd
　Ellesmere Port CH66 . . . . .69 C5
　Golborne WA3 . . . . .3 F7
Furber St CW1 . . . . .190 C5
Furne Rd CH1 . . . . 117 E4
Furness Cl
　Holmes Chapel CW4 . . . .130 A3
　Poynton SK12 . . . . .36 D4
　Winsford CW7 . . . . .149 B8
Furness Ct WA7 . . . . .24 F4
Furness Lodge Cl SK23 . . . .39 D3
Furness Rd WA8 . . . . .13 E3
FURNESS VALE 39 C3
Furness Vale Bsns Ctr
　SK23 . . . . .39 D4
Furness Vale Prim Sch
　SK23 . . . . .39 D3
Furness Vale Sta SK23 . . . .39 D4
Furnival St 175 B7
Furnival St CW2 . . . . .190 C2
Furrocks Cl CH64 . . . . .66 F5
Furrocks La CH64 . . . . .66 F5
Furrocks Way CH64 . . . . . .66 F5
Furrows The CW4 . . . . .94 E8
Fylde Ave SK8 . . . . .34 C8
Fytton Cl SK11 . . . . .111 D1

G

Gable Ave SK9 . . . . .60 A7
Gable Ct **5** CW5 . . . . . . .204 E6
Gables Cl WA2 . . . . .8 F3
Gable St WA12 . . . . .2 A3
Gables The ST7 . . . . .193 C3
Gabriel Bank CW8 . . . . . . .76 A1
Gadbrook Bsns Ctr CW9 . . 104 D5
Gadbrook Pk CW9 . . . . . . .104 D5
Gadbrook Rd CW9 . . . . . . 104 D6
Gail Cl SK9 . . . . .60 B2
Gainford CW8 . . . . .12 C3
Gainsborough Cl SK9 . . . . .60 C8
Gainsborough Cl WA8 . . . . .12 B1
Gainsborough Prim Sch
　CW2 . . . . .190 B2
Gainsborough Rd
　Crewe CW2 . . . . .190 B3
　Warrington WA4 . . . . 16 B2
Gairloch Cl WA2 . . . . .8 F4
Gaisgill Ct WA8 . . . . .12 C4
Galbraith Cl WA2 . . . . 129 C3
Galbraith Cl CW12 . . . . . . 156 C2
Gale Ave WA5 . . . . .7 F1
Galion Way WA8 . . . . 12 F3
GALLANTRY BANK 200 B8
Galleys Bank CH7 . . . . . . .195 B3
Gallimore Ho ST7 . . . . . . .210 D8
Galloway Cl
　Holmes Chapel CW4 . . . .130 C2
　Middlewich CW10 . . . . . .128 E2
Galloway Gn CW12 . . . . . .156 E5
Gallowsclough La WA6 . . . 100 F4
Galway Ave WA8 . . . . .12 E3
Galway Cres WA11 . . . . . . .1 D7
Galway Gr CW2 . . . . .206 B4
Game St CW11 . . . . .175 A3
Galway Pl CH1 . . . . .237 A3
Ganton Cl WA8 . . . . .13 B4
Garden Cl SK10 . . . . .87 E1
Garden Ct CH1 . . . . .237 A3
Garden La
　Chester CH1 . . . . .237 A3
　Harthill CH3 . . . . .183 E3
Garden Rd WA16 . . . . .56 F3
Garden St
　Bollington SK10 . . . . .87 F8
　Congleton CW12 . . . . 156 C3
　Macclesfield SK10 . . . . . .87 E1
Gardens The
　Holt LL13 . . . . .180 E1
　Lawton-gate ST7 . . . . . . .194 C4
　Sandbach CW11 . . . . 175 B6
Garden Terr
　Chester, Broughton CH2 . . 118 F2
　Chester CH1 . . . . .237 A3
Garden Wlk **8** M31 . . . . .11 E3
Gardiner Ave WA1 . . . . . . .1 C6
Garfit St CW10 . . . . .128 C2
Garner St WA2 . . . . .16 C7
Garnett Ave WA4 . . . . 17 A4
Garnett Cl CW5 . . . . 204 F4
Garnetts La WA8 . . . . .13 C8
Garrett Field WA3 . . . . .9 D5
Garrigill Cl WA3 . . . . 13 C5
Garsdale Cl WA5 . . . . .14 F7
Garside Ave WA3 . . . . .3 D7
Garth Dr CH2 . . . . .118 C5
Garth Hts SK9 . . . . .60 C7
Garton Dr WA3 . . . . .3 E8
Garven Pl WA1 . . . . 15 C8
Garwood Cl WA3 . . . . .15 C8
Gaskell Ave
　Knutsford WA16 . . . . 56 F2
　Warrington WA4 . . . . 17 A3
Gaskell St WA4 . . . . .16 C1
Gas Rd SK11 . . . . .112 D8
Gas Works Ind Est ST7 . . . .194 E2
Gatcombe Mews **1** SK9 . . .60 A6
Gateacre Ct CH66 . . . . . . .69 F8
Gatefield St CW1 . . . . . . .190 D3
Gatehouse The **7** CW5 . . 204 E5
Gateley Cl WA3 . . . . .17 E3
GATESHEATH 165 E5
Gatesheath Dr CH2 . . . . . .118 E7
Gatesheath La CH3 . . . . . .165 F5
Gatewarth Ind Est WA5 . . . 15 D3
Gate Warth St WA5 . . . . . . 15 D4
Gateway
　Crewe CW1 . . . . .190 F2
　Newcastle-under-Lyme
　ST5 . . . . .210 D2
Gateway Theatre* CH1 . . . .237 A2
Gateway Trad Pk WA5 . . . .16 A7
Gathurst Ct WA8 . . . . .22 B8
Gauntlet Birds of Prey, Eagle
　& Vulture Park* WA16 . . .56 D5
GAUNTONS BANK 215 E4
Gaunts Way WA7 . . . . .49 E6
Gavin Rd WA8 . . . . .22 B7
Gaw End La CW11 . . . . . . .131 C6
Gawer Pk CH2 . . . . .118 C4
GAWSWORTH 135 E8
Gawsworth Ave CW2 . . . . .189 F3
Gawsworth Cl
　Alsager ST7 . . . . .193 C3
　Bramhall SK7 . . . . .35 E6
　Holmes Chapel CW4 . . . .130 B3
　Macclesfield SK11 . . . . . .134 E8
　Poynton SK12 . . . . .36 F2
Gawsworth Ct WA3 . . . . . . .9 F5
Gawsworth Dr CW11 . . . . .175 C7
Gawsworth Hall* SK11 . . . .134 E8

Gawsworth Prim Sch
　SK11 . . . . .111 D2
Gawsworth Rd
　Ellesmere Port CH66 . . . . .69 E5
　Macclesfield SK11 . . . . . .111 D5
Gawsworth Way SK9 . . . . . .34 E4
Gayhurst Ave WA2 . . . . . . .8 F2
Gaymoore Cl CH2 . . . . . . .237 A4
Gaynor Ave WA11 . . . . . . .1 F7
GAYTON 41 B6
Gayton Cl CH2 . . . . .118 E5
Gayton Farm Rd CH60 . . . .41 A5
Gayton La CH60 . . . . .41 B6
Gayton Mill Cl CH60 . . . . . .41 B7
Gayton Parkway CH60 . . . .41 C5
Gayton Prim Sch CH60 . . . .41 A6
Gayton Rd CH60 . . . . .41 A6
Gayton Sands RSPB
　Reserve* CH60 . . . . .40 E4
Gelli Dderw/Oak Gr
　CH4 . . . . 140 D5
GEMINI 7 D3
Gemini Bsns Pk WA5 . . . . .7 E3
Gemmull Cl CW2 . . . . 229 F4
General St WA1 . . . . .16 C5
Genesis Ctr The WA3 . . . . .9 E5
Geneva Rd WA7 . . . . .126 C1
Geo. Hampson's Bldgs
　WA3 . . . . .5 C8
George Bates Cl ST7 . . . . .193 C3
George Cl WA4 . . . . 17 A3
George Ho CW5 . . . . .204 E7
George Kenyon Mews
　CH4 . . . . 140 E6
George Rd WA5 . . . . .15 C4
George St W SK11 . . . . . . .112 D8
George's Cl SK12 . . . . .36 E3
Georges Cres WA4 . . . . . . .17 B2
Georges Ct **13** SK10 . . . .112 C8
George's La CW9 . . . . .54 D1
George's Prec WA5 . . . . . . 14 D6
George's Road E SK12 . . . . .36 E3
George's Road W SK12 . . . .36 E3
George St
　Alderley Edge SK9 . . . . . .60 A1
　Audley ST7 . . . . .209 D2
　Barnton CW8 . . . . .78 B3
　Chester CH1 . . . . .237 A3
　Ellesmere Port CH65 . . . . .70 C7
　Knutsford WA16 . . . . 57 A2
　Macclesfield SK11 . . . . . .112 D8
　Newton-le-Willows WA12 . . 2 A4
　Sandbach CW11 . . . . 174 C8
　Whaley Bridge SK23 . . . . .65 E7
　Winsford CW7 . . . . .126 E1
George St S ST7 . . . . .209 F2
George's Wlk CW11 . . . . . .175 B6
George VI Ave CW10 . . . . .151 D6
George VI Cl CW10 . . . . . .151 D6
Georgia Pl WA5 . . . . .15 C7
Gerard Dr CW5 . . . . .204 C4
Gerards Gdns CH66 . . . . . 205 D6
Gerosa Ave WA3 . . . . .8 B8
Gerard Ave
　Ellesmere Port CH66 . . . . .69 C4
　Warrington WA5 . . . . 15 F7
Gerrard Dr CW8 . . . . .77 D1
Gerrard Rd WA3 . . . . .9 A7
Gerrards Ave CH3 . . . . . . .119 A1
Gerrard St WA8 . . . . .23 B8
Giantswood La
　Congleton CW12 . . . . . . .156 C6
　Marton CW12 . . . . .132 F1
GIBB HILL 53 D1
Gibb Hill CW9 . . . . .53 D1
Gibbon Dr CW9 . . . . .80 B3
Gibson Cl CW5 . . . . .204 D6
Gibson Cres CW11 . . . . . . 174 D6
Gibson Ct Trad Est CH65 . . .70 C8
Gibson St
　Warrington, Howley WA1 . . 16 C5
　Warrington, Stockton Heath
　WA4 . . . . .16 D1
Gigg La
　Moore WA4 . . . . .25 B5
　Warrington WA4 . . . . 17 E3
Gig La WA1 . . . . .17 E8
Gilbert Cl **2** CW1 . . . . . .195 A2
Gilbert Ct WA4 . . . . .4 F3
Gilbert Ho WA7 . . . . .22 E3
Gilchrist Ave SK11 . . . . . . .111 E7
Gilchrist Rd M44 . . . . .11 F6
Gilderdale Cl WA3 . . . . . . .30 C6
Gillan Ct WA3 . . . . .50 C5
GILLBENT 34 F6
Gilbent Rd SK8 . . . . .35 A7
Gillow Cl CW1 . . . . .190 A8
GILLOW HEATH 179 C2
Giltbrook Cl WA8 . . . . .12 F3
Gilwell Cl WA4 . . . . .17 C2
Gilwern Cl CH2 . . . . .118 C4
GINCLOUGH 88 F6
Gingerbread La CW5 . . . . .205 A5
Gipsy Cnr SY13 . . . . .224 E2
Girton Cl CH65 . . . . .70 D4
Girton Rd CH65 . . . . .70 D4
Girvin Dr CH64 . . . . .66 F6
Glade Dr CH66 . . . . .68 F6
Gladewood Cl **1** SK9 . . . .60 C8
Gladstone Ave CH1 . . . . . .118 B2
Gladstone Mews WA7 . . . . .49 F8
Gladstone Rd
　Broughton CH4 . . . . .139 B3
　Chester CH1 . . . . .118 B3
　Neston CH64 . . . . .66 E8
Gladstone St
　Northwich CW8 . . . . .103 E7
　Warrington WA2 . . . . 16 A6

Gladstone St *continued*
　8 Widnes WA8 . . . . . . .23 B8
　Willaston CW5 . . . . .205 D6
　Winsford CW7 . . . . .149 D8
Gladstone Way WA12 . . . . .2 B4
Glaisdale Cl CW2 . . . . 206 A6
Glamis Cl
　Chester CH3 . . . . .119 A2
　Wistaston CW2 . . . . .205 E8
Glanaber Ct CH4 . . . . .141 A7
Glan Aber Pk CH4 . . . . . . .141 A7
Glandon Dr SK8 . . . . .35 C8
Glastonbury Ave
　Cheadle SK8 . . . . .35 C6
　Chester CH2 . . . . .118 F7
　Golborne WA3 . . . . .4 C8
Glastonbury Cl WA7 . . . . . .24 F3
Glastonbury Dr
　Middlewich CW10 . . . . . .128 B1
　Poynton SK12 . . . . .36 D5
GLAZEBROOK 11 B6
Glazebrook La WA3 . . . . . .11 B5
Glazebrook StaWA3 . . . . . .11 A5
GLAZEBURY 5 B7
Glazebury CE Prim Sch
　WA3 . . . . .4 D2
Glaziers La WA3 . . . . .4 D2
Gleadmere WA8 . . . . .12 C2
GLEADSMOSS 132 B6
Gleaner Cl WA7 . . . . .22 F3
Gleave Ave SK10 . . . . .88 B8
Gleave Rd
　Burtonwood WA5 . . . . . . .6 F6
　Weaverham CW8 . . . . . . .77 D1
Gleave Cl WA5 . . . . .17 C1
Glebe Cl CW5 . . . . 220 A8
Glebecroft Ave CH2 . . . . . .72 A3
Glebe Ct SK12 . . . . .194 D2
Glebe Farm Mews CW7 . . . .71 E2
Glebe Green Dr CW7 . . . . .149 C6
Glebe La WA8 . . . . .13 B5
Glebe Mdw WA6 . . . . .4 E2
Glebelands Rd WA16 . . . . .57 A1
Glebe Mdws CH2 . . . . .96 F1
Glebe Rd CW8 . . . . .102 A4
Glebe St CW7 . . . . 194 D2
Glebe The WA7 . . . . .23 E1
Glebeway Rd CH65 . . . . . . .70 F5
Gleggs Cl CH3 . . . . .142 B7
Glegg St SK11 . . . . .112 E7
Glenathol Rd CH66 . . . . . . .69 C4
Glenbourne Pk SK7 . . . . . .35 D5
Glenburn Ave CH62 . . . . . .43 E4
Glen Cl WA3 . . . . .11 B2
Glencoe Cl CW4 . . . . .130 C2
Glencoe Rd CH66 . . . . .69 C4
Glencourse Rd WA8 . . . . . .13 A1
Glendale Ave
　Elton CH2 . . . . .72 A3
　Sandycroft CH5 . . . . 116 A3
Glendale Bsns Pk CH5 . . . .116 A3
Glendale Cl
　Buerton CW3 . . . . .230 F4
　Crewe CW2 . . . . .189 D3
　Glendale Pk CH5 . . . . . . .116 A3
Glendene Ave SK7 . . . . . . .35 D5
Glenfield Rd CH66 . . . . . . .69 C4
Glenholme Rd SK7 . . . . . . .35 D7
Glenmaye Rd CH66 . . . . . .69 C4
Glenn Pl WA8 . . . . .12 E1
Glenorchy Cl CW4 . . . . . . .130 C2
Glen Rd CH66 . . . . .69 C4
Glenside Cl CH1 . . . . .117 D5
Glenside Dr SK9 . . . . .60 E8
Glen The
　Blacon CH1 . . . . 117 E5
　Runcorn WA7 . . . . .49 F5
Glenton Pk CH64 . . . . .66 F6
Glenville Cl
　Cheadle SK8 . . . . .34 F7
　Runcorn WA7 . . . . .49 B8
Glenwood CW7 . . . . .24 C1
Glenwood Cl **3** CH66 . . . .69 C6
Glenwood Gdns CH66 . . . . .69 C6
Glenwood Rd CH66 . . . . . . .69 C6
Gleyve WA16 . . . . .29 C5
Gloucester Ave WA3 . . . . . .3 B8
Gloucester Cl
　Ellesmere Port CH66 . . . . .94 E8
　Macclesfield SK10 . . . . . .87 E4
　Warrington WA1 . . . . 17 D7
Gloucester Ho **13** CH1 . . .237 C3
Gloucester Rd
　Gatley SK8 . . . . .34 C7
　Kidsgrove ST7 . . . . .195 A3
　Knutsford WA16 . . . . 81 F8
　Poynton SK12 . . . . .36 D4
　Widnes WA8 . . . . .13 B3
Gloucester St CH1 . . . . . . .237 B4

Glover Rd WA3 . . . . 9 C4
Glovers Loom CH3 . . . . 142 B7
Glover St
  Crewe CW1 . . . . 190 A5
  Newton-le-Willows WA12 . . 2 C3
Gloverstone Ct CH1 . . . 237 B1
Glyn Ave CH62 . . . . 43 E7
Glyn Garth CH1 . . . . 117 D3
Go Ape! Delamere★
  CW8 . . . . 100 B2
Goathland Way SK11 . . 112 D6
Goddard Ct 13 CW1 . . . 190 B5
Goddard Rd WA7 . . . . 23 E3
Goddard St CW1 . . . . 190 B5
Godfrey St WA2 . . . . 16 D7
Godscroft La WA6 . . . . . . 73 E6
Godshill Ct WA5 . . . . 14 D7
Godstall La CH1 . . . . 237 B2
Godstow WA7 . . . . 24 E4
Godward Rd SK22 . . . . . . 39 B8
GOLBORNE 3 A8
Golborne Cty Prim Sch
  WA3 . . . . 3 A8
Golborne Dale Rd WA3,
  WA12 . . . . 3 A5
Golborne La WA16 . . . . . 28 F3
Golborne Rd
  Golborne WA3 . . . . 3 C8
  Winwick WA1, WA2 . . . . . . 8 A7
Golborne St WA12 . . . . . . 2 E4
Goldcliff Cl WA5 . . . . 7 D3
Goldcrest Cl
  Runcorn WA7 . . . . 49 F5
  Winsford CW7 . . . . 149 C5
Golden Hill CW2 . . . . 207 E3
Golden Sq (Sh Ctr) WA1 . 16 B5
Goldfinch Cl CW12 . . . . . 156 E1
Goldfinch Dr ST7 . . . . . . 193 B3
Goldfinch La WA3 . . . . 9 E4
Goldfinch Rd ST7 . . . . . 195 F1
Goldford La SY14 . . . . . . 199 F6
Goldsmith Dr CW11 . . . 174 D6
Goldsmith La SY13 . . . . 228 A3
Gold Triangle Ind Est
  WA8 . . . . 22 C2
Golf Course Rd CW8 . . . 100 D1
Golftyn Dr CH5 . . . . 91 C1
Golftyn La CH5 . . . . 91 C1
GOLLY 161 B1
Gongar La
  Ashton Hayes CH3 . . . . . 121 E8
  Mouldsworth CH3 . . . . 98 E1
Gonsley Cl CH2 . . . . 237 B4
Gonville Ave SK11 . . . . . 112 F3
Gooch Dr WA12 . . . . 2 D2
Goodall's Cnr CW2 . . . . . 206 C3
Goodall St SK11 . . . . 112 E7
Goode Way CW2 . . . . 190 D1
Goodier Ct WA7 . . . . 49 C7
Goodrington Rd SK9 . . . 34 E3
Goodwin Cres CW2 . . . . 206 C4
Goodwood Cl
  Barnton CW8 . . . . 78 B3
  Chester CH1 . . . . 118 B2
Goodwood Gr CH66 . . . . 69 D3
Goodwood Rise CW10 . . 128 A2
Gooseberry La
  Kelsall CW6 . . . . 122 E3
  Runcorn WA7 . . . . 24 D1
Goosebrook Cl CW9 . . . . 78 D8
Goosebrook La WA4 . . . . 52 F2
Goose La WA4 . . . . 26 A2
Goosetrey Cl SK9 . . . . . . 34 E1
GOOSTREY 107 D1
Goostrey Com Prim Sch
  CW4 . . . . 130 F8
Goostrey Com Prim Sch (The
  Annexe) CW4 . . . . 107 C1
Goostrey Ct 4 CW12 . . 156 F3
Goostrey La CW4 . . . . . . 130 B8
Goostrey Sta CW4 . . . . . 131 A8
Goostry La WA16 . . . . . . 108 A7
Gordale Cl
  Congleton CW12 . . . . . . 157 A5
  Northwich CW8 . . . . 103 D8
  Warrington WA5 . . . . 14 F7
  Winnington CW8 . . . . 78 D1
Gordon Ave
  Bebington CH62 . . . . 43 E7
  Haydock WA11 . . . . 1 F7
  Warrington WA1 . . . . 17 B7
Gordon La CH1 . . . . 95 B5
Gorran Haven WA7 . . . . 50 C5
Gorse Bank Rd WA15 . . 32 C7
Gorse Cl WA6 . . . . 101 A6
GORSE COVERT 10 B5
Gorse Covert CW9 . . . . . . 79 C3
Gorse Covert Prim Sch
  WA3 . . . . 10 B5
Gorse Covert Rd WA3 . . 10 B6
Gorsefield CH3 . . . . 166 A1
Gorsefield Ave CH62 . . . 43 D5
Gorsefield Cl CH62 . . . . . 43 D5
Gorsefield Hey SK9 . . . . 60 E8
Gorse La CW12 . . . . 178 D5
Gorselands SK8 . . . . 35 B5
Gorse Sq M31 . . . . 11 D3
Gorse Stacks CH1 . . . . . 237 B3
Gorse The WA14 . . . . 31 B8
Gorse Way CH3 . . . . 142 A5
Gorsewood Prim Sch
  WA7 . . . . 50 D7
Gorsewood Rd WA7 . . . . 50 D6
GORSEY BANK 231 F2

Gorsey Bank Cres CW5 . . 220 A8
Gorsey Bank Prim Sch
  SK9 . . . . 59 F7
Gorsey La
  Partington WA13 . . . . 20 B7
  St Helens WA5, WA9 . . . . . 6 C5
  Warrington WA1, WA2 . . 16 D7
Gorsey Rd SK9 . . . . 59 F8
Gorseywell La WA7 . . . . . 50 F6
Gorsley Cl CW10 . . . . . . 151 C5
GORSTAGE 102 C6
Gorstage La CW8 . . . . . . 102 C7
GORSTELLA 140 A1
Gorstons La CH64 . . . . . . 67 A6
Gorston Wlk M22 . . . . . . 33 C8
GORSTYHILL 207 E2
Gorsty Hill Cl CW2 . . . . 207 F2
Gorsty Hill Ct CW2 . . . . 207 F2
Gosberryhole La CW12 . 158 A2
Gosforth Ct WA7 . . . . 49 E7
Gosforth Pl CW2 . . . . . . 118 F3
GOSLAND GREEN 169 B1
Gosling Cl WA4 . . . . 26 A1
Gosling Rd WA3 . . . . 9 B7
Gosling Way CW12 . . . . 156 A3
Gosport Cl WA7 . . . . 8 F1
Goss St CH1 . . . . 237 A2
Gough Ave WA4 . . . . 8 B2
Gough's La WA16 . . . . . . 82 C7
Goulden St
  Crewe CW1 . . . . 190 A5
  Warrington WA5 . . . . 15 E6
Goulders Ct WA7 . . . . 50 B5
GOWHOLE 39 E4
Gowy Cl
  Alsager ST7 . . . . 192 F3
  Handforth SK9 . . . . 34 E1
  Sandbach CW11 . . . . . . 174 E8
Gowy Cres CH3 . . . . 121 B2
Gowy Ct
  Calveley CW6 . . . . 169 E2
  Ellesmere Port CH66 . . . 69 E8
Gowy Rd CH2 . . . . 96 F1
Gowy Wlk CW7 . . . . 127 A3
Goyt Forest Walks★
  SK11 . . . . 115 E7
Goyt Pl SK23 . . . . 65 E7
Goyt Rd
  Disley SK12 . . . . 38 D5
  Horwich End SK23 . . . . . 65 E6
  New Mills SK22 . . . . 39 D6
Goytside Mdws Nature
  Reserve★ SK22 . . . . 39 C6
Goyt's La SK17 . . . . 90 F7
Goyt Valley Ind Est SK23 . 39 D4
Goyt Valley Walks★ SK23 . 90 E6
Goyt View SK22 . . . . 39 B6
Grace Ave WA2 . . . . 16 B8
Grace Cl CW1 . . . . 191 C4
Grace Rd CH65 . . . . 70 C7
GRADELEY GREEN 202 F5
Grafton Mews CH2 . . . . 237 B4
Grafton Rd CH65 . . . . 70 C7
Grafton St
  Newton-le-Willows WA12 . . 2 B3
  Warrington WA5 . . . . 15 E6
Graham Ave CH66 . . . . . . 69 D5
Graham Cl WA8 . . . . 22 C1
Graham Cres M44 . . . . . . 11 C3
Graham Dr
  Disley SK12 . . . . 38 C6
  Halewood L26 . . . . 21 A8
Graham Rd
  Blacon CH1 . . . . 117 F3
  Widnes WA8 . . . . 22 C8
Grainger's Rd CW9 . . . . 103 F5
Grammar School Ct WA4 . 16 F3
Grammar School Rd
  Lymm WA13 . . . . 18 F2
  Warrington WA4 . . . . 16 D3
Grampian Way
  Bebington CH62 . . . . 43 E4
  Neston CH64 . . . . 66 E5
  Winsford CW7 . . . . 149 A7
Granary Mews SK12 . . . . 36 E3
Granary Mill WA7 . . . . . . 50 F6
Granby Cl WA7 . . . . 50 C5
Granby Rd
  Cheadle SK8 . . . . 35 B8
  Warrington WA4 . . . . 26 C8
Grandford La CW5 . . . . . 217 D2
Grand Junction Ret Pk
  CW1 . . . . 190 D3
GRANGE
  Runcorn 49 D7
  Warrington 17 E8
Grange Ave
  Barnton CW8 . . . . 78 A3
  Warrington WA4 . . . . 17 E8
Grangebrook Dr CW7 . . 126 C3
Grange Cl
  Chorlton CW2 . . . . 207 E4
  Crewe CW1 . . . . 190 E3
  Golborne WA3 . . . . 3 C6
  Sandbach CW11 . . . . . . 174 F7
Grange Comp Sch WA7 . 23 C1
Grange Cres CH66 . . . . . 44 A1
Grange Ct
  Biddulph ST8 . . . . 179 D2
  14 Knutsford WA16 . . . . 57 A2
  Winsford CW7 . . . . 126 B2
Grange Dr
  Hartford CW8 . . . . 103 A6
  Thornton Hough CH63 . . 42 A7
  Warrington WA5 . . . . 15 A4
  Widnes WA8 . . . . 12 D1
Grange Farm Cl WA5 . . . 15 D6

Grangefields ST8 . . . . . . 179 E4
Grange Green Manor
  WA4 . . . . 25 E7
Grange Inf Sch The WA7 . 23 C1
Grange Jun Sch The
  Hartford CW8 . . . . 103 A6
  Runcorn WA7 . . . . 23 C1
Grange La
  Tilston SY14 . . . . 198 E3
  Weaverham CW8 . . . . . . 102 A7
  Whitegate CW8 . . . . 125 F7
  Winsford CW7 . . . . 126 B5
Grangelands SK10 . . . . . 86 F2
Grange Lea CW10 . . . . . 128 B1
Grangemoor WA7 . . . . . . 49 D8
Grange Park Ave
  Runcorn WA7 . . . . 23 C2
  Wilmslow SK9 . . . . 60 A8
Grange Park Dr ST8 . . . 179 E3
Grange Pl M44 . . . . 11 E5
Grange Prim Sch CW7 . 126 B1
Grange Rd
  Barnton CW8 . . . . 78 A3
  Biddulph ST8 . . . . 179 D3
  Chester CH2 . . . . 118 D4
  Chester, Vicarscross CH3 . 119 C2
  Cuddington CW8 . . . . . . 101 F3
  Ellesmere Port CH65 . . . 70 C4
  Haydock WA11, WA12 . . . 1 D5
  Macclesfield SK11 . . . . . 112 C6
  Mouldsworth CH3 . . . . . . 98 E1
  Northwich, Rudheath CW9 . 104 D6
  Runcorn WA7 . . . . 23 C2
  Sandbach CW11 . . . . . . 175 A7
Grange Road N WA7 . . . 23 C2
Grange Road W CH3 . . . 119 C2
Grange Sch The CW8 . . . 103 B6
Grangeside CH2 . . . . 118 D7
Grange The
  Congleton CW12 . . . . . . 179 B8
  Hartford CW8 . . . . 103 B5
  Macclesfield SK11 . . . . . 112 A6
Grange Valley WA11 . . . . 1 D6
Grange Valley Prim Sch
  WA11 . . . . 1 D5
Grange Villas CH3 . . . . . 142 F6
Grangeway
  Handforth SK9 . . . . 34 D4
  Runcorn WA7 . . . . 49 C8
Grange Way CW11 . . . . . 174 F7
Grangeway Ct WA7 . . . . 49 C8
Grangewood Dr SK11 . . 83 F3
Granston Cl WA5 . . . . 7 D1
Grant Cl WA5 . . . . 7 D1
Grantham Ave
  Warrington, Bruche WA1 . . 16 E7
  Warrington WA4 . . . . 26 B8
Grantham Ct CW9 . . . . . 104 C7
Granville Dr CH66 . . . . . . 69 B7
Granville Rd
  Chester CH1 . . . . 118 B3
  Northwich CW9 . . . . 104 A5
  Wilmslow SK9 . . . . 59 F5
Granville Sq CW7 . . . . . 149 E8
Granville St
  13 Runcorn WA7 . . . . . . 23 A3
  Warrington WA1 . . . . 16 D6
  Winsford CW7 . . . . 149 E8
Grapes St 5 SK11 . . . . 112 D7
GRAPPENHALL 17 A1
Grappenhall Hall Sch
  WA4 . . . . 17 B1
GRAPPENHALL HEYS . . . 27 A8
Grappenhall Heys Prim Sch
  WA4 . . . . 27 E6
Grappenhall La WA4 . . . 27 E6
Grappenhall Rd
  Ellesmere Port CH65 . . . 69 F3
  Warrington WA4 . . . . 16 D1
Grasmere Ave
  Congleton CW12 . . . . . . 155 F2
  Crewe CW2 . . . . 189 F5
  Warrington WA2 . . . . 8 D2
Grasmere Cl CW7 . . . . . 126 D2
Grasmere Cres
  Bramhall SK7 . . . . 35 E8
  High Lane SK12 . . . . 37 E8
Grasmere Dr
  Holmes Chapel CW4 . . . 130 A3
  Runcorn WA7 . . . . 49 D5
Grasmere Rd
  Alderley Edge SK9 . . . . . 60 A1
  Chester CH2 . . . . 118 F5
  Ellesmere Port CH65 . . . 70 C2
  Lymm WA13 . . . . 18 F4
  Neston CH64 . . . . 66 E6
  Partington M31 . . . . 11 E3
Grason Ave SK9 . . . . 34 C3
Grassfield Way WA16 . . 82 A8
Grassmoor Cl CH62 . . . . 43 E8
Grassygreen La ST7 . . . 209 E1
Gratrix Rd CH62 . . . . 43 D8
GRAVEL 127 A1
Gravel La SK9 . . . . 59 E7
Gravel Wlk SY14 . . . . . . 213 D7
Gravenhunger La CW3 . 232 D1
GRAVENHUNGER MOSS . 232 D2
Graveyard La WA16 . . . . 58 F5
Gray Ave WA11 . . . . 1 D6
Graylag Cl WA7 . . . . 49 F5
Graymarsh Dr SK12 . . . . 36 E2
Gray's Cl ST7 . . . . 195 B7
Greasby Dr CH66 . . . . . . 69 E4
Great Ashfield WA8 . . . . 12 D3
GREAT BARROW 120 E6
GREAT BUDWORTH 79 A7

Great Budworth CE Prim Sch
  CW9 . . . . 79 B8
Great Delph WA11 . . . . . . 1 D7
Greater Grace Sch CH1 . 95 B4
Great Hall Pk CH65 . . . . . 70 D4
Great King St SK11 . . . . 112 C8
Great Oak Sq WA16 . . . . 58 A4
Great Queen St SK11 . . 112 C8
Great Riding WA7 . . . . . . 50 C7
GREAT SANKEY 15 A6
Great Sankey High Sch
  WA5 . . . . 14 E8
Great Sankey L Ctr WA5 . 14 E8
Great Sankey Prim Sch
  WA5 . . . . 15 A5
GREAT SUTTON 69 D3
Greaves La 5 SY14 . . . . 222 E6
Greaves Lane E SY14 . . 222 E7
Greaves Rd SK9 . . . . 59 E7
Grebe Cl
  Knutsford WA16 . . . . 57 B3
  Poynton SK12 . . . . 36 B4
Greeba Ave WA4 . . . . 16 B3
Greek St WA7 . . . . 22 F2
Greenacre SK8 . . . . 34 C7
Green Acre Cl WA16 . . . . 82 B8
Greenacre Dr CH63 . . . . 43 C7
Greenacre Rd CH4 . . . . 140 F4
Green Ave
  Alpraham CW6 . . . . 169 D4
  Barnton CW8 . . . . 78 A3
  Davenham CW9 . . . . 103 F3
GREENBANK 103 C7
Greenbank
  Chester CH4 . . . . 141 E6
  Dunham-on-the-Hill WA6 . 97 E6
Green Bank
  Adderley TF9 . . . . 235 A5
  Chester CH4 . . . . 141 E6
Greenbank Ave CH66 . . . 69 C7
Greenbank Cl SK10 . . . . 88 A8
Greenbank Dr SK10 . . . . 88 A8
Greenbank Gdns WA4 . . 16 F2
Greenbank La CW8 . . . . 103 D6
Greenbank Pk CW11 . . . 175 A2
Greenbank Rd
  Chester CH2 . . . . 119 A4
  Warrington WA4 . . . . 16 F2
Greenbank Residential Sch
  CW8 . . . . 103 D6
Greenbank St WA4 . . . . . 16 C2
Greenbank Sta CW8 . . . 103 D6
Green Bridge Cl WA7 . . . 24 A2
Greenbridge Rd WA7 . . . 24 B2
Green Coppice WA7 . . . . 50 C8
Greencourts Bsns Pk M22 . 34 A8
GREENDALE 86 E7
Greendale Dr
  Middlewich CW10 . . . . . . 151 B7
  Newcastle-under-Lyme
  ST5 . . . . 210 D1
Greendale Gdns CW6 . . 190 E5
Greendale La SK10 . . . . . 86 D8
Green Dr
  Alsager ST7 . . . . 193 D4
  Handforth SK9 . . . . 34 D2
Green Farm CH4 . . . . . . 163 B2
Greenfield Ave CH4 . . . . 161 A7
Greenfield Cl SK22 . . . . . 39 A8
Greenfield Cres
  Chester CH3 . . . . 119 B5
  Waverton CH3 . . . . 143 B6
Greenfield Farm Ind Est
  CW12 . . . . 156 B3
Greenfield Gdns CH2 . . . 72 B3
Greenfield La
  Chester CH2 . . . . 119 B5
  Frodsham WA6 . . . . 49 B1
Greenfield Rd
  Bollington SK10 . . . . 88 A7
  Broughton CH4 . . . . 139 C4
  Congleton CW12 . . . . . . 156 B3
  Ellesmere Port CH66 . . . 69 B7
  Waverton CH3 . . . . 143 B6
Greenfields
  Chester CH2 . . . . 95 F1
  Winsford CW7 . . . . 127 B1
Greenfields Ave
  Bebington CH62 . . . . 43 C7
  Shavington CW2 . . . . . . 206 B4
  Warrington WA4 . . . . 26 D8
Greenfields Cl
  Neston CH64 . . . . 66 F5
  Newton-le-Willows WA12 . . 2 C4
  Warrington WA1 . . . . 17 C7
Greenfields Cres CH62 . 43 C7
Greenfields Croft CH66 . 66 E5
Greenfields Dr
  Alsager ST7 . . . . 193 E3
  Neston CH64 . . . . 66 F5
Greenfields La
  Malpas SY14 . . . . 213 B4
  Rowton CH3 . . . . 142 F5
Greenfields Lodge CH3 . 120 D6

Greenfields Prim Sch 6
  CW7 . . . . 126 A1
Greenfield Way CW8 . . . 102 A4
Greengate WA15 . . . . 32 D7
Greengate Rd ST7 . . . . . 193 F5
Greengates Cres CH64 . . 66 E5
Green Hall Mews SK9 . . . 60 B6
Greenhaven Ct CW5 . . . 219 E5
Greenhill La WA4 . . . . . . 52 A5
Greenhills Cl SK11 . . . . 112 E7
Greenhill Wlk SK10 . . . . 38 D6
Greenhouse Farm Rd
  WA7 . . . . 50 B6
Greenhythe Rd SK8 . . . . 34 C6
Greenings Ct WA2 . . . . . 16 C6
Green Jones Brow WA5 . . 6 F6
Green La
  Acton CW5 . . . . 204 B3
  Alderley Edge SK9 . . . . . 59 F1
  Audlem CW3 . . . . 229 F2
  Barbridge CW5 . . . . 187 A7
  Bollington SK10 . . . . 63 B1
  Burtonwood WA5 . . . . 6 E7
  Chester CH4 . . . . 140 E4
  Chester, Vicarscross CH3 . 119 B3
  Christleton CH3 . . . . 120 C2
  Davenham CW9 . . . . 103 F3
  Disley SK12 . . . . 38 D4
  Ellesmere Port, Great Sutton
  CH66 . . . . 69 C4
  Ellesmere Port, Wolverham
  CH65 . . . . 70 C4
  Higher Kinnerton CH4 . . 161 B6
  Higher Wincham CW9 . . . 79 F4
  Irlam M44 . . . . 11 E5
  Kelsall CW6 . . . . 122 D4
  Knutsford WA16 . . . . 56 D4
  Lindow End SK9 . . . . 84 F8
  Over Peover WA16 . . . . . . 83 D1
  Picton CH2 . . . . 96 C3
  Poynton SK12 . . . . 37 C4
  Sandbach CW11 . . . . . . 173 F7
  Saughall CH1 . . . . 117 C2
  Shocklach SY14 . . . . 211 C7
  Tattenhall CH3 . . . . 182 F5
  Tilston SY14 . . . . 212 B8
  Warrington, Dudlow's Green
  WA4 . . . . 26 F5
  Warrington, Paddington
  WA1 . . . . 17 A8
  Widnes WA8 . . . . 12 E1
  Willaston CW5 . . . . 205 E5
  Wilmslow SK9 . . . . 60 B7
  Winwick WA2 . . . . 8 A7
Green Lake La CH3 . . . . 163 F3
Greenland Cl CW6 . . . . . 146 D1
Greenlands CH3 . . . . 166 B3
Green Lane Cl 3 SK8 . . 34 E8
Green Lane Cl WA2 . . . . . 8 A7
Green Lane E
  Connah's Quay CH5 . . . . 93 C1
  Sealand CH5 . . . . 116 D7
Green Lane Est
  Connah's Quay CH5 . . . . 93 C1
  Sealand CH5 . . . . 116 C8
Green Lane Spect Sch
  WA1 . . . . 17 B8
Green Lane W CH5 . . . . . 93 B3
Greenlaw CW9 . . . . 104 A5
Green Lawns Dr 8 CH66 . 94 F8
Greenlea Cl CH3 . . . . 70 B2
GREENLOOMS 1 D2
Green Mdw Ind Prim Sch 7
  WA3 . . . . 3 B8
Green Mdws
  Golborne WA3 . . . . 3 E5
  Macclesfield SK11 . . . . . 111 F6
Greenoaks Farm Ind Est
  WA8 . . . . 23 C8
Green Oaks Path WA8 . . 23 C8
Green Oaks (Sh Ctr) WA8 . 23 B8
Green Oaks Way WA8 . . 23 C8
Greenock Mews WA8 . . 12 E3
Greenore Dr L24 . . . . 21 D2
Green Pk CH4 . . . . 102 E7
Green Rd M31 . . . . 11 E3
Greensbridge La L26 . . . 21 A8
Greenshall La SK12 . . . . 38 F5
Greenshank Cl WA12 . . . 2 C4
Greenside WA6 . . . . 74 D7
Greenside Cl CW9 . . . . . 105 D5
Greenside Dr CW9 . . . . . 105 D5
Green St
  5 Alderley Edge SK9 . . . 60 A1
  Holt LL13 . . . . 180 E1
  Knutsford WA16 . . . . 57 A2
  Macclesfield SK10 . . . . . 112 E7
  Sandbach CW11 . . . . . . 175 A4
  Warrington WA5 . . . . 15 E5
Greens The WA15 . . . . . . 32 D7
Greensway CH4 . . . . 141 E7
Green The
  Cheadle SK8 . . . . 34 F8
  Congleton CW12 . . . . . . 156 C2
  Ellesmere Port CH65 . . . 70 B2
  Hale L24 . . . . 21 D1
  Handforth SK9 . . . . 34 D3
  Hartford CW8 . . . . 103 B5
  Harthill CH3 . . . . 183 E4
  Higher Kinnerton CH4 . . 161 B7
  Lawton-gate ST7 . . . . . . 194 A4
  Middlewich CW10 . . . . . . 151 D6
  Nantwich CW5 . . . . 204 D8
  Neston CH64 . . . . 66 F6
  Partington M31 . . . . 11 E3
  4 Runcorn WA7 . . . . 23 F1
  Saughall CH1 . . . . 94 A2

Green The *continued*
Tarvin CH3 . . . . **121** F7
Thornton Hough CH63 . . . **42** C4
Woore CW3 . . . . **232** C1
Green View WA13 . . . . **19** B5
Green Villa Pk SK9 . . . . . . **59** E4
Greenway
Alsager ST7 . . . . **193** B5
Bramhall SK7 . . . . **35** D6
Congleton CW12 . . . . **156** B3
Crewe CW1 . . . . **190** D7
Farndon CH3 . . . . **180** F1
Neston CH64 . . . . **41** B2
Saughall CH1 . . . . **94** A1
Tilston SY14 . . . . **198** C3
Warrington, Great Sankey
WA5 . . . . **14** E7
Warrington, Paddington
WA1 . . . . **16** F7
Warrington WA4 . . . . **26** D7
Wilmslow SK9 . . . . **60** B6
Greenway Cl
Helsby WA6 . . . . **73** B3
Rode Heath ST7 . . . . **193** F8
Greenway Dr CW9 . . . . . **104** C2
Greenway Rd
Biddulph ST8 . . . . **179** E2
Gatley SK8 . . . . **34** C6
Runcorn WA7 . . . . **23** A1
Speke L24 . . . . **21** A3
Widnes WA8 . . . . **13** B1
Greenways ST7 . . . . **209** F2
Greenways Ct CH62 . . . . **43** C6
Greenway St CH4 . . . . . . **237** C2
Greenway Wlk CW9 . . . **104** C7
Greenwell Rd WA11 . . . . . **1** C6
Green Wlk
Cuddington CW8 . . . . . . **102** B4
Partington M31 . . . . **11** E3
Greenwood Ave
Chester CH4 . . . . **141** D7
Congleton CW12 . . . . **156** F3
Greenwood Cl CW8 . . . . . **77** D1
Greenwood Cres WA3 . . . . **8** E2
Greenwood Ct WA3 . . . . . . **4** F1
Greenwood Dr
Newton-le-Willows WA12 . . **2** D2
Runcorn WA7 . . . . **24** F4
Wilmslow SK9 . . . . **60** D8
Greenwood Rd WA13 . . . . **18** F2
Greenwood Terr WA16 . . . **58** A4
Greenwood The CW6 . . . **168** D8
Greg Ave SK10 . . . . **87** E8
Greg Mews SK9 . . . . **34** B2
Gregory Cl WA5 . . . . **15** C7
Gregorys Row WA3 . . . . . . **4** A8
Gregson Rd WA8 . . . . **13** C1
Grenfell Cl CH64 . . . . **41** C1
Grenfell Ct CH64 . . . . **66** C8
Grenfell Pk CH64 . . . . **41** C1
Grenfell St WA8 . . . . **23** B8
Grenville Cl WA1 . . . . **191** C5
Grenville Cres CH63 . . . . **43** C7
Grenville Rd CH64 . . . . . . **41** F1
Gresford Ave CH2 . . . . . . **237** C2
Gresford Cl WA5 . . . . **7** E1
Gresley Way ST7 . . . . **209** F2
Gresty Bldgs CW5 . . . . . **204** E6
Gresty Green Rd CW2 . . **206** D2
Gresty La CW2 . . . . **206** B2
Gresty Rd CW2 . . . . **190** D1
Gresty Side CW5 . . . . . . **204** C5
Gresty Terr CW1 . . . . **190** E4
Greta Ave SK8 . . . . **34** C8
Greville Dr CW7 . . . . **127** A1
Grey Friars CH1 . . . . **237** A2
Greyfriars Cl WA2 . . . . **9** A3
Greyhound Park Rd CH1 . **118** A3
Greyhound Rd CH1 . . . . . **118** A3
Greyhound Rd SK10 . . . . . **86** B5
Greymist Ave WA1 . . . . . . **17** C7
Greys Ct WA1 . . . . **17** C7
Greysfield Flats CH3 . . . **120** D6
Grey St WA4 . . . . **16** C6
Greystoke Dr SK9 . . . . **60** A2
Greystoke Rd SK10 . . . . . . **87** F2
Greystone Pk CW1 . . . . . **190** D4
Greystones CH6 . . . . **69** D4
Greystones Rd CH3 . . . . **119** C1
Grice St WA4 . . . . **16** C1
Griffin Cl
Blacon CH1 . . . . **117** F6
New Mills SK22 . . . . **39** D6
Norton in Hales TF9 . . . . **236** C2
Griffin La SK8 . . . . **34** D7
Griffin Mews WA8 . . . . **13** B3
Griffith Ave WA3 . . . . **9** E5
Griffiths Dr CW9 . . . . **104** D6
Griffiths Rd
Lostock Gralam CW9 . . . . . **79** F1
Northwich CW8 . . . . **104** E8
Griffiths St WA4 . . . . **16** F4
Grig Pl ST7 . . . . **193** C5
Grimsditch La WA4 . . . . . . **52** B5
Grimshaw Ave SK10 . . . . . **88** A7
Grimshaw La SK10 . . . . . . **88** A7
Grindley Bank CH2 . . . . **119** F8
GRINDLEY BROOK **225** C3
Grindley Gdns CH65 . . . . . **70** C2
Grindley Gn SY13 . . . . . . **228** B3
Grisedale Ave WA2 . . . . **8** B3
Grisedale Cl WA7 . . . . **49** E5
Grisedale Way SK11 . . . **112** A5
Gritstone Dr SK10 . . . . . . **112** A8
Grizedale WA8 . . . . **12** B2

Grizedale Cl CW2 . . . . . . **189** D2
Groarke Dr WA5 . . . . **14** D8
Groby Rd CW1 . . . . **190** E8
Grocotts Row CW5 . . . . **204** E5
Grosvenor Ave
Alsager ST7 . . . . **193** D5
3 Golborne WA3 . . . . **3** D8
Hartford CW8 . . . . **103** A4
Warrington WA1 . . . . **16** F7
Grosvenor Cl
Warrington WA5 . . . . **15** C5
Wilmslow SK9 . . . . **60** A4
Grosvenor Cotts CH4 . . **141** D7
Grosvenor Ct
Chester CH1 . . . . **237** C2
12 Crewe CW1 . . . . **190** B5
7 Winsford CW7 . . . . . . **149** C7
Grosvenor Dr SK12 . . . . . . **36** D3
Grosvenor Gdns WA12 . . . **2** C2
Grosvenor Grange WA1 . . . **9** B1
Grosvenor Mus★ CH1 . . **237** A1
Grosvenor Nuffield Hospl
The CH4 . . . . **141** C6
Grosvenor Pk Rd CH1 . . **237** C2
Grosvenor Pk Terr CH1,
CH3 . . . . **237** C2
Grosvenor Pl CH1 . . . . . . **237** B1
Grosvenor Rd
Chester CH4 . . . . **141** C7
Congleton CW12 . . . . **156** A3
Haydock WA11 . . . . **1** B7
Tarvin CH3 . . . . **121** A2
Widnes WA8 . . . . **13** B5
Grosvenor Sh Ctr
Chester CH1 . . . . **237** B2
17 Macclesfield SK11 . . . **112** D8
Grosvenor St
Chester CH1 . . . . **237** A2
Crewe CW1 . . . . **190** B5
3 Macclesfield SK10 . . . . **112** C8
Runcorn WA7 . . . . **23** B3
Winsford CW7 . . . . **149** C8
Grosvenor Wharf Rd
CH65 . . . . **70** D7
Grotsworth La SY14 . . . . **214** E8
Grotto La WA16 . . . . **108** B7
Grounds St WA2 . . . . **16** B7
Grove Arc SK9 . . . . **60** A2
Grove Ave
Chester CH3 . . . . **119** B3
Kidsgrove ST7 . . . . **194** E1
Lawton-gate ST7 . . . . **194** A4
Lostock Gralam CW9 . . . . . **80** A3
Lymm WA13 . . . . **18** C3
Wilmslow SK9 . . . . **60** B7
Grove Cres CW7 . . . . **149** B8
Grove Ct
Alsager ST7 . . . . **193** E4
Lymm WA13 . . . . **18** C3
Grove Gdns CH3 . . . . **119** E2
Grove Ho SK8 . . . . **35** B6
Grove La SK8 . . . . **35** A6
Grovemount CW9 . . . . . . **103** F2
Grove Park Ave ST7 . . . . **194** A4
Grove Pk WA16 . . . . **57** C2
Grove Rd CH1 . . . . **94** E4
Grove Rise WA13 . . . . **18** E3
Grove St
New Mills SK22 . . . . **39** B7
Runcorn WA7 . . . . **23** B2
Warrington WA4 . . . . **16** C4
Wilmslow SK9 . . . . **60** B7
Groves The
Chester CH1 . . . . **237** C2
Ellesmere Port CH66 . . . . . **95** A8
Grove Terr WA6 . . . . **73** C4
Grove The
Cheadle SK8 . . . . **35** A6
Knutsford WA16 . . . . **57** C4
Lawton-gate ST7 . . . . **194** A4
Lymm WA13 . . . . **18** E3
Tarporley CW6 . . . . **146** C2
Warrington WA5 . . . . **14** F4
Whitchurch SY13 . . . . **225** F1
Grove Way SK9 . . . . **60** B7
Grovewood Mews SK11 . **112** C6
Grub La CW6 . . . . **122** C5
Grundy Cl WA8 . . . . **12** F3
Grundy St WA3 . . . . **3** A7
Guardian St WA5 . . . . **15** F6
Guardian Street Ind Est
WA5 . . . . **15** F6
Guernsey Cl
Congleton CW12 . . . . **157** A2
Middlewich CW10 . . . . . . **128** D2
Warrington WA4 . . . . **26** D8
Guernsey Dr CH65 . . . . . . **70** C1
Guernsey Ho CW1 . . . . . . **119** B5
Guernsey Rd WA8 . . . . **13** E3
Guests Slack WA6 . . . . . **100** B8
Guest St WA8 . . . . **23** A7
Guilden Gn CH3 . . . . **119** F5
GUILDEN SUTTON **119** F5
Guilden Sutton CE Prim Sch
CH3 . . . . **119** D5
Guilden Sutton La CH3 . . **119** D5
Guildford Ave SK8 . . . . **35** A6
Guildford Cl
1 Chester CH4 . . . . **140** F6
Warrington WA2 . . . . **9** A1
Guildhall Mus★ CH1 . . . **237** A2
Guillemot Cl CW1 . . . . . . **190** F5
Gullane Cl SK10 . . . . **87** B4
Gullet The CW6 . . . . **184** D5
Gulliver's World★ WA5 . . . **7** E1
Gulls Way CH60 . . . . **40** E7

Gunco La
Macclesfield SK11 . . . . . . **112** E6
Prestbury SK10 . . . . **87** C8
Gunn Gr CH64 . . . . **66** F8
GURNETT **112** F4
Gutterscroft CW1 . . . . . . **191** D5
Gutticar Rd WA8 . . . . **12** B1
Guy La CH3 . . . . **143** D5
Gypsy La CH1 . . . . **94** F2

H

Hacked Way La SK11 . . . **113** F6
HACK GREEN **218** D5
Hack Green Secret Nuclear
Bunker★ CW5 . . . . **218** D4
Haddon Cl
Alderley Edge SK9 . . . . **59** F2
High Lane SK6 . . . . **37** E6
Holmes Chapel CW4 . . . . **130** B3
Macclesfield SK11 . . . . . . **112** B5
Wistaston CW2 . . . . **206** B7
Haddon Dr WA8 . . . . **12** C3
Haddon Ho 3 CH64 . . . . . **66** E8
Haddon La CH64 . . . . **67** C4
Haddon Rd
Burton CH64 . . . . **67** D2
Gatley SK8 . . . . **34** C7
Hadfield Cl WA8 . . . . **13** E2
Hadfield St CW9 . . . . **79** B1
Hadleigh Cl WA5 . . . . **14** E5
Hadley Ave CH62 . . . . **43** D8
Hadley Dr CW2 . . . . **207** E4
Hadlow La CH64 . . . . **67** F7
Hadlow Rd CH64 . . . . **67** F6
Hadlow Terr CH64 . . . . **67** F7
Hadrian Dr CH1 . . . . **117** E6
Hadrian Way
Cuddington CW8 . . . . **102** B2
Middlewich CW10 . . . . . . **128** C2
Hadyn Jones Dr CW5 . . . **204** F4
Hafod Cl
Blacon CH1 . . . . **117** D3
Connah's Quay CH5 . . . . . **91** C1
Hag Bank La SK12 . . . . . . **38** D7
HAGUE BAR **38** F7
Hague Bar Prim Sch SK22 **38** E8
Hague Bar Rd SK22 . . . . . **39** A7
Hague Fold Rd SK22 . . . . **38** F8
Haig Ave
Irlam M44 . . . . **11** C4
Warrington WA5 . . . . **15** A5
Haig Ct WA16 . . . . **57** C4
Haighton Ct 1 CW5 . . . . **204** E6
Haig Rd
Knutsford WA16 . . . . **57** C4
Widnes WA8 . . . . **13** A1
Hailwood Ho SK10 . . . . . . **88** B8
HALE . . . .
Altrincham **32** B8
Liverpool **21** D1
Hale Ave SK12 . . . . **36** D2
HALE BANK **22** A4
Halebank CE Prim Sch
WA8 . . . . **22** A5
Halebank Rd WA8 . . . . **21** F5
Hale Bank Terr WA8 . . . . . **22** A4
HALE BARNS **32** B8
Hale CE Prim Sch L24 . . . **21** B1
Hale Gate Rd
Hale WA8 . . . . **21** F3
Widnes WA8 . . . . **22** A3
Hale Gr WA5 . . . . **15** A6
HALE HEATH **21** A1
Hale Rd
Hale L24 . . . . **21** B2
Widnes WA8 . . . . **22** C7
Hale Rd Woodland Nature
Reserve★ WA8 . . . . **22** A7
Hale Road Ind Est WA8 . . **22** A4
Hale St WA2 . . . . **16** B7
Hale View WA8 . . . . **48** E8
Hale View Rd WA6 . . . . . . **73** C4
HALEWOOD **21** B8
Halewood Animal Ctr
(RSPCA)★ L26 . . . . **21** B6
Halewood Lane Ends L26 **21** A8
Halewood L Ctr L26 . . . . . **21** A7
HALEWOOD VILLAGE . . **21** A8
Haley Rd N WA5 . . . . **6** E6
Haley Road S WA5 . . . . **6** E5
Halfacre La WA4 . . . . **17** F2
Half St SK11 . . . . **112** D6
Halghton La LL13 . . . . . . **222** B2
Halifax Cl WA2 . . . . **8** D2
Halkett Cl CH4 . . . . **140** F6
Halkyn Rd CH2 . . . . **237** C4
Hall Acres La SK8 . . . . **34** E8
Hallams Dr CW5 . . . . **205** B4
Hallastone Rd WA6 . . . . . . **73** C4
Hall Ave WA8 . . . . **12** A1
Halla-Way WA4 . . . . **16** E3
Hall Bank WA16 . . . . **58** C4
Hall Bank E WA16 . . . . **58** C4
Hall Bank S WA16 . . . . **58** C4
Hall Cl SK10 . . . . **87** D4
Hallcroft WA11 . . . . **1** F4
Hallcroft Pl WA4 . . . . **17** A2
Hall Dr
Alsager ST7 . . . . **193** C4
Marston CW9 . . . . **79** B6
Warrington WA5 . . . . **26** D6
Willaston CW5 . . . . **205** D6
Hallefield Cres 4 SK11 . **112** E7
Hallefield Dr SK11 . . . . . . **112** E7
Hallefield Rd SK10,SK11 . **112** E7

Hall Farm CH62 . . . . **44** A4
Hall Farm Cl SK23 . . . . . . **65** D8
Hallfield Dr CH2 . . . . **72** B3
Hallfield Pk CH66 . . . . **69** D4
Hallfields Rd
Tarvin CH3 . . . . **121** C2
Warrington WA2 . . . . **8** D1
Hall Gr SK10 . . . . **87** D3
HALL GREEN
Sandbach Green **194** E5
Whitchurch **224** E1
Hallgreen La CW12 . . . . . **155** D8
Hall Hill SK10 . . . . **87** E7
Halliday Cl WA3 . . . . **9** F3
Halliwell Jones Stad The
(Warrington Wolves RLFC)
WA2 . . . . **16** A6
Halliwell's Brow WA16 . . . **29** B3
Hall La
Appleton Thorn WA4 . . . . . **27** B8
Audlem CW3 . . . . **230** C7
Brown Knowl CH3 . . . . . . **199** C7
Cronton L35 . . . . **12** C7
Daresbury WA4 . . . . **25** D2
Haughton CH6 . . . . **186** D5
Kelsall CW6 . . . . **122** D6
Little Leigh CW9 . . . . **77** F8
Lostock Gralam CW9 . . . . . **79** F3
Mobberley WA16 . . . . **58** D4
Newton-le-Willows WA5 . . . **7** B8
Ollerton WA16 . . . . **83** B5
Partington M31 . . . . **11** F4
Pickmere WA16 . . . . **55** B1
Sandbach CW11 . . . . **174** B5
Shotwick CH1 . . . . **93** B5
St Helens WA9 . . . . **6** A4
Stretton WA4 . . . . **52** D8
Sutton Lane Ends SK11 . . **112** F3
Utkinton CW6 . . . . **146** C6
Winsford CW7 . . . . **149** B3
Hall La The CW6 . . . . **147** D2
Hall Moss La SK7 . . . . **35** C4
Hall Nook WA5 . . . . **14** F3
Hallows Ave WA2 . . . . **16** D8
Hallows Cl CW6 . . . . **122** C4
HALLOWSGATE **122** C4
Hallowsgate Ct CW6 . . . . **122** C4
Hall Rd
Handforth SK9 . . . . **34** E3
Haydock WA11 . . . . **1** E7
Warrington WA1 . . . . **17** C7
Wilmslow SK9 . . . . **60** A7
Hallsgreen La CH2 . . . . . . **96** F7
Hallshaw Ave CW1 . . . . . **190** E5
Hallside Pk WA16 . . . . **57** C1
Halls Rd
Biddulph ST8 . . . . **179** C1
Mow Cop ST7 . . . . **195** C7
Hall St
Audley ST7 . . . . **209** D2
Macclesfield SK10 . . . . . . **112** C8
New Mills SK22 . . . . **39** B8
Warrington WA5 . . . . **16** C5
Hall Terr WA5 . . . . **14** E7
Hall View CH3 . . . . **166** B1
Hall View Cl CW8 . . . . . . **102** A7
Hall Wood Ave WA11 . . . . . **1** E8
Hallwood Cl WA7 . . . . **49** B6
Hallwood Ct CH64 . . . . **66** F7
Hallwood Dr CH64 . . . . **68** D4
Hallwood Link Rd WA7 . . . **49** F6
HALLWOOD PARK **49** F6
Hallwood Park Ave WA7 . . **49** E6
Hallwood Park Prim Sch
WA7 . . . . **49** E6
Hallwood Rd SK9 . . . . **34** D2
Hallwood Wlk 3 CH65 . . . **70** B7
Halsall Ave WA2 . . . . **16** D8
Halsall Cl WA7 . . . . **50** C5
Halsall's Cotts WA8 . . . . . **21** E5
Halstone Ave SK9 . . . . **59** E4
HALTON BROOK **23** D1
Halton Brook Ave WA7 . . . **23** E1
Halton Castle★ WA7 . . . . **23** F1
Halton Cres CH66 . . . . **69** F2
Halton Ct WA4 . . . . **23** D2
Halton Dr CW2 . . . . **189** D5
Halton General Hospl
WA7 . . . . **49** F7
Halton High Sch WA7 . . . . **50** C6
Halton House WA7 . . . . . . **49** F3
Halton Lea (Sh Ctr) WA7 . **49** E8
Halton Link Rd WA7 . . . . . **49** E8
HALTON LODGE **49** D7
Halton Lodge Ave WA7 . . . **49** D7
Halton Lodge Prim Sch
WA7 . . . . **49** D7
Halton Miniature Railway★
WA7 . . . . **50** B7
Halton Rd
Chester CH2 . . . . **118** F6
Ellesmere Port CH66 . . . . . **69** E2
Runcorn WA7 . . . . **23** D2
Halton Sch WA7 . . . . **23** F1
Halton St WA11 . . . . **1** E6
Halton Station Rd WA7 . . . **49** F5
HALTON VIEW **13** C1
Halton View Rd WA8 . . . . . **13** C1
HALTON VILLAGE **49** F8
Halton Way CH66 . . . . **69** A6
Hambledon CH1 . . . . **118** A5
Hamble Dr WA5 . . . . **14** F3
Hambleton Cl WA8 . . . . . . **12** C3
Hambleton Rd SK8 . . . . . . **34** C8

Gre–Har 257

Hambleton Way CW7 . . . **149** A7
Hambletts Hollow WA6 . . **100** F6
Hamble Way SK10 . . . . **86** E1
Hamilton Ave
Irlam M44 . . . . **11** D4
Sandycroft CH5 . . . . **116** A3
Hamilton Cl
Haslington CW1 . . . . **191** C4
Macclesfield SK10 . . . . . . **113** A8
Neston CH64 . . . . **41** B2
Hamilton Ct CH64 . . . . **66** F8
Hamilton Pl CH1 . . . . **237** A2
Hamilton Rd CH5 . . . . **91** D1
Hamilton St CH2 . . . . **118** F3
Hamlet The CH4 . . . . **141** A7
Hamlin Cl WA7 . . . . **49** A6
Hammersmith Way WA8 . . **13** D4
Hammond Sch CH2 . . . . . **119** B7
Hammond St CW2 . . . . . . **190** C3
Hamnett Ct WA3 . . . . **9** E3
Hampshire Cl CW12 . . . . **156** D4
Hampshire Gdns ST7 . . . **194** F2
Hampshire Rd M31 . . . . . . **11** D2
Hampshire Wlk SK10 . . . . **86** F2
Hampson Ave WA3 . . . . **4** F3
Hampson Cres SK9 . . . . . **34** C4
Hampstead Ct 7 CW7 . . **149** A8
Hampstead Dr CW2 . . . . **221** C8
Hampton Cl
Neston CH64 . . . . **66** E6
Widnes WA8 . . . . **13** E3
Hampton Court Way WA8 **13** D4
Hampton Cres
Neston CH64 . . . . **66** E6
No Man's Heath SY14 . . . **214** A5
Hampton Ct
Gatley SK9 . . . . **34** D5
Runcorn WA7 . . . . **24** C4
Hampton Dr
Cronton WA8 . . . . **12** C5
Warrington WA5 . . . . **15** C4
Hampton Gdns CH65 . . . . **70** A5
HAMPTON GREEN **214** B7
HAMPTON HEATH **213** E7
Hampton Heath Ind Est
SY14 . . . . **213** D7
Hampton Rd
Chester CH4 . . . . **140** F6
Irlam M44 . . . . **11** D4
Hamson Dr SK10 . . . . **63** B1
Hamsterley SY14 A3 . . . . . **10** B6
Hanbury Cl CW2 . . . . **206** B7
Hancock Cl WA4 . . . . **16** C4
Hancock Rd CW12 . . . . . . **156** F4
Handa Dr CH65 . . . . **95** B8
HANDBRIDGE **141** F7
Handbridge CH4 . . . . **237** B1
Handford Ave CH62 . . . . . . **43** F5
Handford Rd CH2 . . . . **118** F6
HANDFORTH **34** C4
Handforth Cl WA4 . . . . **17** C3
Handforth Dean Ret Pk
SK9 . . . . **34** E4
Handforth La WA7 . . . . **49** D6
Handforth Rd
Crewe CW2 . . . . **189** D3
Handforth SK9 . . . . **34** E1
Handforth Sta SK9 . . . . . . **34** D3
HAND GREEN **168** B6
HANDLEY **182** D8
Handley Dr WA2 . . . . **8** E1
Handley Hill CW7 . . . . **149** C8
Handley St WA7 . . . . **22** F3
Hand St SK11 . . . . **112** B8
Hangman's La
Lostock Green CW9 . . . . . **105** C2
Smallwood CW11 . . . . **177** B5
HANKELOW **230** C7
Hankelow Cl
Chester CH2 . . . . **237** B4
Middlewich CW10 . . . . . . **151** C6
Hankey St 2 WA7 . . . . . . **22** F2
Hankins Heys La CW3 . . . **231** A1
Hankinson St M31 . . . . . . **11** E2
Hanley Cl
Disley SK12 . . . . **38** C2
Widnes WA8 . . . . **12** C1
Hanley Rd WA8 . . . . **12** C1
Hannah's Wlk 2 CW10 . . **151** C8
Hanns Hall Farm CH64 . . . **67** E8
Hanns Hall Rd CH64 . . . . . **67** D8
Hanover Ct WA7 . . . . **50** A6
Hanover Dr 2 CW7 . . . . . **149** D6
Hanover Ho 6 CW8 . . . . **103** C5
Hanover St WA1 . . . . **16** A4
Hapsdale View WA6 . . . . . **72** E1
HAPSFORD **72** F1
Hapsford Cl WA3 . . . . **9** C4
Hapsford La WA6 . . . . **97** E8
Hapsford Mews WA6 . . . . **72** E2
Harbord St WA1 . . . . **16** B4
Harbour Cl
Chester CH2 . . . . **118** E7
Runcorn WA7 . . . . **50** D6
Harbour La SK11 . . . . **111** C1
Harburn Wlk M22 . . . . **33** E8
Harbutt's Field CW10 . . . **128** C2
Harcourt Cl WA3 . . . . **9** E3
HARDEN PARK **60** A3
Harden Pk SK9 . . . . **60** A3
Harding Ave
Chester CH2 . . . . **166** C2
Warrington WA2 . . . . **8** E1
Harding Rd
Chester CH2 . . . . **118** B8

Harding Rd continued
Nantwich CW5 . . . . 204 C4
Hardings Mdw ST7 . . . . . 194 F2
Hardings Row ST7 . . . . . 195 D7
HARDING'S WOOD 194 E2
Hardings Wood ST7 . . . . 194 E2
Hardingswood Rd ST7 . . 194 E2
Hardknott Rd CH62 . . . . . 43 E8
Hardwick Cl SK6 . . . . 37 F6
Hardwick Dr SK11 . . . . . . 112 B5
Hardwicke Ct CW1 . . . . . 190 E4
Hardwicke Rd SK12 . . . . . 36 E4
Hardwick Grange WA1 . . 17 E8
Hardwick Rd WA7 . . . . . . 23 D3
Hardy Cl
  Ellesmere Port CH66 . . . . 69 F3
  Wistaston CW2 . . . . 205 F8
Hardy Dr SK7 . . . . 35 D7
Hardy Rd WA13 . . . . 18 C2
Hardy St WA2 . . . . 16 B6
Harebell Cl
  Huntington CH3 . . . . 142 A6
  Widnes WA8 . . . . 12 E4
Harebell Gr ST7 . . . . 195 F1
Harecastle Ave ST7 . . . . 194 E1
Harecastle Ct ST7 . . . . . . 210 E6
Harecastle Villas ST7 . . 194 E2
Harefield Dr SK9 . . . . 60 B5
Harefield Rd SK9 . . . . 34 E4
Hare Hill Gdn★ SK10 . . . 86 B6
Hare La CH3 . . . . 119 D3
Hare's La WA6 . . . . 73 F7
Harewood Ave CH66 . . . . 69 C4
Harewood Cl
  Northwich CW9 . . . . 103 F4
  Winsford CW7 . . . . 126 A1
Harewood Way SK11 . . . 112 B5
Harfield Gdns CH66 . . . . 69 C5
Harford Cl WA5 . . . . 14 F4
HARGRAVE 144 A1
Hargrave Ave CW2 . . . . . 189 F3
Hargrave Dr CH66 . . . . . . 69 E5
Hargrave La
  Bebington CH64 . . . . 43 A4
  Thornton Hough CH63,
    CH64 . . . . 42 F5
Hargreave Ho 6 CH64 . . 66 E8
Hargreaves Ct WA8 . . . . . 13 D1
Hargreaves Ho 5 WA8 . . 13 D1
Hargreaves Rd CW9 . . . . 104 C8
Harington Cl CH2 . . . . . . 118 C8
Harland Gn L24 . . . . 21 A3
Harlech Cl WA5 . . . . 7 E2
Harlech Ct CH65 . . . . 70 D3
Harlech Gr 3 WA7 . . . . . 23 F1
Harlech Way CH65 . . . . . . 70 D3
Harlow Cl WA4 . . . . 17 C3
Harlyn Ave SK7 . . . . 35 F7
Harlyn Gdns WA5 . . . . . . 14 D3
Harn The CH66 . . . . 69 C3
Haroldgate SY13 . . . . . . 225 F1
Harold Rd WA11 . . . . 1 F7
Harper Cl CH66 . . . . 69 D4
Harper Gr CW12 . . . . 156 E4
Harpers Rd WA2 . . . . 9 B2
Harpur Cl SK11 . . . . 112 D6
Harpur Cres ST7 . . . . . . 193 B5
Harrier Rd WA2 . . . . 8 F2
Harriet St M44 . . . . 11 E5
Harrington Dr SK11 . . . . 111 D1
Harris Cl CW1 . . . . 173 B1
HARRISEAHEAD 195 E4
Harriseahead La ST7 . . 195 D4
Harrison Cl WA1 . . . . 16 C6
Harrison Dr
  Crewe CW1 . . . . 190 B4
  Goostrey CW4 . . . . 107 B1
  Haydock WA11 . . . . 1 A6
Harrison Gr CH5 . . . . . . 116 A3
Harrisons Pl 4 CW8 . . . 103 E8
Harrison Sq WA5 . . . . 7 F1
Harrison St WA8 . . . . 22 B6
Harrisons Terr CH66 . . . . 69 C6
Harrison Way WA12 . . . . . 2 C4
Harris Rd CW9 . . . . 80 A2
Harris St WA8 . . . . 13 C1
Harrogate Cl
  Bebington CH62 . . . . 43 D4
  Warrington WA5 . . . . 7 A1
Harrogate Rd CH62 . . . . . 43 D4
Harrop La SK10 . . . . 62 E5
Harrop Rd
  Bollington SK10 . . . . 88 C8
  Runcorn WA7 . . . . 23 B1
Harrow Cl
  Crewe CW2 . . . . 190 A1
  Warrington WA4 . . . . 26 E6
  Wilmslow SK9 . . . . 60 D8
Harrow Dr WA7 . . . . 23 E2
Harrow Gr CH62 . . . . 43 E8
Harrow Rd CH65 . . . . 70 D4
Harrow Way CW9 . . . . . . 103 E3
HARTFORD 103 C4
Hartford Ave SK9 . . . . 59 F5
HARTFORD BEACH 103 A6
Hartford Bsns Ctr CW8 . 102 F4
Hartford Cl CW11 . . . . . . 175 C7
Hartford Dr CH65 . . . . 69 F4
Hartford Gr 4 WA8 . . . . 103 C5
Hartford Hill Pool 8
  CW8 . . . . 103 E7
Hartford Manor Prim Sch
  CW8 . . . . 103 C5
Hartford Mews 3 CH3 . . 119 B1
Hartford Prim Sch CW8 . 103 B4

Hartford Rd CW9 . . . . . . 103 E3
Hartford Sta CW8 . . . . . . 103 A4
Hartford Way CH1 . . . . . . 118 A2
HARTHILL 183 E3
Harthill Cl CW9 . . . . 103 E5
Harthill La CH3 . . . . 183 E4
Harthill Rd
  Blacon CH1 . . . . 117 E6
  Burwardsley CH3 . . . . . . 184 A6
Hartington Dr SK7 . . . . . . 36 E8
Hartington Rd
  Bramhall SK7 . . . . 35 E6
  Gatley SK8 . . . . 34 B8
  High Lane SK12, SK6 . . . . 37 F7
Hartington St CH4 . . . . . 141 E7
Hartland Cl
  Poynton SK12 . . . . 36 D5
  Widnes WA8 . . . . 13 A5
Hartley Cl WA13 . . . . 18 F3
Hartley Gdns CW12 . . . . 179 B8
Hartley Gn SK10 . . . . 87 F8
Harton Cl WA8 . . . . 12 E3
Hartswood CW4 . . . . 26 E3
Hartwell Gr CW7 . . . . . . 126 F4
Harty Rd WA11 . . . . 1 A5
Harvard Cl WA7 . . . . 24 D2
Harvard St WA2 . . . . 8 A3
Harvest Cl CW9 . . . . 126 F8
Harvest Rd SK10 . . . . 87 C3
Harvey Ave
  5 Nantwich CW5 . . . . . . 205 A6
  Newton-le-Willows WA12 . . 1 F3
Harvey Ct WA2 . . . . 8 B3
Harvey La WA3 . . . . 3 A8
Harvey Rd CW12 . . . . . . 157 A5
Harwood Gdns WA4 . . . . 17 A2
Haryngton Ave WA5 . . . . 15 F7
Haseley Cl SK12 . . . . 36 C6
Haslemere Ave WA15 . . . 32 C6
Haslemere Dr WA5 . . . . . 14 D4
Haslemere Way CW6 . . . 190 D6
Haslin Cres CH3 . . . . 142 D7
HASLINGTON 191 D4
Haslington Cl ST5 . . . . . . 210 D1
Haslington Gr L26 . . . . . . 21 A6
Haslington Prim Sch
  CW1 . . . . 191 D4
HASSALL 192 C7
HASSALL GREEN 176 A2
Hassall Rd
  Alsager ST7 . . . . 193 B5
  Haslington CW11 . . . . . . 192 B7
  Sandbach CW11 . . . . 175 C4
  Winterley CW11 . . . . 191 F8
Hassall Way 7 SK9 . . . . . 34 E5
Hassals La CH2 . . . . 96 F3
Hastings Ave WA2 . . . . . . 8 B4
Hastings Rd CW5 . . . . . . 204 F5
Hasty La
  Altrincham WA15 . . . . 32 E8
  Hale WA15 . . . . 32 E8
  Wythenshawe WA15 . . . . 32 F8
Hatchery Cl WA4 . . . . 27 B4
Hatchings The WA13 . . . . 18 E2
HATCHMERE 100 D4
Hatch Mere★ WA6 . . . . . 100 C4
Hatchmere Cl
  Sandbach CW11 . . . . 174 F7
  Warrington WA5 . . . . 15 E5
Hatchmere Dr CH3 . . . . . 142 B8
Hatchmere Pk WA6 . . . . 100 C5
Hatfield Cl CW4 . . . . 130 B3
Hatfield Gdns WA4 . . . . . 26 E4
Hathaway Cl SK8 . . . . 34 B7
Hathaway Dr SK11 . . . . . 112 C5
HATHERTON 219 E3
Hatherton Cl
  Newcastle-under-Lyme
    ST5 . . . . 210 D2
  5 Northwich CW9 . . . . . 103 F4
Hatherton Gr L26 . . . . . . 21 A6
Hatherton Way CH2 . . . . 237 B4
Hatlequin Theatre★
  CW9 . . . . 103 F7
Hatley La WA6 . . . . 73 F7
Hatter St CW12 . . . . 156 E3
HATTON 26 A2
Hatton Ave CH62 . . . . 43 E3
Hatton Bldgs CH2 . . . . . . 237 B4
Hatton Brow Terr SK11 . . 112 F4
HATTON HEATH 143 B1
Hatton La
  Hartford CW8 . . . . 103 D6
  Stretton WA4 . . . . 26 B1
Hatton Rd CH1 . . . . 117 E6
Hatton St SK11 . . . . 112 C7
HAUGHTON 186 C6
Haughton Cl SK10 . . . . . . 86 F1
HAVANNAH 157 A6
Havannah Bsns Ctr 6
  CW12 . . . . 156 F4
Havannah La
  Congleton CW12 . . . . . . 156 F6
  St Helens WA9 . . . . 1 B2
Havannah Prim Sch
  CW12 . . . . 157 A5
Havannah St CW12 . . . . . 156 F4
Haven The
  Crewe CW1 . . . . 190 D7
  Sandbach CW11 . . . . 174 E7
Havergal St 4 WA4 . . . . 22 F1
Haverhill Cl CW12 . . . . . 207 C3
Haverty Prec WA12 . . . . . 2 B1
Havisham Cl WA3 . . . . 9 D5
Hawarde Cl WA12 . . . . . . 2 A4
Hawarden (Chester) Airport
  CH4, CH5 . . . . 139 D7
Hawarden Gdns CH65 . . . 70 D2

Hawarden Ind Pk CH5 . . 139 B6
Haweswater Ave
  Crewe CW1 . . . . 173 B1
  Haydock WA11 . . . . 1 A6
Haweswater Cl WA7 . . . . 50 A5
Haweswater Dr CW7 . . . 126 D2
Hawick Cl CH64 . . . . 66 E7
Hawker Cl CH4 . . . . 139 C4
Hawkins La SK10 . . . . 88 D4
Hawkins Rd CH64 . . . . . . 41 F1
Hawkins View CH3 . . . . . 120 E6
Hawk Rd SK22 . . . . 39 E8
Hawks Ct WA7 . . . . 49 E6
Hawksey Dr CW5 . . . . . . 204 F4
Hawkshead Cl WA7 . . . . . . 9 C4
Hawkshead Cl WA7 . . . . . 50 A4
Hawkshead Rd WA5 . . . . . 6 E6
Hawkshead Way CW7 . . 126 D2
Hawkshaw Cl WA3 . . . . . . 9 C4
Hawk St CW11 . . . . 175 B6
Hawkstone Gr WA6 . . . . . 73 C4
Hawley La WA15 . . . . 32 B8
Hawley Dr WA15 . . . . 32 B8
Hawley La WA15 . . . . 32 B8
Hawley's Ct WA5 . . . . 8 A1
Hawley's Way WA5 . . . . . . 8 A1
Haworth Ave CW12 . . . . 157 A5
Haworth Cl SK11 . . . . . . 112 B5
Hawthorn Ave
  5 Nantwich CW5 . . . . . 204 F5
  Newton-le-Willows WA12 . . 2 D3
  Runcorn WA7 . . . . 23 A1
  1 Widnes WA8 . . . . 13 B2
  Wilmslow SK9 . . . . 60 A7
Hawthorn Bank SK22 . . . 39 B6
Hawthorn Cl
  Holmes Chapel CW4 . . . . 130 D3
  Winsford CW7 . . . . 126 C3
Hawthorn Cotts CH60 . . . 40 F8
Hawthorn Dr M44 . . . . . . 11 D5
Hawthorne Ave
  Audley ST7 . . . . 209 F1
  Fowley Common WA3 . . . . 5 C4
  Warrington WA5 . . . . 15 A6
  Warrington, Woolston WA1 . 17 B7
Hawthorne Bsns Pk WA5 . 16 A8
Hawthorne Cl
  Congleton CW12 . . . . . . 156 A4
  Haydock WA11 . . . . 1 A5
Hawthorne Ct ST7 . . . . . 193 E4
Hawthorne Dr
  Sandbach CW11 . . . . 175 D6
  Willaston CH64 . . . . 43 B1
Hawthorne Gr
  Barnton CW8 . . . . 77 F4
  Poynton SK12 . . . . 37 C4
  Warrington, Bruche WA1 . . 16 F7
  Warrington WA4 . . . . 16 D3
  Winsford CW7 . . . . 127 A1
Hawthorne Rd
  Frodsham WA6 . . . . 49 B1
  Warrington WA4 . . . . 26 C8
Hawthorn Gdns ST7 . . . . 210 D8
Hawthorn Gn SK9 . . . . . . 60 A7
Hawthorn Gr
  Bramhall SK7 . . . . 35 C6
  Warrington WA4 . . . . 16 D1
  Wilmslow SK9 . . . . 60 B7
Hawthorn La
  Bebington CH62 . . . . 43 D8
  Congleton CW12 . . . . . . 155 C6
  Crewe CW2 . . . . 189 F2
  Wilmslow SK9 . . . . 60 A7
Hawthorn Pk SK9 . . . . . . 60 A7
Hawthorn Rd
  Bollington SK10 . . . . 87 F8
  Christleton CH3 . . . . 142 E7
  Ellesmere Port CH66 . . . . 69 D6
  Lymm WA13 . . . . 18 D3
  Neston CH64 . . . . 41 C1
  Newcastle-under-Lyme
    ST5 . . . . 210 E1
  Plumley WA16 . . . . 80 F3
  Weaverham CW8 . . . . . . 102 C8
Hawthorn Rise SK10 . . . . 86 E6
Hawthorn St WA8 . . . . . . 60 A6
Hawthorns The
  Bunbury CW6 . . . . 185 E8
  Ellesmere Port CH66 . . . . 69 F7
  Haslington CW11 . . . . . . 191 D5
  Northwich CW8 . . . . 103 C7
  Tarporley CW6 . . . . 146 D1
  Tarvin CH3 . . . . 121 B1
Hawthorn View
  Conah's Quay CH5 . . . . . 116 A7
  Lindow End WA16 . . . . . . 59 B2
  Wilmslow SK9 . . . . 60 A7
Hawthorn Villas CW4 . . . 130 C3
Hawthorn Way SK10 . . . . 87 E2
Hawthorn Wlk
  3 Partington M31 . . . . . 11 E3
  Wilmslow SK9 . . . . 60 A7
  Wincham CW9 . . . . 79 C3
Haycroft SK8 . . . . 34 E8
Haycroft Cl CH66 . . . . 69 D2
Haydan Ct CH2 . . . . 118 D4
Haydn Mews WA6 . . . . . . 73 B4
Haydn Jones Dr CW5 . . . 204 F3
HAYDOCK 1 D6
Haydock Cl
  Chester CH3 . . . . 118 B2
  Macclesfield SK10 . . . . . . 87 C3
Haydock English Martyrs' RC
  Prim Sch WA11 . . . . 1 C6
Haydock High Sch WA11 . . 1 C6

Haydock La WA11 . . . . 1 C7
Haydock Lane Ind Est
  WA11 . . . . 1 E8
Haydock L Ctr WA11 . . . . . 1 B6
Haydock Park Racecourse
  WA3 . . . . 2 E8
Haydock St
  Newton-le-Willows WA12 . . 2 A3
  Warrington WA2 . . . . 16 B7
Hayes Cl CW5 . . . . 204 E7
Hayes Cres WA6 . . . . 49 C1
Hayes Dr CW8 . . . . 78 C3
Hayes Pk CH1 . . . . 237 A4
Haye's Rd M44 . . . . 11 E5
Hayfield Rd
  New Mills SK22 . . . . 39 D8
  Warrington WA4 . . . . 17 C7
Hayfields WA16 . . . . 57 C3
Hayfields Gr CW3 . . . . . . 229 F3
Haygarth Hts 5 CH1 . . . 237 C3
Hayhead Cl ST7 . . . . 195 B2
Hayhurst Ave CW10 . . . . 151 C8
Hayhurst Cl CW9 . . . . . . 103 F8
Hayle Cl SK10 . . . . 86 D1
Hayling Cl CW1 . . . . 190 B8
Haymakers Cl CH4 . . . . . 140 F7
Haymakers Way CH1 . . . 117 A8
HAYMOOR GREEN 205 E2
Haymoor Green Rd CW5 . 205 E3
Hayscastle Cl WA3 . . . . . . 9 D5
Hayside Wlk SY14 . . . . . 213 A3
Hayton St WA16 . . . . 56 F1
Haywood Cres WA7 . . . . 24 D2

Hazel Ave
  Macclesfield SK11 . . . . . 112 A5
  Runcorn WA7 . . . . 48 D8
Hazelbadge Cl SK12 . . . . 36 C4
Hazelbadge Rd SK12 . . . . 36 C4
Hazelbank CH65 . . . . 69 F3
Hazelborough Cl WA3 . . . 10 B5
Hazel Cl
  1 Ellesmere Port CH66 . . 69 F1
  Kidsgrove ST7 . . . . 195 B3
Hazelcroft SK9 . . . . 85 A8
Hazelcroft Gdns SK9 . . . . 85 A8
Hazeldean Ct 17 SK9 . . . 34 E1
Hazel Dr
  Gatley M22 . . . . 34 A8
  Lymm WA13 . . . . 18 F2
  Poynton SK12 . . . . 36 F3
  Weaverham CW8 . . . . . . 102 D7
  Winsford CW7 . . . . 149 C8
Hazel Gr
  Alsager ST7 . . . . 194 A3
  Crewe CW1 . . . . 190 C7
  Golborne WA3 . . . . 3 B8
  Warrington WA1 . . . . 17 A8
Hazel Grove High Sch
  SK7 . . . . 36 C8
Hazelhurst Dr SK10 . . . . . 88 A8
Hazelmere Cl CW8 . . . . . 103 C5
Hazel Rd CH4 . . . . 140 F6
Hazel St WA1 . . . . 16 D7
Hazel Wlk M31 . . . . 11 E3
Hazelwood Cl WA8 . . . . . 22 A8
Hazelwood Mews WA4 . . 17 C1
Hazelwood Rd
  Barnton CW8 . . . . 78 B4
  Wilmslow SK9 . . . . 60 B7
  Wythenshawe M22 . . . . . 33 D8
Hazlehurst Rd WA6 . . . . . 74 D6
Hazlemere Ave SK11 . . . 112 A6
Headland Cl WA3 . . . . 3 E6
Headlands The CH1, CH3 . 237 C2
Headworth Cl CW9 . . . . . 103 F4
HEALD GREEN 34 B8
Heald Green Sta SK8 . . . . 34 A8
Heald St WA12 . . . . 1 F3
Healey Cl CW1 . . . . 190 A8
Heapy St SK11 . . . . 112 E6
Hearn's La CW5 . . . . 202 E5
HEATH 49 A6
Heath Ave
  Ellesmere Port CH65 . . . . 70 A1
  Rode Heath ST7 . . . . 193 F7
  Sandbach CW11 . . . . 175 E6
Heath Bank CH3 . . . . 119 D5
Heathbank Rd SK8 . . . . . . 34 F8
Heathbrook Cotts CW9 . . 104 F7
Heath Bsns & Technical Pk
  The WA7 . . . . 49 A7
Heath Cl
  Chester CH3 . . . . 142 B8
  Sandbach CW11 . . . . 175 D6
  Tarvin CH3 . . . . 121 B1
Heathcote Cl CH2 . . . . . . 118 C4
Heathcote Gdns CW9 . . . 104 D7
Heathcote St ST7 . . . . . . 195 A2
Heath Ct
  Alsager ST7 . . . . 193 F6
  Ellesmere Port CH66 . . . . 69 B6
Heath Dr
  Knutsford WA16 . . . . 56 F2
  Runcorn WA7 . . . . 49 A7
  Tarvin CH3 . . . . 121 B1
Heath End Rd ST7 . . . . . 193 B5
Heather Ave M44 . . . . 11 D6
Heather Brae WA12 . . . . . 2 A4
Heather Brae Mews
  CW12 . . . . 156 A3
Heather Cl
  Ellesmere Port CH66 . . . . 69 E3
  Macclesfield SK11 . . . . . 112 C3
  Runcorn WA7 . . . . 49 E4
  Warrington WA3 . . . . 9 D5
Heather Ct CH3 . . . . 142 A8
Heather Falls SK22 . . . . . 39 B8

Heatherfield Ct SK9 . . . . . 60 E8
Heathergate Pl CW2 . . . . 206 B8
Heatherside ST7 . . . . 195 C6
Heatherways CW6 . . . . . 146 C3
Heather Wlk M31 . . . . 11 E3
Heathfield SK9 . . . . 60 A5
Heathfield Ave CW1 . . . . 190 C4
Heathfield Cl
  Congleton CW12 . . . . . . 155 F3
  Nantwich CW5 . . . . 204 F6
Heathfield Ct
  Ellesmere Port, Whitby
    CH65 . . . . 70 B5
  Ellesmere Port, Whitbyheath
    CH66 . . . . 95 A8
Heathfield Dr ST5 . . . . . . 210 D1
Heathfield Pk
  Warrington WA4 . . . . 17 A2
  Widnes WA8 . . . . 12 D3
Heathfield Rd
  Audlem CW3 . . . . 230 A5
  Ellesmere Port CH65 . . . . 70 B5
Heathfields Cl CH2 . . . . . 237 B4
Heathgate Ave L24 . . . . . 21 A2
Heath Gn CW6 . . . . 146 C4
Heath Gr CH66 . . . . 69 B7
Heath La
  Chester CH3 . . . . 142 A8
  Culcheth WA3 . . . . 4 A1
  Ellesmere Port, Little Sutton
    CH66 . . . . 69 B7
  Golborne, Kenyon WA3 . . . 3 F2
  Golborne WA3 . . . . 3 D6
  Great Barrow CH3 . . . . . 120 C6
  Great Budworth CW9 . . . . 54 A1
  High Legh WA16 . . . . 28 D5
  Little Leigh WA4, CW8 . . . 77 B7
  Marbury SY13 . . . . 226 E6
  Stoak CH2 . . . . 95 E7
  Swan Green WA16 . . . . . 106 F4
  Willaston CH64, CH66 . . . 68 D7
  Wincham CW9 . . . . 79 C3
Heathlands Ho WA16 . . . . 56 F2
Heathlands Rd CH66 . . . . 69 B7
Heathmoor Ave WA3 . . . . 3 D6
Heath Park Gr WA7 . . . . . 48 F8
Heath Rd
  Bollington SK10 . . . . 87 E6
  Chester CH2 . . . . 118 E7
  Congleton CW12 . . . . . . 156 A2
  Runcorn WA7 . . . . 23 B2
  Sandbach CW11 . . . . 175 D6
  Warrington WA5 . . . . 14 F5
  Weaverham CW8 . . . . . . 77 E1
  Widnes WA8 . . . . 12 D2
Heath Road S WA7 . . . . . 49 B8
Heath Road S WA7 . . . . . 48 F6
Heathside CW5 . . . . 204 F6
Heaths La CW6 . . . . 123 D4
Heath Specialist Tech Coll
  The WA7 . . . . 49 B7
Heath St
  Crewe CW1 . . . . 190 D4
  Warrington WA4 . . . . 26 C8
Heath Terr
  Chester CH2 . . . . 118 E8
  Smallwood CW11 . . . . . . 154 B1
Heathview CW1 . . . . 191 D3
Heath View
  Alsager ST7 . . . . 193 E5
  Weston CW2 . . . . 207 B5
Heathview Cl WA8 . . . . . . 22 A5
Heathview Rd WA8 . . . . . 22 A5
Heathway CH60 . . . . 41 B7
Heath Way CW6 . . . . 168 D8
Heathwood ST7 . . . . 193 F7
Heathwood Dr ST7 . . . . . 193 B5
Heathwood Gr WA1 . . . . . 17 B7
HEATLEY 19 C5
Heatley Cl WA13 . . . . 19 A4
Heatley La CW5 . . . . 217 F3
Heatley Way 5 SK9 . . . . . 34 D4
HEATON 159 E2
Heaton Cl CW10 . . . . 151 C6
Heaton Ct WA3 . . . . 9 F6
Heaton Sq CW7 . . . . 149 C8
Heaton Way CW2 . . . . . . 207 E4
Heaward Cl CW2 . . . . . . 206 B4
Hebden Ave WA3 . . . . 5 B5
HEBDEN GREEN 148 F7
Hebden Green Com Sch
  CW7 . . . . 149 A7
Heber's Cl SY14 . . . . 213 C5
Heber Wlk CW9 . . . . 104 A8
Hedge Hey WA7 . . . . 24 A1
Hedge Row SK10 . . . . 63 A1
Hedgerow Dr CW9 . . . . . 79 C3
Hedgerows The WA11 . . . . 1 C6
Hedingham Cl 7 SK10 . . 111 F8
Hefferston Grange Dr
  CW8 . . . . 102 A7
Hefferston Rise CW8 . . . . 102 A7
Heights The WA6 . . . . 73 C4
Helena Cl WA16 . . . . 57 C2
Helah Wern CW5 . . . . . . 204 E2
Hellyar-Brook Rd ST7 . . . 193 B4
Helmdon Cl CW7 . . . . . . 127 A3
Helmsdale Cl CW1 . . . . . 190 B6
Helmsdale La WA5 . . . . . 15 C6
Helmsley Cl WA5 . . . . 15 E7
HELSBY 73 C3
Helsby Ave CH62 . . . . 43 F3
Helsby High Sch WA6 . . . . 73 D5
HELSBY MARSH 73 B5
Helsby Pk WA6 . . . . 73 E5

Helsby Quarry Nature Reserve* WA6 73 B2
Helsby Rd WA6 73 C1
Helsby St WA1 16 D6
Helsby Sta WA6 73 B4
Helsby Way 4 SK9 34 D4
Helston Cl
Bramhall SK7 35 F7
Runcorn WA7 50 B5
Warrington WA5 14 E5
Helston Gr SK8 34 C8
Helton Cl CW4 130 A3
Hemingford Cl CH66 69 D2
Hemlegh Vale WA6 73 B2
Hemmingshaw La CW11 176 B8
Hemming St CW8 78 D1
Hemswell Cl CW7 149 E8
Hemsworth Ave CH66 69 C5
HENBURY 111 B8
Henbury Cl CW10 151 C7
Henbury Gdns WA4 26 E3
Henbury La SK8 34 F6
HENBURY MOSS 110 D5
Henbury Pl WA7 49 B6
Henbury Rd SK9 34 D4
Henbury Rise SK11 111 C8
Henderson Cl WA5 14 D6
Henderson Rd
Widnes, Lower House WA8 22 F8
2 Widnes WA8 13 A1
Henderson St SK11 112 C7
Hendon Cl
Crewe CW1 190 F5
2 Wilmslow/Alderley Edge SK9 60 D8
Henley Ave M44 11 E6
Henley Cl
Macclesfield SK10 87 B4
Neston CH64 66 E6
Warrington WA4 26 E6
Henley Ct WA7 23 D2
Henley Dr CW7 126 F1
Henley Rd
Chester CH4 140 F6
Chorlton CW2 207 B1
Neston CH64 66 E6
Henrietta St CW12 156 C3
Henry Pl CH1 237 B3
Henry St
Crewe CW1 190 D5
Haslington CW1 191 D4
2 Lymm WA13 18 E3
Tarporley CW6 146 C2
Warrington WA1 16 A5
4 Widnes WA8 13 C1
Henry Wood Ct 1 CH4 140 E6
Henshall Ave WA4 16 F4
Henshall Dr CW11 175 D8
Henshall Hall Dr CW12 157 B1
Henshall La WA14 20 C6
Henshall Rd SK10 87 F7
Henshall St CH1 237 A4
Henshaw La SK11 110 E2
Hepherd St WA5 15 D4
Hepley Rd SK12 37 A3
Herald Dr CW1 190 E3
Herald Pk CW1 190 E3
Herald Pk CW1 190 E3
Heralds Cl WA8 22 C8
Heralds Gn WA5 7 A2
Herberts La CH60 40 F8
Herbert St
Burtonwood WA5 6 E6
Congleton CW12 156 F3
Crewe CW1 191 A5
Lostock Gralam CW9 80 A2
Herbert Swindells Cl CW2 190 D1
Herdman St CW2 190 D2
Hereford Ave
Ellesmere Port CH66 94 E8
Golborne WA3 3 B8
Hereford Cl
Macclesfield SK10 86 F1
Warrington WA1 17 D7
Hereford Dr SK9 34 E3
Hereford Pl CH1 118 A5
Hereford Way CW10 128 E2
Hereward Rd CH3 119 B1
Heritage Ct CH1 237 B2
Hermitage Ct
Holmes Chapel CW4 130 D3
Saughall CH1 117 A8
Hermitage Dr CW4 130 D3
Hermitage Green La WA2, WA12 8 A8
Hermitage La CW4 130 C7
Hermitage Prim Sch CW4 130 D4
Hermitage Rd CH1 117 B7
Hermitage The CH60 40 F7
Heron Bsns Pk WA8 23 D8
Heron Cl
Broughton CH4 139 C4
Farndon CH3 180 F1
Knutsford WA16 57 B3
Runcorn WA7 50 D8
Winsford CW7 149 D5
Heron Cres CW1 190 F5
Heron Ct
Neston CH64 66 C7
Northwich CW9 79 C2
Heron Dr SK12 36 A3
Heron Pl CH2 237 B4
Herons Reach WA3 5 C6
Herons Way
Chester CH4 141 B2
Herons Way continued
Runcorn WA7 24 F4
Herrick Cl CW2 206 A8
Hertford Apartments WA2 9 A3
Hertford Cl
Congleton CW12 156 E4
Warrington WA1 17 E7
Hertford Gr M44 11 C6
Hesketh Cl WA5 14 F4
Hesketh Croft CW1 190 A8
Hesketh Dr CW9 80 A3
Hesketh Grange Cotts CH63 42 A7
Hesketh Meadow La WA3 3 F8
Hesketh Rd L24 21 E2
Hesketh St 5 WA5 15 D4
Hesketh Street N WA5 15 D4
Hesnall Cl WA3 5 C8
Hessle Dr CH60 40 F7
HESWALL 40 D7
Heswall Ave WA3 4 E4
Heswall Point 7 CH60 41 A8
Heswall Rd CH66 69 D4
Heswall Sta CH60 41 D8
HETHERSON GREEN 214 D8
Hetherson Green La SY14 214 D8
Hewetson Cres SK11 111 E7
Hewitt Dr CW7 150 D8
Hewitt Gr CW9 79 F5
Hewitt St
Chester CH2 118 F3
Crewe CW2 190 D2
Northwich CW9 79 D2
Warrington WA4 16 C3
Hexham Ct CH1 118 B2
Hexham Way 4 SK10 87 C4
Heybridge La SK10 87 B6
Heydon Cl
Congleton CW12 156 C3
Halewood L26 21 A7
Heyes Ave WA11 1 D5
Heyes Dr WA13 18 C2
Heyes Farm Rd SK11 111 E8
Heyes Ho SK11 111 E8
Heyes La
Alderley Edge SK9 60 B3
Warrington WA4 26 E8
Heyes Pk CW8 102 F4
Heyes Rd WA8 22 C8
Heyeswood La CW8 103 A4
Heyfield Park Rd CH66 69 B7
Heygarth Prim Sch CH62 43 E5
Heygarth Rd CH62 43 E5
Hey Lock Cl WA12 7 C8
Heys Ave CH62 43 D8
Heysbank Rd SK12 38 D5
Heysham Cl WA7 50 D6
Hey Shoot La WA3 5 C5
Heysoms Ave CW8 103 D7
Heysoms Cl CW8 103 D7
Heys The
Bebington CH62 43 F5
Runcorn WA7 23 E1
Heythrop Dr CH60 41 D8
Heywood Cl SK9 60 B2
Hey Wood Cl WA12 7 C8
Heywood Gn CW2 206 C8
Heywood La CW3, SY13 234 C7
Heywood Rd
Alderley Edge SK9 60 B2
Ellesmere Port CH66 69 D5
Heywoods Ridge CW3 229 E3
Heywood St CW12 156 C2
Heywoods The CH2 118 C4
Hibbert St
New Mills SK22 39 B6
6 Widnes WA8 23 B8
Hibel Rd SK10 87 D1
Hickhurst La CW6 147 D3
Hickmore Heys CH3 119 F5
Hickory Cl WA1 17 E7
Hickson St CW8 78 B3
Hidcote Cl CW2 206 B8
HIDEBANK 39 C8
Hield Brow CW9 79 C7
Hield Gr CW9 79 C8
Hield La CW9 79 C8
Higginbotham Gn SK11 112 E6
Higginson Cl CW12 179 C8
Higham Ave WA5 7 F1
Highbank Cl CW8 78 B3
High Bank Cl M44 11 D6
Highbank Rd
Kingsley WA6 75 C2
Northwich CW8 103 D7
High Bent Ave SK8 35 A6
HIGH CARR 210 F3
High Carr Bsns Pk ST5 210 F2
High Carr Network Ctr ST5 210 F2
Highcliffe Ave CH1 118 B4
Highcroft Ave CW12 156 F2
High Cross La CH3 182 D1
High Ct SK10 88 B8
High Elm Dr WA15 32 C8
High Elm Rd WA15 32 D7
High Elms SK8 35 B5
Higher Ash Rd ST7 210 D8
Higher Ashton WA8 12 F3
HIGHER BUNBURY 168 F1
HIGHER BURWARDSLEY 184 C5
HIGHER CARDEN 198 D7
Higher Carden La SY14 198 D6
HIGHER DISLEY 38 E4
Higher Downs WA16 57 C2
HIGHERFENCE 113 A8
Higher Fence Rd SK10 87 F1
HIGHER FERRY 140 C8
Higher Heyes Dr WA6 75 C1
HIGHER HURDSFIELD 88 A2
HIGHER KINNERTON 161 B8
Higher Knutsford Rd WA4 16 F2
Higher La
Bollington SK10 88 B6
Disley SK12 38 E1
Dutton WA4 51 D4
Kettleshulme SK23 64 E6
Lymm WA13 19 B1
Higherland Ct 6 ST7 195 A2
HIGHER MARSTON 79 C6
HIGHER POYNTON 37 B2
Higher Rd L26, WA8 21 C5
HIGHER RUNCORN 23 A1
HIGHER SHURLACH 104 E6
HIGHER WALTON 25 F7
HIGHER WHITLEY 52 D5
HIGHER WINCHAM 79 F4
Higher Works Cotts SK11 158 C6
HIGHER WYCH 224 D4
Highfield
Elton CH2 72 B4
Prestbury SK10 87 A5
High Field WA14 20 B2
Highfield Ave
Audlem CW3 230 A4
Golborne WA3 2 F8
Kidsgrove ST7 195 B2
Lostock Gralam CW9 80 A3
Warrington, Dudlow's Green WA4 26 D4
Warrington WA5 15 A5
Highfield Cl CH64 66 E8
Highfield Com Prim Sch CH1 117 F4
Highfield Cres
Handforth SK9 34 C1
Widnes WA8 13 A2
Highfield Dr
Lymm WA13 18 C2
Macclesfield SK10 87 A1
Nantwich CW5 205 A6
Highfield Est SK9 34 C1
Highfield La
Coddington CH3 181 E4
Golborne WA3 3 C5
Winwick WA2 8 C7
Highfield Parkway SK7 35 D4
Highfield Pl 1 CW8 103 E8
Highfield Rd
Blacon CH1 117 D5
Bollington SK10 88 A8
Cheadle SK8 34 F8
Congleton CW12 156 E2
Ellesmere Port CH65 70 C5
Ellesmere Port, Little Sutton CH66 69 B6
Lymm WA13 18 C2
Macclesfield SK11 112 C7
Neston CH64 66 F8
Northwich CW8 103 F7
Poynton SK12 36 A4
Widnes WA8 13 A2
Highfield Road N 11 CH65 70 C6
Highfields SY13 224 A2
Highfields Cty Prim Sch CW5 204 F6
Highfield Specl Sch L26 21 A7
Highfield Terr SK22 39 D8
Highgate Cl
Crewe CW1 190 A8
Runcorn WA7 24 D1
High Gates Cl WA5 15 E7
High Gates Lodge WA5 15 E7
Highgrove Mews 2 SK9 60 A6
High Hill Rd SK22 39 D8
Highlands Rd WA7 48 F8
Highlands The CW6 185 E8
Highland Way WA16 82 A7
HIGHLANE 134 C6
HIGH LANE 37 E8
High Lane Prim Sch SK6 37 F8
High Lea Rd SK22 39 A8
HIGH LEGH 29 B5
High Legh Prim Sch WA16 29 C5
High Legh Rd WA13 29 C8
High Lowe Ave CW12 157 A4
Highmarsh Cres WA12 2 B4
High Mdw 2 SK8 34 E8
High Mount CH60 40 F8
High St
Audley ST7 210 A1
Bollington SK10 88 B8
Clotton CW6 145 D4
Congleton CW12 156 D2
Crewe CW2 190 D3
Farndon CH3 180 E2
Frodsham WA6 49 B1
Golborne WA3 3 A8
Great Budworth CW9 79 A7
Hale L24 21 D1
Harriseahead ST7 195 E5
Kidsgrove, The Rookery ST7 195 C4
Macclesfield SK11 112 D6
Malpas SY14 213 B3
Mow Cop ST7 195 D7
Nantwich CW5 204 E5
Neston CH64 66 E7
Newchapel ST7 195 E2
New Mills SK22 39 C8
Newton-le-Willows WA12 2 D4
Norley WA6 100 F5
High St continued
Northwich CW9 103 F8
Runcorn WA7 23 A2
Saltney CH4 140 E7
Sandbach CW11 175 B6
Talke ST7 210 D6
Tarporley CW6 146 C2
Tarvin CH3 121 B2
Tattenhall CH3 166 B1
Warrington WA1 16 C5
Weaverham CW8 77 C1
Winsford CW7 126 D1
High Street Prim Sch CW7 126 D1
Hightown
Crewe CW1 190 C4
Middlewich CW10 128 C1
Sandbach CW11 175 B6
Hightown Appts 6 CW1 190 C4
Hightree Dr SK11 111 C8
High View
Helsby WA6 73 C4
Mount Pleasant ST7 195 B5
HIGH WARREN 26 C6
High Warren Cl WA4 26 C5
Highwood Rd WA4 26 C7
Hignett Ave WA9 1 B2
Hilary Ave SK8 34 D8
Hilary Cl
Chester CH3 119 B1
Warrington WA5 14 D6
Widnes WA8 13 E3
Hilbre Ave CH60 40 E6
Hilbre Bank CW6 169 D4
Hilbre Dr CH65 70 C1
Hilden Pl WA2 16 D8
Hilden Rd WA2 8 E1
Hillary Ave CW12 157 A2
Hillary Dr CW3 230 A4
Hillary Rd
Bebington CH62 43 E5
Kidsgrove ST7 195 B3
Hillberry Cres WA4 16 B3
Hillbre Way 1 SK9 34 D4
Hillbrook Rd SK7 35 D6
Hill Cl
Bunbury CW6 185 E7
Neston CH64 67 B5
HILLCLIFFE 26 C8
Hill Cliffe Rd WA4 26 B8
Hill Cotts CH3 164 A4
Hillcourt Rd SK6 37 F7
Hillcrest WA7 23 D1
Hillcrest Ave CW4 130 B3
Hillcrest Dr CH66 69 A6
Hillcrest Rd
Bollington SK10 87 F7
Ellesmere Port CH66 69 B6
Kelsall CW6 122 E6
Warren SK11 112 A4
Hill Ct CH64 67 B5
Hill Dr
Handforth SK9 34 E3
Whaley Bridge SK23 65 D8
Hillesden Rise CW12 156 F2
Hillfield
Frodsham WA6 74 B7
Runcorn WA7 50 D8
Hillfield Gdns CW5 204 E4
Hillfield Pl CW5 204 E4
Hillfield Rd CH66 69 D7
Hillfields CW12 156 D4
Hill Fields CW12 156 D3
Hill Fields Cl CW12 156 D4
Hillfield View CW5 204 E4
Hillfoot Cres WA4 26 B7
Hillfoot La WA6 74 E3
Hilliards Ct CH4 141 B3
Hillingden Ave L26 21 A7
Hill La
Brown Knowl CH3 199 C8
Peckforton CW6 184 E6
Hillock La WA1 17 C8
Hill Rd CH4 141 E2
Hill Road N WA6 73 D3
Hill Road S WA6 73 C3
Hillsboro Ave WA6 74 C7
Hillsdown Way CH66 69 C2
Hillside
Broomedge WA13 19 E1
Northwich CW8 103 C7
Hillside Ave
Newton-le-Willows WA12 1 F2
Runcorn WA7 48 E8
Hillside Cl
Bramhall SK7 36 A7
Chorlton CW2 207 E3
Helsby WA6 73 D4
Mow Cop ST7 195 D7
Hill Side Cl SK12 38 E6
Hillside Ct
Macclesfield SK10 88 A1
Warrington WA4 26 D3
Hillside Dr
Crewe CW1 190 E5
Ellesmere Port CH66 69 E7
Macclesfield SK10 88 A1
Hillside Gr WA5 14 F4
Hillside Ho 7 CW8 103 C5
Hillside La CW9 126 E7
Hillside Prim Sch WA6 73 D4
Hillside Rd
Blacon CH1 117 E4
Frodsham WA6 74 C7
Heswall CH60 41 A7
Kelsall CW6 122 D4
Knutsford WA16 57 A2
Warrington WA4 26 D3
Hillside View SK22 39 A8
Hill St
Crewe CW1 190 D4
Macclesfield SK11 112 D6
Runcorn WA7 23 A2
Sandbach CW11 174 D7
Warrington WA1 16 B5
Winsford CW7 126 F1
Hill Terr ST7 209 D2
Hill The
Knutsford WA16 82 B8
Sandbach CW11 175 D5
HILLTOP 60 B8
Hilltop WA7 50 C7
Hill Top
Altrincham WA15 32 A8
Barnton CW8 78 B2
Hill Top Ave
Cheadle SK8 35 B8
Wilmslow SK9 60 B8
Winsford CW7 126 C1
Hill Top La
Heswall CH60 41 B8
Neston CH64 67 B5
Hilltop Pk WA16 79 F7
Hilltop Rd
Guilden Sutton CH3 119 F5
Lymm WA13 18 C2
Hill Top Rd
Acton Bridge CW8 76 F2
Dutton WA4 51 C1
Runcorn WA7 50 F6
Warrington, Stockton Heath WA4 16 F2
Warrington, Woolston WA1 17 C7
Hill Top Rise SK23 65 D8
Hill View
Bollington SK10 87 F7
Whaley Bridge SK23 65 C8
Widnes WA8 12 F5
Hill View Ave WA6 73 A1
Hillview Cl WA6 74 C7
Hill View Prim Sch WA7 49 E4
Hillview Rise CW8 78 E1
Hilton Ave WA5 15 B5
Hilton Cl
9 Macclesfield SK11 111 F7
Middlewich CW10 151 B8
Hilton Dr M44 11 C5
Hilton Gr SK12 36 D4
Hilton Rd
Disley SK12 38 B7
Poynton SK12 37 C5
Himalayan Birch Cl CH66 69 E6
Hinchley Cl CW8 103 A5
Hinckley Ct CW12 156 A3
Hinderton Dr CH60 40 F6
Hinderton Gn CH64 66 F8
Hinderton La CH64 67 A8
Hinderton Rd CH64 66 F8
Hinderton Sch CH65 69 F3
Hinde St CW5 204 D4
Hind Heath La CW11 174 F4
Hind Heath Rd CW11 174 E4
Hindle Ave WA5 7 F1
Hindley Cres CW8 78 A3
Hinton Cres WA4 26 E8
Hinton Rd
Crewe CW2 206 D8
Runcorn WA7 23 A1
Hirsch Cl CW5 205 A4
Hitchen's Cl WA7 50 D7
Hitchens La SY14 184 D1
Hitch Lowes SK11 84 A3
Hobart Cl SK7 35 F4
Hobart Way CH1 117 D4
Hobb La WA4 25 C5
Hobbs Cl CW1 191 D4
Hobbs Hill La WA16 28 E1
Hobby Ct WA7 49 E6
Hobcroft La WA16 58 A7
Hob Hey La WA3 4 D3
Hob La
Churton CH3 180 F5
Dunham-on-the-Hill WA6 97 C6
Hobson St SK11 112 D6
Hockenhull Ave CH3 121 B2
Hockenhull Cres CH3 121 B2
Hockenhull La
Tarvin, Broom Bank CH3 121 B1
Tarvin CH3 121 B2
Hocker La
Adder's Moss SK10 85 F4
Nether Alderley SK10 85 C4
Hockerley Ave SK23 65 D8
Hockerley Cl SK23 65 D8
Hockerley La SK23 65 D8
Hockerley New Rd SK23 65 D8
HOCKLEY 37 A2
Hockley Cl SK12 37 A3
Hockley Paddock SK12 36 F3
Hockley Rd SK12 37 A3
HODGEHILL 132 E8
Hodgehill La SK11 132 E5
Hodge La
Hartford CW8 103 A6
Weaverham CW8 102 D5
Hodgkin Cl CW5 204 F4
Hodgkinson Ave WA5 7 F1
Hoghton Rd L24 21 E2
Hogshead La CW8 124 C7
Holbeck WA7 50 C7
Holbein Cl CH4 141 E6
Holborn Ct WA8 12 F3
Holbrook Cl WA5 14 E5

Holbury Cl CW1 . . . . 190 B8
Holcombe Ave WA3 . . . . . . 3 C8
Holcombe Dr SK10 . . . . . . 87 B3
Holcot Ct CW7 . . . . 127 A4
Holcroft La WA3 . . . . 5 D2
Holdings La CW3 . . . . . . 232 F4
Holehouse La
  Langley SK11 . . . . 113 C4
  Scholar Green ST7 . . . . 194 D8
  Whiteley Green SK10 . . 62 D2
Hole House La CW8 . . . . 77 E4
Hole La WA16 . . . . 106 E4
Holes La WA1 . . . . 17 B7
Holford Ave
  Lostock Gralam CW9 . . 80 A3
  Warrington WA3 . . . . . 15 F8
Holford Cres WA16 . . . . . 57 B1
Holford Dr WA3 . . . . 59 C7
Holford Moss WA7 . . . . . 24 D3
Holford St CW12 . . . . . 156 D3
Holford Way WA12 . . . . . . 2 F3
Holgrave Cl WA16 . . . . . . 29 C4
Holkam Cl CW9 . . . . 103 F5
Holker Cl SK12 . . . . 36 F4
Holkham Cl WA8 . . . . 12 F1
Holkham The CH3 . . . . . 119 B1
Holland Cl CW11 . . . . . . 175 C5
Holland Ct SK12 . . . . 36 E3
Holland Rd SK7 . . . . 35 E7
Hollands La WA6 . . . . . 122 C5
Hollands Pl SK11 . . . . . 112 F7
Hollands Rd CW9 . . . . . 103 F7
Holland St
  Crewe CW1 . . . . 190 B6
  5 Macclesfield SK11 . . 112 C7
Holland Wlk CW5 . . . . . 204 D6
Hollies La SK9 . . . . 60 F7
Hollies The
  Moulton CW9 . . . . . . 126 E8
  1 Northwich CW9 . . 103 E6
  Runcorn WA7 . . . . 49 D8
  Shavington CW2 . . . . . 206 B4
HOLLINFARE 11 A3
Hollingford Pl WA16 . . . . 82 A8
HOLLIN GREEN 202 F6
Hollingreen La CW5 . . . . 229 B7
Hollin Green La CW5 . . . 202 E6
Hollinhey Prim Sch SK11 112 F3
Hollin La
  Langley SK11 . . . . 113 A1
  Newhall CW5 . . . . 228 D8
  Styal SK9 . . . . 33 F5
  Sutton Lane Ends SK11 . . 136 C6
Hollin Rd SK10 . . . . 88 A7
HOLLINS 210 E8
Hollins Cres ST7 . . . . . . 194 E1
Hollins Dr WA2 . . . . 8 A6
Hollins Grange ST7 . . . . 210 D8
HOLLINSGREEN 152 D4
HOLLINS GREEN 11 B2
Hollinshead Cl ST7 . . . . 194 F7
Hollins Hill CW6 . . . . . . 146 F8
Hollins La
  Antrobus CW9 . . . . 53 F4
  Marbury SY13 . . . . . . 226 E7
  Winwick WA2 . . . . 7 E6
HOLLINS-LANE 226 E6
Hollins Park Hospl WA2 . . 7 F6
Hollins Rd SK11 . . . . . . 112 F6
Hollins Terr SK11 . . . . . 112 F6
Hollins Way WA8 . . . . . . 22 B5
Hollinwood Ct ST7 . . . . 210 E8
Hollinwood Rd
  Disley SK12 . . . . 38 D6
  Talke ST7 . . . . 210 E8
Holloway WA7 . . . . 22 F1
Hollow Dr WA4 . . . . 16 E1
Hollow La
  Kingsley WA6 . . . . 75 B3
  Knutsford WA16 . . . . . 57 B1
Hollowmoor Heath CH3 . . 121 A4
Hollow Oak La CW8 . . . . 101 D4
Hollowood Rd SY14 . . . . 213 B5
Hollow The ST7 . . . . . . 195 B5
Holly Ave WA12 . . . . 2 D3
Hollybank
  Audlem CW3 . . . . 229 E3
  Moore WA4 . . . . 25 B5
Holly Bank
  Chester CH1 . . . . 237 A4
  Frodsham WA6 . . . . . . 74 C8
  Helsby WA6 . . . . 73 D2
  Lymm WA13 . . . . 18 D2
Hollybank Cl CW8 . . . . . 78 D1
Hollybank Ct
  Chester CH1 . . . . 237 A4
  Widnes WA8 . . . . 12 F1
Hollybank Rd WA7 . . . . . 49 F8
Holly Bank Rd SK9 . . . . 34 B1
Hollybank Cres CW5 . . . 205 D5
Holly Bush La WA16 . . . 10 C2
Holly Cl
  Connah's Quay CH5 . . . 91 C1
  Hale L24 . . . . 21 D2
  Mickle Trafford CH2 . . 119 F8
Holly Cotts CW12 . . . . . 132 C1
Holly Croft CW12 . . . . . 154 F6
Holly Ct
  Helsby WA6 . . . . 73 C5
  Middlewich CW10 . . . . 128 B2
Holly Dr CW7 . . . . 149 D8
Holly Farm Cl WA16 . . . . 12 E4
Hollyfield Rd CH65 . . . . 70 B5
Hollyfields CW11 . . . . . 191 F8

Holly Gr
  Over Tabley WA16 . . . . . 56 A3
  Warrington WA1 . . . . . 17 A7
Holly Heath Cl CW11 . . . 175 C5
Holly Hedge La WA4 . . . 25 D6
Holly House Est CW10 . . 129 C6
HOLLYHURST 227 A5
Hollyhurst Rd SY13 . . . . 227 B7
Holly La
  Alsager ST7 . . . . 193 E3
  Harriseahead ST7 . . . . 195 F5
  Wythenshawe SK9 . . . . 33 C5
Holly Mount CW2 . . . . . 206 E5
Holly Pl CW5 . . . . 205 D6
Holly Rd
  Bramhall SK7 . . . . 35 E5
  Chester CH4 . . . . 140 F5
  Ellesmere Port CH65 . . 70 C5
  Golborne WA3 . . . . 3 C8
  Haydock WA11 . . . . 1 A6
  High Lane SK6 . . . . 37 F7
  Lymm WA13 . . . . 18 B5
  Macclesfield SK11 . . . 112 B7
  Newcastle-under-Lyme
   ST5 . . . . 210 D1
  Poynton SK12 . . . . 36 E3
  Warrington WA3 . . . . . 14 E5
  Weaverham CW8 . . . . 102 C8
Holly Road N SK9 . . . . . 60 B6
Holly Road S SK9 . . . . . 60 B6
Holly Terr
  Tilston SY14 . . . . 198 C3
  Warrington WA5 . . . . . 14 F5
Hollythorn Ave SK8 . . . . 33 C7
Holly Tree Dr
  Biddulph ST8 . . . . 179 C2
  Swan Green SK11 . . . . 106 D7
Hollytree Rd WA16 . . . . 80 F3
Holly Wlk
  Northwich CW8 . . . . . 103 C7
  Partington M31 . . . . . 11 D3
Holm Dr **7** Handforth SK9 . . 34 D5
  Elton CH2 . . . . 72 B4
  Elton CH2 . . . . 72 C3
HOLMES CHAPEL 130 C4
Holmes Chapel Bsns Ctr
  CW4 . . . . 130 D3
Holmes Chapel Comp Sch
  CW4 . . . . 130 A2
Holmes Chapel L Ctr
  CW4 . . . . 130 A2
Holmes Chapel Prim Sch
  CW4 . . . . 130 B3
Holmes Chapel Rd
  Allostock WA16 . . . . . 106 B3
  Brereton Green CW4,
   CW12 . . . . 154 D8
  Congleton CW12 . . . . 155 C4
  Knutsford WA16 . . . . . 82 C3
  Lach Dennis CW9 . . . . 105 E4
  Middlewich CW10 . . . . 128 E2
  Sandbach CW11 . . . . 153 E1
  Sproston Green CW4,
   CW10 . . . . 129 B2
  Withington Green SK11 . . 109 A7
Holmes Chapel Sta CW4 130 D2
Holmes Ct WA3 . . . . 9 C4
Holme St CH3 . . . . 120 F2
Holmesville Ave CW12 . . 156 B3
Holmeswood Cl SK9 . . . 60 C8
Holmfield Ave WA7 . . . . 23 C2
Holmfield Dr
  Cheadle SK8 . . . . 35 B8
  Ellesmere Port CH66 . . 69 D3
Holmlea Dr CW1 . . . . . . 190 F3
Holmlea Way SK10 . . . . 86 D6
Holm Oak Way CH66 . . . 94 F8
Holmsfield Rd WA1 . . . . 16 D5
Holmshaw La CW1 . . . . 192 B3
Holmwood Dr CH65 . . . . 79 C8
HOLT 196 D8
Holt Gdns WA16 . . . . . . 58 E6
Holt Hey CH64 . . . . 67 A5
Holt La WA7 . . . . 49 F8
HOLTRIDGE 215 E6
Holtridge La SY13 . . . . 215 E6
Holt's La SK9 . . . . 33 F3
Holt's Prim Sch LL13 . . 196 D8
Holt St CW1 . . . . 190 D4
Holy Family RC Prim Sch
  WA8 . . . . 12 D5
Holyhead Cl WA5 . . . . . . 7 D3
Holyrood Ave WA8 . . . . 13 A4
Holyrood Dr CW2 . . . . . 205 E8
Holyrood Way CH3 . . . . 119 B2
Holy Spirit Prim Sch WA9 . 1 A3
Holy Spirit RC Aided Prim
  Sch The WA7 . . . . 49 D8
Holywell Cl CH4 . . . . . . 41 B1
Holywell Dr WA1 . . . . . . 16 C5
Holywell La CH3 . . . . . . 182 D2
Home Cl CH3 . . . . 142 E7
Homecrofts CH64 . . . . . 66 E5
Homedene Ho CH1 . . . 237 A3
Home Farm WA16 . . . . 56 B8
Home Farm Ave SK10 . . 86 F1
Home Farm Pk CW5 . . 172 A8
Home Pk CH1 . . . . 94 F1
Homeshire Ho ST7 . . . 193 D3
Homestead Ave WA11 . . 1 A6
Homestead Ct CW4 . . . 104 D7
Homestead Rd SK12 . . 38 C6
Homesteads The CW5 . . 172 A6
Homeway WA6 . . . . 73 C4
Homewood Cres CW8 . . 103 B5
Honey Fields CW6 . . . . 146 C1
Honeysuckle Ave WA5 . . 15 E4

Honeysuckle Cl
  Broughton CH4 . . . . . 139 C3
  Widnes WA8 . . . . 13 B4
Honey Suckle Cl **3** CH4 . . 9 D1
Hong Kong Ave M90 . . . 33 A8
Honister Ave WA2 . . . . 8 C2
Honister Gr WA7 . . . . . 49 E5
Honiton Way
  Middlewich CW10 . . . 128 D2
  Warrington WA5 . . . . 14 E4
HONKLEY 161 C3
Hood La WA5 . . . . 15 C4
Hood Lane N WA5 . . . . 15 C6
HOOD MANOR 15 D5
Hood Rd WA8 . . . . 12 F1
HOOFIELD 145 A2
Hoofield La CH3 . . . . . 145 A1
HOO GREEN 29 F2
Hoo Green La WA16 . . 29 E1
Hooker St CW8 . . . . . . 103 E7
Hook La CW6 . . . . 145 A6
Hookstone Dr CH66 . . . 69 C6
HOOLE 119 A3
HOOLE BANK 119 C4
Hoole CE Prim Sch CH2 119 A3
Hoole Gdns CH2 . . . . . 119 B3
Hoole Ho CH2 . . . . 119 B4
Hoole La CH2 . . . . 119 A3
HOOLE PARK 118 F3
Hoole Pk CH2 . . . . 118 F2
Hoole Rd CH2 . . . . 118 F3
Hoole Way CH1 . . . . . . 237 B3
Hooleyhey La SK10, SK11 . . 89 D4
Hoolpool La WA6 . . . . 119 A2
HOOTON 44 A1
Hooton Gn CH6 . . . . . . 44 B2
Hooton Hey CH66 . . . . 69 D5
Hooton La CH66 . . . . . 44 B3
Hooton Rd CH64, CH66 . . 43 D1
Hooton Sta CH66 . . . . 43 D1
Hooton Way
  7 Handforth SK9 . . 34 D5
  Hooton CH66 . . . . 44 A2
  Hooton Works CH66 . . 43 E1
Hope Ave SK9 . . . . 34 C3
Hope Croft CH66 . . . . . 69 F2
Hope Farm Prec CH66 . . 69 F2
Hope Farm Rd CH66 . . 69 E2
Hopefield Rd WA7 . . . . 23 A1
Hope Green Way SK10 . . 36 D2
Hope La
  Midway SK10 . . . . 36 D1
  Wardsend SK10 . . . . 36 E1
Hope Rd CH4 . . . . 139 B3
Hope St
  Audley ST7 . . . . 209 F3
  Chester CH4 . . . . 140 F7
  Crewe CW2 . . . . 190 D2
  Macclesfield SK10 . . 112 E8
  Newton-le-Willows WA12 . . 2 B3
  Sandbach CW11 . . . . 175 B6
Hope Street W SK10 . . 112 C8
Hopkins Cl CW12 . . . . 156 B3
Hopkinson Ct CH1 . . . 118 B1
Hopwood Cl **1** WA3 . . 3 F8
Horace Black Gdns CH5 . . 70 C6
Horace Lawton Ct **2**
  CW12 . . . . 156 D3
Horbury Gdns CH66 . . 69 C5
Hornbeam Ave CH66 . . 69 F1
Hornbeam Cl
  Chester CH2 . . . . 119 B3
  Runcorn WA7 . . . . 24 C1
Hornbeam Dr CW8 . . . 102 E4
Hornbeam Dr L26 . . . . 21 A7
Hornby Dr
  Congleton CW12 . . . . 156 A3
  Nantwich CW5 . . . . . 205 A5
Hornby La WA2 . . . . 8 A6
Horncastle Cl **4** WA3 . . 3 F8
Horn's Mill Prim Sch WA6 73 A1
Hornsmill Way WA6 . . 73 A3
Horridge Ave WA12 . . . 2 C5
Horrocks La WA1 . . . . 16 B5
Horrocks Rd CH2 . . . . 118 C5
Horsemarket St WA1 . . 16 B5
Horseshoe Cl WA6 . . . 75 B2
Horseshoe Cres WA2 . . 8 B3
Horseshoe Dr SK11 . . 112 B7
Horseshoe La SK9 . . . 60 A2
Horsley La CW6 . . . . . 167 E1
Horstone Cres CH66 . . 69 F2
Horstone Gdns CH66 . . 70 A2
Horstone Rd CH66 . . . 69 F2
HORTON GREEN 212 A8
Horton Way CW5 . . . . 205 A4
NORWICH END 65 D5
Hoscar Ct WA8 . . . . . . 22 D2
Hospital La CW5 . . . . 203 E2
Hospital of St John
  Almhouses CH1 . . . 237 A3
Hospital St
  Crewe CW1 . . . . 190 D6
  Nantwich CW5 . . . . . 204 E5
Hotel Way WA7 . . . . . 49 F7
Hotel Rd M90 . . . . 33 C7
Hotel St WA12 . . . . 2 B3
Hothersall Cl CW1 . . . 173 B1
HOUGH
  Alderley Edge 60 D1
  Crewe 206 F3
Hough Cl SK10 . . . . . . 88 D5
HOUGH COMMON 206 F2
Hough Cotts CW2 . . . . 206 E3
Hougher Wall Rd ST7 . . 209 D1

Hough Gn
  Ashley WA15 . . . . 31 E5
  Chester CH4 . . . . 141 B7
HOUGH GREEN 12 B2
Hough Green Rd WA8 . . 12 B3
Hough Green Sta WA8 . 12 B2
Hough La
  Alderley Edge SK9 . . 60 D3
  Barnton CW8, CW9 . . 78 B4
  Comberbach CW9 . . . 78 A7
  Norley WA6 . . . . 100 F5
Houghley Cl SK10 . . . 87 C2
Hough's La WA4 . . . . . 26 A6
Houghton Cl
  Chester CH2 . . . . 118 F3
  Newton-le-Willows WA12 . . 2 B3
  8 Northwich CW9 . . 103 F4
  Widnes WA8 . . . . 13 D2
Houghton Croft WA8 . . 12 C5
HOUGHTON GREEN . . . 8 E4
Houghton St
  Newton-le-Willows WA12 . . 2 B3
  Warrington WA2 . . . . 16 B6
  Widnes WA8 . . . . 13 D2
Houndings La CW11 . . 175 B4
Hourd Way CH66 . . . . 94 E8
Housesteads Dr CH2 . . 118 F3
Housman Cl CH1 . . . . 118 A5
Houston Gdns WA5 . . 15 A8
Hove Cl CW1 . . . . 190 B8
Hove The WA7 . . . . . . 50 D6
Hovis Mill SK11 . . . . . 112 F7
Howard Ave
  Bebington CH62 . . . . 43 D8
  Lymm WA13 . . . . 19 B4
Howard Ct
  Neston CH64 . . . . 41 F1
  Runcorn WA7 . . . . 24 C4
Howard Rd
  Culcheth WA3 . . . . 5 A2
  Saltney CH4 . . . . 140 D6
Howards Way CH64 . . . 67 A6
Howarth Ct **1** WA7 . . 23 B2
HOWBECK BANK 219 E8
Howbeck Cres CW5 . . 220 A8
Howbeck Wlk CW2 . . 206 D8
Howells Ave CH66 . . . 69 D3
Howe Rd CH4 . . . . 141 B7
Howe St SK10 . . . . 87 F1
Howey Hill CW12 . . . . 156 D1
Howey La
  Congleton CW12 . . . . 156 D2
  Frodsham WA6 . . . . . . 74 B7
Howey Rise WA6 . . . . . 74 B7
Howgill Cl CH66 . . . . . 68 F6
HOWLEY 16 D5
Howley La WA1 . . . . . . 16 E5
Howley Quay Ind Est WA1 16 D5
Howson Rd WA2 . . . . . . 8 C3
Howty Cl SK9 . . . . 34 D1
Hoylake Cl WA7 . . . . . 50 C6
Hoyle St WA5 . . . . 15 F7
Hubert Dr CW10 . . . . . 151 C8
Hubert Worthington Ho **9**
  SK9 . . . . 60 A1
Hudson Cl WA5 . . . . . 15 D8
Hudson Gr **6** WA3 . . . 3 F8
Hudson Rd WA2 . . . . . . 8 E2
Hughes Ave WA2 . . . . . 8 D2
Hughes Dr CW2 . . . . . 189 F4
Hughes Pl WA2 . . . . . . 8 D2
Hughes St WA4 . . . . . 16 C3
Hugh St CH4 . . . . 141 D7
Hulley Pl SK10 . . . . . . 87 F2
Hulley Rd SK10 . . . . . 87 F2
Hullock's Pool Rd ST7 . . 209 E5
HULME 8 B3
Hulme Hall Ave SK8 . . 35 B8
Hulme Hall La WA16 . . 106 B4
Hulme Hall Rd SK8 . . . 35 A8
Hulme La WA16 . . . . . 106 C7
Hulme Sq SK11 . . . . . 112 D5
HULME WALFIELD . . . 156 B7
Hulsehall CW1 . . . . . . 30 A4
Hulseheath La WA16 . . 30 A3
Hulse La CW9 . . . . . . 105 B4
Hulton Cl CW12 . . . . . 157 B1
Humber Cl WA8 . . . . . 13 F3
Humber Dr ST8 . . . . . 179 E1
Humber Rd
  Ellesmere Port CH66 . . 69 F2
  Warrington WA2 . . . . . 8 B3
Humble Bee Bank Cotts
  CW5 . . . . 187 C8
Hume St WA1 . . . . 16 D6
Humphrey's Cl WA7 . . 50 D7
Hungerford Ave CW1 . . 190 E4
Hungerford Pl
  Barthomley CW2 . . . 208 D5
  Sandbach CW11 . . . 175 A5
Hungerford Prim Sch
  CW1 . . . . 190 E4
Hungerford Rd CW1 . . 190 F4
Hungerford Terr CW1 . . 190 F4
Hungerford Villas CW1 . . 190 F4
HUNSTERSON 220 B1
Hunsterson Rd
  Bridgemere CW5 . . 231 D8
  Hatherton CW5 . . . 220 B3
Hunt Cl WA5 . . . . 15 B8
Hunter Ave
  Shavington CW2 . . . 206 D7
  Warrington WA2 . . . . 8 B3

Hunters Cl SK9 . . . . . . 34 F1
Hunter's Cres CH3 . . . 121 C1
Hunters Ct
  Helsby WA6 . . . . 73 D4
  Runcorn WA7 . . . . . . 49 E6
Hunter's Dr CH3 . . . . 121 C1
Huntersfield CW2 . . . 206 B3
Hunters Field CW8 . . 103 D7
Hunters Hill
  Kingsley WA6 . . . . . . 75 C1
  Weaverham CW8 . . . 77 C1
Hunters La CW8 . . . . 102 E4
Hunters Lodge SK9 . . 34 F1
Hunters Mews SK9 . . 60 C7
Hunters Pointe CW12 155 C6
Hunters Pool La SK10 . . 86 C8
Hunters Rise CW7 . . . 126 C1
Hunters View SK11 . . 237 A3
Hunter's View WA5 . . 34 C3
Hunters Way
  Neston CH64 . . . . . . 66 C8
  Talke ST7 . . . . 210 D8
Hunters Wlk CH1 . . . 237 A2
Hunting Lodge Mews
  CW8 . . . . 102 A4
HUNTINGTON 142 A5
Huntington Prim Sch
  CH3 . . . . 142 A5
Huntley St WA5 . . . . . 15 C4
Huntly Chase SK9 . . . 60 C7
Hunt Rd WA11 . . . . 1 E6
Huntsbank Bsns Pk CW2 205 E2
Huntsbank Dr ST5 . . . 210 D1
Hunts Cl CH3 . . . . . . 119 B1
Hunts Field Cl WA13 . . 18 D2
Hunts La WA4 . . . . . . 16 F2
Huntsman Dr M44 . . . 11 F7
HURDSFIELD 87 E2
Hurdsfield Cl CW10 . . 151 C7
Hurdsfield Com Prim Sch
  SK10 . . . . 87 F2
Hurdsfield Grn SK10 . . 87 E3
Hurdsfield Ind Est SK10 87 E3
Hurdsfield Rd SK10 . . 87 F1
Hurford Ave CH65 . . . 69 F3
Hurlbote Cl SK9 . . . . . 34 D5
Hurleston Bldgs CW5 . . 204 E6
Hurlestone Cl CH2 . . . 96 F1
Hurley Cl WA5 . . . . . . 15 C5
Hurn Cl CW1 . . . . 190 B8
HURST 179 F3
Hurst Ave SK8 . . . . . . 35 C6
Hurst Cl
  Bunbury CW6 . . . . . . 185 E8
  Talke ST7 . . . . 210 D8
Hurst Ct CW6 . . . . . . 185 F8
Hurstfield Inf Sch SK8 . . 35 C6
Hursthead Jun Sch SK8 . . 35 C7
Hursthead Rd SK8 . . . 35 B7
Hurst La
  Bollington SK10 . . . . 88 A8
  Glazebury WA3 . . . . . 5 C7
Hurst Lea Ct SK9 . . . . 60 A2
Hurst Lea Rd SK22 . . . 29 C7
Hurst Mews WA6 . . . . 75 C2
Hurst Mill La WA3 . . . . 5 C8
Hurst Rd ST8 . . . . 179 F4
Hurst St WA8 . . . . 23 A4
Hurst The WA6 . . . . . . 75 C2
Hurstwood CH3 . . . . . 143 A4
Hush Ho CH1 . . . . 237 A2
Huskisson Way WA12 . . 2 B4
Hutchins' Cl CW10 . . . 151 C6
Hutchinson St WA8 . . 22 F6
Huttfield Rd L24 . . . . . 21 A1
Hutton Cl WA3 . . . . 4 E5
Hutton Dr CW12 . . . . 157 A2
HUXLEY 167 A8
Huxley CE Prim Sch CH3 167 A7
Huxley Cl
  Bramhall SK7 . . . . . . 35 E7
  Macclesfield SK10 . . 87 B2
Huxley Ct CH66 . . . . . 69 F8
Huxley Dr SK7 . . . . . . 35 E7
Huxley La CW6 . . . . . 168 B6
Huxley St CW1 . . . . . 103 C7
Hyacinth Cl WA11 . . . . 1 F6
Hyde Bank Ct SK22 . . 39 D3
Hyde Bank Mill SK22 . . 39 C8
Hyde Bank Rd SK22 . . 39 C8
Hyde Cl
  Ellesmere Port CH65 . . 69 C4
  Runcorn WA7 . . . . . . 49 D6
Hydrangea Way WA9 . . 6 A7
Hylton Ct CH65 . . . . . 70 E2
Hylton Dr SK8 . . . . . . 35 C8
Hythe Ave CW1 . . . . . 190 B8

I

Ian Rd ST7 . . . . 195 D3
Iberis Gdns WA9 . . . . 6 A7
Ibis Ct WA1 . . . . 16 A3
Ikey La CW5 . . . . 202 F6
Ikins Dr ST7 . . . . 209 F2
Ilex Ave WA2 . . . . 8 B7
Ilford Way WA16 . . . . 58 A4
ILLIDGE GREEN 154 C4
Imperial Ave CH1 . . . 117 C4
Imperial Ct CW5 . . . . 204 F5
Imperial Mews
  Crewe CW2 . . . . . . 190 D3
  Ellesmere Port CH65 . . 70 B6
INCE 71 F6
Ince Ave CH62 . . . . . 43 E3
Ince Dr CH3 . . . . 180 F1
Ince & Elton Sta CH2 . . 72 B4

Ince La
Elton CH2 . . . . 72 B3
Wimbolds Trafford CH2 . . . 96 F5
Ince Orchards CH2 . . . . . 72 B4
Indigo Rd CH65 . . . . 70 F6
Ingersley Ct SK10 . . . . . 88 B8
Ingersley Rd SK10 . . . . . 88 C8
Ingersley Vale SK10 . . . . 88 B8
Ingham Ave WA12 . . . . . 2 C1
Ingham Cl CH3 . . . . 119 A1
Ingham Rd WA8 . . . . 12 F4
Inglegreen CH60 . . . . . . 41 B8
Inglenook Rd WA5 . . . . . 14 F4
Ingleton Cl
  Holmes Chapel CW4 . . . 130 A3
  Newton-le-Willows WA12 . 2 B4
Ingleton Gr WA7 . . . . . . 49 D5
Inglewood Ave CW10 . . . 151 D5
Inglewood Cl
  Partington M31 . . . . . 11 F4
  Warrington WA3 . . . . . 10 B6
Inman Ave WA9 . . . . 1 B2
Inner Gosling Cl WA4 . . . 25 F1
Innisfree Cl CH66 . . . . . 69 C5
Innovation Ho CW7 . . . . 149 A7
Insall Rd WA2 . . . . 8 F2
Intack La WA16 . . . . . . 28 B3
Intake Cl CH64 . . . . 68 A8
International Appr M90 . . 33 C7
Inveresk Rd SY14 . . . . . 198 C3
Inward Way CH65 . . . . . . 70 B7
Iona Cres WA8 . . . . 12 F6
Ion Path CW7 . . . . 127 C1
Irby Cl CH66 . . . . 69 E4
Ireland Blackburne Ho
  WA1 . . . . 16 E7
Ireland Rd
  Hale L24 . . . . 21 E1
  Haydock WA11 . . . . . . 1 C6
Ireland St
  Warrington WA2 . . . . . 16 B8
  Widnes WA8 . . . . 13 D2
Iris Cl WA8 . . . . 12 C2
Iris Wlk ⁊ M31 . . . . . . 11 E2
Irlam & Cadishead Com High
  Sch M44 . . . . 11 F7
Irlam Ind Est M44 . . . . . 11 E7
Irlam Sta M44 . . . . 11 E7
Ironbridge Dr CW4 . . . . 130 C2
Irons La CH3 . . . . 120 F7
Irvin Dr M22, SK8 . . . . . 34 A8
Irving's Cres CH4 . . . . . 140 E6
Irwell La WA7 . . . . 23 B3
Irwell Rd WA4 . . . . 16 B2
Irwell Rise SK10 . . . . . 87 F7
Irwell St WA8 . . . . 23 A4
Irwin Dr SK9 . . . . 34 C5
Isabella Cl CH4 . . . . . . 140 E6
Isherwood Cl WA2 . . . . . 8 F3
Isis Cl CW12 . . . . 156 F1
Islay Cl CH65 . . . . 70 C1
Islington Gn WA8 . . . . . 13 D4
ISYCOED 196 C1
Ivatt Dr CW2 . . . . 190 E1
Iveagh Cl WA7 . . . . 50 A7
Iver Cl
  Chester CH2 . . . . . . 118 E2
  Cronton WA8 . . . . . . 12 C6
Iver Rd CH2 . . . . 118 E2
Ivy Ave WA12 . . . . 2 C1
Ivy Bank Prim Sch SK11 . . 112 A5
Ivychurch Mews WA7 . . . 23 D2
Ivy Cotts SY13 . . . . . . 225 A8
Ivy Ct CW4 . . . . 162 D2
Ivy Dr CW8 . . . . 102 A2
Ivy Farm Ct L24 . . . . . . 21 D1
Ivy Farm Dr CH64 . . . . . 66 F6
Ivy Farm Gdns WA5 . . . . 4 D4
Ivy Farm La CH3 . . . . . 183 C1
Ivy Gdns CW12 . . . . . . 156 C2
Ivy Ho
  Macclesfield SK11 . . . 112 A7
  Nether Alderley SK9 . . 84 C7
Ivy House Rd ST8 . . . . . 179 C2
Ivy La
  Alsager ST7 . . . . . . 193 E2
  Macclesfield SK11 . . . 112 A6
Ivy Meade Cl ⁊⁰ SK11 . . . 111 F7
Ivy Meade Rd SK11 . . . . 111 F6
Ivy Mews CH2 . . . . 119 A5
Ivy Rd
  Golborne WA3 . . . . . . 3 B8
  Macclesfield SK11 . . . 112 A7
  Poynton SK12 . . . . . . 36 E3
  Warrington WA1 . . . . . 17 E7
Ivy St WA7 . . . . 23 A1
Ivy Wlk M31 . . . . 11 D3

J

Jackie Stewart Bsns Ctr
  CW6 . . . . 147 D6
Jack La
  Moulton CW9, CW10 . . . 127 A7
  Weston CW2 . . . . 207 D6
Jackson Ave
  Culcheth WA3 . . . . . . 4 E3
  Nantwich CW5 . . . . . . 204 F5
  Warrington WA1 . . . . . 16 F6
Jackson Ct CH5 . . . . . . 139 B7
Jackson Rd CW12 . . . . . . 18 C3
Jackson's Brickworks Nature
  Reserve* SK12 . . . 37 D6
Jacksons Cl SK10 . . . . . 88 A8
Jacksons Edge Rd SK12 . . 38 B6
Jackson's La SK7 . . . . . 36 C8

Jackson St
  Burtonwood WA5 . . . . . 6 E6
  Haydock WA11 . . . . . . 1 A7
  Macclesfield SK11 . . . 112 D6
Jacobs Way WA16 . . . . . 79 F7
Jamage Ind Est ST7 . . . 210 D5
Jamage Rd ST7 . . . . . . 210 D5
James Atkinson Way
  CW1 . . . . 189 F7
James Ave CH66 . . . . . . 69 C3
James Cl WA8 . . . . 23 A4
James Hall St CW5 . . . . 204 E6
James Pl CH2 . . . . 118 F2
James Rd WA11 . . . . 1 F7
James St
  Chester CH1 . . . . . . 237 B3
  Macclesfield SK11 . . . 112 D6
  Northwich CW9 . . . . . 104 C8
  ⁊ Warrington WA1 . . . 16 B5
Jamieson Cl
  Alsager ST7 . . . . . . 193 E4
  Chester CH3 . . . . . . 119 A2
Jane Maddock Homes
  ST7 . . . . 193 B3
Jan Palach Ave CW5 . . . 204 F4
Japonica Gdns WA9 . . . . 6 A7
Jarman SK11 . . . . 112 F4
Jasmine Cres ST7 . . . . . 195 D2
Jasmine Gdns WA9 . . . . . 6 A7
Jasmine Gr WA8 . . . . . . 22 D8
Jasmine Wlk M31 . . . . . 11 F2
Jasmin Way ST7 . . . . . . 195 F2
Jay Cl WA3 . . . . 10 A4
Jays Cl WA7 . . . . 50 E7
Jedburgh Ave CH66 . . . . 69 A6
Jefferson Dr WA5 . . . . . 15 B7
Jefferson Gdns WA8 . . . . 12 F3
Jellicoe Ave WA4 . . . . . 11 L6
Jennet's La WA3 . . . . . . 5 C8
Jenny La SK7 . . . . 35 E4
Jensen Ct WA7 . . . . 23 C3
Jersey Ave CH65 . . . . . . 70 C1
Jersey Cl CW12 . . . . . . 157 A2
Jersey Way CW10 . . . . . 128 D2
Jervis Cl WA2 . . . . 9 A3
Jesmond Cres CW2 . . . . . 190 B2
Jesmond Gr SK8 . . . . . . 35 B8
Jesmond Rd CH1 . . . . . . 118 B2
Jessop Ho WA7 . . . . 22 E3
Jessop Way CW1 . . . . . . 191 C4
JH Godwin Prim Sch
  CH1 . . . . 117 D4
Jockey St WA2 . . . . 16 B7
JODRELL BANK 108 D2
Jodrell Bank (Granada)
  Arboretum* SK11 . . 108 D3
Jodrell Bank Obsy & Visitor
  Ctr* CW4 . . . . . 108 C3
Jodrell Cl
  Holmes Chapel CW4 . . . 130 A3
  Macclesfield SK11 . . . 112 C7
Jodrell Dr WA4 . . . . . . 27 A7
Jodrell Mdw SK23 . . . . . 65 D8
Jodrell Rd SK23 . . . . . . 65 D8
Jodrell St
  Macclesfield SK11 . . . 112 C7
  New Mills SK22 . . . . . 39 B7
John Bradshaw Ct CW12 . . 156 C4
John Brunner Cres CW9 . . 103 E6
John Ford Way CW11 . . . 154 B1
John Fryer Ave CW9 . . . . 80 A5
John Gresty Dr CW5 . . . . 205 D6
John Lloyd Ct M44 . . . . . 11 F8
John May Ct SK10 . . . . . 87 B2
John Middleton Cl L24 . . 21 E2
John Nicholas Cres CH65 . 70 C6
John Rd WA13 . . . . 18 C3
Johns Ave
  Haydock WA11 . . . . . . 1 E7
  Runcorn WA7 . . . . . . 48 F8
Johns Cl SK10 . . . . 88 D5
Johnson Ave WA12 . . . . . 2 B5
Johnson Cl CW12 . . . . . . 157 B1
Johnsons Cl CH4 . . . . . . 141 B5
Johnson's La WA8 . . . . . 13 E1
Johnson St SK23 . . . . . . 65 E8
John St
  Bollington SK10 . . . . 88 B8
  Congleton CW12 . . . . . 156 C2
  Crewe CW1 . . . . 190 C5
  Ellesmere Port CH65 . . 70 B6
  Golborne WA3 . . . . . . 3 A8
  Irlam M44 . . . . 11 E5
  Macclesfield SK11 . . . 112 D6
  ⁊ Northwich CW9 . . . . 104 A8
  Utkinton CW6 . . . . . . 146 B7
  Warrington WA3 . . . . . 9 C4
  Winsford CW7 . . . . . . 126 C1
Jonathan's Way CH1 . . . . 117 E5
Jones's La CW10 . . . . . . 152 D6
Jonson Rd CH64 . . . . . . 66 E8
Jordangate SK10 . . . . . . 112 D8
Joseph Cres ST7 . . . . . . 193 F2
Joseph Groome Twrs ⁊
  CH65 . . . . 70 C6
Joseph St WA8 . . . . 13 C2
Joyce Ave CW7 . . . . 126 C2
Joy La WA5 . . . . 6 E4
Jubilee Almshouses
  CW5 . . . . 204 E6
Jubilee Ave
  Crewe CW2 . . . . 190 B3
  Warrington, Padgate WA1 . 16 F8
  Warrington WA5 . . . . . 14 E4
Jubilee Cres WA11 . . . . . 1 A7
Jubilee Ct
  ⁊ Handforth SK9 . . . . 34 E5
  Holmes Chapel CW4 . . . 130 A3

Jubilee Gdns
  Nantwich CW5 . . . . . . 204 E4
  New Mills SK22 . . . . . 39 C7
Jubilee Gn CH65 . . . . . . 70 C4
Jubilee Gr WA13 . . . . . . 18 C4
Jubilee Rd CW12 . . . . . . 156 E2
Jubilee St SK22 . . . . . . 39 C7
Jubilee Terr CW5 . . . . . 204 E4
Jubilee Villa CW11 . . . . 175 C2
Jubilee Way
  Widnes WA8 . . . . 12 E1
  ⁊ Winsford CW7 . . . . 126 D1
Jubits La WA8 . . . . 13 A8
Juddfield St WA11 . . . . . 1 A7
Judy La SK11 . . . . 113 A3
Julian Way WA8 . . . . . . 12 F4
July Bglws CW4 . . . . . . 141 E2
Jumper La SK10 . . . . . . 88 F7
Junction Eight Bsns Ctr
  CH65 . . . . 70 A7
Junction Ho CW1 . . . . . . 190 A5
Junction La WA12 . . . . . 2 B3
June Ave CH62 . . . . 43 E8
Juniper Cl ST5 . . . . . . 210 C1
Juniper Ct CH2 . . . . . . 119 B4
Juniper Dr CH66 . . . . . . 69 E1
Juniper Gr CH66 . . . . . . 69 F1
Juniper La WA3 . . . . . . 18 A7
Juniper Rise SK10 . . . . . 86 E1
Jupiter Dr CH1 . . . . . . 117 E2
Jurby Ct WA2 . . . . 8 F1
Justice St SK10 . . . . . . 87 D1

K

Kaleyards CH1 . . . . 237 B2
Kansas Pl WA5 . . . . 15 B7
Karen Cl WA5 . . . . 7 A6
Karen Way CH66 . . . . . . 69 D3
Kaye Ave WA3 . . . . 3 A8
Kay La WA13 . . . . 29 B8
Keats Cl
  Ellesmere Port CH66 . . 94 E8
  Widnes WA8 . . . . 22 F8
Keats Dr
  Macclesfield SK10 . . . 86 F1
  Rode Heath ST7 . . . . . 193 E8
  Wistaston CW2 . . . . . 206 A8
Keats Gr WA2 . . . . 8 F5
Keats La CW9 . . . . 80 A5
Keats Terr CH1 . . . . . . 118 A5
Keble St WA8 . . . . 23 B7
KECKWICK 25 A3
Keckwick La WA4 . . . . . . 25 A3
Keele Cres SK11 . . . . . . 112 B6
Keel Hey CH64 . . . . 43 B1
Keepers Cl
  Knutsford WA16 . . . . . 57 D3
Keepers La WA9 . . . . . . 53 D4
Keeper's La CW8 . . . . . . 102 E8
Keeper's Rd WA4 . . . . . . 27 A7
Keepers Wlk WA7 . . . . . . 27 A7
Keith Ave WA5 . . . . 14 E6
Keith Dr CH63 . . . . 43 D5
Kelburn Ct WA3 . . . . . . 9 F6
Kelmscott Cl CH66 . . . . . 69 D2
KELSALL 122 C4
Kelsall Ave CH62 . . . . . 43 F3
Kelsall Cl
  Bebington CH63 . . . . . 43 E3
  Warrington WA3 . . . . . 9 C3
  Widnes WA8 . . . . 12 D1
Kelsall Com Prim Sch
  CW6 . . . . 122 C4
Kelsall Rd CH3 . . . . . . 121 C4
Kelsall St CW12 . . . . . . 156 E3
Kelsall Way
  Audley ST7 . . . . 209 D1
  ⁊ Handforth SK9 . . . . 34 D5
Kelsborrow Cl CW9 . . . . . 103 E3
Kelsborrow Way CW6 . . . . 122 D4
Kelso Way SK10 . . . . . . 87 C4
Kelstern Cl ⁊ CW9 . . . . 104 B8
KELSTERTON 91 B2
Kelsterton Ct CH5 . . . . . 91 C1
Kelsterton La CH6 . . . . . 91 C1
Kelsterton Rd
  Connah's Quay CH5, CH6 . 91 C2
  Kelsterton CH6 . . . . . 91 A3
Kelvin Cl WA3 . . . . 9 D6
Kelvin Gr CH2 . . . . 118 E4
Kelvin St WA3 . . . . 9 F5
Kemberton Dr WA8 . . . . . 13 A5
Kemble Cl CW2 . . . . 206 B8
Kemmel Ave WA4 . . . . . . 16 C3
Kempsell Way L26 . . . . . 21 A7
Kempsell Wlk L26 . . . . . 21 A7
Kempton Ave CW1 . . . . . . 190 C7
Kempton Cl
  Chester CH1 . . . . . . 118 B2
  Newton-le-Willows WA12 . 2 D5
  Runcorn WA7 . . . . . . 49 C6
Kempton Way SK10 . . . . . 87 C4
Kendal Ave WA2 . . . . . . 8 C2
Kendal Cl
  Chester CH4 . . . . . . 119 A6
  Ellesmere Port CH66 . . 69 D2
  Macclesfield SK11 . . . 111 F6
Kendal Ct CW12 . . . . . . 156 A2
Kendal Dr
  Bramhall SK7 . . . . . . 35 C5
  Ellesmere Port CH66 . . 69 E2
Kendal Rd
  Macclesfield SK11 . . . 111 F6
  Widnes WA8 . . . . 12 C1
Kendal Rise WA7 . . . . . . 49 D5

Kendal Way CW2 . . . . . . 207 C1
Kendrick Cl CW8 . . . . . . 77 C7
Kendrick St WA1 . . . . . . 16 A5
Kenilworth Ave
  Handforth SK9 . . . . . 34 D3
  Knutsford WA16 . . . . . 57 C2
  Runcorn WA7 . . . . . . 49 B8
Kenilworth Cl
  Macclesfield SK11 . . . 111 F6
  Wistaston CW2 . . . . . 206 A7
Kenilworth Ct CH65 . . . . 70 E2
Kenilworth Dr
  Hazel Grove SK7 . . . . 36 D8
  Warrington WA1 . . . . . 16 F8
Kenilworth Gdns WA12 . . . 2 C1
Kenilworth Gr CH66 . . . . 69 C3
Kenilworth Ho ⁊ CH1 . . . 237 C3
Kenilworth Rd
  Golborne WA3 . . . . . . 3 E7
  Macclesfield SK11 . . . 111 F6
  Neston CH64 . . . . . . 66 E5
Kenley Ave WA8 . . . . . . 12 D5
Kenmare Bank CW9 . . . . . 104 A5
Kenmore Gr WA4 . . . . . . 11 D6
Kennedy Ave SK10 . . . . . 86 F2
Kennedy Cl CH2 . . . . . . 119 A5
Kennedy Ct ⁊ WA5 . . . . . 15 B7
Kennel La
  Cuddington CW8 . . . . . 102 A1
  Little Budworth CW8 . . 124 E7
Kennels Gn CW7 . . . . . . 79 E4
Kennelwood Rd CW9 . . . . 78 C7
Kennerley's Ct SK9 . . . . 60 A7
Kennerley's La SK9 . . . . 60 A7
Kennet Cl SK9 . . . . 34 D2
Kennet Dr CW2 . . . . 156 F1
Kenneth Rd WA8 . . . . . . 22 C8
Kennet Rd WA11 . . . . 1 C6
Kennet Way ⁊⁰ SK11 . . . . 111 F8
Kennington Pk WA8 . . . . . 12 E4
Kenrick Cl CW3 . . . . . . 232 C1
Kensington Ave WA4 . . . . 17 C2
Kensington Cl
  Chester CH4 . . . . . . 141 A6
  Widnes WA8 . . . . 13 D4
Kensington Ct
  Alsager ST7 . . . . . . 192 F3
  ⁊ Nantwich CW5 . . . . 204 E6
  Wilmslow SK9 . . . . . . 60 A6
  Winsford CW7 . . . . . . 149 C7
Kensington Dr
  Congleton CW12 . . . . . 156 F4
  Willaston CW5 . . . . . 205 D4
Kensington Gn CH4 . . . . . 140 A6
Kensington Rd
  Chester CH4 . . . . . . 141 A6
  Ellesmere Port CH65 . . 70 A5
Kensington Sq ⁊ SK10 . . . 111 F8
Kensington Way CW9 . . . . 103 E3
Kent Ave SK10 . . . . 87 E6
Kent Cl CH63 . . . . 43 B8
Kent Dr CW12 . . . . 156 A2
Kent Gdns CH2 . . . . 118 F5
Kent Gr WA7 . . . . 23 B1
Kent Ho ST7 . . . . 210 D6
Kentmere Ave CW7 . . . . . 126 D2
Kentmere Pl WA2 . . . . . . 8 A3
Kenton Rd L26 . . . . 21 A7
Kent Rd
  Chester CH4 . . . . . . 118 F5
  Irlam M44 . . . . 11 C5
  Partington M31 . . . . . 11 E2
  Warrington WA5 . . . . . 15 C4
Kentridge Dr CH66 . . . . . 69 D3
Kent's Green La CW1,
  CW11 . . . . 191 E7
Kent's La CW1 . . . . 173 C1
Kent St
  Warrington WA4 . . . . . 16 C4
  Widnes WA8 . . . . 13 B1
Kentwell Dr SK10 . . . . . 87 C3
Kenview Cl WA8 . . . . . . 13 A6
Kenwick Cl CH66 . . . . . . 69 C3
Kenwood Ave SK7 . . . . . . 35 D5
KENYON 3 F3
Kenyon Ave WA5 . . . . . . 14 E5
Kenyon Cl WA3 . . . . 23 A6
Kenyon La
  Culcheth WA3 . . . . . . 4 A4
  Golborne, Kenyon WA3 . . 3 F3
  Golborne WA3 . . . . . . 3 F5
Kenyons Lane N WA11 . . . . 1 F8
Kenyon's Lane S WA11 . . . 1 F7
Kerfoot Bsns Pk WA2 . . . . 16 A7
Kerfoot St WA2 . . . . . . 16 A7
Keristal Ave CH4 . . . . . 142 A7
KERRIDGE 88 A6
Kerridge Cl CW10 . . . . . 151 B8
KERRIDGE-END 88 D3
Kerridge Rd SK10 . . . . . 88 C4
Kerry Croft CH66 . . . . . 69 E1
Kershaw Gr SK11 . . . . . . 112 B8
Kershaw St WA8 . . . . . . 12 D1
Kershaw Way WA12 . . . . . 2 C5
Kestrel Ave WA16 . . . . . 57 B3
Kestrel Cl
  Congleton CW12 . . . . . 156 E1
  Middlewich CW10 . . . . 151 D6
  Winsford CW7 . . . . . . 149 D5
Kestrel Dr CW1 . . . . . . 190 B8
Kestrel La WA3 . . . . . . 9 E4
Kestrel Rd
  Heswall CH60 . . . . . . 41 C7
  Northwich CW8 . . . . . 103 C7
Kestrels Way WA7 . . . . . 49 F6

Keswick Ave
  Bebington CH63 . . . . . 43 C4
  Macclesfield SK11 . . . 111 F5
  Warrington WA2 . . . . . 8 C2
Keswick Cl
  Chester CH2 . . . . . . 119 A5
  Crewe CW2 . . . . 189 E3
  Irlam M44 . . . . 11 D4
  Macclesfield SK11 . . . 111 F6
  Widnes WA8 . . . . 12 C1
  Winsford CW7 . . . . . . 126 D2
Keswick Cres WA2 . . . . . 8 C2
Keswick Ct CW12 . . . . . . 156 A2
Keswick Dr
  Bramhall SK7 . . . . . . 35 C5
  Frodsham WA6 . . . . . . 74 D8
Keswick Gdns CH63 . . . . . 43 C5
Keswick Rd SK6 . . . . . . 37 E8
Ketlan Ct CH4 . . . . 140 E7
Kettell Ave CW1 . . . . . . 190 A6
Kettle La CW3 . . . . 230 C2
KETTLESHULME 64 F4
Kettleshulme St James CE
  Prim Sch SK23 . . . 64 F4
Kettleshulme Way SK12 . . . 37 A3
Kettleshulme Wlk ⁊ SK9 . . 34 E1
Kew Gardens WA8 . . . . . . 13 D4
Keyes Cl WA3 . . . . 9 E4
Keyes Gdn WA3 . . . . 9 F4
KEY GREEN 157 E4
Keysbrook CH3 . . . . 166 C2
Kidderton Cl CW5 . . . . . 202 E7
Kidderton La CW5 . . . . . 202 F7
KIDNAL 212 E8
KIDSGROVE 195 B1
Kidsgrove Ski Ctr ST7 . . . 232 C2
Kidsgrove Sta ST7 . . . . . 194 F1
Kidston Dr CW1 . . . . . . 189 F7
Kilbuck La WA11 . . . . . . 2 A8
Kilburn Ave CH62 . . . . . 43 E6
Kilburn Cl SK8 . . . . . . 34 B7
Kildare Cl L24 . . . . . . 21 F2
Kildonan Rd WA4 . . . . . . 17 A2
Kilford Cl WA5 . . . . . . 7 E2
Killingworth La WA3 . . . . 10 B5
Kilmorey Park Ave CH2 . . . 237 A4
Kilmorey Park Rd CH2 . . . 118 F3
Kilmorey Pk CH2 . . . . . . 118 F4
Kilncroft WA7 . . . . 50 B5
Kiln Croft La SK9 . . . . . 34 E4
Kiln La CW5 . . . . 228 B8
Kilsby Dr WA8 . . . . 13 E2
Kilshaw Rd WA5 . . . . . . 6 F6
Kilsyth Cl WA2 . . . . . . 8 A3
Kimberley Dr WA4 . . . . . 16 C1
Kimberley St WA5 . . . . . 15 E5
Kimberley Terr CH2 . . . . 118 F2
Kinder Dr CW2 . . . . 189 D3
Kinderton Cl WA16 . . . . . 29 C4
Kinderton Mobile Home Pk
  CW10 . . . . 152 A7
Kinderton St CW10 . . . . . 128 D1
Kinder View SK22 . . . . . 39 C7
King Arthur's Wlk WA7 . . . 24 A1
Kingbur Pl CW3 . . . . . . 229 F4
King Charles Ct CH1 . . . . 237 A3
King Edward Bldgs ⁊
  CH3 . . . . 119 A1
King Edward Rd
  ⁊ Macclesfield SK10 . . 112 D8
King Edward St
  Macclesfield SK10 . . . 112 D8
  Northwich CW9 . . . . . 104 C8
  Warrington WA1 . . . . . 16 E7
Kingfisher Cl
  Congleton CW12 . . . . . 156 E1
  Farndon CH3 . . . . . . 180 F1
  Nantwich CW5 . . . . . . 204 E8
  Runcorn WA7 . . . . . . 49 F5
  Warrington WA3 . . . . . 9 F4
Kingfisher Ct
  Chester CH2 . . . . . . 237 A4
  Northwich CW9 . . . . . 79 C2
Kingfisher Dr ⁊ CW7 . . . 149 D6
Kingfisher Gr CW7 . . . . . 149 D5
King George Ave CW9 . . . 104 B8
King George Cres WA1 . . . 16 F7
King George Rd WA11 . . . . 2 A7
King George Way ST7 . . . . 195 F1
Kingham Cl ⁊ WA8 . . . . . 13 D1
King Ho ST7 . . . . 210 D5
King James Ct WA7 . . . . . 49 E6
Kings Pl CW5 . . . . 204 E6
King's Ave WA3 . . . . . . 3 F7
Kingsbury Cl WA4 . . . . . 16 C1
Kingsbury Dr ⁊ SK9 . . . . 34 D1
Kingsbury Rd WA8 . . . . . 13 D4
Kings Cl
  Chester CH4 . . . . . . 140 F5
  Wilmslow SK9 . . . . . . 60 A6
King's Cres CW10 . . . . . 128 C2
King's Crescent E CH3 . . . 119 A1
King's Crescent W CH3 . . . 119 A1
Kings Croft CH5 . . . . . . 91 D1
Kings Ct
  Nantwich CW5 . . . . . . 204 D5
  Runcorn WA7 . . . . . . 24 D4
King's Ct
  Chester CH1 . . . . . . 237 A3
  Middlewich CW10 . . . . 128 D2
Kingsdale Rd WA5 . . . . . 14 F7

Kingsdown Cl CW2..... 207 C1
Kings Dr
  Helsby WA6 .... 73 B3
  Wistaston CW2........ 205 E8
Kingsfield Ct CH4...... 141 C3
King's Gate CW8....... 102 A2
Kingshead Cl WA7...... 24 A2
Kings La CW6.......... 147 D4
King's La
  Allostock CW10, WA16 ... 106 C1
  Nantwich CW5......... 204 D5
Kingsland Grange WA1... 9 D1
Kingslawn Cl 4 CW9... 103 F5
Kings Lea Ho CH3...... 142 A8
KINGSLEY............ 75 C2
Kingsley Ave
  Bebington CH62........ 43 E3
  Handforth SK9........ 34 C2
Kingsley Cl
  Northwich CW8....... 103 C5
  Talke ST7........... 210 D6
Kingsley Com Prim Sch
  WA6................ 74 F2
Kingsley Cres WA7..... 23 A1
Kingsley Ct CW11...... 174 D8
Kingsley Dr
  Northwich CW9....... 104 A6
  Warrington WA4...... 26 C7
Kingsley Gdns CH3..... 142 B8
Kingsley Gn WA6....... 74 E5
Kingsley Rd
  Chester CH3.......... 142 B8
  Congleton CW12....... 157 A3
  Crowton CW8......... 76 B1
  Ellesmere Port CH65... 70 C5
  Frodsham WA6........ 74 E4
  Haslington CW1....... 191 C4
  Runcorn WA7......... 23 A1
  Talke ST7........... 210 D6
Kingsley Wlk CW7...... 126 B2
Kings Mdw
  Hough CW2........... 206 E2
  Runcorn WA7......... 50 C8
KINGSMEAD........... 103 E5
Kingsmead
  Chester CH2......... 118 C8
  Northwich CW9....... 103 F4
Kingsmead Crossroads 10
  CW9............... 103 F4
Kingsmead Ct WA3...... 9 A8
Kingsmead Prim Sch
  CW9............... 103 F4
Kingsmead Sq CW9..... 103 E4
Kings Mews CH66....... 69 C7
Kings Rd
  Connah's Quay CH5.... 91 D1
  Ellesmere Port CH66... 69 C7
  Golborne WA3......... 3 A7
  Irlam M44........... 11 E6
  Warrington WA2....... 9 A2
King's Rd SK9......... 59 E8
King's Sch The
  Chester CH4......... 141 B4
  Macclesfield SK10..... 87 C1
King St
  Audley ST7.......... 209 D1
  Chester CH1......... 237 A3
  Congleton CW12....... 156 F4
  Ellesmere Port CH65... 70 C6
  Hartford CW8........ 103 B5
  Kidsgrove ST7....... 195 A2
  Knutsford WA16...... 57 A2
  Macclesfield SK10.... 112 E8
  Middlewich CW10..... 128 B8
  Newton-le-Willows WA12.. 104 F6
  Runcorn WA7......... 23 A3
  Sandbach CW11....... 174 E8
  Talke ST7........... 210 D5
Kingston Ave
  Macclesfield SK11.... 112 F7
  Warrington WA5...... 14 E6
Kingston Cl WA7....... 23 E2
Kingston Ct
  14 Handforth SK9...... 34 E1
  Saughall CH1........ 94 B2
Kingston Pl ST8....... 179 E2
Kingston Rd SK9....... 34 D5
Kingstreet SK7........ 35 B1
King Street Trad Est
  CW10.............. 128 C2
KINGSWAY........... 23 A8
Kingsway
  Bollington SK10...... 87 E7
  Chester CH2......... 118 F5
  Crewe CW2........... 190 B2
  Frodsham WA6........ 74 B8
  Heswall CH60........ 41 C6
  Newton-le-Willows WA12.. 2 C2
  Northwich CW9....... 104 F6
  Widnes WA8.......... 13 A1
  Winsford CW7....... 126 F1
Kingsway Ho WA4...... 16 F4
Kingsway L 3 WA8..... 23 A7
Kingsway N WA1....... 16 F6
Kingsway S WA1, WA4... 16 F4
Kingsway W CH2....... 118 E4
KINGSWOOD
  Frodsham........... 74 C1
  Warrington.......... 7 B2
Kingswood
  Kidsgrove ST7....... 195 B1
  Warrington WA5...... 7 B2

Kingswood Ave
  Chorlton CW2......... 207 B3
  Saughall CH1......... 94 C1
Kingswood Cres CW10... 151 E5
Kingswood La CH1...... 94 C1
Kingswood Pk WA6..... 99 D7
Kingswood Rd WA5..... 7 A2
Kings Wood Wlk CW6... 122 D5
Kinloch Cl
  Crewe CW1.......... 190 B6
  Halewood L26........ 21 A7
Kinnerley Rd CH65..... 70 A3
Kinnersley Ave CH5.... 57 A8
Kinnersley Rd ST7..... 210 F8
Kinnersley St 1 ST7... 195 A2
Kinnerton Cl CH4...... 140 E5
KINNERTON GREEN..... 161 B7
Kinnerton Hts CH4..... 161 B7
Kinnerton La CH4...... 161 A8
Kinnerton Rd CH4...... 162 A7
Kinnington Way CH1.... 94 F7
Kinnock Pk WA5....... 6 E6
Kinross Cl WA2........ 8 F4
Kinsale Dr WA3........ 9 C4
KINSEY HEATH......... 230 B1
Kinsey Rd CH65....... 70 D1
Kinsey's La CH2....... 71 F6
Kinsey St CW12....... 156 E2
Kintore Cl
  Bebington CH63....... 43 C4
  Winsford CW7....... 127 A3
Kintore Dr WA5........ 14 D6
Kintyre Cl CH65....... 70 C1
Kipling Ave WA2....... 8 C1
Kipling Cres WA8..... 22 F8
Kipling Rd CH1........ 117 F5
Kipling Way CW1...... 190 F4
Kirby Cl CH2......... 118 D5
Kirkacre Ave WA12..... 7 C8
Kirkby Rd WA3......... 4 F3
Kirkcaldy Ave WA5..... 14 D6
Kirkfell Dr SK6....... 37 E8
Kirkham Ave WA3...... 3 E6
Kirkham Cl WA5....... 15 B4
Kirkham Rd
  Gatley SK8.......... 34 C8
  Widnes WA8.......... 13 C2
Kirkstall Cl
  Macclesfield SK10.... 87 B2
  Poynton SK12........ 36 D4
Kirkstead Rd SK8...... 35 C6
Kirkstead Way WA3.... 3 A8
Kirkstone Ave WA2.... 8 C2
Kirkstone Cres WA7... 50 A4
Kirkstone Ct CW12.... 156 A1
Kirkwall Dr WA5...... 15 A3
Kirkwood Cl CH3...... 119 A2
Kishfield La SK23..... 65 A6
Kitchener Ave M44.... 11 C4
Kitchen St CH1........ 118 B1
Kite Gr ST7......... 195 D3
Kitfield Ave CW10..... 151 D7
KITT'S MOSS.......... 35 D6
Kitt's Moss La SK7.... 35 D6
Knap The CH60........ 41 A6
Knebworth Ct CW12.... 179 B8
Knight Rd WA5......... 6 F6
Knightsbridge Ave
  1 Northwich CW9..... 103 E3
  Warrington WA4...... 17 C2
Knightsbridge Cl
  13 Handforth SK9..... 34 D1
  Widnes WA8.......... 13 D4
Knightsbridge Ct
  Chester CH4......... 237 C2
  Warrington WA1...... 16 A5
Knight's Cl SK11...... 112 E7
Knight's Grange (Sports
  Complex) CW7....... 126 B3
Knights La CW6....... 123 E1
Knights Mdw CW7...... 126 C3
Knight St SK11....... 112 E7
Knights Way CW2...... 206 B3
Knightwake Rd SK22... 39 A8
Knole Ave SK12....... 36 F4
KNOLLS GREEN........ 58 E3
Knoll St SK22........ 39 B8
Knoll The WA7........ 49 F7
KNOTBURY........... 138 F5
Knottingley Dr CH66... 69 C5
Knott's Hos WN7...... 4 B8
Knotty La CW7........ 179 F8
Knowe The CH64....... 68 A8
Knowle Cl CH66....... 94 C4
Knowle Gn SK9....... 34 C3
Knowle Pk SK9........ 34 C3
Knowles Ind Est SK23.. 39 D3
Knowles St 2 WA8.... 13 C2
Knowl Hey Rd L26..... 21 A6
Knowl La CH3......... 180 E5
Knowl The CH3........ 180 F5
Knowsley Ave WA3..... 3 B8
Knowsley Ct CH2...... 118 F4
Knowsley Expressway L35,
  WA8.............. 21 F8
Knowsley La ST7...... 194 F4
Knowsley Rd
  Chester CH2......... 118 F4
  Hazel Grove SK7...... 36 F8
  Macclesfield SK11.... 112 C5
KNUTSFORD.......... 57 A3
Knutsford District Com Hosp
  WA16............. 56 F1
Knutsford Her Ctr*
  WA16............. 57 A2
Knutsford High Sch (Lower
  Sch) WA16......... 56 E1
Knutsford High Sch (Upper
  Sch) WA16......... 56 F1

Knutsford L Ctr WA16... 56 A1
Knutsford Old Rd WA4.. 17 A2
Knutsford Rd
  Alsager ST7......... 193 F6
  Antrobus CW9........ 53 D4
  Chelford SK11....... 84 A2
  Grappenhall WA4..... 17 C1
  Great Budworth CW9... 54 A2
  Holmes Chapel CW4... 130 B5
  Mobberley WA16...... 57 E4
  Row-of-Trees SK9, WA16.. 59 D3
  Warrington WA4...... 16 D3
Knutsford Road Wlk 12
  SK11............. 112 E7
Knutsford Sta WA16.... 57 A1
Knutsford View WA15... 32 C8
Knutsford Way CH1.... 117 F2
Kronsbec Ave CH65.... 69 D6
KUS Ind Est CH5...... 139 A6
Kynaston Dr CH4...... 140 C7

L

Laburnum Ave
  Crewe CW2........... 189 F2
  2 Nantwich CW5...... 204 F5
  Warrington WA1...... 17 C7
Laburnum Cl
  Congleton CW12...... 156 A4
  Talke ST7........... 210 E8
Laburnum Cres CW8.... 78 B3
Laburnum Ct
  Lymm WA13.......... 19 B4
  Wistaston CW2....... 205 F7
Laburnum Farm Cl CH64 . 67 A5
Laburnum Gr
  Crewe CW1.......... 190 D6
  Ellesmere Port CH66... 95 A8
  Runcorn WA7......... 49 C7
  Saltney CH4......... 140 E6
  Weaverham CW8...... 108 D8
Laburnum La
  Altrincham WA15...... 31 E8
  Warrington WA5...... 14 C5
Laburnum Pl ST5...... 210 D1
Laburnum Rd
  Davenham CW9....... 103 F3
  Golborne WA3......... 3 F7
  Irlam M44.......... 11 D5
  Macclesfield SK11.... 112 E5
  Northwich CW9....... 104 C6
Laburnum Way LL13... 180 D1
Lacey Ave SK9........ 34 B1
Lacey Ct
  Handforth SK9....... 34 B1
  Widnes WA8.......... 23 B7
Lacey Gn SK9......... 34 B1
Lacey Gr SK9......... 34 B1
LACEY GREEN......... 34 B1
Lacey Green Prim Sch
  SK9.............. 34 B1
Lacey St WA8......... 23 A7
LACH DENNIS......... 105 D5
LACHE.............. 140 F5
Lache Hall Cres CH4... 140 F4
Lache La
  Chester, Westminster Park
  CH4............. 141 B5
  Roughhill CH4....... 140 E3
Lache Park Ave CH4.... 141 A6
Lache Prim Sch CH4... 141 A5
Lacy Ct CW12........ 156 D2
Ladies Mile WA16...... 56 F2
Ladies Wlk CH64...... 66 E8
Lady Acre Cl WA13..... 18 D2
Ladybarn Ave WA3..... 2 F7
Ladybarn Cres SK7.... 35 F6
Ladybarn Manor SK7... 35 E6
Ladybrook Gr 6 SK9... 34 D2
Ladybrook Prim Sch 1
  SK7............. 35 F6
Ladycroft Cl WA1...... 17 E7
Ladyfield St SK9...... 60 B7
Ladyfield Terr SK9.... 60 C7
Lady Helen Wlk CW5... 204 E6
Lady Heyes Crafts & Antiques
  Ctr* WA6......... 74 F4
Lady La
  Croft WA3........... 9 C8
  Culcheth WA3......... 4 C1
  Mobberley WA16...... 58 C6
Lady Mary's Sq WA16.. 30 E3
Ladypit Rd SK23....... 39 E4
Ladypool L24......... 21 C2
Lady Richeld Cl WA7... 24 D3
Ladys Cl SK12........ 36 E4
Ladythorn Ave SK7.... 35 F5
Ladythorn Cres SK7.... 35 F6
Ladythorn Gr SK7..... 35 F5
Ladythorn Rd SK7..... 35 F6
Ladywood Rd WA5..... 7 D1
Lagos Gr CW2........ 126 E2
Laidon Ave CW2...... 206 A7
Laira Ct WA2......... 16 C7
Laira St WA2......... 16 C7
Lake La WA4.......... 52 F5
Lakelands Cl SK10..... 112 F7
Lakemore Ctry Pk*
  CW1............. 174 C1
Lakeside
  Bosley SK11........ 158 D8
  Chester CH4......... 141 A8
  Willmslow/Alderley Edge
  SK9............. 59 C7
Lakeside Cl
  Chester CH4......... 118 F7
  Widnes WA8.......... 22 A8

Lakeside Dr
  Poynton SK12........ 36 E5
  Warrington WA1...... 16 A3
Lakeside Rd WA13..... 18 D2
Lakeside View
  Moulton CW7........ 126 F7
  Nantwich CW5....... 204 E3
Lake View
  Alsager ST7......... 193 C2
  Congleton CW12...... 156 B2
  Furness Vale SK23.... 39 D4
Lakewood CH4........ 141 B2
Laleston Cl WA8...... 22 E8
Lambert Cres CW5..... 204 C6
Lambert's La CW12.... 156 E1
Lambert Way CW8..... 103 A4
Lamb La WA14........ 31 D4
Lambourn Ave WA8.... 12 C5
Lambourn Cl SK12..... 36 D4
Lambourn Dr CW1...... 173 B1
Lambourne Cl
  4 Ellesmere Port CH66.. 94 F8
  Wythenshawe M22..... 33 D8
Lambourne Gr
  5 Middlewich CW10.... 128 C1
  St Helens WA9......... 1 A4
Lambs House Sch CW12. 156 F4
Lambsickle Cl WA7..... 48 F6
Lambsickle La WA7.... 49 A6
Lambs La WA1......... 17 A7
Lamb St ST7.......... 195 A2
Lamerton Cl WA5...... 14 D4
Lamerton Way SK9..... 34 E2
Lampeter Cl WA5...... 14 D4
Lampits La CH3....... 120 E6
Lamport Cl WA8....... 13 E3
Lanark Gdns WA8...... 12 E3
Lanark Wlk SK10...... 86 F2
Lancashire Rd M31.... 11 E2
Lancaster Ave
  Golborne WA3......... 3 C8
  Runcorn WA7......... 48 E8
  Widnes WA8.......... 12 A2
Lancaster Cl
  Hazel Grove SK7...... 36 D8
  Newton-le-Willows WA12... 1 F4
  Warrington WA2....... 8 F2
  Winsford CW7....... 149 D6
Lancaster Ct 3 WA4... 16 E1
Lancaster Dr CH3...... 119 B2
Lancaster Fields CW1.. 191 A2
Lancaster Gdns CH65... 70 D3
Lancaster Pk CH4...... 139 A3
Lancaster Rd
  Handforth SK9....... 34 E1
  Irlam M44.......... 11 D5
  Widnes WA8.......... 13 B3
Lancaster St WA5...... 15 E5
Lancelyn Ct SY14..... 213 B3
Lancelyn Dr SK9...... 60 D8
Lancer Ct WA7........ 23 E3
Lancers Croft CH66.... 69 E1
Lancing Ave WA2...... 8 A4
Lancing Rd CH65...... 70 D4
Land Cut La WA3....... 9 D3
Lander Cl WA5........ 10 F2
Land La SK9.......... 60 C6
Landor Cl WA3......... 3 E8
Landscape Dene WA6... 73 D4
Landseer Ave
  Neston CH64......... 66 F7
  Warrington WA4...... 16 B2
Landseer Dr SK10..... 111 E8
Landswood Pk CW8.... 103 B4
LANE ENDS.......... 173 D3
Lane Ends WA8........ 21 D5
LANE HEAD........... 3 E6
Lane Head Ave WA3.... 3 F8
Lanehead Rd SK23..... 65 C5
Laneside Rd SK22..... 39 E7
Lane The SY13, SY14... 223 C3
Langcliffe Cl WA3..... 4 E3
Langdale Ave WA13.... 18 F4
Langdale Cl
  High Lane SK6....... 37 E8
  Macclesfield SK11.... 111 F5
  Warrington WA2....... 8 E2
  Widnes WA8.......... 22 C8
  Winsford CW7....... 126 D2
Langdale Ct CW12..... 156 A1
Langdale Rd
  Bramhall SK7........ 35 C5
  Crewe CW2.......... 189 D2
  Partington M31...... 11 E3
  Runcorn WA7......... 23 B1
Langdale Way WA6..... 49 C1
Langden Cl WA3....... 4 A8
Langdon Ho CH4...... 141 B7
Langfield WA3......... 3 E7
Langfield Gr CH62..... 43 D5
Langford L24......... 21 C2
Langford Ct CH3...... 121 C2
Langford Rd CW9...... 80 A3
Langford St 21 SK11... 112 C8
Langford Way WA4..... 27 D4
Langland Cl WA5...... 14 F7
LANGLEY............ 113 C3
Langley Ave WA12..... 2 C1
Langley Beck WA8..... 13 C4
Langley Cl
  Newcastle-under-Lyme
  ST5............. 210 D2
  Sandbach CW11...... 175 C8
Langley Ct CH65...... 70 E3
Langley Dr
  Crewe CW2.......... 190 A2
  Handforth SK9....... 34 E3
  Macclesfield SK11.... 112 B4

Langley Hall Cl SK11... 113 B4
Langley Hall Cotts SK11. 113 B4
Langley Rd
  Langley SK11........ 113 A3
  Northwich CW9....... 104 A6
Langport Dr CH3...... 119 C2
Langton Cl
  Newton-le-Willows WA12.. 2 A4
  Widnes WA8.......... 12 B3
Langton Gn WA1....... 17 D7
Langwell Cl WA3...... 10 A5
Lanreath Cl SK10...... 86 D1
Lansbrook Ct WA7..... 23 C2
Lansdown Cl SK8...... 35 C7
Lansdowne
  Culcheth WA3......... 4 E2
  Frodsham WA6........ 74 D6
Lansdowne Gr CH4.... 141 A7
Lansdowne Rd
  Connah's Quay CH5.... 91 D1
  Crewe CW1.......... 190 F5
  Great Barrow CH3.... 120 D3
Lansdowne St SK10.... 87 E1
Lansdown Rd CH4..... 139 B4
Lanyard Way CW11.... 175 C3
Lapwing Cl
  Golborne WA3......... 3 D8
  Newton-le-Willows WA12.. 2 C3
  Packmoor ST7....... 195 E1
  Winsford CW7....... 149 C5
Lapwing Gr WA7...... 50 A6
Lapwing La
  Moore WA4.......... 25 A8
  Whisterfield SK11.... 109 C4
Lapwing Rd ST7...... 195 D3
Lapwing Rise CH60.... 40 F6
Larch Ave
  Hough CW2.......... 206 F5
  Macclesfield SK11.... 112 A5
  Newton-le-Willows WA12.. 2 C2
  Warrington WA5...... 14 E5
  Widnes WA8.......... 13 B2
Larch Cl
  Golborne WA3......... 3 F6
  Poynton SK12........ 36 F3
  Runcorn WA7......... 49 C7
  Weaverham CW8...... 102 D7
Larchdale Cl CH66.... 94 F8
Larches The WA16.... 58 E2
Larchfields CH1...... 117 A8
Larch Rd
  Crewe CW2.......... 189 E2
  Haydock WA11........ 1 E7
  Partington M31...... 11 E3
  Runcorn WA7......... 49 C7
Larch Rise SK10...... 86 D6
Larchtree Cl CW8..... 78 B4
Larchway
  Bramhall SK7........ 35 C7
  High Lane SK6....... 37 F7
Larch Way CH4....... 140 E6
Larchways WA4....... 26 D5
Larchwood Dr SK9..... 60 E8
LARDEN GREEN........ 202 D4
Lark Ave ST7......... 195 D3
Larkfield ST7........ 195 B1
Larkfield Ave WA1.... 17 A7
Lark Hall Cl SK10..... 113 A7
Lark Hall Cres SK10... 113 A8
Lark Hall Rd SK10.... 113 A7
Lark Hill Cotts SK22... 39 A8
Larkspur Cl
  Chester CH4......... 140 F4
  Nantwich CW5....... 204 E8
  Runcorn WA7......... 49 F4
Larkspur Gr WA5...... 15 E3
Larkstoke Cl WA4..... 26 E6
Larkway CH60........ 41 B8
Larkwood Way SK10... 87 E5
Larne Ct WA4......... 12 E2
Larne Dr CH4......... 139 D4
Laskey La WA4........ 17 F4
LATCHFORD.......... 17 C1
Latchford Rd CH60.... 41 B6
Latchford St James CE Sch
  WA4............. 16 B4
Latchford St WA4..... 17 A3
Latham Ave
  Helsby WA6.......... 73 B1
  Newton-le-Willows WA12.. 2 A4
  Runcorn WA7......... 23 C1
Latham Ho WA12....... 2 B4
Latham Rd CW11...... 175 A5
Latham St CW7....... 126 C1
Lathom Ave WA2...... 16 B8
Lathom Rd M44....... 11 F8
Lathom Way SK10..... 87 F2
Latimer Dr CW2...... 190 A4
Latimer Rd WA8...... 13 C4
Launceston Cl
  Runcorn WA7......... 50 C6
  Winsford CW7....... 149 B7
Launceston Dr
  Bramhall SK7........ 35 F7
  Warrington WA5...... 14 E3
Laura St CW2......... 190 D1
Laurel Ave
  Newton-le-Willows WA12.. 2 D3
  Warrington WA1...... 17 D7
Laurel Bank
  Warrington WA4...... 17 C1
  Widnes WA8.......... 13 A3
  Winsford CW7....... 149 D8
Laurel Cl
  Barnton CW8......... 78 A4
  Middlewich CW10..... 128 B2
  Sandbach CW11...... 175 C5

Laurel Dr
Crewe CW2 . . . . **189** F2
Ellesmere Port CH65 . . . . . . **70** B2
Harriseahead ST7 . . . . **195** E4
Willaston CH64 . . . . **43** B1
Laurel Gr
Chester CH2 . . . . **119** A3
Golborne WA3 . . . . **3** D8
Laurel Pk CW6 . . . . **145** A6
Laurels Farm Ct CH2 . . . . . **72** B3
Laurels The
High Lane SK6 . . . . **37** E8
Milton Green CH3 . . . . **165** C2
Laurel Way SK8 . . . . **35** C8
Laurel Wlk M31 . . . . **11** E2
Laurelwood Dr 4 CH66 . . **69** E1
Laureston Ave CW1 . . . . . **190** F4
Lavender Cl WA7 . . . . **23** C1
Lavender Dr CW9 . . . . **104** E7
Lavender Gdns
St Helens WA9 . . . . **6** A7
Warrington WA5 . . . . **15** E4
Lavender Wlk M31 . . . . **11** E2
Lavenham Cl
Hazel Grove SK7 . . . . **36** E8
Macclesfield SK10 . . . . **87** C2
LAVISTER **162** C1
Lavister Cl 6 CW9 . . . . . . **103** F4
Lavister Wlks LL12 . . . . . . **162** C1
Lawford Cl CW1 . . . . **189** F8
Lawford Dr CH60 . . . . **41** C8
Lawn Ave WA1 . . . . **16** F8
Lawn Dr CH2 . . . . **118** D7
Lawns Ave CH63 . . . . **43** B6
Lawnsdale CW8 . . . . **101** D5
Lawns The SK9 . . . . **59** E4
Lawnswood Gr CH2 . . . . . . **72** B3
Lawrence Ave
3 Middlewich CW10 . . . . **128** C1
Moulton CW9 . . . . **126** E8
Lawrence Avenue E 2
CW10 . . . . **128** C1
Lawrence Cl
Cranage CW4 . . . . **130** A5
3 Sandbach CW11 . . . . . . **174** D6
Lawrence Pl SK12 . . . . **36** D2
Lawrence St
Crewe CW1 . . . . **190** C4
Sandycroft CH5 . . . . **116** A3
Laws Gdns CH3 . . . . **142** A8
Lawson Cl WA1 . . . . **17** E7
Lawson Rd WA7 . . . . **49** A8
Law St CH2 . . . . **118** F3
Lawton Ave
Bramhall SK7 . . . . **35** E8
Lawton-gate ST7 . . . . **194** D3
Lawton Cl WA3 . . . . **4** E3
Lawton Coppice ST7 . . . . **194** E4
LAWTON-GATE **194** A4
Lawtongate Est ST7 . . . . . **194** A5
Lawton Hall ST7 . . . . **194** C4
Lawton Hall Dr ST7 . . . . . **194** C4
LAWTON HEATH **193** E6
LAWTON HEATH END **193** C6
Lawton Heath Rd ST7 . . . **193** F5
Lawton Rd ST7 . . . . **193** E4
Lawton St
Congleton CW12 . . . . **156** E2
Crewe CW2 . . . . **190** C3
Kidsgrove ST7 . . . . **195** C4
Lawton Way CW11 . . . . . . **174** E7
Laxey Ave WA1 . . . . **17** D6
Laxton Cl CH66 . . . . **94** F8
Laxton Way CW10 . . . . **128** C2
Layland Ave WA3 . . . . **4** E4
Layton Cl WA3 . . . . **9** E3
Lea Ave
Crewe CW1 . . . . **190** F4
Goostrey CW4 . . . . **107** C1
Lea Bank Cl SK11 . . . . **112** A8
Lea Cl CW11 . . . . **175** C5
Leacroft Rd WA3 . . . . **10** A7
Lea Cross Gr WA8 . . . . **12** C3
Leadbeaters Cl SK11 . . . . **112** F7
Leadbeaters Rd SK11 . . . . **112** F7
Leadgate La CH3 . . . . **144** F2
Lea Dr
Nantwich CW5 . . . . **204** C4
Wimboldsley CW10 . . . . . . **151** A4
Leadsmithy St CW10 . . . . **128** C1
Leadworks La CH1 . . . . . . **237** C3
Leaf Gr CW7 . . . . **126** B1
Leafield Dr SK8 . . . . **34** F6
Leafield Rd SK12 . . . . **38** C6
Leaf La CW7 . . . . **127** A2
Leafy Way CW8 . . . . **102** D7
LEA GREEN **172** A8
Lea Hall Barns CW5 . . . . . **220** E6
Lea Hall Pk CH1 . . . . **95** A3
Lea Homes CW5 . . . . **217** B7
Leahurst Cl CH2 . . . . **118** F4
Lea La CH3 . . . . **164** C3
Leamington Ave WA12 . . . . **2** C1
Leamington Cl
Neston CH64 . . . . **66** E6
Warrington WA5 . . . . **15** A8
Leamington Rd
Congleton CW12 . . . . **155** F3
Macclesfield SK10 . . . . **86** F1
Lear Dr CW2 . . . . **205** F8
Leas Cl 3 CH66 . . . . **69** C5
Leaside WA7 . . . . **23** D1
Leaside Rd CH1 . . . . **117** E6
Leaside Way SK9 . . . . **60** C6
Lea's Pas CW10 . . . . **128** B1
Lea St SK22 . . . . **39** A8
Leatham Cl WA3 . . . . **9** E3
Leathers La L26 . . . . **21** A7
Lea Way ST7 . . . . **193** D3
Leawood Cl CW8 . . . . **103** A6
Ledbury Dr CW2 . . . . **206** A7
Ledge Ley SK8 . . . . **34** E8
Ledger Rd WA11 . . . . **1** A5
Ledley St SK10 . . . . **87** F7
LEDSHAM **68** F2
Ledsham Cl WA3 . . . . **9** C3
Ledsham Ct CH66 . . . . **69** B6
Ledsham Hall La CH66 . . . . **68** E4
Ledsham La CH66 . . . . **68** F3
Ledsham Park Dr CH66 . . . **69** A6
Ledsham Rd CH66 . . . . **69** B6
Ledsham Village CH66 . . . **68** F2
Ledston Cl WA7 . . . . **24** D1
Ledward St CW7 . . . . **127** A1
Ledyard Cl WA5 . . . . **15** D7
Leech Rd SY14 . . . . **213** B3
Lee Cl WA16 . . . . **56** F1
Lee Ct
Runcorn WA7 . . . . **23** D2
Warrington WA2 . . . . **8** C2
Lee Dr CW8 . . . . **103** E7
Lee Green La CW5 . . . . . . **150** A1
Leek Old Rd SK11 . . . . **112** E2
Leek Rd CW12 . . . . **179** A8
Leen La CH1 . . . . **237** B2
Lee Rd WA5 . . . . **15** B6
Lees La
Ellesmere Port CH65 . . . . . . **70** E4
Mottram St Andrew SK10 . . **61** B7
Neston CH64 . . . . **67** A7
Lees Mill 4 SK22 . . . . **39** C7
Lees Rd SK7 . . . . **35** D5
Lees The WA5 . . . . **15** A8
LEFTWICH **104** B5
Leftwich Com Prim Sch
CW9 . . . . **104** A4
Leftwich Warehouse
CW9 . . . . **103** F7
Legh Cl SK12 . . . . **36** E4
Legh Ct
Golborne WA3 . . . . **3** A8
Knutsford WA16 . . . . **57** D4
Legh Gdns WA16 . . . . **57** B1
Legh Ho 2 WA16 . . . . **57** B1
Legh Rd
Adlington SK10 . . . . **62** C5
Haydock WA11 . . . . **1** B6
High Lane SK12 . . . . **38** A6
Knutsford WA16 . . . . **82** B8
Prestbury SK10 . . . . **87** A8
Legh St
Golborne WA3 . . . . **3** A8
3 Lymm WA13 . . . . **18** E3
Newton-le-Willows WA12 . . . **2** A3
Warrington WA1 . . . . **16** A5
Legh Vale Prim Sch WA11 . . **1** B6
Leicester Ave ST7 . . . . **193** D5
Leicester St
Northwich CW9 . . . . **79** A1
Warrington WA5 . . . . **15** F5
Leigh Ave
Knutsford WA16 . . . . **57** C3
Widnes WA8 . . . . **13** A1
Leigh Green Cl 4 WA8 . . . **22** C8
Leigh La CW8 . . . . **77** C5
Leigh Rd
Congleton CW12 . . . . **157** B5
Wilmslow SK9 . . . . **59** D5
Leigh's Brow CW8 . . . . **77** F3
Leigh St SK11 . . . . **112** E7
Leighstone Ct CH2 . . . . . . **237** A4
Leighton Chase CH64 . . . . **41** D1
Leighton Cotts CH64 . . . . . **41** D5
Leighton Ct CH64 . . . . **66** D8
Leighton Dr WN7 . . . . **4** B8
Leighton Hospl CW1 . . . . . **172** E1
Leighton Obsy★ WA8 . . . . . **12** E6
Leighton Pk CH64 . . . . **66** D8
Leighton Prim Sch CW1 . **189** F8
Leighton Rd CH64 . . . . **41** D2
Leighton St 11 CW1 . . . . . **190** B5
Leightons The CH64 . . . . . . **66** D8
Leighton View CW1 . . . . . **190** A8
Leigh Way CW8 . . . . **77** C1
Leinster Gdns WA7 . . . . **22** F3
Leinster St WA7 . . . . **22** F3
Leira Way WA7 . . . . **23** A2
Leiria Way WA7 . . . . **23** B2
Lenham Wlk M22 . . . . **33** D8
Lenthall Ave CW12 . . . . . . **178** F8
Leonard St
Chester CH1 . . . . **118** B3
Runcorn WA7 . . . . **48** D7
Warrington, Stockton Heath
WA4 . . . . **16** C1
Warrington WA2 . . . . **16** C7
Leon Cl WA5 . . . . **14** D7
Leslie Rd CW7 . . . . **149** A7
Lessingham Rd WA8 . . . . . **12** F3
Lester Cl ST7 . . . . **193** D4
Leven Ave CW7 . . . . **126** F2
Levens Cl WA5 . . . . **15** F6
Levens Way 1 WA8 . . . . **22** C8
Leven Wlk CH66 . . . . **70** A7
Leveret Rd L24 . . . . **21** A3
Levisham Gdns WA5 . . . . . **15** E7
Lewin St CW10 . . . . **128** C1
Lewis Ave WA5 . . . . **7** F2
Lewis Cl
Ellesmere Port CH65 . . . . . . **95** C8
Nantwich CW5 . . . . **205** A5
Lewis Cres WA8 . . . . **23** A7
Lewis Gr WA8 . . . . **12** D1
Lewis St CW1 . . . . **190** C3
Lexden St WA5 . . . . **15** E6
Lexington Wlk 2 WA5 . . . **15** C7
Leycester Cl WA16 . . . . **82** C8
Leycester Dr WA16 . . . . **57** F7
Leycester Rd WA16 . . . . . . **82** B8
Leyfield Ct CH4 . . . . **140** F5
Leyland Dr CH4 . . . . **140** C6
Leyland Gr
Haslington CW1 . . . . **191** C4
Haydock WA11 . . . . **1** B6
Leyland Wlk CW7 . . . . **149** C6
Leyton Cl WA7 . . . . **49** B6
Liberty Cl WA5 . . . . **15** C7
Libris Ho 1 WA16 . . . . **57** A1
Libris Pk 2 WA16 . . . . **57** A1
Libris Pl 3 WA16 . . . . **57** A1
Libson Cl WA2 . . . . **9** A3
Lichfield Ave
Golborne WA3 . . . . **3** D8
Grappenhall Heys WA4 . . . . **27** A7
Lichfield Cl WA16 . . . . **57** D2
Lichfield Ct CW7 . . . . **149** D7
Lichfield Dr CH66 . . . . **94** E8
Lichfield Rd
Blacon CH1 . . . . **117** F5
Talke ST7 . . . . **210** D7
Lichfield St CW10 . . . . **128** D2
Lidgetts La SK10 . . . . **88** C3
Lift La CW9 . . . . **78** D3
Light Alders La SK12 . . . . . **38** A6
Lightburn St 6 WA7 . . . . . **22** F1
Lightfoot Cl CH60 . . . . **41** B7
Lightfoot La
Eaton CW6 . . . . **147** A4
Heswall CH60 . . . . **41** B7
Lightfoot St CH2 . . . . **118** F2
Lighthouse Rd L24 . . . . **47** E7
Lightley Cl CW11 . . . . **175** A4
Lightley Ct CW11 . . . . **175** A4
Light Oaks Rd WA3 . . . . **5** C6
LIGHTWOOD GREEN **229** B3
Lightwood Green Ave
CW3 . . . . **229** A2
Lightwood Rd ST5 . . . . **210** D1
Lilac Ave
Knutsford WA16 . . . . **56** E1
Warrington WA5 . . . . **15** A5
Widnes WA8 . . . . **13** B2
Lilac Cl
Kelsall CW6 . . . . **122** E2
Newcastle-under-Lyme
ST5 . . . . **210** D1
Lilac Cres WA7 . . . . **49** C8
Lilac Ct CW12 . . . . **156** E2
Lilac Dr CW8 . . . . **103** D6
Lilac Gr
Ellesmere Port CH66 . . . . . . **95** A8
Warrington WA4 . . . . **16** E1
Lilac Wlk M31 . . . . **11** E3
Lilford Ave WA5 . . . . **15** F8
Lilford Dr WA5 . . . . **14** F6
Lilford Sq SK11 . . . . **112** D5
Lilford St WA5 . . . . **15** F7
Lillyfield CH60 . . . . **40** F6
Lilybrook Dr WA16 . . . . **57** B1
Lily La CW10 . . . . **129** B6
Limbrick Rd ST7 . . . . **209** A1
Lime Ave
Frodsham WA6 . . . . **74** C8
Northwich CW9 . . . . **103** F5
Weaverham CW8 . . . . **102** D8
3 Widnes WA8 . . . . **13** B2
Lime Cl
Hollinfare WA3 . . . . **11** A2
Middlewich CW10 . . . . **128** B2
Sandbach CW11 . . . . **175** A7
Tarporley CW6 . . . . **146** D2
Lime Ct
Leftwich CW9 . . . . **104** A5
Northwich CW9 . . . . **103** F5
Limefield Ave WA13 . . . . . . **18** F2
Lime Gr
Alsager ST7 . . . . **193** E2
Chester CH2 . . . . **119** A3
Elton CH2 . . . . **72** A3
Golborne WA3 . . . . **3** E6
Macclesfield SK10 . . . . **112** E8
Runcorn WA7 . . . . **49** C8
Saltney CH4 . . . . **140** D6
Shavington CW2 . . . . **206** C4
Winsford CW7 . . . . **127** A1
Limehurst Gr CH62 . . . . **43** D6
Limekiln La WA5 . . . . **6** E3
Lime Kiln La ST7 . . . . **194** E2
Limekiln Row WA7 . . . . **50** A8
Limerick Cl WA8 . . . . **12** E3
Limes Cl CW1 . . . . **191** C4
Limes La WA4 . . . . **52** D6
Lime St
Congleton CW12 . . . . **156** D2
Crewe CW1 . . . . **190** C6
Ellesmere Port CH65 . . . . . . **70** C7
Limes The
Culcheth WA3 . . . . **4** D4
Golborne WA3 . . . . **3** D6
Middlewich CW10 . . . . **128** B1
Limetree Ave
Warrington, Stockton Heath
WA4 . . . . **16** E1
Warrington WA1 . . . . **17** A8
Lime Tree Ave
Congleton CW12 . . . . **156** B3
Crewe CW1 . . . . **190** E6
Lime Tree Cl
Ellesmere Port CH66 . . . . . . **95** A8
Winsford CW7 . . . . **149** C8
Lime Tree Dr CH3 . . . . **180** F1
Lime Tree Gr CH60 . . . . **41** C8
Lime Tree La WA16 . . . . **29** D6
Limeways WA4 . . . . **26** E5
Lime Wlk
6 Handforth SK9 . . . . **34** D1
Partington M31 . . . . **11** D3
Lime Wood Cl CH2 . . . . **118** F4
Limewood Cres CW8 . . . . . **78** B4
Limewood Gr CW8 . . . . **78** B4
Linacre La WA8 . . . . **12** E5
Lincoln Ave
Gatley SK8 . . . . **34** B7
Irlam M44 . . . . **11** C4
Lincoln Cl
Golborne WN7 . . . . **4** C8
Macclesfield SK10 . . . . **86** F2
Rainow SK10 . . . . **88** E5
Runcorn WA7 . . . . **49** C6
Warrington WA1 . . . . **17** E6
Lincoln Ct
Helsby WA6 . . . . **73** B3
5 Warrington WA5 . . . . **15** B7
Lincoln Dr CH2 . . . . **119** A5
Lincoln Ho 12 CH1 . . . . . . **237** C3
Lincoln Pl SK10 . . . . **86** F2
Lincoln Rd
Blacon CH1 . . . . **117** F5
Ellesmere Port CH66 . . . . . . **69** D3
Handforth SK9 . . . . **34** E1
Kidsgrove ST7 . . . . **194** F2
Lincoln Sq WA8 . . . . **13** B2
Lincoln St 3 CW1 . . . . **190** B5
Lincoln Wlk SK10 . . . . **86** F2
Lincombe Hey SK10 . . . . . . **87** C8
Lincombe Rd M22 . . . . **33** D8
Lindale Cl CW12 . . . . **157** A5
Linden Cl
Congleton CW12 . . . . **179** A8
Ellesmere Port CH66 . . . . . . **94** F8
Lymm WA13 . . . . **19** A4
Warrington WA1 . . . . **17** D7
Linden Ct
Macclesfield SK10 . . . . **87** B2
Sandbach CW11 . . . . **174** F3
Widnes WA8 . . . . **12** F4
Linden Dr
Biddulph ST8 . . . . **179** C1
Crewe CW1 . . . . **190** F4
Helsby WA6 . . . . **73** B1
Mickle Trafford CH2 . . . . **96** F1
Linden Gr
Biddulph ST8 . . . . **179** C1
Bramhall SK7 . . . . **35** D4
Chester CH2 . . . . **119** A4
Saltney CH4 . . . . **140** D6
Linden Way
High Lane SK6 . . . . **38** A7
Widnes WA8 . . . . **12** F4
Lindfield Cl WA4 . . . . **25** A5
Lindfield Estate N SK9 . . . **60** A6
Lindfield Estate S SK9 . . . **59** F6
Lindfields CH4 . . . . **140** F6
Lindi Ave WA4 . . . . **17** C2
Lindisfarne Ave
Ellesmere Port CH65 . . . . . . **70** C2
Golborne WA3 . . . . **4** C8
Lindisfarne Cl CW10 . . . . **128** B1
Lindisfarne Ct WA8 . . . . . . **12** F6
Lindisfarne Dr SK12 . . . . . . **36** D4
Lindley Ave WA4 . . . . **16** F4
Lindop Cl WA16 . . . . **57** C2
Lindow Comm Nature
Reserve★ SK9 . . . . **59** E7
Lindow Court Pk WA16 . . . **59** B5
Lindow Ct SK9 . . . . **59** E8
LINDOW END **59** B2
Lindow Fold Dr SK9 . . . . . . **59** D5
Lindow La SK9 . . . . **59** E6
Lindow Par SK9 . . . . **59** F6
Lindow Prim Sch SK9 . . . . **59** D3
Lindrick Cl SK10 . . . . **87** C4
Lindrum Ave SK11 . . . . **112** D2
Lindsay Way ST7 . . . . **193** A4
Lindsay Wlk CW8 . . . . **102** A4
Lindsworth Cl WA5 . . . . **15** C6
Linear View WA12 . . . . **2** C1
Linenhall Pl CH1 . . . . **237** A2
Lines Rd M44 . . . . **11** F8
Lingdale Wlk SK11 . . . . . . **112** D5
Lingfield Cl SK10 . . . . **87** C4
Lingfield Dr CW1 . . . . **190** C7
Lingfield Ho WA7 . . . . **48** E8
Lingfield Rd WA7 . . . . **22** E1
LINGLEY GREEN **14** C7
Lingley Green Ave WA5 . . **14** D8
Lingley Mere Bsns Pk
WA5 . . . . **14** D8
Lingley Rd WA5 . . . . **14** D6
Linglongs Ave SK23 . . . . . . **65** C5
Linglongs Rd SK23 . . . . **65** C5
Lingmell Gdns CW4 . . . . . **129** F3
Lingwell Ave WA8 . . . . **12** D2
Lingwell Pk WA8 . . . . **12** E2
Lingwood Rd WA5 . . . . **14** F6
Links Ave CH66 . . . . **69** C7
Links Cl CH63 . . . . **43** B6
Linkside Ave WA2 . . . . **8** B6
Linkside Way CH66 . . . . **94** F8
Links Rd SK9 . . . . **59** E4
Links View CH66 . . . . **69** C7
Linksway
Chester CH2 . . . . **118** C7
Congleton CW12 . . . . **178** E8
Linksway Cl CW12 . . . . . . **178** F8
Link The SK9 . . . . **34** D3
Linkway WA7 . . . . **49** C8
Link Wlk M31 . . . . **11** D2
Linley Gr ST7 . . . . **193** F3
Linley La ST7 . . . . **194** A2
Linley Rd
Alsager ST7 . . . . **193** F2
Linley Rd *continued*
Cheadle SK8 . . . . **35** B8
Talke ST7 . . . . **210** C8
Linley Trad Est ST7 . . . . . . **194** C1
Linmere Visitor Ctr★
CW8 . . . . **100** B2
Linnards La CW9, WA16 . . . **80** B5
Linnet Cl
Newton-le-Willows WA12 . . . **2** C3
Warrington WA2 . . . . **8** D3
Winsford CW7 . . . . **150** B8
Linnet Gr
Macclesfield SK10 . . . . **87** A1
Warrington WA3 . . . . **9** E4
Linnets Pk WA7 . . . . **23** C3
Linnets Way CH60 . . . . **40** E8
Linnett Cl CW1 . . . . **190** A7
Linnett Gr ST7 . . . . **195** E1
Linton Ct CW7 . . . . **127** A3
Linum Gdns WA9 . . . . **6** B7
Linwood CW7 . . . . **150** B8
Linwood Cl WA7 . . . . **50** C5
Lion Salt Works★ CW9 . . . **79** C3
Lion St CW12 . . . . **156** D2
Liskeard Cl WA7 . . . . **50** B6
Liskeard Dr SK7 . . . . **35** F7
Lismore Wlk M22 . . . . **33** E8
Lister Cl CW10 . . . . **151** D6
Lister Rd WA7 . . . . **23** C3
Little Abbey Gateway
CH1 . . . . **237** A3
Little Aston Cl SK10 . . . . . . **87** C4
Little Back La CW11 . . . . . **176** E6
Little Birches CH65 . . . . **70** A6
LITTLE BOLLINGTON **20** B2
Little Bollington CE Prim Sch
WA14 . . . . **20** B2
Littlebourne WA7 . . . . **50** E7
LITTLE BUDWORTH **147** F8
Little Budworth Ctry Pk★
CW6 . . . . **147** C8
Littlecote Gdns WA4 . . . . . **26** D4
Littledale Rd WA5 . . . . **14** F7
Littledales La CW8 . . . . . . **102** E4
Little Delph WA11 . . . . **1** C7
Littlegate WA7 . . . . **49** E8
Little Gn CH66 . . . . **69** D3
LITTLE HEATH **230** A5
Little Heath Cl CW3 . . . . . **230** A5
Little Heath La WA14 . . . . . **20** D5
Little Heath Rd
Chester CH3 . . . . **119** E1
Christleton CH3 . . . . **142** E8
Little La CH64 . . . . **41** C1
Little Lakes CW2 . . . . **207** D2
LITTLE LEIGH **77** C4
Little Leigh Prim Sch
CW8 . . . . **77** D5
Little Meadow Cl SK10 . . . **87** B7
Little Mere CH3 . . . . **142** E8
Little Moreton Hall★
CW12 . . . . **177** E2
LITTLE-MOSS **194** E6
Little Moss Cl ST7 . . . . **194** E5
Little Moss La ST7 . . . . **194** E5
LITTLE NESTON **66** D6
LITTLER **126** A2
Little Rake La CH2 . . . . **95** D5
Littler Grange Ct CW7 . . . **126** A1
Littler La CW7 . . . . **125** F1
Little Roodee CH5 . . . . **139** B7
Little Row 5 ST7 . . . . **195** B2
Littler Rd WA11 . . . . **1** A5
Little St John St CH1 . . . . **237** B2
Little St
Congleton CW12 . . . . **156** D2
4 Macclesfield SK10 . . . . **112** D8
LITTLE STANNEY **70** E1
Little Stanney La CH2 . . . . **95** F8
Littlestone Cl WA8 . . . . **13** A4
LITTLE SUTTON **69** B5
Little Sutton CE Prim Sch
CH66 . . . . **69** A6
Little Sutton Sta CH66 . . . . **69** C6
LITTLETON **119** E1
Littleton Cl
1 Northwich CW9 . . . . **103** F4
Warrington WA5 . . . . **15** D4
Littleton La CH3 . . . . **119** E2
LITTLE TOWN **4** C1
Little Wissage CH66 . . . . . . **69** F2
Littondale Cl CW12 . . . . . . **157** A5
Liverpool Pl WA8 . . . . **12** C1
Liverpool Rd
Backford CH1, CH2 . . . . **95** B4
Chester CH2 . . . . **118** C6
Haydock, Stanley Bank WA11 **1** A7
Haydock WA11 . . . . **1** B8
Irlam, Cadishead M44 . . . . . **11** D4
Kidsgrove ST7 . . . . **195** A1
Neston CH64 . . . . **41** F1
Newcastle-under-Lyme
ST5 . . . . **210** D2
Warrington, Great Sankey
WA5 . . . . **14** E6
Warrington, Penketh WA5 . . **15** B4
Warrington WA5, WA1 . . . . . **15** F5
Widnes WA8 . . . . **12** C1
Liverpool Road E ST7 . . . **194** E2
Liverpool Road W ST7 . . . **194** B4
Liverpool Row WA12 . . . . . . **7** D8
Liverpool St CW9 . . . . **104** C8
Livingstone Cl
Macclesfield SK10 . . . . **111** F8
Warrington WA5 . . . . **15** D7

Livingstone Rd CH65. . . . . . 70 C2
Livingstone Way CW10 .151 D6
Liz Kaye Ho SK11. . . . . . .112 E7
Llandaff Cl CH66. . . . . . . 69 E1
Llandovery Cl CW7. . . . .149 B7
Lloyd Cl CH3. . . . . 180 E2
Lloyd Cres WA12. . . . . . . .1 F3
Lloyd Dr CH65 . . . . 70 D1
Lloyd Pl CH1. . . . . 117 E4
Llyndir La LL12 . . . . 162 B1
Llys Bernsdale/Bernsdale Ct
  CH5. . . . . 116 A3
Llys Cadnant/Cadnant Ct
  CH4. . . . . 139 D5
Llys Caer CH4. . . . . 139 A3
Llys Catrin/Catherine Ct
  CH5. . . . . 139 B6
Llys Derwen CH4. . . . . . 161 A8
Llys Maes Y Ffynnon/
  Springfield Ct CW4 . . . 161 A8
Llys Perenna/Perenna Ct
  CH6. . . . . 91 B2
Llys Rhuddlan/Rhuddlan Ct
  5 CH4. . . . . 140 F6
Llys Sant Iago/St James Ct
  CH5. . . . . 91 D1
Llys Y Faenol CH5. . . . . .139 B7
Lochbrook Ave CW12 . . .156 A2
Lobelia Gr WA7. . . . . . . .49 F4
Lobelia Wlk 6 M31. . . . . .11 E2
Lochinvar Ave CH66. . . . .68 F6
Lochleven Rd CW2. . . . . 206 A3
Lochmaben Cl CW4 . . . .130 B2
Loch St
  4 Runcorn WA7. . . . . .23 A2
  10 Runcorn WA7. . . . . .23 A3
Locke Ho CW1. . . . . . . 190 B4
Locker Ave WA2. . . . . . . .8 B2
Lockerbie Cl
  Holmes Chapel CW4 . .130 C2
  Warrington WA2. . . . . .8 E3
Lockett Rd WA8. . . . . . . 13 B3
Lockett St WA4. . . . . . . .16 F3
Lockgate E WA7. . . . . . .24 C2
Lockgate W WA7. . . . . . .24 C2
LOCKING STUMPS. 9 C3
Locking Stumps La WA3 . .9 B4
Locking Stumps Prim Sch
  WA3. . . . . .9 C3
Lockitt St CW2. . . . . . . .190 D3
Lock La M31. . . . . .11 E3
Lock Rd
  Bebington CH62. . . . . 44 A8
  Warrington WA1. . . . . 16 F6
Locks The
  Grappenhall WA4. . . . .17 B3
  Middlewich CW10. . . .151 D8
Lockton La WA5. . . . . . . 15 E7
Lockwood View WA7. . . .50 F5
Lodge Brow SK10. . . . . . 63 A1
Lodgebury Ct SY14. . . . .211 C2
Lodge Cl WA13. . . . . . . .19 B4
Lodge Dr
  Culcheth WA3. . . . . . . .4 F3
  Moulton CW9. . . . . . .126 F7
  Winsford CW7. . . . . . .127 A1
Lodgefields Dr CW2. . . . 189 E4
Lodge Gdns CH2. . . . . . 118 D6
Lodge Hollow WA6. . . . . 73 B4
Lodge La
  Antrobus CW9. . . . . . .54 A6
  Dutton WA4. . . . . 76 C8
  Hartford CW8. . . . . . .103 B4
  Hatherton CW5. . . . . 220 A4
  Haydock WA11, WA12, WN4 .2 B8
  Lostock Gralam CW9 . . .80 A2
  Runcorn WA7. . . . . . . 49 F8
  Saughall WA7. . . . . . . 94 A2
  Warrington WA5. . . . . 15 F7
  Widnes WA8. . . . . . . 12 B4
Lodge Lane Inte WA7 . . .49 E7
Lodge Rd
  Alsager ST7. . . . . 193 C4
  Knutsford WA16. . . . . 57 C3
  Sandbach CW11. . . . . 174 E5
  Talke ST7. . . . . .210 D6
  Widnes WA8. . . . . . . 22 B8
Lodmore La SY13. . . . . . 233 C6
Lofthouse Gate WA8 . . . 12 F4
Lomas Sq SK11. . . . . . . .112 D5
Lomax Rd CW5. . . . . . . 205 D6
Lomond Gr CH66. . . . . . 69 F3
London Rd
  Adlington SK10. . . . . . 62 C5
  Alderley Edge SK9. . . . 60 A1
  Allostock WA16. . . . . 106 F3
  Bridgemere CW5, CW3 . .232 A5
  Davenham CW9. . . . . 104 A1
  Frodsham WA6. . . . . . 74 C7
  Hatherton CW5. . . . . 220 D4
  Holmes Chapel CW4 . .130 C2
  Macclesfield SK11. . . . 112 D3
  Nantwich CW5. . . . . . 204 F5
  Northwich CW9. . . . . 103 F7
  Northwich, Leftwich CW9 .104 A5
  Sandbach CW11. . . . .174 D8
  Stapeley CW5. . . . . . 205 B3
  Woore CW3. . . . . . . 232 C1
London Road N SK12. . . 36 E5
London Road S SK12. . . 36 D3
London Road Terr SK11 .112 D5
London Row WA12. . . . . .7 D8
Loney St SK11. . . . . .112 C7

Long Acre
  Cuddington CW8. . . . .101 D4
  Weaverham CW8. . . . .77 C1
Longacres Rd WA15. . . .32 D7
Long Acres Rd CH64. . . 41 E2
Longacre St SK10. . . . . 112 C8
LONGBARN. 9 B1
Longbarn Bvd WA2. . . . .9 C2
Longbarn Cty Prim Sch
  WA2. . . . . .9 B1
Long Barn La
  Warrington WA1. . . . . .9 B2
  Warrington, Woolston WA1 .17 D8
Longbenton Way WA7. . .28 B4
Longburgh Cl CH2. . . . .118 F3
Longbutt La WA13. . . . . 19 A2
Longbutts La SK11. . . . .111 E2
Longclough Rd ST5. . . . 210 D2
Long Croft La SK8. . . . . 34 E8
Longcross Ct CW10. . . . 128 C1
Longdale Dr CH1. . . . . . 117 C5
Longden Cl SK7. . . . . . . 35 E5
Longden La SK11. . . . . . 113 A6
Longden St SK10. . . . . . 112 E8
Longdin St WA4. . . . . . . 16 F3
Longdown Rd CW12. . . .155 F4
Longfield Ave
  Chester CH2. . . . . . . 118 E7
  Gatley SK8. . . . . 34 C7
Longfield Gdns WA2. . . .8 C1
Longfield Rd WA2. . . . . .8 C1
LONGFORD. 8 B1
Longford Dr WA8. . . . . . 12 E2
Longford St
  4 Crewe CW2. . . . . . .190 D2
  Warrington WA2. . . . . 16 B7
LONG GREEN. 97 F1
LONGHILL. 230 E5
Long Hill SK23. . . . . 65 F2
Longhill La CW3. . . . . . 230 E5
Longhorn Cl CW10. . . . 128 C3
Long La
  Alpraham CW6. . . . . .169 E4
  Bickerton SY14. . . . . 199 F4
  Bollington SK10. . . . . 63 B2
  Burland CW5. . . . . . .203 A8
  Chester CH2. . . . . . . 118 F7
  Hargrave CH3. . . . . . .143 D2
  Harriseahead ST7 . . . 195 E4
  Haughton CH3. . . . . .186 D4
  Huxley CH3. . . . . 166 C8
  Middlewich CW10. . . .151 C7
  Saughall CH1. . . . . . . 94 B2
  Swan Green WA16. . . .107 D7
  Swettenham CW12. . . .131 F5
  Tilston SY14. . . . . . . 198 B3
  Warrington WA2. . . . . .8 B1
  Wettenhall CW6, CW7 . .170 C6
Longlands Dr SK22. . . . 39 B8
Longlands Rd SK22. . . . 39 B8
Long Lane S CW10. . . . .151 D7
Longley Ave CW6. . . . . 122 D6
Longley La CW6. . . . . . .99 D1
Long Looms CH3. . . . . .120 D6
Longlooms Rd CH65 . . . 70 D1
Longley St WA5. . . . . . . .7 F1
Long Shoot CW4. . . . . .130 D8
Long Shoot Rd SK11. . . 108 E1
Longsides Rd WA15. . . . 32 C7
Longsight La SK8. . . . . .34 F6
Long Spinney WA7. . . . .50 D8
Longster Cl WA6. . . . . . 73 B2
Longstone La CW6. . . . 124 E3
Longton Ave WA3. . . . . .3 C7
Long Valley Rd ST8. . . .179 C2
Longview Ave ST7. . . . .193 E4
Long Wlk M31. . . . . 11 D3
Longsdon Ct SK11. . . . .210 C1
Longshaw St WA5. . . . . .7 F1
Longwood Rd WA4. . . . 26 E5
Lonsdale Cl
  Warrington WA5. . . . . 14 F8
  3 Widnes WA8. . . . . .22 C8
Lonsdale Ct CH4. . . . . . 140 F4
Lon Y Cryddion/Cobbler's La
  LL12. . . . . 116 F7
Lon yr Orsaf/Station App
  CH1. . . . . .116 F7
Lon yr Ywen/Yew Tree Ave
  CH1. . . . . .116 F7
Looe Cl WA8. . . . . 12 E2
Looms The CH64. . . . . . 41 B2
Loont The CW7. . . . . . . 149 C2
Lord Nelson St WA1. . . 16 C5
Lordship La WA6. . . . . . 73 B7
Lordshire Pl ST7. . . . . . 195 F2
Lords La WA3. . . . . .9 C4
Lords Mill Rd CW2. . . . 206 B4
Lord's St M44. . . . . 11 C1
Lord St
  Bollington SK10. . . . . 88 B8
  Chester CH3. . . . . . . 118 F2

Lord St continued
  Crewe CW2. . . . . 190 D3
  Croft WA3. . . . . .9 A8
  Macclesfield SK11. . . . 112 D6
  Newton-le-Willows WA12 .2 A3
  Runcorn WA7. . . . . . . 22 F3
  Warrington WA4. . . . . 16 B4
Lorne St CH1. . . . . .237 A3
Lorraine St ST7. . . . . . . 195 F1
Lostock Ave
  Poynton SK12. . . . . . .36 B4
  Warrington WA5. . . . . 15 F8
Lostock Cl 2 CW9. . . . . 103 E5
Lostock Gn CW9. . . . . . 80 A3
LOSTOCK GRALAM. 80 A3
Lostock Gralam CE Prim Sch
  CW9. . . . . 80 A2
Lostock Gralam Sta CW9 .80 A2
LOSTOCK GREEN. 105 B8
Lostock Hall Prim Sch
  SK12. . . . . 36 B3
Lostock Rd Hd SK12. . . .36 B3
Lostock Hollow CW9. . . 80 A2
Lostock Rd SK12. . . . . . 36 D2
Lostock St WA4. . . . . . . 34 D4
Lotus Gdns WA9. . . . . . 6 A7
Louise St CH1. . . . . 237 A3
Loushers La WA4. . . . . . 16 D2
Lovage Cl WA2. . . . . . . .9 C1
Lovat Dr WA16. . . . . . . 82 B7
Lovatt Ct WA13. . . . . . . 19 B4
Lovatts The ST7. . . . . . .195 A1
Love La
  Hassall Green CW11 . . .176 C3
  Nantwich CW5. . . . . . 204 E5
Love Lane SY14. . . . . . 213 A4
Lovell Ct CW4. . . . . 130 C3
Lovel Terr WA8. . . . . . . 22 B5
Lovely La WA5. . . . . 15 F6
Love St CH1. . . . . .237 B2
Lowcross La SY14. . . . . 198 D3
Lowe Ave
  Congleton CW12. . . . .156 E2
  Warrington WA4. . . . . 16 F4
Lowe Cres CW9. . . . . . .53 C4
Lowe Dr WA16. . . . . . . 57 B2
Lower Appleton Rd WA8 .13 C1
Lower Ash Rd ST7. . . . .194 E1
Lower Bank St 10 SK11 . .112 E7
Lower Beech Cotts SK10 .87 D2
Lower Bridge St CH1. . . 237 B1
Lower Brook St CH5. . . . 91 D1
LOWER BUNBURY. 185 F8
LOWER CARDEN. 198 C6
Lower Church St WA8. . . 23 A5
Lower Cl C 26. . . . . 21 A8
Lower Darwin St CW9. . 103 E6
Lower Exchange St 13
  SK11. . . . . 112 E7
Lower Farm Mews CW6 .147 B3
Lowerfield Rd SK10. . . . 87 E1
Lower Field Rd CH4. . . . 141 A5
Lower Fold Cott SK6. . . 37 D7
Lower Greenshall La SK12 .38 F6
Lower Hague SK22. . . . .38 E6
Lower Haigh St 3 CW7 .149 C8
Lower Hall La WA6. . . . 182 D2
Lower Hall Mews CH1. . 182 C2
Lower Hall Rd SY13. . . . 215 D4
LOWER HEATH. 156 E2
Lower Heath WA12. . . . 156 D4
Lower Heath Ave CW12 .156 E4
Lower Heath Terr CW12 .156 E4
Lower High St ST7. . . . .195 D7
LOWERHOUSE. 87 E8
LOWER HOUSE. 22 E8
Lowerhouse SK10. . . . . 87 E8
Lower House La WA8. . . 22 F8
LOWER KINNERTON. . . 139 D1
Lower La
  Aldford CH3. . . . . . . 164 A2
  Churton CH3. . . . . . . 181 A7
  Eaton CW6. . . . . 147 A3
Lowerlea SK12. . . . . . . 38 A8
Lower Macclesfield Rd
  SK23. . . . . 65 E6
Lower Meadow Dr CW12 .156 C3
Lower Meadow WA9. . . .34 E4
Lower Mersey St CH65 .70 C7
Lower Park Cres SK12. . .36 C6
Lower Park Prim Sch
  SK12. . . . . 36 C4
Lower Park Rd
  Chester CH4. . . . . . . 237 C2
  Poynton SK12. . . . . . .36 B5
Lower Park St CW12. . . 156 E3
LOWER PEOVER. 82 E1
Lower Peover CE VA Prim
  Sch WA16. . . . . 81 E1
Lower Rake La WA6. . . . 73 B4
Lower Rd L26, WA8. . . . 21 C7
Lower Robin Hood La
  WA6. . . . . 73 B3
Lower Rock St 2 SK22 .39 C7
Lower Sandy La CH3. . . 199 C7
LOWER STRETTON. . . . 52 F8
LOWER THREAPWOOD .222 E6
LOWER WALTON. 26 A8
Lower Wash La WA4. . . 16 E3
LOWER WHITLEY. 52 D3
LOWER WITHINGTON .132 A8
LOWER WYCH. 224 B6
Lowe St CW1. . . . . .111 F2
Lowe St
  Golborne WA3. . . . . . .3 A8
  Macclesfield SK11. . . . 112 D7
Loweswater Cl WA2. . . . 8 B3
Loweswater Cres WA11 .1 A6

Lowfield Gdns WA3. . . . .5 C7
Lowfields Ave WA4. . . . 23 E3
Lowfields Cl CH62. . . . . 43 E3
Low Hill WA6. . . . . .97 D5
Lowlands Rd 6 WA7. . . .22 F2
Lowland Way WA16. . . . 82 A8
Low LEIGHTON. 39 D8
Low Leighton Rd SK22 .39 D8
Low Mdw SK23. . . . . . .65 D8
Lownorth Rd M22. . . . . 33 E8
Lowry Cl WA5. . . . . 15 D6
Low St ST7. . . . . .193 E8
Lowther Ave WA3. . . . . 4 F4
Lowther St SK10. . . . . . 88 C8
LOWTON. 3 E8
Lowton Bsns Pk WA3. . . 4 A7
LOWTON COMMON. 4 A8
Lowton Gdns WA3. . . . .3 B5
LOWTON HEATH. 3 C6
Lowton High Sch WA3. . 4 A8
Lowton Jun & Inf Sch WA3 .4 A7
Lowton Rd WA3. . . . . . .3 B8
LOWTON ST MARY'S . . .3 F8
Lowton St Mary's CE Prim
  Sch WA3. . . . . 4 A8
Lowton West Prim Sch
  WA3. . . . . 3 D8
Loxdale Dr CH65. . . . . . 69 F4
Loxley Cl
  Macclesfield SK11. . . . 112 B7
  Warrington WA5. . . . . 15 A8
Loyola Hey L35. . . . . . . 12 E8
Lucerne Cl CH3. . . . . . .142 B6
Ludford Cl ST5. . . . . . . 210 D2
Ludford Cl CW1. . . . . . 190 C5
Ludlow Ave CW1. . . . . .190 F3
Ludlow Cl
  Macclesfield SK10. . . . 87 E2
  Warrington, Paddington
  WA1. . . . . 17 B8
Ludlow Cres WA7. . . . . 49 B8
Ludlow Dr CH65. . . . . . 70 E3
Ludlow Rd CH1. . . . . . .118 A5
Ludwell Cl CH4. . . . . . .141 B6
LUGSDALE. 23 C7
Lugsdale Rd WA8. . . . . 23 B7
Lulworth Cl CW7. . . . . .149 B7
Lumb Brook Mews 5
  WA4. . . . . 16 E1
Lumb Brook Rd
  Appleton Thorn WA4 . .27 A5
  Warrington WA4. . . . . 26 F8
Lumley Cl SK7. . . . . . . .35 C6
Lumber La WA5. . . . . . .6 F8
Lumb La WA5. . . . . 6 F8
Lumley Pl CH1. . . . . . . 237 B2
Lumley Rd
  Chester CH2. . . . . . . 118 C4
  Macclesfield SK11. . . . 111 F7
Lumley Wlk L24. . . . . . 21 E1
Lumpy St CW12. . . . . . .156 C3
Lundy Dr CH65. . . . . . . 95 C8
Lune Cl 1 CW12. . . . . . 157 A1
Lunehurst 8 WA3. . . . . .3 E8
Lune Way WA8. . . . . . . 12 C1
Lunt Ave CW2. . . . . . . .190 C2
LUNTS HEATH. 13 A5
Lunts Heath Prim Sch
  WA8. . . . . 13 B5
Lunt's Heath Rd WA8. . . 13 B5
Lunts Moss ST7. . . . . . 194 C6
Luntswood Gr WA12. . . 2 A4
Lupin Dr
  Haydock WA11. . . . . . 1 F6
  Huntington CH3. . . . .142 B6
Lupus Way CH66. . . . . . 69 F3
Luscombe Cl L26. . . . . 21 A8
Luther Gr WA9. . . . . . . .1 E2
Luton St WA8. . . . . 23 A7
Lutyens Cl SK10. . . . . . 111 F8
Lyceum Cl CW1. . . . . . 190 A8
Lyceum Theatre* 1
  CW1. . . . . 190 D4
Lyceum Way CW1. . . . .190 A8
Lychgate WA4. . . . . . . .25 F7
Lycroft Cl WA7. . . . . . . 49 B6
Lydbury Cl WA5. . . . . . .7 D2
Lydden Rd CH65. . . . . . 70 B7
Lydgate Cl CW2. . . . . . 205 F8
Lydiate La
  Runcorn WA7. . . . . . . 48 D7
  Willaston CH64. . . . . 42 E1
Lydiate The
  Heswall CH60. . . . . . .40 F7
  Willaston CH64. . . . . 42 D1
Lydiat La SK9. . . . . 60 A1
Lydney Ave SK8. . . . . . .34 C7
Lydstep Cl WA5. . . . . . . .7 E2
Lydyett La CW8. . . . . . .78 B3
Lymcote Dr CW8. . . . . .103 A4
Lyme Ave
  Handforth SK9. . . . . . 34 B1
  Macclesfield SK11. . . . 112 D5
Lyme Com Prim Sch WA12 .1 F4
Lyme Gr WA13. . . . . . . 112 D2
LYME GREEN. 112 D2
Lyme Green Bsns Pk
  SK11. . . . . 112 C3
Lyme Green Settlement
  SK11. . . . . 112 D2
Lyme Lea Cl SK8. . . . . . 35 B8
Lyme Park* SK12. . . . . 38 B2
Lyme Park Ctry Pk* SK12 .38 B2
Lyme Rd
  High Lane SK12. . . . . .38 A6
  Poynton SK12. . . . . . .37 C3

Lyme St
  Haydock WA11. . . . . . 1 E6
  Newton-le-Willows WA12 .1 F4
  13 Warrington WA1. . . 16 B5
Lyme View SK11. . . . . . 112 D2
Lymewood Dr
  Disley SK12. . . . . . . .38 C6
  Wilmslow SK9. . . . . . 60 E8
LYMM. 18 E4
Lymm Brook 1 WA13. . 18 E3
Lymm Hall WA13. . . . . 18 E3
Lymmhay La WA13. . . . 18 E4
Lymm High Sch WA13. . 19 B3
Lymmington Ave WA13 .18 E3
Lymm Rd
  Little Bollington WA14 . .20 B1
  Warrington WA4. . . . . 17 F3
Lynalls Cl CW12. . . . . . 155 F3
Lynbrook Rd CW1. . . . .190 F4
Lyncastle Rd WA4. . . . . 27 D4
Lyncastle Way WA4. . . . 27 D4
Lyncombe Cl SK8. . . . . 35 B6
Lyncroft Cl CW1. . . . . . 190 F3
Lyndale 2 WA7. . . . . . . 49 C8
Lyndale Ave
  Bebington CH62. . . . . 43 E4
  Warrington, Fearnhead WA2 .8 F2
  Warrington WA3. . . . . 16 D8
Lyndale Ct CW7. . . . . . 127 A3
Lyndale Sch The CH62. . 43 E4
Lyndale Way WA5. . . . . 59 D5
Lyndon Gr WA7. . . . . . 49 B8
Lyneal Ave CH66. . . . . . 69 C3
Lyngard Cl SK9. . . . . . . 34 E1
Lynham Ave WA5. . . . . 15 B5
Lynmar St ST7. . . . . . . 210 C8
Lynn Cl WA7. . . . . .49 C7
Lynndene CH66. . . . . . . 69 D7
Lynn St SK11. . . . . 112 C6
Lynside Wlk M22. . . . . 33 E8
Lynthorpe Ave M44. . . 11 D6
Lynton Ave M44. . . . . . 11 E6
Lynton Cl
  Chester CH4. . . . . . . 140 F6
  Heswall CH60. . . . . . .41 B6
  Knutsford WA16. . . . . 57 C1
  Warrington WA5. . . . . 14 E4
Lynton Cres WA8. . . . . 12 E2
Lynton Dr SK6. . . . . . . .37 E8
Lynton Gdns WA4. . . . . 26 D4
Lynton Gr CW1. . . . . . 191 D5
Lynton La SK9. . . . . . . 60 A2
Lynton Mews SK9. . . . . 60 A2
Lynton Park Rd SK8. . . .34 F8
Lynton Pl
  Alsager ST7. . . . . 193 D4
  Broughton CH4. . . . . 139 B4
Lynton Way CW2. . . . . 206 A8
Lynwood
  Altrincham WA15. . . . 32 B8
  Wilmslow SK9. . . . . . 60 A6
Lynwood Ave
  Golborne WA3. . . . . . .3 E6
  Warrington WA4. . . . . 26 C7
Lynwood Rd CH1. . . . . 117 F5
Lyon Ct WA4. . . . . 16 F3
Lyon's La WA4. . . . . . . 26 E6
Lyons Rd WA5. . . . . . . 15 A4
Lyon St
  Chester CH1. . . . . . . 237 B3
  Crewe CW1. . . . . 190 D4
  Warrington WA4. . . . . 16 F3
Lysander Com High Sch
  WA2. . . . . .8 F2
Lysander Dr WA2. . . . . 8 E2
Lyster Cl WA3. . . . . . . .9 F3
Lytham Cl WA5. . . . . . . 15 B3
Lytham Dr
  Bramhall SK7. . . . . . . 36 A7
  Winsford CW7. . . . . . 126 C2
Lytham Rd WA4. . . . . . 13 C2
Lytherton Ave M44. . . 11 D4
Lythgoes La WA2. . . . . 16 B6

M

Mableden Cl SK8. . . . . . 34 D8
Mablins La CW1. . . . . . 190 B8
Mablins Lane Com Prim Sch
  CW1. . . . . 190 B8
Macbeth Ho ST7. . . . . .210 C8
McCarthy Cl WA3. . . . . 10 A3
McClellan Pl WA8. . . . . 13 E1
MACCLESFIELD. 112 B4
Macclesfield Coll of FE
  SK11. . . . . 112 B6
Macclesfield District General
  Hospl SK10. . . . . 112 B8
MACCLESFIELD
  FOREST. 114 D5
Macclesfield Forest Walks*
  SK11. . . . . 114 A3
Macclesfield High Sch
  SK11. . . . . 112 B6
Macclesfield L Ctr SK10 .86 C2
Macclesfield Rd
  Alderley Edge SK9. . . . 85 D7
  Congleton CW12. . . . .156 F6
  Eaton CW12. . . . . . . .134 B2
  Hazel Grove SK7. . . . . 36 E4
  Holmes Chapel CW4 . .130 E4
  Kettleshulme SK23, SK10 .64 D3
  Prestbury SK10. . . . . 86 F4
  Rainow SK10. . . . . . . 89 B7
  Wilmslow SK9. . . . . . 60 E6
Macclesfield Sta SK11 .112 D8

Macdermott Rd WA8 . . . . . 22 F5
MacDonald Rd M44 . . . . . . 11 E8
McEllin Cl ST7 . . . . 209 E2
McGarva Way CH65 . . . . . . 70 C4
McGowan Ho ST7 . . . . . . 210 D8
McKeagney Gdns WA8 . . . 22 C7
McKee Ave WA2 . . . . 8 B2
McKinley St WA5 . . . . 15 A7
McKinley Way WA8 . . . . . . 12 F3
McLaren St CW1 . . . . 190 C7
McMinnis Ave WA9 . . . . . . 1 B2
McNeill Ave CW1 . . . . 190 A5
Macon Cl CW1 . . . . 190 E3
Macon Ind Pk CW1 . . . . . 190 E3
Macon Way CW1 . . . . 190 E3
Maddocks Cl CH3 . . . . . . 180 E2
Maddocks Hill WA6 . . . . . 100 F5
Maddock St ST7 . . . . 209 D1
Madeley Cl
  Altrincham WA14 . . . . . . 31 E8
  Broughton CH4 . . . . 139 C4
Madeley St CW2 . . . . 190 C1
Madeline McKenna Ct
  WA8 . . . . 12 C3
Madison Cl WA9 . . . . 1 A2
Madron Ave SK10 . . . . . . 86 D1
Madtor Cl CH63 . . . . 43 C6
Maes-y-Coed CH4 . . . . . 140 E6
Magdala Pl CW9 . . . . 104 C8
Magdalen Cl CW2 . . . . . . 190 A1
Magecroft CW1 . . . . 173 B1
Maggoty La SK11 . . . . . . 111 D1
Mag La WA13, WA16 . . . . 28 F6
Magnolia Cl
  [6] Ellesmere Port CH66 . . 69 F1
  [5] Partington M31 . . . . . 11 E2
  Warrington WA1 . . . . 17 E7
Magnolia Dr WA7 . . . . . . 49 F4
Magnolia Rise SK10 . . . . . 86 E6
Magpie Cres [9] ST7 . . . . 195 B2
Maiden Est CW2 . . . . 228 C8
Maiden Gdns CH65 . . . . . 70 D3
Maidenhills CW10 . . . . . . 128 D1
Maidstone Cl SK10 . . . . . . 87 B2
Maidwell Cl CW7 . . . . . . 127 A4
Main Cl WA11 . . . . 1 A6
Main Dr WA14 . . . . 20 E3
Main La WA3 . . . . 3 F3
Main Rd
  Betley CW2, CW3 . . . . . 221 F8
  Broughton CH4 . . . . 139 B4
  Goostrey CW4 . . . . 107 E1
  Higher Kinnerton CH4 . . 161 A8
  Langley SK11 . . . . 113 C4
  Moulton CW9 . . . . 126 F8
  Norton in Hales TF9 . . . 236 C1
  Shavington CW2 . . . . . . 206 B4
  Weston CW2 . . . . 207 B4
  Worleston CW5 . . . . 188 F5
  Wybunbury CW5 . . . . . . 220 B8
Main St
  Frodsham WA6 . . . . 74 B8
  Great Barrow CH3 . . . . . 120 E5
  Runcorn WA7 . . . . 49 F8
Maintree Cres L24 . . . . . . 21 A4
Mainwaring Cl CW5 . . . . 205 A4
Mainwaring Dr
  Saltney CH4 . . . . 140 C2
  Wilmslow SK9 . . . . 60 D8
Mainwaring Rd
  Bebington CH62 . . . . 43 D8
  Over Peover WA16 . . . . 108 A8
Mairesfield Ave WA4 . . . . 17 B2
Maisterson Ct [7] WA1 . . 16 C6
Maitland Way [6] CH1 . . 117 D4
Maitland-Wood Cl CW9 . . 79 D1
Major Cross St [6] WA8 . . 23 A7
Makepeace Cl CH3 . . . . . 119 C3
Makerfield Dr WA12 . . . . . 2 A5
Malaga Ave M90 . . . . 33 B7
Malahide Cl WA8 . . . . 12 E2
Malam Dr CW9 . . . . 104 D6
Malbank CW5 . . . . 204 E6
Malbank Rd CW2 . . . . . . 189 E4
Malbank Sch & Sixth Form
  Coll CW5 . . . . 204 C6
Malcolm Ave WA5 . . . . . . 8 D1
Malcolm Cres CH63 . . . . . 43 C6
Malcolm St WA7 . . . . 23 B2
Malham Cl WA5 . . . . 7 E7
Malhamdale Rd CW12 . . 157 A5
Malin Cl L24 . . . . 21 D2
Maliston Rd WA5 . . . . . . 15 B5
MALKINS BANK 175 C3
Mallaig Cl CW4 . . . . 130 C2
Mallard Cl
  Knutsford WA16 . . . . . . 57 B3
  Warrington WA2 . . . . 8 D3
Mallard Cres SK12 . . . . . 36 A4
Mallard Ct
  Chester CH2 . . . . 118 F7
  Crewe CW1 . . . . 191 A2
  Gatley SK8 . . . . 34 B8
Mallard La WA3 . . . . 9 F3
Mallard Way
  Crewe CW1 . . . . 191 A2
  Winsford CW7 . . . . 149 D6
Mallory Cl WA16 . . . . . . 58 A4
Mallory Ct
  Congleton CW12 . . . . . 155 F3
  Mobberley WA16 . . . . . . 58 A4
Mallory Rd CH65 . . . . 70 A4
Mallory Wlk CW7 . . . . . . 162 A7
Mallow Cl CH3 . . . . 142 A6
Mallowdale Cl CH62 . . . . 43 F5
Mallow Wlk M31 . . . . 11 F2
Mall The WA1 . . . . 16 A5

Malmesbury Cl
  Middlewich CW10 . . . . . 128 B1
  Poynton SK12 . . . . 36 D4
Malmesbury Pk WA7 . . . 24 E2
Malmesbury Rd SK8 . . . . 35 B6
Malory Cl CW1 . . . . 190 F5
MALPAS 213 B2
Malpas Alport Endowed Prim
  Sch SY14 . . . . 213 B4
Malpas Cl
  Handforth SK9 . . . . 34 E1
  Northwich CW9 . . . . . . 104 B7
Malpas Dr WA5 . . . . 15 C4
Malpas Rd
  Ellesmere Port CH65 . . . 69 F4
  Northwich CW9 . . . . . . 104 C7
  Runcorn WA7 . . . . 49 B7
Malpas Sports Ctr SY14 . 213 C5
Malpas Way CW9 . . . . . . 103 F4
Malta Rd CH2 . . . . 95 B1
Malt Kiln Rd WA16 . . . . . 80 F4
Malt Kiln Way CW11 . . . . 175 B7
Maltmans Rd WA13 . . . . . 18 D3
Malton Ave WA3 . . . . 3 E7
Malton Cl WA8 . . . . 12 C5
Malton Dr SK7 . . . . 36 D7
Malt St WA16 . . . . 57 A2
Malvern Ave CW65 . . . . . 70 D3
Malvern Cl
  Congleton CW12 . . . . . 155 F3
  Shavington CW2 . . . . . . 206 B4
  Warrington WA5 . . . . . . 15 A8
Malvern Dr SK10 . . . . 87 E4
Malvern Rd
  Bacon CH1 . . . . 118 A5
  Haydock WA3 . . . . 1 A4
  Knutsford WA16 . . . . . . 81 F8
Malvern Way CW7 . . . . . 149 B7
Manchester Airport M90 . 33 A7
Manchester Airport Sta
  M90 . . . . 33 B7
Manchester Bridge CW1 . 190 E4
Manchester Bsns Pk M22 . 33 D8
Manchester New Rd M31 . 11 F4
Manchester Rd
  Congleton CW12 . . . . . 156 E5
  Handforth SK9 . . . . 34 C2
  Hollinfare WA3 . . . . 11 A2
  Hollins Green WA3 . . . . 11 B3
  Knutsford WA16 . . . . . . 56 E4
  Macclesfield SK10 . . . . . 87 D4
  Warrington, Bruche WA1 . 16 F7
  Warrington WA3 . . . . . . 18 D7
  Warrington, Woolston WA1 . 17 C7
  Wincham CW9 . . . . 79 D1
Manchester Row WA12 . . . 7 D8
Mancroft Cl WA7 . . . . . . 17 E7
Mandarin Ct WA1 . . . . . . 16 B5
Manhattan Gdns [1] WA5 . 15 B7
Manifold Cl CW11 . . . . . . 174 E8
Manifold Dr SK6 . . . . 37 F6
MANLEY 99 A4
Manley Cl
  Antrobus CW9 . . . . 53 C4
  Holmes Chapel CW4 . . . 130 A3
  Northwich CW9 . . . . . . 104 A5
MANLEY COMMON 99 C5
Manley Cty Prim Sch
  WA6 . . . . 99 C5
Manley Gdns WA5 . . . . . . 15 F5
Manley Gr SK7 . . . . 35 E6
Manley La
  Dunham-on-the-Hill WA6 . 97 F5
  Manley Mere Sail Sports &
    Adventure Trail* WA6 . . 98 B5
Manley Rd
  Frodsham WA6 . . . . 74 B3
  Manley WA6 . . . . 98 E7
  Warren SK11 . . . . 112 A5
Manley View CH2 . . . . . . 72 C3
Manna Dr CH2 . . . . 72 C3
Manners La CH60 . . . . . . 40 E6
Mannings La CH2 . . . . . . 118 F6
Mannings Lane S CH2 . . 119 A5
Manning St CW2 . . . . . . 190 D1
Manora Rd CW9 . . . . . . 104 A8
Manor Cl
  Broughton CH5 . . . . . . 139 C7
  Cheadle SK8 . . . . 35 C8
  Congleton CW12 . . . . . 157 A1
  Great Barrow CH3 . . . . . 120 E6
  Lymm WA13 . . . . 18 E2
  Neston CH64 . . . . 66 C7
  Warrington WA1 . . . . . . 17 C7
  Wilmslow SK9 . . . . 59 F8
Manor Cres
  Broughton CH4 . . . . . . 139 C8
  Knutsford WA16 . . . . . . 82 A8
  Macclesfield SK10 . . . . . 87 D3
  Northwich CW10 . . . . . 151 C7
Manor Dr
  Barnton CW8 . . . . 78 B2
  Chester CH3 . . . . 119 C1
  Northwich, Rudheath CW9 . 104 C7

Manor Farm Cl CH2 . . . . 119 F8
Manor Farm Cres CH1 . . . 94 B8
Manor Farm Ct
  Broughton CH5 . . . . . . 139 B7
  [5] Frodsham WA6 . . . . . 49 C1
Manor Farm Mews WA7 . . 24 D4
Manor Farm Rd WA7 . . . . 24 D4
Manor Fell WA7 . . . . 50 B7
Manorfield Cl CH1 . . . . . . 69 A1
Manor Fields CW10 . . . . . 151 C7
Manor Gdns
  Nantwich CW5 . . . . . . 204 E6
  Wilmslow SK9 . . . . 60 D7
Manor Gr CW8 . . . . 103 C6
Manor Ho
  Bebington CH62 . . . . . . 43 D8
  Ellesmere Port CH66 . . . 69 D2
  Row-of-Trees SK9 . . . . . 59 D3
Memorial Rd CH64 . . . . . 66 C8
Manorial Road S CH64 . . 66 C7
Manor Ind Est WA4 . . . . . 16 E4
Manor La
  Broughton CH5 . . . . . . 139 B7
  Davenham CW9 . . . . . . 104 D2
  Ellesmere Port CH66 . . . 69 D3
  [3] Middlewich CW10 . . 151 C8
  Ollerton WA16 . . . . 82 E6
MANOR PARK
  Middlewich 151 B7
  Runcorn 24 B3
Manor Park Ave WA7 . . . . 24 C4
Manor Park CP Sch WA16 . 57 C2
Manor Park Dr CH66 . . . . 69 D2
Manor Park N WA16 . . . . 57 C2
Manor Park Rd CW12 . . . 134 D2
Manor Park S WA16 . . . . 57 C1
Manor Pk CH65 . . . . 139 B7
Manor Pk CH3 . . . . 120 E6
Manor PI
  Hatherton CW5 . . . . . . 220 B1
  Widnes WA8 . . . . 12 B1
Manor Rd
  Bebington CH62 . . . . . . 43 E6
  Chester CH4 . . . . 141 B5
  Cuddington CW8 . . . . . 101 F2
  Frodsham WA6 . . . . 49 C1
  Haydock WA11 . . . . 1 F7
  Horwich End SK23 . . . . . 65 E5
  Lymm WA13 . . . . 18 E2
  Mow Cop ST7 . . . . 195 D7
  Nantwich CW5 . . . . . . 204 E6
  Runcorn WA7 . . . . 23 D2
  Sandbach CW11 . . . . . 175 D6
  Sealand CH5 . . . . 116 A6
  Thornton Hough CH63 . . 42 A7
  Widnes WA8 . . . . 12 B1
  Wilmslow SK9 . . . . 59 E8
Manor Road N CW5 . . . . 204 E7
Manor Sq CW7 . . . . 149 A8
Manor St CW8 . . . . 103 D6
Manor Terr SK11 . . . . . . 113 B3
Manor The WA1 . . . . 17 F7
Manor Way
  Crewe CW2 . . . . 190 C1
  Sandbach CW11 . . . . . 175 C6
Manse Field Rd WA6 . . . . 75 B1
Manse Gdns WA12 . . . . . . 2 D4
Mansell Cl WA3 . . . . 13 C5
Mansfield Apartments
  WA2 . . . . 9 A3
Mansfield Cl WA3 . . . . . . 10 A4
Mansfield Rd CH65 . . . . . 70 A2
Mansion Ct [5] WA5 . . . 204 F5
Mansion Dr WA16 . . . . . . 57 C2
Mansion Rd WA5 . . . . . . 14 F3
Manuel Perez Rd WA5 . . . 15 B6
Manx Rd WA1 . . . . 16 B3
Maori Dr WA6 . . . . 74 A8
Maple Ave
  Alsager ST7 . . . . 193 E2
  Aston WA7 . . . . 50 C2
  Disley SK12 . . . . 39 A6
  Ellesmere Port CH66 . . . 69 D6
  Golborne WA3 . . . . 3 F7
  [4] Sandbach CW11 . . . 175 B6
Maple Cl
  Brereton Green CW11 . . 153 F5
  Congleton CW12 . . . . . 155 F4
  Holmes Chapel CW4 . . . 130 D4
  Sandbach CW11 . . . . . 175 C6
Maple Cres WA3 . . . . 14 F3
Maple Ct CW7 . . . . 127 A3
Maple Gr
  Barnton CW8 . . . . 78 B4
  Bebington CH62 . . . . . . 43 C8
  Chester CH2 . . . . 119 B4
  Crewe CW1 . . . . 190 E6
  Ellesmere Port CH66 . . . 95 A8
  Northwich, Greenbank
    CW9 . . . . 103 C7
  Saltney CH4 . . . . 140 D5
  Warrington WA4 . . . . . . 16 D3
  Winsford CW7 . . . . 127 A1
Maple La CW8 . . . . 101 F2
Maple PI ST7 . . . . 193 F7
Maple Rd
  Alderley Edge SK9 . . . . . 60 B3
  Bramhall SK7 . . . . 35 E6
  Partington M31 . . . . 11 B3

Maple Rd continued
  Warrington WA1 . . . . . . 17 E7
  Winwick WA2 . . . . 8 B6
Maples SK9 . . . . 59 F6
Maples The
  Mobberley WA16 . . . . . . 58 E1
  Winsford CW7 . . . . 127 A3
Mapleton Dr WA7 . . . . . . 49 F3
Maplewood SK11 . . . . . . 112 D5
Maplewood Cl WA8 . . . . . 22 A7
Maplewood Gr CH1 . . . . 117 B8
Maplewood Rd SK9 . . . . . 60 E8
Mapplewell Cres WA5 . . . 15 A6
Marble Arch [5] WA16 . . . 57 A2
MARBURY 226 D8
Marbury Ctry Pk* CW9 . . 78 E5
Marbury Gdns CH65 . . . . 70 D3
Marbury House Farm
  WA4 . . . . 52 E5
Marbury La CW9 . . . . 78 E5
Marbury Rd
  Chester CH3 . . . . 119 C2
  Comberbach CW9 . . . . . 78 D6
  Handforth SK9 . . . . 34 B1
  Norbury SY13 . . . . 215 B3
Marbury St WA4 . . . . 16 C3
March St CW1 . . . . 190 E4
Marchwiel Rd CH65 . . . . . 70 D4
Marcien Way WA8 . . . . . . 12 F3
Marcliff Gr WA16 . . . . . . 57 A1
Marcross Cl WA5 . . . . 7 E1
Mardale Ave WA2 . . . . 8 C3
Mardale Cl CW12 . . . . . . 157 B5
Mardale Cres WA13 . . . . . 18 F3
Mardale Ct CW4 . . . . . . 130 A2
Mardon Cl WA16 . . . . 57 C1
Marford Cl CW9 . . . . 103 E5
Marfords Ave CH63 . . . . . 43 C7
Margaret Ave WA1 . . . . . 17 B7
Margaret Ct WA8 . . . . . . 23 B7
Margaret's La CH66 . . . . . 69 A7
Margaret Ave SY17 . . . . . 194 E7
Marian Ave WA12 . . . . 1 F3
Marian Dr CH3 . . . . 142 B8
Marian Rd WA11 . . . . 1 E7
Marie Cl CW5 . . . . 216 F4
Marie Dr WA4 . . . . 17 D2
Marigold Cl SK11 . . . . . . 111 F8
Marigold Pl WA5 . . . . . . 15 D3
Marigold Way WA9 . . . . . . 6 A7
Marina Ave WA5 . . . . 15 C4
Marina Cl SK9 . . . . 34 D5
Marina Dr
  Chester CH2 . . . . 118 E7
  Ellesmere Port CH65 . . . 70 B5
  Warrington WA2 . . . . 8 C1
Marina Flats CH3 . . . . . . 142 E7
Marina Gr WA7 . . . . 23 B1
Marina La WA7 . . . . 50 E7
Marina Village WA7 . . . . . 50 E7
Marina Wlk CH65 . . . . . . 70 B5
Marine App [19] CW9 . . . 103 F8
Marine Ave M31 . . . . 11 D3
Marine Dr CH60 . . . . 40 D6
Mariner Cl WA7 . . . . 50 D6
Mariners Way M44 . . . . . . 11 F8
Marion Dr
  Mobberley WA16 . . . . . . 58 A4
  Runcorn WA7 . . . . 48 F6
Maritime Cl WA12 . . . . 2 C5
Mark Ave CH66 . . . . 69 C4
Mark Cl CW2 . . . . 118 F2
Market Cl CW1 . . . . 190 D5
Market Sq WA4 . . . . 26 D8
Market Ctr The CW1 . . . . 190 D4
Market Gate WA1 . . . . . . 16 B5
Market PI
  Bollington SK10 . . . . . . 88 B8
  Hampton Heath SY14 . . 213 D7
  Macclesfield SK10, SK11 . 112 D8
  Winsford CW7 . . . . 126 F1
Market Sq
  Chester CH1 . . . . 237 A2
  Congleton CW12 . . . . . 156 D2
  Crewe CW1 . . . . 190 D4
  Disley SK12 . . . . 38 D6
  Kidsgrove ST7 . . . . 195 A1
  Nantwich CW5 . . . . . . 204 E5
  New Mills SK22 . . . . . . 39 B7
  Newton-le-Willows WA12 . 2 A3
  [9] Northwich CW9 . . . 103 F8
  Whaley Bridge SK23 . . . 65 E7
  Widnes WA8 . . . . 23 A7
Market Way [7] CW9 . . . 103 F8
Marketgate Ave
  Alderley Edge SK9 . . . . . 60 B2
  Winsford CW7 . . . . 126 C3
Markham Cl
  Knutsford WA16 . . . . . . 57 C4
  Macclesfield SK10 . . . . . 87 D4
  Wistaston CW2 . . . . . . 205 E8
Marlborough Cres
  Warrington WA4 . . . . . . 16 F2
  Widnes WA8 . . . . 13 A5
Marlborough Ct
  [1] Chester CH3 . . . . . 119 B2
  [3] Macclesfield SK10 . . 112 D7
Marlborough Dr
  Helsby WA6 . . . . 73 B2
  Macclesfield SK10 . . . . . 87 D4
  Sandbach CW11 . . . . . 175 B8
Marlborough Ho [8]
  SK11 . . . . 111 F8

Marlborough Prim Sch The
  SK10 . . . . 87 D4
Marlborough Rd CH65 . . . 70 D3
Marlborough Way WA11 . . 1 E8
Marlborough Wlk CH65 . . 70 C3
Marl Cl CW8 . . . . 102 A4
Marl Croft CH63 . . . . 43 B7
Marl Edge SK10 . . . . 87 A5
Marley Ave CW1 . . . . . . 190 E3
Marley Gr SY13 . . . . 227 C8
MARLEY GREEN 227 C8
Marley Rd SK12 . . . . 36 E2
Marley Way CH4 . . . . . . 140 E7
Marlfield Ave WA13 . . . . . 19 A2
Marlfield Rd
  Altrincham WA15 . . . . . 32 D7
  Warrington WA4 . . . . . . 17 A2
Marlfields Prim Sch
  CW12 . . . . 156 C2
Marl Heys CH2 . . . . 118 F7
Marline Ave CH63 . . . . . . 43 C6
Marling Pk WA16 . . . . . . 74 D6
Marling Pk WA8 . . . . 12 D2
Marlow Ave CH2 . . . . . . 118 F7
Marlow Cl
  Sandbach CW11 . . . . . 174 D5
  Warrington WA3 . . . . 9 C5
Marlow Dr
  Altrincham WA14 . . . . . . 20 F2
  Handforth SK9 . . . . 34 C5
Marlowe Cl
  Blacon CH1 . . . . 118 A5
  Widnes WA8 . . . . 12 F1
  Wistaston CW2 . . . . . . 206 A8
Marlowe Ct SK11 . . . . . . 112 C5
Marlowe Dr CW5 . . . . . . 204 F3
Marlowe Rd
  [1] Neston CH64 . . . . . . 66 E8
  Northwich CW9 . . . . . . 104 C6
Marlston Ave CH4 . . . . . 141 A6
Marlston Cl CH4 . . . . . . 140 E1
Marlston Pl WA7 . . . . 49 B6
Marlwood Pl CH4 . . . . . . 139 A3
Maroon Rd M22 . . . . 33 F7
Marple Cres CW2 . . . . . . 189 E2
Marple Dr SK8 . . . . 34 D7
Marquis Dr SK8 . . . . 34 D7
Marriott Rd CW11 . . . . . 174 F3
Marron Ave WA2 . . . . 8 B2
Marryat Cl WA3 . . . . 8 A6
Marsden Ave WA4 . . . . . . 17 A4
Marsden Cl WA8 . . . . 12 E4
Marsden Terr [3] SK11 . . 112 C7
Marshall Ave WA5 . . . . . . 1 C7
Marshall Gr WA5 . . . . . . 179 B8
Marshall La CW5 . . . . . . 103 D6
Marshall Rd WA1 . . . . . . 17 D7
Marshall's Arm Nature
  Reserve* CW8 . . . . . . 103 D5
Marshalls Ct [2] CW8 . . 103 C5
Marsh Ave ST7 . . . . 195 E2
Marsh Brook Cl WA3 . . . 12 A6
Marsh Cl ST7 . . . . 193 A3
Marsh Farm La CW5 . . . 189 D4
MARSHFIELD BANK 189 C4
Marshfield Bank CW2 . . 189 D4
Marshfield La ST7 . . . . . 179 C2
Marshgate WA8 . . . . 22 B6
Marshgate Pl WA6 . . . . . 49 D2
Marsh Gr ST8 . . . . 179 C3
MARSH GREEN
  Biddulph 179 D3
  Frodsham 74 A8
Marsh Green Cl ST8 . . . 179 D2
Marshgreen Rd ST8 . . . . 179 D3
Marsh Green Rd CW11 . . 174 E8
Marsh Hall Pad WA1 . . . . 13 B4
Marsh House La WA1,
  WA4 . . . . 16 C7
Marsh La
  Alsager ST7 . . . . 193 A3
  Churton CH3 . . . . 181 B5
  Dutton WA4 . . . . 51 E3
  Frodsham WA6 . . . . 74 A8
  Holmes Chapel CW4 . . . 130 E2
  Ince CH2 . . . . 72 D6
  Mere WA16 . . . . 30 F3
  Nantwich CW5 . . . . . . 204 C5
  New Mills SK22, SK23 . . 39 C6
  Norley CW8, WA6 . . . . 101 B7
  Ravensmoor CW5 . . . . 203 F2
  Runcorn WA7 . . . . 23 F3
  Warrington, Penketh WA5 . 14 C2
Marshlands Rd CH64 . . . . 66 E5
Marsh Lane Trad Est
  SK22 . . . . 39 D7
Marsh Rd WA4 . . . . 27 B4
Marsh St
  Warrington WA1 . . . . . . 16 D7
  Widnes WA8 . . . . 23 A6
Marshway Dr WA12 . . . . . 2 A3
Marson St WA2 . . . . 16 A6
MARSTON 79 B4
Marston Cl CH62 . . . . . . 43 E3
Marston Gdns CH65 . . . . 69 F6
Marston La CW9 . . . . 79 C6
Marten Ave CH63 . . . . . . 43 C7
Martens Rd M44 . . . . 11 E5
MARTHALL 83 E4
Marthall La WA16 . . . . . . 83 B7
Marthall Way [6] SK9 . . 34 E5
Marthall La WA16 . . . . . . 83 B7
Martin Ave
  Newton-le-Willows WA12 . 2 C5
  Warrington WA2 . . . . 8 E1

Martin Cl
Chester CH2 . . . . 118 C8
Runcorn WA7 . . . . 50 A7
Martindale Gr WA7 . . . . 49 D5
Martin Rd
Chester CH2 . . . . 118 C8
Frodsham WA6 . . . . 74 B8
MARTIN'S ASH 227 B2
MARTINSCROFT 17 F7
Martinscroft Gn WA1 . . 17 F7
Martinsfields WA5 . . . . . 77 A5
Martin's La CH3 . . . . . . 143 F3
Martins Mill CW12 . . . . 179 C8
MARTIN'S MOSS 176 E6
Martland Ave WA3 . . . . . . 3 E7
Martlet Ave SK12 . . . . . . 38 C6
MARTON 133 B5
Marton Cl
Congleton CW12 . . . . . . 156 E5
Culcheth WA3 . . . . 4 E4
Hough CW2 . . . . 206 E3
Macclesfield SK10 . . . . . . 86 F1
Marton & District CE Prim
Sch SK11 . . . . 133 C5
MARTON GREEN 125 C4
Marton Hall La SK11 . . . 133 B3
Marton La
Marton SK11 . . . . 133 D7
Warren SK11 . . . . 111 B1
Marton Rd CH4 . . . . 139 C3
MARTONSANDS 125 F4
Marton Way 5 SK9 . . . . . 34 E5
Martree Ct CW11 . . . . . . 174 D8
Mary Dendy Unit (Hospl)
SK10 . . . . 84 C6
Maryfield Cl WA3 . . . . 3 A7
Maryhill Cl ST7 . . . . 195 A3
Maryhill High Sch ST7 . . 195 A3
Maryhill Prim Sch ST7 . . 195 A3
Maryhill Rd WA7 . . . . 49 A8
Maryland Cl WA5 . . . . . . 15 C7
Marys Gate CW2 . . . . . . 205 E8
Mary St
Crewe CW1 . . . . 190 E5
Widnes WA8 . . . . 23 D7
Maryville Cl 3 CH3 . . . . . 70 C6
Masefield Ave WA8 . . . . 22 F8
Masefield Dr
Blacon CH1 . . . . 117 E6
Crewe CW1 . . . . 190 F4
Winwick WA2 . . . . 8 A5
Masefield Way CW11 . . . 174 D5
Maskery Pl CW12 . . . . . . 156 E4
Mason Ave
Warrington WA1 . . . . 16 E8
Widnes WA8 . . . . 13 B4
Mason Cl CH66 . . . . 69 D2
Masons La SK10 . . . . 87 F1
Mason's Row CW6 . . . . . 169 E2
Mason St
Chester CH2 . . . . 237 A3
Runcorn WA7 . . . . 23 C3
Warrington WA1 . . . . 16 C5
Massey Ave
Hartford CW8 . . . . 103 A4
Lymm WA13 . . . . 18 B2
Warrington WA5 . . . . 7 F2
Winsford CW7 . . . . 126 F1
Massey Brook La WA13. . . 18 B2
Masseyfield Rd WA7 . . . . 50 B5
Massey St 6 SK9 . . . . . . 60 A1
Masters Cl WA1 . . . . 56 F1
Mastiff La SY14 . . . . 213 B1
Mates La SY14 . . . . 213 B6
Mather Ave
Golborne WA3 . . . . 3 E6
Runcorn WA7 . . . . 48 D7
Mather Cl CW10 . . . . 151 C8
Mather Dr
Comberbach CW9 . . . . 78 C8
Northwich CW9 . . . . 104 D7
Mathers Cl WA2 . . . . 9 A4
Mathieson Rd WA8 . . . . . 22 E5
Matlock Cl WA5 . . . . 15 A8
Matlock Dr SK7 . . . . 36 E8
Matlock Rd SK8 . . . . 34 C7
Matterdale Cl WA6 . . . . . 74 D7
Matterhorn Rd CH66 . . . . 69 F7
Matthew Cl CH2 . . . . 118 F2
Matthews Pl CW12 . . . . . 157 A2
Matthews St WA1 . . . . . . 16 D7
Matthews Way CW3 . . . . 229 F3
Matty's La WA6 . . . . 74 A7
Mavor Ct CW1 . . . . 190 B4
Mawdsley Ave WA1 . . . . . 17 E7
Mawdsley Cl ST7 . . . . . . 193 A3
MAW GREEN 190 E7
Maw Green Cl CW1 . . . . . 190 E7
Maw Green Rd CW1 . . . . 190 F7
Maw La CW1 . . . . 191 C7
Mawson Ct WA5 . . . . 15 D8
Maxfield Cl SK11 . . . . . . 111 F8
Maxwell Cl CH65 . . . . 70 A2
Maxwell Rd CW12 . . . . . 179 A8
Maxwell St
Crewe CW2 . . . . 190 C3
Warrington WA3 . . . . 9 E6
May Ave SK8 . . . . 35 B6
Mayberry Gr WA2 . . . . 9 A1
Maybrook Pl WA4 . . . . . . 16 F3
Maydor Ave CH4 . . . . . . 140 C7
Mayfair Cl
Poynton SK12 . . . . 36 E4
Warrington WA5 . . . . 14 D7

Mayfair Ct CH4 . . . . 162 E5
Mayfair Dr
Crewe CW1 . . . . 190 F6
Northwich CW9 . . . . 103 F3
Mayfair Gr WA8 . . . . 12 D1
Mayfield Ave
Macclesfield SK11 . . . . . 112 C5
Widnes WA8 . . . . 12 B1
Mayfield Cl CW4 . . . . . . 130 D3
Mayfield La WA13 . . . . . 13 A2
Mayfield Dr
Bebington CH62 . . . . 44 B6
Cuddington CW8 . . . . . . 102 A4
Golborne WN7 . . . . 4 C8
Winsford CW7 . . . . 127 A3
Mayfield Gdns CH64 . . . . 41 E1
Mayfield Gr
Cuddington CW8 . . . . . . 102 A4
Wilmslow SK9 . . . . 59 E5
Mayfield Mews CW1 . . . 189 F6
Mayfield Rd
Blacon CH1 . . . . 117 D5
Bramhall SK7 . . . . 35 E4
Mobberley WA16 . . . . 57 F4
Northwich CW9 . . . . 104 C8
Warrington WA4 . . . . 17 A2
Mayfield Terr SK11 . . . . . 112 C5
Mayfield View WA13 . . . . 18 F2
Mayflower Rd CW5 . . . . 204 E3
May Rd
Cheadle SK8 . . . . 35 B6
Heswall CH60 . . . . 41 A8
Maythorn Ave WA3 . . . . . 4 A7
Maytree Ave CH3 . . . . . 119 B2
May Wlk 2 M31 . . . . 11 E3
Mead Ave ST7 . . . . 194 E7
Mead Cl WA16 . . . . 56 F1
Meade The SK9 . . . . 60 C8
Meadow Ave
Congleton CW12 . . . . . . 156 C1
Goostrey CW4 . . . . 107 C1
Warrington WA4 . . . . 16 B2
Weston CW2 . . . . 207 B5
MEADOWBANK 126 D5
Meadow Bank
Adderley TF9 . . . . 235 A4
Kelsall CH6 . . . . 122 C4
Meadowbank Dr CH66. . . . 69 A6
Meadowbank Gdns WA5 . . 5 C7
Meadow Brow SK9 . . . . . 60 A2
Meadow Cl
Cuddington CW8 . . . . . . 102 A4
Farndon CH3 . . . . 180 F1
Goostrey CW4 . . . . 107 E1
Helsby WA6 . . . . 73 B3
High Lane SK6 . . . . 37 F8
Neston CH64 . . . . 66 E6
Newton-le-Willows WA12 . . 1 F3
Shavington CW2 . . . . . . 206 D5
Tarvin CH3 . . . . 121 B2
Whaley Bridge SK23 . . . . 65 C8
Widnes WA8 . . . . 12 D3
Wilmslow SK9 . . . . 59 E4
Winsford CW7 . . . . 126 C3
Meadow Com Prim Sch
CH66 . . . . 69 E2
Meadow Cotts 5 CW12 . . 156 D3
Meadowcroft
Higher Kinnerton CH4 . . . 161 A7
Saughall CH1 . . . . 94 B1
Meadow Croft
Alsager ST7 . . . . 193 E2
Ellesmere Port CH66 . . . . 67 E8
Macclesfield SK10 . . . . . . 87 A6
Meadowcroft Ct WA7 . . . 50 A8
Meadow Ct
Frodsham WA6 . . . . 49 C1
Mollington CH1 . . . . 94 F1
Newchapel ST7 . . . . 195 E2
No Man's Heath SY14 . . . 214 A5
Meadow Dr
Barnton CH64 . . . . 78 A3
Knutsford WA16 . . . . 81 F8
Prestbury SK10 . . . . 87 B7
Wistaston CW2 . . . . 205 F7
Meadowfield
Tarporley CW6 . . . . 146 C1
Whaley Bridge SK23 . . . . 65 D8
Meadow Field Rd CH4. . . 141 A5
Meadow Gate CW9 . . . . . 79 F5
Meadow Home Pk CW7 . . 126 D6
Meadow House Pk CW6 . 185 D5
Meadow La
Comberbach CW9 . . . . . . 78 C7
Disley SK12 . . . . 38 D6
Ellesmere Port CH65 . . . . 70 D6
Huntington CH3 . . . . 142 A5
Moulton CW9 . . . . 126 F8
Warrington WA2 . . . . 9 A2
Willaston CH64 . . . . 67 F8
Meadow Lane Ind Pk
CH65 . . . . 70 D5
Meadow Mill Ct CW12. . . 156 E3
Meadow Rd
Broughton CH4 . . . . 139 B4
Weaverham WA6 . . . . . . 102 E7
Meadow Rise
Clutton CH3 . . . . 182 D2
Winsford CW7 . . . . 126 A1
Meadow Row WA1 . . . . . . 24 A1
Meadowside
Disley SK12 . . . . 39 A6
Fourlane-ends SK10 . . . . 63 B8

Meadowside continued
Frodsham WA6 . . . . 74 A8
Northwich CW8 . . . . 103 D7
Whaley Bridge SK23 . . . . 65 D8
Meadowside Ave ST7 . . . 209 D2
Meadowside Com Prim Sch
WA2 . . . . 8 B1
Meadowside La ST7 . . . . 195 B7
Meadowside Mews CH1 . . 118 B4
Meadowside Rd CH62 . . . 43 E8
Meadows La
Chester CH4 . . . . 237 C1
Saughall CH1 . . . . 117 A8
Tilston SY14 . . . . 212 B6
Meadows Pl CH4 . . . . . . 141 E7
Meadows Rd
Cheadle SK8 . . . . 34 F8
Glazebury ST7 . . . . 194 F1
Meadow St
New Mills SK22 . . . . 39 C8
3 Northwich CW9 . . . . . . 104 A8
Meadows The
Ashton Hayes CH3 . . . . . 121 E8
Congleton CW12 . . . . . . 156 E3
Irlam M44 . . . . 11 E6
Neston CH64 . . . . 66 F6
Meadowsway CH2 . . . . . 118 D8
Meadowsweet Rd WA16. . . 57 F3
Meadow The CW4 . . . . . 130 D8
Meadowvale Cl CW5 . . . . 204 E7
Meadow View
Chester CH3 . . . . 118 F1
Ellesmere Port CH2 . . . . . 70 E1
Elton CH2 . . . . 72 A3
Lymm WA13 . . . . 18 D4
Middlewich CW10 . . . . . 128 B2
Sealand CH5 . . . . 116 A6
Meadow View Dr WA6 . . . 74 A7
Meadow Way
Lawton-gate ST7 . . . . . . 194 A5
Macclesfield SK10 . . . . . . 87 E2
Wilmslow SK9 . . . . 59 E4
Meadow Wlk
Partington M31 . . . . 11 E3
4 Runcorn WA7 . . . . 49 F7
Mead Rd WA1 . . . . 17 A8
Meadscroft Dr SK9 . . . . . 59 F1
Meads Rd ST7 . . . . 193 D4
Meadway
Bramhall SK7 . . . . 35 E5
Ellesmere Port CH66 . . . . 69 B7
Golborne WA3 . . . . 3 D8
Heswall CH60 . . . . 40 F6
High Lane SK6 . . . . 37 F8
Poynton SK12 . . . . 36 B4
Runcorn WA7 . . . . 49 E8
Meakin Cl CW12 . . . . 157 B1
Mealors New Cotts CH64 . 62 A4
Mealors Weint CH64 . . . . 41 B1
Meal St SK22 . . . . 39 C8
Meddings Cl SK9 . . . . . . 85 A8
Medina Ave CW9 . . . . . . 126 F2
Medina Way ST7 . . . . . . 195 B2
Medlar Cl CH4 . . . . 140 F5
Medway Cl
Golborne WN7 . . . . 4 C8
Handforth SK9 . . . . 34 D2
Warrington WA2 . . . . 8 E2
Medway Dr ST8 . . . . 179 D1
Medway Rd WA3 . . . . 5 A2
Meeanee Dr CW5 . . . . . . 204 D4
Mee St SK11 . . . . 112 E5
Meeting House La WA6 . . 74 E2
Meeting La WA5 . . . . 14 E5
MEGACRE 210 A1
Megacre ST7 . . . . 210 A1
Megg La CW9 . . . . 53 B4
Meg La
Langley SK11 . . . . 113 D1
Macclesfield SK10 . . . . . 111 E8
Melbourne Ave WA9 . . . . 33 A8
Melbourne Gr CW1 . . . . 191 C5
Melbourne Rd
Blacon CH1 . . . . 117 D4
Bramhall SK7 . . . . 35 F5
Melbury Ct WA3 . . . . 9 F6
Melbury Rd SK8 . . . . 35 B6
Melchett Cres CW9 . . . . 104 D7
Meldon Cl CW2 . . . . 206 C8
Melford Ct WA1 . . . . 17 D8
Melford Dr
Macclesfield SK10 . . . . . . 87 C2
Runcorn WA7 . . . . 23 C1
Meliden Gr WA6 . . . . 73 B1
Melksham Cl SK11 . . . . . 112 A7
Mellard St ST7 . . . . 209 D1
Mellock Cl CH64 . . . . 66 F6
Mellock La CH64 . . . . 66 F7
Mellor Cl WA7 . . . . 24 D1
Mellor Cres WA16 . . . . . . 56 E1
Mellors Bank ST7 . . . . . 195 D6
Mellor St
Crewe CW1 . . . . 190 B8
Packmoor ST7 . . . . 195 F2
Mellor View SK12 . . . . . . 38 E6
Melrose Ave
Burtonwood WA5 . . . . 6 F7
Chester CH3 . . . . 119 B2
Warrington WA4 . . . . 26 D8
Melrose Cres SK12 . . . . . 37 D5
Melrose St 15 SK9 . . . . . 34 E1
Melrose Way
Crewe CW1 . . . . 190 B8
Ellesmere Port CH66 . . . . 94 F8
Melton Ave WA4 . . . . 26 B8

Melton Cl CW12 . . . . . . 155 F3
Melton Dr CW12 . . . . . . 155 F3
Melton Rd WA7 . . . . 49 C7
Melverly Dr CH1 . . . . . . 117 C4
Melville Cl
Warrington WA2 . . . . 16 B7
2 Widnes WA8 . . . . 13 D1
Melville Rd M44 . . . . 11 C5
Mendell Cl CH62 . . . . 43 E8
Mendell Prim Sch CH62 . . 43 E8
Mendip Ave WA2 . . . . 8 B3
Mendip Cl
Ellesmere Port CH66 . . . . 69 E3
Gatley SK8 . . . . 34 B7
Winsford CW7 . . . . 149 B8
Menin Ave WA4 . . . . 16 C3
Menlow Cl WA4 . . . . 17 C1
Mentmore Gdns WA4 . . . 26 F5
Meols Cl
Ellesmere Port CH66 . . . . 69 E4
Hale L24 . . . . 21 E2
Mercer Cl SY14 . . . . 213 B3
Mercer Rd WA1 . . . . 1 D6
Mercer St
Burtonwood WA5 . . . . 6 E6
Newton-le-Willows WA12 . . 2 D4
Mercer Way
Chester CH4 . . . . 140 F6
Nantwich CW5 . . . . 204 E7
Mercer Wlk CH65 . . . . . . 70 C4
Merchants Ct CW1 . . . . . 190 C7
Mercian Cl CW2 . . . . . . 206 B4
Mercury Ct CH1 . . . . 117 E2
MERE 56 B8
Mere Ave CH63 . . . . 43 B6
Mere Bank CW9 . . . . 127 A8
Merebank Rd CW2 . . . . . 190 B1
Merebrook Cl SK11 . . . . 112 A8
Merebrook Rd SK11 . . . . 111 F8
Mere Brook Wlk CW2 . . . 190 C1
Mere Cl
Ellesmere Port CH66 . . . . 69 D2
Haslington CW1 . . . . 191 D4
Pickmere WA16 . . . . 80 A7
Mere Cres CW8 . . . . 123 F6
Merecroft 1 CH3 . . . . . . 119 A1
Mere Ct
Alsager ST7 . . . . 193 D4
Chelford SK11 . . . . 83 F3
6 Knutsford WA16 . . . . . . 57 A2
Weston CW2 . . . . 207 B5
Winsford CW7 . . . . 149 E8
Meredith Ave WA4 . . . . . 17 B2
Meredith St CW1 . . . . . . 190 C5
Mere Hall WA16 . . . . 56 A8
Merehaven Cl WA16 . . . . 80 A7
Mereheath Dr WA16 . . . . 56 E7
Mereheath La WA16 . . . . 56 E5
Mereheath Pk WA16 . . . . 56 F3
Mere Ho ST7 . . . . 193 C3
Mere La
Cuddington CW8 . . . . . . 102 A2
Pickmere WA16 . . . . 79 F7
Merelake Rd ST7 . . . . . . 210 B8
Meremere Dr ST5 . . . . . . 210 D2
Mere Rd
Marston CW9 . . . . 79 B6
Newton-le-Willows WA12 . . 2 F4
Warrington WA2 . . . . 9 A2
Weston CW2 . . . . 207 B5
Mereside Ave CW12 . . . . 156 B3
Mereside Cl SK10 . . . . . . 87 A1
Mereside Gdns SK23 . . . . 65 D6
Mereside Rd WA16 . . . . . 30 C2
Mere St CW1 . . . . 190 C8
Merevale Cl WA7 . . . . 49 E6
Mere View WA6 . . . . 73 A2
Mere View Gdns WA4 . . . 26 E5
Merewood Cl WA2 . . . . . . 8 D3
Mereworth Dr CW9 . . . . 103 F5
Meriton Rd SK9 . . . . 34 D4
Merlin Ave WA16 . . . . . . 57 B3
Merlin Cl
Runcorn WA7 . . . . 24 A1
Winsford CW7 . . . . 150 A8
Merlin Ct 4 CW1 . . . . . . 190 A8
Merlin Way
Crewe CW1 . . . . 190 A8
Kidsgrove ST7 . . . . 195 D3
Merrick Cl WA2 . . . . 8 E3
Merridale The WA15 . . . . 32 A8
Merriden Rd SK10 . . . . . . 87 B2
Merrill's Ave CW2 . . . . . 189 E5
Merriman Ave WA16 . . . . 57 C3
Merrivale Rd CW2 . . . . . 206 B8
Merrydale Cl SK10 . . . . . 86 F1
Merryman's La SK9 . . . . . 84 B7
Mersey Pl CW7 . . . . 127 B1
Mersey Rd
Runcorn WA7 . . . . 23 A3
Widnes WA8 . . . . 23 A4
Mersey St
St Helens WA9 . . . . 1 A3
Warrington WA1 . . . . 16 B5
Merseyton Rd CH65 . . . . 70 B8
Merseyton Road Workshops
CH65 . . . . 70 C7
Mersey View WA7 . . . . . . 48 D7
Mersey View Rd WA8 . . . 22 B4
Mersey Wlk WA4 . . . . . . 16 F5
Mersham Ct WA8 . . . . . . 12 F4
Merton Ave SK7 . . . . 36 F8
Merton Cl CH64 . . . . 66 E6
Merton Dr CH4 . . . . 141 A4
Merton House Sch CH2 . . 118 C4

Merton Rd
Bebington CH65 . . . . 44 B3
Ellesmere Port CH66 . . . . 69 F3
Poynton SK12 . . . . 36 B4
Mertoun Rd WA4 . . . . . . 16 B1
Mervyn Rd CW8 . . . . 77 E1
Merwood Ave SK8 . . . . . . 34 D8
Messuage La CW12 . . . . 132 E4
Meteor Cres WA2 . . . . 8 D2
Mevagissey Rd WA7 . . . . 50 C5
Mevril Rd SK23 . . . . 65 E5
Mevril Springs Way SK23. . 65 E5
Mews The
Barnton CH64 . . . . 78 B2
Burtonwood WA5 . . . . 6 E6
Holmes Chapel CW4 . . . . 130 C3
New Mills SK22 . . . . 39 D8
Tarporley CW6 . . . . 168 C8
Willaston CH64 . . . . 68 A8
Wilmslow SK9 . . . . 33 D4
Meynell Cl CW2 . . . . 190 A1
Meynell Pl CH1 . . . . 118 A5
Meyrick Cl WA2 . . . . 2 A3
Miami Cl 9 WA5 . . . . 15 B7
Micawber Rd SK12 . . . . . 36 E2
Michigan Pl WA5 . . . . . . 15 C7
Micklegate
Mickle Trafford CH2. . . . . 119 E8
Runcorn WA7 . . . . 50 D7
MICKLE TRAFFORD 119 E8
Mickle Trafford Village Sch
CH2 . . . . 119 E8
Micklewright Ave CW1 . . 190 D5
Mickley Hall La CW5 . . . 218 A3
Mid-Cheshire Coll (Hartford
Campus) CW8 . . . . 103 C8
Mid Cheshire Coll (London
Road Site) CW9. . . . . . . 103 F5
Mid Cheshire Coll (Verdin
Ctr) CW7 . . . . 126 D1
Middlecroft CH3 . . . . . . 119 E5
Middlehills SK11 . . . . . . 113 A6
Middlehurst Ave CW8 . . . 102 E8
Middlehurst Rd WA4 . . . . 17 A2
Middle La
Aldford CH3 . . . . 163 F3
Congleton CW12 . . . . . . 157 D4
Kingsley WA6 . . . . 74 F2
MIDDLEWICH 128 D3
Middlewich High Sch 5
CW10 . . . . 151 C8
Middlewich L Ctr CW10 . . 151 C8
Middlewich Prim Sch
CW10 . . . . 151 B8
Middlewich Rd
Allostock WA16 . . . . 106 D5
Church Minshull CW1,
CW10 . . . . 172 E5
Cranage CW4, CW10 . . . 129 E6
Crewe CW1 . . . . 189 D6
Delamere CW6, CW8 . . . 123 D5
Holmes Chapel CW4 . . . . 130 B3
Knutsford WA16 . . . . 82 A3
Lower Peover WA16 . . . . . 81 F2
Nantwich CW5 . . . . 189 B1
Nantwich CW5 . . . . 204 F7
Northwich CW9 . . . . 104 D7
Sandbach CW11 . . . . 174 E7
Winsford CW7, CW10 . . . 127 C8
Middlewich Road Ind Est
CW10 . . . . 129 A6
Middlewich St CW1 . . . . 190 D6
Middle Wlk
Frodsham WA6 . . . . 74 B7
Knutsford WA16 . . . . 57 B2
MIDDLEWOOD 37 C5
Middlewood WA3 . . . . 3 E8
Middlewood Rd
Hazel Grove SK7, SK12 . . 37 C7
High Lane SK6 . . . . 37 C7
Poynton SK12 . . . . 37 B4
Middlewood Sta SK12 . . . 37 D6
Middlewood View SK6 . . . 37 D7
Midfield Cl ST8 . . . . 179 C2
Midhurst Cl SK8 . . . . 34 F8
Midland St WA8 . . . . 13 B1
Midland Terr SK22 . . . . . 39 C7
Midland Way WA1, WA5 . . 16 B5
Midlothian Ho 6 CH1 . . . 237 C3
Midpoint 18 Motorway Ind
Est CW10 . . . . 128 E1
MIDWAY 36 D2
Midway SK8 . . . . 35 D6
Midway Dr SK12 . . . . 36 D2
Midwood St 14 WA8 . . . . 23 B8
Milborne Ct CW2 . . . . . . 118 E5
Mildenhall Cl WA5 . . . . . 15 B6
Mile Bank Rd SY13 . . . . 226 D3
Miles Cl WA3 . . . . 9 F3
Milford Gdns WA4 . . . . . . 26 D4
Milk St CW12 . . . . 156 D3
Millar Cres WA8 . . . . 23 A7
Mill Ave WA5 . . . . 14 E7
Millbank WA13 . . . . 18 E3
Mill Bank CH64 . . . . 67 A5
Millbank Cl SK11 . . . . . . 84 A3
Millbank Cotts CH33 . . . 166 C2
Millbank Ct WA4 . . . . 74 A8
Millbank Dr SK10 . . . . . . 86 F1
Millbeck Cl CW2 . . . . . . 207 B5
Mill Bridge Cl CW1 . . . . 190 F3
Millbridge Gdns WA12 . . . 2 E3
Millbrook Cl
Fowley Common WA3 . . . . 5 C5
Winsford CW7 . . . . 148 F8
Millbrook Ct
Middlewich CW10 . . . . . . 128 D1
Warrington WA2 . . . . 8 B2

Millbrook End CH3 . . . . 166 A2
Millbrook Fold SK7 . . . . . . 36 F8
Millbrook Gr ▊ SK9 . . . . . . 34 D1
Mill Brow WA8 . . . . 13 C1
Millbuck Pk CW11 . . . . 174 C5
Millbuck Way CW11 . . . . . 174 C6
Mill Cl
  Chester CH2 . . . . 118 D6
  Knutsford WA16 . . . . 57 D4
  Warrington WA2 . . . . 8 E4
Mill Cotts
  Bollington SK10 . . . . 88 B8
  Christleton CH3 . . . . 142 D8
  Willaston CH64 . . . . 42 F1
Millcroft
  Neston CH64 . . . . 41 E1
  Sandbach, Wheelock
  CW11 . . . . 191 F8
Mill Cross CH3 . . . . 143 B5
Mill Ct CH65 . . . . 69 F6
Milldale Rd WN7 . . . . 4 B8
Millend CW12 . . . . 209 C5
Millend La ST7 . . . . 209 C5
Millennium Way ▊ WA8 . . . 15 B7
Millennium Ct CH64 . . . . . . 41 E2
Millennium Way ST5 . . . . . 210 F2
Millers Cl CH3 . . . . 143 A4
Millers Croft ▊ SK10 . . . . . 112 C8
Millers Ct ▊ SK10 . . . . 112 C8
Millersdale Cl CH62 . . . . . . 43 F5
Millersdale Gr WA7 . . . . 50 A5
Millers La WA13 . . . . 19 B5
Millers Mdw SK10 . . . . 88 E5
Miller St WA4 . . . . 16 C4
Millers View ST7 . . . . 195 A1
Millers Wharf ST7 . . . . 193 E7
Milley La WA16 . . . . 80 C7
Mill Farm La WA16 . . . . 8 E3
Mill Farm Cotts CW7 . . . . . 149 B3
Mill Farm Est CW5 . . . . 217 A3
Millfield
  Holt LL13 . . . . 196 D7
  Neston CH64 . . . . 41 E1
Millfield Bsns Ctr WA11 . . . 1 E8
Mill Field Cl CH3 . . . . 180 F2
Millfield La
  Haydock WA11 . . . . 1 E8
  Saighton CH3 . . . . 142 F1
  Tarporley CW6 . . . . 146 C2
Millfield Rd WA8 . . . . 13 C2
Millfields CW5 . . . . 204 D4
Millfields Prim Sch
  Bebington CH62 . . . . 43 E4
  Nantwich CW5 . . . . 204 C5
Millfield Terr CH66 . . . . 69 C7
Millgate CW8 . . . . 101 F4
Mill Gn
  Congleton CW12 . . . . 156 D3
  Willaston CH64 . . . . 67 F8
Mill Gr
  Bulkeley SY14 . . . . 184 E2
  Kidsgrove ST7 . . . . 194 D1
Mill Green La WA8 . . . . 13 E5
Mill Green Sch WA12 . . . . . . 2 E3
Mill Hill Ave SK12 . . . . 36 D7
Mill Hill Dr CW1 . . . . 175 A5
Mill Hill Hollow SK12 . . . . . 36 D7
Mill Hill La CW11 . . . . 175 A4
Mill Ho CW5 . . . . 204 D5
Millhouse Ave WA4 . . . . 16 D1
Millhouse La WA3 . . . . 9 A6
Milling Field The CW4 . . . . 130 C2
Millingford Ind Est WA3 . . . 3 A8
Millington Cl
  Runcorn WA7 . . . . 49 F3
  Widnes WA8 . . . . 22 F8
Millington Gdns WA13 . . . . 19 C4
Millington Hall La WA14 . . 30 B5
Millington La
  Rostherne WA14 . . . . 30 B6
  Weaverham CW8 . . . . 102 B6
Mill La
  Adlington SK10 . . . . 62 B6
  Aldford CH3 . . . . 163 F3
  Alsager CW11 . . . . 192 E8
  Altrincham WA15 . . . . 32 E4
  Audlem, Little Heath CW3 230 A4
  Audlem, Swanbach CW3 . . 229 E2
  Barthomley CW2 . . . . 208 C2
  Blakenhall CW5 . . . . 221 B4
  Bold Heath WA8 . . . . 13 D6
  Bollington SK10 . . . . 88 C8
  Brereton Green CW4 . . . . . 153 E8
  Bulkeley SY14 . . . . 184 E2
  Burton CH64 . . . . 67 C1
  Chester CH4 . . . . 118 D6
  Christleton CW3 . . . . 120 D2
  Congleton CW12 . . . . 179 C8
  Cronton WA8 . . . . 12 D6
  Cuddington CW8 . . . . 101 F4
  Duddon CW6 . . . . 145 A2
  Eaton CW6 . . . . 147 B2
  Ellesmere Port CH66 . . . . . 69 E5
  Frodsham WA6 . . . . 49 F2
  Goostrey CW4 . . . . 107 E2
  Great Barrow CH3 . . . . 120 E5
  Hazel Grove SK7 . . . . 36 F8
  Heswall CH60 . . . . 41 B8
  Higher Walton WA4 . . . . . . 25 E7
  Holmes Chapel CW4 . . . . . 154 A8
  Huxley CH3 . . . . 144 C1
  Kelsall CW6 . . . . 122 E5
  Kingsley WA6 . . . . 75 E3
  Lindow End SK9 . . . . 84 A7
  Little Budworth CW6 . . . . . 148 A8
  Lymm WA13 . . . . 19 C4
  Macclesfield SK11 . . . . . . 112 D7
  Marton CW12 . . . . 132 F2

Mill La continued
  Middlewich CW10 . . . . 128 D1
  Middlewich, Stud Green
  CW11 . . . . 152 C1
  Mobberley WA16 . . . . 58 B4
  Mottram St Andrew SK10 . . 61 C5
  Neston CH64 . . . . 67 C5
  Newton-le-Willows WA12 . . . 2 E3
  Over Peover WA16, SK11 . 108 D8
  Prestbury SK10 . . . . 61 F6
  Sandbach CW11 . . . . 174 C8
  Sandbach, Wheelock
  CW11 . . . . 175 B2
  Siddington SK11 . . . . 109 F6
  Smallwood CW11 . . . . 176 D7
  Tarvin CH3 . . . . 121 C4
  The Bank ST7 . . . . 195 A7
  Warrington, Houghton Gn
  WA2 . . . . 8 E4
  Warrington, Stockton Heath
  WA4 . . . . 16 E1
  Warrington WA2 . . . . 7 F4
  Weston CW2 . . . . 207 B8
  Whitegate CW7, CW8 . . . . 126 B6
  Willaston CH64 . . . . 42 F1
Mill Lane Cotts CW11 . . . . 120 E5
Mill Lane End CW5 . . . . . . 204 E5
Mill Lane Ind Est CH22 . . . . 70 F2
Mill Mdw WA12 . . . . 2 E3
Millmead ST7 . . . . 193 F7
Mill Park Dr CH62 . . . . 43 E3
Mill Pool La CW5 . . . . 187 C6
Millport Cl WA2 . . . . 9 A2
Millrace Dr CW2 . . . . 206 B8
Mill Rd
  Macclesfield SK11 . . . . . . 112 D6
  Wilmslow SK9 . . . . 60 B7
Mill Rise
  Helsby WA6 . . . . 73 C4
  Kidsgrove ST7 . . . . 195 A1
Mill Row CW11 . . . . 175 C5
Mill St
  Chester CH4 . . . . 237 B1
  Congleton, Buglawton
  CW12 . . . . 156 F4
  Congleton CW12 . . . . 156 D3
  Crewe CW2 . . . . 190 D3
  Golborne WA3 . . . . 3 A8
  Macclesfield SK11 . . . . . . 112 D7
  Nantwich CW5 . . . . 204 E5
  Neston CH64 . . . . 66 D8
  Wilmslow SK9 . . . . 60 B7
Millstone Ave ST7 . . . . 194 E1
Millstone Cl SK12 . . . . 36 F5
Millstone La CW5 . . . . 204 E5
Millstone Pas SK11 . . . . . . 112 E6
Mill Stream Cl WA4 . . . . . . 107 E1
Mills Way CW1 . . . . 173 B1
Mill The ST7 . . . . 195 C5
Mill View Cl SY14 . . . . 184 E2
Mill View Prim Sch CH2 . . 118 E6
Millway
  Altrincham WA15 . . . . 32 C7
  Waverton CH3 . . . . 143 B5
Mill Way CW5 . . . . 204 F5
Millway Rd L24 . . . . 21 A4
Mill Wharf CH3 . . . . 143 B5
Millwood WA7 . . . . 24 C1
Mill Wood & Alder Wood
  Nature Reserve* L24 . . . . 21 B4
Millwood Cl ▊ SK8 . . . . 34 E8
Millwood Ct L24 . . . . 21 A4
Millwood Dr CW8 . . . . 102 E4
Millyard The CH4 . . . . 162 C1
Milne Cl CW2 . . . . 189 F1
Milner Cop CH60 . . . . 41 A8
Milner Rd
  Heswall CH60 . . . . 41 A8
  Northwich CW8 . . . . 103 C6
MILNERS GREEN 143 C2
Milner St WA5 . . . . 15 F5
Milnthorpe Rd WA5 . . . . 6 E6
Milton Ave
  Irlam M44 . . . . 11 E6
  Newton-le-Willows WA12 . . . 2 B3
  Widnes WA8 . . . . 22 E8
Milton Cl
  Ellesmere Port CH65 . . . . . 70 D4
  Higher Wincham CW9 . . . . 80 A5
  Middlewich CW10 . . . . 151 D5
Milton Cres ST7 . . . . 210 C8
Milton Ct SK7 . . . . 35 F6
Milton Dr
  Poynton SK12 . . . . 36 D4
  Wistaston CW2 . . . . 206 A8
Milton Gr
  Helsby WA6 . . . . 73 A1
  Warrington WA4 . . . . 16 D3
MILTON GREEN 165 C2
Milton Rough CW8 . . . . 76 E2
Milton St
  Chester CH1 . . . . 237 B3
  Widnes WA8 . . . . 23 A5
Milton Way CW11 . . . . 174 D6
Milvain Dr WA2 . . . . 9 A1
Milverton Dr SK7 . . . . 35 B5
Mimosa Cl CH2 . . . . 72 C4
Miners Way
  Speke L24 . . . . 21 A3
  Widnes WA8 . . . . 21 F2
Minerva Ave CH1 . . . . 117 E2
Minerva Cl WA4 . . . . 16 D2

Minerva Ct CH1 . . . . 117 E2
Mine Way WA11 . . . . 1 F7
Minn-End-La SK11 . . . . 159 B6
Minor Ave SK11 . . . . 112 D3
Minshull La CW5, CW7 . . . 171 C4
Minshull New Rd CW1 . . . 189 F7
Minshull St WA16 . . . . 57 A2
MINSHULL VERNON 172 E5
Minster Cl CW7 . . . . 149 D5
Minster Ct
  Runcorn WA7 . . . . 48 E8
  Wistaston CW2 . . . . 205 E8
Minster Dr WA14 . . . . 31 A8
Minster Rd CW2 . . . . 190 A2
Minton Way WA8 . . . . 13 B5
Mirfield Cl WA3 . . . . 3 D7
Mirion St CW1 . . . . 190 D4
Mission Mews CH2 . . . . . . 118 F2
Missouri Dr WA5 . . . . 15 A7
Misty Cl WA8 . . . . 12 C2
Mitchell Ave
  Burtonwood WA5 . . . . 6 E5
  Kidsgrove ST7 . . . . 194 D1
Mitchell Dr ST7 . . . . 194 D1
Mitchell Fold
  Fourlane-ends SK10 . . . . . . 63 D8
  High Lane SK6 . . . . 37 D1
Mitchell St
  Golborne WA3 . . . . 3 A8
  Warrington WA4 . . . . 26 C8
Mitton Cl WA8 . . . . 13 E3
Mitton Cl WA3 . . . . 4 E5
MMU Institute of Education
  (Alsager) ST7 . . . . 193 A5
MMU Institute of Education
  (Crewe) CW1 . . . . 190 F3
Moat Ho ▊ CW8 . . . . 103 F8
Moat Ho Dr CW2 . . . . 190 A2
Moat La
  Audley ST7 . . . . 209 B3
  Hollins Green WA3 . . . . 10 E2
MOBBERLEY 58 A4
Mobberley CE Prim Sch
  WA16 . . . . 58 C5
Mobberley Rd
  Ashley WA14, WA15,
  WA16 . . . . 31 E3
  Knutsford WA16 . . . . 57 B3
  Wilmslow SK9 . . . . 33 D1
  Mobberley Sta WA16 . . . . . 57 F7
MOBLAKE 230 D4
Modyn CH2 . . . . 118 C4
Moelfre Dr SK8 . . . . 35 C7
Moelwyn Dr CH66 . . . . 69 F7
Moggie La SK10 . . . . 36 F1
Mold Rd CH4 . . . . 139 A3
MOLLINGTON 94 E2
Mollington Ct CH1 . . . . 94 F3
Mollington Grange Bsns Pk
  CH1 . . . . 117 F8
Mollington Rd M22 . . . . 33 E8
Molly Potts Cl WA16 . . . . . . 82 B8
Molyneux Ave WA5 . . . . 15 F8
Monarch Cl
  Crewe CW2 . . . . 189 F4
  Irlam M44 . . . . 11 E6
Monarch Dr CW9 . . . . 103 E5
Monck Dr CW5 . . . . 204 D6
Mond Rd WA8 . . . . 23 A8
Mond St WA1 . . . . 78 B3
Monica Dr WA8 . . . . 13 A5
Monks Coppenhall Prim Sch
  CW1 . . . . 190 E7
Monks Gr CH65 . . . . 70 B6
MONKS HEATH 85 A1
Monk's Heath Crossroads
  SK10 . . . . 85 A1
Monks Heath Hall Wrkshps
  SK10 . . . . 85 B1
Monks La
  Acton CW5 . . . . 203 F7
  Crewe CW1 . . . . 189 F5
  Nantwich CW5 . . . . 204 E5
Monk's La CW3 . . . . 230 C5
Monks Orch CW5 . . . . 204 F5
Monks Pl WA2 . . . . 16 E6
Monks St WA3 . . . . 3 A8
Monk St CW1 . . . . 190 A5
Monks Way CW8 . . . . 103 B4
Monkswood Cl WA5 . . . . 7 E2
Monmouth Cl WA1 . . . . 17 E7
Monmouth Dr CH65 . . . . . . 70 D3
Monroe Cl WA1 . . . . 17 B8
Monsall Cl SK11 . . . . 112 F7
Monsall Dr SK11 . . . . 112 F7
Montague Rd WA8 . . . . 22 A6
Montana Cl ▊ WA3 . . . . 15 C7
Montclare Cres WA4 . . . . . 16 F2
Montcliffe Cl WA3 . . . . 9 C5
Montgomery Cl
  Knutsford WA16 . . . . 57 C4
  Warrington WA5 . . . . 15 C7
Montgomery Rd WA8 . . . . . 22 D8
Montgomery Way CW7 . . . 149 B7
Montmorency Rd WA16 . . . 57 D3
Montpelier Ave WA7 . . . . . . 48 F6
Montrose Cl
  Macclesfield SK10 . . . . 87 A1
  Shavington CW2 . . . . 206 B3
  Warrington WA3 . . . . 8 F4
Montrose Ct
  Chester CH4 . . . . 140 F7
  Holmes Chapel CW4 . . . . . 130 B2
Monument Rd ST7 . . . . 210 D6
Monument View ST7 . . . . . 209 F2
Moody St CW12 . . . . 156 D2
Moor Cl ST8 . . . . 179 E1
Moor Cres CH4 . . . . 139 D1

Moorcroft WA16 . . . . 80 F3
Moorcroft Ave CH3 . . . . . . 119 B1
Moorcroft Cres CH3 . . . . . 119 C4
Moorcroft Ct CH3 . . . . 119 B1
Moorcroft Mews CH4 . . . . 140 D6
Mordale Rd WA16 . . . . 57 B2
Moorditch La WA6 . . . . 48 F1
MOORE 25 B6
Moore Ave
  St Helens WA9 . . . . 1 B3
  Warrington WA4 . . . . 17 D3
Moore Cl WA8 . . . . 13 D2
Moore Dr WA11 . . . . 1 F6
Moore Gr WA13 . . . . 19 B5
Moore La WA4 . . . . 25 C7
Moore Prim Sch WA4 . . . . . 25 A5
Moore Reserve* WA4 . . . . 25 C8
Moorfield Cres WA3 . . . . 4 A7
Moorfield Dr
  Neston CH64 . . . . 41 C1
  Wilmslow SK9 . . . . 59 E5
Moorfield Prim Sch WA8 . 13 D3
Moorfield Rd WA8 . . . . 13 D3
Moorfields CW5 . . . . 205 E6
Moorhead La CW11 . . . . . . 154 D3
Moorhill Rd SK11 . . . . 112 C4
Moor Ho WA6 . . . . 74 B8
Moorhouse Ave ST7 . . . . . 193 C4
Mooring Cl CH2 . . . . 118 D5
Mooring Cl WA7 . . . . 50 D6
Moorings CW12 . . . . 156 E1
Moorings Cl WA4 . . . . 41 B1
Moorings The
  Christleton CH3 . . . . 142 E7
  Disley SK12 . . . . 38 E6
  Heswall CH60 . . . . 40 C8
  Middlewich CW10 . . . . 128 C1
Moorland Cl CH60 . . . . 41 A7
Moorland Dr
  Cheadle SK8 . . . . 34 F8
  Runcorn WA7 . . . . 50 E7
Moorland Pk CH60 . . . . 41 A7
Moorland Rd
  Biddulph ST8 . . . . 179 D1
  Ellesmere Port CH66 . . . . . 69 E8
  Mow Cop ST7 . . . . 195 D7
Moorlands Ave CW8 . . . . . 102 A4
Moorlands Cl SK10 . . . . 87 C3
Moorlands Dr CW5 . . . . . . 206 A1
Moorlands Pk CW8 . . . . . . 102 A4
Moor Lane Bsns Ctr ▊
  WA8 . . . . 23 A7
Moor Lane SK9 . . . . 34 E1
Moor-Park Way CW9 . . . . 103 F4
Moorsbrook Gr ▊ SK9 . . . . 34 E1
Moorsfield Ave WA3 . . . . . 229 F3
MOORSIDE 66 C7
Moorside
  Knutsford WA16 . . . . 57 A2
  Warrington WA4 . . . . 16 E4
Moorside Ave CH64 . . . . . . 66 C8
Moorside Ct WA8 . . . . 22 F7
Moorside La
  Neston CH64 . . . . 66 D8
  Pott Shrigley SK10 . . . . 63 E4
Moors La CW7 . . . . 149 B5
Moorson Ave ST7 . . . . 194 F8
Moor St SK12 . . . . 156 E2
Moorview Gdns ST7 . . . . . 195 E6
Moorway CH60 . . . . 41 B8
Moran Cl SK9 . . . . 34 E2
Moran Cres SK11 . . . . 112 B7
Moran Rd SK11 . . . . 112 B7
Moran Rd SK11 . . . . 15 A6
Moran Rd SK11 . . . . 112 B7
Morcott La L24 . . . . 21 D2
Moresby Cl WA7 . . . . 50 E7
Moreton Ave SK7 . . . . 35 E5
Moreton Cl CW11 . . . . 175 C7
Moreton Dr
  Alsager ST7 . . . . 193 C3
  Handforth SK9 . . . . 34 E3
  Holmes Chapel CW4 . . . . . 130 B3
  Poynton SK12 . . . . 36 F4
Moreton Pl ST7 . . . . 194 E6
Moreton Rd CW2 . . . . 189 F3
Moreton St CW8 . . . . 78 D1
Moreton Terr WA4 . . . . 74 A8
Moreville Cl CW9 . . . . 103 E3
Morgan Ave WA2 . . . . 8 C2
Morgan Cl
  Blacon CH1 . . . . 117 F6
  Crewe CW2 . . . . 190 A4
Morgans Way WA3 . . . . 4 A8
Morgan Wlk CW5 . . . . 204 D6
Morland Ave
  Bebington CH62 . . . . 43 D6
  Neston CH64 . . . . 66 F7
MORLEY 33 C2
Morley Cl CH2 . . . . 119 F8
Morley Ct WA1 . . . . 16 B5
MORLEY COMMON 15 F1
Morley Dr CW12 . . . . 157 A1
MORLEY GREEN 33 C1
Morley Green Rd SK9 . . . . . 33 C1
Morley Rd
  Runcorn WA7 . . . . 23 A1
  Warrington WA3 . . . . 16 A1
Morley St WA1 . . . . 16 D6

Mornant Ave CW8 . . . . 103 A3
Mornington Ave CH65 . . . . 70 C5
Mornington Cl CW11 . . . . . 174 D7
Morphany La WA4 . . . . 51 E6
Morreys La CW6 . . . . 122 F6
Morris Ave WA4 . . . . 16 F4
Morris Cl WA11 . . . . 1 A5
Morris Dr CW8 . . . . 77 D1
Morrison Cl WA5 . . . . 15 A5
Morris Pk CW8 . . . . 103 B4
Mort Ave WA4 . . . . 17 A5
Mortimer Ave WA2 . . . . 16 B8
Mortimer Dr CW5 . . . . 175 C5
Mortlake Cl WA8 . . . . 12 C3
Mortlake Cres CH3 . . . . . . 119 A1
Morton Ave WA6 . . . . 73 B1
Morton Cl WA5 . . . . 15 C8
Morton Dr SK11 . . . . 112 F3
Morton Gdns CH1 . . . . 117 E4
Morton Rd
  Blacon CH1 . . . . 117 C4
  Runcorn WA7 . . . . 50 D8
Morval Cres WA7 . . . . 23 D1
Morven Cl WA2 . . . . 8 E3
Mosedale Gr WA7 . . . . 49 E5
Moseley Ave WA4 . . . . 17 A3
Moses Ct CH1 . . . . 237 C3
MOSS BANK 23 D8
Moss Bank
  Bramhall SK7 . . . . 35 C5
  Chester CH2 . . . . 118 C4
  Winsford CW7 . . . . 126 C1
Moss Bank Rd WA8 . . . . . . 23 D7
Moss Bower Rd SK11 . . . . 112 C4
MOSSBROW 19 E7
Moss Brow SK10 . . . . 87 E7
Moss Brow La WA16 . . . . . . 28 D4
Moss Cl
  Warrington WA4 . . . . 16 E2
  Willaston CH64 . . . . 68 A8
Moss Croft CW1 . . . . 190 A8
Mossdale Cl
  Crewe CW2 . . . . 189 E4
  Warrington WA5 . . . . 15 A7
Moss Dr
  Manley WA6 . . . . 98 F4
  Middlewich CW10 . . . . 151 D6
MOSSEND 154 E1
MOSS END 54 C2
Moss End La CW11 . . . . . . 176 E8
Moss Farm Barns CW8 . . . 102 D4
Moss Farm Rest Ctr
  CW8 . . . . 103 D8
Mossfield Cres ▊ ST7 . . . . 195 B2
Moss Fields
  Alsager CW1 . . . . 193 A3
  Crewe CW1 . . . . 173 A1
Moss Gate WA3 . . . . 10 A5
Moss Gr
  Lymm WA13 . . . . 19 B4
  Newcastle-under-Lyme
  ST5 . . . . 210 D3
  Saltney CH4 . . . . 140 D3
Moss Green Way WA9 . . . . . 1 A1
Mosshall La WA4 . . . . 26 F1
Moss Hey Prim Sch SK7 . . 35 C5
MOSS HOUSES 111 F2
Moss La
  Alderley Edge SK9 . . . . 60 B1
  Bollington SK10 . . . . 87 E8
  Bramhall SK7 . . . . 35 D5
  Brereton Green CW12 . . . 154 F5
  Byley CW10 . . . . 129 B7
  Congleton CW12 . . . . 156 E6
  Crewe CW1 . . . . 173 A2
  Cuddington CW8 . . . . 102 A3
  Dunham Woodhouses WA13 20 B8
  Fowley Common WA3 . . . . . 5 D5
  Golborne WA3 . . . . 3 B5
  Higher Wincham CW9 . . . . 79 E6
  High Legh, Sink Moss WA16 28 D4
  High Legh WA16 . . . . 29 E6
  Hollins Green WA3 . . . . 10 E5
  Irlam M44 . . . . 11 D5
  Lawton-gate ST7 . . . . 194 F4
  Lostock Green CW9 . . . . . 105 D8
  Macclesfield SK11 . . . . . . 112 C4
  Manley WA6 . . . . 99 A4
  Mere WA16 . . . . 56 C5
  Mobberley WA16 . . . . 58 F4
  Moore WA4 . . . . 25 A6
  Mottram St Andrew SK10 . . 61 A2
  Norbury SY13 . . . . 215 C5
  Norley WA6 . . . . 101 B5
  Northwich CW8 . . . . 103 D7
  Over Peover WA16 . . . . 83 C3
  Partington SK11 . . . . 11 F3
  Partington, Mossbrow
  WA13 . . . . 11 F1
  Sandbach CW11 . . . . 174 C7
  Siddington SK11 . . . . 109 E2
  St Helens, Moss Nook WA9 . . 1 A1
  Tarporley WA6 . . . . 146 B2
  Warmingham CW1 . . . . 173 C3
  Warrington WA3 . . . . 9 E1
  Wythenshawe SK9 . . . . 33 E6
Mosslands Cl CH66 . . . . . . 69 E2
Moss Lane CW5 . . . . 206 A1
Moss Lane Bsns Ctr
  CW11 . . . . 174 D6
Moss Lane Ind Est CW11 174 D7
MOSSLEY 179 A8
Mossley Ave CH62 . . . . 43 D8

Mossley CE Prim Sch
CW12 . . . . **179** B8
Mossley Ct CW12 . . . . **178** F8
Mossley Garth Cl 4
CW12. . . . . **157** A1
Moss Mere CW11 . . . . **176** F7
MOSS NOOK **33** F7
Moss Pl ST17 . . . . **195** B3
Moss Rd
Alderley Edge SK9 . . . . **60** C2
Congleton CW12 . . . . . . **178** F7
Irlam M44 . . . . **11** C7
Northwich CW8 . . . . . . **103** D8
Warrington WA4 . . . . . . **17** A3
Moss Rose SK9 . . . . . . **60** B2
Moss Rose (Macclesfield
Town FC) SK11 . . . . . **112** C4
Moss Side La
Antrobus CW9 . . . . **53** D7
Hollins Green WA3 . . . . **10** F3
Moore WA4 . . . . **24** F7
Moss Side Rd M44 . . . . **11** E6
Moss Sq
Crewe CW1 . . . . **190** D4
Macclesfield SK11. . . . . **112** D4
Moss St
Weaverham CW8 . . . . . . **77** D1
Widnes WA8 . . . . **23** D7
Moss Terr
Warren SK11 . . . . **112** A5
Wilmslow SK9 . . . . **60** F8
Winnington WA8 . . . . . . **78** D1
Moss The CW9 . . . . **78** D7
Mossvale CH66 . . . . **69** D8
Moss View Rd WA13 . . **112** A4
Moss Way ST7 . . . . **193** A3
Mossways Gn SK9. . . . . **59** C7
Mossways Pk SK9 . . . . . **59** C7
Mosswood SK9 . . . . **34** E1
MOSTON **95** C1
Moston Ct 5 CW12 . . . **156** F3
Moston Gr WA13. . . . . . . **18** D3
MOSTON GREEN **174** B8
Moston Rd
Chester CH2 . . . . **118** D8
Sandbach CW11 . . . . . . **174** D6
Moston Way CH66 . . . . . **69** F3
Mostyn Ave CH60 . . . . . **40** C8
Mostyn Gdns CH64 . . . . **41** B1
Mostyn House Sch CH64 . **66** C8
Mostyn PI CH1 . . . . **117** E6
Mostyn Sq CH64 . . . . **41** B1
Mote Hill Ct WA1 . . . . . **16** D6
Motherwell Cl WA8 . . . . **12** E3
Mottershead Cl 1 WA8 . **23** A8
Mottershead Rd WA8 . . . **23** A8
Mottram Cl
Middlewich CW10 . . . . **151** B7
Warrington WA4 . . . . . . **17** B3
Mottram Dr CW5. . . . . . **205** A4
Mottram Rd SK9 . . . . . . **60** D1
MOTTRAM ST ANDREW . **61** B2
Mottram St Andrew Prim Sch
SK10 . . . . **61** B1
Mottram St Andrew Stud
Farm* SK10. . . . . **61** A2
Mottram Way SK10 . . . . **87** E2
Moughland La WA7 . . . . **49** A8
Moulders La WA1 . . . . . **16** B4
MOULDSWORTH **98** F7
Mouldsworth La 2 CW9. **103** E4
Mouldsworth Motor Mus*
CH3. . . . . **98** E1
Mouldsworth Sta CH3. . . **99** A2
Moulton Cl
Knutsford WA16. . . . . . . **57** C1
Northwich CW8 . . . . . . **103** E4
Runcorn WA7. . . . . **49** F4
Moulton Ct CW9. . . . . . **126** F8
Mountain View
Helsby WA6 . . . . **73** B3
Saltney CH4 . . . . **140** E6
Mount Ave CH60 . . . . . . **40** F8
Mount Barns CH2 . . . . . **95** C6
Mountbatten Ct CW2 . . **190** A3
Mountbatten Way CW12 . **156** E3
Mount Cl CW5 . . . . **204** F6
Mount Ct 3 CH60 . . . . . **40** F8
Mount Dr CW5. . . . . **204** F6
Mount Farm Way CH66 . **69** C2
Mountfield Rd SK7. . . . . **35** E5
Mount Mews CH60 . . . . . **40** F8
Mount Pl CH2 . . . . **118** F2
MOUNT PLEASANT
Mow Cop **195** B6
Winsford **149** A7
Mount Pleasant
Audlem CW3 . . . . **230** B4
Chester CH4 . . . . **140** F7
Congleton CW12 . . . . . **156** E2
Crewe CW1 . . . . **190** B6
Elton CW1 . . . . **72** A4
Haslington CW1. . . . . . **191** D4
Kidsgrove ST7 . . . . **195** A1
Macclesfield SK10 . . . . . **87** B1
Rainow SK10 . . . . **88** D3
Widnes WA8 . . . . **13** A2
Wilmslow SK9 . . . . **60** A8
Mount Pleasant Ave WA9. .**1** B3
Mount Pleasant Dr CW7. **149** A7
Mount Pleasant Gdns*
CW6 . . . . **122** E7
Mount Pleasant Rd
Davenham CW9 . . . . . . **103** F2

Mount Pleasant Rd continued
The Bank ST7. . . . . **195** B7
Mount Pleasant Residential
Pk CW4 . . . . **130** D8
Mount Rd
Kidsgrove ST7 . . . . **195** B2
Runcorn WA7. . . . . **49** F8
Mount St WA8 . . . . **13** B1
Mount Terr SK11. . . . . . **112** F7
Mount The
Chester CH3 . . . . **118** F1
Congleton CW12 . . . . . **156** A2
Great Budworth CW9 . . . **79** A7
Hale WA15. . . . . **32** C8
Heswall CH60 . . . . **40** F8
Kidsgrove ST7 . . . . **195** A1
Scholar Green ST7. . . . . **194** E7
Mount Way CH3 . . . . . . **143** A4
Mourne Cl CH66 . . . . . . **69** A6
Mousley Bottom Nature
Reserve* SK22 . . . . **39** A7
MOW COP **195** C7
Mow Cop Rd ST7. . . . . . **195** D6
Mowcroft La WA5. . . . . . **14** B3
Mow La
Mount Pleasant ST7. . . **195** A5
Mow Cop ST7 . . . . **179** B2
Mowpen Brow WA16 . . . . **29** B6
Moxon Ave WA4 . . . . **16** F5
Moyles Cl WA8 . . . . **12** D2
Mudhouse La CH64 . . . . **67** F2
Muhlrach La SK12 . . . . . **38** E3
Muirfield Cl
Northwich CW9 . . . . . . **104** A5
Warrington WA2 . . . . **9** A3
Wilmslow SK9 . . . . **60** F8
Muirfield Dr
Macclesfield SK10 . . . . . **87** D4
Winsford CW7. . . . . **126** C2
Muirfield Mews CW7. . . **126** C2
Muir Rd CH1 . . . . **117** E3
Mulberry Ave
Golborne WA3 . . . . **3** F7
Windess WA8. . . . . **23** C7
Mulberry Cl
Elton CH2. . . . . **72** C3
Gatley SK8. . . . . **34** C7
Warrington WA1 . . . . . . **17** E7
Mulberry Ct
Macclesfield SK11 . . . . **112** D4
Warrington WA4 . . . . . . **16** D1
Mulberry Dr SK10 . . . . . **87** E1
Mulberry Gdns CW11. . . **174** D7
Mulberry Rise CW8 . . . **103** C7
Mulcaster Ct CW1. . . . . **191** D5
Mull Cl CH65. . . . . **70** C1
Mullein Cl WA3. . . . . **3** D8
Mullen Cl WA5. . . . . **7** F1
Mullins Ave WA12. . . . . . **2** C5
Mullion Cl WA7 . . . . **50** B6
Mullion Gr WA2 . . . . **9** A1
Mulsford Cl LL13. . . . . . **222** A8
Mulsford La LL13, SY14. . **222** B8
MURDISHAW **50** D7
Murdishaw Ave WA7 . . . . **50** D6
Murdishaw West CP Sch
WA7 . . . . **50** D6
Murdishaw Wood & Valley
Nature Reserve* WA7 . . **50** E6
Muriel Cl WA5 . . . . **14** D6
Murray Cl SK10 . . . . **87** A1
Murrayfield SK10 . . . . . . **87** A5
Murrayfield Dr CW5. . . . **205** D5
Museum St WA1 . . . . **16** B5
Music Hall Pass CH1 . . **237** B2
Muslin Row CW5. . . . . . **172** A5
Mustard La WA3 . . . . **4** B1
Myddleton La WA2. . . . . . **8** C6
Myrica Gr CH2 . . . . **119** B3
Myrtle Ave
Haydock WA11. . . . . **1** B7
Higher Kinnerton CH4 . . **161** A7
Newton-le-Willows WA12 . . **2** C2
Myrtle Gr
Warrington WA4 . . . . . . **16** D3
Widnes WA8 . . . . **22** D8
Myrtle Rd M31. . . . . **11** D3
Myrtle St
Crewe CW2 . . . . **190** C3
Ellesmere Port CH65 . . . **70** C7
Mytholme Ave M44 . . . . . **11** C3
Mytton Dr CW5. . . . . . . **204** D6

N

Nabbs Cl ST7 . . . . **195** B2
Nabbswood Rd ST7. . . . **195** B2
Nab Cl SK10 . . . . **63** C1
Nab Headey SK10 . . . . . . **63** C1
Nab La SK10 . . . . **63** C1
Nairn Ave CW4 . . . . **130** D2
Nairn Cl
Bebington CH63. . . . . . . **43** D4
Warrington WA2 . . . . **9** B3
Nancy View SK10 . . . . . . **88** B8
Nansen Cl WA5 . . . . **15** D7
Nansmoss La SK9 . . . . . . **33** D5
Nant Peris CH1 . . . . **117** D3
NANTWICH **204** D6
Nantwich Mus* CW5 . . **204** E5
Nantwich Rd
Audlem ST7. . . . . **209** B1
Barbridge CW5 . . . . . . **187** B8
Betley ST7 . . . . **208** E1
Broxton CH3 . . . . **183** C1
Chorley Bank CW5. . . . . **201** E2

Nantwich Rd continued
Crewe CW2 . . . . **190** C2
Ellesmere Port CH66. . . . **69** F3
Middlewich CW10 . . . . **151** A7
Sound CW5 . . . . **217** B5
Tarporley CW6 . . . . **168** D7
Wimboldsley CW10 . . . **150** F5
Wistaston CW2, CW5 . . **189** C2
Woore CW3 . . . . **232** B1
Nantwich Sta CW5. . . . . **204** E4
Nantwich Trade Yd CW5 . **204** F7
Nantwich Way 6 SK9. . . **34** E5
Naomi Cl CH1. . . . . **117** D5
Napier Gdns 3 ST7. . . . **195** A2
Napier Rd CH2 . . . . **118** C8
Napier St WA1 . . . . **16** C5
Napley Dr TF9 . . . . **236** C2
NAPLEY HEATH **236** F1
Napley Rd TF9 . . . . **236** D1
Nares Cl WA5. . . . . **7** C1
Narrow La
Crewe, Crewe Green
CW1. . . . . **191** C3
Wardsend SK10. . . . . . . **37** A1
Naseby Rd CW12. . . . . . **156** A3
Nathan Dr WA11. . . . . **1** E6
Nathans Mdw CW12 . . . **156** A4
National Waterways Mus*
CH65. . . . . **70** C7
Nat La CW7. . . . . **126** F2
Nat Lane Ret Pk CW7 . . **126** F2
Naughton Lea WA8 . . . . . **12** D2
Naughton Rd 3 WA8. . . . **23** A8
Navan Ct CW1 . . . . **190** B5
Navigation Cl WA7. . . . . **50** D6
Navigation Ho 10 CW9. . **103** F8
Navigation Rd WA8 . . . **103** F7
Navigation St WA1. . . . . **16** D5
Naylor Ave WA13 . . . . **3** B8
Naylor Ct CH66. . . . . **69** E6
Naylor Cres
Ellesmere Port CH66. . . . **69** E6
Nantwich CW5 . . . . **205** A4
Naylor Ct
Ellesmere Port CH66 . . . **69** E6
Northwich CW9 . . . . . . **103** F8
Naylor Gn CH66. . . . . . . **69** E6
Naylor PI CH66. . . . . **69** E8
Naylor Rd
Overpool CH66 . . . . **69** F7
Widnes WA8 . . . . **13** D1
Naylor St WA1. . . . . **16** B5
Naylor Wlk CH66. . . . . . . **69** F7
Nazareth House La WA8 . . **22** C7
Neal Ave SK8 . . . . **34** A8
Neath Cl SK12 . . . . **36** D5
Needham Cl WA7 . . . . . . **23** D2
Needham Dr
Cranage CW4. . . . . **130** A5
Hartford CW8 . . . . **103** A4
Needhams Bank CW11 . **174** C6
Needhams Wharf Cl SK10 **88** A1
Neills Rd WA5 . . . . **6** B6
Neil St WA8 . . . . **13** C2
Nelson Ave SK12 . . . . . . **37** A3
Nelson Bldgs ST17 . . . . **195** A1
Nelson Cl SK12 . . . . **37** A3
Nelson Dr M44. . . . . **11** E6
Nelson Gr ST7 . . . . **193** F2
Nelson Ind Est ST7 . . . **194** C1
Nelson Rd CH65. . . . . . . **70** C7
Nelson St
Chester CH1 . . . . **237** C3
Congleton CW12 . . . . . **156** D2
Crewe CW2 . . . . **190** C2
Macclesfield SK11 . . . . **112** D7
Newton-le-Willows WA12 . . **2** A3
Widnes WA8 . . . . **23** A6
Nemos Cl WA6. . . . . **73** C2
Neptune Cl WA7 . . . . **50** D7
Nesfield Ct CW11 . . . . . **191** F7
Nesfield Dr CW11 . . . . . **191** F7
NESS **67** B4
Ness Acre La CH64 . . . . **67** E8
Ness Botanic Gdns*
CH64. . . . . **67** A8
NESS HOLT **66** F5
Nessina Gr CW2 . . . . . . **205** F8
NESTON. **66** D7
Neston Cl WA6. . . . . **73** A2
Neston Dr CH2. . . . . **118** C5
Neston Gn CH66 . . . . **69** F3
Neston High Sch CH64 . . **41** F1
Neston Prim Sch CH64 . . **66** E7
Neston Rd
Heswall CH63, CH64. . . . **41** F5
Neston CH64. . . . . **67** A8
Willaston CH64 . . . . **67** F8
Neston Recn Ctr CH64 . . **41** F1
Neston Road Cotts CH63. . **42** A6
Neston Sta CH66 . . . . . . **66** E8
Neston Way SK9 . . . . . . **34** D3
NETHER ALDERLEY **85** A5
Nether Alderley Mill*
SK10. . . . . **85** A5
Nether Alderley Prim Sch
SK10. . . . . **85** A6
Netherfield WA8. . . . . . . **22** E8
Netherfields SK9. . . . . . . **85** A8
Nether Fold SK10 . . . . . . **87** A8
Nether Lea CW4 . . . . . . **130** C8
Netherley Rd WA8 . . . . . **12** A2
Netherpool Rd CH66 . . . . **69** F8
NETHER TABLEY **80** F8
NETHERTON **74** A6
Netherton Dr WA6 . . . . . **74** A7

Netherton Farm Cotts
WA6. . . . . **74** A7
Neumann St CW9 . . . . . **104** B8
Nevada Cl WA5 . . . . **15** C8
Neville Ave
St Helens WA9 . . . . **1** B2
Warrington WA2 . . . . **8** D1
Neville Cl CH3 . . . . **119** B1
Neville Cres WA5 . . . . . . **15** A3
Neville Dr CH3. . . . . **119** B1
Neville Rd
Bebington CH62. . . . . . . **43** E8
Chester CH3 . . . . **119** B1
Neville St
Crewe CW2 . . . . **190** D1
Newton-le-Willows WA12 . . **2** A3
Nevin Cl SK7. . . . . **36** A7
Nevin Rd CH1 . . . . **117** D3
Nevis Dr CW2 . . . . **189** D3
New Albert Terr WA7 . . . **23** B3
Newall Ave CW11 . . . . . **175** A5
Newall Cl CH3 . . . . **166** B1
Newall Cres CW7 . . . . . **127** A1
Newarth Dr WA13 . . . . . **19** A2
New Bank Pl WA8 . . . . . **12** B1
New Bank Rd WA8 . . . . . **12** B1
New Barnet WA8. . . . . . . **12** F4
Newbiggin Way 10 SK10. **112** C8
Newbold Ct 9 CW12. . . **156** F3
New Bold Ct WA9 . . . . . . **6** A7
Newbold Way CW5 . . . . **204** E3
Newbold Gr WA5. . . . . **7** E2
NEW BOSTON **1** E7
Newbridge Cl
Runcorn WA7. . . . . **50** C6
Warrington WA5 . . . . **7** D2
Newbridge Rd CH65. . . . **70** F4
New Bridge Rd CH65, CH2. **70** F3
Newbridge Rd WA7 . . . . **24** D1
Newbury Ave
Crewe CW1 . . . . **190** C2
5 Winsford CW7 . . . . **149** A8
Newbury Cl
Cheadle SK8 . . . . **35** A6
Widnes WA8 . . . . **13** A3
Newbury Ct SK9 . . . . **60** A6
Newbury Rd
Chester CH4 . . . . **140** F6
Gatley SK8. . . . . **34** C7
Newby Ct CW12 . . . . . . **156** A1
Newcastle Rd
Astbury CW12 . . . . **178** A7
Brereton Green CW11 . . **153** F4
Congleton CW12 . . . . . **156** A2
Hassall Green CW11 . . . **176** A3
Nantwich CW5 . . . . **204** F6
Shavington CW2, CW5. . **206** C3
Smallwood CW11 . . . . . **176** D6
Talke ST7 . . . . **210** F2
Willaston CW5 . . . . **205** E4
Woore CW3 . . . . **232** E1
Newcastle Road N CW11 **153** E5
Newcastle Road S CW11 **153** F5
Newcastle St CW1 . . . . **190** A5
NEWCASTLE-UNDER-
LYME **210** D3
NEWCHAPEL. **195** E2
Newchapel Obsy & Natural
Science Ctr* ST7 . . . . **195** E2
Newchapel Rd ST7. . . . . **195** C3
New Chester Rd CH62. . . **43** E7
Newchurch Com Prim Sch
WA3 . . . . **4** E2
Newchurch La WA3 . . . . . **4** F2
Newcombe Ave WA2 . . . . **16** E8
New Cotts
Hampton Heath SY14 . . **213** E7
Manley WA6. . . . . **99** C7
New Crane Bank CH1 . . **118** B1
New Crane St CH1 . . . . **118** B1
New Cswy CW8 . . . . **101** F7
New Cut Ind Est WA1. . . **17** C7
New Cut La WA1 . . . . **17** B7
Newdigate St CW1 . . . . **190** C4
New Farm Cotts WA3 . . . **11** A7
New Farm Ct
Great Barrow CH3. . . . . **120** E5
Malpas SY14. . . . . **213** A5
NEWFIELD. **172** E8
Newfield Ct WA13. . . . . . **19** A5
Newfield Dr CW1 . . . . . **190** E5
Newfield Rd WA13 . . . . . **18** D3
Newfield St WA1 . . . . . . **175** B7
Newfield Terr WA6 . . . . . **73** B2
Newgate
1 Macclesfield SK11. . **112** D7
Wilmslow SK9 . . . . **59** E7
Newgate Rd SK9 . . . . . . **59** D7
Newgate St CH1 . . . . . . **237** B2
Newgate Wlk CH1. . . . . **237** B2
New Grosvenor Rd CH65 . **70** B7
New Hall Ave SK8 . . . . . . **34** B7
New Hall La CH66 . . . . . **44** B1
Newhall Rd CH2 . . . . . . **118** E6
New Hall St SK10 . . . . . . **87** D1
Newham Cl SK11. . . . . . **112** F3
New Hampshire Cl 7
WA5. . . . . **15** B7
Newhaven Ct CW5 . . . . **204** F5
Newhaven Rd WA2 . . . . . . **8** B4
Newheyes CH64. . . . . **41** E1
New Hey La CH64 . . . . . **68** A6
New Home Farm Cotts
CH64 . . . . **93** A7

NEW HORWICH **65** E6
New Horwich Rd SK23. . . **65** E6
New Hos CW5 . . . . **187** D6
New Houses CH3. . . . . . **143** B7
New Inn Cotts WA16 . . . **108** C2
New Inn La CW11 . . . . . **176** A2
New King St
Audley ST7. . . . . **209** C1
Middlewich CW10 . . . . **128** C2
New La
Appleton Thorn WA4 . . . **27** B5
Churton CH3 . . . . **180** F6
Croft WA3 . . . . **9** B7
Harthill CH3. . . . . **183** F3
Winsford CW7 . . . . **149** F8
Newland Cl WA8 . . . . . . **12** C3
Newland Mews WA3 . . . . **4** E5
Newlands SK9 . . . . **59** C7
Newlands Ave
Bramhall SK7. . . . . **35** F8
Cheadle SK8 . . . . **35** A7
Newlands Cl
Cheadle SK8 . . . . **35** A7
Frodsham WA6. . . . . **74** C6
Newlands Dr
Golborne WA3 . . . . **3** D8
Wilmslow SK9 . . . . **59** E5
Newlands Rd
Macclesfield SK10 . . . . **111** E7
Warrington WA4 . . . . . . **16** F2
New Lands CW5 . . . . . . **205** B4
NEW LANE END **4** A2
New Lane End WA3 . . . . . **4** A2
Newlyn Ave
Congleton CW12 . . . . . **178** E8
Macclesfield SK10 . . . . . **86** D1
Newlyn Cl WA7 . . . . **50** B6
Newlyn Gdns WA5 . . . . . **14** D3
New Manchester Rd WA1 **17** A7
Newman Cl CW12 . . . . . **156** B3
New Manor Rd WA4 . . . . **51** B6
Newman's La CW5 . . . . **219** D8
Newman St WA4 . . . . **16** F3
Newmarket Cl 1 SK10. . **87** C4
New Market Wlk 10 WA1 . **16** B5
New Meadowside Residential
Cvn Pk CW5 . . . . **217** E5
NEW MILLS **39** D7
New Mills Central Sta
SK22. . . . . **39** B7
New Mills Heritage Ctr*
SK22. . . . . **39** C8
New Mills L Ctr SK22. . . **39** C8
New Mills Newtown Sta
SK22. . . . . **39** B6
New Mills Prim Sch 1
SK2 . . . . **39** B8
New Mills Sch Bsns & Ent
Coll 1 SK22 . . . . **39** C8
Newmoore La WA7. . . . . **24** F4
New Moss Rd M44 . . . . . **11** D6
Newnham Dr CH65. . . . . **70** C4
New Pale Rd WA6. . . . . . **99** C6
New Park Ct SK22. . . . . . **39** D7
New Platt La CW12 . . . . **107** B1
Newport Gr ST5. . . . . . . **210** E2
Newquay Cl WA7 . . . . . . **50** B6
Newquay Ct CW12 . . . . **178** E8
Newquay Dr
Bramhall SK7. . . . . **35** F7
Macclesfield SK10 . . . . **111** D8
New Rd
Anderton CW9 . . . . **78** D4
Antrobus CW9 . . . . **27** D1
Astbury CW12 . . . . **178** B4
Audley ST7. . . . . **209** E3
Buxton SK17 . . . . **138** F1
Duddon CW6 . . . . **145** B6
Ellesmere Port CH66. . . . **69** A8
Horwich End SK23. . . . . **65** E6
Lymm WA13. . . . . **18** E3
Marton CW12 . . . . **132** D1
Mossend CW11 . . . . . . **154** F2
Prestbury SK10 . . . . **87** A7
Rosthern WA16 . . . . **30** E3
Warrington WA4 . . . . . . **16** C4
Whaley Bridge, Bridgemont
SK23 . . . . **39** F1
Winsford CW7 . . . . **126** E2
Wrenbury CW5 . . . . **216** D3
New Road Bsns Ctr CW7 **126** E2
New Russia Hall (Gt
Northern Architectural
Antiques)* CH3 . . . . . . **165** E5
Newry Ct CH2. . . . . **118** D4
Newry Park E CH2 . . . . **118** D4
Newry Pk CH2 . . . . **118** D4
NEWSBANK **132** F1
New School La CH66 . . . **44** B1
Newsham Cl WA8 . . . . . . **12** B4
Newsholme Cl WA3. . . . . . **4** F3
Newspaper House WA5 . . **14** F8
New St
Congleton CW12 . . . . . **156** E2
Haslington CW1. . . . . . **191** C5
Neston CH64. . . . . **66** E7
New Mills SK22 . . . . **39** D7
8 Runcorn WA7 . . . . . . **23** A2
Sandbach CW11 . . . . . **174** D7
Widnes WA8 . . . . **23** B8
Wilmslow SK9 . . . . **59** E5
Newstead Cl SK12. . . . . . **36** F3
Newstead Rd WA8 . . . . . **21** F6
New Street Cotts CW12. . **157** A6
Newtech Sq CH5. . . . . . . **92** F2
NEWTON
Chester **118** F5
Frodsham. **74** D3

NEWTON continued
Tattenhall 166 E4
Newton Ave WA3 . . . . .9 E5
Newton Bank
Middlewich CW10 . . . . . . 128 B1
Preston on the Hill WA4 . . 51 B8
Newton Bank Prep Sch
WA12 . . . . .2 B2
Newton Com HosplWA12 . .2 B2
Newton Cotts CH3 . . . . . 166 C4
Newton Gdns WA3 . . . . . . 4 A8
Newton Gr WA2 . . . . .8 F3
Newton Hall CH2 . . . . . . 118 F5
Newton Hall Ct CH2 . . . . 118 F5
Newton Hall Dr CH2 . . . . 118 F5
Newton Hall La WA16 . . . .58 E5
Newton Hall Mews 🔢
CW10 . . . . 151 C8
Newton Heath CW10 . . . 128 B1
Newton Ho CH2 . . . . 118 F5
Newton Hollow WA6 . . . .74 D1
NEWTONIA 128 B1
Newton La
Chester CH2 . . . . 118 F4
Daresbury WA4 . . . . .51 C8
Golborne WA12 . . . . .2 E6
Tattenhall CH3 . . . . 166 D4
NEWTON-LE-WILLOWS . .2 B2
Newton-le-Willows Com
High SchWA12 . . . . 2 D5
Newton-le-Willows Prim Sch
WA12 . . . . 2 E2
Newton-le-Willows Sta
WA12 . . . . 2 A2
Newton Park Dr WA12 . . . .2 F3
Newton Park View CH2 . .118 F4
Newton Pl CW12 . . . . . . 156 F2
Newton Prim SchCH2 . . 118 E4
Newton Rd
Ellesmere Port CH65 . . . .70 C5
Golborne, Lowton Common WA3,
WN7 . . . . .4 A8
Golborne, Town of Lowton WA12,
WA3 . . . . .3 D5
Handforth SK9 . . . . .34 A1
St Helens WA9 . . . . .1 A3
Winwick WA2 . . . . 8 A5
Newtons Cres CW11 . . . . 191 F7
Newtons Gr CW11 . . . . . 191 E7
Newton St
Crewe CW1 . . . . 190 D5
Macclesfield SK11 . . . . . 112 C7
NEWTOWN
Burwardsley 183 D8
Frodsham 49 D1
New Mills 39 B7
Poynton 37 A3
Sound 217 E4
Widnes 23 A6
Newtown
Neston CH64 . . . . .66 F7
Newchapel ST7 . . . . 195 F2
Newtown Cl CH1 . . . . . . 237 B3
Newtown Prim Sch 🔢
SK22 . . . . 39 B6
New Warrington Rd CW9 .79 C2
New William Cl M31 . . . . . 11 F4
NEW WOODHOUSES . . . 227 E1
New York Cotts CW9 . . . .29 F2
Nicholas Ave CW9 . . . . . 104 C6
Nicholas Ct CH1 . . . . . . 237 A2
Nicholas Rd
Weaverham CW8 . . . . . . .77 D1
Widnes WA8 . . . . .22 C8
Nicholas St Mews CH1 . . 237 A2
Nicholas St CH1 . . . . . . 237 A2
Nicholls St WA4 . . . . .17 B2
Nicholson Ave SK10 . . . . 87 E1
Nicholson Cl SK10 . . . . . .87 E1
Nicholson St WA1 . . . . . . 15 F5
NICK I' TH' HILL 179 B4
Nickleby Rd SK12 . . . . . . 36 E3
Nickleford Hall Dr WA8 . . 12 F6
Nickolson Cl CH2 . . . . . . 119 F8
Nicol Ave WA1 . . . . 17 F8
Nidderdale Cl CW12 . . . . 157 A5
Niddries Ct CH1 . . . . 117 E5
Niddries La CW9 . . . . . . 126 F7
Nield Ct CH2 . . . . 118 D7
Nigel Gresley Cl CW1 . . .191 A4
Nigel Rd CH60 . . . . 41 C8
Nightingale Cl
Farndon CH3 . . . . 180 F1
Handforth SK9 . . . . .34 B1
Middlewich CW10 . . . . . 151 D6
Runcorn WA7 . . . . 49 F5
Warrington WA3 . . . . .9 F4
Nightingale Ct 🔢 CW7 . . 149 D6
Nightingale Way ST7 . . . 193 B3
Nile St CW2 . . . . 190 C2
Nine Hos The CH3 . . . . . 166 B1
Nixon Dr CW7 . . . . 126 B2
Nixon Rd CW8 . . . . 101 F3
Nixon's Row CW5 . . . . . 204 C5
Nixon St
Crewe CW1 . . . . 189 F5
Macclesfield SK11 . . . . . 112 B8
No 1 Road N CW2 . . . . . 192 F1
No 1 Road S CW2 . . . . . 192 F1
No 2 Road N CW2 . . . . . 192 F1
No 2 Road S CW2 . . . . . 192 F1
No. 216 CW2 . . . . 192 F1
Noahs Ark La WA16 . . . . .58 F1
Noble Cl WA3 . . . . .9 E3
NO MAN'S HEATH 214 B4
Nook La
Antrobus CW9 . . . . 53 E6

Nook La continued
Golborne WA3 . . . . 3 B8
Warrington, Fearnhead WA2 . 9 B2
Warrington WA4 . . . . 17 A3
Nook The
Backford CH1 . . . . .95 B4
Bramhall SK7 . . . . .35 D5
Chester CH2 . . . . 118 E4
Guilden Sutton CH3 . . . . 119 F5
Hankelow CW3 . . . . 230 C8
Saltney CH4 . . . . 140 E6
Noon Ct WA12 . . . . .2 B1
Noonsun Farm WA16 . . . . 58 E1
Nora St WA1 . . . . 16 C5
Norbreck Ave CW2 . . . . 190 B2
Norbreck Cl WA5 . . . . . . .15 A8
NORBURY 215 D4
Norbury Ave WA2 . . . . . . 16 D8
Norbury Cl
Hough CW2 . . . . 206 E3
Knutsford WA16 . . . . . . .57 C3
Widnes WA8 . . . . .13 E1
NORBURY COMMON . . . 215 C6
Norbury Dr
Congleton CW12 . . . . . . 156 E4
Middlewich CW10 . . . . . 151 B8
Norbury St
Macclesfield SK11 . . . . . 112 C7
Northwich CW9 . . . . 104 B8
Norbury Town La SY13 . .215 C3
Norbury Way 🔢 SK9 . . . .34 D5
Norcott Ave WA4 . . . . . . 16 D2
NORCOTT BROOK 52 C6
Norcott Dr WA5 . . . . .6 F6
Norden Cl WA3 . . . . .9 C5
Norfolk Cl M44 . . . . 11 C5
Norfolk Dr WA5 . . . . 14 E6
Norfolk Gr ST8 . . . . 179 C1
Norfolk Ho ST7 . . . . 210 D6
Norfolk House Prep Sch
CW11 . . . . 175 B7
Norfolk Pl WA8 . . . . .22 C8
Norfolk Rd
Chester CH2 . . . . 118 F4
Congleton CW12 . . . . . . 156 E4
Ellesmere Port CH65 . . . .70 C5
Kidsgrove ST7 . . . . 194 F2
Norfolk St WA7 . . . . 23 B3
Norfolk Wlk SK10 . . . . . . 86 F2
Norgrove Cl WA7 . . . . . . 50 E8
Norland's La L35, WA8 . . 12 F7
Norlands Pk WA8 . . . . . . 12 F6
Norland St WA8 . . . . 13 D1
NORLEY 100 F6
Norleane Cres WA7 . . . . .49 B8
Norley Ave
Bebington CH62 . . . . 43 E3
Ellesmere Port CH65 . . . .69 F6
Norley CE Prim Sch
WA6 . . . . 100 F5
Norley Cl WA5 . . . . 15 E6
Norley Dr CH3 . . . . 119 C1
Norley La CW8 . . . . 101 A8
Norley Pl CW9 . . . . 103 E5
Norley Rd
Cuddington CW8, WA6 . . 101 E4
Kingsley WA6 . . . . .75 A1
Norley WA6 . . . . 100 D7
Sandiway CW8 . . . . 102 A3
Norman Ave
Haydock WA11 . . . . 2 A7
Newton-le-Willows WA12 . 2 E3
Normandy Cl WA5 . . . . . . 15 E7
Normandy Ct CH66 . . . . . 94 F8
Normandy Dr CW7 . . . . . 149 D8
Normandy Ave 🔢 CW7 . . 149 D8
Normandy Rd CH2 . . . . . .95 C1
Norman Ho 🔢 CW8 . . . . 103 C5
Norman Rd WA3 . . . . . . .23 A1
Normans Cotts 🔢 CH64 . . 66 F7
Norman's Hall Farm SK10 .63 B5
Norman's La WA4 . . . . . . 52 F4
Norman St WA4 . . . . 16 B6
Norman Way CH1 . . . . . . 117 E5
Norreys Ave WA5 . . . . . . 15 F8
Norris Gr WA8 . . . . 22 C5
Norris Rd CH1 . . . . 117 E5
Norris St WA2 . . . . 16 D8
North Ave WA2 . . . . 16 B8
Northbank Ind Pk M44 . . 11 F6
North Brook Rd CW6 . . . 146 B7
Northcote Rd SK7 . . . . . . 35 F7
Northdale Rd WA1 . . . . . . 17 A8
North Downs WA16 . . . . . 57 D2
North Dr
Heswall CH60 . . . . 41 A7
High Legh WA16 . . . . 29 C4
Northwich CW9 . . . . 104 E7
Northern La WA8 . . . . . . 12 A3
Northern Pathway CH4 . .237 C1
Northern Rise CH66 . . . . . 69 E4
Northfield Dr
Biddulph ST8 . . . . 179 E2
Wilmslow SK9 . . . . .60 D8
Northfield Pl CW2 . . . . . 206 C8
Northfields WA16 . . . . . . 57 C3
NORTH FLORIDA 1 D8
North Florida Rd WA11 . . . 1 D8
Northgate CW6 . . . . 146 B7
Northgate Arena CH2 . . .237 B3
Northgate Ave
Chester CH2 . . . . 237 B4
Macclesfield SK10 . . . . . .87 B1
Northgate Row CH1 . . . . 237 B2
Northgate St CH1 . . . . . 237 A3

NORTHGATE VILLAGE . . 237 B4
North Gn CH5 . . . . 116 A6
Northlands CW3 . . . . . . 232 C1
Northmead SK10 . . . . . . .87 A5
Northolt Ct WA2 . . . . .8 E1
North Par CH64 . . . . 41 B2
North Park Brook Rd WA5 .7 E1
North Rd
Altrincham WA15 . . . . . . 32 A8
Bebington CH65 . . . . 44 E3
Connah's Quay CH5 . . . . .91 F2
Ellesmere Port CH65 . . . .70 B8
Halewood L26 . . . . 21 A5
NORTH RODE 134 E2
North St
Chester CH3 . . . . 119 A1
Congleton CW12 . . . . . . 156 D3
Crewe CW1 . . . . 190 C7
Haydock WA11 . . . . .1 E6
Mount Pleasant ST7 . . . . 195 B6
Newton-le-Willows WA12 . .1 F4
Saltney CH4 . . . . 140 B7
Sandycroft CH5 . . . . 116 A3
North Stafford St CW1 . . 190 E4
Northumberland Rd M31 . 11 E2
North View
Crewe CW1 . . . . 190 A6
Ellesmere Port CH66 . . . .69 C7
Middlewich CW10 . . . . . 128 B2
Warrington WA5 . . . . 14 E7
Northward Rd SK9 . . . . . .59 F6
Northway
Chester CH4 . . . . 141 A7
Lymm WA13 . . . . .18 D4
Runcorn WA7 . . . . 49 F8
Widnes WA8 . . . . .12 D1
Winnington CW8 . . . . . . .78 D1
North Way
Holmes Chapel CW4 . . . 130 C3
Shavington CW2 . . . . . . 206 D5
North West Wing CW8 . . 102 A8
NORTHWICH 103 D8
Northwich Rd
Allostock CW4, WA16 . . . 106 C1
Antrobus CW9 . . . . 53 B2
Dutton WA4 . . . . 51 B2
Great Budworth CW9 . . . .78 F8
Higher Kinnerton CH4 . . . 161 A7
Knutsford WA16 . . . . 56 D1
Runcorn, Brookvale WA7 . 50 C5
Weaverham CW8 . . . . . . 102 E7
Northwich Ret Pk CW9 . . 79 C1
Northwich Sta CW9 . . . . 104 B8
Northwood Ave
Middlewich CW10 . . . . . 151 C6
Newton-le-Willows WA12 . .2 F3
Northwood Rd WA16 . . . . 23 F2
Northwood Way WA7 . . . .23 E2
NORTON 24 C1
Norton Ave
Saltney CH4 . . . . 140 D6
Warrington WA5 . . . . 14 E5
Norton Cotts WA7 . . . . . . 50 E7
Norton Gate WA7 . . . . . . 50 C8
Norton Hill WA7 . . . . 24 C2
NORTON IN HALES 236 C1
Norton in Hales CE Prim Sch
TF9 . . . . 236 C2
Norton La
Runcorn, Norton WA7 . . . 24 D1
Runcorn, Town Park WA7 . 50 A8
Norton's La CH3 . . . . 98 B2
Norton St SK10 . . . . 112 E8
Norton Station Rd WA7 . .50 D8
Norton View WA7 . . . . . . .50 A8
Norton Village WA7 . . . . .24 D1
Norton Way CW11 . . . . . 174 D7
Nortonwood La WA7 . . . . 24 C1
Norville CH66 . . . . 69 D7
Norwich Ave WA3 . . . . . . .3 D8
Norwich Dr CH66 . . . . . . 94 E8
Norwood Ave
Bramhall SK7 . . . . .35 D5
Golborne WA3 . . . . .3 F7
High Lane SK6 . . . . 37 D7
Norwood Dr CH4 . . . . . . 141 B6
Nottingham Cl WA7 . . . . .17 E6
Nova Ct 🔢 CW1 . . . . . . 190 B5
Nova Scotia 125 C6
Nun House Cl CW7 . . . . . 127 B2
Nun House Dr CW7 . . . . 127 B2
Nunsmere Cl CW7 . . . . . 127 B2
Nuns Rd CH1 . . . . 237 A1
Nursery Ave WA15 . . . . . 31 E8
Nursery Cl
Crewe CW2 . . . . 190 A2
Kidsgrove ST7 . . . . 194 D1
Shavington CW2 . . . . . . 206 C3
Widnes WA8 . . . . .13 D3
Nursery Dr
Biddulph ST8 . . . . 179 C2
Poynton SK12 . . . . 36 D4
Nursery Gr M31 . . . . 11 F4
Nursery La
Congleton CW12 . . . . . . 156 E2
Nether Alderley SK10 . . . 84 D5
Siddington SK11 . . . . . . 110 A3
Wilmslow SK9 . . . . 59 F5
Nursery Pk WA6 . . . . . . 100 B7
Nursery Rd
Barnton CW8 . . . . 78 B3
Bollington SK10 . . . . 87 E7

Nursery Rd continued
Oakhanger CW1, ST7 . . . 192 D3
Scholar Green ST7 . . . . . 194 E5
Nursery The CW8 . . . . . 103 C6
Nutfield Ave CW1 . . . . . 190 B7
Nuthurst Gdns 🔢 CW5 . 204 F5
Nuttall Cl WA3 . . . . .9 C4
Nuttall St M44 . . . . 11 E6

O

Oak Ave
Alsager ST7 . . . . 193 E2
Disley SK12 . . . . 39 A6
Golborne WA3 . . . . .3 B8
Haydock WA11 . . . . .1 D5
Irlam M44 . . . . 11 D5
Macclesfield SK11 . . . . . 112 A5
Newton-le-Willows WA12 . .2 D3
Wilmslow SK9 . . . . 59 F5
Winsford CW7 . . . . 149 D2
Oak Bank
Alderley Edge SK9 . . . . . 60 A2
Disley SK12 . . . . 39 A6
Oak Bank Cl CW5 . . . . . 205 E4
Oak Bank Dr SK10 . . . . . .63 B1
Oak Bank La CH2 . . . . . . 119 C6
Oak Brow Cotts SK9 . . . . 33 E4
Oak Cl SK9 . . . . 59 F6
Oak Cotts
Styal SK9 . . . . .33 E4
Wybunbury CW5 . . . . . . 216 F4
Oakdale Ave
Frodsham WA6 . . . . .74 D6
Warrington WA4 . . . . 16 D1
Oakdale Cl
Broughton CH4 . . . . 139 B3
Chorlton CW2 . . . . 207 B3
Oakdene Ave
Ellesmere Port CH66 . . . .69 C5
Gatley SK8 . . . . .34 C7
Warrington WA1 . . . . 17 C7
Oakdene Cl CH62 . . . . . . 43 D5
Oakdene Ct SK9 . . . . 34 F4
Oakdene Way CW6 . . . . 168 D8
Oak Dr
Cheadle SK8 . . . . .35 C7
Higher Kinnerton CH4 . . . 161 A7
Middlewich CW10 . . . . . 151 D7
Runcorn WA7 . . . . 49 C7
Scholar Green ST7 . . . . . 194 E6
Oakefield Prim Sch CW1 190 B6
Oakenbank La SK10 . . . . 88 D7
Oakenclough Cl SK9 . . . . 34 D2
Oakes Cnr CW5 . . . . 219 E3
Oak Farm CW6 . . . . 186 C5
Oakfield Ave
Chester CH2 . . . . 118 E8
Knutsford WA16 . . . . . . .57 C3
Wrenbury CW5 . . . . 216 F3
Oakfield Com Prim Sch
WA8 . . . . .22 B8
Oakfield Dr
Chester CH2 . . . . 118 E8
Widnes WA8 . . . . .22 A8
Oakfield Rd
Alderley Edge SK9 . . . . . 60 B2
Bebington CH62 . . . . 43 C8
Blacon CH1 . . . . 117 D4
Ellesmere Port CH66 . . . .68 E8
Plumley WA16 . . . . 80 F3
Poynton SK12 . . . . 36 F4
Oakfield Rise CW4 . . . . . 130 B3
Oakfield Terr CH66 . . . . . 68 E8
Oakfold SK10 . . . . .88 A6
Oak Gr
Ellesmere Port CH65 . . . .70 A3
Nantwich CW5 . . . . 204 E3
Poynton SK12 . . . . 36 D4
Oak Gr/Gelli Dderw
CH4 . . . . 140 D5
OAKGROVE 135 D7
Oakgrove SchSK8 . . . . . 34 C7
OAKHANGER 192 C2
Oakhill Cl SK10 . . . . 87 B4
Oak Ho
Chester CH2 . . . . 118 C5
🔢 Northwich CW9 . . . . 175 B6
Oak House La CW7 . . . . 149 B8
Oakhurst Chase SK9 . . . 60 A2
Oakhurst Dr CW2 . . . . . 206 B7
Oak La
Astbury CW12 . . . . 178 B4
Cuddington CW8 . . . . . . 101 F2
Kerridge SK10 . . . . 88 A5
Marton SK11 . . . . 133 C5
Wilmslow SK9 . . . . 59 F6
Oakland Ave CW1 . . . . . 191 C4
Oakland Ct SK12 . . . . . . 36 D4
Oakland Gdns WA1 . . . . 16 E7
Oaklands
Bebington CH62 . . . . 43 D6
Guilden Sutton CH3 . . . . 119 F4
Oaklands Ave CH3 . . . . . 166 B2
Oaklands Cl SK9 . . . . 34 E1
Oaklands Cres CH3 . . . . 166 B2
Oaklands Dr WA13 . . . . . 18 D2
Oaklands Rd
Golborne WA3 . . . . .3 F7
Ollerton WA16 . . . . 82 F6
Oaklands Specl Sch
CW7 . . . . 149 B7

NEW–O'C 269

Oakland St
Warrington WA1 . . . . 16 E7
Widnes WA8 . . . . .23 A4
Oaklea Ave CH2 . . . . 118 F4
Oak Lea Ave SK9 . . . . . . 60 A5
Oakleaf Lodge SK11 . . . . 112 D5
Oakleigh WA1 . . . . 82 C7
Oakleigh Ct CW12 . . . . . 155 F3
Oakleigh Ho SK10 . . . . . . 88 B8
Oakleigh Rd SK8 . . . . 34 E8
Oakleigh Rise CW8 . . . . . 78 E1
Oakley Cl CW11 . . . . 175 A8
Oakley Ct CH65 . . . . 70 C4
Oakley St CW1 . . . . 190 C5
Oak Lo SK7 . . . . 35 D7
Oak Mdw WA8 . . . . 102 E7
OAKMERE 124 A4
Oakmere Barns CW8 . . . 124 A7
Oakmere Cl CW11 . . . . . 174 F7
Oakmere Dr
Chester CH3 . . . . 142 B8
Ellesmere Port CH66 . . . .69 F1
Warrington WA5 . . . . 14 F3
Oakmere Hall CW8 . . . . . 101 E1
Oakmere Pl 🔢 CW1 . . . 190 B5
Oakmere Rd
Handforth SK9 . . . . 34 D5
Winsford CW7 . . . . 149 B8
Oakmere St 🔢 WA7 . . . . 23 A2
Oakmoore WA5 . . . . .34 C1
Oakmoore WA7 . . . . .24 F4
Oak Rd
Chelford SK11 . . . . 84 A3
Chester CH4 . . . . 140 F6
Hooton CH66 . . . . 43 E1
Lymm WA13 . . . . .18 C3
Mottram St Andrew SK10 . 86 B7
Paddockhill WA16 . . . . . 59 B5
Partington M31 . . . . 11 D2
Warrington WA5 . . . . 14 F3
Oaks Com Prim Sch The
CH65 . . . . .70 D3
Oaks Dr The CH2 . . . . . . 118 D7
Oaks Gdns WA5 . . . . 14 E4
Oaks Pl WA8 . . . . .23 A7
Oak St
Crewe CW2 . . . . 190 D3
Croft WA3 . . . . .9 A7
Ellesmere Port CH65 . . . .70 C7
Northwich CW9 . . . . 79 A1
Rode Heath ST7 . . . . 193 E8
Sandbach CW11 . . . . . . 174 D8
Oaks The
Bebington CH62 . . . . 43 C8
Goostrey CW4 . . . . 130 D8
Mobberley WA16 . . . . . . 58 E1
🔢 Northwich CW9 . . . . 103 E3
Stoke-on-Trent ST7 . . . . 194 E2
Widnes WA8 . . . . .13 D4
Oaksway CH60 . . . . 41 C6
Oakthorn Gr WA11 . . . . . .1 C6
Oaktree Cl
Barnton CW8 . . . . 78 B4
Tarporley CW6 . . . . 146 D2
Oak Tree Cl CW11 . . . . . 190 F5
Oak Tree Ct CH2 . . . . . . 119 A3
Oak Tree Cr CW6 . . . . . . 122 E2
Oak Tree Dr CW1 . . . . . . 190 F5
Oak Tree Gate CW3 . . . . 229 F3
Oaktree La ST7 . . . . 210 D3
Oak Tree La CW10 . . . . . 129 E7
Oak View
Knutsford WA16 . . . . . . .57 C1
Speke L24 . . . . 21 A3
Oak Villas CW5 . . . . 216 F4
Oakways WA4 . . . . 26 D5
OAKWOOD
Alderley Edge SK9 . . . . . 85 B8
Barnton CW8 . . . . 78 A2
Oakwood La
Altrincham WA14 . . . . . . 31 B8
Barnton CW8 . . . . 78 A2
Sandbach CW11 . . . . . . 174 B8
Oakwood Pk CH62 . . . . . 43 D5
Oakwood Rd
Disley SK12 . . . . 38 D6
Rode Heath ST7 . . . . 193 F8
Oak Wood Rd WA16 . . . . 29 F2
Oakworth Cl CW12 . . . . . 156 C3
Oathills SY14 . . . . 213 B5
Oathills Cl CW6 . . . . 146 D1
Oathills Dr CW6 . . . . 146 D1
Oathills La CW6 . . . . 146 D1
Oatlands SK9 . . . . .85 B8
Oat Market 🔢 CW5 . . . . 204 E5
Oban Dr CH60 . . . . 41 A8
Oban Gr WA2 . . . . .9 A3
Obelisk Way CW12 . . . . . 156 C3
OCCLESTON GREEN . . . 151 B2
O'Connell Cl WA11 . . . . . .1 C6

Oddfellows Pas CW10 . . . . . . 128 B1
Odeon Bldg CH1 . . . . 237 A3
Offal Pit La WA6 . . . . 74 F2
Offley Ave CW11 . . . . 175 B7
Offley Prim Sch CW11 . . 175 B7
Offley Rd CW11 . . . . 175 B7
Off Spring Bank SK22 . . . 39 C8
Ogden Rd SK7 . . . . 35 D5
Oglet La L24 . . . . 45 C6
Ohio Gr WA5 . . . . 15 C6
Oil Sites Rd CH65 . . . . . . 71 C5
Okell St WA7 . . . . 23 A2
Old Albert Terr WA7 . . . . 23 B3
Old Alder La WA8 . . . . 7 D5
Old Applecroft CW11 . . . 174 C5
OLD BOSTON 2 A8
Old Boston WA11 . . . . 2 A7
Old Boston Trad Est WA11 . . 2 B8
Old Brickworks Ind Est
  SK10 . . . . 63 E4
Old Butt La ST7 . . . . 194 D2
OLDCASTLE HEATH 223 E8
Oldcastle La SY14 . . . . . 222 E8
Old Cherry La WA13 . . . . 28 A7
Old Chester Ct CW5 . . . . 187 D6
Old Chester Rd
  Barbridge CW5 . . . . . . 187 D6
  Ellesmere Port CH66 . . 69 D4
  Helsby WA6 . . . . 73 C4
  Higher Walton WA4 . . . 25 F7
Old Church Cl CH65 . . . . 70 C7
Old Coach Rd
  Brown Knowl SY14, CH3 . . 199 B6
  Kelsall CW6 . . . . 122 D5
  Runcorn WA7 . . . . 22 F3
Old Constabulary The ①
  CW5 . . . . 204 D5
Old Court Ho The ⑨
  WA16 . . . . 57 A2
Olde George The CH1 . . . 237 B3
Old Farm Cl
  Macclesfield SK10 . . . . 87 A2
  Willaston CH64 . . . . . . 68 A8
Old Farm Cotts CH1 . . . 116 E3
Old Farm Mews SK8 . . . . 35 C7
Oldfield Cres CW4 . . . . . 140 F5
Oldfield Cty Prim Sch
  CH3 . . . . 119 C3
Oldfield Dr
  Chester CH3 . . . . 119 C2
  Mobberley WA16 . . . . . 58 A4
Oldfield La WA14 . . . . . . 20 F4
Oldfield Rd
  Ellesmere Port CH65 . . 70 B5
  Lymm WA13 . . . . 18 C4
  Sandbach CW11 . . . . . 174 F3
Oldgate WA8 . . . . 22 C7
Old Gate Cl CW10 . . . . . 151 B7
Old Gorse Cl CW2 . . . . . 189 C3
OLD HALL 15 C8
Old Hall Cl WA4 . . . . 26 A8
Oldhall Cres SK9 . . . . . . 34 E3
Old Hall Ct
  Ashton Hayes CH3 . . . 121 F7
  Malpas SY14 . . . . 213 B3
Old Hall Dr
  Ellesmere Port CH65 . . 70 B4
  Horwich End SK23 . . . . 65 E4
Old Hall Gdns CH2 . . . . 237 C4
Old Hall La
  Elton CH2 . . . . 72 B3
  Hargrave CH3 . . . . . . 144 A1
  Over Tabley WA16 . . . . 55 E4
  Woodford SK7 . . . . 35 D1
Old Hall Pk CH3 . . . . 119 F5
Old Hall Pl CH1 . . . . 237 A2
Old Hall Rd
  Northwich CW9 . . . . . . 104 A5
  Warrington WA5 . . . . . 15 D7
Oldhall St SY14 . . . . 213 B3
Old Hall St SK10 . . . . . . 87 D1
Oldhams Hill
  Kingsmead CW8 . . . . . 103 F8
  Winnington CW8 . . . . . 78 F1
Oldham's Rise SK10 . . . . 87 D3
Oldham St
  Bollington SK10 . . . . . . 88 B8
  Warrington WA4 . . . . . 16 D3
Old Hey Wlk WA12 . . . . . . 2 C1
Old Higher Rd WA8 . . . . . 21 D5
Oldhill Cl ST7 . . . . 210 E5
Old Hutte La L26 . . . . . . 21 A6
Old Knutsford Rd ST7 . . 194 A3
Old La
  Acton Bridge CW8 . . . . 76 F3
  Antrobus CW9 . . . . 53 C3
  Davenham CW9 . . . . . 104 D2
  Heswall CH60 . . . . 41 D8
  Mouldsworth CH3 . . . . 99 C2
  Pulford CH4 . . . . 162 E2
Old Library The CW7 . . . 126 C1
Old Liverpool Rd WA5 . . 15 E4
Old Man of Mow★ ST7 . . 195 D8
Old Market Pl
  ① Knutsford WA16 . . . . 57 A2
  ⑫ Warrington WA1 . . . . 16 B5
Old Marsh Farm Ho CH5 . 116 A4
Old Mill Cl
  Heswall CH60 . . . . 41 B7
  Lymm WA13 . . . . 19 C6
Old Mill Ct CH2 . . . . 118 D6
Old Mill La
  Hazel Grove SK7 . . . . . 37 A8
  Higher Whitley WA4 . . . 52 F3
  Macclesfield SK11 . . . . 112 E6

Old Mill Pl CH3 . . . . 166 B1
Old Mill Rd CW11 . . . . . 175 C6
Old Mill The
  Crowton CW8 . . . . 76 B2
  Ellesmere Port CH66 . . 69 C7
OLD MOSS 144 D7
Old Moss La
  Fowley Common WA3 . . 5 E6
  Tarvin CH3 . . . . 146 D7
Old Newcastle Rd CW5 . . 205 D4
Old Orchard SK9 . . . . . . 60 A7
Old Orchard The
  Antrobus CW9 . . . . 53 C4
  Cuddington CW8 . . . . . 101 F4
Old Paddock The CW4 . . 130 F8
Old Pale Cotts CW6 . . . . 123 C7
Old Pale Hts CW8 . . . . . 123 C7
Old Park Rd CW1 . . . . . . 207 D8
Old Pearl La CH3 . . . . . . 119 B1
Old Penny La WA11 . . . . . 2 A7
Old Pewterspear La WA4 . 26 E4
Old Port Sq CH1 . . . . . . 118 B2
Old Pump Ho The CH66 . . 68 E8
Old Quay Cl CH65 . . . . . 66 C7
Old Quay La CH64 . . . . . 66 D7
Old Quay St WA7 . . . . . . 23 B3
Old Quays The WA4 . . . . 16 E3
Old Rd
  Anderton CW9 . . . . 78 D3
  Audley ST7 . . . . 209 D3
  Furness Vale SK23 . . . . 39 D4
  Handforth SK9 . . . . . . 34 D3
  Horwich End, New Horwich
    SK23 . . . . 65 E6
  Horwich End SK23 . . . . 65 E4
  Warrington WA4 . . . . . 16 B4
  Wilmslow SK9 . . . . 60 B8
Old Ribbon Mill The
  SK11 . . . . 112 D6
Old School Cl
  Barnton CW8 . . . . 78 B2
  Farndon CH3 . . . . 180 E2
  Kidsgrove ST7 . . . . . . 195 A1
  Neston CH64 . . . . 66 F5
Old School House La WA3 . 8 A7
Old School La SK8 . . . . . 35 A8
Old Seals Way CH1 . . . . 118 A3
Old Smithy La WA13 . . . . 18 E2
Old Smithy Row SK10 . . . 39 C7
Old Stack Yd CH3 . . . . . 120 E6
Old Tannery CW5 . . . . . 204 F6
Old Upton La WA8 . . . . . 12 E4
Old Vicarage Gdn CW3 . . 230 A3
Old Vicarage La CW8 . . . 103 C5
Old Vicarage Rd CH64 . . 68 A8
Old Wargrave Rd WA12 . . 2 C3
Old Warrington Rd CW9 . . 79 A2
Old Wesleyan Schoolhouse
  The SK22 . . . . 39 B6
Old Whint Rd WA11 . . . . . 1 A6
Old Woman's La CH3 . . . 142 D7
OLD WOODHOUSES . . . 227 C2
Old Wrexham Rd CH4 . . . 141 C7
O'leary St WA2 . . . . 16 C7
Olive Dr CH66 . . . . 66 F8
Olive Gr ST5 . . . . 210 D1
Oliver Cl SK10 . . . . 87 F7
Oliver Rd CH66 . . . . 66 E8
Oliver Ho CH66 . . . . 69 D4
Oliver St WA2 . . . . 16 B6
Ollersett Ave SK22 . . . . . 39 D8
Ollersett Dr SK22 . . . . . . 39 D8
Ollersett Ho SK22 . . . . . . 39 D8
Ollershaw La CW9 . . . . . 79 C4
OLLERTON 82 F6
Ollerton Cl WA4 . . . . 17 B3
Ollerton Pk WA5 . . . . 6 E7
Ollerton Rd SK9 . . . . 34 E5
Ollier St ① WA8 . . . . 23 A7
Olympia Pl WA5 . . . . 15 B7
Omega Bvd WA5 . . . . 6 D1
One Oak La SK9 . . . . 60 F7
ONNELEY 232 F3
Onslow Rd CH1 . . . . 117 D4
ONSTON 76 E1
Onston La CW8 . . . . 101 E8
Openshaw La M44 . . . . . 11 E6
Orange Gr WA2 . . . . 8 E2
Orchard Ave
  Acton Bridge WA8 . . . . 76 E4
  Lymm WA13 . . . . 18 F3
  Partington M31 . . . . . . 11 F4
  Whaley Bridge SK23 . . 65 D7
Orchard Brow WA3 . . . . . 11 A2
Orchard Cl
  Barnton CW8 . . . . 78 B3
  Bunbury CW6 . . . . . . 185 F8
  Cheadle SK8 . . . . 35 C7
  Chester CH2 . . . . 118 D5
  Ellesmere Port CH66 . . 69 F1
  Frodsham WA6 . . . . . . 74 A6
  Frodsham WA6 . . . . . . 75 E2
  Goostrey CW4 . . . . . . 107 E1
  Higher Wincham CW9 . . 80 A6
  Macclesfield SK11 . . . . 112 B6
  Poynton SK12 . . . . 36 E3
  Weaverham CW8 . . . . . 77 D1
  Wilmslow SK9 . . . . 59 F5
  Winsford CW7 . . . . . . 126 D2
Orchard Cotts CW6 . . . . 146 D1
Orchard Cres
  Kidsgrove ST7 . . . . . . 194 D1
  Nantwich CW5 . . . . . . 204 E3
  Nether Alderley SK10 . . 84 F6
Orchard Croft CH3 . . . . . 119 E5

Orchard Ct
  Alsager ST7 . . . . 193 E4
  Croft WA3 . . . . 9 A8
  Frodsham WA6 . . . . . . 74 A8
  Haslington CW1 . . . . . 191 D4
Orchard Dene CW8 . . . . 101 D5
Orchard Dr
  Handforth SK9 . . . . . . 34 E2
  Little Leigh CW8 . . . . . 77 D5
  Neston CH64 . . . . 66 E5
Orchard Gdns
  Congleton CW12 . . . . . 156 A3
  Tarporley CW6 . . . . . . 168 D8
  Weaverham CW8 . . . . . 77 B1
Orchard Gn SK9 . . . . 60 B1
Orchard Gr CH3 . . . . . . 180 F1
Orchard Haven CH66 . . . 69 E1
Orchard Ho SK10 . . . . . . 86 E1
Orchard La CH66 . . . . . . 69 A8
Orchard Park La CH2 . . . 72 B4
Orchard Pk CH2 . . . . 72 B4
Orchard Pl
  Helsby WA6 . . . . 73 C4
  Poynton SK12 . . . . 36 D4
Orchard Rd
  Ellesmere Port CH65 . . 70 B2
  Lymm WA13 . . . . 19 B5
  Whaley Bridge SK23 . . 65 D7
Orchard Rise CW9 . . . . . 126 E8
Orchard St
  Chester CH1 . . . . 237 A3
  Crewe CW1 . . . . 190 C5
  Northwich CW9 . . . . . 104 B8
  Warrington, Fearnhead WA2 . 9 A2
  Warrington, Stockton Heath
    WA4 . . . . 26 C8
  Warrington WA1 . . . . . 16 C5
  Willaston SK9 . . . . . . 205 D6
Orchard The
  Alderley Edge SK9 . . . . 85 B8
  Chester CH3 . . . . 142 A8
  Disley SK12 . . . . 38 D6
  Malpas WA6 . . . . 73 B2
Orchard Way
  Congleton CW12 . . . . . 156 A3
  Kelsall CW6 . . . . 122 D5
  Widnes WA8 . . . . 12 A3
Orchard Wlk
  Neston CH64 . . . . 66 E8
  ② Runcorn WA7 . . . . . 49 F7
Orchid Cl
  Huntington CH3 . . . . . 142 A6
  Irlam M44 . . . . 11 E8
Orchil Cl CH66 . . . . 69 A6
Ordnance Ave
  Warrington, Birchwood
    WA3 . . . . 10 A5
  Warrington WA3 . . . . . . 9 F4
Ordsall Cl CW11 . . . . . . 174 F3
ORFORD 8 D2
Orford Ave
  Disley SK12 . . . . 38 D6
  Warrington WA1, WA2 . . 16 C7
Orford Cl
  Golborne WA3 . . . . 3 A7
  Hale L24 . . . . 21 E2
  High Lane SK6 . . . . 37 E7
Orford Gn WA2 . . . . 8 D1
Orford La WA2 . . . . 16 B7
Orford Rd WA2 . . . . 16 E8
Orford St WA1 . . . . 16 B5
Organsdale Cotts CW6 . . 123 B5
Oriel Ho CH2 . . . . 118 C4
Orion Bvd WA5 . . . . 6 E1
Orkney Cl
  ③ Ellesmere Port CH65 . 70 C1
  Widnes WA8 . . . . 13 E3
Orlando Dr WA5 . . . . 15 C7
Orme Cl
  Macclesfield SK10 . . . . 87 B3
  Prestbury SK10 . . . . . . 87 A8
Orme Cres SK10 . . . . 87 D3
Ormerod Cl CW11 . . . . . 175 C5
Ormesby Gr CH63 . . . . . 43 B6
Orme St SK9 . . . . 60 A1
Ormond Cl WA8 . . . . 12 C2
Ormonde Rd CH2 . . . . . 118 C4
Ormonde St CH1 . . . . . . 237 C3
Orrell Cl WA5 . . . . 15 A6
Orton Cl CW7 . . . . 127 A4
Orwell Cl SK9 . . . . 34 D2
Osborne Ave WA2 . . . . . . 1 A1
Osborne Cl CW11 . . . . . 174 D5
Osborne Gr CW2 . . . . . . 206 C5
Osborne Rd
  Golborne WA3 . . . . 3 E7
  Warrington WA4 . . . . . 16 B1
Osbourne Cl
  Bebington CH62 . . . . . 43 E7
  Wilmslow SK9 . . . . 60 D6
OSCROFT 121 E2
Osier Cl CH2 . . . . 72 C3
Osmere Cl SY13 . . . . . . 226 B1
Osnath Wks WA2 . . . . . . 16 B6
Osprey Ave CW7 . . . . . . 149 D5
Osprey Cl
  Middlewich CW10 . . . . 151 D5
  Runcorn WA7 . . . . 49 F5
  Warrington WA3 . . . . . . 9 F3
Osprey Ct CH2 . . . . 237 A4
Osprey Dr SK9 . . . . 60 C8

Osprey View ST7 . . . . . . 195 D3
Ossett Cl WA7 . . . . 50 D8
Ossmere Cl CW11 . . . . . 174 F8
Ostler's La WA16 . . . . . . 58 E7
Oteley Ave CH62 . . . . . . 43 D8
Otters Bank ② CW7 . . . 126 A1
Ottersbank Mews CW8 . . 123 F3
OUGHTRINGTON 19 C4
Oughtrington Cres WA13 . 19 B4
Oughtrington La WA13 . . 19 A2
Oughtrington Prim Sch
  WA13 . . . . 19 B4
Oughtrington View WA13 . 19 B4
Oulton Ave CH2 . . . . . . 118 E7
Oulton Cl WA7 . . . . 50 B8
Oulton Dr CW12 . . . . . . 155 F3
Oulton Mill La CW6 . . . . 147 B7
Oulton Pl CH1 . . . . 237 B3
Our Lady Mother of the
  Saviour RC Prim Sch
  WA7 . . . . 50 A6
Our Lady of Lourdes RC Prim
  Sch M31 . . . . 11 E3
Our Lady of Perpetual
  Succour RC Prim Sch
  WA8 . . . . 22 A8
Our Lady's RC Prim Sch
  WA4 . . . . 16 E3
Our Lady's Star of the Sea RC
  Prim Sch CH65 . . . . . 70 A3
Ousel Nest CW8 . . . . . . 101 D4
Out La CH3 . . . . 184 C6
Outwood Dr SK8 . . . . . . 34 A8
Outwood La M90 . . . . . . 33 C7
Outwood Lane W M90 . . . 33 B8
Outwood Prim Sch SK8 . . 34 D7
Outwood Rd SK8 . . . . . . 34 B7
Oval The
  Ellesmere Port CH65 . . 70 C3
  Gatley SK8 . . . . 34 B8
Ovenhouse La SK10 . . . . 87 E7
Oven La SK11 . . . . 114 D5
OVER 149 B8
Overdale La CW8 . . . . . 101 D1
Overdale Rd
  New Mills SK12 . . . . . . 38 F6
  Willaston CH64 . . . . . . 43 A1
Overdene Rd CW7 . . . . . 149 D8
Overfields WA16 . . . . . . 57 D3
Over Hall Com Sch CW7 . 149 B7
Overhall Dr SK9 . . . . 60 E7
Overhill La SK9 . . . . 60 E7
Overhill Rd SK9 . . . . 60 D7
OVER KNUTSFORD 57 C1
Overleigh Cl CH4 . . . . . 141 D7
Overleigh Rd CH4 . . . . . 141 C7
Overleigh St Mary's CE Prim
  Sch CH4 . . . . 141 D6
Overleigh Terr CH4 . . . . 141 C7
OVER PEOVER 83 A1
Over Pl WA16 . . . . 82 C8
OVERPOOL 69 F7
Overpool Gdns CH66 . . . 69 F3
Overpool Rd
  Ellesmere Port CH66 . . 70 A2
  CH65, CH66 . . . . 69 F5
Overpool Sta CH66 . . . . 69 E6
Over Rd
  Church Minshull CW5 . . 172 A7
  Winsford CW7 . . . . . . 149 F1
Over St John's CE Prim Sch
  ① CW7 . . . . 126 B1
OVER TABLEY 56 A5
OVERTON 74 C7
Overton Cl
  Congleton CW12 . . . . . 156 C3
  Middlewich CW10 . . . . 151 B8
Overton Dr WA6 . . . . 74 C6
Overton Heath La SY14 . . 212 F5
Overton Rd ST8 . . . . . . 179 F6
Overton Way ② SK9 . . . 34 D5
Overway WA7 . . . . 126 E1
Overwood Ave CH1 . . . . 94 E1
Overwood La
  Blacon CH1 . . . . 117 C4
  Mollington CH1 . . . . . . 94 E1
Ovington Gr WA7 . . . . . . 49 F3
Owen Cl CH1 . . . . 117 E6
Owens Cnr WA4 . . . . . . 26 D3
Owen St
  Crewe CW1 . . . . 190 C2
  Northwich CW9 . . . . . 104 B8
  Warrington WA2 . . . . . 16 A7
Owlers The SK23 . . . . . . 65 E6
Owley Wood Rd CW8 . . . 77 E1
Owlhurst The SK10 . . . . 88 B8
Owl Ind Est The CH5 . . . 116 B6
Owlsfield WA12 . . . . 2 E3
Oxborough Cl WA8 . . . . 12 F4
Oxenham Rd WA2 . . . . . . 8 A3
Oxford Cl CH66 . . . . 94 E8
Oxford Ct WA1 . . . . 16 D6
Oxford Dr
  Halewood L26 . . . . 21 A8
  Heswall CH60 . . . . 41 F6
Oxford Gr M44 . . . . 11 C6
Oxford Rd
  Chester CH4 . . . . 140 F6
  Macclesfield SK11 . . . . 112 B7
  Runcorn WA7 . . . . 49 A8
Oxford St
  Crewe CW1 . . . . 190 B5
  Newton-le-Willows WA12 . 2 B3
  Warrington WA4 . . . . . 16 C4
  Widnes WA8 . . . . 23 B7

Ox-Hey Cres ST8 . . . . . 179 D1
Ox-Hey Dr ST8 . . . . 179 D1
Oxhey Fst Sch ST8 . . . . 179 E1
Oxheys WA7 . . . . 50 C8
Oxheys La CW6 . . . . . . 169 C8
Oxmead Cl WA2 . . . . 9 B1
Oxmoor Wood Nature
  Reserve★ WA7 . . . . . 50 A5
Oxmoor Wood Nature
  Reserve★ WA7 . . . . . 24 D5
Oxney Cl SK17 . . . . 111 F8
Oxton Cl WA8 . . . . 12 C4
Oxton Gn CH66 . . . . 69 D4

P

PACKMOOR 195 F1
Packmoor Prim Sch ST7 . 195 F1
Packsaddle Pk SK10 . . . 86 E5
Padarn Cl CH4 . . . . 140 D5
PADDINGTON 17 A8
Paddington Bank WA1 . . 16 F6
Paddington Mdws Nature
  Reserve★ WA1 . . . . . 17 A6
Paddock Brow SK10 . . . . 87 A5
Paddock Chase SK12 . . . 36 F1
Paddock Cl CW3 . . . . . . 223 C5
Paddock Dr CH64 . . . . . 41 D2
PADDOCKHILL 59 A4
Paddockhill La WA16 . . . 59 A4
Paddock La
  Audlem CW3 . . . . 230 B2
  Horwich End SK23 . . . . 65 F5
  Kettleshulme SK23 . . . 64 F4
  Lymm WA13 . . . . 19 C7
  Partington WA13, WA14 . 20 B5
Paddock Rd CH4 . . . . . . 141 E1
Paddock Rise WA7 . . . . . 49 E4
Paddock Row CH1 . . . . . 237 B2
Paddocks Gn CW12 . . . . 178 F8
Paddocks The
  Chester CH1 . . . . 94 B5
  Prestbury SK10 . . . . . . 87 A5
  Whitegate CW8 . . . . . 125 B6
Paddock The
  Chester CH4 . . . . 141 B7
  Ellesmere Port CH66 . . 69 D3
  Elton CH2 . . . . 72 A3
  Handforth SK9 . . . . . . 34 C4
  Hartford CW8 . . . . . . 103 C3
  Hassall Green CW11 . . 175 F2
  Helsby WA6 . . . . 73 C2
  Heswall CH60 . . . . 41 C8
  Horwich End SK23 . . . . 65 F6
  Lymm WA13 . . . . 19 C4
  Sandbach CW11 . . . . . 175 B7
  Tarporley CW6 . . . . . . 146 D1
  Willaston CW5 . . . . . . 205 D4
Paddock View CW10 . . . 128 C2
Paddock Way CH4 . . . . . 161 A2
Paddock Wlk CW8 . . . . . 150 A4
PADGATE 8 F1
Padgate Bsns Ctr WA1 . . 17 B8
Padgate La
  Warrington, Padgate WA1 . 16 F8
  Warrington WA1 . . . . . 16 D7
Padgbury Cl CW12 . . . . 156 A1
Padgbury La CW12 . . . . 156 A1
Padge La CH3 . . . . 183 C2
Padmore Cl CW1 . . . . . 190 A7
Padstow Dr ST7 . . . . . . 193 B3
Padstow Cl
  Crewe CW1 . . . . 190 B8
  Macclesfield SK10 . . . . 111 E8
  Warrington WA5 . . . . . 14 E3
Padstow Dr SK7 . . . . . . 35 F7
Padstow Sq WA7 . . . . . . 50 B5
Padworth Pl CW1 . . . . . 173 B1
Page Gr CW2 . . . . 206 B3
Paige La WA8 . . . . 13 C1
Paignton Cl WA5 . . . . . . 14 E4
Painswick Rd CH66 . . . . 69 E2
Paisley Ave CH62 . . . . . 43 E4
PALACE FIELDS 50 A6
Palace Fields Ave WA7 . . 50 A6
Palace Fields Local Ctr
  WA7 . . . . 50 A6
Palacefields Prim Sch
  WA7 . . . . 50 A6
Palace Ney CH64 . . . . . . 67 A5
Palatine Cl CH1 . . . . . . 117 D6
Palatine Ind Est WA4 . . . 16 C3
Palgrave Cl CH1 . . . . . . 118 A5
Palin Dr WA5 . . . . 14 E6
Palliser Cl WA3 . . . . 10 A3
Pall Mall CW5 . . . . 204 E5
Palma Ave M90 . . . . 33 B8
Palmarsh Rd WA8 . . . . . 22 B5
Palmer Cl ③ CW9 . . . . . 103 F5
Palmer Cres WA5 . . . . . 15 D8
Palmer Rd CW11 . . . . . 175 C5
Palmerston Cl CW1 . . . . 191 C5
Palmerston Cl CH65 . . . 59 B8
Palmerston Rd SK11 . . . 112 A7
Palmerston St CW10 . . . 88 B8
Palmerston Way ST8 . . . 179 D1
Palm Gr CH66 . . . . 70 D1
Palmyra Square N WA1 . . 16 A5
Palmyra Square S WA1 . . 16 A5
PANDY 222 A3
Pangbourne Cl WA4 . . . 26 E6
Panton Pl CH2 . . . . 118 F3
Panton Rd CH2 . . . . 118 F3
Parade Rd M90 . . . . 33 C7
Parade The
  ① Alderley Edge SK9 . . 60 A1
  Blacon CH1 . . . . 117 E5

Parade The *continued*
Culcheth WA3 4 E3
Neston CH64 41 B1
Paradise CH4 237 B1
PARADISE GREEN 171 E6
Paradise La CW5 171 E7
Paradise Mill Silk Mus* 15 SK11 112 D7
Paradise St SK11 112 C7
Paragon Cl WA8 13 B5
Parbold Ct WA8 22 D8
Parc Ddiwydiannol Glannau Dyfrdwy/Deeside Ind Pk CH5 92 E2
Parc Ddiwydiannol Y Ffin/Borders Ind Pk The CH4 140 C7
Parchments The WA12 2 D4
Parish Cl ST7 193 B4
Park Ave
Bramhall SK7 35 D5
Furness Vale SK23 39 D3
Haydock WA11 1 A6
Poynton SK12 36 E4
Saltney CH4 140 E6
Saughall CH1 94 A2
Talke ST7 210 E8
Tattenhall CH3 166 B2
Warrington WA4 16 D3
Weaverham CW8 77 D1
Widnes WA8 13 B1
Wilmslow SK9 60 C8
Winsford CW7 127 A3
Park Avenue N WA12 2 C2
Park Avenue S WA12 2 C2
Park Bank CW12 156 F2
Park Brook Rd SK11 112 A8
Park Bvd WA1 16 B4
Park Cl CH3 121 B2
Park Cres
Cuddington CW8 101 F4
Furness Vale SK23 39 D3
Handforth SK9 34 B1
Warrington WA4 26 D6
Park Ct
Chester CH1 237 C2
Frodsham WA6 74 A8
Runcorn WA7 49 A8
1 Warrington WA1 16 A5
Parkdale Ind Est WA1 16 C4
Parkdale Rd WA1 17 A7
Park Dr
Chester CH2 119 A4
Ellesmere Port CH65 70 B3
Handforth SK9 34 B1
Wistaston CW2 205 F8
Park Drive Gdns CW2 205 F8
Park Drive S CH2 119 A4
PARK END 209 A4
Parker Ave CW8 103 A6
Parker Dr CH3 180 E1
Parker Drive S CH3 180 F1
Parker's Bldgs CH1 237 C3
Parkers Ct WA7 49 E6
Parker's Rd CW1 190 A8
Parker's Row CH3 180 F6
Parker St
Macclesfield SK11 112 E7
Runcorn WA7 23 B3
Warrington WA1 16 A5
Parker Way CW12 156 A3
Park Est CW2 206 D5
Parkett Heyes Rd SK11 111 E7
Parkfield CW1 173 A1
Parkfield Ave WA4 17 A4
Parkfield Dr
Ellesmere Port CH65 70 A3
Helsby WA6 73 B3
Nantwich CW5 204 E4
Parkfield Rd
Broughton CH4 139 C3
Knutsford WA16 82 B8
Northwich CW9 104 C8
Parkfields La WA2 8 F2
PARKGATE
Neston 41 C1
Over Peover 108 B8
Parkgate WA16 57 C3
Parkgate Ave WA16 108 B8
Parkgate Ct
Chester CH1 118 B4
Warrington WA4 16 C2
Parkgate Ho CH64 41 B1
Parkgate La
Heswall CH64 41 F5
Knutsford WA16 57 C3
Parkgate Prim Sch CH64 41 C1
Parkgate Rd
Blacon CH1 118 A6
Macclesfield SK11 112 C4
Neston CH64 66 D8
Puddington CH66 68 C2
Saughall CH1 94 C3
Warrington WA4 16 D1
Woodbank CH1 93 E7
Parkgate Trad Est WA16 57 C4
Parkgate Way
7 Handforth SK9 34 D4
Runcorn WA7 50 D7
Park Gn SK11 112 D7
Park Gr SK11 112 C6
Parkhill Ct WA16 57 B1
Park House Dr
Prestbury SK10 87 A8
Sandbach CW11 175 C8
Parkhouse Ind Est ST5 210 F1
Park House La SK10 87 A8
Park House Mews CW11 175 D8
Parkhouse Road E ST5 210 F1
Parkhouse Road W ST5 210 E1
Park La
Audley ST7 209 B4
Congleton CW12 156 F2
5 Congleton CW12 157 A1
Frodsham WA6 74 B8
Hargrave CH3 144 E3
Hartford CW8 103 B4
Hatherton CW5 219 E4
Higher Walton WA4 25 F5
Little Bollington WA14 20 B2
Littleton CH3 119 F3
Macclesfield SK11 112 C6
Moulton CW9 126 F7
Pickmere CW9, WA16 79 E8
Poynton SK12 36 F3
Pulford CH4 162 E5
Sandbach CW11 174 F6
Parkland Cl WA4 27 B4
Parkland Dr CH2 72 B3
Parklands
Ellesmere Port CH66 69 D6
Kidsgrove ST7 195 B1
Widnes WA8 12 C3
Parklands Com Prim Sch CH66 69 D5
Parklands Dr
Chorlton CW2 207 E3
Heswall CH60 41 C6
Parklands Gdns CH66 69 D6
Parklands The
Congleton CW12 157 A2
Middlewich CW10 151 B7
Parklands View CH66 69 D5
Parklands Way SK12 36 E4
Parkland View CW5 204 D4
Park Lane Sch SK11 112 B6
Parklea CH66 69 D6
Parkleigh CW12 156 E2
Park Mills Cl CW5 205 D5
Park Mount Cl SK11 112 A6
Park Mount Dr SK11 112 A6
Park Prim Sch The WA7 24 A1
Park Rd
Bebington, Eastham CH62 43 F6
Congleton CW12 156 E3
Ellesmere Port CH65 70 C4
Golborne WA3 3 A7
Haslington CW1 191 D5
Heswall CH60 41 B8
High Lane SK12 38 A6
Horwich End SK23 65 D6
Little Budworth CW6 124 F1
Lymm WA13 29 D8
Middlewich CW10 128 C1
Nantwich CW5 204 E3
New Mills SK22 39 C7
North Rode CW12 134 F2
Partington, Warburton WA13 19 C8
Runcorn WA7 49 A8
Tarporley CW6 146 D2
Thornton-le-Moors CH2 71 E1
Warrington, Orford WA2 8 D1
Warrington WA5 14 E6
Widnes WA8 13 B1
Willaston CH64 68 B8
Willaston (nr Nantwich) CW5 205 C5
Wilmslow SK9 59 F7
Winnington CW8 78 D1
Park Road Com Prim Sch WA5 14 E6
Park Road N WA12 2 E4
Park Road S WA12 2 D2
Park Road W CH4 141 A7
Parkroyal Com Sch 9 SK11 112 C7
Parkside Bsns Pk WA3 3 A8
Parkside Cl
High Lane SK6 37 D8
Neston CH64 66 D8
Parkside Ct WA8 13 A2
Parkside Rd WA12, WA2 3 B2
Park St
Bollington SK10 88 B8
Chester CH1 237 B2
Congleton CW12 156 E2
Haydock WA11 1 A6
Macclesfield SK11 112 D7
Neston CH64 66 E8
Northwich CW8 103 E7
Parkstone Dr CW1 190 B8
Parksway WA1 17 D7
Park The
Christleton CH3 142 E8
Warrington WA5 14 D3
Park Vale Rd SK11 112 C6
Park View
Audlem CW3 230 C8
Bebington CH62 43 C8
Congleton CW12 156 E3
Hazel Grove SK7 37 B8
Little Bollington WA14 20 B2
Nantwich CW5 204 F6
Newton-le-Willows WA12 2 E3
Warrington WA2 8 E3
Parkview Ct CH60 40 F8
Park View Ct SK12 36 E4
Parkview Pk WA13 29 D8
Park View Rd ST7 195 B3
Park W CH60 40 E7
Parkway
Connah's Quay CH5 92 E1
Holmes Chapel CW4 130 C3
Wilmslow SK9 60 B6
Park Way CH1 94 A2
Parkway Bsns Ctr CH5 92 E1
Park Wlk CH2 118 E4
Parkwood Cl
Bebington CH62 43 E8
Lymm WA13 18 D2
Parliament St 4 CW8 103 E7
Parliament Way 9 CH66 94 F8
Parlington Cl WA8 22 C7
Parnell Sq CW12 157 A2
PARRAH GREEN 231 E7
Parr Gr WA11 1 A6
Parr St
Macclesfield SK11 112 C8
Warrington WA1 16 C4
1 Widnes WA8 13 C1
Parrs Wood View WA4 17 B1
Parry Dr WA4 17 E3
Parsonage Gn
Hale L24 21 E1
Wilmslow SK9 60 B7
Parsonage Rd WA8 23 A4
Parsonage St SK11 112 D7
Parsonage Way WA5 15 A5
Parsons La CH2 118 B7
Parson St CW12 156 C2
PARTINGTON 11 F4
Partington L Ctr M31 11 F2
Partington Prim Sch M31 11 F3
Partington Sh Ctr M31 11 F3
Partington Sq WA7 24 F4
Partridge Cl
Congleton CW12 156 E1
Warrington WA3 9 E4
Winsford CW7 149 D5
Partridge Way CW9 79 F5
Parvey La SK11 112 E2
Pasture Cl
Kelsall CW6 122 C4
Macclesfield SK10 87 C3
Pasture Dr WA3 9 B7
Pasture La WA2 9 B1
Pastures Dr CW2 207 D3
Pastures The WA9 6 A7
Patch La SK7 35 D5
Patmos La WA16 105 F8
Patrivale Cl WA1 16 F6
Patten La WA1 16 B5
Patterdale Ave WA2 8 C2
Patterdale Cl CW2 189 D3
Patterdale Rd M31 11 E3
Patterson Cl WA3 9 E3
Patterson St WA12 2 B3
Patton Dr WA5 15 B6
Paul Cl WA5 14 D6
Paulden Rd CW9 80 A2
Paul St WA2 16 A6
Pavement La WA16 57 F3
Pavilion Ct WA12 2 A3
Pavilions The
Chester CH4 141 B3
Davenham CW9 103 E2
Pavilion Way
Congleton CW12 156 C3
Macclesfield SK10 86 F1
Paxford Pl SK9 60 A5
Payne Cl WA5 15 D6
Paythorne Cl WA3 4 F3
Peace Ctr WA5 15 D5
Peace Dr WA5 15 D5
Peach Field CH3 142 B7
Peach Gr WA11 1 E7
Peach La CW5 189 A1
Peach Tree Cl L24 21 E2
Peacock Ave
Warrington WA1 16 E6
Winsford CW7 149 C5
Peacock Dr SK8 34 B6
Peacock Hay Rd ST7 210 F4
Peacock La WA16 29 E6
Peacock Way 5 SK9 34 D5
Peak Rd SK22 39 D8
Pearle St SK10 87 D1
Pearlings The CH3 119 B1
Pearl La
Chester CH3 119 C1
Littleton CH3 119 D1
Pearl St SK10 87 A7
Pearson Ave WA4 16 D2
Pearson St 9 SK11 112 E7
Pear Tree Ave
Crewe CW1 190 B7
Runcorn WA7 49 C7
Pear Tree Bank CW12 156 E2
Peartree Cl CW11 175 E6
Pear Tree Cl
Frodsham WA6 49 D1
Hale L24 21 E1
Weaverham CW8 77 C1
Winsford CW7 149 D7
Peartree Cres WA12 2 C2
Pear Tree Dr CW9 80 A6
Pear Tree Farm Cotts CW9 104 F4
Pear Tree Field CW5 205 A4
Peartree La SY14 222 D1
Pear Tree La
Acton Bridge CW8 76 E4
Whitchurch SY13 225 D1
Peartree Pl WA4 16 C4
Pear Tree Prim Sch CW5 205 A4
Pear Tree Rd ST7 209 F1
Pear Tree Way
Chester CH2 118 F6
5 Ellesmere Port CH66 69 E1
Pearwood Cl CW6 146 D1
Peasley Cl WA2 9 B1
Pebble Brook Cty Prim Sch CW2 190 C1
Peckfield Cl WA7 50 A5
PECKFORTON 184 F5
Peckforton Castle* CW6 167 E1
Peckforton Cl CW11 174 E7
Peckforton Dr
Ellesmere Port CH66 69 E3
Runcorn WA7 49 F4
Peckforton Hall Farm CW6 185 A6
Peckforton Hall La CW6 185 B6
Peckforton Rd CW6 168 A2
Peckforton Way
Chester CH2 118 F6
2 Northwich CW8 103 E7
Peckforton Wlk 11 SK9 34 E1
Peckmill Cl SK9 34 E2
Peck Mill La WA6 98 A7
Peckmill Rdbt CW9 127 B8
Pedley Hill
Booth Green SK10 62 F7
Rainow SK10 88 E4
Pedley House La WA16 58 E1
Pedley La
Chelford WA16 83 D8
Congleton CW12 157 F4
Pedley St CW2 190 D2
Peebles Cl
Ellesmere Port CH66 68 F6
Holmes Chapel CW4 130 B2
Peel Cl WA1 17 D6
Peel Cres CH3 121 E7
Peel Ct 4 ST7 195 A2
Peel Dr CW12 178 B7
Peel Hall La CH3 121 E7
Peel Hall Pk CH3 121 D8
Peel Hollow ST7 209 A2
Peel House La WA8 13 B2
Peel La CW12 178 D7
Peel Sq 1 CW1 190 B5
Peel St
Crewe CW1 190 B5
Macclesfield SK11 112 D6
Newton-le-Willows WA12 2 A3
Runcorn WA7 22 F3
Peel Terr CH1 237 C3
Peerswood Ct CH64 66 E5
Peewit Cl CW7 149 D5
Peggie's La SK10 62 E2
Pelham Cl CW1 191 C5
Pelham Rd WA4 17 C3
Pelican Cl CW1 191 A5
Pemberton Cl CH64 68 A8
Pemberton Rd CH1 237 A3
Pembridge Ct CH65 70 E3
Pembridge Gdns CH65 70 E3
Pembroke Apartments WA2 9 A3
Pembroke Cl CH4 141 E6
Pembroke Ct WA7 24 D5
Pembroke Dr CH65 70 A3
Pembroke Gdns WA4 26 D4
Pembroke Gr M44 11 C6
Pembroke Rd SK11 111 F7
Pembroke Way CW7 149 B7
Penare WA7 50 C6
Penbrook Cl CW2 189 D3
Penda Way CW11 175 B6
Pendine Cl WA5 7 C2
Pendlebury Gdns SK11 112 D2
Pendlebury St WA4 17 A3
Pendle Cl
Crewe CW1 191 A5
Ellesmere Port CH66 68 F6
Pendle Gdns WA3 4 E2
Penfold Cl CH1 94 B8
Penfold Hey CH2 118 D7
Penfolds WA7 23 D1
Penfold Way CH4 162 A7
Penhale Mews SK7 35 F7
Peninsula Ho WA2 16 C7
Penistone Dr CH66 69 B5
PENKETH 14 D4
Penketh Ave WA5 15 F8
Penketh Bsns Pk WA5 15 B4
Penketh Com Prim Sch WA5 14 D4
Penketh Ct
1 Runcorn WA7 23 B2
Warrington WA5 14 D4
Penketh Cty High Sch WA5 15 A5
Penketh Rd WA5 15 A4
Penketh's La 10 WA7 23 A3
Penketh South Com Prim Sch WA5 14 E3
Penkford La WA5 1 D2
Penkford Sch WA12 1 E2
Penkford St WA12 1 E3
Penkmans La WA6 74 C6
Penlington Ct CW5 204 F6
Penmann Cres L26 21 A7
Penmark Cl WA5 7 C2
Penmon Cl CH1 117 D3
Pennant Cl WA3 10 A3
Penn Bridge SK11 158 E6
Penn Gdns CH65 70 B5
Penn House Cl SK7 35 E8
Pennine Ct SK10 87 E2
Pennine Rd WA2 8 E2
Pennine Way
Biddulph ST8 179 E1
Winsford CW7 149 B8
Pennine Wlk CH66 69 B6
Pennington Cl WA6 49 D2
Pennington Dr WA12 2 E3
Pennington Gn CH66 69 C3
Pennington La WA5, WA9 1 D2
Penningtons La SK11 111 F5
Penn La WA7 22 F1
Penny Bank Cl CH4 139 A3
Pennyfields Rd ST7 195 D2
Penny La
Collins Green WA5 1 D1
Cronton L35, WA8 12 B6
Haydock WA11 2 B7
Rainow SK10 88 D3
Pennymoor Dr CW10 128 D2
Pennypleck La CW9 28 A2
Penny's La
Northwich CW9 104 F7
Rudheath CW9 105 B5
Penrhyn Cres
Hazel Grove SK7 36 C8
Runcorn WA7 49 B7
Penrhyn Rd CW8 103 E8
Penrith Ave
Macclesfield SK11 111 F5
Warrington WA2 8 C2
Penrith Cl
Frodsham WA6 49 D1
Partington M31 11 E4
Penrith Ct CW12 156 A2
Penrose Gdns WA5 14 D3
Penry Ave M44 11 E6
Penryn Cl WA5 14 E3
Pensarn Gdns WA5 7 D2
Pensby Ave CH2 118 D5
Pensby Dr CH66 69 D4
Pensby Rd CH60 40 F8
Penshaw Ct WA7 49 E7
Pentland Ave WA2 8 B3
Pentland Cl
Chester CH3 119 A2
Winsford CW7 149 B8
Pentland Pl WA2 8 B3
Pentre Cl CH3 121 F7
Pentre La CH3 121 F7
Penzance Cl SK10 111 E8
Peony Gdns WA9 6 B7
Peover Hall & Gardens* WA16 107 E8
PEOVER HEATH 108 C8
Peover La
Chelford SK11 108 F8
Congleton CW12 157 F6
Peover Rd SK9 34 E5
Peover Superior Endowed Prim Sch WA16 108 B8
Pepper Ct SK9 60 A6
Pepper St
Appleton Thorn WA4 27 B3
Ashley WA16 31 F1
Chelford SK11 83 E2
Chester CH1 237 B2
Christleton CH3 142 D8
Hale L24 21 D1
Henbury SK11 111 B8
Lymm WA13 18 F3
Middlewich CW10 128 C1
Nantwich CW5 204 E5
Peppers The WA13 18 F3
Percival Cl CH2 118 C8
Percival La
Ollerton WA16 83 B3
Runcorn WA7 22 E2
Percival Rd
Chester CH2 118 C8
Ellesmere Port CH65 70 B6
Percival St WA1 16 C5
Percy James Cl ST7 193 E4
Percy Rd CH4 141 D7
Percy St
Northwich CW9 104 A8
Warrington WA5 15 E5
Percyvale St SK10 112 E8
Peregrine Cl CW7 149 D5
Perenna Ct/Llys Perenna CH6 91 B2
Perrin Ave WA7 48 E8
Perrins Rd WA5 6 F6
Perry Fields CW1 173 B1
Perry St WA7 23 B2
Perth Cl
Bramhall SK7 35 F5
Holmes Chapel CW4 130 B2
Warrington WA2 8 F3
Peterborough Cl
Ellesmere Port CH66 94 F7
Macclesfield SK10 87 A2
Peter Destapleigh Way CW5 205 A3
Peter Ellson Cl CW2 190 D1
Peter House Rd SK11 112 F3
Peter Pl 7 CW1 190 B5
Peters Cl SK10 87 A7
Petersfield Gdns WA3 4 E4
Petersfield Way CW2 207 D3
Petersgate WA7 50 D7
Petersham Dr WA4 26 E5
Peter St
Golborne WA3 3 A8
Macclesfield SK11 112 C7
Northwich CW9 79 B1
Peterstone Cl WA5 7 D2
Peter Street W 1 SK11 112 C7
Petham Ct WA8 12 E4
Petrel Ave SK12 36 B4
Petrel Cl CW7 149 D5
Pettypool Activity Ctr* CW8 102 C1

Petunia Cl WA9	6 A7
Petunia Gr SK11	112 B5
Petworth Ave WA2	8 B3
Petworth Cl CW2	206 B8
Pevensey Dr WA16	82 A8
Peveril Cl WA4	26 D8
Peveril Dr SK7	36 F8
Peveril Gdns SK12	39 A6
Peveril Mews SK12	39 A6
Peveril Wlk ❸ SK11	111 F7
Pewithall Prim Sch WA7	49 B7
Pewit La CW5	231 C7
PEWTERSPEAR	26 E4
Pewterspear Green Rd WA4	26 E3
Pewterspear La WA4	26 E4
Pexall Rd SK11	134 C3
Pex Hill Ct WA8	12 E5
Pexhill Dr SK10	111 E7
Pexhill Rd SK11	111 C5
Pheasant Cl WA3	9 F4
Pheasant Dr CW9	79 F5
Pheasant Field L24	21 C2
Pheasant Way CW7	149 D5
Pheasant Wlk WA16	29 C4
Philip Rd WA8	22 B8
Philips Dr WA5	14 E7
Philips La CH66	69 C4
Philip St CH5	116 A2
Phillips Rd CH1	117 D3
Phillip St CH2	118 F3
Phillips Way CH60	40 E8
Phipps' La WA5	6 F7
Phoenix Ave WA5	7 F2
Phoenix Cl ST7	195 C2
Phoenix Ctr The CW7	127 C1
Phoenix L Pk CW1	190 C3
Phoenix Pl WA3	15 A7
Phoenix St CH5	116 A3
Phythian Cres WA5	14 F4
Pichael Nook WA4	17 A4
Pickenham Cl SK11	111 F6
Pickering Cres WA3	17 D3
Pickerings Cl WA7	49 C6
Pickerings O The Boat CW8	76 B5
Pickering's Pasture Nature Reserve★ WA8	22 B3
Pickerings Rd WA8	22 B3
Pickering Sq CW7	237 C4
Pickering Way CW5	204 F4
Pickford St SK11	112 D7
PICKMERE	80 A7
Pickmere Cl CW11	174 F7
Pickmere Ct Crewe CW1	190 C5
❿ Handforth SK9	34 D5
Pickmere Dr Bebington CH62	43 F3
Bebington CH62	43 F4
Chester CH3	142 B8
Runcorn WA7	50 C5
Pickmere La Higher Wincham CW9	79 F6
Pickmere Rd WA16	55 D2
Pickmere SK9	34 D5
Pickmere St WA5	15 E5
Pickwick Cl CW11	175 C8
Pickwick Pl ST7	194 D2
Pickwick Rd SK12	36 D3
Picow Farm Rd WA7	22 E1
Picow St ❷ WA7	22 F1
PICTON	96 C3
Picton Ave Ellesmere Port CH65	70 C5
Runcorn WA7	23 B2
Picton Cl Bebington CH62	43 E3
❷ Northwich CW9	103 F4
Warrington WA3	9 C4
Picton Dr Handforth SK9	34 E2
Winsford CW7	126 B2
Picton Gorse La CH2	119 B7
Picton La CH2	96 C4
Picton Sq CW4	130 C3
Piele Rd WA11	1 E8
Pierce St SK11	112 C8
Pierpoint La CH1	237 B2
Pierpoint St WA5	15 F3
Pigginshaw SK9	59 E8
Pigot Pl WA4	16 F5
Pike La WA6	75 A3
Pikemere Prim Sch ST7	193 B5
Pikemere Rd ST7	193 B5
Pikenall La CW8	76 D3
Pike Rd SK10	89 B6
Pike St WA4	16 C1
Pike The CW5	204 E3
Pilgrim Cl WA2	8 A6
Pilgrims Way WA7	24 D2
Pillar Box La CW11	153 B3
Pillmoss La WA4	52 B8
Pillory St CW5	204 E5
Pimblett Rd WA11	1 E7
Pimblett St WA3	3 A7
Pimlico Rd WA7	22 E2
Pinders Farm Dr WA1	16 C5
Pineapple Pk CW7	127 B2
Pine Ave Newton-le-Willows WA12	2 D2
❹ Widnes WA8	13 B2
Pine Cl Haydock WA11	1 C6
Macclesfield SK10	87 F1

Pine Cl continued Talke ST7	210 D7
Pine Ct ST7	193 E4
Pinedale Cl CH66	95 A8
Pine Gdns CH2	118 C6
Pine Gr Chester CH2	119 B4
Ellesmere Port CH66	70 A1
Golborne WA3	3 C8
Sandbach CW11	175 C6
Warrington WA1	17 A7
Winsford CW7	127 A1
Pinehey CH64	41 D1
Pine Ho CH2	118 C5
Pinehurst SK10	86 E6
Pinellas WA7	23 B3
Pine Lo SK7	35 F7
Pine Rd Bramhall SK7	35 F8
Heswall CH60	41 C8
Macclesfield SK10	87 F1
Poynton SK12	36 F3
Runcorn WA7	49 C8
Pines The Mobberley WA16	58 E1
❽ Northwich CW9	103 E6
Widnes WA8	13 D4
Pinetree Cl Barnton CW8	78 B4
Winsford CW7	127 A1
Pine Tree Cl CH4	139 C3
Pine Trees WA16	57 F8
Pineways WA4	26 D5
Pine Wlk Nantwich CW5	204 F4
❸ Partington M31	11 E3
Pinewood Ave WA1	16 E7
Pinewood Cl CH2	72 C3
Pinewood Ct CW2	206 B7
Pinewood Dr CH60	41 B8
Pinewood Gr ST5	210 C1
Pinewood Rd Burtonwood WA5	6 F7
Wilmslow SK9	60 E8
Winsford CW7	126 B2
Pinfold Cl WA15	32 D7
Pinfold Ct CH4	141 E6
Pinfold La Alpraham CW6	169 D5
Chelford WA16	83 D6
Chester CH4	141 D6
Little Budworth CW6	147 E7
Middlewich CW10	128 B1
Plumley WA16	81 B4
Wythenshawe M90, WA15	32 F6
Pinfold St ❿ SK11	112 C8
Pinfold Way CW8	77 D1
Pingard's La CW8	101 C6
Pingate Dr SK8	35 A6
Pingate La SK8	35 A6
Pingate Lane S SK8	35 A6
Pingot Croft CH3	142 B7
Pingot La WA6	99 A5
Pingot Rd SK22	39 D8
Pinmill Brow WA6	74 B7
Pinmill Cl WA6	74 C7
Pinners Brow WA2	16 B6
Pinners Brow Ret Pk WA2	16 B6
Pinners Fold WA7	24 B1
PINSLEY GREEN	216 D2
Pinsley Green Rd CW5	216 E2
Pinsley View CW5	216 E4
Pintail Pl CW7	149 D6
Pinwood Ct ❿ SK9	34 E1
PINTS' ASH	119 D4
Pipers Ash CW7	126 A1
Piper's Cl CH60	40 D8
Pipers Ct CH2	119 B4
Piper's End CH60	40 D8
Pipers La Chester CH2	119 B4
Puddington CH64	93 A8
Piper's La CH60	40 D8
Pipers The Golborne WA3	3 F8
Heswall CH60	40 D8
Pipit Ave WA12	2 C3
Pipit La WA3	9 E3
Pippin Cl CW10	151 C7
Pippits Row WA7	49 E4
Pirie Cl CW12	157 A4
Pirie Rd CW12	157 A4
Pitcher La CW11	177 A8
Pit La Hough CW2	206 E2
Talke ST7	210 C6
Widnes WA8	13 A4
Pitt La SK11	132 B8
Pitts Cl CH3	121 C2
Pitts Heath La WA7	24 F1
Pitt St Macclesfield SK11	112 D6
Warrington WA5	15 F7
Widnes WA8	23 A5
Pitville Terr WA4	22 C7
Plaistow Ct WA7	49 E7
Plane Gr ST5	210 E1
Plane Tree Dr CW1	190 E6
Plane Tree Gr WA11	2 A7
Plane Tree Rd M31	11 D3
Planewood Gdns WA3	3 F7
Plantagenet Cl ❸ CW7	149 D6
Plantation Cl WA4	24 A1
Plantation Dr CH66	69 C7
Plant La CW11	174 B7
Plant St CW11	175 A7
Plas Dinas CH1	117 D3

Plas Newton La CH2	118 F5
Plas Newydd CH4	161 B6
Platt Ave CW11	175 A7
Platts La Christleton CH3	143 D8
Duddon CH3, CW6	144 E7
Tarvin, Broom Bank CH3	144 B8
Tarvin CH3	121 B2
Tattenhall CH3	183 F7
Platt's La CH3	164 E5
Platts St WA11	1 A6
Pleasance Way WA12	2 D4
Pleasant St Macclesfield SK10	87 F1
Northwich CW8	103 E7
Pleasant View SK10	111 C8
Pleasant Way SK8	35 C6
Pleck Rd CH65	70 A2
PLEMSTALL	97 B1
Plemstall Cl CH2	119 F8
Plemstall La CH2	97 A1
Plemstall Way CH2	96 F1
Plemston Ct CH66	69 F8
Plex The ST7	193 D4
Plinston Ave WA4	16 F4
Plough Croft ST7	193 A3
Plough La CH3	143 B7
Ploughmans Cl CH66	94 E8
Ploughmans Way Ellesmere Port CH66	94 E8
Macclesfield SK10	87 B3
Plover Ave CW7	149 D5
Plover Cl Farndon CH3	180 F1
Macclesfield SK10	87 B4
Newton-le-Willows WA12	2 C2
Plover Dr WA7	50 D8
Plovers La WA6	73 C5
Plover Way WA3	3 E8
Plumbs Fold CW8	78 A2
Plumley Cl WA7	80 F3
PLUMLEY	
Plumley Cl Chester CH3	119 C1
❶❻ Macclesfield SK11	112 E7
Plumley Gdns WA8	12 A1
PLUMLEY MOOR	81 C2
Plumley Moor Rd WA16	81 C2
Plumley Rd SK9	34 D5
Plumley Sta WA16	81 A3
Plumpstons La WA6	49 B1
Plumpton Cross ❸ WA8	13 B2
Plumpton Mews ❼ WA8	13 C2
Plum Terr CH1	237 A3
Plumtre Ave WA5	15 F8
Plymouth Cl WA7	50 E6
Plymouth Dr SK7	35 F7
Plymyard Ave CH62	43 D5
Plymyard Cl CH62	43 D5
Plymyard Ct CH62	43 D5
Poachers' La WA4	16 F3
Pochard Ave CW7	149 D6
Pochard Dr SK12	36 A4
Pochard Rise WA7	50 D8
Pochin Way CW10	128 E1
Pocket Nook La WA3	4 B7
Pocklington Ct WA2	8 F1
Points Ho CW1	190 A5
Polden Cl CH66	69 A6
Poleacre Dr WA8	12 D2
Pole La CW9	53 E2
Pole Lane Ends CW9	53 C4
Pollard Ave WA6	74 D7
Pollard Dr CW5	205 B4
Polperro Cl Macclesfield SK10	86 D1
Warrington WA5	14 E3
Pond Cotts CH2	72 A3
Pond St WA3	4 A8
Pond View Cl CH60	41 C8
Pond Wlk WA9	1 A1
Pool Bank Bsns Pk CH3	121 C3
Pool Bank Cotts CH3	121 C3
Poole Ave WA2	8 B2
Poole Cres WA2	8 B2
Pool Hall La CH66	69 E8
Pool Hall Rd CH66	69 F8
POOLEHILL	188 A2
Poole Hill Rd CW5	188 A2
Poole La CH2	72 E2
Pool End Cl SK10	87 D4
Pool End Rd SK10	87 D4
Poole Old Hall La CW5	188 D4
Pooles La CW11	177 B5
POOLFOLD	179 F4
Poolford La CW4	129 E2
Pool Hall Ind Est CH65, CH66	70 A8
Pool House Rd SK12	37 D5
Pool La Cuddington CW8	102 B2
Haslington CW11	192 A7
Ince CH2	71 F4
Lymm WA13	18 B4
Malpas SY14	212 D1
Runcorn WA7	23 B3
Tarvin CH3	121 C4
Warrington WA4	16 A1
Pool Meadows Rd CW1	191 B4
Pool Side ST7	194 A3
Poolside Cl ST7	193 E4
Poolside Rd WA7	23 B1
Pools Platt La CW9	53 E6
Pool St Macclesfield SK11	112 E6
Widnes WA8	23 B7
Pooltown Rd CH65	69 F5
Pool View CW11	191 F7

Poplar Ave Culcheth WA3	4 F3
Moulton CW9	126 F8
Newton-le-Willows WA12	2 D3
Runcorn WA7	49 C7
Warrington WA5	14 E3
Wilmslow SK9	59 F5
Poplar Cl Congleton CW12	156 A4
❷ Ellesmere Port CH65	70 B4
Runcorn WA7	49 C7
Winsford CW7	149 B8
Poplar Ct CW5	205 A4
Poplar Dr Alsager ST7	193 E2
Kidsgrove ST7	195 A1
Middlewich CW10	151 D7
Poplar Gr Bollington SK10	88 A8
Crewe CW1	190 E5
Elton CH2	72 A3
Haydock WA11	1 C6
Irlam M44	11 D6
Poplar Hall La CH2	95 C6
Poplar La TF9	236 F5
Poplar Rd Chester CH4	140 F5
Haydock WA11	1 C6
Macclesfield SK11	112 D6
Weaverham CW8	102 D8
Poplars Ave Warrington, Hulme WA2	8 C3
Warrington, Winwick Quay WA2	8 A4
Poplars Pl WA2	8 D2
Poplars The Golborne, Wash End WN7	4 C8
Lymm WA13	18 D4
Wistaston CW2	205 F7
Poplar View WA4	25 A7
Poplar Way SK6	38 A7
Poplar Weint ❷ CH64	66 E8
Poplar Wlk M31	11 D3
Poppy Cl CW2	207 C5
Poppyfields Alsager ST7	193 B3
Warrington WA5	15 D3
Porlock Cl Heswall CH60	41 B6
Warrington WA5	14 E3
Port Arcades Sh Ctr CH65	70 C5
Porter Ave WA12	2 C5
Porter Dr CW9	104 C6
Porters Croft CH3	119 F5
Porter St WA7	23 C2
Porter Way CW9	104 C6
Portford Cl SK10	86 F1
Porthcawl Cl WA8	12 C3
Porthleven Rd WA7	50 B5
Portland Dr Biddulph ST8	179 D2
Scholar Green ST7	194 E6
Winsford CW7	149 B8
Portland Pl WA6	73 C4
Portland St Macclesfield SK11	112 D7
Newton-le-Willows WA12	1 F4
Runcorn WA7	22 F3
Portland Trad Pk WA2	16 A6
Portland Wlk ❹ SK11	111 F7
Portloe Rd SK8	34 B7
Portman Pl ❸ CW7	149 A8
Portmarnock Cl SK10	87 B3
Portola Cl WA4	26 E8
Portree Ave CH63	43 D5
Portree Dr CW4	130 B2
Portrush Cl Macclesfield SK10	87 C4
Widnes WA8	12 E3
Portside WA7	50 E7
Portside Bsns Pk CH65	70 B8
Portsmouth Pl WA7	50 E6
Portway M22	33 E8
Postles Pl CW9	103 F6
Post Office La Betley CW2	207 F1
Hampton Heath SY14	213 D7
Norley WA6	100 E5
Runcorn WA7	48 D7
Post Office Pl ❶ CW9	79 A1
Potter Cl CW5	205 D4
Potters Barn The★ CW11	176 A1
Potters End ST8	179 C1
Potters La WA8	21 F5
Pott Hall SK10	63 D3
POTT SHRIGLEY	63 C3
Pott Shrigley CE Prim Sch SK10	63 C3
POULTON	163 B2
Poulton Cres WA1	17 D8
Poulton Dr WA8	22 D8
Poulton Hall Rd CH63	43 A7
Poulton Rd CH63	43 A8
Pound Rd CH66	69 C7
Powder Mill Rd WA4	17 A3
Powell's Orch CH4	141 C7
Powell St WA4	16 F3
Powey Cl CH1	94 B5
Pownall Ave SK7	35 F7
Pownall Ct SK9	59 E8
POWNALL GREEN	35 E6
Pownall Green Prim Sch SK7	35 E7
Pownall Hall Sch SK9	59 F8

POWNALL PARK	59 F7
Pownall Pl SK7	35 E7
Pownall Rd SK9	59 F8
Pownall Sq SK11	112 C8
Pownall St SK10	87 D1
Powy Dr ST7	195 B2
Powys Cl CH1	237 A3
Powys St WA5	15 F5
POYNTON	36 E4
Poynton Cl WA4	17 B3
Poynton Coppice Nature Reserve★ SK12	37 B2
Poynton High Sch & Performing Arts Coll SK12	36 F2
Poynton Ind Est SK12	36 D1
Poynton L Ctr SK12	36 F2
Poynton St ❿ SK10	112 C8
Poynton Sta SK12	36 C4
Pratchitts Row CW5	204 E5
Precinct The CW2	189 F2
Preece Cl WA8	12 D4
Preesall Ave SK8	34 B8
Premier Pk CW7	127 B3
Prenton Pl CW4	141 E7
Prescot Rd WA8	12 D2
Prescot St CH2	118 F3
Prescott Rd SK9	34 B1
Prescott St WA4	16 E3
PRESTBURY	87 B7
Prestbury CE Prim Sch SK10	86 F7
Prestbury Cl ❽ Northwich CW9	103 F4
Widnes WA8	22 E8
Prestbury Dr WA4	17 D4
Prestbury La SK10	87 B7
Prestbury Rd Adder's Moss SK10	85 F6
Macclesfield SK10	87 B1
Nether Alderley SK10	86 A5
Wilmslow SK9	60 E5
Prestbury Sta SK10	87 A7
Preston Ave M44	11 F7
PRESTON BROOK	50 F5
PRESTON ON THE HILL	51 A6
Preston Street W SK11	112 B6
Prestwich Ave WA3	4 E3
Prestwick Cl Macclesfield SK10	87 C5
Widnes WA8	12 F3
Winsford CW7	126 C2
Prestwood St ❸ M44	10 A7
Pretoria St CH4	141 D7
Price Ave CW11	175 A5
Price Dr CW11	175 A5
Price Gr WA9	1 A2
Pride Cl WA12	2 C2
Priestfield Rd CH65	70 C5
Priest La SK10	61 B1
Priestley Bsns Ctr WA5	15 F5
Priestley Coll WA4	16 C3
Priestley Ct WA4	16 C3
Priestley St WA5	15 F5
Priestly Ct ❺ CW5	204 E5
Priestner Dr WA6	73 B4
Priestway La CH64	67 E1
Priesty Ct CW12	156 D2
Priesty Fields CW12	156 D2
Primary St M44	11 D5
Primitive St ST7	195 C7
Primrose Ave Haslington CW1	191 C5
Macclesfield SK11	112 B5
Primrose Chase CW4	130 D8
Primrose Cl Huntington CH3	142 A6
Runcorn WA7	50 A8
Warrington WA2	8 D2
Widnes WA8	12 E1
Primrose Gr WA11	1 E7
PRIMROSE HILL	28 C6
Primrose Hill Crewe CW2	189 E5
Cuddington CW8	101 F4
Kelsall CW6	122 C6
Primrose La WA6	73 B1
Primula Cl WA9	6 A7
Primula Dr WA3	3 D8
Prince Albert St CW1	190 D4
Prince Edward St CW5	204 E6
Prince Henry Sq ❸ WA1	16 B5
PRINCE HILL	231 F6
Prince Rd SK12	37 C5
Princes Ave Bebington CH62	43 E6
Chester CH1	237 C3
Northwich CW9	104 B8
Princes Cl WA7	23 F1
Princes Cres CW5	204 E7
Princes Pk CW8	78 A2
Princes Pl WA8	12 E1
Princes Rd CH65	70 B6
Princess Ave Audley ST7	209 D1
Haydock WA11	2 A7
Warrington, Bruche WA1	16 F6
Warrington, Great Sankey WA5	14 E7
Warrington, Padgate WA1	17 A8
Princess Cl CW2	205 F8
Princess Cres Middlewich CW10	151 D6
Warrington WA1	16 F6
Princess Ct ST7	210 D5

Princess Dr
Bollington SK10 . . . . 87 E7
Nantwich CW5 . . . . 205 A6
Sandbach CW11 . . . . 175 A7
Wistaston CW2 . . . . 205 F8
Princess Gr CW2 . . . . . . 205 F8
Princess Rd
Allostock WA16 . . . . 106 E3
Lymm WA13 . . . . 18 C3
Wilmslow SK9 . . . . 59 F5
Princess St
Bollington SK10 . . . . 87 F7
Chester CH1 . . . . 237 A2
Congleton CW12 . . . . . . 156 D3
Crewe CW1 . . . . 190 C6
Knutsford WA16 . . . . 57 A2
Northwich CW9 . . . . 79 E2
1 Runcorn WA7 . . . . 23 A3
Talke ST7 . . . . 210 D5
2 Warrington WA5 . . . . . . 15 D4
Winsford CW7 . . . . 127 A2
Princes St WA1 . . . . 2 B3
Prince's St WA8 . . . . 23 A8
Princess Wlk SK7 . . . . 36 A7
Princes Way SK11 . . . . . . 111 E7
Princeway WA6 . . . . 74 B8
Prince William Ave CH5 . 116 B3
Prior Cl CW7 . . . . 189 F1
Priory Ave CW9 . . . . 103 F4
Priory Cl
Chester CH1 . . . . 118 C4
Congleton CW12 . . . . . . 179 B7
Crewe CW1 . . . . 190 A8
Runcorn WA7 . . . . 24 A1
Winsford CW7 . . . . 126 C3
Priory Ct SK10 . . . . 86 F1
Priory Dr SK10 . . . . 86 E2
Priory Hospl Altrincham The
WA15 . . . . 32 A2
Priory La SK10 . . . . 86 E2
Priory Pl
Chester CH1 . . . . 237 B2
Kidsgrove ST7 . . . . 195 B3
Priory Rd
Altrincham WA14 . . . . 31 B8
Runcorn WA7 . . . . 24 C2
Wilmslow SK9 . . . . 59 E8
Priory St
Northwich CW9 . . . . 104 A8
Warrington WA4 . . . . 16 B3
Priory The
Neston CH64 . . . . 41 E1
Winwick WA2 . . . . 8 A7
Priory Way WA8 . . . . 103 B4
Pritchard Dr CW9 . . . . . . 103 E2
Private WIk CH3 . . . . 142 A8
Probert Cl CW2 . . . . 190 A4
Proctors Cl WA11 . . . . 13 D2
Proctors La CW11 . . . . . . 174 E5
Proffits La WA6 . . . . 73 E4
Promised Land La CH2 . . 142 E5
Prospect Ave M44 . . . . . . 11 E6
Prospect Dr
Altrincham WA15 . . . . 32 D8
Davenham CW9 . . . . 103 E2
Prospect La WA3 . . . . 10 D3
Prospect Rd M44 . . . . 11 E6
Prospect Row WA7 . . . . . . 48 F7
Prospect St CW12 . . . . . . 156 C2
Prosperity Ct CW10 . . . . . 128 D1
Prosperity Way CW10 . . . 128 D1
Prosser Rd CH2 . . . . 95 C1
Protector Way M44 . . . . . . 11 F8
Provan Way CH1 . . . . 117 D5
Provident St WA9 . . . . 1 A3
Prunus Rd CW1 . . . . 190 E6
Pryors The CH3 . . . . 121 C3
Ptarmigan Pl CW7 . . . . . 149 D5
Public Hall St **1** WA7 . . . 23 A3
Pudding La CW6 . . . . 168 A7
PUDDINGLAKE 129 A8
PUDDINGTON 92 F8
Puddington La WA7 . . . . . 74 B8
Puddle Bank La CW12 . . . 178 F5
Puffin Ave SK12 . . . . 36 B4
Puffin Cl CH65 . . . . 95 C8
PULFORD 162 D3
Pulford App
Aldford CH3 . . . . 163 D3
Pulford CH4 . . . . 162 E2
Pulford Cl
Northwich CW9 . . . . 103 E4
Runcorn WA7 . . . . 49 E6
Pulford Ct CH4 . . . . 162 D2
Pulford La CH4 . . . . 162 A6
Pulford Rd
Blacon CH1 . . . . 117 C5
Ellesmere Port CH65 . . . . 69 F4
Winsford CW7 . . . . 126 C1
Pullman Cl CH60 . . . . 40 C8
Pullman Dr CW9 . . . . 104 C8
Pump Ct ST7 . . . . 209 E2
Pumping Station Hos
CW6 . . . . 184 E3
Pump La
Churton CH3 . . . . 181 A1
Runcorn WA7 . . . . 49 F8
Tattenhall CH3 . . . . 182 C6
Pumptree Mews SK11 . . . 111 E7
Purdy Cl WA5 . . . . 7 D1
Puritan Bldgs WA7 . . . . . . 23 C2
Purley Dr M44 . . . . 11 C5
Purser La SY14 . . . . 211 E4
Puss Bank Sch SK10 . . . . 112 F8
Putney Ct WA7 . . . . 49 F7
Pye Cl WA11 . . . . 2 B8
Pyecroft Cl WA5 . . . . 14 D6
Pyecroft Rd WA5 . . . . 14 D6

Pyecroft St CH4 . . . . 141 D7
Pye Rd CH60 . . . . 41 A8
Pym's La CW1 . . . . 189 E6
Pyramid Theatre * WA1 . . 16 A4
Pyrus Ave CW1 . . . . 190 E6
Pyrus Gr WA6 . . . . 73 C4
Pytcheley Hollow WA6 . . 100 F6

Q

Quadrant Cl WA7 . . . . 50 D6
Quadrant The CH1 . . . . . 117 E2
Quadrant The WA3 . . . . . . 9 F5
Quad The CH1 . . . . 117 E2
Quail Cl WA2 . . . . 8 D3
Quaintways CW8 . . . . 103 C4
Quakers Coppice CW1 . . 191 A2
Quakers Way LL13 . . . . . 180 E1
Quantock Cl
Ellesmere Port CH66 . . . . 69 A6
Winsford CW7 . . . . 149 A7
Quarry Ave CH3 . . . . 180 F1
QUARRYBANK 146 C8
Quarrybank CW6 . . . . . . 184 F6
Quarry Bank CW6 . . . . . . 146 C8
Quarry Bank Cotts CW6 . 184 F6
Quarry Bank Mill * SK9 . . 34 B3
Quarry Bank Rd SK9 . . . . . 34 C3
Quarry Bank Rise CW7 . . 149 B8
Quarry Cl
Chester CH4 . . . . 141 C7
Runcorn WA7 . . . . 23 D1
Quarry Ct
Farndon CH3 . . . . 180 F1
Widnes WA8 . . . . 12 C1
Quarry Hill CH3 . . . . 180 F1
Quarry La
Christleton CH3 . . . . 142 E7
Kelsall CW6 . . . . 122 D5
Warrington WA4 . . . . 26 C6
Quarry Rd
Neston CH64 . . . . 42 C7
New Mills SK22 . . . . 39 D7
Quarry Terr ST7 . . . . 195 A1
Quarter The CH1 . . . . . . 237 B3
Quay Fold WA5 . . . . 15 F4
Quayle Cl WA11 . . . . 1 C6
Quay Pl WA7 . . . . 50 E7
Quayside
Congleton CW12 . . . . . . 156 E1
Neston CH64 . . . . 66 E5
Quay Side WA6 . . . . 49 D1
Quayside Mews WA13 . . . 18 E3
Quayside Way SK11 . . . . . 112 E7
Quay The WA6 . . . . 49 D2
Queastybirch La
Hatton WA4 . . . . 25 F1
Hatton WA4 . . . . 26 A1
Quebec Rd WA2 . . . . 16 D7
Queen Anne Ct SK9 . . . . . 60 C6
Queen Annes Ct **5** SK8 . . 34 E1
Queen Elizabeth Ho CW9 . 79 A1
Queens Ave
Ellesmere Port CH65 . . . . 70 A3
Warrington WA1 . . . . 16 E7
Queen's Ave
Chester CH1 . . . . 237 C3
Connah's Quay CH5 . . . . . 91 D1
Glazebury WA3 . . . . 5 C7
Macclesfield SK10 . . . . . . 87 E2
Sandycroft CH5 . . . . 116 A3
Widnes WA8 . . . . 22 B8
Queensbury Cl
3 Handforth SK9 . . . . . . 34 D1
1 Wilmslow SK9 . . . . . . 60 D8
Queensbury Way WA8 . . . 12 E3
Queens Cl SK10 . . . . 87 E6
Queen's Cl
Macclesfield SK10 . . . . . . 87 E6
Runcorn WA7 . . . . 22 F1
Queens Cres
Chester CH2 . . . . 118 E7
Warrington WA1 . . . . 17 A8
Queen's Cres CW1 . . . . . 172 E2
Queens Ct
Chester CH2 . . . . 237 C1
Winsford CW7 . . . . 126 D1
Queen's Ct CW10 . . . . . . 128 D1
Queens Dr
Golborne WA3 . . . . 3 C8
Helsby WA6 . . . . 73 B3
Heswall CH60 . . . . 40 E8
Newton-le-Willows WA12 . . 2 C5
Warrington WA4 . . . . 17 A2
Queen's Dr
Chester CH4 . . . . 237 C1
Middlewich CW10 . . . . . . 151 D7
Nantwich CW5 . . . . 204 D4
Sandbach CW11 . . . . 175 A8
Queensford LL13 . . . . . . 222 A8
Queensgate
Bramhall SK7 . . . . 35 E5
Chester CH1 . . . . 118 C4
Northwich CW8 . . . . 103 E8
Queensgate Prim Sch
SK7 . . . . 35 E4
Queens Gdns
Ellesmere Port CH65 . . . . 70 B5
Talke ST7 . . . . 210 D6
Queen's Par **1** CW7 . . . 126 D1
QUEEN'S PARK 141 F8
Queen's Park Dr CH4 . . . 189 F3
Queen's Park Gdns CW2 . 189 F4
Queen's Park High Sch
CH4 . . . . 237 B1
Queen's Park Ho CH4 . . . 237 B1

Queen's Park Rd CH4 . . . 237 B1
Queen's Park View CH4 . 237 B1
Queens Pk CH6 . . . . 40 D8
Queens Pl CH1 . . . . 237 B3
Queens Rd
Chester CH3 . . . . 119 B3
Ellesmere Port CH66 . . . . 69 C7
Haydock WA11 . . . . 2 A7
Queen's Rd
Chester CH1 . . . . 237 C3
Runcorn WA7 . . . . 22 F1
Wilmslow SK9 . . . . 60 A6
Queen's Sch (Lower) The
CH2 . . . . 118 C7
Queen's Sch The CH1 . . . 237 A2
Queen St
Audley ST7 . . . . 209 C1
Bollington SK10 . . . . 88 B8
Bunbury CW6 . . . . 185 E8
Chester CH1 . . . . 237 B2
Congleton, Buglawton
CW12 . . . . 156 F4
Congleton CW12 . . . . . . 156 C2
Crewe CW1 . . . . 190 E5
Ellesmere Port CH65 . . . . 70 C7
Golborne WA3 . . . . 3 B8
Kidsgrove ST7 . . . . 195 A2
Knutsford WA16 . . . . 56 F2
Macclesfield SK10 . . . . . 112 D8
Middlewich CW10 . . . . . . 128 C1
Nantwich CW5 . . . . 204 E5
Newton-le-Willows WA12 . . 2 B3
Northwich CW9 . . . . 103 F7
8 Runcorn WA7 . . . . 23 A3
Shavington CW2 . . . . 206 C4
Widnes WA8 . . . . 22 F6
Queens Terr SK9 . . . . 34 D3
Queensway
Alsager ST7 . . . . 193 B5
Chester CH2 . . . . 118 F5
Crewe CW1 . . . . 190 C4
Frodsham WA6 . . . . 74 B8
Gatley SK8 . . . . 34 C8
Heswall CH60 . . . . 41 A8
Knutsford WA16 . . . . 56 E3
Partington M31 . . . . 11 F4
Poynton SK12 . . . . 36 D3
Runcorn WA7 . . . . 22 F3
Widnes WA8 . . . . 22 F6
Winsford CW7 . . . . 149 D8
Queen's Way CH4 . . . . . . 139 B4
Queensway Trad Est WA8 . 23 A5
Queen Victoria St **14**
SK11 . . . . 112 D8
Quill Ct M44 . . . . 11 E6
Quillet The CH64 . . . . 66 F7
Quinn St **19** WA8 . . . . . . 23 B8
Quinta Prim Sch The
CW12 . . . . 156 A2
Quinta Rd CW12 . . . . 156 A3
QUOISLEY 226 B8

R

RABY 42 C4
Raby Ave CH63 . . . . 43 B6
Raby Cl
Bebington CH63 . . . . 43 A7
Heswall CH60 . . . . 40 F7
Widnes WA8 . . . . 13 E2
Raby Ct CH65 . . . . 70 D3
Raby Dr CH63 . . . . 43 A6
RABY MERE. 43 B7
Raby Mere Rd CH63 . . . . . 43 B6
Raby Park Cl CH64 . . . . . 66 E8
Raby Park Rd CH64 . . . . . 41 F1
Raby Rd
Neston CH64 . . . . 66 E8
Thornton Hough CH63 . . . 42 B5
Racecourse La CW6 . . . . 124 A1
Racecourse Pk SK9 . . . . . 59 F6
Racecourse Rd SK9 . . . . . 59 E6
Racefield Cl WA13 . . . . . . 18 F3
Racefield Rd WA16 . . . . . . 56 F2
Race The SK9 . . . . 34 D2
Radbroke Cl CW11 . . . . . 175 D8
Radcliffe Ave WA3 . . . . 4 E3
Radcliffe Cl SK12 . . . . 36 F4
Radcliffe Rd
Sandbach CW11 . . . . 174 F3
Sutton Lane Ends SK11 . . 135 D7
Winsford CW7 . . . . 149 B6
Raddel La WA4 . . . . 52 C5
Raddle Wharf CH65 . . . . . 70 C7
Raddon Pl WA4 . . . . 16 E3
Radford Cl WA8 . . . . 22 C7
Radley Cl CH43 . . . . 14 E3
Radley Dr CH63 . . . . 41 F6
Radley La WA2 . . . . 8 E4
RADMORE GREEN 186 E3
RADNOR 155 E6
Radnor Cl
Congleton CW12 . . . . . . 156 B3
Sandbach CW11 . . . . 174 E7
Radnor Dr
Chester CH4 . . . . 141 A4
Widnes WA8 . . . . 12 D2
Radnor Park Ind Ctr
CW12 . . . . 156 A4
Radnor Park Trad Est
CW12 . . . . 156 B4
Radnor St WA5 . . . . 15 E6
Radway Gn CH66 . . . . 69 E1
RADWAY GREEN 192 F1
Radway Green Bsns & Tech
Ctr CW2 . . . . 192 F1

Radway Green Rd
Alsager CW2 . . . . 208 E8
Barthomley CW2 . . . . . . 208 D6
Raeburn Ave
Bebington CH62 . . . . 43 E6
Neston CH64 . . . . 66 F7
Raeburn Prim Sch CH62 . 43 D6
Raglan Cl WA3 . . . . 9 F6
Raglan Rd SK10 . . . . 87 F2
Ragley Cl SK12 . . . . 36 F4
Railbrook Ct CW2 . . . . . . 190 D2
Railton Ave CW1 . . . . 190 A7
Railway Cotts
Congleton CW12 . . . . . . 157 A1
Hollinfare WA3 . . . . 11 B5
Hooton CH66 . . . . 43 E1
Wimboldsley CW10 . . . . . 150 F1
Railway St
Crewe CW1 . . . . 190 D2
Newton-le-Willows WA12 . . 2 B3
Railway Terr
Disley SK12 . . . . 38 D6
Sandycroft CH5 . . . . 116 B3
Railway View WA5 . . . . 1 D1
Rainbow Cl WA8 . . . . 12 C3
Rainbow St CW1 . . . . 190 D4
Rainford Cl ST7 . . . . 195 F1
RAINOW. 88 D5
Rainow Cl CW10 . . . . 151 B7
Rainow Dr SK10 . . . . 37 A2
Rainow Prim Sch SK10 . . 88 D4
Rainow Rd SK10 . . . . 88 B8
Rainow View SK10 . . . . . . 63 C1
Rainow Way **1** SK9 . . . . . 34 E1
Rajar Cotts WA16 . . . . 57 F4
Rajar WIk WA16 . . . . 58 A4
Rake House Mews WA6 . . 73 B4
Rake La
Backford CH2 . . . . 95 D6
Broughton CH5 . . . . 139 A8
Christleton CH3 . . . . 143 A7
Dunham-on-the-Hill WA6 . . 97 B7
Dunham-on-the-Hill WA6 . . 97 E7
Eccleston CH4 . . . . 141 C1
Helsby, Helsby Marsh WA6 . 73 A5
Helsby WA6 . . . . 73 C4
Rake The
Bebington CH62. . . . . 43 C8
Burton CH64 . . . . 67 D1
Rake Way CH1 . . . . 94 A1
Raleigh Cl WA5 . . . . 7 D1
Raleigh Rd WA5 . . . . 6 F6
Ramany's Caravan * SK9 . 60 B6
Rampit Cl WA11 . . . . 1 F7
Ramp Road E M90 . . . . . . 33 C7
Ramp Road S M90 . . . . . . 33 C7
Ramp Road W M90. . . . . . 33 B7
Ramsay Cl WA3 . . . . 9 E3
Ramsbottom St **2** CW1 . 190 B5
Ramsbrook La L24, WA8 . 21 C3
Ramsdale Rd SK7 . . . . 35 E8
Ramsden Ct CH4 . . . . 140 F4
Ramsey Cl
Warrington WA5 . . . . 14 F3
Ramsey Rd CH65 . . . . 70 C1
Ramsfield Rd L24 . . . . 21 A4
Randal Cres SK23 . . . . . . 65 E5
Randall Cl WA12 . . . . 2 B4
Randle Bennett Cl CW11 . 174 E7
Randle Mdw CH66 . . . . . . 69 F1
Randle Meadow Ct CH66 . 69 F2
Randle's View CW12 . . . . 179 C8
Range Ct SK10 . . . . 87 E1
Rangemoor Cl WA3 . . . . . 10 A6
Rannoch Cl CH66 . . . . 69 F3
Ranulph Cl WA6 . . . . 74 C7
Ranworth Ct CW2 . . . . . . 237 B4
Ranworth Dr WA3 . . . . 3 E8
Ranworth Rd WA5 . . . . . . 14 E6
Rappax Rd WA15. . . . . 32 A8
Raquets Ct The CW10 . . . 127 D5
Rathbone Pk CW6. . . . . . 146 D2
Rathlin Cl WA8 . . . . 13 E3
Rathmell Cl WA3 . . . . 4 E3
Rathvale Dr M22 . . . . 33 C8
Ravenbank Com Prim Sch
WA13 . . . . 18 F3
Raven Cl CW11 . . . . 175 A8
Raven Cotts TF9 . . . . 235 A5
Ravendale Cl CW7 . . . . . . 149 E8
Ravenfield Dr WA8 . . . . . . 12 C3
Ravenho La SK10 . . . . 88 B2
Ravenhurst Ct WA3 . . . . . . 9 F5
Ravenoak Park Rd SK8 . . . 35 B8
Ravenoak Rd SK8 . . . . 35 B8
Ravenscar Cres M22 . . . . 33 D8
Ravens Cl ST7 . . . . 209 E3
Ravenscliffe Rd ST7 . . . . 195 A1
RAVENSCLOUGH 101 E3
Ravens Cnr CW5 . . . . 203 E2
Ravenscroft CW4 . . . . . . 130 A3
Ravenscroft Cl
Middlewich CW10 . . . . . . 128 C2
Sandbach CW11 . . . . 175 C7
Ravenscroft Rd CW2 . . . . 189 E3
Ravensdale WA2 . . . . 8 D3
Ravenscroft CW8 . . . . . . 101 D4
Ravensholme La CH3 . . . 166 A2
Ravens La CW5 . . . . 203 E5
Raven's La ST7 . . . . 209 E3
Ravensmead Prim Sch
ST7 . . . . 209 E3
RAVENSMOOR 203 E2
Ravenswood CW8 . . . . . . 103 B4
Ravenswood Dr SK8 . . . . . 35 B8
Ravenswood Rd SK9 . . . . . 59 E4
Ravenswood Dr WA15. . . . 32 D7
Rawcliffe Cl WA8 . . . . 12 F4

Pri–Red **273**

Rawdon Cl WA7 . . . . 50 A7
Rawlings Cl WA3 . . . . 9 F3
Rawlinson Cres L26 . . . . . 21 B8
Rawson Rd CH1 . . . . 117 E3
Ray Ave CW5 . . . . 204 F7
Raycliffe Cl WA7 . . . . 49 D5
Rayleigh Ave CW9 . . . . . 127 A8
Rayleigh Way SK10 . . . . . 86 E1
Raymond Ave WA4 . . . . . . 16 D2
Raymond St CH1 . . . . . . 237 A3
Rays Brow CW8 . . . . 78 B2
Readesdale Ave CW2 . . . 189 F2
Reade's La CW12 . . . . . . 156 F5
Reading Room La SY14,
CH3 . . . . 199 D8
Rean Mdw CH3 . . . . 166 B2
Reaper Cl WA5 . . . . 15 D6
REASE HEATH. 188 C1
Reaseheath Coll CW5 . . . 188 C1
Reay St WA8 . . . . 13 C2
Rectory Ave WA3 . . . . 3 C8
Rectory Cl
Farndon CH3 . . . . 180 E1
Heswall CH60 . . . . 40 F7
8 Nantwich CW5 . . . . . . 204 E5
Winwick WA2 . . . . 8 A6
Wistaston CW2 . . . . 205 E8
Rectory Gdns
Lymm WA13 . . . . 18 E3
Talke ST7 . . . . 210 D6
Rectory La
Adderley TF9 . . . . 235 B5
Capenhurst CH1 . . . . 94 A8
Heswall CH60 . . . . 40 E7
Lymm WA13 . . . . 18 E3
Winwick WA2 . . . . 8 A6
Rectory View ST7 . . . . . . 210 D6
Redacre SK12 . . . . 36 F6
Redacre Cl WA4 . . . . 51 A3
Red Bank Ave WA12 . . . . . 2 F1
Redbourne Dr
Chorlton CW2 . . . . 207 D1
Widnes WA8 . . . . 12 B4
Redbrook Cl CH62 . . . . . . 43 D6
Redbrook Gr **2** SK9 . . . . . 34 D1
Redbrook Rd M31 . . . . . . 11 E2
Redbrook Way SK10 . . . . . 62 C5
Red Brow La WA7, WA4 . . 50 F8
RED BULL. 194 E3
Redcar Dr CH62 . . . . 43 D5
Red Cow Yd **11** WA16 . . . 57 A2
Reddish Ave SK23 . . . . . . 65 D6
Reddish Cres WA13 . . . . . 18 F4
Reddish La
Horwich End SK23 . . . . . . 65 D6
Lymm WA13 . . . . 19 A5
Reddish Rd SK23 . . . . 65 D6
Reddy La WA14 . . . . 30 B8
Redesdale Cl WA7 . . . . 8 E2
Redesmere Cl
Macclesfield SK10 . . . . . . 87 A1
Northwich CW9 . . . . 104 A5
Sandbach CW11 . . . . 174 F7
Redesmere Dr SK9 . . . . . . 60 A1
Redesmere La SK11 . . . . . 110 B3
Redesmere Rd SK9 . . . . . . 34 D5
Redfern Ave CW12 . . . . . 156 F4
Red Gables WA4 . . . . 27 B3
Redgate SK9 . . . . 103 D7
Redhill Cl WA5 . . . . 15 B6
Redhill Mews CH65 . . . . . 70 B6
Redhill Rd
Chester CH4 . . . . 140 F6
Kelsall CW6 . . . . 122 C5
Red Ho SK10 . . . . 87 E1
Redhouse La SK12 . . . . . . 38 E7
Red House La WA14 . . . . . 20 C8
Redhouses SK11 . . . . 113 D3
Red La
Disley SK12 . . . . 38 C5
Frodsham WA6 . . . . 74 C7
Huxley CH3 . . . . 166 D6
Lower Whitley WA4 . . . . . . 52 C1
Sandbach CW11 . . . . 174 C6
Warrington WA4 . . . . 26 C7
Redland Cl CH4 . . . . 141 A7
Redland Ho CH4 . . . . 141 B7
Red Lion Cl ST7 . . . . 210 D7
Red Lion La
Ellesmere Port CH66. . . . . 69 C7
Nantwich CW5 . . . . 204 D5
Red Lodge SK12 . . . . 38 A6
Redmain Gr WA3 . . . . 3 E8
Redmayne Cl WA12 . . . . . . 2 B4
Redmere Dr CH60 . . . . . . 41 D8
Redmoor La
Disley SK12 . . . . 39 A4
New Mills SK22 . . . . 39 B6
Red Pike CH66 . . . . 69 D8
Redpoll La WA3 . . . . 9 E1
Redrock Cres ST7 . . . . . . 195 C1
Red Row SK7 . . . . 37 B8
Redruth Ave SK10 . . . . . . 86 E1
Redruth Cl WA7 . . . . 50 C6
Redshank Ave CW7 . . . . . 149 C5
Redshank Cl WA12 . . . . . . 2 C4
Redshank Dr SK10 . . . . . . 87 C5
Redshank La WA3 . . . . 9 F3
Redshaw Cl CW10 . . . . . . 151 C6
Redstart Cl **7** WA3 . . . . . . 3 E8
Redstone Dr **8** SK9. . . . . . 34 D1
Red Stone Hill WA6 . . . . . 73 C4
RED STREET. 210 E3
Redtail Cl WA7 . . . . 22 F3

Redvales Ct WA3.......... 9 C4
Redvers Ave CH66........ 44 A2
Redway La SK10 .... 88 B7
Redwing Cl ST7........... 195 F1
Redwood Cl
  Barnton CW8............ 78 B4
  Holt LL13.............. 196 D8
  Saltney CH4............ 140 E6
  Warrington WA1........ 17 E7
Redwood Ct SK10.......... 87 E5
Redwood Dr
  Crewe CW1............. 189 F7
  Ellesmere Port CH66.... 69 F1
  Elton CH2.............. 72 C4
Reece Cl CH2............. 119 E8
Reedgate La CW7......... 27 F1
Reed La CW9............. 53 C6
Reedsmere Cl WA4....... 16 E2
Reedsmere Wlk CW9...... 78 D8
Reeman St WA4.......... 34 B2
Rees Cres CW4.......... 130 C3
Reeves Rd CH3........... 142 B8
Reeve St WA3............ 4 B8
Regal Cl
  Ellesmere Port CH66.... 69 E3
  Northwich CW9......... 103 E4
Regal Cres WA8........... 22 B8
Regency Cl ST7........... 210 D5
Regency Ct
  Chester CH2............ 119 E8
  Winsford CW7........... 149 C7
Regency Gdns SK8........ 34 E8
Regency Hospl (Private)
  SK11.................. 112 B8
Regency Pk
  Wilmslow SK9.......... 59 F5
  Widnes WA8............ 12 E3
Regency Sq WA5......... 15 F6
Regency Way CW9........ 103 E4
Regency Wlk CW10....... 128 D1
Regent Ave
  Haydock WA11.......... 1 B7
  Macclesfield SK11...... 112 B6
  Warrington WA1........ 17 A8
Regent Bank SK9......... 59 F5
Regent Cl
  Bramhall SK7........... 35 D4
  Shavington CW2........ 206 B3
  Wilmslow SK9.......... 59 F5
Regent Ct WA15.......... 32 C8
Regent & Foundry Ct **19**
  SK11.................. 112 C8
Regent Rd WA8........... 13 B1
Regents Cl CH3.......... 119 B2
Regents Gate CW5....... 205 A5
Regent St
  Ellesmere Port CH65.... 70 A5
  Moulton CW9........... 126 F8
  Newton-le-Willows WA12. 2 A3
  12 Runcorn WA7...... 23 A3
  Warrington WA1........ 16 A5
Regents The SK9......... 60 C8
Regents Way **4** CW7... 149 A8
Reginald Mitchell Prim Sch
  The ST7............... 194 D1
Registry Cl CW9......... 103 E4
Reid Ave WA5............ 15 F8
Reid Ct CH66............ 69 C7
Reid St CW1............. 190 C6
Reins Croft CH64........ 41 E1
Rembury Pl WA4.......... 51 A3
Remer St CW1............ 190 B3
Renaissance Way CW1.... 191 A3
Rendel Cl WA12.......... 2 D2
Rendlesham Cl WA3...... 10 B6
Renfrew Ave CH62........ 43 E5
Renfrew Cl SK10......... 86 F7
Renown Cl WA3........... 9 D4
Renshaw St CW9......... 79 D2
Rensherds Pl WA16...... 29 C5
Renton Ave WA7......... 23 D2
Repton Cl WA16......... 29 C4
Repton Dr CW9.......... 191 D5
Repton Rd CH65......... 70 D4
Reservoir Rd SK23...... 65 D7
Reservoir Terr CH2..... 118 F2
Retreat The CW1......... 190 C6
Revesby Cl WA8......... 12 D2
Rex Bldgs SK9........... 60 B6
Reynolds Ave
  St Helens WA9......... 1 B2
  Warrington WA3........ 9 E5
Reynold's La CW11...... 175 F6
Reynolds Mews SK9...... 60 E8
Reynolds St WA4........ 16 F3
Rhoden St CW1.......... 191 A6
Rhodes Cl CW1.......... 191 D4
Rhodes St WA2.......... 16 C7
Rhodesway CH60......... 41 B7
Rhodfa Llyn **2** CH4... 140 E6
Rhodfar Bont **6** CH4.. 140 F6
Rhona Cl CH63.......... 43 C4
Rhona Dr WA5........... 14 E6
Rhone Ct CH53.......... 187 F4
RHUDDALL HEATH........ 146 E1
Rhuddlan Cl CH65....... 70 D2
Rhuddlan Ct/Llys Rhuddlan
  5 CH4............. 140 F6
Rhuddlan Rd CH1........ 117 D3
Rhum Cl CH65........... 70 C1
Rhyl St WA8............ 22 F7
Ribble Ave CW7......... 127 B1
Ribble Cl
  Culcheth WA3.......... 4 F2
  Widnes WA8............ 13 F3

Ribble Dr ST8........... 179 E1
Ribble Pl CW7.......... 127 B1
Ribblesdale CH65........ 70 B3
Ribblesdale Ave CW12... 157 A5
Ribblesdale Cl CH62..... 43 F5
Ribchester Gdns WA3.... 5 A3
Richard Cl WA7......... 24 A2
Richard Moon St CW1.... 190 B4
Richard Reynolds St M44. 11 E6
Richards Croft CH3...... 142 A7
Richards Gr CW12....... 156 A3
Richardson Cl
  4 Sandbach CW11... 174 D6
  Shavington CW2........ 206 D3
Richardson St WA2...... 16 C8
Richard St
  Crewe CW1............. 190 B5
  Northwich CW9......... 104 C7
Richbell Cl M44......... 11 F7
Richmond Ave
  Grappenhall WA4....... 17 C3
  Handforth SK9......... 34 D4
  Haydock WA11.......... 1 B7
  Runcorn WA7........... 23 E2
  Warrington WA4....... 17 A4
Richmond Cl
  Chorlton CW2.......... 207 D1
  Culcheth WA3.......... 4 D4
  Lymm WA13............ 19 B4
  Sandbach CW11........ 174 E7
Richmond Cres CH3...... 119 C2
Richmond Ct
  Chester CH3........... 118 F2
  Ellesmere Port CH65... 70 D3
  Warrington WA4....... 17 A3
  Widnes WA8............ 13 D4
Richmond Dr
  Lymm WA13............ 19 B4
  Northwich CW9......... 104 A4
Richmond Gdns WA12.... 2 C2
Richmond Gr SK7........ 35 F6
Richmond Hill
  11 Knutsford WA16. 57 B1
  Macclesfield SK11..... 112 E6
Richmond Mews CH2..... 118 F2
Richmond Pl CW1....... 112 E6
Richmond Rd CW1...... 190 E5
Richmond St
  Warrington WA4....... 17 A3
  Widnes WA8............ 13 C1
Richmond Village CW5... 205 A5
Rickaby Cl CH63........ 43 C8
Ridding La WA7......... 50 B5
Riddings Ct CW8........ 103 B4
Riddings La
  Hartford CW8.......... 103 B4
  Wybunbury CW5........ 220 A8
Ridge Ave WA16........ 57 A1
Ridgeborne Cl WA5...... 7 D2
Ridge Hill
  Langley SK11.......... 113 B2
  Utkinton SK11......... 146 B5
Ridge Pk SK7........... 35 D6
Ridge The CW8......... 123 D7
Ridge View SK11....... 112 C5
Ridgeway
  Golborne WA3.......... 3 E7
  Wilmslow SK9.......... 60 F7
Ridgeway Cl CH66...... 69 C2
Ridgeway Ho CH3....... 121 C7
Ridgeway The
  Alvanley WA6......... 74 A1
  Cronton WA8.......... 12 C6
  Disley SK12.......... 38 C6
  Heswall CH60........ 41 B7
  Runcorn WA7........ 50 D6
  Tarvin CH3........... 121 C3
Ridgewell Ave **4** WA3. 3 D8
Ridgmont Rd SK7...... 35 E5
RIDGWARDINE.......... 235 E1
Ridgway Gdns WA13... 18 D3
Ridgway St
  Crewe CW1............. 190 D5
  Warrington WA2...... 16 B6
Ridings Inf Sch The CH1. 94 A1
Ridings The
  Haydock WA11......... 1 D6
  Saughall CH1......... 117 B8
  Wilmslow SK9......... 59 D4
Ridley Cl CW2......... 206 E2
Ridley Dr WA5........ 15 C4
Ridley Gn CW5........ 185 D1
Ridley Hill Farm CW6... 185 D3
Ridley Rd SK10....... 87 E8
RIDLEYWOOD........... 196 C3
Ridley Wood Rd LL13... 196 A3
Ridsdale **2** WA8.... 22 C8
Rigby Ave CW1......... 190 A7
Rigby Rd ST7.......... 195 B3
Rigby's Row CW5...... 204 E5
Rigby St WA3.......... 3 A8
Rigg St **5** CW1..... 190 B5
Riley Bank Mews WA6... 74 B1
Riley Cl CW11......... 174 C5
Riley Dr WA7.......... 49 A9
Riley's Way ST7...... 209 F2
Rilshaw La CW7....... 150 B8
Rixton Ave WA3....... 4 D3
Rimington Cl WA3..... 4 E3
Rimsdale Cl CW2...... 206 A4
Ring-o'Bells La SK12.. 38 D6
Ring Rd
  Chester CH2, CH3..... 119 C3
Ringfield Rd L24..... 21 A2
Ringstead Cl SK9..... 34 D1
Ringstead Dr SK9..... 34 D1

Ringstone Way SK3.... 65 D8
Ringway
  Ellesmere Port CH66... 69 E4
  Neston CH64.......... 41 E1
  Waverton CH3........ 143 B5
Ringway Cl SK10...... 87 B4
Ringway Prim Sch **5**
  M22.................. 33 D8
Ringway Rd
  Runcorn WA7.......... 23 D2
  Wythenshawe M22, M90. 33 D7
Ringway Road W M22,
  M90.................. 33 D8
Ringway Trad Est M22.. 33 E8
Ringwood Cl WA3...... 10 B5
Ripley Ave SK8....... 35 B5
Ripley Cl SK7........ 36 E8
Ripley St WA5........ 15 E6
Ripon Ave
  Ellesmere Port CH66... 69 C5
  Golborne WA3......... 3 D8
Ripon Cl
  Macclesfield SK10.... 87 C3
  Newton-le-Willows WA12. 2 C5
Ripon Dr CW2......... 206 A7
Ripon Row CW7....... 49 D6
Riseley St SK10...... 112 C8
Rise The SK23........ 65 C6
Rising Sun Cl SK11... 112 A5
Rising Sun Rd SK11... 112 A4
RISLEY............... 9 E6
Risley Moss Nature
  Reserve * WA3...... 10 B5
Risley Rd WA3........ 9 F6
Rivacre Brow CH66... 69 E8
Rivacre Bsns Ctr CH66. 69 E5
Rivacre Rd CH62, CH65,
  CH66................ 69 E8
Rivacre Valley CP Sch
  CH66................ 69 E7
Rivacre Valley Ctry Pk *
  CH66................ 69 D8
Rivacre Valley Nature
  Reserve * CH66..... 69 C8
Rivenmill Cl WA8..... 13 C5
Riverbank Cl
  Bollington SK10..... 87 F8
  Heswall CH60........ 40 F6
  Nantwich CW5....... 204 E8
Riverbank Rd CH60... 40 E6
Riverbank Rd CW12... 156 F4
River La
  Chester CH4......... 141 C7
  Farndon CH3........ 180 E2
  Partington M31...... 11 F4
  Saltney CH4......... 140 E7
Rivermead Ave WA15.. 32 C7
River Rd
  Connah's Quay CH5... 91 F1
  Warrington, Latchford WA4. 16 B3
  Warrington, Wilderspool
  WA4................ 16 C2
Riversdale
  Frodsham WA6....... 49 C1
  Warrington WA1...... 17 F7
Riversdale Rd WA7.... 49 E8
Rivershill Gdns WA15.. 32 D6
River St
  Congleton CW12..... 156 D3
  Macclesfield SK11... 112 E6
  Wilmslow SK9....... 60 B8
River View CW7...... 126 E1
Riverview Rd CH64.... 66 F5
River Wlk **8** WA7... 49 F7
Rivington Cl WA1..... 17 E8
Rivington Gr M44.... 11 D6
Rivington Rd
  Ellesmere Port CH65.. 70 C5
  Runcorn WA7........ 50 F3
Rixton Ave WA3...... 15 F8
Rixton Clay Pits Nature
  Reserve * WA3..... 10 F2
Rixton Park Homes WA3. 10 F2
Roaches The SK11.... 112 B5
Road Beta CW10...... 151 D8
Road Four CW7....... 127 C2
Road Four CW7....... 127 B2
Road One
  Weston CW1.......... 207 D8

Road One continued
  Winsford CW7......... 127 B3
Roadside Cl WA3...... 3 C8
Road Three CW7...... 127 D1
Road Two
  Anderton CW9........ 78 C3
  Weston CW1.......... 207 C8
  Winsford CW7........ 127 B2
Roan Cl SK11......... 112 F7
Roan House Way SK11.. 112 F7
Roan Mews SK11...... 112 F7
Robert Moffat WA16... 29 C5
Roberts Ave WA3...... 1 A5
Roberts Ct WA7...... 49 F6
Roberts Dr CW9...... 104 D6
Roberts Fold WA3.... 9 D4
Roberts Rd CW9...... 80 A2
Robert St
  Northwich CW9....... 103 A6
  Runcorn WA7......... 23 C2
  Warrington WA5..... 15 F6
  Widnes WA8.......... 13 B1
Robert's Terr CH1.... 118 B1
Robin Cl
  Chelford SK11....... 84 A2
  Rainow SK10........ 88 E5
  Runcorn WA7........ 50 D7
  Sandbach CW11...... 175 A8
Robin Cres SK11..... 112 C6
Robin Hood Ave SK11. 112 D5
Robin Hood La WA6... 73 B2
Robin La
  Chelford SK11....... 84 A3
  Sutton Lane Ends SK11. 112 D2
Robinsbay Rd M22.... 33 E8
Robins Cl SK7....... 35 D7
Robins Croft CH66... 69 F2
Robins La WA3...... 4 D2
Robin's La SK7...... 35 E7
Robinsons Croft CH3.. 142 B7
Robins Way SK10.... 88 A7
Rob La WA12........ 2 E5
Robson St WA1...... 16 D6
Robson Way **3** WA3. 3 A8
Roby Gr WA5....... 15 A8
Roche Gdns SK8.... 35 B6
Rochester Cl
  Golborne WA3...... 3 A8
  Warrington WA5.... 15 C5
Rochester Cres CW1.. 190 F6
Rochester Dr CH65... 70 D3
Rochester Ho SK10... 86 F1
Rock Bank SK23.... 65 G6
Rock Cotts CH5.... 91 D1
Rock Dr WA6....... 49 C1
Rock Farm Cl CH64. 67 A6
Rock Farm Gr CH64. 67 A6
Rockfield Cl WA8... 12 D2
Rockfield Dr WA6... 73 C2
Rockfield Mews WA4. 16 F2
Rockford Gdns WA5.. 15 A8
Rockford Lodge WA16. 57 C1
Rockhouse La ST7... 210 C2
Rockingham Cl WA3.. 10 B6
Rock La
  Burwardsley CH3... 184 C6
  Chester CH2....... 237 A4
  Widnes WA8....... 12 F4
Rocklands La CH63. 42 C8
Rocklee Gdns CH64. 67 A6
Rockliffe La CH6... 91 A3
Rock Mill La SK22.. 39 B7
Rock Rd
  Connah's Quay CH5. 91 F1
  Warrington WA1.... 16 E4
ROCKSAVAGE....... 49 B4
Rock Savage Rdbt WA7. 49 E4
Rockside ST7...... 195 C6
Rock St SK22...... 39 C7
Rock The WA6..... 73 C2
Rock Villas LL13.. 180 E1
Rockwood Ave CW2. 190 A3
Rockwood Cl CW2.. 190 A3
Rocky La
  Heswall CH60.... 40 F8
  Tattenhall CH3... 182 F7
Rock Lane S CH60. 41 A8
Roddy La WA6.... 75 E2
Rode Cl **7** CW12. 156 F3
Rode Hall & Gdns* ST7. 194 B7
RODEHEATH....... 134 B3
RODE HEATH....... 193 E7
Rode Heath Prim Sch
  ST7.............. 193 F7
Rodehouse Cl ST7. 193 F7
Rode Mill Ct ST7. 193 F6
Rodepool Cl WA3.. 34 D2
Rode St CW6...... 146 A3
Rode The ST7..... 193 D4
Rodgers Cl WA3... 4 B8
Rodney St SK11... 112 D7
Roebourne Rise **4** CH1. 117 D4
Roebuck St CW1... 190 C5
Roedean Wlk CW1.. 190 D6
Roehampton Dr WA7. 49 E2
Roehurst La CW7.. 126 D2
Roemarsh Ct WA7. 49 E6
Roe Pk CW12..... 178 E1
Roe St
  Congleton CW12... 156 E2
  Macclesfield SK11.. 112 D7
Roewood La
  Higher Hurdsfield SK10. 88 A1

Roewood La continued
  Macclesfield SK10... 113 A8
Roften Ind Est CH66. 43 D1
Rokeby Ct WA7.... 24 D5
Rokeden WA12..... 2 D4
Roklis Grange **9** CH4. 66 E8
Roland Ave WA7... 22 F1
Rolands Wlk WA7.. 23 F2
Rolleston St WA2.. 16 A6
Rolls Ave CW1.... 190 A6
Rolt Cres CW10... 151 C7
Roman Cl
  Newton-le-Willows WA12. 2 C2
  Runcorn WA7...... 23 E2
Roman Ct CH64.... 66 F7
Roman Dr CH1..... 117 D6
Romanes St CW8... 103 E7
Roman Rd WA4.... 16 C1
Roman Way CW11.. 174 E7
Romiley Rd CH66.. 69 E6
Romney Cl
  Neston CH64..... 66 E7
  Widnes WA8...... 13 E2
Romney Croft CH64. 66 F7
Romney Way CH64. 66 F7
Romsey Dr SK8.... 35 C6
Rona Ave CH65.... 70 C1
Ronald Dr WA2.... 9 B2
Ronaldsway WA8... 13 E2
Ronaldsway
  Halewood L26.... 21 A4
  Heswall CH60.... 40 A6
  Roman Rd WA8... 22 E5
ROODEE........... 237 A1
Rood Hill CW12... 156 D3
Rood La CW12.... 156 E4
Rookery Cl
  1 Nantwich CW5.. 204 F5
  Sandbach CW11.... 174 C5
  Tarporley CW6.... 122 C4
Rookery Ct CW11.. 174 C5
Rookery Dr
  Nantwich CW5.... 204 E4
  Tattenhall CH3... 166 B2
Rookery Farm Rd CW6. 169 A6
Rookery Gdns CW9. 103 E3
Rookery La SY13.. 228 E4
Rookerpool Cl SK9. 34 D2
Rookery Rd
  Kidsgrove ST7.... 195 C3
  Tilston SY14..... 198 B3
Rookery Rise CW7. 150 A8
ROOKERY THE..... 195 C3
Rookery The
  Broughton CH4... 139 B3
  Newton-le-Willows WA12. 2 D4
Rook St CW2..... 190 C2
Rooks Way CH40.. 40 E8
Roome St WA2.... 16 C7
Rope Bank Ave CW2. 206 A7
Rope La
  Shavington CW2... 206 A5
  Wistaston CW2.... 205 F7
Ropewalk The CH64. 66 C8
Rope Wlk CW12... 156 D3
Ropeworks The CH1. 118 B2
Rosam Ct WA7.... 49 E6
Roscoe Ave
  Newton-le-Willows WA12. 3 A4
  Warrington WA3... 16 D8
Roscoe Cres WA7.. 48 E7
Roscoe Rd M44... 11 F8
Roscoes Yd **8** WA16. 57 A2
Roscommon Way WA8. 12 E3
Roscote Cl CH60.. 40 F7
Roscote The CH60. 40 F7
Rose Ave WA11... 1 E6
Rose Bank
  Bollington SK10... 87 F7
  Lymm WA13...... 18 E3
Rosebank Cl CW7. 149 F8
Rosebank Mews CW10. 129 E5
Rosebank Rd M44. 11 C4
Rosebank Sch CW8. 78 A3
Rosebank Wlk CW8. 78 A4
Rosebery Way CW1. 191 C4
Rose Cl
  5 Blacon CH1.. 117 D4
  Halewood L26... 21 A7
  Runcorn WA7.... 50 D5
Rose Cnr CH3.... 166 A1
Rose Cotts CW12. 154 F6
Rose Cres WA8... 22 F7
Rosecroft CH62.. 43 C6
Rosedale Ave
  Golborne WA3.... 3 C7
  Warrington WA1.. 17 C7
Rosedene Cl CH2. 118 E8
Rose Farm Cl CW9. 79 E4
Rose Farm Mews WA6. 73 B4
Rose Gdns CH64.. 66 F6
Roseheath Dr L26. 21 A6
Rosehill Ave WA9. 6 B5
Rosehill Rd CW2. 190 B1
Roselands Ct LL12. 162 C1
Rose Lea Cl WA8. 13 A4
Rosemary Ave
  Runcorn WA7.... 49 F4
  Warrington WA4.. 16 E2
Rosemary Cl
  Broughton CH4... 139 C3
  Warrington WA5.. 15 C6
Rosemary Dr WA2. 9 B2
Rosemary La LL12. 161 D1
Rosemary Row CH3. 166 A1
Rosemary Wlk M31. 11 F2
Rosemere Dr CH1. 94 F7
Rosemoor Gdns WA4. 26 F5

Rosemount CW10 . . . . 128 C1
Rosemount Cotts WA2 . . . . .8 B8
Rose St WA8 . . . . 22 F7
Rose Terr
  6 Blacon CH1 . . . . 117 D4
  Crewe CW1 . . . . 190 C5
Rosetree Mdw CW9 . . . . . 80 A2
Rosevale Rd ST5 . . . . . . 210 F1
Rose View Ave WA8 . . . . . 13 A2
Roseville Dr CW12 . . . . . 179 B8
Roseway SK11 . . . . 112 D5
Rose Wharf WA1 . . . . . . 112 E7
Rose Wlk 3 M31 . . . . . . 11 E3
Rosewood Ave
  Chester CH2 . . . . 118 D5
  Frodsham WA6 . . . . . . 74 D7
  Warrington WA1 . . . . . 16 E7
Rosewood Cl CW1 . . . . . 190 E6
Rosewood Dr CW7 . . . . . 126 A1
Rosewood Farm Ct WA8 . . 12 E4
Rosewood Gr
  Saughall CH1 . . . . . . 117 B8
  Widnes WA8 . . . . 22 B8
Rosewood Ho CW12 . . . . 156 A3
Rossall Cl L24 . . . . 21 E2
Rossall Ct SK7 . . . . 35 E6
Rossall Dr SK7 . . . . 35 E6
Rossall Gr CH66 . . . . . . 69 D6
Rossall Rd
  Warrington WA5 . . . . . 15 B4
  Widnes WA8 . . . . 13 D2
Rossbank Rd CH65 . . . . . 70 A7
Ross Cl WA5 . . . . 15 D7
Rosscliffe Rd CH65 . . . . . 70 A6
Ross Dr CH66 . . . . 69 C5
Rossenclough Rd SK9 . . . 34 D1
Rossendale Dr WA3 . . . . . 10 A6
Rossendale Rd SK8 . . . . . 34 C8
Rossett Ave 1 M22 . . . . . 33 D8
Rossett Bsns Village
  LL12 . . . . 162 B1
Rossett Cl
  Northwich CW9 . . . . . 103 E4
  Warrington WA5 . . . . . 7 E2
Rossett Pk LL12 . . . . . . 162 C1
Rossett Rd LL13 . . . . . . 180 A1
Rossfield Rd CH65 . . . . . 70 A7
Rossfield Road N CH65 . . 70 B7
Rosslyn Cl CH5 . . . . . . 116 A2
Rosslyn La CW8 . . . . . . 102 A3
Rosslyn Rd CH3 . . . . . . 119 B3
Rossmill La WA15 . . . . . 32 B7
Rossmore Bsns Pk CH65 . . 70 B7
Rossmore Ct CH66 . . . . . 69 E6
Rossmore Gdns CH66 . . . . 69 D6
Rossmore Ind Est CH65 . . 70 A7
Rossmore Prim Sch CH66 . 69 C7
Rossmore Road E CH65 . . 69 F7
Rossmore Road W CH66 . . 69 D7
Rossmore Terraced
  Factories CH65 . . . . . 70 A4
Rossmount Rd CH65 . . . . 70 A6
Ross Rd CH65 . . . . 70 A6
Ross St WA8 . . . . 13 B1
Rosswood Rd CH65 . . . . . 70 A6
ROSTHERNE 30 E4
Rostherne Ave
  Ellesmere Port CH66 . . . 69 E4
  Golborne WA3 . . . . . . 3 D8
  High Lane SK6 . . . . . . 37 E8
Rostherne Cl 1 WA5 . . . . 15 D4
Rostherne Cres WA8 . . . . 12 D2
Rostherne Dr WA16 . . . . 30 F1
Rostherne La WA16 . . . . 30 E4
Rostherne Mere National
  Nature Reserve* WA14 . 30 E5
Rostherne Rd SK9 . . . . . 59 F6
Rostherne Way CW7 . . . . 174 F7
Rosyth Cl WA2 . . . . 8 F3
Rothay Dr WA5 . . . . 14 D3
Rothbury Cl WA7 . . . . . . 49 D6
Rother Dr CH65 . . . . . . 70 A7
Rother Dr Bsns Ctr CH65 . 70 A7
Rotherhead Dr SK11 . . . . 112 B5
Rothersgreen Rd SK9 . . . 59 D6
Rothesay Cl WA7 . . . . . . 23 F2
Rothesay Dr CH62 . . . . . 43 E4
Rothesay Rd CH4 . . . . . 141 A7
Rough Bank CW12 . . . . . 179 E8
Rough Heys La SK11 . . . . 111 A8
ROUGHHILL 140 E1
Roughlea Ave WA3 . . . . . 4 D4
Roughley Ave WA5 . . . . . 15 D4
Roughlyn Cres CH4 . . . . 140 E1
Roughwood La
  Alsager CW11, ST7 . . . 193 B7
  Hassall Green CW11 . . . 176 A1
Roundabout The WA8 . . . 12 D6
Round Gdns SK10 . . . . . 88 A8
Roundhey SK8 . . . . 34 C8
Round Hill Mdw CH3 . . . 142 B7
Round Mdw SK10 . . . . . 88 E5
Round Thorn WA3 . . . . . 9 A8
Roundway SK7 . . . . 35 D6
Round Way SK22 . . . . . . 39 D8
Roundy La SK10 . . . . . . 62 F6
Routledge St WA8 . . . . . 13 B1
Rowan Ave WA3 . . . . . . 3 F7
Rowan Cl
  Alsager ST7 . . . . 193 D3
  Delamere CW8 . . . . . 123 D7
  Lawton Heath ST7 . . . . 193 D6
  Middlewich CW10 . . . . 151 E6
  Runcorn WA7 . . . . . . 49 C7
  Sandbach CW11 . . . . . 174 F7
  Warrington WA5 . . . . . 14 F6
  Winsford CW7 . . . . . . 126 D3
Rowan Ct SK9 . . . . 60 B7

Rowan Dr SK8 . . . . 35 C8
Rowan Gr CH5 . . . . 91 C1
Rowan Ho CH2 . . . . 237 C4
Rowan Lo SK7 . . . . 35 F7
Rowan Pk CH3 . . . . 142 E7
Rowan Pl CH2 . . . . 119 B4
Rowan Rd CW8 . . . . . . 102 D8
Rowan Rise CW8 . . . . . . 78 A3
Rowans Cl CW1 . . . . . . 189 F7
Rowanside WA8 . . . . . . 86 E6
Rowanside Dr SK9 . . . . . 60 E8
Rowans The
  Broughton CH4 . . . . . 139 B3
  4 Northwich CW9 . . . . 103 E6
  Widnes WA8 . . . . 13 D2
Rowan Tree Rd WA16 . . . 59 B5
Rowan Way SK10 . . . . . 87 E1
Rowan Wlk M31 . . . . . . 11 E2
Rowcliffe Ave CH4 . . . . . 141 A4
Rowena Ct CH2 . . . . . . 118 F3
Rowland Cl WA2 . . . . . . 9 A3
Rowlands Hts 1 CH1 . . . 237 C3
Rowlands View CW6 . . . . 146 B7
Rowley Bank La WA16 . . . 29 B1
ROWLEYHILL 181 B1
Rowley Rd SK7 . . . . 36 E8
Rowley Way WA16 . . . . . 82 B7
ROWLINSON'S GREEN . . . 28 C5
ROW-OF-TREES 59 D3
Rowson Dr M44 . . . . . . 11 D6
Rowswood Ctyd WA4 . . . . 25 E5
Rowswood Farm WA4 . . . 25 E5
Row The
  3 Winsford CW7 . . . . . 126 D1
  Wrenbury CW5 . . . . . 217 B5
Rowthorn Cl WA8 . . . . . . 22 E8
ROWTON 142 E5
Rowton Bridge Rd CH3 . . 142 E7
Rowton Cl 7 CW9 . . . . . 103 F4
Rowton La CH3 . . . . . . 142 F6
Rowton Rd WA5 . . . . . . 189 D4
Roxborough Cl WA5 . . . . . 7 A6
Roxburgh Cl SK10 . . . . . 87 A1
Roxburgh Rd CH66 . . . . . 68 F6
Roxby Way WA16 . . . . . . 82 A7
Roxholme Wlk M22 . . . . . 33 C8
Royal Arc 5 CW1 . . . . . 190 C4
Royal Ave WA8 . . . . . . 12 A1
Royal Ct 3 WA16 . . . . . 57 A2
Royal Gdns
  Altrincham WA14 . . . . . 20 F7
  Northwich CW9 . . . . . 103 E3
Royal La CW6 . . . . 147 B7
Royal Manchester Sch
  SK8 . . . . 34 D6
Royal Mdws SK10 . . . . . 87 A1
Royal Mews CW9 . . . . . 104 D5
Royal Pl WA8 . . . . 12 A1
Royal Pl SK12 . . . . 38 D5
Royal St SK10 . . . . 228 E1
ROYAL'S GREEN 228 C1
Royal Sh Arc The 8 CH64 . 66 E8
Royce Cl CW1 . . . . 190 A7
Royce Cl WA16 . . . . 56 F2
Royden Ave
  Irlam M44 . . . . 11 F8
  Runcorn WA7 . . . . . . 49 A8
Royds Cl CW8 . . . . 103 B4
Royds Ct CW11 . . . . . . 174 D5
Roylance Dr CW10 . . . . . 151 C8
Royleen Dr WA6 . . . . . . 74 D6
Royle Pk CW12 . . . . . . 156 D3
Royle's Pl CW8 . . . . . . 103 D6
Royles Sq 2 SK9 . . . . . . 60 A1
Royle St
  Congleton CW12 . . . . . 156 D3
  Northwich CW9 . . . . . 104 B8
  Winsford CW7 . . . . . . 126 E1
Royston Ave WA1 . . . . . 17 A7
Royston Cl
  Ellesmere Port CH66 . . . 69 F3
  2 Golborne WA3 . . . . . 3 E8
Rozel Cres WA5 . . . . . . 15 B5
Rubin Dr CW1 . . . . 189 F7
Rudd Ave WA9 . . . . 1 B2
RUDHEATH 104 D6
Rudheath Cl CW2 . . . . . 189 D5
Rudheath Cty High Sch
  CW9 . . . . 104 D7
Rudheath La WA7 . . . . . 24 D3
Rudheath L Ctr CW9 . . . 104 D7
Rudheath Prim Sch
  CW9 . . . . 104 D6
Rudheath Way CW9 . . . . 104 E5
Rudloe Ct WA3 . . . . 8 F1
Rudstone Cl CH66 . . . . . 69 B5
Rudyard Cl SK11 . . . . . 112 B6
Rue De Bohars CH66 . . . 168 D8
Rufford Cl
  Widnes WA8 . . . . 12 C2
  Wistaston CW2 . . . . . 206 B8
Rufford Ct WA11 . . . . . . 17 E8
Rufus Ct CH1 . . . . 237 A3
Rugby Cl SK10 . . . . 87 E4
Rugby Dr SK10 . . . . 87 E4
Rugby Ho SK10 . . . . . . 87 D3
Rugby Rd CH65 . . . . . . 70 D3
Rugby Wlk CH65 . . . . . . 70 D3
Ruislip Ct WA2 . . . . 8 F1
RULOE 101 D7
RUNCORN 23 C1
Runcorn Docks Rd WA7 . . 22 E2
Runcorn East Sta WA7 . . 50 D7
Runcorn Hill Nature
  Resetve* WA7 . . . . . . 48 F8
Runcorn Mkt WA7 . . . . . 23 A3
Runcorn Rd
  Barnton CW8 . . . . . . 78 B2
  Higher Walton WA4 . . . 25 D6

Runcorn Rd continued
  Little Leigh CW8 . . . . . 77 D5
Runcorn Spur Rd WA7 . . . 23 B1
Runcorn Sta WA7 . . . . . 23 B2
Runcorn Swim Pool WA7 . 23 A3
Runger La M90, WA5 . . . 32 F8
Runnell The CH64 . . . . . 41 D4
Runnymede WA1 . . . . . . 17 D7
Runnymede Ct 2 WA8 . . 13 C1
Runnymede Dr WA11 . . . . 1 A6
Runnymede Wlk 3 WA8 . . 13 C2
Rupert Row WA7 . . . . . . 50 A8
Ruscoe Ave CW11 . . . . . 174 E6
Ruscolm Cl WA5 . . . . . . 14 D7
Rushes Mdw WA13 . . . . . 19 B5
Rushey Cl WA15 . . . . . . 32 D7
Rushfield Cres WA7 . . . . 50 B5
Rushfield Rd
  Cheadle SK8 . . . . 35 A6
  Chester CH4 . . . . 141 B5
Rush Gdns WA13 . . . . . . 19 A4
RUSHGREEN 19 A4
Rushgreen Rd WA13 . . . . 19 A4
Rushmere Cl SK10 . . . . . 62 F2
Rushmere La CH3 . . . . . 163 F3
Rushmore Gr WA1 . . . . . 17 A7
Rushholme Cl WA5 . . . . . 15 B4
Rushside Rd SK8 . . . . . . 35 A6
RUSHTON 147 C5
Rushton Ave WA12 . . . . . 2 B4
Rushton CE Prim Sch
  SK11 . . . . 159 B2
Rushton Cl
  Burtonwood WA5 . . . . . 6 F7
  Northwich CW9 . . . . . 104 C7
  Widnes WA8 . . . . 12 F3
Rushton Dr
  Chester CH2 . . . . 118 E7
  Hough CW2 . . . . 206 E2
  Middlewich CW10 . . . . 151 C7
Rushton Fold SK10 . . . . . 61 A2
Rushton La CW6 . . . . . . 147 D6
Rushton Rd SK8 . . . . . . 35 A6
RUSHTON SPENCER 159 B2
Rushy View WA12 . . . . . . 2 A4
Ruskin Ave
  Newton-le-Willows WA12 . 2 C4
  Warrington WA2 . . . . . 8 C2
Ruskin Ct WA14 . . . . . . 57 A2
Ruskin Dr CH65 . . . . . . 70 D3
Ruskin Rd
  Congleton CW12 . . . . . 156 C2
  Crewe CW2 . . . . 190 C2
Ruskin Sports & Language
  Coll CW7 . . . . 190 C2
Ruskin Way WA16 . . . . . 57 A3
Russel Ct WA8 . . . . 13 B4
Russell Ave
  Alsager ST7 . . . . 193 C5
  High Lane SK6 . . . . . . 37 C7
Russell Cl CW12 . . . . . . 179 A8
Russell Dr CW1 . . . . . . 191 C5
Russell Rd
  Runcorn WA7 . . . . . . 48 B8
  Winsford CW7 . . . . . . 149 C8
Russell St CH1, CH3 . . . 237 C3
Russet Cl CW10 . . . . . . 151 D6
Russet Rd CW8 . . . . . . 102 D8
Russet Specl Sch CW8 . . 102 E8
Russet Way SK9 . . . . . . 59 E3
Rutherford Dr WA16 . . . . 82 C7
Ruthin Cl WA5 . . . . 7 E3
Ruthin Ct CH65 . . . . . . 70 D3
Ruthin Wlk WA5 . . . . . . 73 A1
Rutland Ave
  Golborne WA3 . . . . . . 3 D7
  Halewood L26 . . . . . . 21 A8
  Warrington WA4 . . . . . 26 B8
Rutland Cl
  Congleton CW12 . . . . . 156 E4
  Sandbach CW11 . . . . . 174 C5
Rutland Dr
  Middlewich CW10 . . . . 151 C7
  Weaverham CW8 . . . . . 77 C1
Rutland Pl CH2 . . . . . . 119 A5
Rutland Rd
  Hazel Grove SK7 . . . . . 36 E8
  Irlam M44 . . . . 11 D5
  Kidsgrove ST7 . . . . . . 195 A2
  Macclesfield SK11 . . . . 112 D4
  Partington M31 . . . . . 11 E2
Rutland St 1 WA7 . . . . . 22 F2
Rutter Ave WA5 . . . . . . 7 F2
Ryburn Cl CW2 . . . . . . 207 B3
Ryburn Rd SK11 . . . . . . 112 A5
Rydal Ave
  High Lane SK6 . . . . . . 37 E8
  Warrington WA4 . . . . . 16 A2
Rydal Cl
  Ellesmere Port CH65 . . . 70 C2
  Holmes Chapel CW4 . . . 130 B2
  Neston CH64 . . . . 66 F6
  Winsford CW7 . . . . . . 126 D3
Rydal Ct CW12 . . . . . . 156 A2
Rydal Dr WA15 . . . . 32 D8
Rydal Gr
  Chester CH4 . . . . 141 A6
  Helsby WA6 . . . . 73 B1
  Runcorn WA7 . . . . . . 49 B8
Rydal Mount CW1 . . . . . 173 B1
Rydal Pl SK11 . . . . 112 A6
Rydal Way
  Alsager ST7 . . . . 193 C5
  Widnes WA8 . . . . 12 C1
Ryde Cl CW1 . . . . 190 B8

Ryder Rd
  Warrington WA1 . . . . . 17 C7
  Widnes WA8 . . . . 13 B4
Ryders St CW8 . . . . . . 103 E8
Ryebank Ave CW1 . . . . . 190 B7
Ryebank Way SK10 . . . . . 87 C3
Rye Cl ST7 . . . . 193 B3
Ryecroft CH2 . . . . 72 B3
Ryecroft Cl CW10 . . . . . 151 B7
Ryecroft La
  Duddon CH3, CW6 . . . 144 C6
  Mobberley WA16 . . . . . 57 E4
Ryecroft Rd CH60 . . . . . 41 C7
Ryedale Way CW12 . . . . 179 C8
Ryelands St CW1 . . . . . 190 B5
RYE HILLS 209 E1
Ryehills ST7 . . . . 209 E1
Ryelands Cl SY14 . . . . . 213 B4
Rylands Dr WA2 . . . . . . 16 C7
Rylands St
  Warrington WA1 . . . . . 16 B5
  5 Widnes WA8 . . . . . 23 B8
Ryles Cl SK11 . . . . 112 C5
Ryles Cres SK11 . . . . . . 112 C5
Ryles Ho SK11 . . . . 112 C5
Ryle's Park Rd SK11 . . . . 112 C6
Ryle St SK11 . . . . 112 D6
Ryleys Farm SK9 . . . . . . 59 F1
Ryleys La SK9 . . . . 59 F1
Ryleys Sch The SK9 . . . . 59 F1

S

Sabre Cl WA7 . . . . 50 D7
Sack La CW9 . . . . 54 F6
Sacred Heart RC Prim Sch
  WA5 . . . . 15 E5
Saddleback Dr SK10 . . . . 86 F7
Saddlers Rise WA7 . . . . . 50 C8
Saddlery Way CH1 . . . . . 118 B1
Sade Ct 4 CW1 . . . . . . 190 B5
Sadler Cl CW7 . . . . 126 D1
Sadler Rd CW7 . . . . . . 126 D1
Sadler's Cl CW4 . . . . . . 130 B3
Sadlers La CW6 . . . . . . 124 A1
Sadler St WA8 . . . . 13 C1
Sadlers Wells CW6 . . . . 185 E8
Saffron Cl
  Golborne WA3 . . . . . . 3 E8
  Warrington WA2 . . . . . 9 B1
Saffron Wlk M31 . . . . . . 11 F2
Sagars Rd
  Handforth SK9 . . . . . . 34 C3
  Styal SK9 . . . . 34 B4
Sage Cl WA2 . . . . 9 C2
SAIGHTON 142 E1
Saighton CE Prim Sch
  CH3 . . . . 142 E1
Saighton La CH3 . . . . . 142 F2
St Aelred's RC Tech Coll
  WA12 . . . . 2 D4
St Alban Rd WA5 . . . . . 14 E5
St Albans Cl WA11 . . . . . 2 A7
St Albans Dr CW5 . . . . . 204 F3
St Alban's RC Prim Sch
  Macclesfield SK10 . . . . 86 F1
  Warrington WA5 . . . . . 15 F6
St Albans St SK22 . . . . . 39 C8
St Ambrose Coll WA15 . . 32 B8
St Ambrose Ct WA4 . . . . 16 B2
St Ambrose RC Prim Sch
  L24 . . . . 21 A2
St Andrew's Ave WA8 . . . 13 C1
St Andrew's CE Prim Sch
  WA2 . . . . 8 C3
St Andrews Cl
  Crewe CW2 . . . . 190 C1
  Ellesmere Port CH65 . . . 70 E2
  Macclesfield SK10 . . . . 86 F1
St Andrews Dr
  Holmes Chapel CW4 . . . 130 B2
  Kidsgrove ST7 . . . . . . 195 C3
St Andrew's Gdns ST7 . . 193 E2
St Andrew's Rd
  Ellesmere Port CH65 . . . 70 E2
  Macclesfield SK11 . . . . 112 B7
St Andrews Wlk
  Mickle Trafford CH2 . . . 96 F1
  New Mills SK22 . . . . . 39 D8
St Annes Cl WA8 . . . . . . 12 E1
St Annes Ave WA4 . . . . . 17 B2
St Anne's Ave CW10 . . . . 151 D8
St Annes Avenue E WA4 . . 17 B2
St Anne's Fulshaw CE Prim
  Sch SK9 . . . . 59 F6
St Anne's La CW5 . . . . . 204 D5
St Anne's RC Prim Sch
  CW5 . . . . 204 E3
St Anne's Rd WA8 . . . . . 13 B2
St Anne St CH1 . . . . . . 237 B3
St Ann's CE Prim Sch
  WA2 . . . . 16 C8
St Ann's Rd CW10 . . . . . 151 C8
St Ann's Rd S SK8 . . . . . 34 C8
St Ann's Sq SK8 . . . . . . 34 C8
St Anthony Pl WA2 . . . . . 8 B6
St Anthony's RC Prim Sch
  CH4 . . . . 140 E6
St Asaph Dr WA5 . . . . . . 7 E3
St Asaph Rd CH66 . . . . . 94 E8
St Augustine's Ave WA4 . . 16 F4
St Augustines Dr CW2 . . 207 E3
St Augustine's RC Prim Sch
  Runcorn WA7 . . . . . . 24 A2

St Augustine's RC Prim Sch
continued
  Warrington WA4 . . . . . 16 F4
St Austell Cl WA5 . . . . . 14 E3
St Austell Ave SK10 . . . . 86 E1
St Austell Cl
  Macclesfield SK10 . . . . 86 E1
  Runcorn WA7 . . . . . . 50 B6
St Austell Dr SK8 . . . . . 34 B8
St Austins La WA1 . . . . . 16 B4
St Barnabas CE Prim Sch
  WA5 . . . . 15 F5
St Barnabas Ct SK11 . . . 112 C6
St Barnabas Pl WA5 . . . . 15 F6
St Bartholomews Ct CH5 . 116 E6
St Basil's RC Prim Sch
  WA8 . . . . 13 A2
St Bede's Ave CW8 . . . . . 77 D1
St Bede's RC Inf Sch WA8 13 A1
St Bede's RC Jun Sch
  WA8 . . . . 13 A1
St Bede's RC Prim Sch
  CW8 . . . . 102 F7
St Benedicts Cl WA2 . . . 16 B7
St Benedict's RC Prim Sch
  Handforth SK9 . . . . . . 34 D3
  Warrington WA2 . . . . . 16 D7
St Bernard's RC Prim Sch
  CH65 . . . . 70 D3
St Berteline's CE Prim Sch
  WA7 . . . . 50 C8
St Brannocks Rd SK8 . . . 35 B7
St Brides Cl WA5 . . . . . 14 E3
St Bridget's CE Prim Sch
  WA5 . . . . 8 F3
St Bridgets Ct CH4 . . . . 141 B6
St Bridget's RC Prim Sch
  WA2 . . . . 8 E3
St Catherine Dr CW8 . . . 103 A4
St Catherine's RC Prim Sch
  WA3 . . . . 3 E7
St Chad's CE Prim Sch
  Newcastle-under-Lyme
  ST5 . . . . 210 D2
  Winsford CW7 . . . . . . 149 E8
St Chads Cl CW5 . . . . . 220 A8
St Chad's Fields CW7 . . . 149 C5
St Chad's RC High Sch
  WA7 . . . . 49 D7
St Chad's Rd CH1 . . . . . 117 F4
St Chads Way TF9 . . . . . 236 C2
St Chad's Terr ST5 . . . . 210 D2
St Christophers Ct CH2 . . 118 D8
St Clair St CW2 . . . . . . 190 D1
St Clare's RC Prim Sch
  CH4 . . . . 141 A5
St Clements Cl CW2 . . . . 207 B1
St Clement's RC Prim Sch
  WA7 . . . . 49 A8
St David Rd CH62 . . . . . 44 A6
St Davids Dr
  12 Ellesmere Port CH66 . 94 F8
  Warrington WA5 . . . . . 7 F2
St David's High Sch CH4 140 C6
St David's Rd CH4 . . . . . 140 D7
St David's Terr CH4 . . . . 140 C6
St Edwards Cl SK11 . . . . 112 D6
St Edward's RC Prim Sch
  WA2 . . . . 23 B3
St Elmo Pk SK12 . . . . . 37 C4
St Elphin Fairfield CE Prim
  Sch WA1 . . . . 16 C5
St Elphins Cl WA1 . . . . . 16 C5
SS Peter & Paul RC High Sch
  WA8 . . . . 12 F2
St Gabriels Ct ST7 . . . . 193 C3
St Gabriel's RC Prim Sch
  ST7 . . . . 193 C3
St George's CH1 . . . . . 237 B3
St Georges Ave 13 CH66 . 94 F8
St George's Cl WA4 . . . . 26 E3
St George's Cl WA16 . . . . 82 C8
St George's Cres
  Chester CH4 . . . . 237 C1
  Waverton CH3 . . . . . . 143 A5
St George's Ct WA8 . . . . 22 D8
St George's Pl 1 SK11 . . 112 D7
St George's Rd SK22 . . . 39 C8
St George's Rd CW7 . . . . 149 C8
St George's St SK11 . . . 112 D6
St George's Way
  Northwich CW9 . . . . . 103 F5
  Thornton Hough CH63 . . 42 A7
St Gerard's RC Prim Sch
  WA8 . . . . 23 B7
St Gregory's RC High Sch
  WA5 . . . . 15 D5
St Gregory's RC Prim Sch
  SK10 . . . . 87 F1
ST HELENS 1 A1
St Helens CE Prim Sch
  WA3 . . . . 11 B2
St Helens Cl WA3 . . . . . 11 B3
St Helens Coll Newton
  Campus WA12 . . . . . . 2 B4
St Helens Rd
  Golborne WN7 . . . . . . 4 B8
  5 Northwich CW9 . . . . 104 A8
St Hilarys Pk SK9 . . . . . 85 A8
St Hilda's Dr WA6 . . . . . 49 C1
St Ives Cl SK10 . . . . . . 86 E1
St Ives Pk CH5 . . . . . . 116 A3

St Ives Way CH5 . . . . 116 A3
St James Ave
　Chester CH2 . . . . 118 F7
　Congleton CW12 . . . . . . 156 C2
　Warren SK11 . . . . 111 E2
St James CI
　Audlem CW3 . . . . 230 A4
　1 Frodsham WA6 . . . . . . 49 C1
St James Ct
　Audley ST7 . . . . 209 D2
　Cheadle SK8 . . . . 34 F6
　Chester CH2 . . . . 118 F3
St James' Ct
　Biddulph ST8 . . . . 179 E3
　Warrington WA4 . . . . 16 B3
St James Ct/Llys Sant Iago
　CH5 . . . . 91 D1
St James' Dr SK9 . . . . 60 A6
St James' Prim Sch WA11 . . 1 E6
St James' RC High Sch
　SK8 . . . . 34 F6
St James Sq SK22 . . . . . . 39 C8
St James St CH1 . . . . 237 B3
St James Terr **9** CW7 . . . 149 A8
St James Way **10** CW8 . . 103 C5
St James' Way SK8 . . . . . . 34 F6
St James Wlk **11** CW8 . . 103 E7
St John Ave WA4 . . . . 16 B2
St John Fisher RC Prim Sch
　WA8 . . . . 13 D1
St John's Ave
　Knutsford WA16 . . . . 56 F1
　Lostock Gralam CW9 . . . . 79 F3
St John's Brow WA7 . . . . . 23 B3
St John's CE Prim Sch
　Bollington SK10 . . . . 88 A7
　Kingsley WA6 . . . . 75 C2
　Sandbach CW11 . . . . . . 175 E6
St John's CI CW9 . . . . . . 104 E8
St Johns Ct
　Chester CH1 . . . . 237 B2
　Winsford CW7 . . . . 126 B1
St John's Ct
　Knutsford WA16 . . . . 57 C2
　Warrington WA1 . . . . 16 F7
St Johns Dr CW7 . . . . 149 A8
St John's Dr
　Bebington CH62 . . . . 44 A5
　Chester CH4 . . . . 237 C1
　Congleton CW12 . . . . . . 156 C2
　Knutsford WA16 . . . . 57 A1
　7 Macclesfield SK11 . . . 112 C7
　Wilmslow SK9 . . . . 59 E5
St John's Rear Rd CH4 . . 237 C1
St John's St WA7 . . . . 23 B3
St John St
　Chester CH1 . . . . 237 B2
　Newton-le-Willows WA12 . . 2 A3
Saint Johns Vale WA16 . . 57 D3
St John's Way
　Cuddington CW8 . . . . . . 102 B2
　Sandbach CW11 . . . . . . 175 E6
St John's Wood ST7 . . . . 194 F1
St John's Wood Com Sch
　WA16 . . . . 57 D2
St John The Evangelist CE
　Aided Prim Sch SK11 . . 112 A7
St John The Evangelist RC
　Prim Sch **2** ST7 . . . . . 194 F1
St Joseph's CI WA5 . . . . . 14 E5
St Joseph's RC Prim Sch
　Warrington WA5 . . . . 14 E5
　Winsford CW7 . . . . 149 B8
St Josephs Way CW5 . . . . 205 A5
St Katherines Way WA3 . . . 3 A8
St Kilda CI CH65 . . . . 70 C1
St Lawrence Ct CW5 . . . . 204 F6
St Lawrence Rd WA8 . . . . 74 B8
St Leonard's Way CW3 . . 232 C1
St Lewis RC Prim Sch WA3 . 4 A1
St Luke's Ave WA3 . . . . 3 D8
St Luke's CE Prim Sch
　CW12 . . . . 130 D3
St Luke's Cres WA8 . . . . . 13 B4
St Luke's Ho **3** SK10 . . . 111 F8
St Luke's RC Prim Sch
　WA6 . . . . 74 C8
St Luke's Way WA6 . . . . . 49 B1
St Margaret's Ave WA3 . . . 8 D1
St Margaret's CE Prim Sch
　WA2 . . . . 8 D1
St Marks CI CH66 . . . . . . 94 F8
St Mark's Prim Sch CW9 . . 53 C4
St Mark's RC Prim Sch
　L26 . . . . 21 A8
St Marks Rd CH4 . . . . . . 140 F6
St Mark's St WA11 . . . . 1 A6
St Martins Dr CH66 . . . . . 69 D2
St Martins La WA7 . . . . . . 50 D7
St Martins RC Prim Sch
　WA7 . . . . 50 D7
St Martin's Rd ST7 . . . . . 210 E6
St Martin's Way CH1 . . . . 237 A3
St Mary of the Angels RC
　Prim Sch CW8 . . . . 69 D6
St Mary's Ave CW8 . . . . . 77 D1
St Mary's CE Prim Sch
　Bosley SK11 . . . . 158 D8
　Lymm WA13 . . . . 11 C5
　Runcorn WA7 . . . . 50 A8
St Mary's CI
　Alsager ST7 . . . . 193 C5
　Hale L24 . . . . 21 E2
　Warrington WA4 . . . . 26 C6
St Marys Ct CW5 . . . . . . 204 A7

St Mary's Ct
　Congleton CW12 . . . . . . 156 A2
　Golborne WA3 . . . . 4 B8
　Partington M31 . . . . 11 F4
St Mary's Dr CW8 . . . . . . 126 A8
St Mary's Hill CH1 . . . . . . 237 B1
St Mary's Hospl WA2 . . . . . 8 B1
St Mary's RC Jun Sch
　WA12 . . . . 2 B3
St Mary's RC Prim Sch
　Congleton CW12 . . . . . . 156 D3
　Crewe CW2 . . . . 190 A1
　Middlewich CW10 . . . . . 151 C8
　2 New Mills SK22 . . . . . 39 B8
St Mary's RC Sch WA12 . . . 2 C4
St Mary's Rd
　Disley SK12 . . . . 38 D5
　Dodleston CH4 . . . . 162 A4
　Nantwich CW5 . . . . 204 E7
　New Mills SK22 . . . . 39 B8
　Runcorn WA8 . . . . 23 F1
　Warrington WA5 . . . . 14 F5
　Widnes WA8 . . . . 23 A4
St Mary's St
　Crewe CW1 . . . . 190 C4
　Warrington WA4 . . . . 16 D3
St Mary's Way CH4 . . . . . 139 C5
St Matthews CE Prim Sch
　WA4 . . . . 26 E2
St Matthews CI
　Haslington CW1 . . . . . . 191 D4
　Warrington WA4 . . . . 26 D7
St Mawes CI WA8 . . . . . . 12 E2
St Mawes Ct SK10 . . . . . . 86 E1
St Mawgan Ct WA2 . . . . . . 8 F2
St Michael's Ave SK7 . . . . 35 E8
St Michael's CI
　Little Leigh CW8 . . . . . . 77 D5
　Widnes WA8 . . . . 22 C7
St Michael's Cotts CW2 . . 156 B2
St Michael's Ind Est WA8 . 22 C7
St Michael's RC Prim Sch
　WA8 . . . . 22 C7
St Michael's Rd WA8 . . . . . 22 C7
St Michael's Row CH1 . . . 237 B2
St Michael's Sq CH1 . . . . 237 B2
St Michaels Terr **10**
　SK11 . . . . 112 D8
St Michael's View CW1 . . 190 B5
St Michael's Way CW10 . . 128 C1
St Monicas CI WA3 . . . . . . 4 A8
St Monica's RC Prim Sch
　WA3 . . . . 26 D7
St Nicholas CI CW5 . . . . 204 F5
St Nicholas RC High Sch
　CW8 . . . . 103 D6
St Nicholas Rd WA3 . . . . . 4 A8
St Olave St CH1 . . . . 237 B1
St Oswalds CI CH1 . . . . . 237 B3
St Oswald's CE Aided Prim
　Sch CH1 . . . . 94 F2
St Oswalds CI
　Malpas SY14 . . . . 213 B3
　Winwick WA2 . . . . 8 B6
St Oswald's Cres CW11 . . 153 F5
St Oswalds La
　Lower Whitley WA4 . . . . 52 D1
　Windyharbour SK11 . . . . 109 D1
Salter's La
　Bickerton SY14 . . . . 199 F8
　Broxton CH3, SY14 . . . . 183 E1
　Hoole Bank CH2 . . . . . . 119 C8
SALTERSWALL 125 F3
Salt Line Way CW5 . . . . . 174 D6
Salt Mdws CW5 . . . . 204 C5
Salt Mus The * CW9 . . . . 103 F7
SALTNEY 140 D6
Saltney Bsns Ctr CH4 . . . 140 E7
Saltney Ferry Prim Sch
　CH4 . . . . 140 B6
Saltney Ferry Rd CH4 . . . 140 B7
Saltney Terr CH4 . . . . . . 140 B7
Salton Gdns WA5 . . . . . . 15 E7
Saltwood Dr WA7 . . . . . . 50 C5
Saltworks CI WA6 . . . . . . 49 D2
Samian CI CW10 . . . . . . 128 C2
Samphire Gdns WA9 . . . . . 6 B7
Samuel St
　Crewe CW1 . . . . 190 B5
　Macclesfield SK11 . . . . . 112 D7
　Packmoor ST7 . . . . 195 F1
　Warrington WA5 . . . . 15 E4
Sanbec Gdns WA8 . . . . . 12 D5
Sandalwood WA7 . . . . . . 24 C1
Sandalwood CI WA2 . . . . . 8 D2
SANDBACH 175 B5
Sandbach Com Prim Sch
　CW11 . . . . 175 A6
Sandbach Crosses * 175 B6
Sandbach Dr CW9 . . . . . 103 E6
SANDBACH HEATH 175 D6
Sandbach High Sch & Sixth
　Form Coll CW11 . . . . . 175 A7
Sandbach L Ctr CW11 . . . 175 A7
Sandbach Rd
　Congleton CW12 . . . . . . 156 A2
　Rode Heath ST7 . . . . . . 193 E7
Sandbach Road N ST7 . . 193 C4
Sandbach Road S ST7 . . 193 D3
Sandbach St CW11 . . . . . 175 A6
Sanderling Rd WA12 . . . . 2 C4
Sanders Hey CI WA7 . . . . 50 B5
Sanderson CI
　Crewe CW2 . . . . 206 A2
　Warrington WA5 . . . . 14 D6
Sanderson Way CW10 . . . 128 C1
Sanders Sq SK11 . . . . . . 112 D5
Sandfield Ave CW5 . . . . . 216 F3

St Teresa's RC Prim Sch
　M44 . . . . 11 E8
St Theresa's RC Prim Sch
　CH1 . . . . 117 F5
St Thomas CE Prim Sch
　1 Kidsgrove ST7 . . . . . 195 A1
　Warrington WA4 . . . . 16 D1
St Thomas St WA8 . . . . . . 12 E1
St Thomas More RC High Sch
　CW2 . . . . 190 A2
St Thomas of Canterbury CE
　Jun Sch CH1 . . . . 237 A4
St Thomas's Pathway
　CH1 . . . . 237 B2
St Thomas St ST7 . . . . . . 195 E7
St Thomas Terr WA8 . . . . 12 E1
St Thomas' View CH65 . . . 70 B4
St Vincent Dr CW8 . . . . . 102 F3
St Vincent Rd WA5 . . . . . 14 F5
St Vincent's RC Prim Sch
　Knutsford WA16 . . . . 57 C1
　Warrington WA5 . . . . 14 F5
St Wenefredes Gn SY13 . 214 F6
St Werburgh's & St
　Columba's RC Prim Sch **1**
　CH2 . . . . 118 F2
St Werburgh St CH1 . . . . 237 B2
St Wilfrid's CE Aided Prim
　Sch WA4 . . . . 25 C5
St Wilfrids CI CW9 . . . . . 104 A3
St Wilfrid's Dr WA4 . . . . . 17 C1
St Wilfrid's RC Prim Sch
　CW8 . . . . 103 D5
St Winefride's RC Prim Sch
　CH64 . . . . 66 F7
Salander Cres CW2 . . . . . 206 A7
Salerno Rd CH2 . . . . 95 B1
Salesbrook La CW5 . . . . . 228 C7
Salford CW7 . . . . 230 A4
Salford PI CW12 . . . . 156 E3
Salisbury Ave
　Crewe CW2 . . . . 190 C1
　Saltney CH4 . . . . 140 E6
Salisbury CI
　Crewe CW2 . . . . 190 C1
　10 Ellesmere Port CH66 . 94 F8
Salisbury PI SK10 . . . . . . 87 E4
Salisbury Rd WA11 . . . . . . 1 E8
Salisbury St
　Chester CH1 . . . . 118 B3
　Golborne WA3 . . . . 3 A8
　Runcorn WA7 . . . . 23 A1
　Warrington WA1 . . . . 16 D6
　4 Widnes WA8 . . . . 23 B8
Salkeld St **8** CW9 . . . . . 104 B8
Salmon Leap CH4 . . . . . . 237 B1
Salop PI ST7 . . . . 195 A3
Salop Wlk SK10 . . . . 86 F2
Saltash CI WA7 . . . . 50 B6
Saltersbrook Gr **12** SK9 . . 34 E1
Salters Ford CW8 . . . . . . 77 F3
Saltersford Cnr CW4 . . . . 130 E3
Saltersgate CH66 . . . . . . 69 F2

Sandfield Cres WA3 . . . . . . 5 C7
Sandfield CI
　3 Frodsham WA6 . . . . . . 74 B8
　Wrenbury CW5 . . . . 216 F4
Sandfield Hall WA3 . . . . . . 3 A4
Sandfield La
　Acton Bridge CW8 . . . . . 76 E1
　Hartford CW8 . . . . 103 C4
Sandfield Pk CH60 . . . . . . 40 D8
Sandfield Terr WA8 . . . . . 76 F1
Sandford Cres CW2 . . . . 207 D2
Sandford Rd CW5 . . . . . 204 F7
Sandgate Rd SK10 . . . . . . 87 F2
Sandham Gr CH60 . . . . . . 41 D7
Sandham Rd L24 . . . . 21 A4
Sandheys CH64 . . . . 41 C1
Sandhill Terr WA4 . . . . . . 16 E3
Sandhole Cotts **2** CW7 . 149 B8
Sandhole La
　Chelford WA16 . . . . 83 D4
　Crowton CW8 . . . . 101 B7
Sandhurst Ave CW2 . . . . 190 A1
Sandhurst Dr **2** SK9 . . . . 60 C8
Sandhurst Rd L26 . . . . . . 21 A6
Sandhurst St WA4 . . . . . . 16 F3
Sandicroft CI WA3 . . . . . . 9 C5
Sandiford Rd CW4 . . . . . 130 C3
Sandiford Sq CW9 . . . . . 104 A8
Sandileigh Ave WA14 . . . . 56 F2
Sandington Dr CW8 . . . . 101 F2
SANDIWAY 102 B3
Sandiway
　Bebington CH63 . . . . 43 C6
　Knutsford WA16 . . . . 57 B2
　Warrington WA8 . . . . 12 A1
　Warrington WA1 . . . . 16 D6
Sandiway CI CW8 . . . . . . 102 A2
Sandiway La CW9 . . . . . . 53 A2
Sandiway Pk CW8 . . . . . . 102 E4
Sandiway Prim Sch CW8 102 B3
Sandiway Rd
　Crewe CW1 . . . . 190 A7
　Handforth SK9 . . . . 34 D5
Sand La SK10 . . . . 84 F5
Sandlebridge Farm SK9 . . 83 F6
Sandle Bridge La WA16,
　SK9 . . . . 83 E5
Sandle Bridge Rise WA16 . 83 F6
SANDLOW GREEN 131 B1
Sandmoor PI WA13 . . . . . 19 A2
Sandon Cres CH64 . . . . . 66 E5
Sandon Park Gdns CW2 . 189 D4
Sandon PI WA8 . . . . 13 D1
Sandon Rd CH2 . . . . 118 E4
Sandon St CW1 . . . . 190 D4
Sandown CI
　Culcheth WA3 . . . . 4 F4
　Middlewich CW10 . . . . . 151 C8
　Runcorn WA7 . . . . 49 C6
　Wilmslow SK9 . . . . 60 A6
Sandown Cres CW8 . . . . 102 A3
Sandown Dr WA15 . . . . . . 32 D6
Sandown PI SK11 . . . . . . 111 F7
Sandown Rd CW1 . . . . . . 190 C7
Sandown Reach CW5 . . . 229 D7
Sandown Terr CH3 . . . . . 118 F1
Sandpiper CI
　Macclesfield SK10 . . . . . 87 B4
　Newton-le-Willows WA12 . . 2 C4
Sandpiper Ct
　Chester CH4 . . . . 141 B2
　Kidsgrove ST7 . . . . 195 C2
Sandpiper Way CH4 . . . . 141 B3
Sandra Dr WA12 . . . . 2 E3
Sandringham Ave
　Chester CH3 . . . . 119 A2
　Helsby WA6 . . . . 73 B4
Sandringham CI
　Altrincham WA14 . . . . . . 20 F1
　Northwich CW9 . . . . . . 103 E4
　Winsford CW7 . . . . 126 C3
Sandringham Ct
　Golborne WA3 . . . . 3 E7
　5 Wilmslow SK9 . . . . . . 60 A6
Sandringham Dr
　Poynton SK12 . . . . 36 D3
　Warrington WA5 . . . . 15 C4
　Wistaston CW2 . . . . 205 E8
Sandringham Gdns **2**
　CH65 . . . . 70 D2
Sandringham Rd **11** CW8 103 C5
Sandringham Rd
　Congleton CW12 . . . . . . 156 F4
　Macclesfield SK10 . . . . . 87 F1
　Widnes WA8 . . . . 13 A4
Sandringham Way **4** SK9 60 A6
Sandrock Rd CH3 . . . . . . 142 E7
Sandsdown CI ST8 . . . . . 179 C1
Sandside Rd ST7 . . . . . . 193 B3
Sands Rd ST7 . . . . 195 E6
Sandstone Mews WA8 . . . 12 E4
Sandstone Wlk CH60 . . . . 41 A7
Sandwich Dr SK10 . . . . . . 87 C4
Sandwood Ave CH4 . . . . 139 B3
Sandybank CW8 . . . . 78 D1
Sandy Brow La WA3 . . . . . 3 E2
Sandy CI SK10 . . . . 87 F2
SANDYCROFT 116 B2
Sandycroft Ind Est CH5 . 116 A2
Sandyfield Ct ST8 . . . . . . 179 C1
Sandyhill PI **1** CW7 . . . 149 D6
Sandyhill Rd CW7 . . . . . 149 D6
Sandy La
　Allostock CW4 . . . . 106 C1
　Astbury CW12 . . . . 177 E6
　Aston CW5 . . . . 217 C2
　Bold Heath WA8 . . . . . . 14 B6

Sandy La continued
　Brown Knowl CH3 . . . . . 199 C7
　Bulkeley SY14 . . . . 184 C1
　Chester CH3 . . . . 119 A1
　Congleton, Astbury Marsh
　CW12 . . . . 156 B2
　Congleton CW12 . . . . . . 155 D3
　Croft WA3 . . . . 9 A8
　Cronton WA8 . . . . 12 D5
　Golborne, Lowton Common
　WA3 . . . . 4 A8
　Golborne WA3 . . . . 2 F8
　Goostrey CW4 . . . . 107 D1
　Haslington CW11 . . . . . 192 B7
　Hatherton CW5 . . . . 219 F5
　Helsby WA6 . . . . 73 B2
　Higher Kinnerton CH4 . . 161 A6
　Huntington CH3 . . . . . . 141 F8
　Knutsford WA16 . . . . 82 D3
　Lymm WA13 . . . . 19 B4
　Macclesfield SK10 . . . . . 86 C2
　Neston CH64 . . . . 67 A7
　Runcorn, Preston Brook
　WA7 . . . . 50 F6
　Runcorn WA7 . . . . 48 E7
　Saighton CH3 . . . . 142 C3
　Saltney CH4 . . . . 140 D6
　Sandbach CW11 . . . . . . 174 D5
　Swan Green WA16 . . . . 106 E6
　Swettenham CW12 . . . . 131 F3
　Tarvin CH3 . . . . 121 C4
　Threapwood SY14 . . . . . 222 E8
　Warrington, Longford WA2 . . 8 C2
　Warrington, Penketh WA5 . . 15 A4
　Warrington, Stockton Heath
　WA4 . . . . 26 D8
　Weaverham CW8 . . . . . . 77 C2
　Whitegate CW8 . . . . . . 125 D6
　Wilmslow SK9 . . . . 59 E8
Sandylands Cres ST7 . . . 193 F5
Sandylands Pk CW2 . . . . 205 D2
Sandylane Mews CW12 . 156 C5
Sandy Lane W WA2 . . . . . 8 B3
Sandymere Ct CW7 . . . . 126 B1
Sandymoor La WA7 . . . . . 24 D2
Sandy Rd ST8 . . . . 179 C2
Sandy Way CW7 . . . . 149 B8
SANKEY BRIDGES 15 C4
Sankey Bridges Ind Est
　WA5 . . . . 15 C4
Sankey for Penketh Sta
　WA5 . . . . 14 F6
Sankey La WA4 . . . . 25 F1
Sankey St
　Golborne WA3 . . . . 3 A8
　Newton-le-Willows WA12 . . 2 A3
　Warrington WA1 . . . . 16 A5
　Widnes WA8 . . . . 23 A6
Sankey Valley Ind Est
　WA12 . . . . 2 A2
Sankey Valley Pk *
　Newton-le-Willows WA5 . . 1 D3
　Warrington WA5 . . . . 15 D5
Sankey Valley St James Prim
　Sch WA5 . . . . 15 C6
Sankey Way WA5 . . . . . . 15 D5
Santa Rosa Bvd WA5 . . . . 15 A7
Santon Dr WA3 . . . . 3 E8
Sapling La CW6 . . . . 146 F3
Sarah Bartholomew Sch
　WA6 . . . . 97 E6
Sark Ave CH65 . . . . 95 B8
Sark Ho CH2 . . . . 119 B4
Sarl Williams Ct CH1 . . . 237 A3
Sarn Bank Rd SY14 . . . . 222 E6
Sarn Rd SY14 . . . . 222 D8
Sarra La CH3 . . . . 184 B5
Sarsfield Ave **1** WA3 . . . . 3 D8
Sarus Ct WA7 . . . . 24 B4
SAUGHALL 117 B8
Saughall CI CW9 . . . . . . 103 E4
Saughall Hey CH1 . . . . . . 94 A1
Saughall Rd
　Blacon, Abbot's Meads
　CH1 . . . . 118 A4
　Blacon CH1 . . . . 117 E5
Saughall Thomas Wedge CE
　Jun Sch CH1 . . . . 94 A1
Saundersfoot CI WA5 . . . . 7 E2
Saunders St CW1 . . . . . . 190 B4
Saunderton CI WA11 . . . . . 1 C7
Saunton CI CW7 . . . . 126 A2
Savannah PI **4** WA5 . . . . 15 C7
Saville Ave WA5 . . . . 15 F7
Saville Rise CW7 . . . . . . 126 E1
Saville St SK11 . . . . 112 E7
Savoy Rd CW1 . . . . 207 A8
Sawley CI
　Culcheth WA3 . . . . 5 A2
　Runcorn WA7 . . . . 50 E7
Sawley Dr SK8 . . . . 35 C6
Sawpit St WA13, WA14 . . . 20 A6
Sawyer Dr ST8 . . . . 179 C1
Saxon CI WA4 . . . . 26 B5
Saxon Crossway CW7 . . . 126 B1
Saxon Rd WA7 . . . . 23 C2
Saxons La CW8 . . . . 103 D7
Saxon Terr **4** WA8 . . . . . 13 B1
Saxon Way
　Blacon CH1 . . . . 117 E6
　6 Ellesmere Port CH66 . 94 F8
　Sandbach CW11 . . . . . . 175 C6
Sayce St WA8 . . . . 13 B1
Scafell Ave WA2 . . . . 8 C3
Scafell CI
　Bebington CH62 . . . . 43 D3
　High Lane SK6 . . . . 37 E8
Scaife Rd CW5 . . . . 204 F5

Scaliot Cl SK22 . . . . 39 B8
Scar La SY14 . . . . 198 F1
Sceptre Cl WA12 . . . . 2 A3
SCHOLAR GREEN 194 E8
Scholar Green Prim Sch
  ST7 . . . . 194 E6
Scholar Rise CW7 . . . . . . 127 A2
Scholars Cl SK10 . . . . 111 D8
Scholar's Ct 10 CH64 . . . . 66 E8
Scholars Green La WA13 . 18 F2
School Ave CH64 . . . . 66 F6
School Bank
  Norley WA6 . . . . 101 A6
  Wybunbury CW5 . . . . . . 220 B8
School Brow WA1 . . . . 16 C6
School Cl
  Audley ST7 . . . . 210 A1
  Knutsford WA16 . . . . 56 E1
  Marbury SY13 . . . . 226 E8
  Poynton SK12 . . . . 36 F3
School Cotts
  Bradwall Green CW11 . . 153 B4
  Wimboldsley CW10 . . . . 150 F4
School Cres CW1 . . . . 190 E4
School Dr
  Barnton CW8 . . . . 78 A3
  Lymm WA13 . . . . 19 C5
School Field Cl CW3 . . . . 230 F4
Schoolfold La SK10 . . . . . . 62 A1
School Grn CH3 . . . . 182 C1
SCHOOL GREEN 149 C5
School Hill CH60 . . . . 40 F7
School Hos SK11 . . . . 109 A1
School House Cotts CH66. 69 B6
School La
  Aldford CH3 . . . . 163 F2
  Antrobus CW9 . . . . 53 C3
  Astbury CW12 . . . . 178 B8
  Audlem CW3 . . . . 230 A4
  Bold Heath WA8 . . . . . . 13 E7
  Brereton Green CW11 . . 153 F5
  Bunbury CW6 . . . . 168 E1
  Burwardsley CH3 . . . . . 184 B6
  Cuddington CW8 . . . . . 102 A2
  Eaton (nr Congleton)
    CW12 . . . . 156 E8
  Ellesmere Port CH66 . . . 69 A8
  Elton CH2 . . . . 72 B3
  Frodsham WA6 . . . . 74 C7
  Great Budworth CW9 . . . 79 B8
  Guilden Sutton CH3 . . . 119 E5
  Hartford CW8 . . . . 103 C4
  Henbury SK11 . . . . 111 B6
  Higher Whitley WA4 . . . . 52 E6
  Hollinfare WA3 . . . . 11 C2
  Hooton CH66 . . . . 43 F1
  Irlam, Cadishead M44 . . 11 D5
  Lostock Gralam CW9 . . . 80 A2
  Manley WA6 . . . . 99 A5
  Marton SK11 . . . . 133 C5
  Mickle Trafford CH2 . . . 119 E8
  Moulton CW9 . . . . 126 F8
  Nantwich CW5 . . . . 204 E6
  Neston CH64 . . . . 42 B2
  Neston, Little Neston CH64. 66 F6
  Neston, Parkgate CH64 . . 41 B1
  Nether Alderley SK10 . . . 86 A6
  Norbury SY13 . . . . 215 E2
  Norley WA6 . . . . 100 D5
  Ollerton WA16 . . . . 83 B4
  Onneley CW3 . . . . 232 E1
  Partington WA14 . . . . . . 20 D5
  Poynton SK12 . . . . 36 F4
  Runcorn WA7 . . . . 49 F8
  Sandbach CW11 . . . . . . 174 D7
  Sandbach Heath CW11 . 175 E6
  Smallwood CW11 . . . . . 176 F5
  Warmingham CW11 . . . 173 E7
  Warrington WA3 . . . . 10 D5
School Mews SK7 . . . . 35 E7
School Rd
  Ellesmere Port CH65 . . . 70 B5
  Handforth SK9 . . . . 34 D4
  Higher Shurlach CW9 . . 104 D5
  Warrington WA2 . . . . 8 C1
  Winsford, Meadowbank
    CW7 . . . . 126 E5
  Winsford, Wharton CW7 . 127 A2
School Road N CW9 . . . . 104 E6
School Road S CW9 . . . . 104 E6
School Terr WA3 . . . . 3 A8
School Way
  Northwich CW9 . . . . . . 104 A8
  Widnes WA8 . . . . 13 D3
Schooner Cl WA7 . . . . 50 D6
Scilly Cl CH65 . . . . 70 C1
Scope Ho CW1 . . . . 190 E1
Scotch Hall La CW9 . . . . . 53 A3
Scotia Wlk 图 WA3 . . . . 3 F8
Scotland Rd WA1 . . . . 16 B5
Scott Ave
  Crewe CW1 . . . . 190 F4
  Widnes WA8 . . . . 22 F8
Scott Cl
  Macclesfield SK10 . . . . 113 A7
  Rode Heath ST7 . . . . . . 193 E8
  图 Sandbach CW11 . . . 174 D6
Scott Ct WA2 . . . . 16 B6
Scotthope Cl SK11 . . . . . 111 F6
Scotton Ave CH66 . . . . 69 B5
Scott Rd SK10 . . . . 87 A7
Scotts Ind Est WA5 . . . . . . 16 A7

Scott St WA2 . . . . 16 C6
Scott Wlk WA1 . . . . 16 C5
Scroggins La M31 . . . . 11 F4
Sea Bank CW10 . . . . 128 D1
Seabank Rd CH60 . . . . 40 E6
Seabury St WA4 . . . . 17 A3
Seacombe Dr CH66 . . . . . . 69 E3
Seafield Ave CH60 . . . . 40 E6
Seaford Cl WA2 . . . . 24 D1
Seaford Pl WA2 . . . . 8 A4
Seagrave St CW9 . . . . . . 103 F5
Seagull Cl CW1 . . . . 190 F5
Seahill Rd CH1 . . . . 116 F8
Sea La WA7 . . . . 23 D2
SEALAND 116 E6
Sealand Cl WA2 . . . . 8 E1
Sealand Ind Est CH1 . . . . 117 F2
Sealand Rd
  Blacon CH1 . . . . 117 C3
  Chester CH1 . . . . 118 A2
  Sealand CH1, CH5 . . . . 116 D6
Sealand Trad Pk CH1 . . . 117 F2
Sealand Way 图 SK9 . . . . 34 D4
Sea Rd SK7 . . . . 36 A7
Seathwaite Cl WA7 . . . . . . 49 E5
Seaton Cl WA1 . . . . 190 B8
Seaton Pk WA7 . . . . 24 E3
Seaton St CW7 . . . . 127 D1
Seattle Cl 图 WA5 . . . . 15 B7
Sea View CH64 . . . . 66 E4
Seaview Ave CH62 . . . . . . 44 B6
Seaville St CH3 . . . . 237 C3
Secker Ave WA4 . . . . 16 D2
Secker Cl WA4 . . . . 16 D2
Second Ave
  Connah's Quay CH5 . . . . 92 F3
  Crewe CW1 . . . . 190 F2
  Kidsgrove ST7 . . . . 194 E1
  Poynton SK12 . . . . 36 D1
  Runcorn WA7 . . . . 49 F8
  Sandbach CW11 . . . . . 175 A5
Second Dig La CW5 . . . . 219 C8
Second Wood St CW5 . . 204 D5
Sedberg Cl CW4 . . . . 130 A3
Sedbergh Ave WA2 . . . . . 49 E5
Seddon St CW10 . . . . 128 C2
Sedgefield Cl 图 SK10 . . . 87 C4
Sedgefield Rd CH1 . . . . . 118 B2
Sedgeford Cl SK9 . . . . 34 D1
Sedgewick Cres WA5 . . . . 6 E6
Sedgmere Ave CW1 . . . . 190 A8
Sedum Cl CH3 . . . . 142 A6
Sefton Ave
  Congleton CW12 . . . . . 157 A1
  Widnes WA8 . . . . 13 A3
Sefton Dr SK9 . . . . 34 C2
Sefton Rd CW2 . . . . 119 A4
Sefton St WA12 . . . . 1 F3
Selby Cl
  Poynton SK12 . . . . 36 D5
  Runcorn WA7 . . . . 24 F4
Selby Gdns SK8 . . . . 35 C6
Selby Gn CH66 . . . . 69 B5
Selby St WA5 . . . . 15 E5
Selkirk Ave
  Bebington CH62 . . . . . . 43 E4
  Warrington WA4 . . . . 17 A3
Selkirk Cl
  Ellesmere Port CH66 . . . 68 F5
  Macclesfield SK10 . . . . . 86 F2
Selkirk Dr
  Chester CH4 . . . . 141 A7
  Holmes Chapel CW4 . . 130 B2
Selkirk Rd CH4 . . . . 141 A7
Seller St CH1 . . . . 237 C3
Selsdon Ct CH4 . . . . 141 C7
Selsey Cl CW1 . . . . 190 B8
Selworthy Dr
  Cheadle SK8 . . . . 35 C7
  Sutton Lane Ends SK11 . 112 F3
Selwyn Jones Sport Ctr
  WA12 . . . . 2 D5
Selwyn Cl
  Newton-le-Willows WA12 . 2 B5
  Widnes WA8 . . . . 13 E3
Selwyn Dr
  Cheadle SK8 . . . . 35 C7
Semper Cl WA7 . . . . 157 A4
Seneschal Ct WA7 . . . . . . 49 E6
Senna La CW9 . . . . 78 C8
Sennen Cl WA7 . . . . 50 C5
Sens Cl CH1 . . . . 237 A2
Sephton Ave WA3 . . . . 4 E3
Serin Cl WA12 . . . . 2 C3
Serpentine The CH4 . . . . 141 B7
Servite Cl CH65 . . . . 69 F6
Servite Pl CH64 . . . . 66 E5
Sett Cl SK22 . . . . 39 B8
Sevenoaks Cl SK10 . . . . . 87 B2
Seven Row CH64 . . . . 66 E5
Seven Sisters La WA16 . . 82 E5
Severn Cl
  Biddulph ST8 . . . . 179 E1
  Congleton CW12 . . . . . 157 A1
  Macclesfield SK10 . . . . . 86 F2
  Warrington WA8 . . . . 22 F6
  Widnes WA8 . . . . 13 F3
Severn Dr SK7 . . . . 35 C6
Severn Rd
  Culcheth WA3 . . . . 5 A3
  Haydock WA11 . . . . 1 E6
  Macclesfield SK11 . . . . 112 C8
  Runcorn WA7 . . . . 22 F2
Severnvale CH65 . . . . 70 B3
Severn Wlk CW7 . . . . 127 A2
Sewell St 图 WA7 . . . . 23 B2
Sextant Cl WA7 . . . . 50 D6
Sexton Ave WA9 . . . . 1 A2
Seymour Chase WA16 . . . 82 A8
Seymour Cl WA7 . . . . 24 C4

Seymour Dr
  Ellesmere Port CH66 . . . 69 E6
  Warrington WA1 . . . . 17 A8
Seymour Ho 图 SK9 . . . . . 34 E1
Seymour Rd SK8 . . . . 35 A8
Shackleton Cl WA5 . . . . . . 15 D8
Shacklock Cl WA1 . . . . 17 E1
Shade Terr SK6 . . . . 37 F7
Shadewood Cres WA4 . . . 17 B2
Shadewood Rd SK11 . . . . 112 A6
Shadowmoss Rd M22 . . . 33 E8
Shady Brook La CW8 . . . . 77 C1
Shady Gdr ST7 . . . . 193 D4
Shaftesbury Ave
  Chester CH3 . . . . 119 C2
  Warrington WA5 . . . . 14 E2
Shaftesbury Way WA5 . . . 6 F7
Shaftway Cl WA11 . . . . 1 F7
Shakerley Ave WA12 . . . 156 F3
Shakespeare Gr WA7 . . . 104 C7
Shakespeare Dr CW1 . . . 191 A4
Shakespeare Gr WA2 . . . . 8 C2
Shakespeare Rd
  Neston CH64 . . . . 41 E1
  Widnes WA8 . . . . 13 A1
Shalcombe Cl L26 . . . . . . 21 A7
Shallacres CH65 . . . . 69 F7
Shallcross Ave SK23 . . . . 65 F4
Shallcross Cres SK23 . . . 65 E4
Shallcross Hall Barns
  SK23 . . . . 65 F4
Shallcross Mill Rd SK23 . 65 E5
Shallcross Rd SK23 . . . . . 65 F4
Shambles The WA16 . . . . 57 B1
Shanklin Cl WA5 . . . . 14 C6
Shannon Cl
  Chester CH4 . . . . 140 E5
  Willaston CW5 . . . . 205 D6
Shannon Gr WA8 . . . . 12 C3
Shargate Cl SK9 . . . . 34 C1
Sharnbrook Dr CW2 . . . . 189 D4
Sharon Park Cl WA4 . . . . 17 C1
Sharpley St 图 SK10 . . . . 112 C8
Sharp St
  Warrington WA2 . . . . 16 C6
  Widnes WA8 . . . . 23 A8
Sharston Cres WA16 . . . . 57 B1
SHAVINGTON 206 C4
Shavington Ave CW2 . . . 118 F4
Shavington Cty High Sch
  CW2 . . . . 206 A5
Shavington L Ctr CW2 . . 206 A5
Shavington Prim Sch
  CW2 . . . . 206 C4
Shavington Way CW9 . . . 103 F4
Shawbury Gr WA1 . . . . 17 A8
Shaw Cl CH66 . . . . 69 F4
Shaw Dr WA11 . . . . 1 C6
Shawell Ct WA8 . . . . 13 E2
Shaw Entry L35, WA8 . . . 12 A7
Shaw Heath View WA16 . . 57 C2
Shaw's Ave WA2 . . . . 16 C8
Shaws Fold SK9 . . . . 33 F3
Shaw St
  Culcheth WA3 . . . . 5 A3
  Haydock WA11 . . . . 1 E6
  Macclesfield SK11 . . . . 112 C8
  Runcorn WA7 . . . . 22 F2
Shay La
  Ashton Hayes CH3 . . . . 121 F7
  Hampton Heath SY14 . . 200 A1
  Tarvin CH3 . . . . 121 E3
Shay's La CW6 . . . . 124 E4
Sheaf Cl CH3 . . . . 121 C2
Sheardhall Ave SK12 . . . . 38 E5
Sheath St CW9 . . . . 104 A8
Shed La CH3 . . . . 119 B2
Sheepfield Cl CH66 . . . . . 69 C7
Sheerwater Cl WA1 . . . . . 16 F7
Sheffield Cl WA5 . . . . 15 C5
Sheffield Row WA12 . . . . . 7 D8
Sheilings The WA3 . . . . . . 3 F8
Shelagh Ave WA8 . . . . 13 A1
Shelbourne Mews 图
  SK10 . . . . 111 F8
Shelburne Dr CW1 . . . . . 191 C5
Sheldon Ave
  Chester CH3 . . . . 119 B2
  Congleton CW12 . . . . . 157 A1
Sheldon Cl M31 . . . . 11 F3
Sheldon Dr SK11 . . . . 112 B4
Sheldon Pl SK10 . . . . 88 B8
Sheldon Rd
  Hazel Grove SK7 . . . . . . 36 E8
  Poynton SK12 . . . . 37 C2
Sheldrake Gr CH64 . . . . . 66 E5
Shellbrook Gr 图 SK9 . . . 34 D1
Shelley Ave CW9 . . . . 80 A5
Shelley Cl
  Crewe CW1 . . . . 190 F4
  Middlewich CW10 . . . . . 151 E5
  Rode Heath ST7 . . . . . . 193 E8
Shelley Ct 图 CW11 . . . . 174 D6
Shelley Dr CW2 . . . . 189 F1
Shelley Gr WA4 . . . . 16 F4
Shelley Rd
  Blacon CH1 . . . . 117 F6
  Widnes WA8 . . . . 13 A1
SHELL GREEN 13 E1
Shell Green Est WA8 . . . . 23 E8
Shellow La CW11, SK11 . 134 C5
Shellway Rd CH2 . . . . 71 A3
Shelton Cl WA8 . . . . 13 F3

Shenhurst Cl SK9 . . . . 59 E4
Shepcroft La WA4 . . . . 26 C3
Shepherds Fold Dr CW7 . 126 C3
Shepherd's La CH2 . . . . . 118 D5
Shepherds Row WA7 . . . . 23 F2
Shepherds View CW8 . . . 78 B2
Shepley Cl SK7 . . . . 36 D8
Sheppard Cl CW1 . . . . . . 190 D5
Sheppenhall Gr CW5 . . . 217 C1
Sheppenhall La CW5,
  SY13 . . . . 228 D5
Shepsides Cl CH66 . . . . . 69 C3
Shepton Rd CH66 . . . . 69 F2
Sheraton Rd CH3 . . . . . . 143 B5
Sherborne Cl WA7 . . . . . . 24 F3
Sherborne Rd CW1 . . . . . 190 D6
Sherbourne Ave CH4 . . . 141 B5
Sherbourne Cl SK8 . . . . . 35 B6
Sherbourne Rd
  Ellesmere Port CH65 . . . 70 D3
  Macclesfield SK11 . . . . 111 F7
Sherbourne Way WA5 . . . 14 E6
Sherbrooke Rd SK12 . . . . 38 D6
Sherbrook Rise SK9 . . . . . 60 C6
Sheridan Ave WA3 . . . . . . 3 D7
Sheridan Cl CW1 . . . . . . 173 B1
Sheridan Pl WA2 . . . . 8 A5
Sheridan Way WA7 . . . . . . 24 D2
Sheri Dr WA12 . . . . 2 E2
Sheringham Cl CH4 . . . . . 140 E5
Sheringham Dr CW1 . . . 190 B8
Sheringham Rd WA5 . . . . 14 E6
Sherlock Ave WA11 . . . . . . 1 E7
Sherratt Cl
  Congleton CW12 . . . . . 156 E2
  Nantwich CW5 . . . . 204 F4
Sherrington's La CH3 . . . 199 D8
Sherwin St CW2 . . . . 190 C1
Sherwood Cl WA8 . . . . . . 12 C1
Sherwood Cres WA5 . . . . 6 E6
Sherwood Gr WA3 . . . . . . 73 A3
Sherwood Rd
  Blacon CH1 . . . . 117 E5
  Macclesfield SK11 . . . . 112 D5
Shetland Cl
  Warrington WA2 . . . . 8 E4
  Widnes WA8 . . . . 13 E3
Shetland Dr
  Bebington CH62 . . . . . . 43 E8
  Ellesmere Port CH65 . . . 70 C1
Shevington Cl WA8 . . . . . 13 E3
Shevington Wlk WA8 . . . . 13 E3
Shiggins Cl WA5 . . . . 15 D6
Shillingford Cl WA4 . . . . . 26 E5
Shilton Cl CW10 . . . . 151 E5
Shipbrook Rd
  Chester CH2 . . . . 118 F6
  Davenham CW9 . . . . . . 104 A5
Shipgate St CH1 . . . . 237 B1
Shipgate The CH1 . . . . . . 237 B1
Shipley Gdns ST7 . . . . . . 210 D6
Ship St WA6 . . . . 49 C1
Shipton Cl
  Warrington WA5 . . . . 15 B8
  Widnes WA8 . . . . 12 D3
Shirley Ave SK8 . . . . 34 C6
Shirley Dr WA4 . . . . 17 A2
Shirleys Cl SK10 . . . . 87 A6
Shirley Dr SK10 . . . . 87 A6
SHOCKLACH 211 D7
SHOCKLACH GREEN . . . 211 C7
Shocklach Oviatt CE Prim
  Sch SY14 . . . . 211 C7
Shocklach Rd CH2 . . . . . 118 F6
Shones Croft CH64 . . . . . . 67 A5
Shop La
  Congleton CW12 . . . . . 156 E1
  Little Budworth CW6 . . . 124 F2
Shoreham Dr WA5 . . . . . . 15 A3
Shores Green Dr CW9 . . . 79 F5
Shores La CW5 . . . . 203 D7
Short Cl WA12 . . . . 1 E3
Shorthorn Cl CW10 . . . . . 128 D2
Short St
  Haydock WA11 . . . . 1 A2
  图 Macclesfield SK11 . . 112 D8
  Newton-le-Willows WA12 . 1 E3
  Widnes WA8 . . . . 23 A5
Shorwell Cl WA5 . . . . 14 C7
Shot Tower Cl CH1 . . . . . 237 C3
SHOTWICK 93 B4
Shotwick La CH1 . . . . 93 D6
Shotwick Rd CH5 . . . . 92 E7
SHRALEYBROOK 209 A1
Shrewbridge Cres CW5 . 204 E4
Shrewbridge Rd CW5 . . . 204 D4
Shrewsbury Dr ST5 . . . . . 210 E2
Shrewsbury Gdns SK8 . . . 35 C6
Shrewsbury Rd CH3 . . . . . 70 C5
Shrewsbury St 图 CH65 . . 70 C5
Shrewsbury Way CH4 . . . 140 F6
Shropshire Cl
  Middlewich CW10 . . . . . 151 C8
  Warrington WA1 . . . . 17 E6
Shropshire La SY13 . . . . 227 E2
Shropshire St CW3 . . . . . 229 F4
Shuldham Cl WA16 . . . . . . 29 C4
Shurlach Rd CW9 . . . . . . 104 D5
Shutley La CW8 . . . . 77 D6

Shutlingsloe Way SK10 . . 112 A8
Sibbersfield La CH3 . . . . 180 F4
Sibell St CH1 . . . . 237 C3
Siddall St 图 CW7 . . . . . . 104 B8
Siddals Ct CW5 . . . . 204 C5
Siddeley Cl CH4 . . . . 139 C4
Siddeley Dr WA12 . . . . 1 F4
SIDDINGTON 110 A3
Siddington Ave CW4 . . . 104 A4
SIDDINGTON HEATH . . . 109 E1
Siddington Rd
  Handforth SK9 . . . . 34 D5
  Poynton SK12 . . . . 36 F2
Siddorn St CW7 . . . . 126 E1
Side End La SK23 . . . . 64 F3
Side La CW6 . . . . 144 E6
Sidings Cl WA1 . . . . 16 C6
Sidings The SK23 . . . . 65 E8
Sidlaw Cl CH66 . . . . 69 A6
Sidmouth Cl WA5 . . . . 14 E4
Sidmouth Gr SK8 . . . . 34 F2
Sidney Cl CH64 . . . . 41 F1
Sidney Rd CH64 . . . . 41 F1
Siemens Rd M44 . . . . 11 E5
Sienna Cl M44 . . . . 11 E6
Signal Ct CH2 . . . . 118 F2
Silk Heritage Mus ✻
  SK11 . . . . 112 D7
Silk Hill SK23 . . . . 65 F8
Silk Mill
  Macclesfield SK11 . . . . 112 D6
  Poynton SK12 . . . . 36 C4
Silk Mus & Her Ctr ✻ 14
  SK11 . . . . 112 D7
Silk Rd The
  Bollington SK10 . . . . . . 87 E4
  Macclesfield SK10 . . . . 112 E7
Silk St CW12 . . . . 156 C2
Silkstone Cres WA7 . . . . . 50 B7
Silsden Ave WA3 . . . . 4 B8
Silvan Ct SK10 . . . . 87 B1
Silver Ave WA11 . . . . 1 A5
Silverbirch Croft CH4 . . . 139 B3
Silverbirch Way CH66 . . . 94 F8
Silverdale Cl WA8 . . . . . . 103 D7
Silverdale
  Chorlton CW2 . . . . 207 C2
  Frodsham WA6 . . . . 74 C7
  High Lane SK6 . . . . 37 E8
Silverdale Dr SK9 . . . . 60 A4
Silverdale Rd
  Newton-le-Willows WA12 . 2 B4
  Warrington WA4 . . . . 16 B2
Silvergate Ct CW12 . . . . 178 E8
Silver La
  Croft WA3 . . . . 9 F7
  Warrington WA3 . . . . 10 C6
Silvermine Cl 图 ST7 . . . 195 B2
Silvermuir CH1 . . . . 117 C3
Silverne Dr CH65 . . . . 70 A2
Silver St
  Bollington SK10 . . . . 88 B8
  Congleton CW12 . . . . . 156 E2
  Warrington WA2 . . . . 16 B6
Silver Terr CW11 . . . . 175 D6
Silverwood ST7 . . . . 195 B1
Simkin Ave WA4 . . . . 16 F4
Simmonds Cl CW9 . . . . . 103 E3
SIMM'S CROSS 23 B8
Simms Cross Prim Sch
  WA8 . . . . 23 A8
Simonside WA8 . . . . 12 C2
Simons La WA6 . . . . 74 B5
Simonstone Rd CH4 . . . . 139 D4
Simonswood Cl CW10 . . 151 B8
Simpson Cl CH2 . . . . 95 C1
Simpson Ct CW1 . . . . 173 B1
Simpson La SK10 . . . . 63 D7
Simpson Rd CH2 . . . . 95 C1
Simpson's Ct 图 SK11 . . 112 C8
Simpson St CW9 . . . . 59 F6
Simpsons Way CH4 . . . . . 139 B3
Sinclair Ave
  Alsager ST7 . . . . 193 B3
  Warrington WA2 . . . . 8 B2
  Widnes WA8 . . . . 23 A8
Sinderland La
  Partington WA13 . . . . . . 20 B8
  Partington WA13 . . . . . . 20 E8
Singapore Ave M90 . . . . . 33 A8
Singleton Ave CW1 . . . . . 190 C6
Singleton Rd CH65 . . . . . . 69 F4
SINK MOSS 28 D3
Sir John Deane's Coll
  CW9 . . . . 103 F4
Sir Thomas Boteler High Sch
  WA4 . . . . 16 E3
Sir William Stanier Com Sch
  CW1 . . . . 190 C6
Siskin Cl WA12 . . . . 2 C3
Six Acre Gdns WA5 . . . . . 25 A5
Six Acre La WA4 . . . . 25 A5
Sixth Ave CH5 . . . . 92 E1
Skeath Cl WA5 . . . . 175 E6
Skellern St ST7 . . . . 194 D2
SKELLORN GREEN 62 E8
Skellorn Green La SK10 . 62 E8
Skiddaw Cl WA7 . . . . 50 A4
Skip's La CH3 . . . . 142 F7
Skipton Cl
  Hazel Grove SK7 . . . . . . 36 C8
  图 Runcorn WA7 . . . . . . 23 F1
Skipton Dr CH66 . . . . 69 C5

Skye Cl
Ellesmere Port CH65 . . . . . . 70 C1
Widnes WA8 . . . . 13 E3
Skylark Cl SY1 . . . . 189 F7
Sky Lark Rise WA9 . . . . 1 A3
Slacken La ST7 . . . . 194 D2
Slack St SK11 . . . . 112 E6
Slackswood Cl 1 CH65 . . . 70 B7
Slade La
Mobberley WA16 . . . . 58 A7
Nether Alderley SK10 . . . . . 85 E5
Slade St 5 CW9 . . . . 104 B8
Slag La
Golborne WA3 . . . . 3 D8
Haydock WA11 . . . . 1 B7
Slater St
Macclesfield SK11 . . . . 112 C6
Warrington WA4 . . . . 16 D3
Slicks Bsns Ctr CW8 . . . . 78 C2
Slincon Cl ST5 . . . . 210 D1
Slutchers La WA1 . . . . 16 A3
Small Ave WA2 . . . . 8 C2
Smallbrook Wlk CW2 . . . 206 C8
Small Cres WA2 . . . . 8 C2
Small La WA16 . . . . 58 A8
Smallman Rd CW2 . . . . . . 190 C1
SMALLWOOD 176 F5
Smallwood CE Prim Sch
CW11 . . . . 176 F5
Smallwood Cl
4 Middlewich CW10 . . . . 151 C8
Newcastle-under-Lyme
ST5 . . . . 210 D1
Smallwood Forge 1 CW12 . 156 F3
Smallwood Forge WN11 176 D5
Smeaton Wood CW5 . . . . 216 E2
SMETHWICK GREEN . . . 154 F4
Smethwick La CW11,
CW12 . . . . 154 E4
Smith Cl ST7 . . . . 193 B4
Smith Cres WA2 . . . . 16 D8
Smith Dr WA2 . . . . 16 D8
Smithers Cl CW5 . . . . 204 F4
Smithfield Dr/Ffordd
Smithfield LL13 . . . . 196 D8
Smithfield Gn LL13 . . . . . 196 D8
Smithfield La CW11 . . . . . 175 C6
Smithfields CH3 . . . . 166 C2
Smithfield St LL13 . . . . . 196 D8
Smith Gr CW1 . . . . 190 A6
Smithills Cl WA3 . . . . 9 D5
Smith La
Mobberley WA16 . . . . 57 F6
Rainow SK10 . . . . 89 A5
Smith Rd WA8 . . . . 22 F7
Smiths Cotts CH64 . . . . . 66 E5
SMITHS GREEN 109 A2
SMITH'S GREEN 208 B7
Smith's La CW8 . . . . 77 C1
Smith's Lawn SK9 . . . . . . 60 A5
Smith St
Macclesfield SK11 . . . . . . 112 D6
Warrington WA1 . . . . 16 B5
Smith's Terr SK11 . . . . . . 112 E6
Smithy Bank
Acton CW5 . . . . 204 A6
Winsford CW7 . . . . 149 A3
Smithy Brow
Bollington SK10 . . . . 88 C8
Winwick WA3 . . . . .8 F7
Smithy Cl
Cronton WA8 . . . . 12 C5
Neston CH64 . . . . 67 A4
Saughall CH1 . . . . 94 A1
Shocklach SY14 . . . . 211 E7
Smithy Cotts SY14 . . . . . 213 A2
Smithy Ct
Christleton CH3 . . . . 142 E7
Duddon CW6 . . . . 145 C5
6 Ellesmere Port CH66 . . 69 C6
Smithy Dr WA14 . . . . 20 D3
Smithy Gn
Cheadle SK8 . . . . 35 A8
Gatesheath CH3 . . . . 165 E5
Smithy Gr CW11 . . . . 176 A2
SMITHY GREEN
Cheadle Hulme 35 B7
Lower Peover 81 E2
Smithy Hill CH63 . . . . 42 A6
Smithy La
Alsager CW2 . . . . 208 D7
Altrincham WA14 . . . . 20 D3
Barthomley CW2 . . . . 208 A7
Biddulph ST8 . . . . 179 D2
Bosley SK11 . . . . 158 E6
Broxton CH3 . . . . 183 D1
Congleton CW12 . . . . 156 C2
Crewe CW1 . . . . 189 E8
Croft WA3 . . . . 9 A7
Cronton WA8 . . . . 12 C5
Cuddington CW8 . . . . 102 A5
Ellesmere Port CH66 . . . . 69 C6
Great Budworth CW9 . . . . 79 A8
Helsby WA6 . . . . 73 C5
Kingsley WA6 . . . . 75 B2
Little Leigh CW8 . . . . 77 B6
Lostock Gralam CW9 . . . . 80 A2
Malpas SY14 . . . . 213 A2
Mottram St Andrew SK10 . 61 C2
Mouldsworth CH3 . . . . . . 119 F7
Partington M31 . . . . 11 F3
Rainow SK10 . . . . 88 E5
Utkinton CH6 . . . . 146 C6
Weston CW2 . . . . 207 C5
Willaston CH64 . . . . 68 A7

Smithy Pathway CH4 . . . 140 F4
Smithy The CH2 . . . . 118 E8
Smithy Wlk CW11 . . . . . . 174 F3
Smokehall La CW7, CW9 . 126 F6
Smokehall Lane Ind Est
CW7 . . . . 127 A5
Smokey La SY13 . . . . 224 A1
Smokies Way ST8 . . . . . . 179 C1
Smyth Rd WA8 . . . . 13 D2
Snab La
Neston CH64 . . . . 66 F4
Norbury SY13 . . . . 215 B5
Snabwood Cl CH64 . . . . . 66 E5
Snaefell Rise WA4 . . . . . . 26 C7
Snapebrook Gr 6 SK9 . . 34 E1
Snape Hollow CW2 . . . . . 207 F4
Snape La CW2 . . . . 207 E4
Snape Rd
Crewe CW2 . . . . 206 D8
Macclesfield SK10 . . . . . . 87 E2
Snelson La
Chelford, Marthall WA16,
SK9 . . . . 83 D3
Chelford SK11 . . . . 108 E3
Snipe Cl SK12 . . . . 36 A4
Snowberry Cl WA8 . . . . . . 13 E4
Snowberry Cres WA5 . . . . 15 E3
Snowberry Gn 5 CH66 . . 94 F8
Snowberry Wlk M31 . . . . 11 E3
Snowdon Cl
Ellesmere Port CH66 . . . . 69 A6
Warrington WA5 . . . . 14 E6
Snowdon Cres CH4 . . . . 141 A5
Snowdon Dr CW2 . . . . . . 189 D3
Snowdonia Way CW7 . . . 149 B7
Snowdon St CW8 . . . . . . 77 F3
Snowdrop Cl WA7 . . . . . . 49 F4
SNOW HILL 204 D6
Snow Hill SK11 . . . . 112 E6
Solly Cres CW12 . . . . 156 A2
Solvay Rd CW8 . . . . 78 D1
Solway Cl WA2 . . . . .8 F4
Solway Ct CW1 . . . . 191 A2
Solway Gr WA7 . . . . 49 D5
SOMERFORD 154 F7
Somerford Ave CW2 . . . . 190 A3
Somerford Cl CW11 . . . . 175 C8
Somerford Ct 2 CW12 . . 156 F3
Somerford Ho SK12 . . . . . 36 E4
Somerford Rd CH4 . . . . . 139 C4
Somerford Wlk WA8 . . . . 13 E3
Somerley Cl CW1 . . . . 190 B8
Somerset Ave ST7 . . . . . 194 F2
Somerset Cl
Congleton CW12 . . . . 156 D4
Irlam M44 . . . . 11 D6
Somerset Rd CH2 . . . . . . 118 F5
Somerset St CH1 . . . . . . 237 B4
Somerset Way WA1 . . . . . 17 B8
Somerton Cl 6 SK11 . . . 111 F7
Somerton Rd SK11 . . . . . 111 F7
Somerville Cl
Bebington CH63 . . . . 43 B6
High Legh WA16 . . . . 28 B6
Neston CH64 . . . . 66 E5
Somerville Cres CH65 . . . 70 C4
Somerville Rd WA8 . . . . . 22 D8
Somerville St CW2 . . . . . 190 B2
Soot Hill CW8, CW9 . . . . . 78 C3
Sorbus Cl CH2 . . . . 72 C3
Sorbus Dr CW1 . . . . 190 E6
Sorby Rd M44 . . . . 11 F7
Sorrel Cl
Huntington CH3 . . . . 142 A6
Warrington WA2 . . . . 9 C2
Sossmoss La SK10 . . . . . 84 D6
SOUND 217 F5
Sound Common Nature
Reserve ★ CW5 . . . . . . 217 D4
Sound & District Prim Sch
CW5 . . . . 217 F5
SOUND HEATH 217 E5
Sound La
Ravensmoor CW5 . . . . . . 203 E1
Sound CW5 . . . . 217 D7
Souter's La CH1 . . . . 237 B2
South Acre Dr
Handforth SK9 . . . . 34 D3
Macclesfield SK11 . . . . . . 113 A7
Southampton Way WA7 . . 50 E6
South Ave
Chester CH2 . . . . 237 C4
Haslington CW1 . . . . 191 D4
Warrington, Stockton Heath
WA4 . . . . 16 C1
Warrington WA4 . . . . 16 B8
Southbank CW9 . . . . 79 A7
South Bank CH2 . . . . 118 C4
Southbank Ave CW2 . . . . 206 C5
South Bank Cl SK9 . . . . . . 60 B2
South Bank Gr CW12 . . . 156 F2
South Bank Terr WA7 . . . 22 F3
South Cheshire Coll
CW2 . . . . 190 B2
South Cheshire Private Hospl
The CW1 . . . . 172 E1
South Cl
Tarporley CW6 . . . . 146 C2
Wilmslow SK9 . . . . 59 F6
South Crescent Rd CH4 . 237 C1
South Croft CW6 . . . . 185 D6
South Crofts CW5 . . . . . . 204 F5
South Dale WA5 . . . . 14 F5
Southdale Rd WA1 . . . . . . 17 A7
Southdown Cl SK10 . . . . . 87 D4
Southdown Cres SK8 . . . . 34 F8
South Downs WA16 . . . . . 57 C1

South Downs Dr WA14 . . . 31 D8
South Downs Rd WA14 . . . 31 E8
South Dr
Heswall CH60 . . . . 41 A7
Northwich CW9 . . . . 104 D6
Plumley WA16 . . . . 80 F3
Wilmslow SK9 . . . . 60 B6
Southern St WA4 . . . . 16 C1
Southey Cl
8 Sandbach CW11 . . . . . 174 D6
Widnes WA8 . . . . 22 F8
Southfield SK10. . . . . 87 A4
Southfield Cl SK9 . . . . 34 C3
Southfield Rd CH66 . . . . . 69 C7
Southfields WA16 . . . . 57 C3
Southfields Ave WA5 . . . . 14 F6
Southfields Cl CW5 . . . . . 220 A8
South Gr CW5 . . . . 116 A6
South Gr 10 SK9 . . . . 60 A1
South La
Warrington WA5, WA8 . . . . 14 E5
Widnes WA8 . . . . 13 F4
Southlands CW4 . . . . 130 C2
Southlands Ave WA5 . . . . 14 F3
Southlands Ct WA7 . . . . . 48 F8
Southlands Mews 8 WA7 . 22 F1
Southlands Rd CW12 . . . 157 A1
Southlands View CW7 . . . 107 E1
South Lane Entry WA8 . . 13 F5
Southm+an SK9 . . . . 60 A5
South Lodge CW6 . . . . . . 168 D8
South Mead SK12 . . . . 36 B5
South Meadway SK6 . . . . 37 F7
South Oak La SK9 . . . . . . 59 F5
South Par WA7 . . . . 48 D7
South Park Ct Bsns Ctr
SK11 . . . . 112 D6
South Park Dr SK12 . . . . . 36 E5
South Park Rd SK11 . . . . 112 C7
South Pier Rd CH65 . . . . . 70 D7
Southport St WA9 . . . . 1 A3
South Rd
Altrincham, Ashley Heath
WA14 . . . . 31 B8
Ellesmere Port CH65 . . . . 70 C3
Halewood L24 . . . . 21 A4
Runcorn WA7 . . . . 48 D7
Stanlow CH65 . . . . 70 F4
South St
Alderley Edge SK9 . . . . . . 60 A1
Chester CH3 . . . . 119 A1
Congleton CW12 . . . . 156 D3
Crewe CW2 . . . . 190 D2
Mount Pleasant ST7 . . . . 195 B6
3 Widnes WA8 . . . . 23 B8
South Terr 14 SK9 . . . . . . 60 A1
South View
Chester CH4 . . . . 141 D7
Christleton CH3 . . . . 142 F7
Lower Withington SK11 . . 132 A8
New Mills SK22 . . . . 39 B8
South View Ave SK11 . . . 111 D2
South View Cotts ST7 . . . 193 F4
South View La CW7 . . . . . 170 F2
South View Rd CH1 . . . . . 118 B2
Southward Rd WA11 . . . . . 2 A7
Southwark Pl CW7 . . . . . 149 A8
Southway
Middlewich CW10 . . . . . . 128 C5
Runcorn WA7 . . . . 49 F7
Widnes WA8 . . . . 22 D8
South Way CH1 . . . . 117 F4
Southway Ave WA4 . . . . . 26 D7
Southwell Cl WA3 . . . . 3 C8
South West Ave SK10 . . . 87 F6
South Wirral High Sch
CH62 . . . . 43 D4
Southwold Cres WA5 . . . . 14 E5
Southwood Ave WA7 . . . . 24 C2
Southwood Rd CH62 . . . . 43 F8
Southworth Ave WA5 . . . . 15 F8
Southworth La WA2, WA3 . .8 E7
Southworth Rd WA3 . . . . . 9 C4
Sovereign Cl
Golborne WA3 . . . . 3 E7
Northwich CW9 . . . . 104 F6
Runcorn WA7 . . . . 50 A7
Sovereign Way CW3 . . . . . 9 C4
Sovereign Way CH1 . . . . 117 E2
Sowcar Way SK10 . . . . . . 88 C8
Spark Hall Cl WA4 . . . . . . 26 E1
Spark La
Runcorn WA7 . . . . 23 F1
Smallwood CW11 . . . . . . 154 C2
Sparks Cl CH3 . . . . 142 B7
Sparrowbutts Gr ST7 . . . 195 C2
Sparrowhawk Cl WA7 . . . . 50 A7
Sparrow La WA16 . . . . 57 B1
Spath La SK8 . . . . 34 F5
Spath Lane E SK8 . . . . . . 35 B5
Spath Wlk SK8 . . . . 35 B5
Spawell Cl WA3 . . . . 3 E8
Speakman Ave WA12 . . . . 2 C5
Speakman St WA7 . . . . . . 22 F3
Speed's Way CW3 . . . . . . 180 E2
Speedwell Cl
11 Golborne WA3 . . . . . . 3 E8
Heswall CH60 . . . . 41 C8
Huntington CH3 . . . . 142 A5
Speedwell Dr CH60 . . . . . 41 C8
Speke 21 A1
Speke Bvd L24, L26, WA8 . . 21 B5
Speke Ho L24 . . . . 21 A2
Speke Rd WA8 . . . . 22 C6
Spencer Brook SK10 . . . . 86 F6
Spencer Cl
Alsager ST7 . . . . 192 F4

Spencer Cl continued
Wistaston CW2 . . . . 206 A8
Spencer Mews SK10 . . . . 86 F6
Spencer St
Barnton CW8 . . . . 78 B3
Northwich CW8 . . . . 103 E7
SPEN GREEN 177 B6
Spenlow Cl SK12 . . . . 36 E1
Spennymoor Ct WA7 . . . . 49 E7
Spenser Cl WA8 . . . . 12 F1
Spenser Rd CH64 . . . . . . 41 E1
Spey Cl
Middlewich CW10 . . . . . . 128 D3
Winsford CW7 . . . . 126 F2
Spey Dr ST7 . . . . 195 C2
Spike Island ★ WA8 . . . . . 23 A5
Spindle Cl SK12 . . . . 156 E2
Spink La WA16 . . . . 80 A6
Spinnaker Cl WA7 . . . . . . 50 D5
Spinner Cres CW9 . . . . . . 78 D7
Spinners Cl La SK12 . . . . . 36 C4
Spinners Pl WA1 . . . . 16 C6
Spinners Way SK10 . . . . . 87 F7
Spinney Ave
Goostrey CW4 . . . . 107 F1
Widnes WA8 . . . . 12 A1
Spinney Cl
Handforth SK9 . . . . 34 C3
Winsford CW7 . . . . 150 A8
Spinney Dr
Ellesmere Port CH66 . . . . 69 D2
Weston CW2 . . . . 207 B5
Spinney End CH3 . . . . . . 166 A1
Spinney Gdns WA4 . . . . . 27 B4
Spinney La WA16 . . . . 56 E3
Spinney Mead SK10 . . . . 87 E2
Spinney The
Cuddington CW8 . . . . 101 D5
Heswall CH60 . . . . 41 C5
Lawton-gate ST7 . . . . 194 E4
Neston CH64 . . . . 41 D1
Norley WA6 . . . . 100 E5
Sandbach CW11 . . . . 175 C6
Willaston CW5 . . . . 205 D6
Spinney Wlk WA7 . . . . 24 A1
Spires Gdns WA2 . . . . .8 A7
Spital Wlk CH2 . . . . 118 F2
Spodegreen La WA14 . . . 30 C8
Spout La WA16 . . . . 58 B4
Spragg St CW12 . . . . 156 E3
Spring Ave 2 CH66 . . . . . 69 C6
Springbank SK10 . . . . 87 F7
Spring Bank ST7 . . . . 195 B4
Springbank CW7 . . . . 49 B6
Springbank Cres CW7 . . 149 C8
Springbank Gdns
Lymm WA13 . . . . 19 B5
New Mills SK22 . . . . 39 C8
Spring Bank Rd SK22 . . . 39 C8
Springbourne WA6. . . . . . 74 D6
Springburn Gdns WA1 . . 17 F7
Spring Cl ST7 . . . . 193 E8
Springcroft CH64 . . . . 41 C1
Spring Ct 2 WA7 . . . . 23 B2
Springe La CW5 . . . . 203 B5
Springfield Ave
Golborne WA3 . . . . 2 F8
Grappenhall WA4 . . . . 17 B3
Helsby WA6 . . . . 73 B3
Lymm WA13 . . . . 19 B5
Malpas SY14 . . . . 213 C3
Warrington, Padgate WA1 . 17 A8
Springfield Cl CH4 . . . . . 161 A7
Springfield Cres CW8 . . . 77 F3
Springfield Ct/Llys Maes Y
Ffynnon CH4 . . . . 161 A8
Springfield Dr
Talke ST7 . . . . 210 E8
Wilmslow SK9 . . . . 59 D5
Wistaston CW2 . . . . 205 F7
Springfield Pk WA11 . . . . . 1 C7
Springfield Rd
Macclesfield SK11 . . . . . . 111 F8
Malpas SY14 . . . . 213 B3
Mobberley WA16 . . . . 57 F4
Widnes WA8 . . . . 22 A8
Springfields
Cuddington CW8 . . . . 101 D4
Helsby WA6 . . . . 73 B3
Knutsford WA16. . . . . 57 C3
Mickle Trafford CH2 . . . . . 119 E8
Prestbury SK10 . . . . 87 A7
Springfields Sch WA1 . . . 191 A3
Springfields Dr CW12 . . . 156 D3
Springfield St WA1 . . . . . . 16 A5
Spring Gdns
Crewe CW1 . . . . 190 E5
Ellesmere Port CH66 . . . . 69 C6
Macclesfield SK11 . . . . . . 87 D1
Nantwich CW5 . . . . 58 D5
Nantwich CW5 . . . . 204 F5
Springhead Cl ST7 . . . . . 210 D6
Springhead Prim Sch
ST7 . . . . 210 D6
Springhill SK10 . . . . 88 A1
Spring Hill CW6 . . . . 168 C8
Springhill Ave CH62 . . . . 43 D6
Springholm Dr WA4 . . . . . 26 D3
Spring La
Coddington CH3 . . . . 181 E6
Croft WA3 . . . . .9 B6
Lymm WA13 . . . . 19 F3
Spring Mdw CW8 . . . . 78 E1
Springmount WA3 . . . . 3 E7
Spring Mount SK22 . . . . . 39 C8
Spring Rd SK12 . . . . 36 F2
Spring St
Congleton CW12 . . . . 156 E2

Spring St continued
Widnes WA8 . . . . 23 A6
Wilmslow SK9 . . . . 60 A7
Springvale Bsns Ctr
CW11 . . . . 174 D6
Springvale Cl CW11 . . . . . 174 D6
Springvale Ind Pk CW11 174 C6
Springwater Dr CW2 . . . . 207 C1
Springwell Cl CW2 . . . . . 206 C8
Springwood Ave WA8 . . . . 57 C3
Springwood Cl
Blacon CH1 . . . . 117 C4
Macclesfield SK10 . . . . . . 87 D5
Springwood Way SK10 . . 87 D5
Sprink La CW12 . . . . 157 D5
SPROSTON GREEN 129 C2
Sproston Way CW9 . . . . . 103 E4
Spruce Ave CW8 . . . . 102 B3
Spruce Cl
Golborne WA3 . . . . .3 F7
Warrington WA1 . . . . 17 E7
Spruce Gr SK12 . . . . 193 F7
Spuley La SK10 . . . . 63 D2
Spunhill Ave CH66 . . . . . . 69 D2
Spurling Rd WA5 . . . . 14 E3
Spurston Cl WA16 . . . . . . 29 C4
SPURSTOW 185 D6
Spurstow Mews SK8 . . . . 35 C8
Square St SK11 . . . . 112 E6
Square The
Altrincham WA15 . . . . 32 C8
Audlem CW3 . . . . 229 F4
Chester CH1 . . . . 237 C3
Christleton CH3 . . . . 142 E8
Holmes Chapel CW4 . . . . 130 C3
Ince CH2 . . . . 71 F5
6 Lymm WA13 . . . . 18 E3
Woore CW3 . . . . 232 C1
Squires Ave WA8 . . . . 23 A8
Squires Cl WA11 . . . . 1 B6
Squirrel Cl CW8 . . . . 103 C7
Squirrels Chase SK10 . . . 86 F5
Squirrel's Jump SK9 . . . . 60 C1
Stable La
Mouldsworth CH3 . . . . . . 99 A3
Utkinton CW6 . . . . 123 F1
Stables The
Bostock Green CW10. . . . 127 D5
Brereton Heath CW12 . . . 155 A7
Guilden Sutton CH3 . . . . . 119 F5
Lawton-gate ST7 . . . . 194 C4
Stablings The SK9 . . . . . . 60 A5
Stadium Way CH1 . . . . . . 118 B3
Stadmorslow La ST7 . . . 195 F4
Stafford Ave CH65 . . . . . . 95 B8
Stafford Cl SK10 . . . . 86 F2
Stafford Gdns CH65 . . . . . 70 B5
Stafford Rd WA4 . . . . 16 C2
Stafford St
Audlem CW3 . . . . 230 A4
Crewe CW1 . . . . 190 C5
Stafford Wlk SK10 . . . . . . 86 F2
Stag La WA13 . . . . 19 C4
Stage La WA13 . . . . 19 C4
Stainer Cl WA12 . . . . 2 B5
Staines Cl WA4 . . . . 26 E5
Stainforth Cl WA3 . . . . .3 B8
Stainmore Cl WA3 . . . . . . 10 B6
Staithes Rd M22 . . . . 33 D8
Stalbridge Dr WA7 . . . . . . 24 F4
Stalbridge Rd CW2 . . . . . 190 C2
Stallard Way CW10 . . . . . 151 C8
Stalmine Ave SK8 . . . . . . 34 B8
Stamford Ave CW2 . . . . . 190 C3
Stamford Cl
Chester CH3 . . . . 119 C2
Lymm WA13 . . . . 18 F3
Macclesfield SK11 . . . . . . 112 C5
Stamford La CH3 . . . . 120 A1
Stamford Rd
Alderley Edge SK9 . . . . . . 60 B1
Blacon CH1 . . . . 117 C6
Handforth SK9 . . . . 34 A1
Little Bollington WA14 . . . 20 B2
Macclesfield SK11 . . . . . . 112 C4
Stamford St CH65 . . . . . . 70 A5
Stamp Ave CW1 . . . . 190 D6
Stamp Cl CW1 . . . . 190 D6
Stanbridge Cl WA5 . . . . . 15 B6
Standford Dr CW9 . . . . . . 104 A5
Standinwood Rd 2 CH65 . 70 B7
Standish St WA8 . . . . 22 D8
Standon Ave ST5 . . . . . . 210 C2
Stanford Cl 2 CW9 . . . . . 103 F5
Stanhope Ave CW1 . . . . . 190 E3
Stanhope St SK9 . . . . 60 D8
Stanier Cl
Crewe CW1 . . . . 191 A4
Sutton Lane Ends SK11 . . 112 D2
Stanlaw Rd CH65 . . . . 70 C4
Stanley Ave
Warrington, Stockton Heath
WA4 . . . . 16 F2
Warrington WA5 . . . . 14 D7
STANLEY BANK 1 A7
Stanley Bank Rd WA11 . . . 1 A7
Stanley Bank Way WA11. . 1 A7
Stanley & Brocklehurst Ct 5
SK10 . . . . 87 A2
Stanley Cl
Hartford CW8 . . . . 103 A4
Widnes WA8 . . . . 13 C2
Stanley Ct ST7 . . . . 193 C4
Stanley Dr
Gatley SK8, SK9 . . . . 34 D6
Newcastle-under-Lyme
ST5 . . . . 210 D1

Stanley Gr CW9 . . . . 79 E2
STANLEY GREEN 34 E6
Stanley Green Ind Est
   SK8 . . . . 34 E5
Stanley Green Ret Pk SK8 34 F6
Stanley Hall La SK12 . . . 38 C6
Stanley La CH62 . . . . . . 43 A8
Stanley Park Ct CH4 . . . 140 E5
Stanley Park Dr CH4 . . . 140 E5
Stanley Pl
   Chester CH1 . . . . 237 A2
   Warrington WA4 . . . . . 16 F2
Stanley Place Mews
   CH1 . . . . 237 A2
Stanley Rd
   Biddulph ST8 . . . . . . 179 C2
   Ellesmere Port CH65 . . 70 C7
   Handforth SK8, SK9 . . 34 E6
   Knutsford WA16 . . . . . 56 F2
Stanley Road Ind Est
   WA16 . . . . 57 A1
Stanley St
   Chester CH1 . . . . 237 A2
   2 Crewe CW1 . . . . . . 190 C4
   7 Macclesfield SK11 . . 112 D8
   Newton-le-Willows WA12 . 2 A3
   Northwich CW9 . . . . . 104 C8
   Runcorn WA7 . . . . 23 B3
   Warrington WA1 . . . . . 16 B4
Stanley Villas 7 WA7 . . . 22 F1
STANLOW 71 B5
Stanlow Abbey Bsns Ctr
   CH65 . . . . 70 D2
Stanlow & Thornton Sta
   CH2 . . . . 71 D5
Stanmore Rd WA7 . . . . . 23 D2
Stannage La CH3 . . . . . 180 F5
Stanner Cl WA5 . . . . 7 D2
Stannerhouse La CW11 . 175 E4
Stanneybrook Cl WA6 . . 101 A6
Stanney Cl
   Bebington CH62 . . . . . 43 E3
   Neston CH64 . . . . 66 E7
Stanney La
   Ellesmere Port CH65 . . 70 C3
   Stoak CH2 . . . . 70 E1
Stanneylands Cl SK9 . . . 34 C2
Stanneylands Dr SK9 . . . 34 B2
Stanneylands Rd SK9 . . . 34 B2
Stanney Mill Ind Est CH2 70 F3
Stanney Mill La CH2 . . . 70 F2
Stanney Oaks L Ctr CH65 70 D1
Stanney Ten Ind Est CH2 70 F1
Stanney Woods Ave CH65 70 C1
Stanney Woods Nature
   Reserve* CH65 . . . . . . 70 B1
Stansfield Ave WA1 . . . . 16 F6
Stansfield Dr WA4 . . . . . 27 A7
Stanstead Ave WA5 . . . . 14 F3
Stanthorne Ave WA7 . . . 190 A3
Stanthorne Park Mews
   CW10 . . . . 150 E6
Stanton Cl WA11 . . . . . . 1 C6
Stanton Ct CH64 . . . . . . 66 E8
Stanton Dr CH2 . . . . 118 D5
Stanton Rd WA4 . . . . . . 17 D3
Stanyer Ct CW5 . . . . . . 204 D5
STAPELEY 219 D8
Stapeley Broad Lane Prim
   Sch CW5 . . . . 205 A1
Stapeley Cl CW9 . . . . . . 103 E4
Stapeley Ct CW1 . . . . . . 190 B5
Stapeley Gdns L26 . . . . . 21 A6
Stapeley Terr CW5 . . . . . 205 A4
Stapeley Water Gdns*
   CW5 . . . . 205 A3
Stapleford Ct CH66 . . . . 69 F8
Stapleton Ave WA2 . . . . 16 D8
Stapleton Cl WA5 . . . . . . 74 C8
Stapleton Rd SK10 . . . . . 87 B2
Stapleton Way WA8 . . . . 22 B5
Stapley Cl WA7 . . . . 22 F1
Starbeck Dr CH66 . . . . . 69 B5
Starkey Gr WA4 . . . . 16 F4
Star La
   Lymm WA13 . . . . 18 C4
   Macclesfield SK11 . . . . 112 D4
Starling Cl
   Farndon CH3 . . . . 180 F1
   Kidsgrove ST7 . . . . . . 195 D3
   Runcorn WA7 . . . . 50 D7
Start La SK23 . . . . 65 E6
STATHAM 18 C4
Statham Ave
   Lymm WA13 . . . . 18 D3
   Warrington WA2 . . . . . . 8 C2
Statham Cl WA13 . . . . . 18 D3
Statham Dr WA13 . . . . . 18 D3
Statham La WA13 . . . . . 18 A5
Statham Prim Sch WA13 . 18 C4
Statham St SK11 . . . . . . 112 D7
Station App/Lon yr Orsaf
   CH1 . . . . 116 F7
Station Ave
   Ellesmere Port CH66 . . 69 C7
   Helsby WA6 . . . . 73 B4
Station Cl CH64 . . . . 66 F7
Station Cotts
   Mouldsworth CH3 . . . . 99 A2
   Saughall CH1 . . . . 116 F7
Station Gn CH66 . . . . . . 69 C7
Station Hill CW8 . . . . . . 76 F2
Station La
   Dunham-on-the-Hill CH3 . 97 D3
   Guilden Sutton CH2, CH3 . 119 F7
   Rushton Spencer SK11 . 159 B2

Station Rd
   Adderley TF9 . . . . 235 A5
   Alsager ST7 . . . . 193 D3
   Astbury ST7, CW12 . . . 178 B1
   Aston WA7 . . . . 50 B4
   Backford CH1 . . . . 95 A3
   Biddulph ST8 . . . . 179 C1
   Bosley CW12 . . . . 135 A2
   Burton CH64 . . . . 67 B1
   Calveley CW6 . . . . 169 E2
   Chelford SK11 . . . . . . 84 A2
   Ellesmere Port CH65 . . 70 C6
   Crowton CW8 . . . . 76 D2
   Delamere CW8 . . . . . . 123 D8
   Ellesmere Port CH65 . . 70 C6
   Ellesmere Port, Little Sutton
      CH66 . . . . 69 C6
   Elton CH2 . . . . 72 A5
   Furness Vale SK23 . . . . 39 D4
   Goostrey CW4 . . . . . . 131 A8
   Handforth SK9 . . . . . . 34 D3
   Haydock WA11 . . . . . . 1 C6
   Heswall CH60 . . . . 40 F6
   Holmes Chapel CW4 . . 130 D2
   Irlam M44 . . . . 11 E7
   Kidsgrove ST7 . . . . . . 194 F1
   Lostock Gralam CW9 . . 80 A2
   Mobberley WA16 . . . . . 57 F7
   Mouldsworth CH3 . . . . 99 A2
   Mow Cop ST7 . . . . 195 C8
   Nantwich CW5 . . . . . . 204 E5
   Neston CH64 . . . . 66 F7
   Neston, Parkgate CH64 . 66 C8
   Newchapel ST7 . . . . . . 195 E2
   New Mills SK22 . . . . . . 39 B7
   Northwich CW9 . . . . . . 79 B1
   Partington WA14 . . . . . 20 B5
   Runcorn WA7 . . . . 22 F2
   Sandbach CW11 . . . . . 174 D7
   Sandycroft CH5 . . . . . . 116 A2
   Scholar Green ST7 . . . . 194 F7
   Styal SK9 . . . . 34 A4
   Warrington, Fearnhead WA2 9 A2
   Warrington, Great Sankey
      WA5 . . . . 14 F6
   Warrington, Penketh WA5 . 14 E3
   Warrington WA4 . . . . . 16 E2
   Weaverham CW8 . . . . . 77 A1
   Wilmslow SK9 . . . . . . 60 B7
   Winsford CW7 . . . . . . 127 A1
   Worleston CW5 . . . . . . 188 E6
   Wrenbury CW5 . . . . . . 216 F3
Station Road Ind Est WA4 16 F2
Station Road N WA2 . . . . 9 A1
Station Road S WA2 . . . . 9 A1
Station St SK10 . . . . 87 D1
Station Terr WA7 . . . . . . 50 B4
Station View
   Chester CH2 . . . . 118 F2
   Hampton Heath SY14 . . 213 D7
   Nantwich CW5 . . . . . . 204 E4
   Sandbach CW11 . . . . . 174 D8
Station Yard Trad Est
   CW4 . . . . 130 D3
Staveley Dr CW7 . . . . . . 126 D2
Steadings Rise WA16 . . . 56 D6
Steadings The CH3 . . . . 120 A4
Steam Mill Bsns Ctr CH1 237 C3
Steam Mill St CH1, CH3 . 237 C3
Stearns Cl CH1 . . . . 118 A5
Stearns Ho CH1 . . . . . . 118 A5
Steele Rd CW10 . . . . . . 151 D5
Steele St CH1 . . . . 237 B2
Steel St WA1 . . . . 16 D7
Steeple Ct CH4 . . . . 66 E7
Steeple St SK10 . . . . . . 87 E1
Stein Ave WA3 . . . . 3 E8
Stendall Rd CH1 . . . . . . 118 A3
Stephens Ct WA7 . . . . . . 23 C2
Stephens Gdns CH66 . . . 69 B6
Stephen's Gr WA7 . . . . . 73 B2
Stephenson Dr CW1 . . . 191 A4
Stephenson Rd WA12 . . . 2 D2
Stephenson Wlk CW7 . . . 149 A8
Stephen St WA1 . . . . . . 16 D7
Stephens Terr CH66 . . . . 69 B6
Stephens Way ST7 . . . . . 209 F2
Sterling Cl 1 CW9 . . . . . 103 F5
Sterne Cl CW11 . . . . . . 174 D6
Stetchworth Rd WA4 . . . 16 B1
Steuber Dr M44 . . . . 11 F5
Stevenage Cl SK11 . . . . 112 B7
Stevenage Dr SK11 . . . . 112 B7
Steven Ct CH3 . . . . 237 C3
Stevens Rd CH60 . . . . . . 41 C7
Stevens St SK9 . . . . 60 A1
Steventon WA7 . . . . 24 E4
Steward's Ave WA8 . . . . 22 F8
Stewart St CW7 . . . . . . 190 A3
Stile End CH2 . . . . 119 F8
Stiles The CW8 . . . . 101 D5
Stiperstones Cl CH66 . . . 69 A6
Stirling Cl
   Chester CH4 . . . . 119 A2
   Congleton CW12 . . . . . 156 C3
   Macclesfield SK10 . . . . 86 F2
   Warrington WA1 . . . . . 16 F7
   Winsford CW7 . . . . . . 127 A3
Stirling Ct
   Ellesmere Port CH65 . . 70 D3
   Holmes Chapel CW4 . . 130 B2
Stirrup Cl WA2 . . . . 9 A3
Stirrup Field WA3 . . . . . . 3 A8
STOAK 96 A7
Stoak Lodge CH65 . . . . . 70 C4
Stobart Stad Halton (Widnes
   Vikings fc) WA8 . . . . . . 22 F8
Stockdale Cres WA5 . . . . 14 E7

Stockdale Ct WA5 . . . . . 14 E7
Stockdale Dr WA5 . . . . . 14 E7
Stockham Cl WA7 . . . . . 50 A8
Stockham La WA7 . . . . . 50 B7
Stock La CW2, CW5 . . . . 206 B2
Stockley Farm* CW9 . . . 54 E7
Stockley La WA4 . . . . . . 52 F7
Stockport Rd WA4 . . . . . 17 E3
Stocks Ave 4 CH3 . . . . . 119 A1
Stocks Ct The WA3 . . . . . 3 D8
Stocks Hill CW7 . . . . . . 149 F7
Stocks La
   Chester CH3 . . . . 119 A1
   Ollerton WA16 . . . . . . 82 E1
   Rainow SK10 . . . . 88 E5
   Warrington WA5 . . . . . 14 D5
Stockswell Rd WA8 . . . . 12 A3
STOCKTON HEATH 16 D1
Stockton Heath Prim Sch 7
   WA4 . . . . 16 C1
Stockton La WA4 . . . . . . 16 F1
Stockton Rd SK10 . . . . . 59 F4
Stockton View WA4 . . . . 16 B2
Stockwell Farm Ct WA8 . 12 E4
Stoke Abbott Cl SK7 . . . 35 F7
Stoke Cl CH62 . . . . 43 E3
Stoke Gdns CH65 . . . . . 70 C4
Stokehall La CW5 . . . . . 187 E6
Stoke Rd CH65 . . . . 70 E3
Stokes St WA3 . . . . 9 E5
Stoke Wlk CH65 . . . . . . 70 C4
Stoneacre Gdns WA4 . . . 26 C4
Stonebank Dr CH64 . . . . 67 A6
Stone Bank Rd ST7 . . . . 195 B1
Stone Barn La WA7 . . . . 49 F6
Stonebridge Rd CW5 . . . 204 E3
Stone Chair La ST7 . . . . 194 E7
Stonechat Cl
   10 Golborne WA3 . . . . . 3 E8
   Runcorn WA7 . . . . 49 E5
Stone Cotts CW12 . . . . . 157 E2
Stone Croft
   Chester CH3 . . . . 142 B7
   Kingsmead CW9 . . . . . 103 F5
Stonecrop Cl
   Runcorn WA7 . . . . 49 F4
   Warrington WA3 . . . . . . 9 C4
Stone Cross Dr WA8 . . . . 12 E5
Stone Cross Lane N WA3 . 3 C7
Stone Cross Lane S WA3 . 3 C6
Stone Cross Pk WA3 . . . . 3 B7
Stonehaven Dr WA2 . . . . 9 A3
Stone Hayes Lane Lane
   CW8 . . . . 77 F4
Stoneheads SK23 . . . . . 65 D8
Stoneheads Rise SK23 . . 65 D8
Stone Heyes La CW8, CW9 77 F5
Stonehill Cl WA4 . . . . . . 26 D4
Stonehills La WA7 . . . . . 23 C2
Stonehills La WA7 . . . . . 23 C2
Stone House La CW6 . . . 184 E4
Stonelea WA7 . . . . 24 B2
Stoneleigh Cl SK10 . . . . 87 C2
Stoneleigh La WA4 . . . . . 17 D1
Stoneleigh Gdns WA4 . . 17 D1
Stoneley Ave CW1 . . . . . 190 D7
Stoneley Rd CW1 . . . . . 190 D8
STONELEY GREEN 203 D4
Stone Mead Ave WA15 . . 32 C7
Stone Pit La WA3 . . . . . . 3 F2
Stone Pl CH2 . . . . 118 F3
Stones Manor La CW8 . . 78 B8
Stoneway Ct 1 CH60 . . . 40 F8
Stoneyfold La SK11 . . . . 113 A6
Stoneyford La CW8 . . . . 101 C2
Stoney Holt WA7 . . . . . . 50 C8
Stoney La
   Delamere CW6 . . . . . . 123 C6
   Wilmslow SK9 . . . . . . 59 F5
Stoneyland Dr SK22 . . . . 39 B8
Stonyhurst Cres WA3 . . . 4 D5
Stony La CW12 . . . . 156 C1
Stopsley Cl CW12 . . . . . 155 F4
Stores Rd M90 . . . . 33 A6
Stor St SK10 . . . . 88 B8
Stour Ct CH65 . . . . 70 B7
STOWFORD 207 C8
Stradbroke Cl WA3 . . . . . 4 A7
Straight Length WA4 . . . 73 E7
Straight Mile CH4 . . . . . 162 F5
Straker Ave CH65 . . . . . 69 F6
Stratford Gdns CH1 . . . . 117 E4
Stratford Rd
   Blacon CH1 . . . . 117 E4
   Neston CH64 . . . . 66 D6
Stratford Sq SK8 . . . . . . 34 C7
Stratford Way SK11 . . . . 112 C5
Strathaven Ave CW7 . . . 205 E8
Strathearn Rd CH60 . . . . 40 F7
Strathmore Ct CW4 . . . . 130 B2
Stratton Cl WA7 . . . . 50 B6
Stratton Dr WA8 . . . . . . 12 E3
Stratton Rd WA5 . . . . . . 15 B5
Strawberry Cl WA3 . . . . . 9 C4
Strawberry Dr CH66 . . . . 95 A8
Strawberry Fields CH3 . . 142 B7
Strawberry Gn CH66 . . . 95 A8
Strawberry La
   Acton Bridge CW8 . . . . 76 F3
   Mobberley WA16 . . . . . 58 D1
   Wilmslow SK9 . . . . . . 59 E6
Strawberry Pk CH66 . . . . 95 A8
Street Hey La CH64 . . . . 43 B1
Street La
   Lower Whitley WA4 . . . . 52 C3
   Rode Heath ST7 . . . . . 176 F2
   Skellorn Green SK10 . . . 62 D8

Street The
   Mickle Trafford CH2 . . . 119 D8
   Whaley Bridge SK10, SK17 . 90 C5
STRETTON
   Farndon 197 F6
   Warrington 26 E2
Stretton Ave WA3 . . . . . . 3 E7
Stretton Cl CH62 . . . . . . 43 E3
Stretton Hall Mews WA4 . 52 E8
Stretton Rd WA4 . . . . . . 26 E2
Stretton Watermill*
   SY14 . . . . 198 A7
Stretton Way 3 SK9 . . . . 34 D5
Stretton Wlk CW9 . . . . . 103 F4
Strickland Cl WA4 . . . . . 27 A7
Strines Rd SK6 . . . . 38 D8
Stringer Ave CW11 . . . . . 175 C5
Stringer Cres WA4 . . . . . 16 F4
Stringer's La LL12, CH4 . . 161 B4
Stroma Ave CH65 . . . . . 95 B8
Stromness Cl WA2 . . . . . 9 B3
Stuart Cl
   Chester CH3 . . . . 119 C3
   Winsford CW7 . . . . . . 149 C5
Stuart Ct SK10 . . . . 87 B2
Stuart Dr WA4 . . . . 16 F2
Stuart Pl CH1 . . . . 237 B3
Stuart Rd WA7 . . . . 24 C4
Stubbs La
   Lostock Gralam CW9 . . 80 A2
   Mobberley WA16 . . . . . 58 E4
Stubbs Pl CH1 . . . . 117 E3
Stubbs Terr 17 SK11 . . . . 112 E7
Stubby La SK10 . . . . 84 E2
STUD GREEN 152 C1
Stud Green Ind Pk CW11 152 C1
Sturgess St WA12 . . . . . 1 F3
STYAL 34 A3
Styal Cl 4 CW9 . . . . 103 F4
Styal Cross SK9 . . . . 33 E4
Styal Ctry Pk* SK9 . . . . . 33 E3
Styal Gn SK9 . . . . 33 F3
STYAL GREEN 34 A3
Styal Prim Sch SK9 . . . . 33 E4
Styal Rd
   Wilmslow SK9 . . . . . . 60 B8
   Wythenshawe M22 . . . . 33 F7
   Styal Sta SK9 . . . . . . 34 A4
Styal View SK9 . . . . 34 B2
Styperson Way SK12 . . . 36 E3
Sudbrook Cl WA3 . . . . . . 3 E8
Sudbury Dr SK8 . . . . . . 34 C8
Sudbury Rd SK7 . . . . . . 36 E8
Sudlow La
   Knutsford WA16 . . . . . 56 D1
   Plumley WA16 . . . . . . 81 C7
Suez St
   Newton-le-Willows WA12 . 2 B3
   Warrington WA1 . . . . . 16 B5
Suffolk Ave CH65 . . . . . . 69 F5
Suffolk Cl
   Congleton CW12 . . . . . 156 D4
   Macclesfield SK10 . . . . 86 F1
   Warrington WA11 . . . . . 17 E6
Suffolk Dr SK9 . . . . 34 C1
Suffolk Ho 3 CH1 . . . . . 237 C3
Suffolk Pl WA8 . . . . 22 C7
Suffolk St WA7 . . . . 22 F3
Sugar La
   Bollington SK10 . . . . . 63 A3
   Frodsham WA6 . . . . . . 99 A5
   Manley WA6 . . . . 98 E5
   Rainow SK10 . . . . 88 D5
Sugar Pit La WA16 . . . . . 56 E3
Sugar St SK11 . . . . 159 C2
Sulby Ave WA4 . . . . 16 B3
Sulgrave Ave SK12 . . . . 36 F4
Summer Cl 4 WA7 . . . . . 23 B2
Summercroft Cl WA3 . . . 3 A7
Summer Dr CW1 . . . . . . 175 C6
Summerfield ST7 . . . . . . 195 B1
Summerfield Ave WA5 . . . 7 F2
Summerfield Cl CH4 . . . . 139 A3
Summerfield Dr CW9 . . . 126 F8
Summerfield Ho CH3 . . . 119 F5
Summerfield Rd SK9 . . . . 60 A5
Summerfield Rd
   Guilden Sutton CH3 . . . 119 F5
   Mobberley WA16 . . . . . 57 F4
Summerfields WA16 . . . . 57 C3
Summerfields Ctr 10 SK9 34 D1
Summerhill Dr ST5 . . . . . 210 D1
Summerhill Rd SK10 . . . . 86 F4
Summer La
   Daresbury WA4 . . . . . . 51 D7
   Hatton WA4 . . . . 25 F1
   Runcorn WA7 . . . . 23 F1
Summerlea SK8 . . . . 35 B8
Summerlea Cl SK10 . . . . 87 D1
Summers Cl WA8 . . . . . . 22 A7
Summers Way WA16 . . . . 82 A7
Summertrees Rd CH66 . . 69 E3
Summerville Gdns WA4 . . 16 F1
Summerville Wlk WA5 . . . 15 C7
Summit Cl WA4 . . . . 26 E1
Sumner Rd CH1 . . . . . . 117 E4
Sumner St WA11 . . . . . . 1 A6
Sumpter Pathway CH2 . . 118 F3
Sunart Cl CW2 . . . . 206 B6
Sunbank La WA15 . . . . . 32 E6
Sunbank Rd CH66 . . . . . 95 C8
Sunbeam St WA12 . . . . . 2 C3
Sunbury Cl SK9 . . . . 34 E2
Sunbury Cres 3 CH4 . . . 140 F6
Sunbury Gdns WA4 . . . . 26 E7
Suncroft Cl WA1 . . . . . . 17 E7
Suncroft Rd CH60 . . . . . 41 C7
Sundale Dr CW2 . . . . . . 189 D4

Sunderland St SK11 . . . . 112 D7
Sundial Ho WA3 . . . . 4 F3
Sundown Cl SK22 . . . . . 39 A8
Sunfield Cl CH66 . . . . . . 69 D3
Sunflower Cl WA9 . . . . . . 6 A7
Sunningdale Ave WA8 . . 12 B1
Sunningdale Cl
   Burtonwood WA5 . . . . . 6 F6
   Northwich CW9 . . . . . . 104 E7
   Winsford CW7 . . . . . . 126 A2
Sunningdale Dr
   Bebington CH63 . . . . . 43 B6
   Bramhall SK7 . . . . 36 A7
Sunningdale Rd
   Cheadle SK8 . . . . 35 A7
   Macclesfield SK11 . . . . 112 A6
Sunningdale Way CH64 . 66 E4
Sunninghey Ct SK9 . . . . 59 F2
Sunnybank SK9 . . . . 60 B6
Sunny Bank SK11 . . . . . 112 D5
Sunny Bank Cl WA12 . . . 2 C4
Sunny Bank SK11 . . . . . 112 D5
Sunny Bank Cotts
   Ashton Hayes CH3 . . . . 121 E7
   Warrington WA8 . . . . . 14 A4
Sunnybank Dr SK9 . . . . . 59 D4
Sunny Bank Rd CW1, CW2 189 B1
Sunny Bank Rd WA4 . . . . 31 C8
Sunny Lea Mews SK9 . . . 60 A6
Sunnymill Dr CW11 . . . . 175 A6
Sunnyside
   Alsager ST7 . . . . 193 A4
   4 Ellesmere Port CH65 . 70 C6
   Malpas SY14 . . . . 212 F2
Sunnyside La WA7 . . . . . 24 E4
Sunnyside Wlk CW11 . . . 154 B1
Sunset Bsns Ctr WA8 . . . 23 A5
Sunset Bvd WA8 . . . . . . 15 B6
Sunset Cotts CH64 . . . . 67 A4
Surrey Dr CW12 . . . . . . 156 E5
Surrey Rd
   Chester CH2 . . . . 119 A5
   Kidsgrove ST7 . . . . . . 195 A2
   Warren SK11 . . . . 112 A4
Surrey St
   Crewe CW1 . . . . 190 E4
   7 Runcorn WA7 . . . . . 23 A2
   Warrington WA4 . . . . . 16 D5
Surridge WA16 . . . . 29 C5
Susan Dr WA5 . . . . 14 D5
Susan St WA8 . . . . 13 C2
Sussex Ave SK11 . . . . . . 112 A5
Sussex Dr ST7 . . . . 194 F2
Sussex Pl CW12 . . . . . . 156 E5
Sussex Rd
   Chester CH2 . . . . 118 F4
   Irlam M44 . . . . 11 C6
   Partington M31 . . . . . . 11 E3
   Sussex St WA8 . . . . . . 13 D1
   Sussex Way CH2 . . . . . 118 F4
Sutch La WA13 . . . . 19 A3
Sutherland Ct 5 WA7 . . . 23 B2
Sutherland Dr
   Bebington CH62 . . . . . 43 D4
   Macclesfield SK10 . . . . 87 A1
Sutherland Way CH3 . . . 119 B3
Sutton Ave
   Culcheth WA3 . . . . 4 F4
   Neston CH64 . . . . 66 E6
Sutton Cl
   Bebington CH62 . . . . . 43 E3
   Higher Wincham CW9 . . 79 F6
   Macclesfield SK11 . . . . 112 D5
   Mickle Trafford CH2 . . . 119 F8
   Nantwich CW5 . . . . . . 204 C5
Sutton Cswy WA6, WA7 . . 49 E2
Sutton Dr CH2 . . . . 118 E5
Sutton Field CW8 . . . . . 126 A7
SUTTON GREEN 69 C3
Sutton Green Prim Sch
   CH66 . . . . 69 C5
Sutton Hall Dr CH66 . . . . 69 A6
Sutton Hall Gdns CH66 . . 69 A6
Sutton La CW10 . . . . . . 151 C7
SUTTON LANE ENDS . . . 112 E2
Sutton Quays Bsns Pk
   WA7 . . . . 49 E3
Sutton Rd
   Alderley Edge SK9 . . . . 59 F2
   Poynton SK12 . . . . 37 A2
Sutton's La 4 WA8 . . . . . 23 B7
Sutton St
   Runcorn WA7 . . . . 23 B2
   Warrington WA1 . . . . . 16 C4
Sutton Way
   1 Ellesmere Port CH65 . 69 E4
   1 Handforth SK9 . . . . . 34 E5
SUTTON WEAVER 50 B3
Swale Cl SK9 . . . . 34 E2
Swaledale Ave CW12 . . . 157 A5
Swaledale Cl
   Bebington CH62 . . . . . 43 E5
   Warrington WA5 . . . . . 14 F7
Swale Rd CH65 . . . . 70 A7
Swallow Cl
   1 Kidsgrove ST7 . . . . . 195 B2
   Northwich CW8 . . . . . . 113 A7
   Warrington WA3 . . . . . . 9 F4
Swallow Ct
   Handforth SK9 . . . . . . 34 B1
   Winsford CW7 . . . . . . 149 D5
Swallow Dr
   Alsager ST7 . . . . 193 B3
   Kelsall CW6 . . . . 122 D5

Swallow Dr continued
Sandbach CW11 . . . . 175 A8
Swallowfield Cl CW2 . . . . . . 206 A8
Swallowfield Gdns WA4 . . 26 F5
Swallowfields CH3 . . . . 180 E2
Swallowmore View ST7 . . 210 C1
Swallow Rd ST7 . . . . 195 F1
Swanage Cl WA4 . . . . 16 E2
Swanage Ct 6 CW7 . . . . . . 149 D6
Swan Ave WA9 . . . . 1 A2
SWANBACH 229 E1
Swan Bank
Congleton CW12 . . . . 156 D2
Talke ST7 . . . . 210 D7
Swan Cl
Bunbury CW6 . . . . 185 E8
Crowton CW8 . . . . 101 E2
Swan Farm La CW3 . . . . . . 232 B1
Swan Gr WA16 . . . . 106 D7
Swan Ho ST7 . . . . 210 D7
Swan La
Bunbury CW6 . . . . 185 E8
Cheadle SK8 . . . . 35 B8
SWANLEY 203 C5
Swanley La CW5 . . . . 203 D4
Swanlow Ave CW7 . . . . 149 D5
Swanlow Dr CW7 . . . . 149 D6
Swanlow La CW7 . . . . 149 D5
Swan Rd WA12 . . . . 1 E4
Swanscoe Ave SK10 . . . . 88 A7
Swanscoe Cl CW10 . . . . . . 151 B8
Swanscoe La SK10 . . . . 88 B3
Swan St
Congleton CW12 . . . . 156 D2
Wilmslow SK9 . . . . 60 B7
Swanwick Cl CW4 . . . . 107 C1
Swanwick Gn SY13 . . . . . . 215 C5
Swanwick Ho WA16 . . . . . . 57 A2
Swanwick No SK10 . . . . 86 F6
Sweet Briar Cres CW2 . . . 189 F3
Sweet Brier Cl CW8 . . . . 78 B4
Sweetfield Gdns CH66 . . . . 69 D7
Sweetfield Rd CH66 . . . . 69 D7
Sweettooth La CW11 . . . . . 175 A2
SWETTENHAM 131 E3
Swettenham Cl
Alsager ST7 . . . . 193 C3
Sandbach CW11 . . . . 175 D7
SWETTENHAM HEATH . . 132 B3
Swettenham La CW12 . . . 131 E3
Swettenham St SK11 . . . . 112 E7
Swift Cl
Kidsgrove ST7 . . . . 195 B2
Warrington WA2 . . . . 8 E3
Wistaston CW2 . . . . 205 F8
Swinburne Dr CW1 . . . . . . 190 F4
Swindale Ave WA2 . . . . 8 B3
Swinden Cl WA2 . . . . 24 D2
Swine Market 2 CW5 . . . . 204 E5
Swineyard La WA16 . . . . . . 28 C4
Swinford Ave WA8 . . . . 13 E2
Swinhoe Pl WA3 . . . . 4 D3
Swinley Chase SK9 . . . . 34 F1
Swinleys Hey CH3 . . . . 142 A7
Swinnerton St CW2 . . . . . . 190 C2
Swinton Sq 8 WA16 . . . . . . 57 A2
Swireford Rd WA6 . . . . 73 B2
Swiss Cott
Alderley Edge SK9 . . . . 60 C1
Macclesfield SK10 . . . . 87 B2
Swiss Hill SK9 . . . . 60 B1
Swithin Rd M22 . . . . 33 E8
SWORTON HEATH 28 E5
Swynnerton Way WA8 . . . . 13 B5
Sycamore Cl
Audlem CW3 . . . . 230 A4
Biddulph ST8 . . . . 179 E2
Handforth SK9 . . . . 34 B2
Holmes Chapel CW4 . . . . . 130 D3
Nantwich CW5 . . . . 204 F7
Talke ST7 . . . . 210 E8
Sycamore Cres
Barnton CW8 . . . . 78 B4
Hollinfare WA3 . . . . 11 B2
Macclesfield SK11 . . . . 112 A7
Sycamore Ct WA7 . . . . 24 D5
Sycamore Dr
Aston WA7 . . . . 50 B4
Chester CH4 . . . . 140 F5
Ellesmere Port CH66 . . . . . . 70 A1
Lymm WA13 . . . . 18 D4
Middlewich CW10 . . . . 151 E5
Sycamore Gr
Broughton CH4 . . . . 139 B3
Sandbach CW11 . . . . 175 A8
Sycamore La WA5 . . . . 15 B6

Sycamore Lane Com Prim
Sch WA5 . . . . 15 B5
Sycamore Lo SK7 . . . . 35 F7
Sycamore Rd
Paddockhill WA16 . . . . 59 B5
Partington M31 . . . . 11 E3
Runcorn WA7 . . . . 49 D8
Sycamore Rise SK11 . . . . . 112 B6
Sycamores The WA16 . . . . 58 E2
Syddal Cl SK7 . . . . 35 D5
Syddal Cres SK7 . . . . 35 D4
Syddal Gn SK7 . . . . 35 D5
Syddal Ave SK8 . . . . 34 D8
Syddal Rd SK7 . . . . 35 D5
SYDNEY 191 A5
Sydney Ave M90 . . . . 33 A8
Sydney Rd
Bramhall SK7 . . . . 35 F5
Chester CH1 . . . . 118 B3
Crewe CW1 . . . . 190 F6
Sydney St
Northwich CW8 . . . . 103 C7
Runcorn WA7 . . . . 48 D7
Syers Ct WA1 . . . . 16 E8
Sylvan Ave SK7 . . . . 59 F5
Sylvan Cl CW8 . . . . 103 C7
Sylvan Mews CH1 . . . . 117 E6
Sylvia Cres WA2 . . . . 8 D1
Symondley Rd SK11 . . . . . 112 F2
Synge St WA2 . . . . 16 C7
Sytch Croft CH64 . . . . 66 E8

T

Tabley Ave WA8 . . . . 12 D2
Tabley Cl
Knutsford WA16 . . . . 56 E3
Macclesfield SK10 . . . . 112 A8
Sandbach CW11 . . . . 174 E7
Tabley Ct WA16 . . . . 56 E1
Tabley Gr WA16 . . . . 56 E1
Tabley Hill La WA16 . . . . . . 56 B2
Tabley Rd
Crewe CW2 . . . . 189 E3
Handforth SK9 . . . . 34 D5
Knutsford WA16 . . . . 56 E3
Tabley St CW9 . . . . 79 A1
Tabley Stables WA16 . . . . . 81 A8
Tabor St SK11 . . . . 112 E6
Tailors View CW5 . . . . 204 E6
Talbot Ave CH64 . . . . 66 F6
Talbot Cl
Neston CH64 . . . . 66 F6
Shavington CW2 . . . . 206 B4
Warrington WA3 . . . . 9 E3
Talbot Gdns CH64 . . . . 66 F6
Talbot Rd
Alderley Edge SK9 . . . . 60 B1
Dunham-on-the-Hill WA6 . . 97 E7
Ellesmere Port CH66 . . . . . . 69 F3
Talbot St
Chester CH1 . . . . 237 B4
Golborne WA3 . . . . 3 A8
Talbot Way CW5 . . . . 205 A3
Talfryn Cl CH5 . . . . 91 D1
Talisman Cl WA7 . . . . 50 D7
TALKE 210 C2
Talke Rd
Alsager ST7 . . . . 193 E3
High Carr ST5 . . . . 210 F2
Newcastle-under-Lyme ST1,
ST5 . . . . 210 D4
TALLARN GREEN/TALLWRN
GREEN 222 D3
Tall Ash Ave CW12 . . . . . . 157 A4
Tall Chimneys CW11 . . . . . 175 D4
Tall Trees CW8 . . . . 103 C6
Tally Ho La CW5 . . . . 203 E3
Tamar Cl
Haydock WA11 . . . . 1 C6
Kidsgrove ST7 . . . . 195 B2
Tamar Wlk CW7 . . . . 127 A2
Tame Cl
Biddulph ST8 . . . . 179 D1
Sandbach CW11 . . . . 174 E8
Tame Wlk 8 SK9 . . . . 34 D2
Tamworth Cl SK7 . . . . 36 D8
Tamworth St WA12 . . . . 2 A3
Tanhouse WA7 . . . . 23 E1
Tanhouse Ind Est WA8 . . . 23 C7
Tan House La
Burtonwood WA5 . . . . 7 A5
Widnes WA8 . . . . 23 D8
Tankersley Gr WA5 . . . . . . 15 B6
Tanners La WA3 . . . . 16 A6
Tanner's La WA3 . . . . 3 B8
Tanner St CW12 . . . . 156 E2
Tannery CW5 . . . . 204 E4
Tannery La
Neston CH64 . . . . 66 E8
Warrington WA5 . . . . 14 D3
Tanning Court Ind Est
WA1 . . . . 16 C4
Tanning Ct 8 WA1 . . . . 16 C4
Tanyard Fin WA5 . . . . 15 C2
Tanyard La WA15 . . . . 32 A5
Tapley Ave SK12 . . . . 36 E2
Taplow Cl WA4 . . . . 26 E6
Target Cl ST7 . . . . 210 E6
Target Life Sports Ctr
SK8 . . . . 34 B8
Target Rd CH60 . . . . 40 C8
Tarnbeck WA7 . . . . 50 D8

Tarn Cl CW7 . . . . 126 C3
Tarn Ct WA1 . . . . 17 F7
Tarn Mount SK11 . . . . 112 A5
Tarnway WA3 . . . . 3 F7
TARPORLEY 146 C1
Tarporley Bsns Ctr CW6 . 168 C8
Tarporley CE Prim Sch
CW6 . . . . 146 D2
Tarporley High Sch & Sixth
Form Coll 2 CW6 . . . . . . 146 D1
Tarporley Rd
Duddon CH3 . . . . 144 E7
Ellesmere Port CH66 . . . . . . 69 E4
Little Budworth CW6, CW8 . 124 C5
Lower Whitley WA4 . . . . 52 C4
Tarvin CH3 . . . . 121 C1
Utkinton CW6 . . . . 146 E6
Whitchurch SY13 . . . . 225 F3
Tarporley War Memorial
Hospl CW6 . . . . 146 D2
Tarporley Wlk SK9 . . . . 34 E2
Tarrant Ct CH1 . . . . 94 F1
TARVIN 121 C3
Tarvin Ave CW2 . . . . 189 D4
Tarvin Bridge CH3 . . . . . . 119 A2
Tarvin Cl
Ellesmere Port CH65 . . . . . . 70 C4
Golborne WA3 . . . . 3 F7
Macclesfield SK11 . . . . 112 E5
Middlewich CW10 . . . . 151 D5
Northwich CW9 . . . . 103 F5
Runcorn WA7 . . . . 49 C6
Tarvin Prim Sch CH3 . . . . 121 B1
Tarvin Rd
Alvanley WA6 . . . . 73 F4
Bebington CH62 . . . . 43 F3
Chester, Boughton CH3 . . . 119 A2
Chester, Vicarscross CH3 . 119 E2
Christleton CH3 . . . . 120 C3
Manley WA6 . . . . 99 A4
Tarvin Rdbt CH3 . . . . 121 A2
Tarvin Sands Industries
CH3 . . . . 121 B4
Tarvin Way
1 Handforth SK9 . . . . 34 D5
Winsford CW7 . . . . 126 C2
Tasman Cl WA5 . . . . 15 C8
Tate Cl WA8 . . . . 12 D2
Tate Dr CW1 . . . . 191 C4
TATTENHALL 166 B1
Tattenhall La
Beeston CW6 . . . . 167 F2
Tattenhall CH3 . . . . 167 A3
Tattenhall Park Prim Sch
CH3 . . . . 166 B2
Tattenhall Rd CH3 . . . . 166 C4
Tatton Cl
Alsager ST7 . . . . 193 C3
Chester CH4 . . . . 140 E5
Northwich CW9 . . . . 103 F4
Winsford CW7 . . . . 126 C1
Tatton Dr
4 Handforth SK9 . . . . 34 E5
2 Knutsford WA16 . . . . 57 A2
Warrington WA1 . . . . 9 D1
TATTON DALE 30 E1
Tatton Dr CW11 . . . . 175 C7
Tatton Lodge 17 WA16 . . . 57 A2
Tatton Park★ WA16 . . . . . . 56 F7
Tatton Rd
Crewe CW2 . . . . 189 F2
Handforth SK9 . . . . 34 E5
Warrington WA16 . . . . 57 A2
Tatton Stile WA16 . . . . 58 A4
Taurus Pk WA5 . . . . 7 D3
Tavener Cl CH63 . . . . 43 C5
Tavistock Rd WA5 . . . . 14 F4
Tavlin Ave WA5 . . . . 7 F1
Tawney Ct ST7 . . . . 195 B2
Tawny Ct WA7 . . . . 49 E7
TAXAL 38 C3
Taxal & Fernilee Prim Sch
SK23 . . . . 65 D6
Taxal Moor Rd SK23 . . . . . . 65 C3
Taxi Rd M90 . . . . 33 B7
Taximere Cl CW8 . . . . 102 A3
Tay Cl ST8 . . . . 179 E1
Taylor Bsns Pk WA3 . . . . . . 4 F1
Taylor Dr CW5 . . . . 204 C5
Taylor Rd
Altrincham WA14 . . . . 20 F5
Haydock WA11 . . . . 1 F7
Taylor's La
Oakhanger CW1 . . . . 192 C3
Warrington WA5 . . . . 14 A2
Taylors Row WA7 . . . . 23 C2
Taylor St
Warrington WA4 . . . . 16 A1
Widnes WA8 . . . . 13 C1
Teal Ave
Knutsford WA16 . . . . 57 B2
Poynton SK12 . . . . 36 A4
Tealby Cl CW9 . . . . 104 B8
Teal Cl
Warrington WA2 . . . . 8 E3
Winsford CW7 . . . . 149 D5
Teal Gr WA3 . . . . 9 F3
Teals Way CH60 . . . . 40 E8
Tebay Rd CH62 . . . . 43 E8
Tebay Rd PS CH62 . . . . 43 E8
Technology Ctr The CH65 . 70 B7
Tedder Dr M22 . . . . 33 F7
Tedder Sq WA8 . . . . 22 D8
Teddington Cl WA4 . . . . 26 E5
Tees Ct CH65 . . . . 70 A7
Teesdale Cl WA5 . . . . 14 F7
Teesdale Rd WA11 . . . . 1 C7

Tegg's Nose Ctry Pk★
SK11 . . . . 113 D6
Teggsnose La SK11 . . . . . . 113 C6
Tegid Way CH4 . . . . 140 D5
Tegsnose Mount SK11 . . . 113 C4
Telegraph Rd CH60 . . . . . . 41 A7
Telfer Cl CW10 . . . . 151 E6
Telford Cl
Congleton CW12 . . . . 157 B2
Macclesfield SK10 . . . . 88 A1
Talke ST7 . . . . 210 E8
Warrington WA4 . . . . 17 A3
Widnes WA8 . . . . 12 D4
Telford Ct CH1 . . . . 94 D6
Telford Gdns CW11 . . . . . 174 F3
Telford Ho ST7 . . . . 195 B3
Telford Pl CW5 . . . . 204 C5
Telford Rd CH65 . . . . 70 E4
Telford's Quay CH65 . . . . . 70 D7
Telford Way
Audlem CW3 . . . . 230 A3
Chester CH4 . . . . 140 F6
Middlewich CW10 . . . . 128 E1
Tempest Rd SK9 . . . . 60 C1
Templar Ct SK10 . . . . 87 A1
Temple Chambers CH1 . . . 237 B3
Temple Ct WA3 . . . . 9 E6
Templeton Dr WA2 . . . . 9 A3
Tenbury Cl WA5 . . . . 15 A8
Tenby Cl WA5 . . . . 7 F2
Tenby Dr WA7 . . . . 23 D2
Tenby Rd SK11 . . . . 111 F6
Tenchersfield CW5 . . . . . . 205 A4
Tennyson Ave CW1 . . . . . . 190 F4
Tennyson Cl
Crewe CW2 . . . . 190 A1
Macclesfield SK11 . . . . 111 E6
Northwich CW9 . . . . 104 C6
Rode Heath ST7 . . . . 193 E8
Tennyson Dr WA2 . . . . 8 C2
Tennyson Rd
Ellesmere Port CH65 . . . . . . 70 A4
Widnes WA8 . . . . 13 A1
Tennyson Wlk CH1 . . . . . . 118 A5
Tensing Cl WA5 . . . . 15 B8
Tenth Ave CH5 . . . . 92 D3
Terence Ave WA1 . . . . 16 F6
Terminal Road E M90 . . . . 33 C7
Terminal Road W M90 . . . . 33 B7
Tern Ave CW5 . . . . 195 C2
Tern Cl WA8 . . . . 13 B4
Tern Dr SK12 . . . . 36 B4
Terrace Rd WA8 . . . . 23 A5
Terra Nova Sch CW4 . . . . 108 D1
Terrick Mews SY13 . . . . . . 226 B2
Terrick Rd SY13 . . . . 226 A2
Tetchill Cl
Ellesmere Port CH66 . . . . . . 69 D2
Runcorn WA7 . . . . 50 D8
Tetton Cl 8 CW12 . . . . . . 156 F3
Tetton La CW11 . . . . 151 E3
Tewkesbury Cl
Cheadle SK8 . . . . 35 B6
Chester CH2 . . . . 118 F7
Ellesmere Port CH66 . . . . . . 94 E8
Middlewich CW10 . . . . 128 B1
Poynton SK12 . . . . 36 D4
Tewkesbury Dr SK10 . . . . . 87 E4
Tewkesbury Rd WA3 . . . . . . 3 B8
Thackeray Dr CH3 . . . . 119 C3
Thackeray Twrs 2 CH1 . . 237 C3
Thackery Ct 6 CW11 . . . . 174 D6
Thames Cl
Congleton CW12 . . . . 156 F1
Warrington WA2 . . . . 8 D2
Thamesdale CH65 . . . . 70 B4
Thames Dr ST8 . . . . 179 C1
Thames Gdns CH65 . . . . . . 70 B3
Thames Pl CW7 . . . . 127 B1
Thames Rd WA5 . . . . 5 A2
Thames Side CH65 . . . . 70 B3
Thames Trad Ctr M44 . . . . 11 F7
Thatchers Mount WA5 . . . . 1 D1
Thaxted Wlk M22 . . . . 33 C8
Theatre Ct CW9 . . . . 103 F8
THELWALL 17 E3
Thelwall Com Jun Sch
WA4 . . . . 17 D3
Thelwall Inf Sch WA4 . . . . . 17 C3
Thelwall La WA4 . . . . 17 B3
Thelwall New Rd WA4 . . . . 17 C3
Thelwall New Rd Ind Est
WA4 . . . . 17 C3
Thetford Rd CH66 . . . . 69 E4
Thetford Cl SK10 . . . . 87 C3
Thetford Rd WA5 . . . . 14 E6
Thewlis St WA5 . . . . 15 D4
Thingwall Rd CH60 . . . . 40 E7
Third Ave
Connah's Quay CH5 . . . . 92 F1
Crewe CW1 . . . . 190 F1
Kidsgrove ST7 . . . . 194 F1
Poynton SK12 . . . . 36 D1
Runcorn WA7 . . . . 49 F8
Sandbach CW11 . . . . 175 A5
Thirlmere SK11 . . . . 111 F5
Thirlmere Ave WA2 . . . . 8 C3
Thirlmere Cl
Alderley Edge SK9 . . . . 59 F1
Frodsham WA6 . . . . 49 D1
Holmes Chapel CW4 . . . . . 130 A3
Winsford CW7 . . . . 126 F3
Thirlmere Ct CW12 . . . . . . 156 A2
Thirlmere Dr WA13 . . . . 18 F3
Thirlmere Lodge 5 WA13 18 E3
Thirlmere Rd
Chester CH2 . . . . 119 A5

Thirlmere Rd continued
Crewe CW2 . . . . 190 A2
Ellesmere Port CH65 . . . . . . 70 C2
Neston CH64 . . . . 66 E6
Partington M31 . . . . 11 E4
Thirlmere Way WA8 . . . . . . 22 C8
Thirsk Cl WA7 . . . . 49 C6
Thirsk Way SK10 . . . . 87 C3
Thistle Cl WA16 . . . . 79 F7
Thistle Sq M31 . . . . 11 E2
Thistleton Cl SK11 . . . . . . 112 D6
Thistle Wlk 4 M31 . . . . 11 E2
Thistlewood Dr SK9 . . . . . . 60 D8
Thomas Ave CW5 . . . . 205 A3
Thomas Brassey Cl CH2 . 237 C4
Thomas Cl
Alsager ST7 . . . . 193 E4
Blacon CH1 . . . . 117 F6
Ellesmere Port CH65 . . . . . . 70 B2
Mickle Trafford CH2 . . . . . . 119 F8
Thomas Ct WA7 . . . . 49 F7
Thomas Ho CH1 . . . . 118 A5
Thomas Hodges Ct CW8 . 123 D3
Thomas Jones Way WA7 . 23 A3
Thomasons Bridge La
WA4 . . . . 25 E6
Thomas Row 6 CW5 . . . . . 204 E6
Thomas St
Biddulph ST8 . . . . 179 D1
Congleton CW12 . . . . 156 E3
Crewe CW1 . . . . 190 D4
Golborne WA3 . . . . 3 A8
Packmoor ST7 . . . . 195 F1
Runcorn WA7 . . . . 23 B3
Talke ST7 . . . . 210 D8
2 Widnes WA8 . . . . 23 A7
Thompson Ave WA3 . . . . . . 4 E3
Thompson Cl CW12 . . . . . . 2 C1
Thomson Gdns CW12 . . . . 156 A3
Thomson St WA3 . . . . 9 E5
Thoresway Rd SK9 . . . . 59 F5
Thorlby Rd WA3 . . . . 4 F3
Thorley Gr CW2 . . . . 190 A1
Thorley La M90 . . . . 33 A8
Thorley Mews SK7 . . . . 35 F7
Thornberry Cl CH1 . . . . 117 B8
Thornbrook Way CW11 . . 174 D5
Thornbury Ave WA3 . . . . . . 4 F4
Thorn Cl
Runcorn WA7 . . . . 49 C7
Warrington WA5 . . . . 14 F3
Thorn Dr M22 . . . . 34 A8
Thorne Cl SK10 . . . . 87 A5
Thorne Dr CH66 . . . . 69 B4
Thorneycroft Dr WA1 . . . . 16 C6
Thorney Dr SK8 . . . . 35 C5
Thorneyholme Dr WA16 . . 57 B2
Thornfield SK9 . . . . 60 A4
Thornfield Cl WA3 . . . . 3 C8
Thornfield Hey SK9 . . . . . . 60 E8
Thornfields CW1 . . . . 173 B1
Thorn Gr SK8 . . . . 35 A7
Thorngrove Dr SK9 . . . . . . 60 C6
Thorngrove Hill SK9 . . . . . 60 C6
Thorn Grove Prim Sch
SK8 . . . . 35 A7
Thorngrove Rd SK9 . . . . . . 60 C6
Thornhills WA8 . . . . 12 A3
Thorn Ho CH4 . . . . 141 A5
Thorn La CW8 . . . . 103 C5
Thornleigh Ave CH62 . . . . . 43 F3
Thornleigh Dr CH66 . . . . . . 69 E6
Thornley Cl 1 WA13 . . . . . 18 C3
Thornley Rd WA13 . . . . 18 C3
Thorn Rd
Bramhall SK7 . . . . 35 E5
Runcorn WA7 . . . . 49 C7
Warrington WA1 . . . . 17 A8
THORNS GREEN 32 C5
Thornsgreen Rd M23 . . . . . 33 D8
Thornton WA8 . . . . 22 E8
Thornton Ave WA5 . . . . 15 A5
Thornton Bank CW6 . . . . . 169 D4
Thornton Cl CW7 . . . . 127 A3
Thornton Common Rd
CH63 . . . . 42 B7
Thornton Cres CH60 . . . . . . 41 B6
Thorntondale Dr WA5 . . . . 14 F7
Thornton Dr
Chester CH2 . . . . 118 D5
Handforth SK9 . . . . 34 D3
Wistaston CW2 . . . . 206 A7
Thornton Green La CH2 . . 71 E1
Thornton Ho
Audlem CW3 . . . . 230 A5
Thornton Hough CH63 . . . . 42 B6
THORNTON HOUGH 42 A7
Thornton Hough Prim Sch
CH63 . . . . 42 B7
THORNTON-LE-MOORS . . 71 F1
Thornton Mews CH66 . . . . 69 B8
Thornton Rd
Ellesmere Port CH65 . . . . . . 70 C3
Gatley SK8 . . . . 34 C8
Warrington WA5 . . . . 15 B4
Thornton Sq SK11 . . . . 112 A5
Thorntree Bglws SK11 . . . 132 A8
Thorn Tree Cl L24 . . . . 21 E2
Thorn Tree Dr CW1 . . . . . . 173 A1
Thorntree Gn WA4 . . . . 27 B5
Thornway
Bollington SK10 . . . . 88 A7
Bramhall SK8 . . . . 35 C7
High Lane SK6 . . . . 37 F7
Thorn Wlk M31 . . . . 11 E2
Thornwythe Gr CH66 . . . . . 69 E4
Thornycroft CW7 . . . . 126 A1
Thornycroft Cl SK11 . . . . . 111 E1

Thornycroft St **7** SK11 . . . . 112 E7
Thorpe Cl CW1 . . . . 189 F8
Thorp St SK10 . . . . 112 D8
Thowler La WA14 . . . . 30 A5
Threaphurst La SK12 . . . . . 37 C8
THREAPWOOD 222 E7
Three Acres La SK8 . . . . . . 34 E7
Three Fields Cl CW12 . . . . 156 B3
Threeways CW8 . . . . 101 D4
Thrush Way CW7 . . . . 126 F4
Thurlow WA3 . . . . 3 E7
THURLWOOD 193 E7
Thursfield Ave ST7 . . . . . . 195 C3
Thursfield Cl CH1 . . . . 118 B1
Thursfield Prim Sch ST7 195 E3
Thurstaston Rd CH60 . . . . 40 F8
Thurston Ave WA3 . . . . 15 D6
Thurston Gn SK9 . . . . 60 A1
Thurston Rd CH4 . . . . 140 E5
Thynne St WA1 . . . . 16 A4
Tibbs Cross La WA8 . . . . . . 13 B8
Tibb St ST7 . . . . 209 F2
Tickford Bank WA8 . . . . . . 12 E2
Tidal La WA8 . . . . 16 F8
Tideswell Cl SK8 . . . . 34 D8
Tideswell Rd SK7 . . . . 36 E8
Tidnock Ave CW12 . . . . . . 156 E5
Tiffield Ct CW7 . . . . 127 A4
Tilbey Dr WA6 . . . . 74 A8
Tilbury Pl WA7 . . . . 50 F6
Tildsley Cres WA7 . . . . 48 F6
Tilewright Cl ST7 . . . . 195 B2
Tilley St WA1 . . . . 16 C6
Tilman Cl WA5 . . . . 15 B8
TILSTON 198 B3
Tilston Ave WA4 . . . . 17 A4
TILSTONE BANK 168 F4
Tilstone Cl
   Hough CW2 . . . . 206 E2
   Northwich CW9 . . . . . . 104 A5
TILSTONE FEARNALL 168 F6
Tilston Parochial CE Prim
   Sch SY14 . . . . 198 B3
Tilston Rd SY14 . . . . 213 A5
Tilston Wlk SK9 . . . . 34 E1
Timberfields Rd CH1 . . . . 117 A8
Timber La **2** CW9 . . . . . . 103 F8
TIMBERSBROOK 157 F2
Timbersbrook Gr **5** SK9 . . 34 D2
Timberscombe Gdns WA1 17 E6
Timber St SK10 . . . . 87 F1
Timbrell Ave CW1 . . . . . . 190 A6
Timmis Cl WA2 . . . . 9 A3
Timmis Cres WA8 . . . . 13 A1
Timperley Ave WA4 . . . . . . 17 A4
Tinkersfield CW5 . . . . 205 A4
Tinkwood La SY14 . . . . . . 211 F1
Tinsley St WA4 . . . . 16 F3
Tintagel Cl
   Macclesfield SK10 . . . . 111 E8
   Runcorn WA7 . . . . 50 B6
Tintern Ave CH2 . . . . 118 F6
Tintern Cl
   Poynton SK12 . . . . 36 D5
   Warrington WA5 . . . . . . 7 E2
Tintern Rd SK8 . . . . 35 B6
Tipping Brow WA16 . . . . . . 58 C4
Tirley La WA6 . . . . 123 A2
Titherbarn Cl WA6 . . . . . . 40 F7
Titherbarn Rd WA15 . . . . . 32 C8
Tithings The WA7 . . . . 23 E1
TIVERTON 168 C6
Tiverton Cl
   Chester CH4 . . . . 118 F5
   Sandbach CW11 . . . . . 175 C2
   Widnes WA8 . . . . 12 C3
Tiverton Ct **6** CW9 . . . . . 103 E5
Tiverton Dr SK9 . . . . 34 D1
Tiverton Sq WA5 . . . . 14 E4
Tiveton Ct CW9 . . . . 103 F5
Tobermory Cl WA1 . . . . 1 A5
Todbrook Cl SK23 . . . . 65 D6
Todds Bldgs WA8 . . . . 23 A6
Toft Cl
   Chester CH4 . . . . 140 E5
   Widnes WA8 . . . . 12 F1
Toft Rd WA16 . . . . 82 B7
Toft Way SK9 . . . . 34 E4
Tolland La WA15 . . . . 31 F8
Tollard Cl SK8 . . . . 35 B6
Toll Bar Ave SK11 . . . . . . 112 F7
Toll Bar Pl WA2 . . . . 8 A4
Toll Bar Rd
   Chester CH3 . . . . 142 C8
   Macclesfield SK11 . . . . 111 F8
   Warrington WA2 . . . . . . 8 A3
Tollemache Cotts CW5 . . . 203 C8
Tollemache Dr CW1 . . . . . 190 A8
Tollemache Terr CH2 . . . . 118 F2
Tollgate Cl ST7 . . . . 210 C8
Tollgate Dr CW3 . . . . 229 F4
Tollitt St CW1 . . . . 190 C4
Tom Brads Croft SK23 . . . . 65 E8
Tom Fields ST7 . . . . 209 F1
Tomkinson Cl CW7 . . . . . . 189 F7
Tomkinson St CH2 . . . . . . 237 C4
Tom La WA14 . . . . 30 E6
Tomlinson Ave WA2 . . . . . . 16 D8
Tomlins Terr CH1 . . . . 117 E5
Tommy's La
   Congleton CW12 . . . . . 156 F4
   Crewe CW1 . . . . 190 E2
Tonbridge Cl SK10 . . . . . . 87 B2
Toogood Cl CH2 . . . . 119 F8
Top Farm La CW7 . . . . . . 170 F2
Topgate Cl CH60 . . . . 41 B8
Top Park Cl WA13 . . . . 11 E1

Topping Ct WA3 . . . . 9 B4
Top Rd
   Frodsham WA6 . . . . 74 D5
   Kingsley WA6 . . . . 75 B1
Top Station Rd ST7 . . . . . . 195 C7
Torbrook Gr **1** SK9 . . . . . . 34 D2
Torkington Rd SK9 . . . . . . 60 D6
Toronto Ave M90 . . . . 33 B7
Torr Dr CH62 . . . . 44 A7
Torridon Gr CH66 . . . . 69 F3
Torr Rd SK11 . . . . 112 C4
Torr Rise CW6 . . . . 146 D1
Torrs Valley SK22 . . . . 39 C7
Torrvale Rd SK22 . . . . 39 B7
Total Fitness Wilmslow L
   Club SK9 . . . . 35 A4
Totland Cl WA5 . . . . 14 C7
Totland Gr CH2 . . . . 118 E4
Tourney Gn WA5 . . . . 7 A2
Towcester Ct CW1 . . . . . . 118 B1
TOWER HILL 88 D4
Tower Hill SK10 . . . . 88 D4
Tower Hill Rd ST7 . . . . . . 195 F7
Tower Ho The **20** SK11 . . 112 C8
Tower La
   Lymm WA13 . . . . 18 F2
   Runcorn WA7 . . . . 50 D7
   Weaverham WA8 . . . . . 77 B1
Tower Rd CH1 . . . . 118 B2
Towers Cl
   Poynton SK12 . . . . 36 F5
   Wistaston CW2 . . . . . . 206 A7
Towers Ct WA5 . . . . 15 E7
Towers La WA6 . . . . 98 C7
Towers Rd SK12 . . . . 36 F5
Towers The **6** SK10 . . . . . 111 F8
Towers Yard Barns SK12 . . 36 F5
Tower Way WA1 . . . . 190 C4
Townbridge Ct **14** CW8 . . 103 F8
Towneley Ct WA8 . . . . 13 A1
TOWN END 12 C6
Town Farm La WA4 . . . . . 100 D7
Townfield Ave CH3 . . . . . . 180 E2
Townfield Cl ST7 . . . . 194 D2
Townfield Ct WA8 . . . . 78 A3
Townfield La
   Barnton CW8 . . . . 78 A3
   Blacon CH1 . . . . 117 F8
   Farndon CH3 . . . . 180 D2
   Frodsham WA6 . . . . 74 D7
   Lymm WA13 . . . . 19 B7
   Mollington CH1 . . . . . . 94 D2
   Swan Green WA16 . . . . 106 E5
   Tarvin CH3 . . . . 121 B2
   Tiverton CW6 . . . . 168 C6
Townfield Rd
   Mobberley WA16 . . . . . . 58 A4
   Runcorn WA7 . . . . 24 C2
TOWN FIELDS 149 D7
Townfields WA16 . . . . 57 C2
Town Fields CW11 . . . . . . 175 B5
Townfields Cotts **8**
   CW7 . . . . 149 C7
Townfields Cres CW7 . . . . 149 D7
Townfields Dr CW7 . . . . . 149 D7
Townfields Gdns CW7 . . . 149 D7
Townfields Rd CW7 . . . . . 149 D7
Townsfield Dr WA6 . . . . . . 24 C2
Townsfield Villas CW12 . . . 72 B3
Towngate Bsns Ctr WA8 . . 22 B7
Town Gn The WA4 . . . . . . 52 D5
Town Hill WA1 . . . . 16 B5
Town La
   Hale L24,WA8 . . . . 21 E2
   Mobberley WA16 . . . . . . 58 B4
   Neston CH64 . . . . 66 F6
Townley Mill **6** SK11 . . . 112 D7
Townley Pl **5** SK11 . . . . 112 D7
Townley St **4** SK11 . . . . 112 D7
TOWN OF LOWTON 1 F1
Town Park 50 B8
Townsend Farm ST7 . . . . 193 E2
Townsend La ST7 . . . . . . 194 A8
Townsend Rd CW12 . . . . . 156 E2
Townsfield Dr CW6 . . . . . 147 F7
Townsfield La WA2 . . . . 8 A5
Townshend Rd CW9 . . . . . 80 A3
Township Cl CH3 . . . . 182 C1
Town Sq
   4 Northwich CW9 . . . . 103 F8
   6 Runcorn WA7 . . . . . 49 F7
Town Well WA4 . . . . 25 C2
Townwell Ct CW5 . . . . 204 D5
Town Wlk **9** WA7 . . . . . . 49 F7
Trackside Bsns Pk CW11 174 C6
Tracy Dr WA1 . . . . 17 D6
Trafalgar Ave SK12 . . . . . . 37 A3
Trafalgar Cl
   Northwich CW9 . . . . . . 103 E3
   Poynton SK12 . . . . 37 A3
Trafalgar Ct
   3 Macclesfield SK11 . . 112 D7
   Widnes WA8 . . . . 23 A6
Trafford Ave WA5 . . . . 15 F7
Trafford Cres WA7 . . . . . . 49 C6
Trafford Pl SK9 . . . . 60 D6
Trafford Rd
   Alderley Edge SK9 . . . . 60 B1
   Handforth SK9 . . . . 34 B1
Trafford St CH1 . . . . 237 B3
Tragan Dr WA5 . . . . 14 D3
Tramway Rd M44 . . . . 11 F7
Tramway St CH1 . . . . 237 C3
Tranmere Dr SK9 . . . . 34 E2
Trap Rd CW12 . . . . 132 C3
Trap St SK11 . . . . 132 B6

TRAP STREET 132 C5
Travers' Entry WA9 . . . . . . 6 A7
Travis St **10** WA8 . . . . . . 23 B8
Treborth Rd CH1 . . . . 117 D3
Tree Bank Cl WA7 . . . . . . 49 A8
Tree Cl SK10 . . . . 88 D1
Tree Tops CH64 . . . . 66 E4
Treetops Cl WA1 . . . . 16 F7
Tree Way WA16 . . . . 82 A7
Trefoil Cl
   Huntington CH3 . . . . . 142 B6
   Warrington WA3 . . . . . . 9 C5
Tregele Cl CH1 . . . . 117 D3
Trenance Cl WA7 . . . . 50 C5
Trenchard Dr M22 . . . . . . 33 F7
Trent Ave CW7 . . . . 127 B1
Trent Cl
   Bramhall SK7 . . . . 35 C6
   Culcheth WA3 . . . . 5 A2
   Widnes WA8 . . . . 13 B4
   Winsford CW7 . . . . . . 127 B1
Trentdale CH65 . . . . 70 B3
Trentham Cl WA8 . . . . 13 B4
Trentham St WA7 . . . . 22 F3
Trent Way CH60 . . . . 41 C6
Tresham Dr WA4 . . . . 27 A8
Tresilick CI CW1 . . . . 191 A4
Trevone Cl WA16 . . . . 57 A1
Trickett La CW8 . . . . 102 A3
Tricketts La CW5 . . . . . . 205 E5
Tricketts Mews CW5 . . . . 205 E5
Trident Bsns Pk WA3 . . . . . 9 E4
Trident Ind Est WA3 . . . . . . 9 E4
Trident Ret Pk WA7 . . . . . . 49 E7
Trident Way SK11 . . . . . . 112 A5
Trinity Cl CW2 . . . . 190 A1
Trinity Ct
   Congleton CW12 . . . . . 157 B1
   1 Knutsford WA16 . . . . 57 A2
   Warrington WA3 . . . . 9 F5
Trinity Gdns **3** WA6 . . . . 49 C1
Trinity Ho **3** WA6 . . . . . . 49 C1
Trinity La SK11 . . . . 112 F3
Trinity Pl
   Congleton CW12 . . . . . 179 B8
   1 Widnes WA8 . . . . . . 23 B7
Trinity Sq SK10 . . . . 87 F1
Trinity St
   Chester CH1 . . . . 237 A2
   Runcorn WA7 . . . . 23 B3
Trinity Terr **2** CW8 . . . . 103 E8
Troon Cl
   Bebington CH63 . . . . . . 43 C5
   Bramhall SK7 . . . . 36 A7
   Haydock WA11 . . . . 1 A5
   Holmes Chapel CW4 . . 130 C2
Trossach Cl WA2 . . . . 8 E2
Troutbeck Ave
   Congleton CW12 . . . . . 156 A2
   Newton-le-Willows WA12 . 1 E4
   Warrington WA3 . . . . . . 15 F8
Troutbeck Cl WA7 . . . . . . 50 A5
Troutbeck Gr WA12 . . . . . . 2 C1
Trouthall La WA16 . . . . . . 81 A2
Trubshaw Ct ST7 . . . . . . 195 C3
Trubshaw Pl ST7 . . . . . . 195 B3
Truman Cl WA8 . . . . 12 F3
Truman Ct **6** WA5 . . . . . . 15 B7
Trumans La CH66 . . . . . . 69 C7
Truro Cl
   Bramhall SK7 . . . . 35 F7
   Congleton CW12 . . . . . 178 E8
   Ellesmere Port CH66 . . 94 F8
   Macclesfield SK10 . . . . 86 E1
   Runcorn WA7 . . . . 50 C6
   Warrington WA1 . . . . . . 17 B8
Tudor Cl
   Ellesmere Port CH66 . . 94 F8
   Middlewich CW10 . . . . 128 D3
   Northwich CW9 . . . . . . 104 E6
   Warrington WA4 . . . . . . 17 A2
   Winsford CW7 . . . . . . 149 D6
Tudor Ct
   Congleton CW12 . . . . . 156 D2
   4 Warrington WA4 . . . . 16 E1
   Dr SK10 . . . . 86 D7
Tudor Gn
   Blacon CH1 . . . . 117 E6
   Handforth SK9 . . . . 34 E1
Tudor Rd
   Handforth SK9 . . . . 34 E1
   Runcorn WA7 . . . . 24 C3
Tudorway CH60 . . . . 41 B8
Tudor Way
   Chester CH3 . . . . 142 A7
   Congleton CW12 . . . . . 156 D1
   Nantwich CW5 . . . . . . 204 E3
Tue La WA8 . . . . 12 B6
Tulip Gr WA5 . . . . 15 E3
Tulip Rd
   Haydock WA11 . . . . 1 F6
   Partington M31 . . . . . . 11 E2
Tully Ave WA12 . . . . 1 F3
Tulworth Rd SK12 . . . . . . 36 D4
Tunbridge Cl
   Warrington WA5 . . . . . . 15 A8
   Wistaston CW2 . . . . . . 206 A8
Tunnel Rd CW8 . . . . 78 B2
Tunnicliffe Rd SK11 . . . . . 112 D7
Tunnicliffe St **1** SK10 . . 112 D8
Tuns La CH64 . . . . 66 F7
Turf La SK11 . . . . 112 C3
Turnall Rd WA8 . . . . 22 B7
Turnberry Cl
   Lymm WA13 . . . . 18 C4
   Macclesfield SK10 . . . . 87 C4

Turnberry Cl continued
   Northwich CW9 . . . . . 104 E7
   Winsford CW7 . . . . . . 126 C2
Turnberry Dr SK9 . . . . 60 D8
Turner Ave ST7 . . . . 210 A1
Turner Cl
   Crewe CW1 . . . . 190 A8
   Widnes WA8 . . . . 12 D3
Turner Rise SK10 . . . . . . 88 C8
Turner St
   Bollington SK10 . . . . . . 88 B8
   Nantwich CW5 . . . . . . 204 F5
Turner's View CH64 . . . . . 41 D2
Turnhurst Rd ST7 . . . . . . 195 F1
Turnock St SK11 . . . . 112 E7
Turnstone Ave WA12 . . . . . 2 C4
Turnstone Bsns Pk WA8 . . 23 C7
Turret Hall Dr **1** WA3 . . . . 3 E8
Turriff Dr CH63 . . . . 43 C4
Turrocks Cl CH64 . . . . . . 66 E5
Turrocks Croft CH64 . . . . 66 E5
Turton Cl
   Hale L24 . . . . 21 E1
   Warrington WA3 . . . . . . 9 C5
Turton St WA3 . . . . 3 A8
Turville Rd SK9 . . . . 34 D2
Tuscan Cl WA8 . . . . 12 F4
Tushingham Cl CH3 . . . . 142 B7
Tushingham-with-Grindley
   CE Prim Sch SY13 . . . 224 C1
Tuson Dr WA8 . . . . 12 F4
Tutor Bank Dr WA12 . . . . . 2 D3
Tweedsmuir CH3 . . . . . . 119 A2
Tweedsmuir Cl WA2 . . . . . . 9 A4
Twemlow Ave CW11 . . . . 175 B7
Twemlow Green La CW4 . 130 D6
Twenty Acre Rd WA5 . . . . 15 C8
Twinnies Rd SK9 . . . . 34 B1
TWISS GREEN 4 E4
Twiss Green Dr WA3 . . . . . 4 E4
Twiss Green La WA3 . . . . . 4 E4
Twiss Green Prim Sch
   WA3 . . . . 4 E4
Twist Ave WA3 . . . . 3 C8
Two Acre Gr CH66 . . . . . . 69 F1
TWO MILLS 93 E8
Twyford Cl WA8 . . . . 13 B5
Twyford La WA8 . . . . 13 D6
Tyldesley Way CW5 . . . . . 204 D6
Tyler St SK9 . . . . 60 A1
Tyne Cl WA2 . . . . 8 E2
Tynedale Ave CW2 . . . . . . 190 C2
Tynedale Cl SK11 . . . . . . 112 C8
Tynemouth Rd WA7 . . . . . 50 C6
Tynesdale CH65 . . . . 70 B3
Tynwald Cres WA2 . . . . . . 12 F5
Tynwald Dr WA4 . . . . 26 C7
Tyrer Rd WA12 . . . . 2 C1
Tyrer Wlk **2** WA3 . . . . 3 F8
TYTHERINGTON 87 C3
Tytherington Bsns Pk
   SK10 . . . . 87 D5
Tytherington Cl WA10 . . . 151 C6
Tytherington Ct SK10 . . . . 87 D3
Tytherington Dr SK10 . . . . 87 E4
Tytherington Gn SK10 . . . 87 C4
Tytherington High Sch
   SK10 . . . . 87 D2
Tytherington La SK10 . . . . 87 D5
Tytherington Park Rd
   SK10 . . . . 87 D3
Tytherington Sh Ctr **1**
   SK10 . . . . 87 D3

U

Ullapool Cl CH66 . . . . 68 F6
Ullswater SK11 . . . . 111 F5
Ullswater Ave
   Crewe CW2 . . . . 189 E3
   Warrington WA2 . . . . . . 8 D3
   Winsford CW7 . . . . . . 126 B2
Ullswater Cres CH2 . . . . . 119 A6
Ullswater Dr SK9 . . . . 83 F7
Ullswater Gr WA7 . . . . 49 D5
Ullswater Mans SK11 . . . 111 F5
Ullswater Rd
   Congleton CW12 . . . . . 156 A2
   Ellesmere Port CH65 . . 70 C2
   Handforth SK9 . . . . 34 C4
Ulverston Ave WA2 . . . . . . 8 B4
Ulverston Cl WA11 . . . . . . 1 A6
Ulvet Gate WA10 . . . . 29 C4
Underbridge La WA4 . . . . . 25 E6
Undercliffe Ho WA4 . . . . . 26 D8
Under Rainow Rd CW12 . 157 E1
Underway The WA7 . . . . . . 49 F8
Underwood Bsns Pk
   CW1 . . . . 190 A6
Underwood Cl WA16 . . . . . 82 A8
Underwood Ct WA1 . . . . . 190 B6
Underwood Dr CH65 . . . . . 70 C2
Underwood La CW1 . . . . . 190 B6
Underwood Rd SK9 . . . . . 60 C1
Underwood West Prim Sch
   CW1 . . . . 190 A6
Unicorn Gateway **8**
   SK10 . . . . 112 D8
Union Ind Est SK11 . . . . . 112 E7
Union Pl CH1 . . . . 237 A2
Union Rd
   Macclesfield SK11 . . . . 112 E7
   New Mills SK22 . . . . . . 39 C7
Union Sq WA5 . . . . 15 A8

Union St
   Chester CH1 . . . . 237 C2
   Congleton CW12 . . . . . 156 D3
   Crewe CW2 . . . . 190 D3
   Macclesfield SK11 . . . . 112 D7
   Runcorn WA7 . . . . 23 B2
   Sandbach CW11 . . . . . 175 B6
   Warrington WA1 . . . . . . 16 B5
Union Terr CH1 . . . . 237 B3
Union Wlk CH1 . . . . 237 B2
Unity Way ST7 . . . . 210 D8
University CE Acad (North
   Campus) CH66 . . . . . . 69 E6
University CE Acad (South
   Campus) CH65 . . . . . . 70 C2
University of Liverpool,
   Faculty of Veterinary
   Science (Leahurst)
   CH64 . . . . 67 D8
University Way CW1 . . . . . 191 B2
Univ of Chester (Chichester
   House) CH1 . . . . 237 A3
Univ of Chester (Warrington
   Campus) WA2 . . . . 9 B3
Unsworth Ct WA2 . . . . 8 F1
Upcast La SK9 . . . . 59 E3
Uplands CW8 . . . . 101 D4
Uplands Rd CW9 . . . . 78 E4
Uplands The
   Biddulph ST8 . . . . 179 E2
   Macclesfield SK11 . . . . 112 A8
   Runcorn WA7 . . . . 50 A7
Upper Cambrian Rd CH1 118 B2
Upper Haigh St CW7 . . . . 149 C8
Upper Mersey Rd WA8 . . . 23 A5
Upper Mersey St CH65 . . . 70 C7
Upper Northgate St CH1 . 237 A3
Upper Raby Rd CH64 . . . . 42 A2
UPPER THREAPWOOD . . . 222 E7
UPTON
   Chester 118 D6
   Widnes 12 A8
Upton Ave SK8 . . . . 35 A8
Upton Bridle Path WA8 . . . 12 F4
Upton-by-Chester High Sch
   CH2 . . . . 118 F6
Upton Cl
   Golborne WA3 . . . . 3 D8
   Winsford CW7 . . . . . . 126 F4
Upton Dr
   Chester CH2 . . . . 118 C6
   Warrington WA5 . . . . . . 14 F5
Upton Grange
   Chester CH2 . . . . 118 C6
   Widnes WA8 . . . . 12 A4
UPTON HEATH 118 F8
Upton Heath CE Prim Sch
   CH2 . . . . 118 D8
Upton La
   Chester CH2 . . . . 118 D7
   Widnes WA8 . . . . 12 F4
Upton Mount SK10 . . . . . . 87 A1
Upton Pk CH2 . . . . 118 D6
Upton Priory Sch SK10 . . . 86 F2
Upton Rd CH66 . . . . 69 D4
UPTON ROCKS 12 E4
Upton Rocks Ave WA8 . . . 12 E4
Upton Rocks Mews WA8 . . 12 E4
Upton Way **12** SK9 . . . . . 34 D5
Upton Westlea Prim Sch
   CH2 . . . . 118 E7
Upwood Rd WA3 . . . . 3 D7
Ure Ct CH65 . . . . 70 A7
Urmston Ave WA12 . . . . . . 2 B5
Ursuline Way CW2 . . . . . 190 B1
UTKINTON 146 B7
Utkinton La CH66 . . . . . . 146 E7
Utkinton Rd CW6 . . . . . . 146 C5
Utkinton St Paul's CE Prim
   Sch CW6 . . . . 146 B8

V

Vahler Terr WA7 . . . . 23 C2
Vale Ave WA2 . . . . 16 B8
Valebrook Dr CW5 . . . . . . 220 A8
Vale Bsns Ctr CW12 . . . . 156 D2
Vale Cl CH4 . . . . 139 C3
Vale Ct WA4 . . . . 51 A3
Vale Gdns
   Alsager ST7 . . . . 193 E4
   Ellesmere Port CH65 . . 70 B4
   Helsby WA6 . . . . 73 B4
Vale Head SK9 . . . . 34 D2
Valentine Rd
   Kidsgrove ST7 . . . . . . 195 A1
   Newton-le-Willows WA12 . 1 F3
Vale Owen Rd WA2 . . . . . . 8 D1
Vale Rd
   Alpraham CW6 . . . . . . 169 A4
   Ellesmere Port CH65 . . 70 B4
   Hartford CW8 . . . . 103 C4
   Marston CW9 . . . . 79 B6
   Wilmslow SK9 . . . . 59 E8
Vale Royal Ctyd CW8 . . . 126 B8
Vale Royal Dr
   Northwich CW8 . . . . . . 103 C2
   Whitegate CW8 . . . . . . 126 B6
Vale Royal River Park Cvn
   Site CW9 . . . . 126 E6
Vale View WA6 . . . . 79 C1
Vale Wlk CW12 . . . . 156 D2
Valiant Cl WA2 . . . . 8 F2

Valley Brook Bsns Ctr CW2 190 D3
Valley Cl
Alsager ST7 192 F3
Knutsford WA16 82 A7
Valley Ct
Crewe CW2 190 B3
Middlewich CW10 128 E1
Warrington WA2 8 F1
Valley Dr
Chester CH2 118 C5
Ellesmere Port CH66 69 D5
Handforth SK9 34 C3
Valley La
Cuddington CW8 101 F3
Sandiway CW8 102 A3
Valley Rd
Bebington CH62 43 D8
Bramhall SK7 35 F8
Crewe CW2 189 F1
Macclesfield SK11 112 A6
Weaverham CW8 77 C1
Wilmslow/Alderley Edge SK9 59 C7
Valley Sch SK7 35 C5
VALLEY THE 190 A4
Valley View
Congleton CW12 156 C3
Ellesmere Port CH66 69 D5
Newton-le-Willows WA12 2 B1
Northwich CW9 104 C7
Valley Way WA16 82 A7
Vanguard Ct WA3 9 D4
Varden Rd SK12 36 E3
Varden Town Cotts SK10 86 A4
Vardon Dr SK9 60 D6
Varey Rd CW12 156 F4
Vaudrey Cres CW12 156 F3
Vaudrey Dr WA1 17 D7
Vaughan Rd SK23 65 E5
Vaughans La CH3 142 A8
Vauxhall Cl WA5 14 F4
Vauxhall Rd CW5 204 E7
Vauxhall Way CW7 149 C6
Vearows Pl 1 CW8 103 F7
Venables Rd CW9 79 A1
Venable's Rd CH1 117 F4
Venables Way
High Legh WA16 29 C4
Middlewich CW10 151 E6
Venns Rd WA2 16 D7
Ventnor Cl
Middlewich CW10 151 C8
Warrington WA5 14 D7
Venture Ho SK11 112 D6
Venture Way SK12 36 F3
Verbena Cl
Partington M31 11 F3
Runcorn WA7 49 F4
Verdin Ave CW8 78 F1
Verdin Cl
Moulton CW9 126 F7
Winsford CW7 126 C2
Verdin Ct CW1 190 A8
Verdin High Sch The CW7 126 C1
Verdin St CW9 104 C8
Vere St CW1 190 C5
Verity Cl CW1 191 C4
Verity Ct CW10 128 E2
Vermont Cl WA5 15 C7
Vermont Gdns SK7 35 B5
Vernay Gn CH4 141 B5
Vernon Ave
Audley ST7 209 D2
Congleton CW12 178 F8
Hooton CH66 44 A2
Vernon Cl
Audley ST7 209 D2
Poynton SK12 36 D2
Saughall CH1 117 A8
Vernon Dr CW3 230 F4
Vernon Prim Sch SK12 36 E3
Vernon Rd
Chester CH1 118 B2
Poynton SK12 36 E2
Vernon St
Crewe CW1 190 B5
Macclesfield SK10 112 F8
Warrington WA1 16 B4
Vernon Way CW1 190 D4
Veronica Mews WA8 12 D1
Veronica Way CH66 69 D7
Vetch Cl WA3 11 B5
Vetches The CH3 119 F5
Viaduct St WA12 2 A3
Vicarage Ave SK8 35 B7
Vicarage Cl
Guilden Sutton CH3 119 F5
Hale L24 21 E1
Vicarage Ct LL13 196 E8
Vicarage Dr WA11 1 B7
Vicarage Gdns CW11 174 E8
Vicarage Gr CW7 149 D5
Vicarage Hill WA6 73 C4
Vicarage La
Audlem CW3 230 A4
Bunbury CW6 168 F1
Burton CH64 67 D2
Frodsham WA6 74 C7
Helsby WA6 73 C4
Little Budworth CW6 147 F7
Poynton SK12 36 E5
Sandbach CW11 174 E8
Vicarage Rd
Chester CH2 118 F3
Haslington CW1 191 D6
Haydock WA11 1 A7
Northwich CW9 104 B8
Widnes WA8 23 A7
Vicarage Row CH62 44 A5
Vicarage Way 1 SK11 111 F7
Vicarage Wlk
Northwich CW9 104 B7
Warrington WA4 26 C8
Vicar's Cl CH3 121 F7
VICARSCROSS 119 E2
Vicars Cross Ct 2 CH3 119 B2
Vicars Cross Rd CH3 119 C2
Vicar's La CH1 237 B2
Vickers Rd WA8 22 F4
Vickers Way CW9 104 A7
Victoria Ave
Crewe CW2 190 A4
Grappenhall WA4 17 A2
Haslington CW1 191 C4
Heswall CH60 41 A6
Holmes Chapel CW4 130 C2
Kidsgrove ST7 194 F2
Warrington WA5 14 D6
Widnes WA8 13 A3
Victoria Cl SK7 35 D6
Victoria Com Tech Sch CW1 190 C5
Victoria Cres
Chester CH2 237 A4
Chester, Queen's Park CH4 237 C1
Victoria Ct
Chester CH2 237 A4
3 Crewe CW1 190 C4
Haslington CW1 191 C4
8 Kidsgrove ST7 195 A2
Knutsford WA16 56 F1
2 Widnes WA8 23 A8
Victoria Gr WA8 13 A3
Victoria Infirmary CW8 103 E8
Victoria Inf Sch CH1 237 A4
Victoria Mews CH65 70 B5
Victoria Mill Dr CW5 205 D6
Victoria Pathway CH4 237 C1
Victoria Pk CW8 78 F1
Victoria Pl
Chester CH1 237 B3
Warrington WA4 16 C1
Victoria Promenade WA8 23 A4
Victoria Rd
Chester CH1, CH2 237 B3
Ellesmere Port CH65 70 C5
Macclesfield SK10 87 A1
Neston CH64 67 A6
Newton-le-Willows WA12 2 C3
Northwich CW9 104 B8
Runcorn WA7 23 A2
Saltney CH4 140 D5
Warrington, Great Sankey WA5 15 B4
Warrington, Penketh WA5 14 D4
Warrington, Stockton Heath WA4 16 D1
Warrington WA4 16 F2
Widnes WA8 23 A6
Wilmslow SK9 60 A6
Victoria Road Prim Sch
10 Northwich CW9 104 B8
Runcorn WA7 23 A2
Victoria Sq
Warrington WA4 16 C1
8 Widnes WA8 23 A7
Winsford CW7 149 A8
Victoria St
Congleton CW12 156 D2
Crewe CW1 190 C4
Knutsford WA16 56 F2
New Mills SK22 39 B6
Northwich CW9 79 E2
Sandbach CW11 175 B7
Warrington WA1 16 C5
Widnes WA8 23 B7
Victoria Stad (Northwich Victoria FC) CW9 79 D3
Victoria Trad Ctr WA8 23 A6
Victoria Way SK7 35 D6
Victoria Wlk SK10 112 E8
Victory Rd M44 11 C4
Viewlands Dr SK9 34 D2
Viking Way CW12 156 C4
Villa Farm CW11 176 B8
Village Cl
Lostock Green CW9 105 A8
Northwich CW8 77 D1
Runcorn WA7 50 A8
Warrington WA4 17 E4
Village Ct 8 SK9 34 D1
Village Farm CW5 172 A5
Village La WA4 52 D4
Village Mews SK10 87 A6
Village Rd
Christleton CH3 142 E8
Great Barrow CH3 120 E6
Heswall CH60 40 F7
Waverton CH3 143 C4
Village Square Sh Ctr, Bramhall SK7 35 E6
Village St WA7 24 E2
Village Terr The 6 WA4 16 C1
Village The
Astbury CW12 178 B8
Burton CH64 67 D1
Prestbury SK10 86 F6
Village Way 11 SK9 34 D1
Villa Rd CH5 116 B7
Villars St WA1 16 C5
Villas The CW4 131 A8
Villiers Russell Cl CW1 190 D5
Vincent Cl WA5 15 C8
Vincent Dr CH4 141 C6
Vincent St
Crewe CW1 190 E4
Macclesfield SK11 112 D7
Vine Bank Rd ST7 195 A1
Vine Cl SK11 112 A6
Vine Cres WA5 14 F6
Vine Rd CH66 69 F1
Vine St
Bollington SK10 88 B8
10 Runcorn WA7 23 A2
Widnes WA8 23 A7
Vine Terr WA8 12 A2
Vine Tree Ave
Crewe CW2 190 B1
Shavington CW2 206 B5
Vine Tree Prim Sch CW2 190 A1
Vineyard The CW2 206 B4
Violet Cl WA3 9 C5
Violet St WA8 23 A7
Virginia Chase SK8 34 F8
Virginia Dr CH1 117 C4
Virginia Gdns WA5 15 B8
Virginia Terr CH66 69 B8
Virtual Bsns Ctr CH1 117 E2
Viscount Dr
Gatley SK8 34 D7
Wythenshawe M90 32 F7
Viscount Rd WA2 8 E2
Vista Ave WA12 2 A4
Vista Rd
Newton-le-Willows WA11, WA12 2 A6
Runcorn WA7 49 A8
Vista The M44 11 C4
Vista Way WA12 2 A4
Vixen Gr WA8 12 F4
Volunteer Ave 7 CW5 204 E6
Volunteer Fields CW5 204 E6
Volunteer St
Chester CH1 237 B2
Frodsham WA6 49 D1
Vose Cl WA5 15 D6
Vulcan Cl
Newton-le-Willows WA12 2 C1
Warrington WA2 8 F2
Vulcan Ind Est WA12 2 D1
VULCAN VILLAGE 7 C8
Vyrnwy Rd CH4 140 D6

W

Waddington Cl WA3 3 F8
Wadebrook Gr 4 SK9 34 D1
Wadebrook Trad Est CW9 104 C8
Wade Cres CW8 78 A3
Wade Ct ST7 195 A1
Wade Deacon High Sch WA8 13 A2
WADES GREEN 171 F5
Wades La CW7 126 D3
Wadeson Way WA3 9 B7
Wade St CW9 79 B1
Wadsworth Cl SK9 34 E3
Waggon Cotts ST7 208 E1
Waggs Rd CW12 156 C1
Wagg St CW12 156 D2
Wagon La WA11 1 B6
Waine St CW1 190 D5
Wain Ho CH1 94 A1
Wain Lee ST7 195 F4
Wakefield Cl CW1 189 F7
Wakefield Ct CW9 104 A5
Wakefield Ho WA5 15 F6
Wakefield Rd CH66 69 E1
Wakefield St WA3 3 A7
Wakes Mdw CW6 185 E8
Walden Cl WA4 17 D3
Walden Dr CH1 93 D8
Waldon Rd SK11 112 A5
Waldron Gdns CW2 189 F1
Waldron Rd CW1 191 D3
Waldron's La CW1 173 D1
Walfield Ave CW12 156 D5
Walford Ave CW2 190 B3
WALGHERTON 220 B6
Walgrave Cl CW12 156 A3
Walker Cl CW1 191 D4
Walker Dr CW10 151 C8
Walker La SK11 112 E2
WALKER'S GREEN 152 D7
Walkersgreen Rd ST5 210 D2
Walkers La
Ellesmere Port CH66 69 C6
Farndon CH3 180 F2
Scholar Green ST7 177 B2
Tarporley CW6 146 D1
Warrington WA5 14 E3
Walker St
Chester CH2 237 C4
Crewe CW1 190 B5
2 Macclesfield SK10 112 C8
Warrington WA2 16 A6
Wallace Ct CW7 127 D1
Wallace St
Northwich CW8 103 E7
Widnes WA8 23 A8
Wallcroft CH64 68 A7
Wallcroft Gdns CW10 128 C1
Walled Gdn The CW10 127 D5
Wallerscote Cl CW8 102 E8
Wallerscote Prim Sch CW8 102 E8
Wallerscote Rd CW8 102 E8
Waller St SK11 112 E6
WALLEY'S GREEN 172 E7
Walleys La CW5 203 C7
Wallfields Cl CW5 204 E7
Wall Fields Rd CW5 204 E7
Wallhill La CW11 177 D7
Wall Hill Way CW8 76 F3
Wallingford Rd SK9 34 C5
Wallis St
Crewe CW1 190 D4
Warrington WA4 16 B3
Wall La CW5 204 E6
Wallrake CH60 40 F7
Walls Ave CH1 118 B1
Wallsend Ct WA8 12 F3
Wallworth's Bank CW12 156 E2
Wallworth Terr SK9 59 E8
Walmer Pl CW7 149 C6
Walmoor Pk CH3 119 A1
Walmsley St
Newton-le-Willows WA12 2 D4
Widnes WA8 23 C8
Walnut Ave CW8 102 D7
Walnut Cl
Chester CH2 118 D7
Warrington WA1 17 E7
Wilmslow SK9 60 E8
Walnut Cotts LL13 196 D8
Walnut Croft CH3 180 F6
Walnut Dr CW7 127 A1
Walnut Gr CH66 70 A1
Walnut La CW8 103 A5
Walnut Rd M31 11 D3
Walnut Rise CW12 156 B2
Walnut Tree La
Bradwall Green CW11 153 A4
Warrington WA4 26 F4
Walpole Cl CW1 191 C5
Walpole Gr WA2 8 C2
Walpole Rd WA7 49 C6
Walpole St CH1 237 A4
Walsh Cl WA12 2 C5
Walsingham Dr WA7 24 D2
Walsingham Rd WA5 14 F5
Walter St
Chester CH1 237 B4
Warrington WA1 16 E7
Widnes WA8 13 D1
Walters Wood SK23 65 F5
Walthall St CW2 190 C2
Waltham Ave WA3 5 C7
Waltham Ct WA7 24 E4
Waltham Dr SK8 35 B6
Waltham Pl CH4 141 A6
Walton Ave WA5 14 E5
Walton Gr ST7 210 C8
Walton Hall & Gdns* WA4 25 F7
Walton Heath Dr SK10 87 B4
Walton Heath Rd WA4 16 B1
Walton La WA3 9 E5
Walton Lea Rd WA4 26 A7
Walton New Rd WA4 26 B8
Walton Pl CH1 117 E4
Walton Rd
Culcheth WA3 4 F3
Warrington WA4 26 C8
Walton St 13 WA7 23 A2
Waltons The CH4 141 E6
Walton Way ST7 210 C8
Wandsworth Way WA8 22 F5
Wansfell Pl WA2 8 A3
WARBURTON 19 C8
Warburton Bridge Rd WA13, WA3 11 A1
Warburton Cl
Altrincham WA15 32 D6
Barnton CW8 77 F4
Lymm WA13 19 A4
Warburton Dr WA15 32 D6
WARBURTON GREEN 32 D6
Warburton La M31, WA13 11 E2
Warburton Rd SK9 34 D4
Warburton St WA4 16 D1
Warburton View WA3 11 A2
Ward Ave SK10 88 A8
Ward Cl WA5 7 B1
Ward La SK12 38 F4
Wardle Ave CW5 187 C7
Wardle Cotts CW5 187 C7
Wardle Cres SK11 111 E1
Wardle Ind Est CW5 187 A7
Wardle Mews CW10 151 D8
Wardle St 7 SK11 112 D7
Wardley Rd WA4 16 B1
Wardour Cl 6 SK11 111 F7
Wardour St WA5 15 E6
WARDSEND 37 A1
Wards La CW12 179 C8
Ward's La CW11 153 C5
Ward's Terr CH2 118 F3
Wareham Cl
Haydock WA11 1 C7
Warrington WA1 17 C8
Wareham Dr CW1 190 B8
Wareham St SK9 60 B7
Warford Ave SK12 37 A2
Warford Cres SK9 84 B7
Warford Hall Dr SK9 84 B6
Warford La WA16 59 B1
WARFORD PARK 58 E1
Warford Terr WA16 59 B2
WARGRAVE 2 D3
Wargrave House Sch WA12 2 C1
Wargrave Mews WA12 2 C1
Wargrave Prim Sch WA12 2 C1
Wargrave Rd WA12 2 C2
Waring Ave
St Helens WA9 1 B2
Warrington WA4 16 F5
Warkworth Cl WA8 12 C3
Warkworth Ct CH65 70 E3
WARMINGHAM 173 D7
Warmingham CE Prim Sch CW11 173 E8
Warmingham Ct CW10 151 D7
Warmingham La
Middlewich CW10 151 D5
Sandbach CW11 174 B8
Warmingham Rd CW1 173 D4
Warnley Cl WA8 12 D3
WARREN 111 D1
Warren Ave
Knutsford WA16 56 E2
Lostock Gralam CW9 80 A3
Warren Cl
Knutsford WA16 56 F2
Middlewich CW10 151 B7
Poynton SK12 36 B4
Warren Croft WA7 50 D7
Warren Ct
Ellesmere Port CH66 69 D3
Frodsham WA6 74 D6
Warren Dr
Altrincham WA15 32 D7
Broughton CH4 139 A3
Ellesmere Port CH66 69 E7
Newton-le-Willows WA12 2 F4
Warren SK11 111 D1
Warrington WA4 26 D8
Warren Gr SK11 111 D1
Warren Hey SK9 60 E8
Warren La
Hartford CW8 103 A4
Warrington WA1 17 D8
Warren Lea SK12 36 E5
Warren Rd
Warrington, Orford WA2 8 D1
Warrington WA4 26 C7
Warren The
Cuddington CW8 101 D5
Newton-le-Willows WA12 2 A3
Warren Way CW6 168 D8
Warrilow Heath Rd ST5 210 C1
WARRINGTON 16 E6
Warrington Ave
Crewe CW1 190 C6
Ellesmere Port CH65 70 B2
Warrington Bank Quay Sta WA1 15 F4
Warrington Bsns Ctr WA2 16 A6
Warrington Bsns Pk WA2 8 C1
Warrington Central Sta WA2 16 B6
Warrington Collegiate WA2 8 B1
Warrington Hospl WA5 15 F6
Warrington La WA13 19 E2
Warrington Mus & Art Gallery* WA1 16 A4
Warrington Rd
Bold Heath L35, WA8 13 D7
Comberbach CW9 78 D7
Cronton L35 12 E8
Cuddington CW8 102 A5
Fowley Common WA3, WN7 5 C5
Golborne WA3, WA12 3 A6
Hatton WA4 25 F4
Little Leigh CW8 77 A5
Lymm WA13 18 B4
Mere WA16 56 B7
Mickle Trafford CH2 119 E7
Northwich CW9 53 E1
Runcorn, Castlefields WA7 23 E2
Runcorn, Manor Park WA7 24 B4
Warrington, Risley WA3 9 E7
Warrington WA5 14 F4
Widnes WA8 13 D1
Warrington Trad Est WA2 16 A6
Warton Cl
Bramhall SK7 36 A7
Warrington WA5 15 A3
Warwick Ave
Newton-le-Willows WA12 2 E2
Warrington, Bewsey WA5 15 F7
Warrington, Great Sankey WA5 14 D7
Warwick Cl
Kidsgrove ST7 195 A3
Knutsford WA16 57 C1
Macclesfield SK11 111 F6
Neston CH64 66 E5
Warwick Ct
Ellesmere Port CH65 70 E2
Warrington WA1 16 E7
Warwick Dr SK7 36 D8
Warwick Gate CW5 217 C2
Warwick Gr 1 WA7 23 F1
Warwick Mews SK11 111 F6
Warwick Pl CW7 149 C6
Warwick Rd
Blacon CH1 117 F5
Irlam M44 11 D5
Macclesfield SK11 111 E6
Warwick Wlk SK11 111 F6
Wasdale Gr CW1 173 B1
WASH END 4 C8
Washington Cl
Biddulph ST8 179 C2
Cheadle SK8 34 F8
Widnes WA8 12 F3

Wash La
Allostock WA16 . . . . 106 E3
Warrington WA4 . . . . 16 E3
Wasley Cl WA2 . . . . .8 F3
Waste La
Cuddington CW8 . . . . 101 E3
Delamere CW8 . . . . 123 F6
Kelsall CW6 . . . . 122 F4
Watch La CW11 . . . . 174 A6
Waterbank Row CW9 . . . . 103 F7
Waterbridge Ct
2 Lymm WA13 . . . . 18 C3
Warrington WA4 . . . . 26 D8
Waterbridge Mews WA7 . . 24 A2
Waterfoot La SK23 . . . . 65 D6
Waterford Dr CH46 . . . . . . 67 A7
Waterford Pl SK8 . . . . 34 B8
Waterford Way WA7 . . . . . 50 C6
Waterfront Dr WA4 . . . . . . 50 F6
Waterfront St CH3 . . . . 237 B3
Watergate Row N CH1 . . . 237 A2
Watergate Row S CH1 . . . . 237 A2
Watergate Sq CH1 . . . . . . 237 A2
Watergate St CH1 . . . . 237 A2
Waterhouse Ave SK10 . . . . 87 F8
Water La SK9 . . . . 60 A7
Water~Lode CW5 . . . . 204 E5
Waterloo Ctr 5 CH65 . . . . . 70 C5
Waterloo Cotts WA6 . . . . . 99 F8
Waterloo Gr ST7 . . . . 195 A2
Waterloo Ho 16 CW8 . . . . 103 F8
Waterloo La WA6 . . . . 74 F1
Waterloo Rd
Bramhall SK7 . . . . 35 F8
Chester CH2 . . . . 118 C4
Haslington CW1 . . . . 191 D4
Northwich CW8 . . . . 103 E7
Poynton SK12 . . . . 37 A2
8 Runcorn WA7 . . . . 22 F3
Runcorn WA7 . . . . 22 F3
Widnes WA8 . . . . 23 A5
Waterloo Street W SK11 . 112 C8
Watermead Dr WA7 . . . . . 50 F5
Watermill Dr SK11 . . . . . . 112 F7
Watersedge WA6 . . . . 49 D2
Waters Edge
Anderton CW9 . . . . 78 D3
Chester CH1 . . . . 118 B2
Waters Edge Mews
CW10 . . . . 151 C8
Watersfield Cl SK8 . . . . . . 34 F8
Waters Gn SK11 . . . . 112 D8
Waterside
Disley SK12 . . . . 38 E7
Furness Vale SK23 . . . . . . 39 E3
Macclesfield SK11 . . . . . . 112 E7
Warrington WA4 . . . . 26 D8
Waterside Cotts CW5 . . . . 216 E5
Waterside Ct WA7 . . . . 22 E3
Waterside Dr WA6 . . . . . . 49 D2
Waterside La WA4 . . . . . . 22 C5
Waterside Mews CW11 . . 174 F3
Waterside Rd SK12, SK22. . 38 E7
Waterside View
Chester CH1 . . . . 237 B3
Northwich CW9 . . . . 104 E6
Waterside Way CW10 . . . . 128 B2
Waters Reach SK12 . . . . . . 36 F5
Water's Reach SK6 . . . . . . 37 E7
Waters Reams CH3. . . . . . 142 B8
Water St
Bollington SK10 . . . . 88 B8
Macclesfield SK11 . . . . . . 112 C8
Newcastle-under-Lyme
ST5 . . . . 210 D2
Newton-le-Willows WA12 . 2 C4
Northwich CW9 . . . . 104 A7
Runcorn WA7 . . . . 23 A3
Widnes WA8 . . . . 23 A3
Water Tower (Mus)★
CH1. . . . . 118 B2
Water Tower St CH1 . . . . . 41 E1
Water Tower St CH1 . . . . 237 A3
Watertower View CH2 . . . 118 F2
Waterway CH3. . . . . 143 B5
Waterways WA5 . . . . 15 D6
Waterworks La
Ellesmere Port CH66 . . . . . 68 E8
Hooton CH66 . . . . 43 E1
Winwick WA2 . . . . 8 B7
Watery La
Astbury CW12 . . . . 178 C5
Frodsham WA6 . . . . 74 E6
Winwick WA2 . . . . 7 E6
Watkins Ave WA12 . . . . 1 F3
Watkinson Way WA8 . . . . . 13 C5
Watkin St
Sandycroft CH5 . . . . 116 A3
Warrington WA2 . . . . 16 B7
Watlands Rd ST7 . . . . 209 E2
Watling Cres CH4 . . . . 141 E7
Watling Ct
Chester CH3 . . . . 119 C2
Cuddington CW8 . . . . 102 B2
Watling Dr CW6 . . . . 123 C6
Watling St CW9 . . . . 103 F8
Watson's Cl CH4 . . . . 139 C3
Watton Cl WA4 . . . . 17 C3
Wavell Ave WA8 . . . . 22 D8
Waveney Dr SK9 . . . . 34 D2
Waverley Ave WA4 . . . . . . 26 D8
Waverley Cl SK10 . . . . 113 A8
Waverley Ct 1 CW2 . . . . . 190 D2
Waverley Dr SK8 . . . . 35 B7
Waverley Terr CH2 . . . . . . 118 E4
WAVERTON 143 B4
Waverton App CH3. . . . . . 164 E6

Waverton Bsns Pk CH3. . . 142 F4
Waverton Cl
Hough CW2 . . . . 206 E2
Northwich CW9 . . . . 103 E4
Waverton Com Prim Sch
CH3. . . . . 143 A5
Waverton Mill Quays
CH3 . . . . 143 B5
Waverton Pk CH66 . . . . . . 69 E5
Wavertree Ave
Scholar Green ST7. . . . . . 194 E7
Widnes WA8 . . . . 23 A8
Wavertree Ct CH66 . . . . . . 69 F7
Wavertree Dr CW10 . . . . . 151 B7
Wavertree Rd CH1 . . . . . . 117 C5
Waybutt La CW2 . . . . 221 D8
Wayfarers Ct CW9 . . . . 79 F7
Wayfarers Dr WA12 . . . . . . 2 E2
Wayford Cl WA6 . . . . 49 B1
Wayford Mews CW11 . . . . 49 B1
Wayles St CW11 . . . . 149 E8
WAY'S GREEN 149 E8
Wayside Cl WA13 . . . . 18 D2
Wayside Ct CH1 . . . . 118 A5
Wayside Dr SK12. . . . . 36 C4
Wayside Linley ST7 . . . . . 193 F2
Wayside Rd SK10 . . . . . . 112 C8
Waystead Cl CW9 . . . . . . 103 F4
Waywell Cl WA2 . . . . 8 F3
Weald Dr CH66 . . . . 69 A6
Wealstone Ct CH2. . . . . . . 118 E5
Weal Stone La CH2. . . . . . 118 E6
Wearhead Cl WA3 . . . . 2 F7
Weaste Ave WA4 . . . . 17 E2
Weates Cl WA8 . . . . 13 F3
Weathercock La CW12 . . . 157 D3
Weatherstones Cotts
CH64 . . . . 67 D8
Weatherstones Mews
CH64 . . . . 67 C8
Weaver Bank CW5 . . . . . . 204 D5
Weaver Cl
Alsager ST7. . . . . 193 A3
Biddulph ST8 . . . . 179 D1
Sandbach CW11 . . . . 174 E7
Weaver Cres WA6. . . . . . . 49 D1
Weaver Ct SK11. . . . . 112 C7
Weaverdale Pk CW8 . . . . . 77 A6
Weaver Gr
Mickle Trafford CH2. . . . . 119 F8
St Helens WA9. . . . . 1 A3
Winsford CW7 . . . . 126 E1
Weaver Grange CW9 . . . . 126 E8
Weaverhall La CW7 . . . . . 150 B5
WEAVERHAM 77 C2
Weaverham High Sch
CW8 . . . . 102 C8
Weaverham Prim Sch
CW8 . . . . 102 B4
Weaverham Way SK9 . . . . 34 E4
Weaver Ho 18 CW8. . . . . 103 F8
Weaver La 49 B2
Weaver Park Ind Est WA6 49 D2
Weaver Prim Sch The
CW5 . . . . 204 E3
Weaver Rd
Culcheth WA3 . . . . 5 A2
Ellesmere Port CH65 . . . . 70 C2
Frodsham WA6 . . . . 49 D1
Moulton CW9 . . . . 126 E7
Nantwich CW5. . . . . 204 E6
Northwich CW8 . . . . 103 E7
Runcorn, Heath WA7 . . . . 49 A6
Weavers Cotts 3 CW12 156 D3
Weavers Fold WA1 . . . . . . 16 C6
Weaverside CW5. . . . . 204 E2
Weaverside Ave WA7. . . . . 49 F4
Weavers La SK7. . . . . 35 D6
Weaver Square Sh Ctr 22
CW9 . . . . 103 F8
Weaver St
Chester CH1 . . . . 237 A2
Winsford CW7 . . . . 126 E1
Weavervale Pk CW8 . . . . . 77 A6
Weaver Valley Rd CW7 . . 126 F3
Weaver View
Audlem CW3 . . . . 229 E3
Church Minshull CW5 . . . 172 A6
Northwich CW8 . . . . 103 F7
Weaverham CW8 . . . . 77 D1
Weaver Way CW9 . . . . 78 F1
Webb Dr WA5 . . . . 6 F6
Webb's Ct CW9 . . . . 103 F7
Webb's La CW10 . . . . 128 C2
Webbs Orch SK23 . . . . . . 65 D8
Webster Cl CH4 . . . . 139 C3
Webster Ct WA5 . . . . 7 B2
Websters La CH66. . . . . . . 69 C5
Weddell Cl WA5 . . . . 15 D7
Wedge Ave WA11 . . . . 1 A5
Wedgwood Ave ST7. . . . . 210 A1
Wedgwood Dr WA8 . . . . . 13 B8
Wedgwood La ST8 . . . . . . 179 C2
Wedgwood Rd ST7. . . . . . 210 D7
Wednesbury Dr WA5 . . . . 14 F6
Weedon Ave WA12 . . . . . . 2 B5
WEETWOOD COMMON . . 122 C2
Weighbridge Rd CH65. . . . 92 A4
Weint The WA3 . . . . 11 B3
Weir Gr ST7 . . . . 195 B2
Weir La WA1 . . . . 17 E6
Weir St
Northwich CW9 . . . . 103 F7
Warrington WA4 . . . . 16 A1
Welbeck Ave WA3 . . . . 3 C7
Welbeck Cl WA12 . . . . 2 D2
Welbeck Cl CW10 . . . . . . 128 B1
Welford Ave WA3 . . . . 3 C7
Welford Cl SK9 . . . . 60 E8

Welland Cl CW11 . . . . 174 C5
Well Ave SY14 . . . . 213 B3
Well Bank CW11 . . . . 175 B6
Well Bank Cotts WA16. . . 108 C8
Wellbank Ct CW12 . . . . . . 156 C2
Well Bank La WA16, SK11 108 C7
Wellbrook Gr WA7. . . . . . . 50 C5
Well Cl CH64 . . . . 67 A4
Wellcroft Cl CW2 . . . . 206 B7
Wellcroft Gdns WA13 . . . . 19 A2
Weller Ave SK12 . . . . 36 E2
Weller Cl SK12. . . . . 36 D2
Wellesbourne Cl
Macclesfield SK10 . . . . . . 86 F1
Neston CH64. . . . . 66 D6
Wellesley Ave
Ellesmere Port CH65. . . . . 70 C5
Haslington CW1. . . . . 191 C4
Wellesley Cl WA1. . . . . 9 B5
Wellesley Wlk 6 CH65 . . . 70 C5
Wellfarm Cl WA1 . . . . 9 B5
Well Farm Cl
Malpas SY14 . . . . 213 B3
Warrington WA1 . . . . 17 D8
Wellfield
Runcorn WA7 . . . . 50 E5
Widnes WA8 . . . . 13 A3
Winsford CW7 . . . . 127 A2
Wellfield Cl WA16. . . . . . . 80 A7
Wellfield Rd WA3 . . . . 4 F4
Wellfield St WA5. . . . . 15 E5
Wellfield Way SY13 . . . . . 225 F1
Wellingford Ave WA8 . . . . 22 B5
Wellington Cir SK10. . . . . 112 E8
Wellington Cl
Congleton CW12 . . . . . . 156 D4
3 Ellesmere Port CH65 . . 70 C5
Knutsford WA16. . . . . 57 C4
Newton-le-Willows WA12 . 2 A3
Warrington WA2 . . . . 8 F2
Wellington Gate L24 . . . . . 21 E2
Wellington Gdns WA12. . . . 2 A3
Wellington Pl CH1 . . . . . . 237 B3
Wellington Rd
Bollington SK10 . . . . 87 F8
Broughton CH4 . . . . 139 B4
Ellesmere Port CH65. . . . . 70 B4
Hazel Grove SK7 . . . . 37 B8
Kidsgrove ST7 . . . . 195 A2
Nantwich CW5. . . . . 204 E4
Wellington Road N CH65 . 70 C5
Wellington St
15 Macclesfield SK11 . . . 112 C8
Newton-le-Willows WA12 . 2 A3
Northwich CW8 . . . . 103 F7
3 Runcorn WA7 . . . . 23 A3
Warrington WA1 . . . . 16 C5
Weston CW2 . . . . 207 B5
Widnes WA8 . . . . 23 A4
Wellington Street Ind Est
WA8. . . . . 23 A4
Wellington Street Wrkshps
WA1. . . . . 16 C5
Well La
Alsager ST7. . . . . 193 C3
Antrobus CW9 . . . . 53 A4
Biddulph ST8 . . . . 179 D3
Chester CH2 . . . . 118 E5
Heswall CH60 . . . . 41 B6
Kingsley WA6. . . . . 75 C2
Little Budworth CW6 . . . . 147 F7
Macclesfield SK10 . . . . . . 88 B2
Manley WA6. . . . . 98 F3
Mollington CH1 . . . . 94 F2
Neston CH64. . . . . 66 F5
Prestbury SK10 . . . . 87 C8
Stretton WA4. . . . . 52 E8
Warrington WA5 . . . . 14 F3
Weaverham CW8. . . . . 77 C1
Wells Ave CW1 . . . . 191 D5
Wells Ct
Ellesmere Port CH66 . . . . 94 E8
Gatley SK8. . . . . 34 C7
Mickle Trafford CH2. . . . . 119 F8
Warrington WA1 . . . . 17 B8
WELLS GREEN 205 F8
Well St
Malpas SY14 . . . . 213 B3
Mow Cop ST7 . . . . 195 D7
New Mills SK22 . . . . 39 B8
Winsford CW7 . . . . 126 C1
Wellstood Dr CW2 . . . . . . 205 F7
Wellwood Rd CH66. . . . . . 69 E7
Welsby Cl WA2 . . . . 8 F3
Welsh La CW7 . . . . 149 D6
Welshmen's La CW5 . . . . 204 C7
Welshpool Cl WA5 . . . . . . 7 D2
Welsh Rd
Connah's Quay CH5 . . . . 116 A7
Ellesmere Port CH66 . . . . 68 E4
Woodbank CH1 . . . . 93 D3
Welsh Road Cotts CH1 . . . 93 D8
Welsh Row
Nantwich CW5. . . . . 204 D5
Nether Alderley SK10 . . . . 84 F6
Welton Cl SK9 . . . . 59 F4
Welton Dr SK9 . . . . 59 F4
Welton Gr SK9 . . . . 59 E4
Welwyn Cl WA4. . . . . 17 C3
Wemyss Rd CH1 . . . . 117 D7
Wendover Cl WA11 . . . . . . 1 D7
Wenger Rd WA8 . . . . 13 B5
Wenlock Cl
Macclesfield SK10 . . . . . . 87 B2
Newcastle-under-Lyme
ST5 . . . . 210 E2

Wenlock Cl continued
Warrington WA1 . . . . 17 A8
Wenlock Gdns CH66. . . . . 69 F2
Wenlock La CH66 . . . . 69 F2
Wenlock Rd WA7 . . . . 50 A4
Wenlock Way CH4 . . . . . . 140 F6
Wensleydale Ave
Bebington CH62. . . . . 43 E5
Congleton CW12 . . . . . . 157 A5
Wensleydale Cl WA5 . . . . 14 F8
Wensley Dr SK7. . . . . 36 D7
Wensley Rd WA3. . . . . 3 E7
Wentworth Ave
Macclesfield SK11 . . . . . . 111 F6
Warrington WA1 . . . . 17 B7
Wentworth Cl
Northwich CW9 . . . . 104 E7
Widnes WA8 . . . . 13 A5
Wentworth Dr
Bebington CH63. . . . . 43 C5
Bramhall SK7. . . . . 36 A7
Wentworth Gr CW7 . . . . . 126 A2
Werburgh Cl WA13 . . . . . . 19 C8
WERETON 209 C1
Wereton Rd ST7 . . . . 209 D1
WERVIN 96 A4
Wervin Rd CH2 . . . . 96 A3
Wesleyan Mus★ ST7 . . . . . 195 D7
Wesley Ave
Alsager ST7. . . . . 193 D4
Haydock WA11. . . . . 1 F7
2 Sandbach CW11. . . . . . 175 B6
Wesley Cl
Nantwich CW5. . . . . 204 E5
Neston CH64. . . . . 66 D8
Wesley Ct
Congleton CW12 . . . . . . 156 D2
Winsford CW7 . . . . 126 F1
Wesley Gdns 7 ST7 . . . . . 195 A2
Wesley Pl
Crewe CW2 . . . . 190 D2
4 Northwich CW9 . . . . . 104 A8
Wesley St ST7 . . . . 210 A1
Wessex Cl
Shavington CW2 . . . . 206 C3
Warrington WA1 . . . . 17 E7
Wessex Dr CW9 . . . . 104 C6
Westage La CW9. . . . . 79 B8
West Ave
Crewe CW1 . . . . 190 B4
Kidsgrove ST7 . . . . 194 C1
Middlewich CW10 . . . . . . 128 C2
Northwich CW9 . . . . 104 D7
Warrington, Stockton Heath
WA4 . . . . 16 C1
Warrington WA2 . . . . 16 B8
Weston CW2 . . . . 207 B5
WEST BANK 23 A4
West Bank
Alderley Edge SK9. . . . . . 85 A8
Chester CH2 . . . . 118 F3
West Bank Dock Est WA8. 22 E5
West Bank Prim Sch WA8 23 A4
West Bank Rd SK10 . . . . . 87 B1
West Bank St WA8 . . . . . . 23 A5
West Bond St SK11 . . . . . 112 C7
Westbourne Ave CW1 . . . 190 A6
Westbourne Dr 10 SK9 . . 34 D1
Westbourne Ho CW12. . . . 156 B2
Westbourne Mews
CW12. . . . . 156 B2
Westbourne Rd
Blacon CH1 . . . . 118 A4
Warrington WA4 . . . . 26 B7
Westbridge Mews WA1. . . 16 F7
Westbrook Ave WA4 . . . . . 16 D2
WESTBROOK CENTRE . . . 7 B1
Westbrook Cres WA5 . . . . 7 B2
Westbrook Cr WA5 . . . . . . 7 C1
Westbrook Dr SK10 . . . . . 87 C1
Westbrook Old Hall Prim Sch
WA5 . . . . 15 D8
Westbrook Way WA6 . . . . 75 B2
Westbrook Way WA5 . . . . . 7 B1
Westbury Cl
Crewe CW2 . . . . 206 C7
Middlewich CW10 . . . . . . 151 B8
Warrington WA1 . . . . 17 A8
Westbury Ct SK11 . . . . . . 112 A7
Westbury Dr SK11 . . . . . . 112 A7
Westbury Way CH4. . . . . . 140 F6
Westby Cl SK7 . . . . 36 A7
West Cheshire Coll
Chester CW1 . . . . 69 C1
Chester CH4 . . . . 141 D7
Ellesmere Port CH65 . . . . 70 B5
West Cl SK10 . . . . 87 F7
Westcliffe Ct WA8 . . . . . . 13 B4
Westcliff Gdns WA1. . . . . . 26 E3
Westdale Rd WA1 . . . . 17 A7
West Dr
Heswall CH60 . . . . 41 A7
Neston CH64. . . . . 66 E6
Winsford CW7 . . . . 127 A2
West Dudley St CW7 . . . . 126 F1
West End CH3 . . . . 121 E7
West End Cotts CW12 . . . 156 C2
West End Ct LL13 . . . . . . 196 D8
West End La WA11 . . . . . . 1 A6
Westenra Ave CH65 . . . . . 69 F6
Westerham CH3 . . . . 121 E7
Westerhope Way WA8. . . . 12 F3
Westerings The CH62 . . . . 43 C6
Western App CH2 . . . . . . 118 E4

Western Ave
Blacon CH1 . . . . 117 D4
Macclesfield SK11 . . . . . . 112 C5
Milton Green CH3 . . . . . . 165 C2
Nantwich CW5. . . . . 204 E3
Western Ave Sh Mall 7
CH1. . . . . 117 D4
Western Ct CH2 . . . . 118 E4
Western Dr SK11. . . . . 112 C5
Western Pk CW11 . . . . . . 191 F8
Westfield Ave ST7 . . . . . . 209 C2
Westfield Cl
Chester CH4 . . . . 141 B7
Winsford CW7 . . . . 149 C5
Westfield Cres WA7. . . . . . 22 E1
Westfield Dr
Knutsford WA16. . . . . 56 E1
Willaston CW9 . . . . 205 E8
Westfield Gr CW8 . . . . 77 F4
Westfield Mews WA7. . . . . 22 E1
Westfield Prim Sch WA7 . 22 E1
Westfield Rd
Cheadle SK8 . . . . 34 F8
Mow Cop ST7 . . . . 195 C7
Northwich CW9 . . . . 104 B7
Runcorn WA7 . . . . 22 E1
Westfields WA15. . . . . 31 F8
Westfields SK10 . . . . 87 B1
Westfields Rise CW3 . . . . 232 C1
Westford Rd WA3. . . . . . . 16 A1
Westgate
Widnes WA8 . . . . 22 B7
Wilmslow SK9 . . . . 60 A5
Westgate Ave CW7 . . . . . 126 A1
Westgate Pk CW2. . . . . . . 206 E2
West Gn CH5 . . . . 116 A6
West Gr
Alsager ST7. . . . . 193 E4
Heswall CH60 . . . . 40 F8
West Hall St WA16 . . . . . . 7 Z
Westhay Cres WA3. . . . . . 10 A5
WEST HEATH
Congleton 156 A4
Crewe 221 D8
West Heath Gr WA13. . . . 18 C4
West Heath Sh Ctr
CW12 . . . . 156 A3
Westholme Cl
Congleton CW12 . . . . . . 156 C3
Crewe CW2 . . . . 206 C8
Westhouse Cl CH63 . . . . . 43 C5
West House Cl WA13. . . . . 18 C3
West La
Cuddington CW8 . . . . 101 F3
High Legh WA16 . . . . 29 C6
Runcorn WA7 . . . . 49 F8
Westland Dr CW12 . . . . . 156 C2
Westland Dr WA3 . . . . 8 E2
Westlands CW7 . . . . 209 F2
Westlands Cl CH64 . . . . . . 41 F1
Westlands Rd CW10 . . . . 128 B1
Westlands The CW8 . . . . . 156 B1
West Lorne St CW8 . . . . . 237 A3
West Mains L24. . . . . 21 A3
West Mere CW2 . . . . 207 B5
Westmere Dr CW1 . . . . . . 190 F2
Westminster Ave CH44 . . . 141 B7
Westminster Cl
Middlewich CW10 . . . . . . 128 B1
9 Northwich CW9 . . . . . 103 C5
Warrington WA4 . . . . 17 C2
Widnes WA8 . . . . 22 B8
Westminster Ct CH2 . . . . 118 F2
Westminster Dr
Bebington CH62. . . . . 43 D7
Cheadle SK8 . . . . 35 B6
Haydock WA11. . . . . 1 F7
Wilmslow SK9 . . . . 60 A4
Westminster Gn CH65 . . . 70 C6
6 Winsford CW7 . . . . . . 149 A8
WESTMINSTER PARK . . . 141 B6
Westminster Pl 1 WA1 . . 16 B5
Westminster Prim Sch
CH65. . . . . 70 B6
Westminster Rd
Broughton CH4 . . . . 139 B3
Chester CH2 . . . . 118 F3
Ellesmere Port CH65 . . . . 70 C6
Macclesfield SK10 . . . . . . 87 C1
4 Macclesfield SK10 . . . 87 C1
Westminster Ret Pk CH65 70 D6
Westminster St
Crewe CW2 . . . . 190 C2
10 Warrington WA1 . . . . 16 B5
Westminster Terr CH4 . . . 141 C7
Westmorland Cl WA14 . . . 31 B8
Westmorland Ave
Talke ST7. . . . . 210 F7
Widnes WA8 . . . . 13 B1
Westmorland Cl SK10 . . . . 86 F2
Westmorland Rd M31 . . . . 11 E2
Westmorland Terr CW4 . . 130 B3
WESTON
Crewe 207 C5
Macclesfield 111 F8
Weston Cl
Middlewich CW10 . . . . . . 151 C7
Northwich CW9 . . . . 103 F5
Weston Cres WA7. . . . . . . 49 A6

Weston Ct
Runcorn WA7 . . . . 48 F7
Weston Gr
Chester CH2 . . . . 118 E7
Halewood L26 . . . . 21 A6
Weston La CW2 . . . . 206 E5
Weston Link WA7 . . . . 49 D6
WESTON POINT 48 D7
Weston Point Expressway
Runcorn, Rocksavage
WA7 . . . . 49 B5
Runcorn WA7 . . . . 48 E7
Runcorn, Weston WA7 . . . 49 A6
Weston Point Prim Sch
WA7 . . . . 48 E7
Weston Prim Sch WA7 . . . 49 A6
Weston Rd
Crewe CW1 . . . . 190 F1
Runcorn WA7 . . . . 48 E7
Weston CW1, CW2 . . . . . 207 B7
Wilmslow SK9 . . . . 60 E6
Weston Sq SK11 . . . . 111 F7
Weston View WA9 . . . . 49 D4
WESTON VILLAGE 48 E7
Weston Village Prim Sch
CW2 . . . . 207 C5
Westover Rd WA1 . . . . 16 F8
West Park Ave SK12 . . . . . 36 A4
West Park Dr 7 WA6 . . . . 94 F8
West Quay Rd WA2 . . . . . . .7 F3
West Rd
Congleton CW12 . . . . . . 156 C3
Ellesmere Port CH65 . . . . 70 C3
Runcorn WA7 . . . . 48 D7
Weaverham CW8 . . . . 77 B1
Westrees WA8 . . . . 101 D5
West Side Ave WA11 . . . . . . 1 A6
West St
Alderley Edge SK9 . . . . . . 60 A1
Chester CH2 . . . . 237 C4
Congleton CW12 . . . . . . 156 D3
Crewe CW1 . . . . 190 B5
Haslington CW1 . . . . 191 C5
Macclesfield SK11 . . . . . 112 B8
Middlewich CW10 . . . . . . 128 C1
Mount Pleasant ST7 . . . . 195 B6
Warrington WA2 . . . . 16 B7
West Vale CH64 . . . . 66 E6
West View
Antrobus WA4 . . . . 53 A5
Ellesmere Port CH66 . . . . 69 A8
Northwich CW9 . . . . 104 B8
Warrington WA2 . . . . 9 A1
West View Rd WA6 . . . . . . 101 A6
Westville Dr CW12 . . . . . . 156 A2
Westward Rd
Chester CH3 . . . . 142 B8
Shavington SK9 . . . . 59 F6
Westway CH60 . . . . 40 F6
West Way
Holmes Chapel CW4 . . . . 130 B3
Sandbach CW11 . . . . . . 174 F4
Shavington CW2 . . . . . . 206 D5
West Wing The CW10 . . . . 127 D5
Westwood WA3 . . . . .3 C8
Westwood Cl CW2 . . . . . . 207 B1
Westwood Ct CH64 . . . . . . 41 E2
Westwood Rd SK8 . . . . . . 34 B8
WESTY 16 F5
Westy La WA4 . . . . 16 F4
Wet Gate La WA13 . . . . . . 19 E4
Wetheral Rd SK10 . . . . . . 87 B2
Wetherby Cl
Macclesfield SK11 . . . . . 118 B2
Newton-le-Willows WA12 . . 2 C5
Wetherby Way CH66 . . . . . 69 B5
Wetreins La SY14, CH3 . . 197 D6
WETTENHALL 170 F7
WETTENHALL GREEN 170 F6
Wettenhall Rd CW5 . . . . . 188 B4
Wetton La CW8 . . . . 76 E4
Wetton Way SK11 . . . . . . 113 D2
Wexford Ave L24 . . . . 21 D2
Wexford Cl WA11 . . . . 1 D7
Weybourne Cl CH4 . . . . . . 140 E5
Weybridge Cl WA4 . . . . . . 26 E7
Weybridge Dr SK10 . . . . . . 87 B3
Weygates Dr WA15 . . . . . . 32 C7
Weymouth Cl WA7 . . . . 50 E6
Weymouth Rd WA5 . . . . . . .6 F6
Whaddon Dr CH4 . . . . 140 F4
WHALEY BRIDGE 65 D7
Whaley Bridge Prim Sch
SK23 . . . . 65 E2
Whaley Bridge Sta SK23 . . 65 E8
Whaley Ct CH1 . . . . 117 A8
Whaley La SK23 . . . . 65 C8
Whalley Dr CW6 . . . . 147 B3
Whalley Gr WA8 . . . . 13 D3
Whalley Hayes SK10 . . . . 112 C8
Whalley Rd CW9 . . . . 104 A8
Whalley St WA1 . . . . 16 C6
Wharams Bank CW11 . . . . 176 F5
Wharburton Cl WA8 . . . . . 101 F2
Wharf Cl SK23 . . . . 65 E7
Wharfdale Ave CW1 . . . . . 173 B1
Wharfdale Cl WA5 . . . . 15 A7
Wharfe Cl CW12 . . . . 156 F1
Wharfedale WA5 . . . . 50 B6
Wharfedale Dr CH66 . . . . . 43 F5
Wharfedale Rd CW12 . . . . 157 A5
Wharfe La CH65 . . . . 70 A7

Wharf Ind Est The WA1 . . . 16 C4
Wharf La CW12 . . . . 178 B3
Wharf Mill CW12 . . . . 156 F1
Wharford La WA7 . . . . 24 E3
Wharf Rd
Collins Green WA12 . . . . . . 1 E2
Whaley Bridge SK23 . . . . 65 E7
Wharfside Cl 6 WA4 . . . . . 16 E1
Wharf St WA1 . . . . 16 C4
Wharf The
Chester CH1 . . . . 118 B1
Runcorn WA7 . . . . 50 F6
Wharmby Rd WA11 . . . . 1 E6
WHARTON 127 A2
Wharton CE Prim Sch
CW7 . . . . 126 F1
Wharton Ct CH2 . . . . 118 F2
Wharton Gdns CW7 . . . . . 127 A3
Wharton Gn CW7 . . . . 127 A4
WHARTON GREEN 127 B4
Wharton Hall CW7 . . . . . . 127 A2
Wharton Ind Est CW7 . . . 126 F2
Wharton Park Rd CW7 . . . 126 F2
Wharton Rd CW7 . . . . 127 A2
Wharton Ret Pk CW7 . . . . 126 F3
Whatcroft Cl WA7 . . . . 49 D6
Whatcroft Hall La CW9 . . 104 F1
Whatcroft La CW9 . . . . . . 127 E8
Wheatcroft Cl WA5 . . . . . . 15 C6
Wheatfield Cl
Barnton CW8 . . . . 78 A3
Ellesmere Port CH66 . . . . 69 C3
Macclesfield SK10 . . . . . 87 C3
Wheatfield Rd WA8 . . . . . . 12 C5
Wheatland Rd CH60 . . . . . 41 C7
Wheatlands WA7 . . . . 23 E1
Wheatley Ave WA12 . . . . . . 2 C5
Wheatley Rd CW1, CW6 . . . 190 E6
Wheat Moss SK11 . . . . 84 B3
Wheatsheaf Cl SK23 . . . . . 65 E6
Wheatsheaf Rd SK23 . . . . . 65 E6
Wheelman Rd CW1 . . . . . . 190 A7
WHEELOCK 174 F4
Wheelock Cl
Alsager ST7 . . . . 193 A3
Handforth SK9 . . . . 34 D1
Kingsmead CW9 . . . . . . 103 F6
Wheelock Ct CW1 . . . . 175 A2
Wheelock Dr CW7 . . . . 127 B1
WHEELOCK HEATH 192 A8
Wheelock Prim Sch
CW11 . . . . 175 A4
Wheelock St CW10 . . . . . . 128 C1
Wheelock Way 2 ST7 . . . 195 B2
Wheldon Cl CW2 . . . . 118 E8
Wheldon Rd WA8 . . . . 21 F7
Wheldrake Cl CH66 . . . . . . 69 B5
Whernside WA8 . . . . 12 C3
Whetstone Hey CH66 . . . . 69 D5
Whetstone Rd ST8 . . . . . . 179 C2
Wheycroft Mews CW1 . . . . 190 C5
Whickham Cl WA4 . . . . 17 A3
Whimbrel Ave WA12 . . . . . . 2 C3
Whimbrel Cl WA7 . . . . 49 F5
Whinchat Ave WA12 . . . . . . 2 C4
Whinchat Cl WA3 . . . . 3 E7
Whinchat Dr WA3 . . . . 9 F3
Whinfell Gr WA7 . . . . 49 E5
Whipcord La CH1 . . . . 118 B2
Whirley Cl CW10 . . . . 151 C7
WHIRLEY GROVE 86 D3
Whirley La SK10 . . . . 85 F1
Whirley Prim Sch SK10 . . 86 C1
Whirley Rd SK10 . . . . 86 C1
Whirlow Rd CW2 . . . . 206 B7
WHISTERFIELD 109 D3
Whisterfield La SK11 . . . . 109 E3
Whiston Cl
Macclesfield SK11 . . . . . 112 B4
Winsford CW7 . . . . 127 A4
Whiston Mews SK11 . . . . . 113 B4
Whiston St SK11 . . . . 112 C7
Whitbarrow Rd WA13 . . . . 18 D4
WHITBY 70 A4
Whitby Ave
Chester CH2 . . . . 118 D5
Warrington WA2 . . . . 8 D2
Whitby Cl
Crewe CW1 . . . . 190 B8
Poynton SK12 . . . . 36 D4
WHITBYHEATH 70 B1
Whitby Heath Prim Sch
CH65 . . . . 70 B3
Whitby High Sch The
CH65 . . . . 70 A2
Whitby La CH1 . . . . 95 B6
Whitby Park Nature
Reserve* CH65 . . . . 70 B3
Whitby Rd
Ellesmere Port CH65 . . . . 70 C5
Runcorn WA7 . . . . 23 A1
Whitby's La CW7 . . . . 126 B1
WHITCHURCH 226 A1
Whitchurch Cl WA1 . . . . . . 17 A8
Whitchurch Gr ST5 . . . . . 210 E2
Whitchurch Rd
Audlem CW3 . . . . 229 C3
Broxton CH3 . . . . 183 A3
Chester CH3 . . . . 119 B1
Christleton CH3 . . . . 142 E7
Edge Green SY14, CH3 . . 199 B4
Handley CH3 . . . . 182 D8
Milton Green CH3 . . . . . 165 C4
Newhall CW5, SY13 . . . . 228 A6
Royal's Green CW3, SY13 228 C2
Sound CW5 . . . . 217 E3
Waverton CH3 . . . . 143 A3
Whitchurch Way WA7 . . . . 49 D7

White Ave CW2 . . . . 189 F4
Whitebarn Rd WA5 . . . . . . 85 B8
Whitebeam Ave 5 CH66 . . 69 F1
Whitebeam Cl
Newcastle-under-Lyme
ST5 . . . . 210 D1
Runcorn WA7 . . . . 24 C1
Whitebeam Row CW8 . . . . 102 E7
White Bear Yd 13 WA16 . . 57 A2
White Clover Sq WA13 . . . 19 A2
White Ct SK10 . . . . 87 E2
Whitecroft Heath Rd
SK11 . . . . 109 B3
Whitecroft Rd CH66 . . . . . . 69 E2
Whitecroft Villas M31 . . . . 11 E2
WHITECROSS 15 E6
Whitecross Rd WA5 . . . . . 15 E5
Whitecross WA13 . . . . 19 A4
Whitefield Ave WA12 . . . . . 2 E2
Whitefield Cl
Golborne WA3 . . . . 3 A8
Lymm WA13 . . . . 19 A5
Whitefield Ct WA3 . . . . 4 F2
Whitefield Gr WA13 . . . . . 19 A4
Whitefield Rd WA4 . . . . . . 26 B8
Whitegate CH2 . . . . 72 B3
White Friars CH1 . . . . 237 A2
Whitefriars Wlk 4 M22 . . 33 D8
WHITEGATE 126 C8
Whitegate Ave WA3 . . . . . . 4 F2
Whitegate CE Prim Sch
CW8 . . . . 125 F7
Whitegate Cl CW10 . . . . . 151 C6
Whitegate Fields LL13 . . . 180 D1
Whitegate La CH3 . . . . . . 121 E7
Whitegate Rd CW7 . . . . . 125 F3
Whitegates CW12 . . . . . . 179 D4
Whitegates Cl CH64 . . . . . 42 E1
Whitegates Cres CH64 . . . 42 E1
Whitegates Rd CW9 . . . . . 189 E2
Whitehall Ave ST7 . . . . . . 194 F2
Whitehall Cl
Barnton CW8 . . . . 78 A4
Wilmslow SK9 . . . . 60 A5
Whitehall Ct 3 CW5 . . . . 204 D5
Whitehall Dr CW8 . . . . . . 103 C5
Whitehall La CW6 . . . . . . 124 E1
White Hall La CW5 . . . . . . 151 E1
White Hart Gdns CW8 . . . 102 F4
White Hart La CW2 . . . . . 205 E8
Whitehaven La CW5 . . . . . 203 A7
Whitehaven Rd SK7 . . . . . . 35 C5
WHITE HILL 195 B2
Whitehill Rd SK7 . . . . 195 B2
White House Cl WA11 . . . . .1 B6
White House Dr WA15 . . . . 32 B8
White House Dr WA1 . . . . . 17 E7
Whitehouse Expressway
WA7 . . . . 50 B5
Whitehouse Ind Est WA7 . . 50 E4
Whitehouse La
Nantwich CW5 . . . . 204 F7
Partington WA14 . . . . . . 20 D8
Plumley WA16 . . . . 80 F5
Whitehouse Rd WA16 . . . . 30 B3
White La CH3 . . . . 142 D8
Whiteleas Rd SK23 . . . . . . 65 D3
Whitelegg La WA13 . . . . . . 19 E1
WHITELEY GREEN 62 E2
White Lodge Cl CH62 . . . . 43 D5
White Lodge Mews CW8 . 102 A3
Whitemere Ct CH65 . . . . . 70 C7
WHITEMOOR 179 D6
Whitemore Rd CW10 . . . . 151 C6
Whitepark Cl CW10 . . . . . 128 D2
Whiteridge Rd ST7 . . . . . . 195 B2
Whitesands Rd WA13 . . . . 18 C4
Whiteside Rd WA11 . . . . . . 1 B6
Whites La CW2 . . . . 207 B6
Whites Mdw CH3 . . . . 142 A7
Whitesmead Cl SK12 . . . . 38 D5
White St
Macclesfield SK11 . . . . . 112 D6
Warrington, Stockton Heath
WA4 . . . . 16 A5
Warrington WA1 . . . . 16 A5
Widnes WA8 . . . . 23 A5
Whitethorn Ave WA5 . . . . . 14 F5
Whitethorn Way ST5 . . . . 210 E1
Whitethroat Wlk WA3 . . . . .9 F3
Whitewell Cl CW5 . . . . . . 204 F5
Whitewood La SY14 . . . . . 212 D7
Whitfield Ave WA1 . . . . . . 16 F7
Whitfield Dr SK11 . . . . . . 112 B4
Whitfield Rd WA11 . . . . 1 A6
Whitfields The SK10 . . . . . 87 A1
Whitley Ave
Barnton WA8 . . . . 78 B3
Warrington WA1 . . . . 17 A4
Whitley Cl
Middlewich CW10 . . . . . 151 B7
Runcorn WA7 . . . . 48 F8
Whitley Dr CW8 . . . . 103 A4
Whitley La WA16 . . . . 55 B8
Whitley Prim Sch WA4 . . . 52 D1
WHITLEY REED 53 D8
Whitlow Ave CW5 . . . . . . 204 F8
Whitney Cl WA16 . . . . 126 F8
Whitney Croft SK10 . . . . . 113 A8
Whitson Cl WA16 . . . . 29 C4
Whitstable Rd WA8 . . . . . . 12 E4
Whittaker Ave WA2 . . . . . . 8 D2
Whittaker Cl
Congleton CW12 . . . . . . 156 E5
Crewe CW1 . . . . 190 A7

Whittington Gdns CW9 . . 104 A2
Whittle Ave
Haydock WA11 . . . . 1 A5
Warrington WA5 . . . . 15 A7
Whittle Cl CH5 . . . . 116 A3
Whittle Hall La WA5 . . . . . 14 F6
Whittlewood Cl WA3 . . . . . 10 A5
Whitton Dr CH2 . . . . 118 E5
Whitwell Cl WA5 . . . . 15 D6
Whitworth Ct WA3 . . . . 9 E3
Wicker La
Altrincham WA15 . . . . 32 C8
Guilden Sutton CH3 . . . . 120 A4
Wicklow Cl CH66 . . . . 69 A6
Wickson La CH3, CW6 . . . 167 D3
Wickstead Cl CW5 . . . . . . 205 A4
Wicksten Dr WA7 . . . . 23 C2
Widdale Cl WA5 . . . . 14 F7
Widgeon Cl SK12 . . . . 36 B4
Widgeons Covert CH63 . . . 41 F5
WIDNES 22 E7
Widnes Rd
Cuerdley Cross WA5, WA8 . 13 F2
Warrington WA5 . . . . 14 C3
Widnes WA8 . . . . 23 B8
Widnes Sh Pk 16 WA8 . . . 23 B8
Widnes Sta WA8 . . . . 13 A3
Widnes Trade Pk WA8 . . . 23 C8
Widnes Waterfront WA8 . . 23 C7
Wiend The CW7 . . . . 118 D4
Wigg Island Nature
Reserve* WA7 . . . . 23 E4
Wight Cl CH65 . . . . 70 C1
Wightman Ave WA12 . . . . . 2 C5
Wigmore Cl WA3 . . . . 10 A6
Wigsey La WA13 . . . . 19 A7
WIGSHAW 4 D2
Wigshaw La WA3 . . . . 4 D2
Wigwam Cl SK12 . . . . 36 C4
Wilbraham Cl
Acton CW5 . . . . 204 A7
Mickle Trafford CH2 . . . . 119 F8
Wilbraham Rd
Acton CW5 . . . . 204 A7
Congleton CW12 . . . . . . 156 F3
Weaverham CW8 . . . . 77 E1
Wilbrahams Way ST7 . . . . 193 D4
Wilbraham's Wlk ST7 . . . 209 D2
Wilcock Rd WA11 . . . . .2 B8
Wilcote Cl WA8 . . . . 12 F3
Wilcott Dr SK9 . . . . 59 F4
Wild Arum Cl 3 WA3 . . . . .3 E8
WILDBOARCLOUGH 137 E6
Wilderhope Cl CW2 . . . . . 206 C7
WILDERSPOOL 16 C2
Wilderspool Cres WA4 . . . 16 B1
Wilderspool Cswy WA4 . . . 16 C3
Wild Goose Ave ST7 . . . . 195 D3
Wilding Ave 8 WA7 . . . . . 23 B2
Wildings Old La WA3 . . . . .9 A8
Wilding St CW1 . . . . 190 E4
Wildmoor La CH3 . . . . 97 D1
Wildwood Gr WA1 . . . . 17 B7
WILKESLEY 233 F7
Wilkin Croft 5 SK8 . . . . . 34 E8
Wilkins La SK9 . . . . 33 E5
Wilkinson Ave WA1 . . . . . . 16 F6
Wilkinson Cl WA8 . . . . 23 A5
Wilkinson St CW7 . . . . . . 149 B6
Wilkinson St
Ellesmere Port CH65 . . . . 70 C6
Warrington WA2 . . . . 16 C7
Wilkinson Street Mews 1
CH65 . . . . 70 C6
Wilkinson Street N CH65 . 70 C6
Wilkinson Way CW7 . . . . . 149 B7
Willan Rd CH1 . . . . 117 D4
WILLASTON
Ellesmere Port 68 A8
Nantwich 205 D8
Willaston Dr L26 . . . . 21 A6
Willaston Farm CH64 . . . . 67 F8
Willaston Green Mews
CH64 . . . . 67 F8
Willaston Hall Gdns
CW5 . . . . 205 C6
Willaston Prim Sch
Willaston CH64 . . . . 67 F8
Willaston CW5 . . . . 205 D6
Willaston Rd CH63, CH64 . 42 D4
Willaston Way 6 SK9 . . . . 34 D5
Willbank La CW5 . . . . 202 D5
Willeymoor La SY13 . . . . . 225 D8
William Barker Cl 7
CW11 . . . . 175 B6
William Beamont Com High
Sch & Specialist Sports
Coll WA2 . . . . 8 C1
William Foden Cl CW11 . . 174 D7
William Johnson Gdns
CH65 . . . . 70 C6
William Penn Cl WA5 . . . . 14 E5
William Rd ST7 . . . . 195 A1
Williams Ave WA12 . . . . . . 2 C5
Williams Cl CH2 . . . . 118 C4
Williamson Cres SK23 . . . 65 D8
Williamson Dr CW5 . . . . . 204 C5
Williamson Rd SK23 . . . . . 65 D8
William St
Chester CH1 . . . . 237 B3
Chester, Hoole Park CH2 . 118 F3
Congleton CW12 . . . . . . 157 A4
Macclesfield SK10 . . . . . 112 F8
6 Northwich CW9 . . . . 104 B8
Widnes WA8 . . . . 13 C1

William St continued
Winsford CW7 . . . . 126 E1
William Stockton Cty Prim
Sch CH65 . . . . 70 B5
Williams Way
Frodsham WA6 . . . . 74 A8
Henbury SK11 . . . . 111 C8
Willington Ave CH62 . . . . . 43 E3
Willington Cnr CW6 . . . . . 122 E2
Willington La
Duddon CW6 . . . . 145 E7
Kelsall CW6 . . . . 122 D4
Willington Rd
Duddon CW6 . . . . 145 B7
Kelsall CW6 . . . . 122 C2
Willis St WA1 . . . . 16 D6
Willmer Cres ST7 . . . . . . 195 B6
Willotts Hill Rd ST5 . . . . . 210 D1
Willoughby Cl WA5 . . . . . . 7 C1
Willow Ave
Newton-le-Willows WA12 . . 2 E4
2 Widnes WA8 . . . . 13 B2
Willoway Rd CH3 . . . . 119 B2
Willow Bank
Cheadle SK8 . . . . 35 A6
Helsby WA6 . . . . 73 D2
Nantwich CW5 . . . . 204 F6
Willowbank Dr SK10 . . . . . 88 C8
Willow Bank Est WA12 . . . 2 F4
Willowbrook CH5 . . . . . . 116 B4
Willowbrow Rd CH63,
CH64 . . . . 42 D3
Willow Cl
Chester CH2 . . . . 118 C3
Lymm WA13 . . . . 18 E4
Newcastle-under-Lyme
ST5 . . . . 210 D1
Paddockhill WA16 . . . . . 59 B5
Poynton SK12 . . . . 36 E3
Runcorn WA7 . . . . 49 C7
Winsford CW7 . . . . 126 D3
Willow Cres
Chester CH2 . . . . 119 A4
Crewe CW2 . . . . 189 F2
Moore WA4 . . . . 25 A7
Warrington WA1 . . . . 17 B8
Willowcroft Way ST7 . . . . 195 E4
Willow Ct
Alsager ST7 . . . . 193 E4
Connah's Quay CH5 . . . . 91 D1
Higher Kinnerton CH4 . . . 161 A7
Macclesfield SK10 . . . . . 87 B2
Middlewich CW10 . . . . . 128 C2
Nantwich CW5 . . . . 204 F7
Newton-le-Willows WA12 . . 2 D4
Warrington WA2 . . . . 7 F3
Winsford CW7 . . . . 127 B2
Willowdale WA12 . . . . 2 E3
Willowdale Way CH66 . . . . 94 F8
Willow Dr
Blacon CH1 . . . . 117 D5
Bunbury CW6 . . . . 185 E8
Handforth SK9 . . . . 34 D3
Sandbach CW11 . . . . . . 175 E7
Warrington WA4 . . . . 16 E1
Willow Gn
Knutsford WA16 . . . . 56 F3
Weaverham CW8 . . . . . . 102 D8
Willow Gr
Barnton CW8 . . . . 78 B4
Chester CH2 . . . . 119 B4
Ellesmere Port CH66 . . . . 95 A8
Elton CH2 . . . . 72 A3
WILLOW GREEN 77 B5
Willow Green La CW8 . . . . 77 B5
Willow Hayes CH3 . . . . . . 121 F7
Willowherb Cl CH3 . . . . . . 142 A6
Willow La
Goostrey CW4 . . . . 107 E1
Thornton Hough CH63,
CH64 . . . . 42 D3
Warrington WA4 . . . . 26 E4
Willow Lea CH1 . . . . 94 F2
Willowmead Dr SK10 . . . . . 87 A5
Willow Rd
Chester CH4 . . . . 140 F6
Haydock WA11 . . . . 1 E7
High Lane SK6 . . . . 37 F7
Newton-le-Willows WA12 . . 2 E4
Partington M31 . . . . 11 E3
Willows SK9 . . . . 59 F6
Willows Cl CW2 . . . . 206 B7
Willow Sq CW7 . . . . 127 A2
Willow St CW12 . . . . 156 E3
Willows The
Frodsham WA6 . . . . 74 C8
Higher Wincham CW9 . . . 79 F6
Newton-le-Willows WA12 . . 2 D4
2 Northwich CW9 . . . . 103 C6
Partington M31 . . . . 11 F3
Sandbach CW11 . . . . . . 175 B7
Warrington WA1 . . . . 14 F5
Willow Stream SK22 . . . . . 39 D8
Willow Tree Cl WA8 . . . . . 13 D2
Willow Tree Gr ST7 . . . . . 193 F7
Willowview Sch CW1 . . . . 173 D2
Willow Way
Bramhall SK7 . . . . 35 D7
Broughton CH4 . . . . 139 B3
Prestbury SK10 . . . . 87 A5
Willow Wood Com Prim Sch
CW7 . . . . 127 A2
Wilmere La WA8 . . . . 13 A6
Wilmot Ave WA5 . . . . 14 F6
Wilmot Dr WA3 . . . . 2 F7
WILMSLOW 60 C5
Wilmslow Ave CH66 . . . . . 69 E5
Wilmslow Cres WA4 . . . . . 17 D4

Wilmslow Ct SK9 . . . . 34 D3
Wilmslow Dr CH66 . . . . . . 69 E5
Wilmslow Grange Prim Sch
SK9 . . . . 34 A2
Wilmslow High Sch SK9 . . 60 B6
Wilmslow L Ctr SK9 . . . . . . 60 B7
Wilmslow Old Rd
Mottram St Andrew SK10 . 61 A2
Wythenshawe M90 . . . . . . 33 A6
WILMSLOW PARK 60 D7
Wilmslow Park N SK9 . . . . 60 C7
Wilmslow Park S SK9 . . . . 60 C7
Wilmslow Prep Sch for Girls
SK9 . . . . 60 B7
Wilmslow Rd
Adlington SK10 . . . . 61 D6
Alderley Edge SK9 . . . . . . 60 A2
Gatley SK8 . . . . 34 D7
Gatley SK8, SK9 . . . . 34 D8
Handforth SK9 . . . . 34 D4
Mottram St Andrew, Greendale
SK10 . . . . 86 D8
Mottram St Andrew SK10 . 61 A3
Woodford SK7 . . . . 35 C7
Wythenshawe M90, SK9,
WA15 . . . . 32 F5
Wilmslow Sta SK9 . . . . 60 C7
Wilmslow Wlk ⁵ SK11 . . 112 E7
Wilsburg Grange CW8 . . 103 A5
Wilsden Rd WA8 . . . . 12 B1
Wilshaw Terr CH63 . . . . . . 42 B6
Wilson Cl
Warrington WA4 . . . . 17 D3
⁴ Widnes WA8 . . . . 13 D1
Wilson Cres CW9 . . . . 80 B3
Wilson Dr CW9 . . . . 126 F7
Wilson Patten St WA1 . . . 16 A4
Wilsons La CH65 . . . . 70 A3
Wilson St
Warrington, Bewsey WA5 . 16 A7
Warrington, Birchwood WA3 . 9 E5
New Mills SK8 . . . . 34 C7
Wilton Cl CW9 . . . . 103 E4
Wilton Cres
Alderley Edge SK9 . . . . . . 59 F2
Macclesfield SK11 . . . . . 111 E6
Wilton Dr WA15 . . . . 32 C8
Wilton La WA3 . . . . 4 B5
Wiltshire Cl
Macclesfield SK10 . . . . . . 86 E2
Warrington WA1 . . . . 17 D6
Wiltshire Dr CW12 . . . . . 156 E4
Wiltshire Rd M31 . . . . 11 E2
Wiltshire Wlk SK10 . . . . . 86 F2
Wilwick La SK11 . . . . 111 F7
Wimberry Dr ST5 . . . . . . 210 D1
WIMBOLDSLEY 150 F4
Wimboldsley Prim Sch
CW10 . . . . 150 F4
WIMBOLDS TRAFFORD . . 96 F6
WINCHAM 79 C3
Wincham Ave CW9 . . . . . . 79 D3
Wincham Bsns Pk CW9 . . 79 D3
Wincham Cty Prim Sch
CW9 . . . . 79 F5
Wincham La CW9 . . . . 79 D3
Wincham Park (Witton
Albion FC) CW9 . . . . 79 C2
Winchester Ave
Ellesmere Port CH65 . . . . 70 D4
Warrington WA5 . . . . 15 C5
Winchester Cl
Shavington CW2 . . . . 206 B3
Wilmslow SK9 . . . . 59 E5
Winchester Ct CW2 . . . . . 207 B3
Winchester Dr SK10 . . . . 111 F8
Winchester Ho ⑫ SK6 . . 111 F8
Winchester Pl WA8 . . . . . 22 C8
Winchester Sq CH4 . . . . . 140 F5
WINCLE 160 A7
Wincle Ave SK12 . . . . 36 F2
Wincle CE Prim Sch
SK11 . . . . 136 F1
Windermere Ave
Chester CH2 . . . . 119 A6
Warrington WA2 . . . . 8 D3
Widnes WA8 . . . . 13 B4
Windermere Cl CH64 . . . . 66 F7
Windermere Dr
Alderley Edge SK9 . . . . . . 59 F1
Congleton CW12 . . . . 156 F2
Windermere Rd
Crewe CW2 . . . . 189 E2
Ellesmere Port CH65 . . . . 70 C2
Handforth SK9 . . . . 34 C4
Haydock WA11 . . . . 1 B6
High Lane SK6 . . . . 37 E8
Winsford CW7 . . . . 126 C2
Windermere St WA8 . . . . 13 B4
Windess Sta Pk ⑯ WA8 . 23 B8
Windfield Gdns 69 D7
Windings The CW10 . . . . 128 B2
Windle Ct
Neston CH64 . . . . 41 E2
Warrington WA3 . . . . 9 C4
WINDLE HILL 67 C7
Windlehurst Ct SK6 . . . . . 37 D7
Windlehurst Rd SK12 . . . . 37 D8
Windmill Cl
Buerton CW3 . . . . 230 E4
Warrington WA4 . . . . 26 C6
Windmill Dr CW3 . . . . . . 229 F3
WINDMILL HILL 24 C1
Windmill Hill Ave W AE . 24 D2
Windmill Hill Avenue E
WA7 . . . . 24 D1
Windmill Hill Avenue N
WA7 . . . . 24 D3

Windmill Hill Avenue S
WA7 . . . . 24 D2
Windmill Hill Avenue W
WA7 . . . . 24 C2
Windmill Hill Prim Sch
WA7 . . . . 24 D2
Windmill La
Bollington SK10 . . . . 88 B6
Christleton CH3 . . . . 142 D8
Hankelow CW3 . . . . 230 F4
Preston on the Hill WA4 . . 51 A6
Warrington, Penketh WA5 . 14 E5
Warrington WA4 . . . . 26 C6
Windmill Rise CH2 . . . . . 118 D7
Windmill St
Macclesfield SK11 . . . . . 112 C6
Runcorn WA7 . . . . 23 B2
Windscale Rd WA2 . . . . 9 A2
Windsor Ave
Crewe CW1 . . . . 190 B6
Nantwich CW5 . . . . 204 F3
Newton-le-Willows WA12 . 2 D2
⑪ Tarporley CW6 . . . . . 146 D1
Winsford SK9 . . . . 59 F7
Windsor Cl
Bollington SK10 . . . . 87 E6
Cuddington CW8 . . . . . . 101 F4
Middlewich CW10 . . . . . 151 D7
Poynton SK12 . . . . 36 D4
Windsor Ct
Chester CH1 . . . . 237 B1
⑪ Warrington WA4 . . . . 16 E1
Windsor Dr
Alsager ST7 . . . . 192 F4
Altrincham, Bowdon WA14 . 20 F1
Broughton CH4 . . . . 139 A3
Ellesmere Port CH65 . . . . 70 A3
Faddiley CW5 . . . . 202 E2
Haydock WA11 . . . . 2 A7
Helsby WA6 . . . . 73 B2
Warrington WA4 . . . . 17 B2
Winsford CW7 . . . . 149 C5
Windsor Gr
Cheadle SK8 . . . . 34 F8
Runcorn WA7 . . . . 49 B8
Windsor Ho
⑤ Northwich CW8 . . . . 103 C5
Talke ST7 . . . . 210 D1
Windsor Pl CW12 . . . . . . 156 F2
Windsor Rd
Golborne WA3 . . . . 3 C8
Widnes WA8 . . . . 13 A1
Wistaston Green CW2 . . 205 E8
Windsor Sq SK11 . . . . . . 112 D4
Windsor St WA5 . . . . 15 D4
Windsor Way WA16 . . . . . 56 F2
Windways CH66 . . . . 69 D7
Windy Bank Ave WA3 . . . . 3 E8
Winfield Way WA8 . . . . . . 23 B8
Winfrith Rd WA2 . . . . 9 A2
Wingate Rd CH62 . . . . 43 E5
Wingfield Ave SK9 . . . . . . 59 E6
Wingfield Dr SK9 . . . . 59 E6
Wingfield Pl CW7 . . . . . . 149 B6
Winghay Rd ST7 . . . . 195 B2
Winifred St WA2 . . . . 16 C7
Winkwell Dr CH4 . . . . 141 A5
Winlowe ⑱ SK11 . . . . . . 112 E7
Winmarth Dr WA15 . . . . . 32 D7
Winmarleigh St WA1 . . . . 16 A4
WINNINGTON 78 D1
Winnington Ave CW8 . . . 103 C8
Winnington Cl ⑫ CW8 . . 103 F8
Winnington Hill CW8 . . . 103 F8
Winnington La CW8 . . . . . 78 D1
Winnington Park Prim Sch
CW8 . . . . 103 D7
Winnington St
Northwich CW8 . . . . 103 F8
Winsford CW7 . . . . 126 E1
Winscombe The WA7 . . . . 23 D1
Winscombe Ct ⑥ CW8 . . 103 C8
Winsfield Rd SK7 . . . . 36 E8
WINSFORD 126 E2
Winsford Cross Sh Ctr
CW7 . . . . 126 D1
Winsford Cl WA11 . . . . 1 F7
Winsford Gr CH66 . . . . . . 69 C3
Winsford Ind Est CW7 . . 127 E1
Winsford Lifestyle Ctr
CW7 . . . . 149 D8
Winsford Rd WA7 . . . . . . 170 F6
Winsford Sta CW7 . . . . . 127 C1
Winsford Way CH1 . . . . . 117 F2
Winslow Cl WA7 . . . . 50 D8
Winstanley Cl WA5 . . . . . 15 C5
Winstanley Ho WA16 . . . . 56 F2
Winstanley Ind Est WA2 . . 8 B1
Winstanley Rd CH64 . . . . 66 E5
Winston Ave
Alsager ST7 . . . . 193 C5
Newton-le-Willows WA12 . 2 C3
St Helens WA9 . . . . 1 B2
Winston Ct CH2 . . . . 119 A5
Winterbottom La WA16 . . 55 E8
Winterford La CW6 . . . . . 147 B2
Winter Gr WA9 . . . . 1 B3
Wintergreen Wlk ⑬ M31 . 11 F3
Winterlea Dr L26 . . . . 21 A6
WINTERLEY 191 F7
Winterside Cl ST5 . . . . . . 210 D1
Winterton Way SK11 . . . 112 D3
Winton Gr WA7 . . . . 24 D1
Winton Rd WA3 . . . . 3 E6
WINWICK 8 A6

Winwick CE Prim Sch WA2 .8 B6
Winwick La WA3 . . . . 3 E3
Winwick Link Rd WA2, WA3 8 C6
Winwick Park Ave WA2 . . . 8 A3
WINWICK QUAY 8 A3
Winwick Quay WA2 . . . . . . 8 A3
Winwick Rd
Newton-le-Willows WA12 . . 2 F1
Warrington WA2 . . . . 8 A2
Winwick St WA2 . . . . 16 B6
Winwick View WA5 . . . . . . 1 D1
Winksmoor Rd SK22 . . . . 39 B7
Wirral Cl WA3 . . . . 4 E4
Wirral Cres CH64 . . . . 66 F5
Wirral Ctry Pk* CH64 . . . 67 C7
Wirral Metropolitan Coll
CH62 . . . . 44 A7
WIRSWALL 226 A5
Wirswall Rd SY13 . . . . . . 226 C8
Wisdom Wlk CH1 . . . . . . 174 D7
Wisenholme Cl WA7 . . . . 49 E5
WISTASTON 205 D8
Wistaston Ave CW2 . . . . 189 F2
Wistaston Church Lane Prim
Sch CW2 . . . . 205 E8
WISTASTON GREEN . . . 189 D2
Wistaston Green Cl CW2 189 E2
Wistaston Green Prim Sch
CW2 . . . . 189 F2
Wistaston Green Rd
CW2 . . . . 189 E2
Wistaston Pk CW2 . . . . . 189 F1
Wistaston Rd
Crewe CW2 . . . . 190 C3
Wistaston CW5 . . . . 205 E6
Wistaston Road Bsns Ctr
CW2 . . . . 190 B4
Wisterdale Cl CW2 . . . . . 206 A7
Wisteria Way WA9 . . . . 6 A7
Witham Cl CW2 . . . . 206 A8
Witham Way ST8 . . . . 179 E1
Withens Cl CW8 . . . . 102 D8
Withenshaw La SK11 . . . 136 E5
Withens La CW8 . . . . 102 D8
Withers Ave WA2 . . . . 16 D8
Wither's La
High Legh, Primrose Hill
WA16 . . . . 28 C3
High Legh, Rowlinson's Green
WA16 . . . . 28 B4
Witherwin Ave WA4 . . . . . 26 F7
Withington Ave WA3 . . . . . 5 A3
Withington Cl
Northwich CW9 . . . . 104 A5
Sandbach CW11 . . . . 175 C7
WITHINGTON GREEN . . 108 E3
Withinlee Rd SK10 . . . . . . 86 D6
Withins Rd
Culcheth WA3 . . . . 4 F8
Haydock WA11 . . . . 1 F8
Within Way L24 . . . . 21 E1
Withnall Dr WA7 . . . . 206 B4
Withy Cl WA6 . . . . 74 C8
Withycombe Rd WA5 . . . . 14 E4
Withy Croft CH3 . . . . 142 B7
Withyfold Dr SK10 . . . . . . 87 E1
Witney Gdns WA4 . . . . . . 26 E6
Witney La SY14 . . . . 213 D8
Wittenham Ho SK9 . . . . . 34 D2
Wittering La CH60 . . . . . . 40 D7
Witterings The CH64 . . . . 41 E1
Witton Church Walk CE Prim
Sch CW9 . . . . 104 A8
Witton St CW9 . . . . 79 A1
Witton Wlk ⑥ CW9 . . . . 103 F8
Witt Rd WA8 . . . . 23 A2
Wivern Pl WA7 . . . . 23 B3
Wobbs La SY13 . . . . 225 C5
Woburn Ave WA12 . . . . . . 2 D2
Woburn Cl
Haydock WA11 . . . . 1 F7
Macclesfield SK10 . . . . . . 87 C2
Northwich CW9 . . . . 103 E5
Woburn Ct SK12 . . . . 36 F4
Woburn Dr
Chester CH2 . . . . 118 F7
Congleton CW12 . . . . . . 179 B8
Cronton WA8 . . . . 12 D6
Woburn Rd WA2 . . . . 8 A4
Woking Rd SK8 . . . . 35 A7
Wolfe Cl
Grappenhall Heys WA4 . . 27 A8
Knutsford WA16 . . . . 57 C3
Wolstanholme Cl CW2 . . 156 F1
WOLVERHAM 70 D4
Wolverham Prim Sch
CH65 . . . . 70 D4
Wolverton Dr
Handforth SK9 . . . . 34 D1
Runcorn WA7 . . . . 24 D1
Wolverton Ho ⑪ SK9 . . . 60 A1
Wolvesey Pl CW1 . . . . . . 149 B6
Woodacre Gr CH66 . . . . . 69 F8
Woodacre Rd CH66 . . . . . 69 F8
Woodacres Ct SK9 . . . . . . 59 F6
Woodale Cl WA5 . . . . 14 E7
Woodall Ave CH4 . . . . . . 140 E6
Woodall Dr WA7 . . . . 23 B1
Woodavens Gr CW3 . . . . 229 A2
WOODBANK 93 F6
Woodbank SK9 . . . . 60 A2
Woodbank Cl CW2 . . . . . 206 A7
Woodbank La CH1 . . . . . . 93 D5
Woodbank Rd
Ellesmere Port CH65 . . . . 70 B2
Warrington WA5 . . . . 15 A4
Woodbine Ave M44 . . . . . 11 D4

Woodbine Rd WA13 . . . . . 19 B4
Woodbourne Rd SK22 . . . 39 A5
Woodbridge Cl WA4 . . . . 26 E4
Woodbrook SK23 . . . . 65 E8
Woodbrook Cl CW2 . . . . 205 E7
Woodbrook Rd SK9 . . . . . 60 C1
Woodburn Dr CH60 . . . . . 40 F6
Woodchurch La CH66 . . . 69 E6
Woodclose CH66 . . . . 44 A1
Woodcock La ST7 . . . . . . 195 C6
Woodcock's Well CE Prim
Sch ST7 . . . . 195 C6
Woodcote Ave CH65 . . . . 70 B1
Woodcote Cl WA2 . . . . 8 D1
Woodcote Pl CW11 . . . . . 191 F8
Woodcotes The CH62 . . . . 43 D6
Woodcote View SK9 . . . . . 34 F1
Woodcott Ave CW7 . . . . . 126 B1
Woodcott Cl CW2 . . . . . . 206 E2
Woodcott Gr ⑧ SK9 . . . . 34 E1
Woodcotthill La CW5 . . . 217 B3
Woodcroft ST7 . . . . 210 A1
Wood Croft CH3 . . . . 119 F4
Woodcroft Gdns WA4 . . . 26 E6
Wood Dr ST7 . . . . 193 A4
WOODEND 38 E8
Woodend WA7 . . . . 50 E7
Woodend Cl CW10 . . . . . 151 C6
Wood End La WA8 . . . . . . 13 D2
Woodend La
Hollins Green WA3 . . . . . . 10 D2
Mobberley WA16 . . . . 58 E8
Wood End La CH64 . . . . . 67 A4
Woodfall Cl CH64 . . . . 67 A6
Woodfall Gr CH64 . . . . . . 67 A6
Woodfall La CH64 . . . . 67 B6
Woodfall Prim Sch CH64 . 67 A6
Wood Farm CW2 . . . . 189 B4
Woodfield Cl CH4 . . . . . . 139 A3
Woodfield Gr CH2 . . . . . . 119 B5
Woodfield Ho CH2 . . . . . . 119 A5
Woodfield Rd
Cheadle SK8 . . . . 35 B7
Ellesmere Port CH65 . . . . 70 C5
Woodfield Road N ②
CH65 . . . . 70 C5
Woodfields CH3 . . . . 142 E7
Woodfin Croft SK11 . . . . . 84 A3
WOODFORD 35 E2
Woodford Aerodrome
SK7 . . . . 36 A1
Woodford Cl
Crewe CW2 . . . . 189 F2
Helsby WA6 . . . . 73 B2
Runcorn WA7 . . . . 49 B6
Warrington WA4 . . . . 17 C3
Woodford Court Ind Est
CW7 . . . . 149 A8
Woodford Ct CW7 . . . . . . 149 A7
Woodford La
Prestbury SK10 . . . . 61 D7
Winsford CW7 . . . . 149 B8
Woodford Lane W CW7 . . 149 A7
Woodford Lo SK12 . . . . . . 36 C4
Woodford Lodge City High
Sch CW7 . . . . 149 A7
Woodford Lodge Sports Ctr
CW7 . . . . 149 A7
Woodford Mews SK9 . . . . 34 D4
Woodford Park Ind Est
CW7 . . . . 148 F8
Woodford Rd
Bramhall SK7 . . . . 35 E4
Poynton SK12 . . . . 36 B6
Wilmslow SK9 . . . . 60 B2
Woodgate Ave ST7 . . . . . 194 A5
Wood Gdns SK9 . . . . 60 B2
Woodgreen La CW5 . . . . 171 D5
Woodhall Cl
Bramhall SK7 . . . . 35 E3
Warrington WA5 . . . . 15 A8
Woodhall Rd CH65 . . . . . 195 C3
Woodham Gr CH64 . . . . . 66 F5
Woodhatch Rd WA7 . . . . . 50 B5
Wood Heath Way CH62 . . 44 A7
WOODHEY GREEN 202 B6
Woodhey Hall La CW5 . . 202 B6
Woodhey La CW5 . . . . . . 202 C5
Woodhouse ⑮ CW9 . . . . 79 F3
WOODHOUSE-END 135 C8
Woodhouse End Rd
SK11 . . . . 135 C8
WOODHOUSE GREEN . . 158 D2
Woodhouse La
Biddulph ST8 . . . . 179 F2
Buerton CW3 . . . . 235 D8
Partington WA14 . . . . 20 C4
Warren SK11 . . . . 111 E1
Wythenshawe M90 . . . . . 33 D7
Woodhouse Mid Sch
ST8 . . . . 179 E2
Woodhouse Rd M22 . . . . 33 D8
WOODHOUSES 73 E4
Woodhouses Pk WA6 . . . 73 F5
Wood La
Bradwall Green CW10,
CW11 . . . . 152 E3
Broughton CH4 . . . . 139 B4
Burton CH64 . . . . 67 C3
Duddon CW4 . . . . 145 E2
Goostrey CW4 . . . . 107 C1
Neston CH64 . . . . 67 C3
Partington M31 . . . . 11 E3
Runcorn, Brookvale WA7 . 50 C6
Runcorn WA7 . . . . 49 F5

Wood La continued
Sutton Weaver WA7 . . . . . 49 F4
Tattenhall CH3 . . . . 167 A1
Warrington WA4 . . . . 26 E8
Weaverham CW8 . . . . . . 102 E8
Wilmslow WA16 . . . . 32 D1
Wood La CH66 . . . . 146 B6
Woodland Ave
Crewe CW1 . . . . 190 F4
Lymm WA13 . . . . 19 A2
Nantwich CW5 . . . . 205 A5
Newton-le-Willows WA12 . 2 F3
Widnes WA8 . . . . 12 F1
Woodland Bank CH2 . . . . 96 F1
Woodland Cl SK11 . . . . . . 84 A3
Woodland Ct ST7 . . . . . . 193 D4
Woodland Dr WA13 . . . . . 19 A2
Woodland End SK11 . . . . 84 A3
Woodland Gdns CW1 . . . 190 D6
Woodland Rd
Ellesmere Port CH65 . . . . 70 B2
Rode Heath ST7 . . . . 193 D8
Woodlands CW8 . . . . 103 B5
Woodlands Ave
Chester CH1 . . . . 118 B4
Congleton CW12 . . . . . . 156 D4
Kidsgrove ST7 . . . . 194 D1
Woodlands Cl
Cheadle SK8 . . . . 35 A8
Cotebrook CW6 . . . . 147 A8
Neston CH64 . . . . 66 D8
Woodlands Cres WA16 . . 29 C4
Woodlands Ct
Alderley Edge SK9 . . . . . . 85 A8
Knutsford WA16 . . . . 57 B2
Woodlands Dr
Chester CH2 . . . . 118 E4
Chorlton CW2 . . . . 207 C3
Goostrey CW4 . . . . 107 E1
Knutsford WA16 . . . . 57 B2
Warrington WA4 . . . . 17 D3
Woodlands Gr CW8 . . . . . 77 F3
Woodlands Ind Est WA12 . 2 C6
Woodlands La CH3 . . . . . 119 A2
Woodlands Pk
Congleton CW12 . . . . . . 156 C3
Newton-le-Willows WA12 . 2 C6
Woodlands Prim Sch
CH66 . . . . 69 F7
Woodlands Rd
Chester CH4 . . . . 141 A7
Handforth SK9 . . . . 34 E3
High Lane SK12 . . . . 38 A6
Huntington CH3 . . . . 142 A6
Macclesfield SK11 . . . . . 112 C6
Neston CH64 . . . . 66 D8
New Mills SK22 . . . . 39 A8
Northwich CW8 . . . . 103 C5
Wilmslow SK9 . . . . 33 F1
Woodlands Road E ①
CW8 . . . . 103 C5
Woodlands The
Higher Wincham CW9 . . . 80 A6
Kidsgrove ST7 . . . . 194 E3
Northwich CW8 . . . . 78 E1
Woodlands Way CW6 . . . 146 D2
Woodland View
Ellesmere Port CH66 . . . . 69 B8
Horwich End SK23 . . . . . . 65 F2
Woodland Wlk
Bebington CH62 . . . . 43 C8
Runcorn WA7 . . . . 24 A1
WOOD LANE 210 A1
Wood Lane E SK10 . . . . . 63 B8
Wood Lane N
Fourlane-ends SK10 . . . . 63 B8
Wardsend SK10 . . . . 37 B1
Wood Lane Prim Sch ①
ST7 . . . . 210 A1
Wood Lane S SK10 . . . . . 63 B7
Wood Lane W SK10 . . . . . 63 A8
Woodlark Cl CW7 . . . . . . 150 A8
Woodlea Ave CH4 . . . . . . 118 F7
Woodlea Cl CH62 . . . . 43 D5
Woodlea Ct SK8 . . . . 103 D7
Woodlea Dr SK10 . . . . 87 E8
Woodleigh Ct SK9 . . . . . . 60 A2
Woodley Fold WA5 . . . . . . 14 F4
Wood Memorial CP Sch SK9
CH4 . . . . 140 E6
Woodnoth Dr CW2 . . . . . 206 C5
Wood Orchard La CW3 . . 230 A2
Woodpecker Cl WA3 . . . . . 9 F4
Woodpecker Dr
Northwich CW9 . . . . 103 F4
Packmoor ST7 . . . . 195 E1
Woodridge WA7 . . . . 24 C1
Woodrow Ct ⑫ WA15 . . . 15 C7
Woodrow Way
Irlam M44 . . . . 11 F8
Newcastle-under-Lyme
ST5 . . . . 210 F1
Woodruff Cl ST7 . . . . 195 F1
Woodruff Wlk ⑦ M31 . . . 11 F3
Woods Cl WA12 . . . . 82 F6
Woodsfin La CH3 . . . . . . 183 F7
Woods Gr SK8 . . . . 35 B7
WOODSHUTTS 194 E1
Woodshutt's St ST7 . . . . 194 E1
WOODSIDE 99 C2
Woodside
Ellesmere Port CH65 . . . . 70 C2
Knutsford WA16 . . . . 57 B1
Lawton-gate ST7 . . . . 194 E4

Woodside continued
Poynton SK12 . . . . 36 F4
Siddington SK11 . . . . 110 A3
Wilmslow/Alderley Edge
SK9 . . . . 59 C7
Woodside Ave
Alsager ST7 . . . . 193 E4
Crewe CW2 . . . . 189 F2
Frodsham WA6 . . . . 74 D7
Kidsgrove ST7 . . . . 195 A1
Woodside Ct CH2 . . . . 118 C4
Woodside Cty Prim Sch
WA7 . . . . 49 D7
Woodside Dr
High Lane SK6 . . . . 37 F7
Sandbach CW11 . . . . 175 C6
Woodside La
Crewe CW2 . . . . 189 F1
Lymm WA13 . . . . 19 B1
Poynton SK12 . . . . 36 E4
Woodside Rd
Blacon CH1 . . . . 117 C5
Haydock WA11 . . . . 1 E7
Warrington WA5 . . . . 14 F6
Woodside St SK22 . . . . 39 B6
Woodside Terr CW9 . . . . . . 104 B4
Woods La SK8 . . . . 35 B7
Wood's La CW8 . . . . 101 C5
Woodsome Cl CH65 . . . . . . 70 B1
Woodsome Dr CH65 . . . . . . 70 B1
Wood Sorrel Way WA3 . . . . 3 E8
Woods Rd M44 . . . . 11 F8
Wood St
Audley ST7 . . . . 209 E3
Congleton CW12 . . . . 156 D3
Crewe CW2 . . . . 190 D2
Golborne WA3 . . . . 3 B8
Macclesfield SK11 . . . . 112 D7
Mow Cop ST7 . . . . 195 D7
New Mills SK22 . . . . 39 B7
Sandycroft CH5 . . . . 116 A2
Warrington WA1 . . . . 16 D6
Widnes WA8 . . . . 13 C1
Woodstock Ave
Cheadle SK8 . . . . 35 A7
Newton-le-Willows WA12 . . . 2 D2
Woodstock Cl SK10 . . . . . . 87 A2
Woodstock Dr CW10 . . . . . 151 E5
Woodstock Gdns WA4 . . . . . 26 F6
Woodstock Gr WA8 . . . . . . 12 D2
Woodthorn Cl WA4 . . . . 24 F4
Woodvale Cl WA2 . . . . 8 E1
Woodvale Rd
Ellesmere Port CH66 . . . . . 69 D6
Knutsford WA16 . . . . 82 A8
Wood View ST7 . . . . 210 A1
Woodview Cres WA8 . . . . . . 22 A8
Woodview Rd WA8 . . . . 22 A8
Woodville Ave SK9 . . . . 59 C7
Woodville Pl WA8 . . . . 12 D1
Woodville Rd SK9 . . . . 59 C7
Woodwards Cotts CH64 . . . 66 E7
Woodward St CW8 . . . . 77 D1
Woodward Wlk CH3 . . . . . 121 C3
WOODWORTH GREEN . . 186 B8
Woodyear Rd CH62 . . . . . . 43 E7
Woolacombe Cl WA4 . . . . . 16 D2
Woolaston Dr ST7 . . . . 193 D3
Woolden Rd M44, WA3 . . . . 11 B8
WOOLFALL 230 E6
Woollam Dr CH66 . . . . 69 D7
Woolley Ave SK12 . . . . 36 D2
Woolley Cl WA6 . . . . 49 D2

Woolmer Cl WA3 . . . . 10 B6
WOOLSTANWOOD 189 E3
WOOLSTON 17 C8
Woolston Ave CW12 . . . . . 157 A2
Woolston CE Prim Sch
WA1 . . . . 17 D8
Woolston Com High Sch
WA1 . . . . 17 B7
Woolston Com Prim Sch
WA1 . . . . 17 C7
Woolston Dr CW2 . . . . 206 E2
Woolston Eyes Bird Reserve
The* WA1/WA4 . . . . 17 D5
Woolston Grange Ave
Warrington WA1 . . . . 9 D1
Warrington, Woolston WA1 . 17 F8
Woolston Hall WA1 . . . . . . 17 D7
Woolston L Ctr WA1 . . . . . 17 D7
Woolston Rd WA11 . . . . 1 C7
Woolton Ct CH66 . . . . 69 F8
WOORE 232 B1
Woore Prim Sch CW3 . . . . 232 C1
Woore Rd CW3 . . . . 230 D3
Worcester Ave WA3 . . . . 3 B8
Worcester Cl
Talke ST7 . . . . 210 D7
Warrington WA5 . . . . 15 C5
Worcester Pl CH1 . . . . 118 A4
Worcester St CH65 . . . . . . 70 C6
Worcester Wlk 6 CH65 . . . 70 C6
Wordsworth Ave
Warrington WA4 . . . . 16 B2
Widnes WA8 . . . . 22 F8
Wordsworth Cl
Crewe CW2 . . . . 189 F1
7 Sandbach CW11 . . . . . . 174 D6
Wordsworth Cres CH1 . . . . 118 A5
Wordsworth Dr CW1 . . . . . 190 F4
Wordsworth Ho SK10 . . . . . 86 F1
Wordsworth Mews CH1 . . . 118 A5
Wordsworth Sq CH1 . . . . . 118 A5
Wordsworth Way
Alsager ST7 . . . . 193 D4
Ellesmere Port CH66 . . . . . 69 E1
Works Cotts WA7 . . . . 49 E3
Works La CW9 . . . . 79 E1
World Freight Terminal
M90 . . . . 32 F7
World Way M90 . . . . 33 B8
WORLESTON 188 F5
Worleston Cl CW10 . . . . . . 151 C6
Worley Ct CH3 . . . . 183 A8
Worrall St CW12 . . . . 156 E3
Worsborough Ave WA5 . . . . 15 B5
Worsdell Cl CW2 . . . . 190 E1
Worsley Ave
Saughall CH1 . . . . 117 A8
Warrington WA4 . . . . 16 F4
Worsley Dr CW12 . . . . 157 B1
Worsley Rd WA4 . . . . 16 B1
Worsley St
Golborne WA3 . . . . 3 A8
Warrington WA5 . . . . 15 F7
Worth Ct SK12 . . . . 36 D2
WORTHENBURY 211 A1
Worthing St CW9 . . . . 104 C8
Worthington Ave 9 M31 . . 11 F3
Worthington Ct
Henbury SK11 . . . . 111 C8
Nantwich CW5 . . . . 205 A5
Runcorn WA7 . . . . 50 A7
Worthington Ct CH2 . . . . . 118 D4
Worth Prim Sch SK12 . . . . . 36 F2
Wrekin Ho 8 CW8 . . . . . . 103 C5
Wrekin Way CH4 . . . . 140 F6
Wren Ave CW4 . . . . 129 C2

Wrenbury Cl ST5 . . . . 210 D1
WRENBURY 216 F4
Wrenbury Dr 8 CW9 . . . . 103 E5
WRENBURY FRITH 216 C6
Wrenbury Frith CW5 . . . . . 216 B7
Wrenbury Green CW5 . . . . 216 E4
Wrenbury Hall Dr CW5 . . . 217 A5
WRENBURY HEATH 217 B5
Wrenbury Heath Rd
CW5 . . . . 217 D5
Wrenbury Ind Est CW5 . . . 217 A3
Wrenbury Prim Sch
CW5 . . . . 216 F4
Wrenbury Rd
Aston CW5 . . . . 217 B3
Chorley Bank SY14 . . . . . . 201 D1
Marbury SY13 . . . . 226 E8
Wrenbury SY13, CW5 . . . . 216 B1
Wrenbury Sta CW5 . . . . . . 217 A3
Wren Cl
Macclesfield SK10 . . . . 87 A1
Runcorn WA7 . . . . 50 A6
Warrington WA3 . . . . 9 F4
Wrenmere Cl CW11 . . . . . 174 E8
Wrens Cl CW5 . . . . 204 F3
Wrenshot La WA16 . . . . 29 D4
Wrexham Cl
Biddulph ST8 . . . . 179 D1
Warrington WA5 . . . . 7 E1
**Wrexham Ind Est/Ystad
Ddiwidiannol Wrecsam**
LL13 . . . . 196 A1
Wrexham Rd
Bickerton SY14 . . . . 200 A8
Bulkeley SY14, CW6 . . . . . 184 E1
Burland CW5 . . . . 203 C8
Chester CH4 . . . . 141 B4
Faddiley CW5, CW6 . . . . . 202 D6
Holt LL13 . . . . 196 B7
Malpas SY14 . . . . 212 E2
Pulford CH4 . . . . 162 E5
Roughhill CH4 . . . . 140 F1
Worthenbury SY14 . . . . . . 211 C1
Wright Ave CW9 . . . . 104 D6
Wright Cres WA8 . . . . 23 A5
Wright Ct CW5 . . . . 204 F5
Wright Lodge 6 CW5 . . . . 204 F5
WRIGHT'S GREEN 27 A6
Wrights La WA5 . . . . 13 F2
Wright's La
Burtonwood WA5 . . . . 6 F3
Sandbach CW11 . . . . 175 D6
Wright St ST7 . . . . 194 D1
Wright Tree Villas M44 . . . 11 D5
Wrigley La SK10 . . . . 86 B3
Wrigley Rd WA11 . . . . 1 E6
Wrinehill Rd CW5 . . . . 220 E7
Wroxham Cl
Chester CH2 . . . . 237 B4
Helsby WA6 . . . . 73 B4
Wroxham Rd WA5 . . . . 14 E6
Wrynose Rd CH62 . . . . 43 E8
Wybersley Rd SK6 . . . . 38 A8
WYBUNBURY 220 A8
**Wybunbury Delves CE Prim
Sch** CW5 . . . . 220 B7
Wybunbury La CW5 . . . . . 205 E3
**Wybunbury Moss National
Nature Reserve*** CW5 . 206 B1
Wybunbury Rd
Willaston CW5 . . . . 205 D4
Wybunbury CW5 . . . . 220 B7
Wyche Ave CW5 . . . . 204 D5
Wyche Cl CW9 . . . . 104 E6
Wyche La CW6 . . . . 185 F8
Wychelm Rd M31 . . . . 11 F3

Wyche Prim Sch The
CW5 . . . . 204 E6
Wyche Rd CW6 . . . . 185 F8
Wych House Bank CW5 . 204 D5
Wych-House La CW10 . . . 128 C1
Wych La SK10 . . . . 62 D5
Wychwood Ave WA13 . . . . 18 C3
Wychwood Pk CW2 . . . . . 207 C1
Wycliffe Ave SK9 . . . . 60 A7
Wycliffe Ct CH2 . . . . 119 A2
Wycliffe Rd
Ellesmere Port CH65 . . . . . 69 F3
Haydock WA11 . . . . 1 E7
Wyedale CH65 . . . . 70 B3
Wyedale Rd WA11 . . . . 1 C6
Wykeham Chase 8
SK11 . . . . 111 F7
Wyncroft Cl
Ellesmere Port CH65 . . . . . 70 B3
Widnes WA8 . . . . 22 C7
Wyncroft Ct CW8 . . . . 77 C1
Wyncroft Rd WA8 . . . . 22 C7
Wyndham Cl
Bramhall SK7 . . . . 35 E7
Northwich CW9 . . . . 103 F5
Wyndham Cres CH4 . . . . . . 62 A2
Wyndham Rd CH1 . . . . . . 117 C4
Wynd The CW6 . . . . 122 C4
Wynfield Ave M22 . . . . 33 F7
Wyngate Rd WA15 . . . . . . 31 F8
Wynnstay Rd CH4 . . . . . . 139 C4
Wynter Cl SY14 . . . . 198 B3
Wynter La SY14 . . . . 198 B3
Wythburn Gr WA7 . . . . 49 E5
Wythens Rd SK8 . . . . 34 B8
Wythin St CW6 . . . . 168 D1

Y

Yardley Ave WA5 . . . . 15 F8
Yarmouth Rd WA5 . . . . 14 E6
Yarrow Cl CW4 . . . . 139 C3
Yarwood Cl CW8 . . . . 103 F7
Yarwoodheath La WA14 . . 30 E7
YATEHOUSE GREEN 128 D6
Yatehouse La CW10 . . . . . 128 D7
Yates Cl WA5 . . . . 15 C5
Yates Rd
New Mills SK22 . . . . 39 C7
Thornton-le-Moors CH2 . . . 71 E1
Yates St CW2 . . . . 190 C2
**Y Berllan Geirios/Cherry
Orch** LL13 . . . . 196 D8
Yeald Brow WA13 . . . . 18 B3
Yeardsley Ave SK23 . . . . . . 39 D3
Yeardsley Gn SK23 . . . . . . 65 D8
Yeardsley La SK23 . . . . 39 D3
Yearsleys La WA6 . . . . 101 A5
Yeld La CW6 . . . . 122 E8
Yeoman Way CH66 . . . . . . 69 F1
Yeovil Cl WA1 . . . . 17 C8
Yerburgh St CH2 . . . . 118 D4
Yewdale Dr CH66 . . . . 69 F1
Yewlands CW8 . . . . 101 D5
Yewlands Dr WA16 . . . . . . 57 C2
Yew Tree Ave/Lon yr Ywen
CH1 . . . . 116 F7
Yew Tree Bank CW6 . . . . . 145 B5
Yewtree Cl CH64 . . . . 66 F7
Yew Tree Cl
Broughton CH4 . . . . 139 C3
Bulkeley SY14 . . . . 184 D2
Little Budworth CW6 . . . . . 147 F7
Lymm WA13 . . . . 18 E4

Yew Tree Cl continued
Macclesfield SK11 . . . . . . 112 A6
Middlewich CW10 . . . . 128 B2
Prestbury SK10 . . . . 87 B7
Thornton-le-Moors CH2 . . . 71 E1
Wilmslow SK9 . . . . 60 D7
Yew Tree Ct
Alsager ST7 . . . . 193 E2
Chester CH4 . . . . 163 B2
6 Heswall CH60 . . . . 41 A8
Wimboldsley CW10 . . . . . . 150 F3
Yew Tree Dr
Barnton CW8 . . . . 78 B3
Nantwich CW5 . . . . 204 D5
Yew Tree Farm Trad Est
WA11 . . . . 2 A8
Yew Tree La
Appleton Thorn WA4 . . . . . 27 C5
Astbury CW12 . . . . 178 C3
Bridgemere CW5 . . . . 232 A6
Poynton SK12 . . . . 36 F3
Yew Tree Park Rd SK8 . . . 35 B6
Yewtree Rd WA16 . . . . 80 F3
Yew Tree Rd
Wardsend SK10 . . . . 37 B1
Wistaston CW2 . . . . 206 A8
Yew Tree Way
Golborne WA3 . . . . 3 B7
Prestbury SK10 . . . . 87 C6
Yew Wlk 1 M31 . . . . 11 E2
Yonne The CH1 . . . . 237 A2
York Ave
Culcheth WA3 . . . . 4 F2
Warrington WA5 . . . . 14 E7
York Cl
Biddulph ST8 . . . . 179 C2
Talke ST7 . . . . 210 D7
York Cres SK9 . . . . 60 D8
York Ct 2 WA4 . . . . 16 E1
York Dr
Mickle Trafford CH2 . . . . . 119 E8
Warrington WA4 . . . . 17 A2
Winsford CW7 . . . . 149 D6
Wythenshawe M90 . . . . . . 32 F7
York Ho 4 CW8 . . . . 103 C5
York Pl WA7 . . . . 23 A2
York Rd
Connah's Quay CH5 . . . . . . 91 C1
Ellesmere Port CH65 . . . . . 70 C5
Irlam M44 . . . . 11 D5
Warrington WA4 . . . . 17 A2
Widnes WA8 . . . . 22 C8
Yorkshire Rd M31 . . . . 11 E2
York St
Chester CH1 . . . . 237 B3
Macclesfield SK10 . . . . . . 112 E8
Runcorn WA7 . . . . 23 A2
Warrington WA4 . . . . 16 C4
Yorston Lodge Sch WA16 . 56 F1
Ysgol Borderbrook SY14 222 F5
Ystad Ddiwidiannol Wrecsam/
Wrexham 1nd Est LL13 . 196 A1

Z

Zan Dr CW11 . . . . 175 A3
Zan Ind Pk CW11 . . . . 175 A3
Zara Ct WA4 . . . . 1 C7
Zinnia Dr M44 . . . . 11 E8
Zion St 3 CW8 . . . . 103 E7